Politics and Power

AN INTRODUCTION TO AMERICAN GOVERNMENT

AN INTRODUCTION TO
AMERICAN GOVERNMENT

Politics and Power

Sam C. Sarkesian and Krish Nanda

LOYOLA UNIVERSITY OF CHICAGO

ALFRED PUBLISHING CO., INC., NEW YORK

Published by Alfred Publishing Co., Inc.,
75 Channel Drive, Port Washington, N.Y. 11050
© Copyright 1976 by Alfred Publishing Co., Inc.
All rights reserved.
Printed in the United States of America

Library of Congress Cataloging in Publication Data

Sarkesian, Sam Charles. 1927–
   Politics and power: introduction to American government.

   Includes index.
   1. United States—Politics and government—Handbooks, manuals, etc. I. Nanda, Krish, 1930– joint author. II. Title.
JK274.S35   320.4′73   75-1244
ISBN 0-88284-026-6

To our students and colleagues at
Loyola University of Chicago

CONTENTS

Introduction xiii

CHAPTER 1
People and Politics: The Prevailing Issues 1

The Meaning of a Democratic Society 2
The Individual and the Government 4
Changing Society and the Relevance of Democracy 5
The Political Climate 9
Potential for the Political System 16

Selected Readings 19
Crisis of American Political Legitimacy, *Walter Dean Burnham* 21
What America Thinks of Itself, *Newsweek* 31
Race, Revolution and Women, *Shirley Chisholm* 36
Good Things About America, *U.S. News and World Report* 42

CHAPTER 2
Politics, Power and the Political System 49

The Meaning of Politics 49
The Meaning of Power 53
Political Actors 56
Power Relationships 59

Selected Readings 60

Influence, Power, Authority, Coercion, *Robert A. Dahl* 61
The Nature of Social Power, *R.M. MacIver* 65
What Is Political Power?, *Hans J. Morgenthau* 69

CHAPTER 3
The Constitution: Basis for Power 75

The Constitutional Convention 75
Compromises 77
Constitutional Principles 78
Democratic Ideology 83
Political Actors, the Constitution, and Democracy 87
The American Political System: An Overview 89

Selected Readings 92

Letter to Thomas Jefferson, *from James Madison* 93
Our Obsolete System, *Kevin P. Phillips* 103

CHAPTER 4
The Presidency: The Burden and the Glory 109

An Overview of the Presidency 111
Presidential Models 112
The Presidential Personality 115
Presidential Roles 118
Limits on Executive Power 125
Power in the Presidency 128

Selected Readings 134

Out Textbook President, *Thomas E. Cronin* 135
Time for Healing and The Decline and Fall, *Time* 145

CHAPTER 5
The Presidency in Domestic Politics 157

Vietnam and the Presidency 158
The Presidential Mandate 161
Who Affects the President 162
The Presidential Constituencies 166
The Presidential Veto 178
The Economy and Presidential Power 179

The Vice-President   183

Selected Readings   186

The Constraining of the President, *Richard E. Neustadt*   187

CHAPTER 6
The Presidency in Foreign Affairs   201

Constitutional Provisions   201
Treaties and Executive Agreements   202
The Department of State   205
The Department of Defense   206
The President as Commander-in-Chief   208
The National Security Council   209
The Central Intelligence Agency   210
Other Agencies and Individuals   211
Political Aspects of Presidential Power   212
Symbolic Role   213
Countervailing Power   214

Selected Readings   217

The Misuse of Power, *Henry Steele Commager*   218

CHAPTER 7
Congressmen and Their Constituents: Representing the People   227

The Composition of Congress   227
Representational Styles   229
Local v. National Orientation   231
Communication with Constituents   233

Selected Readings   240

On Becoming a United States Senator, *James L. Buckley*   241

CHAPTER 8
Authority, Leadership and Policy-Making in Congress   255

Party Leadership in the House   256
Party Leadership in the Senate   258
The Committee System   260
The 94th Congress   265
Patterns of Policy-Making   266

How a Bill Becomes Law 269

Selected Readings 273

Why Congress Won't Fight, *Elizabeth Drew* 274

CHAPTER 9
The Supreme Court and Society 289

Inside the Supreme Court 290
Role and Function of the Court 292
Court Structure 296
Major Periods of the Supreme Court 303

Selected Readings 311

On the Supreme Court, *Arthur J. Goldberg* 312
From Gideon's Trumpet, *Anthony Lewis* 316

CHAPTER 10
Politics, Society and the Judicial System 321

Power of the Judiciary 321
Historical View of the Legal System 322
Dual Court System 324
Administration of the System 330
Courtroom Practices and Processes: A Case Study 331
Legal Basis of Judicial Power 334
Mass Media and the Courts 335
Limits to Judicial Power 337
Changing the Court System 338
Criminal Justice 340
Courts and Society 342
Problems of Judicial Power 343

Selected Readings 345

The "Fight" Theory versus the "Truth" Theory, *Jerome Frank* 346
Chaos In Our Courts, *Lois Willie* 350

CHAPTER 11
The Bureaucracy: The Fourth Branch of Government 361

Who are the Bureaucrats? 361
Knowledge and Power 363
The Fourth Branch of Government 367

Institutional Characteristics 368
Types of Government Bureaucracies 375
The Bureaucracy, Congress and Interest Groups 377
Internal Conflicts 379
Problems in a Democracy 380

Selected Readings 382

Down the Bureaucracy, *Mathew P. Dumont* 384
Backstabbing, Inc., *Peter Chew* 392

CHAPTER 12
Political Parties—Power to the Bosses 399

The Role of Political Parties 399
Parties and Power 400
Development of the Party System 404
Characteristics of Political Parties 409
Parties and Federalism 411
Party Organization 412
Party National Conventions and Campaign Organizations 413
The Party in Government 415
The Party in the Electorate 416
Limits of the Two-Party System 417

Selected Readings 420

The Irrelevance of American Politics, *Allan C. Brownfeld* 422

CHAPTER 13
Political Interest Groups 433

The Concept of Interest Groups 433
What is an Interest Group? 436
Activities of Interest Groups 438
Categorizing Interest Groups 443
Conflicts Between Interest Groups 445
Interest Groups and Power 446
Importance of Group Spirit and Resources 447
Interest Groups and the Public 448
Campaign Financing and Campaign Reform 449
The Lobbyist and His Role 451
Limiting Interest Groups 452
Interest Groups and Abuses 454

Selected Readings 457

Washington Lobby Employs Many Methods to Attain Objectives, *Congressional Quarterly* 458

The Night the Dairymen Produced Grade-A Clout, *Richard Orr* 463

CHAPTER 14
People and Politics 469

Public Opinion 470
Representation for the Lawmaker 471
More Responsive Public Policy 472
Presidential Conduct and Public Opinion 475
Elections and Public Policy 476
Public Opinion and Power 477
American Voter Behavior 479
Role of the Mass Media 483

Selected Readings 487

Campaigns and the New Technology, *James Moriarity* 488

CHAPTER 15
The American Political System: What Direction? 493

Problems in the 1970s 494
Three Themes of American Politics 495
Need for Balance 498
The System Continues 499
Cleansing the Body Politic 500
Power Struggle Continues 502

Appendix 503

A. Voting Data For Presidential Elections 505
B. Data On Government Operations 509
C. Campaign Expenditures 514
D. Population Data 515
E. Composition Of Congress 519
F. The Government Of The United States 522
G. Data Analysis And Statistical Exercise 523
H. United States Constitution 528

Index 549

Introduction

". . . I shall resign the Presidency effective at noon tomorrow. Vice President Ford will be sworn in as President at that hour, in this office." Thus spoke Richard M. Nixon in a televised broadcast to the nation on August 8th, 1974. Gerald Ford was sworn in as 38th President of the United States on August 9th, ending what everyone hoped was the "long nightmare" of America.

The year 1974 was one of the most astonishing years in the history of the United States. For over a two year period, the Watergate affair had occupied the attention of the American people, Congress, and the President. As revelation after revelation unfolded regarding wrongdoings within the executive branch of government, it became increasingly clear that something was amiss with the political system. Once the House Judiciary Committee completed its hearings and voted three articles of impeachment of the President, the country was faced with agonizing months of proceedings involving the highest office in the land. Then, on August 4th, 1974, President Nixon announced that he had not previously revealed his involvement in the cover-up of the Watergate break-in. The reaction was immediate: Republican supporters of the President felt betrayed and announced support for impeachment. The mood of the nation and of Congress made it clear to most that President Nixon had little chance of avoiding impeachment and trial in the Senate. From August 4th until August 9th, the nation and the world watched as one President resigned under pressure and another was sworn in—a peaceful transfer of power that most nations would envy. Most Americans sighed in relief and congratulated themselves on the fact that the Constitution really worked.

Anyone writing about the American political system in 1975 is faced with a difficult task, not only in trying to develop some coherent theme about the momentous events of August, 1974, but also in assessing the changing domestic values, new international issues and environment, and domestic and international economic problems which may prove more damaging than Watergate. One can easily argue that nothing less than an encyclopedia of details about institutions, behavior, and policy will suffice. We suspect, however, that this cannot be done in any single volume. More important, no one can be sure of what will evolve in the decade of the 1970's. No crystal ball of politics is yet available to untangle the web of issues that have characterized the first half of the 1970's.

With these considerations in mind, our purpose here is modest. We hope to develop in the student an intellectual curiosity and inquisitiveness about the workings of the American political system. While accepting the premise that there is a need to understand the formalities of the American political system, we feel that attempts to tell it all can only lead to an uninspiring and uninteresting book. The "heaviness" with which some textbooks address the student completely submerges the dynamics and realities of the American political system. But more important, we feel that an introductory textbook on American politics should not try to provide all of the details, even if it could. Rather it should focus on the realities of the system while providing the student with fundamental tools to assess the system, reference points which balance the formalities of government institutions with the realities and dynamics of politics.

With this in mind, we have focused on the power theme in assessing American politics. Using power as the framework, we will examine the manner in which political actors in the American system acquire, maintain and use power for their own goals and for those associated with the system.

Our explanation of this theme is set forth in Chapter 2. We understand some of the difficulties of defining power and its application to political systems. However we feel that most students understand power, what it can accomplish, and the dynamics behind it, even though they may not subscribe to its intellectual definition and assessment.

Although its focus is on power, the book is generally divided into more-or-less standard chapters, i.e., the presidency, Congress, the

Introduction

judiciary, etc. We feel that the student is probably more comfortable with this type of approach and better able to understand the relationships between the various institutions and political actors. However, the substance of these chapters provides a unique and more realistic perspective within the familiar textbook framework. The text begins with the identification of the fundamental issues facing the American political system, followed by some discussion of the power theme and how political systems can be studied. Subsequently, this power framework is applied to the study of the American political system. The text concludes with identification of trends and prognostications about the future.

In order to provide a number of views and opinions and bring the student into contact with noted authors in the field of American politics, we have included specially selected readings at the end of each chapter. These readings vary from the highly critical to the optimistic. The student should be careful to note that the readings are representative and certainly do not exhaust the kinds of material and viewpoints that exist in the study of American politics. Nevertheless, they are an integral part of the book and should be read as part of each chapter. Not only do the readings give the student an opportunity to sample various views on American politics, but they provide substance to each of the chapters and complement what is provided by the authors of this text. Through serious study of each chapter and the accompanying readings the student will gain a balanced view of the American political system.

A bibliography and some major questions regarding the subject matter are also included in each chapter. We hope that this will help to develop an intellectual curiosity while stimulating the student to engage in more detailed study of the American political system.

Specific answers to current problems or policy alternatives will not necessarily be found. However, we feel that our power perspective provides the basis for explaining what is happening in American society today and suggesting policy directions. For example, although the reasons behind the Watergate affair are not discussed in detail, they are implicit in our power theme and the student will see how such situations can develop. Answers to Watergate are also inherent in our discussion and the student will clearly see where some of them lie. While answers are not necessarily to be found in this textbook, the basis for the search is here.

The Watergate issue is one of the most difficult things to deal with in writing a textbook at this time. Some authors place Watergate in the preface of their book, suggesting that it may well be the context within which American politics should be viewed. Others discuss it in the postscript, assuming that that's exactly what Watergate is—a postscript to American politics. Still others intersperse explanations of Watergate throughout their textbooks, suggesting that it is an inherent part of the American political problem. In our book we do mention Watergate in a number of appropriate places, but there is very little specific discussion of the Watergate issue per se. As already noted, the power theme itself provides a basic understanding of how such affairs can develop.

Nevertheless there is a need to put Watergate in the proper perspective before we begin. Watergate means different things to different people. The repercussions from it have affected and will affect a number of institutions in the political system as well as the behavior of many political actors. No one scholar, politician, journalist, or citizen can possibly foresee the total impact of the Watergate affair. Indeed, there is even disagreement as to when it began, who was involved, and what it included. From our perspective it demonstrates one result of unchecked and unaccountable power. The presidency was used as the basis for expansion of power to cover questionable activities of the executive branch, which are rationalized in the name of national security and law and order. This circumvented the concepts of separation of powers and checks and balances, diminished the power of other political actors and their ability to check presidential power, and in the final analysis disregarded the power and autonomy of the individual.

Although the Watergate issue was intermingled with the problems of the economy in the 1974 Congressional elections, the results of that election could be interpreted as the first major reaction against Watergate by the voters. Virtually all Republican incumbents running to retain office were defeated. The Democrats won sweeping victories in Congress and in state legislatures and governorships. Some observers felt that the election results represented a negative vote against the Republican party and presidential power rather than a positive vote for the Democratic party. Indeed, in an election thought by many to be one of the most important in a number of years, the light voter turnout seemed to indicate a protest vote against the system itself. Nevertheless, a Congress controlled by large majorities of Democrats could prove to be an effective counterbalancing power to a Republican president, and the years 1975 and 1976 could prove to be difficult ones for the person occupying the presidential office.

Watergate was unique only in that it was exposed, publicized, and hopefully, rectified. The aggrandizement of power and its misuse has been a continuing theme in all political systems. In a democracy the

Introduction

problem of power is particularly sensitive, since its misuse or unauthorized acquisition is destructive of the very premise upon which the political system rests—accountability and responsibility of political actors to the individual citizen.

In this book we have tried, both implicitly and explicitly, to portray Watergate as epitomizing a tendency inherent in all power situations. We have tried neither to overlook it nor to consider it from a panic position, but rather to view it as a phenomenon that is always possible in political systems. At this writing it is still not clear what the total impact of the Watergate affair will be—yet students of American politics must appreciate its implications in terms of power, the potential of political actors, and the substance of democratic ideology. At the minimum the Watergate affair has caused and is causing public suspicion and congressional scrutiny of presidential and democratic power. Moreover, the implications are not limited to the executive office, but extend to virtually all political actors and the political process itself. As a result, public scepticism of politics in general has diminished trust in political institutions. On the other hand, the power of the people, both individually and collectively, asserted itself through the political fog and became a primary factor in the attempt at cleansing the body politic. One can only wonder what would have happened to the democratic condition had a security guard not noticed a small strip of telltale adhesive tape dangling from a door of a room at the Watergate apartments in our capital.

In viewing the problems of our political system, we are reminded of the insights of Alexis de Tocqueville, a Frenchman writing over a century ago about the American system.

> Democratic liberty is far from accomplishing all the projects it undertakes with the skill of adroit despotism. But in the end it produces more than any absolute government and, if it does fewer things well, it does a greater number of things. Democracy does not confer the most skillful kind of government upon the people, but it produces that which the most skillful governments are frequently unable to awaken, namely an all pervading and restless activity, a superabundant force, and an energy which is inseparable from it, and which may, under favorable circumstances, beget the most amazing benefits.[1]

Note

1. J. P. Mayer (ed), *Alexis De Tocqueville, Democracy in America* (New York: Anchor Books, 1969), p. 244. Translated by George Lawrence.

Politics and Power
AN INTRODUCTION TO AMERICAN GOVERNMENT

CHAPTER 1
People and Politics: The Prevailing Issues

By the mid-1970s it had become clear to many that the American way of life was undergoing drastic changes. Americans were becoming disenchanted not only with themselves, but with the way the political system was operating. Yet the abundance of material goods and availability of consumer services had never been greater. More Americans were attending school than ever before; the Vietnam War had been brought to an end; significant advances had been made in medicine and technology; more opportunities existed for minority groups; we had gone to the moon and beyond.

Nevertheless, there was an underlying restiveness and suspicion that all was not well with the American system. Most black Americans were still not convinced that they were being treated as full-fledged citizens; women were still struggling for equal rights; American Indians and Spanish-speaking people felt that they were outside the fold of American citizenship; and middle Americans felt that they were paying heavily for the advancement of others. Problems of ecology and economics had become hard and serious issues. Divisions had appeared between the suburbs and the cities, between the poor and the rich, between races, between ethnic groups and, most significantly, between the people and their leaders.

These issues can be termed characteristic of the American political system in the 1970s, although there is vast disagreement about their relative importance. Each of these issues is directly associated with the power and autonomy of the individual and his relationship and impact on the political system. Once we can identify and understand these fundamental issues, we can better comprehend the realities of the American political system and the character of the American people.

The Meaning of a Democratic Society

A democratic society is based on accepted ideological beliefs, and customs rooted in historical precedent and law. These accepted beliefs presuppose the existence of certain basic values and procedures which form a civic culture based on individual worth, individual power, and reasonable, rational men. Moreover, a democratic society implies the participation of the people in the political system and the ultimate responsibility and accountability of all public officials to the people. Although the phrase "power to the people" has become a cliché, it is nevertheless the essence of a democratic political system. If the people's will is expressed in a meaningful way, the individual does have an impact on the political system and on the politicians and employees of the government. That is, the individual does have power, and the people do have collective power, not only to elect representatives but to make officials, whether elected or administrative, responsible and accountable to them.

The American Ideology

Some observers of American government feel that it is basically nonideological because it has never embraced a hard and fast political creed such as orthodox Marxism, fascism, or Maoism. They point out that the mainstream of politics in America has been characterized by compromise, bargaining, vagueness of political programs, and a series of loose coalitions—all of which are disdained by ideological political creeds.

Others have taken a more lenient view, defining ideology as a system that uses abstract ideas and principles to organize political views into relatively logical patterns. Philip Converse, in his studies of the American electorate, has demonstrated that most people's political beliefs and preferences are organized in a relatively incoherent manner. Their views are a collection of beliefs learned at home, through the media, and in different institutional settings from the public school to the military.[1]

The components of the American ideology include egalitarianism, that is, the belief in the equality of all persons, and liberalism, or, to put it another way, a belief in nonelitism. The American ideology presents many contradictions. The strongly held belief that "all men are created equal" seems odd in light of the nation's history of treatment of minorities. The strong influence of a belief in a supreme deity is coupled with an equally strongly held conviction that there should be a separation of church and state.

American Democracy

American democracy is an outgrowth of 200 years of history. It differs from English democracy, although many of its roots go directly back to the parliamentary system. It is particularly complex, particularly contradictory and unwieldy, and particularly American.

Defined literally, democracy means rule by the people. Pericles, an Athenian statesman, declared: "Our constitution is called a democracy, because it is in the hands not of the few, but of the many." Obviously, it is not possible for 200 million Americans to state their position on each issue of government. For this reason there evolved the present-day system known as "representative democracy." The term simply means that leaders are elected to speak for and represent the people. Implied in this system is the concept of majority rule. Hence, all are free to vote but the person who gets the most votes wins the election. The winner then represents all the people. It is his responsibility in a truly democratic system to represent the rights and views of the minority as well as the majority, and, when necessary, to protect those rights.

"All men are created equal," says the Constitution of the United States. Each is recognized to have basic rights such as freedom of speech, religion, the press, and assembly; the right to vote; and the right of dissent from majority opinion. The importance of human dignity is a basic concept of American democracy.

At this time in American history, these important goals are still far from the realities of political life. Too often majority rule dictates federal and state policy. The plight of the poor and of the minorities, and the enormity of Watergate amply illustrate the shortcomings of the system. President Kennedy declared in a speech at Amherst College in 1963, "men who create power make an indispensable contribution to the Nation's greatness, but the men who question power make a contribution just as indispensable."[2]

It is our belief that the power approach of this text will enable the reader to understand the basis of power in the American system and how this power is used to achieve various purposes. Moreover, we feel that this perspective will show the realities of the American political system.

The Individual and the Government

The day-to-day functioning of our democratic system rests on a number of basic social and cultural assumptions that have been passed on from generation to generation. The American people have been unique in their assumption that the government and its elected officials have the best interests of the populace at heart and, when necessary, will protect the rights of the individual. Each year millions of Americans voluntarily pay their income taxes, register for military service, and arrange to be available for jury duty. The government has had to do little to coerce the people into compliance with these duties. Implicit in the people's support is their belief that they have control over their government and that it is operating efficiently for all the citizens.

Today the old assumptions of an honest government run by responsible, rational men are under investigation. The influence of money interests is thought by many to be more important than the will of the people. Thanks to the tremendous advances in mass communications, especially television, millions of Americans are questioning the quality of life in their country and the role of government. On any given night the six o'clock news may document evidence of irresponsible use of our natural resources, devious behavior by elected officials, or the apparently rapid decay of American cities.

These changes are reshaping the character of our political system. Indeed, some would argue that the essence of the democratic civic culture and the role of the individual have been significantly diminished, and that the individual is powerless now to affect his own political system.

Thomas Jefferson wrote, "to secure these rights, Governments are instituted among men, deriving their just powers from the consent of the governed." Abraham Lincoln put it another way: "Government of the people, by the people and for the people." These are obviously ideals; in the best of all possible worlds all power is not going to be derived from all the people. Nevertheless, as we study the American political system, we will investigate whether or not the individual can still effect responsibility and accountability of his elected officials.

We shall look into the various ways the individual can influence government. There are the established methods of effecting change, such as voting, activity in political parties, organizing interest groups (there is even an association to put trousers on animals), and the marshalling of public opinion. Another method that has been used more frequently in the sixties and seventies is direct action, such as sit-ins, riots, and assassinations. No one would argue the impact of these methods; we shall discuss the causes of such extreme behavior and try to assess its meaning for the future.

Changing Society and the Relevance of Democracy

We are now in what many economists call the postindustrial stage of economic growth in the United States. This means that the replacement of "human power" with machine power has all but been accomplished and we are now searching for meaningful occupations for the mass of citizens who formerly would have found employment in labor. The result has been a massive educational system, increased interdependence within the society, and a lessening of the importance of the individual, as it is now all but impossible to support oneself strictly off the land in an urbanized society. We are witnessing the shaping of a society based on a highly technological orientation. It is a highly integrated society with unlimited alternatives and problems, and with a potential for excellence and for self-destruction that has never before been possible.

It has been predicted, based upon population trends, that by the year 2000 there will be 300 million Americans. The American born in 1950, when the population was just over 150 million, might see the population of the nation double in his lifetime. It should be remembered, and pondered, that the population increase in the United States will not approach that of foreign countries. As of today, the United States is at a zero population growth rate, but that will not have any effect on the growth of population for some time.[3]

It is of some interest to reflect on the current composition of the American population. There are 22.6 million black Americans, 47 percent of whom live in the North and West. Six cities have more blacks than whites. The importance of black voters in the cities of New York, Los Angeles, Philadelphia, Detroit, Chicago, and Cleveland cannot be ignored. The United States is not predominantly white, Anglo-Saxon Protestant; in actuality a majority of Americans stem from other than Anglo-Saxon stock.[4] There are 67 million Protestants, 48 million Catholics, and 6 million Jews.[5] The political persuasions of these people do not necessarily follow any group affiliation, although some patterns cannot be denied. There are blacks for Wallace and for Cleaver, whites for Kennedy and for Goldwater, Jews for Rockefeller and for Nader, and Catholics for Reagan and for Ford. While the fabled "melting pot" of America may not have really brought all the different peoples of the country together, in politics, perhaps more than in any other arena, there is a "melting" of different peoples for common interests.

Who Are We?*

104.3 million	females
98.9 million	males
17.2 million	under five years
20.1 million	sixty-five and over
177.7 million	white
25.5 million	nonwhite
108.5 million	married, divorced, or widowed
140 million[1]	old enough to vote
7 million	in college
52.5 million	in other schools
36.8 million	white-collar workers
27.5 million	blue-collar workers
149.3 million	urban dwellers
40 million	homeowners

*Based on the 1970 census.
[1] Data as of 1972; includes nearly 11 million new voters enfranchised by the Twenty-sixth Amendment, ratified in 1971, which lowered the voting age to 18.
Source: U.S. Bureau of the Census.

Now we must ask ourselves the question: Are the values, perceptions, and differing socialization processes of this vastly varied group of people compatible with a democratic political system? Is a political system based on a document written two hundred years ago relevant to a highly technological, highly mobile, impersonal society? What happens to a system that once prized individual worth when faced with a social system that values technology, control, organization and nonautonomous man? It appears that in such a society politicians and government are responsive to power, in the sense of possession of control over others.

For centuries the concept of power has fascinated man. Montesquieu, an eighteenth-century French philosopher, stated in *The Spirit of the Laws*: "Every man who has power is impelled to abuse it." Lord Acton, the British politician and historian said a hundred years later that "power tends to corrupt and absolute power corrupts absolutely." V. O. Key, a noted political scientist, has observed that power cannot be "poured into a keg, stored, and drawn upon as the need arises."[6] Power, Key writes, is relational—that is, it involves the interactions between the person who exercises power and those whom his actions affect. Finally, it is apparent to all that man, from the beginning of his search for comradeship and society, has found it necessary to accept rulers. Rulers make the difficult decisions for us and in effect decide who gets what, when wars are waged, and the level of taxation. Sometimes we allow certain individuals to govern because they hold a certain office or have a particular blood line. (Note the crowned heads of Europe and, in America, the impact of certain families such as the Rockefellers, Goldwaters, and Kennedys.) To this degree power follows the office.

We shall observe in this book the impact of power on the institutions of government, on the individual as he tries to make his government responsive, and on the ongoing process of change that affects our government daily.

What America Thinks of Itself

In a best seller of a few years ago, Charles A. Reich, a Yale professor, wrote:

> It must be understood in light of the betrayal and loss of the American dream, the rise of the corporate state of the 1960's, and the way in which that state dominates, exploits and ultimately destroys both nature and man. Its rationality must be measured against the insanity of existing reason—reason that makes impoverishment, dehumanization, and even war appear to be logical and necessary. Its logic must be read from the fact that Americans have lost control of the machinery of their society, and only new values and a new culture can restore control.[7]

Reich claimed that a new revolution was coming in America, a revolution that would be non-violent, a revolution that would reshape the culture to return power and autonomy to the individual.

Arthur M. Schlesinger, the noted historian, is not so optimistic. Writing in 1968, Schlesinger stated:

> The crisis of American confidence comes in part from a growing sense of the disassociation between ideas and power. On the one hand, the spread of violence challenges the old belief in the efficacy of reason; on the other hand, new structures brought into existence by modern industrial society intensify the feelings of individual impotence. The great organizations which tower over us seem to have a life and momentum of their own; they consume human beings and human ideas as they

consume steel and electricity. Above all, the accelerating pace of social and technological change heightens the impression of a world out of human control. We all today are constrained to see ourselves as helpless victims of the velocity of history.[8]

Bill Moyers, a noted journalist, writing in 1971, concluded his book with the following:

> There is a myth that the decent thing has almost always prevailed in America when the issues were clearly put to the people. It may not always happen. I found among people an impatience, an intemperance, an isolation which invites opportunists who promise too much and castigate too many. And I came back with questions. Can the country be wise if it hears no wisdom? Can it be tolerant if it sees no tolerance? Can these people I met escape their isolation if no one listens?[9]

Others would suggest that all of the tensions in society, the frustrations, the boredom with work so beautifully portrayed by Studs Terkel in his book, *Working,* the feeling of alienation and disassociation from government and purpose, are simply signs of a dynamic, evolving, participatory democracy. They see the internal clashes as clashes of ideas; they perceive the disagreements as those of concerned responsible people; they see the sporadic violence of our cities and schools as attempts to readjust the system.

Even among those who are critical of themes emerging within American democracy, there is recognition of the necessity for internal struggle to maintain the essence of democracy.

Seymour Martin Lipset has written:

> Only the give and take of a free society's internal struggles offers some guarantee that the products of the society will not accumulate in the hands of a few power holders, and that men may develop and bring up their children without fear of persecution. And, as we have seen, democracy requires institutions which support conflict and disagreement as well as those which sustain legitimacy and consensus.[10]

Freedom and Power of the Individual

At the base of any discussion of the nature of American society is the question of freedom and liberty. In a democratic society it is presumed that the individual will pursue his political goals through a number of activities such as voting, pressure groups, certain voluntary associations, and financial contributions. Thus the individual is able to exercise his freedom and liberty through participation in the political process. Ideally the individual is autonomous in his political activity. We assume that he does not have to deliver his vote to hold a job or to be esteemed in his community. In reality, of course, the individual operates within a cultural setting that values the historical importance of our governmental institutions and strives to maintain a consistency and stability in government.

This balance of the rights and freedom of the individual with the needs of the society is not a scientific balance. It is a balance of values, perceptions, and socialization processes through which the individual's political power reinforces the political system. At the same time the consistency and stability of the system reinforces the political power of the individual. This give and take can be achieved only as long as individual interests coincide to a degree with those of the political system. It is here that the science of politics gives way to the art of politics. To achieve and maintain such a balance is the responsibility of political leaders.

Does American society have the necessary values, perceptions, and socialization processes to operate a democratic political system? Does the meaning of democracy need to be reassessed in light of American experience in a highly technological era and mass society? These are fundamental questions that have become particularly relevant at this time to the American political system.

The Political Climate

Most Americans felt that "something is deeply wrong in America today," according to a Harris survey in late 1973. Of over 1500 Americans surveyed, 55 percent felt that "people running the country don't really care what happens to you." Sixty-one percent agreed that "what you think doesn't count any more." Moreover, the survey indicated that there was a significant gap between the way ordinary citizens saw the country's problems and the way government officials viewed them. This survey clearly showed that a majority of American people were convinced of their impotency—of their lack of power to change or influence the political system.

What caused this? There is no single answer. However, a number of events and issues may have been partially responsible for this feeling of helplessness. The agonies of the Vietnam War and the subsequent adjustments required in the post-Vietnam era, reaction to the Watergate affair, the resignation of Vice President Agnew, the continued pressures on the presidential office, and exposures of corruption and political manipulation in federal, state, and local government —all of these showed the American people their relative isolation from the real centers of political power.

Although the Democratic party claimed an impressive victory in the 1974 congressional elections, most observers felt that it was not an extraordinary one. More important, however, was the light voter turnout—only two out of every five Americans eligible to vote actually voted. Observers claimed that this was a sign of voter apathy, but many Americans felt frustrated and helpless to do anything about the system. At best the light turnout could be construed as a protest not only against Watergate, the economy, and the Republican president, but against the entire system. Even some Democrats cautioned that the vote was not a clear mandate for their party but rather a negative vote against the Republicans and the system. Perhaps a clearer diagnosis can be made in the 1976 presidential elections. In any event, there did not seem to be much joy regarding the results of the election, only a wait-and-see attitude.

In this text we will study the implications of these events and issues with respect to political attitude and the political system. At this point we are primarily concerned with cultural and social factors that created an environment which led to political attitudes and perceptions of impotency by both the individual and groups. These social and cultural considerations go much deeper than the post-Vietnam or Watergate era. They stem directly from the nature of American post-industrial society.

Sacred vs. Secular Society

Sociologists and psychologists long ago recognized the unique values and individual behavior patterns and expectations associated with a modern urbanized industrial society. Such a society is usually based on a secular value system as contrasted to the sacred value system of a traditional, nonurbanized, nonindustrial society.

When we speak of sacred values, we are not necessarily referring to religion, but to those values that stem more or less directly from family and kinship relationships. Such values stress moral and ethical absolutes and give the individual a clear understanding of his expected behavior and social role. These relationships are reinforced by a web of close kinship ties and obligations. Priority is given to tradition and custom within the context of religious duties and sacrifices clearly designed to maintain the status quo. Although there is little social mobility in such societies, there is general individual and social contentment. The individual knows his place in the world and accepts as natural those forces that he cannot understand; he knows what to expect from those around him as well as from the environment.

In a society based on a secular value system, on the other hand, the socialization process is influenced by a large number of forces outside of the immediate family and kinship relationship. Moreover, the values and perceptions in such a society are those associated with achievement, competition, and a scientific orientation that stresses man's control and manipulation of his environment.

This preoccupation with competition is not a new American trait. In 1835, a Frenchman and noted social observer, Alexis de Tocqueville, visited America. His book, *Democracy in America,* has endured as a classic statement on Americans for over one hundred years.

On Americans and competition de Tocqueville wrote:

> It is strange to see with what feverish ardor the Americans pursue their own welfare, and to watch the vague dread that constantly torments them lest they should not have chosen the shortest path which may lead to it. . . . They have swept away the privileges of some of their fellow-creatures which stood in their way; but they have opened the door to *universal competition;* the barrier has changed its shape rather than its position.[11]

In the same vein, Francis J. Grund, a German visitor, discusses the American addiction to "business":

> Active occupation is not only the principal source of their happiness and the foundation of their national greatness, but they are absolutely wretched without it, and instead of the *dolce far niente* [pleasure of idleness], know but the horrors of idleness. . . . the Americans pursue business with unabated vigor till the very hour of death.[12]

Finally, a statement by Gabriel Almond about American values:

> The American is primarily concerned with "private" values, as distinguished from social-group, political, or religious-moral values. His concern with private, worldly success is his most absorbing aim. . . . The "attachment" of the American to his private values is characterized by an extreme degree of competitiveness. American culture tends to be atomistic rather than corporate, and the pressure of movement "upward" toward achievement is intense.[13]

The highly specialized nature of such a society requires a host of special economic skills, social relationships, social organizations, and political institutions. In other words, this type of society is also a highly bureaucratized and organizationally oriented one.

Values and perceptions, particularly in the adolescent and later years, are significantly influenced by mass media and peer groups, to which the family is clearly subordinated. Indeed, the ties and obligations to family and relatives are weak and in some instances nonexistent. Such ties are replaced by mass media imagery and peer group expectations.

Alienation of the Individual

What does all of this mean in terms of power, the individual and the political system? Within the individual, anxiety, alienation, and frustration are created; concern and fear arise because of the continual societal stress on success, competition, and social mobility. The lack of an absolute value system, and the shifting expectations regarding social behavior, create a degree of uncertainty and unpredictability. These in turn reinforce the concern and preoccupation with the achievement of individual interests. Moreover, such anxiety also stimulates the need to do something, to take some action to alleviate prevailing fears. The nature of mass society, with its powerful organizational orientation and bureaucratic structure underlying the political system, i.e., "the establishment," creates a feeling in the individual of isolation from his own political system. The centralized and overpowering nature of the political system leads to a sense of futility and powerlessness in many Americans. Industrial society tends to subordinate man's sense of self-identity to the increasing degree of specialization, and requires the individual to play a series of separate roles.

De Tocqueville commented in 1835:

> In America, the majority raises formidable barriers around the liberty of opinion; within these barriers, an author may write what he pleases; but woe to him if he goes beyond them. Not that he is in danger of an *auto-da-fé*, but he is exposed to continued obloquy and persecution. His political career is closed forever, since he has offended the only authority which is able to open it.... The public therefore, among a democratic people, has a singular power, which aristocratic nations cannot conceive; for it does not persuade others to its beliefs, but it imposes them and makes them permeate the thinking of every one by a sort of enormous pressure of the mind of all upon the individual intelligence.... I think that democratic communities have a natural taste for freedom; left to themselves, they will seek it, cherish it, and view any privation of it with regret. But for equality, their passion is ardent, insatiable, inces-

sant, invincible; they call for equality in freedom; and if they cannot obtain that, they still call for equality in slavery.[14]

In essence, the individual feels he is isolated from the total system or, as David Reisman has suggested, a part of "the lonely crowd."[15] Indeed, the sheer impersonality of the political system may motivate individuals to psychologically withdraw from involvement. Combining these characteristics of anxiety and alienation with the modern environment, the political system creates a sense of frustration in the individual, a feeling that he cannot achieve his values in the existing political system. It is this feeling of frustration to which Schlesinger refers when he states:

> Today as our nation grows more centralized and our energy more concentrated, as our inner tensions grow more desperate and our frustrations in our own land and in the world more embittered, we can no longer regard hatred and violence as accidents and aberrations, as nightmares which will pass away when we awake.[16]

There is a direct connection between these individual factors and the value of conformity that is stressed in both our social and political systems. There seems to be a general feeling that one cannot get anywhere unless he conforms to prevailing social expectations and established rules of the game. Similarly, to succeed politically one must conform to mainstream politics and prevailing values. Indeed, an implicit value in a democratic system is conformity. Egalitarianism implies the "sameness" of individuals. This stress on conformity finds its way into the social and economic system and further diminishes self-identity and individual autonomy or individual power.

Manipulation of the Individual

The loss of power and the diminishment of the individual role in the political system create a condition in which individuals can be manipulated for political ends by a combination of organizational skills and technology. This was clearly demonstrated in the book, *The Selling of the President 1968*.

Here, Joe McGinniss comments on the need for packaging the candidate:

> Let's face it, a lot of people think Nixon is dull. Think he's a bore. . . . They look at him as the kind of kid who always carried a bookbag. Who was forty-two years old the day he was born. They figure other kids got

footballs for Christmas. Nixon got a briefcase and he loved it. He'd always have his homework done and he'd never let you copy.

Now you put him on television, you've got a problem right away. He's a funny-looking guy. He looks like somebody hung him up in a closet overnight and he jumps out in the morning with his suit all bunched up and starts running around saying, "I want to be President." I mean this is how he strikes some people. That's why these shows are important. To make them forget all that.[17]

In 1966, Governor Rockefeller of New York hired an advertising agency to bolster his campaign. Myron McDonald, of the Tinker Agency, commented:

> The agency I work for, as you know, is a consumer goods agency. We peddle Alka-Seltzer, Buick automobiles, Coca-Cola, and so forth. And until 13 or 14 months ago none of us had any political experience. We looked at the Governor in the only way we knew how to look at him; that is as a consumer product. Now, if you don't like to think of him as Alka-Seltzer, why not think of him as a Buick. It's perfectly all right.
>
> But we went to our first meeting and they gave us the results of the current poll, and we all went back home feeling as though we had been appointed purser of the Titanic because the first poll showed that 21 percent of the people would vote for Governor Rockefeller and 79 percent would vote for someone else. It is not apocryphal that the pollster told the Governor that he couldn't be elected dog-catcher. I was there and heard him say that. Of course we're fortunate that he wasn't running for dog-catcher.[18]

The mass media are the transmitters of values and thus become instruments for socialization and setting of political behavior patterns. Through them the individual, consciously or unconsciously, can be placed at the mercy of skilled political organizers, political leaders, special interest groups, and political parties. These institutions and instruments, of course, are part of a democratic system, but in today's environment the individual voice can easily be overwhelmed by organizational and technological dominance. The individual is likely to feel a loss of control over his own destiny. When this occurs there is a concomitant loss of confidence in the political system through which the average American previously exercised his power.

The mass media gave the public deep insights into the operation of the political system in connection with the Watergate affair. Thus Watergate may well have served as a catalytic agent, bringing many Americans face-to-face for the first time, with the stark realities of one aspect of the political system. The question is: Was Watergate typical of politics as normally conducted, or was it an example of extreme use of power?

Political apathy may arise on the assumption that the political system cannot achieve anything for the individual. On the other hand, the environment itself may very well diminish rationality and reasonableness and lead to extremes of action, as exemplified by the violent attacks on public servants in the 1960s. In any case, a feeling of hopelessness is created, a conviction that one cannot achieve anything in the existing political system. The individual may feel that his very existence and well-being are dependent upon forces over which he has absolutely no control.

Dissatisfaction With the Political System

These attitudes ultimately lead to skepticism and cynicism regarding the political system and its officials. In essence, the political system is perceived as operating for the special interests of certain groups, with minimum responsibility to the people as a whole. The credibility and legitimacy of the political system, elected officials, and administrators are diminished. This is hardly an environment that fosters a democratic condition.

Even if one does not accept this view of American society, there appears to be a general consensus that something is decidedly wrong in the body politic. There is a restiveness and a general feeling of unfulfilled promises, and the political system and the major political actors bear the brunt of these criticisms.

In this book we will discuss the importance of the political system remaining legitimate only insofar as it conforms to the perceived ideology and goals of the mass of people. The ideology of the political system must encompass not only the ideals of the system, but also recognize the realities. The gap between the realities, that is, the way the political system actually works, and the ideals, or the way it is supposed to work, must not be so great as to make it unlikely that the system will ever achieve the ideals. Democracy assumes individual worth, autonomy, and power. But the realities of the American political system seem to indicate that power belongs to special interests and selected individuals, with the mass of people restricted to exercising their options once every four years. In the minds of many Americans, therefore, it may be difficult to reconcile their ideas of democracy and democratic society and their increasing knowledge with respect to the actualities of the political system.

We should recognize that this condition need not have been brought about by deliberate scheming of certain political actors. There is much to suggest that America's rush to a better life in terms of material goods has brought with it unanticipated changes and demands on the political and social systems. Now, in retrospect, we can see what has occurred—and many Americans conclude that they do not like what they see.

Power Elite vs. Pluralism

There are two prevalent theories on the basic form of American government today. These are the power elite argument and the pluralist argument.

The power elite argument holds that the distribution of power and wealth in America involves a small, closely knit group of individuals who wield enormous influence in the areas of government and business. The power elite includes politicians, directors of large corporations, military leaders, and other well-placed, wealthy, influential people. According to this viewpoint, first developed by the sociologist C. Wright Mills, the power held by Congress, the courts, and the bureaucracy is not important or decisive on essential matters.[19]

The pluralists argue that political power is rather widely dispersed throughout the society. They claim that power is vested in many conflicting groups that come together in the political arena for the purpose of compromise. Power is never held for long by one faction and the result, according to the pluralists, is a constant give-and-take of different interest groups.

While it is quite likely that both theories have merit, it would seem that power vested in the elite is able to assert itself more quickly and directly in our system.

Potential for the Political System

As we will suggest in this book, the operation of the political system rests primarily on the power of political actors. This is not necessarily an evil—indeed one can argue that the operation of a democratic political system must rest on the existence of some kind of political elite.

Problems stem from this type of system, however, when the activities of political actors become increasingly isolated from the interests and power of individuals. The effective operation of a democratic political system must link individual interests and power of the people to the actions and power of their representatives. Only in this way can individual autonomy be maintained while insuring the stability of the political system. More important, this is the essence of legitimacy in a democratic political system.

The American political system has always been characterized by elected officials and government employees who have acquired power, who attempt to maintain this power, and who ultimately attempt to expand it. What has diminished, is the individual's autonomy and power as a countervailing force to all of the actors of the political system. This power must be expanded and reinforced to insure that politicians and the political system remain within the realm of established policies, which must give priority to individual autonomy and power.

In our assessment of political actors and focus on the power thesis, we will demonstrate the openness of the American political system and the diffusiveness and decentralization of power. We will also show that the political elite is not a closed one; there is significant mobility into and out of political power, providing democratic cleansing action for political leadership. Moreover, the power of the individual remains usable, since all political leaders must ultimately face the nation for reelection.

If attitudes and behavior of the people were to continue along the paths of the "lonely crowd"—apathy, frustration, anxiety, fear, and alienation—then the democratic condition would quickly decay into an authoritarian environment, bringing with it authoritarian politics. In the American political system, the inbred values still stress the worth of the individual and a sufficient number of politicians, administrators, and other political actors still accept individual worth and dignity as the basis for any system. In the early 1970s, there appeared deep stirrings of these values and a rekindled desire to do something about the political system. Rather than accepting the "lonely crowd" attitude, there may be new demands to reshape democracy and provide it with a dynamism that fits the American industrial society. The fundamental issue is whether the individual can restore his autonomy (and ultimately his power) in a political system that has shifted the balance of power to corporate structures, organized special interest groups, and a massive bureaucracy—not to mention political "fat cats" who use money as political power. Among other things, the revelations of Watergate, combined with the general movement toward a more egalitarian society, have produced a volatile mixture. The individual's role in his own political system is at a critical point that will determine whether the system will recapture the humanistic values of democracy while restoring the power of the individual, or whether a *Watergate syndrome* will become imbedded in our system.

Notes

1. See for example, Philip E. Converse, "The Nature of Belief Systems in Mass Publics" in William J. Crofty (ed.), *Public Opinion and Politics: A Reader* (New York: Holt, Rinehart and Winston, Inc., 1970), pp. 129-155.
2. John F. Kennedy, "Remarks at Amherst College," October 26, 1963, in *Public Papers of the Presidents of the United States, John F. Kennedy, 1963* (Washington, D.C.: U.S. Government Printing Office, 1964), p. 816.
3. U.S. Bureau of the Census, *Current Population Reports,* Population Estimates, Series P-25, No. 493, December 1972 (Washington, D.C.: U.S. Government Printing Office, 1972), p. 1. Totals are maximum projected estimates of population.
4. See Ben J. Wattenberg and Richard Scammon, *This U.S.A.*, (Garden City, N.Y.: Doubleday, 1965), pp. 45-46.
5. The Census Bureau does not ask the religion of Americans in the Decennial Census, which is taken every ten years in years that end in zero, but religious groups estimate their own membership. These are round figures based on the *Yearbook of American Churches, 1972* and *The 1973 World Almanac.* Total for Protestants includes only denominations with membership of over one million.
6. V.O. Key, Jr., *Politics, Parties, and Pressure Groups,* 4th ed. (New York: Thomas Y. Crowell Company, 1958), p. 5.
7. Charles A. Reich, *The Greening of America* (New York: Bantam Books, 1971), pp. 2-3.
8. Arthur M. Schlesinger, Jr., *The Crisis of Confidence* (New York: Bantam Books, 1969), p. 41.
9. Bill Moyers, *Listening to America* (New York: Dell Publishing, 1972), p. 377.
10. Seymour Martin Lipset, *Political Man* (Garden City, N.Y.: Doubleday, Anchor Books, 1963), p. 439.
11. Alexis de Tocqueville, *Democracy in America,* ed. J. P. Mayer (Garden City, N.Y.: Doubleday, Anchor Books, 1969), p. 536.
12. Francis J. Grund, *The Americans in Their Moral, Social and Political Relations* (New York: A. M. Kelley, 1971. Reprint of 1837 edition), pp. 202-204.
13. Gabriel A. Almond, *The American People and Foreign Policy* (New York: Harcourt, Brace and Company, 1950), p. 48.
14. de Tocqueville, p. 255.
15. David Reisman, *The Lonely Crowd* (New Haven: Yale University Press, 1961). Abridged Edition.
16. Schlesinger, p. 26.
17. Joe McGinniss, *The Selling of the President 1968* (New York: Trident Press, 1969), p. 103.
18. Public Broadcast Laboratory interview, November 10, 1967.
19. C. Wright Mills, *The Power Elite* (New York: Oxford University Press, 1956).

Selected Readings

In this chapter we have identified a number of major issues facing the American political system. These range from the effects of Watergate and the relevance of American ideology to issues of everyday living. This theme is expanded upon by Burnham in the first reading. He is convinced that beneath the surface of American politics there is a fundamental crisis that goes beyond the headlines of today. Tracing some of the developing problems throughout our history, Burnham believes that a number of "revolutions" have taken and are taking place, fostering a search for new values. He believes that this will culminate in a distinctly different political and social system by the end of the twentieth century. Indeed, he argues that the present struggle within our political system is "for the American soul."

Newsweek magazine conducted an extensive poll late in 1973 to determine "What America Thinks of Itself." The second reading shows the results. The findings generally support Burnham's views: A majority of people felt that there was something deeply wrong in America. Moreover, the poll identified a gap between the views of leaders and those of the average American regarding the working of the political system. The people were more willing to take some kind of action to try to correct what they felt was wrong. This could be interpreted as a reflection of the lack of confidence in the system, or, more optimistically, as a sign of increasing political awareness and involvement. In any case, it suggested a changed political environment and changing political attitudes.

Congresswoman Shirley Chisholm is the first black woman to be elected to Congress in the history of the United States. Writing in 1971, she touches upon many social issues. Congresswoman Chisholm is particularly forceful in supporting equal rights for women. She notes the need for a broad reawakening to the problems of equal rights, especially for the black woman, and black people in general. "The goal though must be more than political freedom. It must be more than economic freedom. It must be total freedom to build a world-wide society predicated on the positive values of human life."

The final reading is from *U.S. News and World Report*, and contains interviews with four recently naturalized U.S. citizens. Because of their experience with other governments, they were able to provide interesting insights on the American system as judged from different standards. In general, they felt that there were many good things about America that overshadowed the bad. The feeling of freedom and social mobility was a common theme in all of the interviews. According to this article, Americans tend to be too pessimistic about their system. Those interviewed felt that Americans ought to be thankful for the way their political system operates in comparison with foreign systems. In light of the peaceful transition of power from Richard Nixon to Gerald Ford in August 1974, perhaps these new U.S. citizens were right about the positive aspects of our system.

In what direction is America going? What kind of political and social system will develop in our lifetime? What kind of political system will there be in America when you reach your middle twenties? We hope that as you study the American political system, this book will help you understand how to assess these questions. Indeed, you may even find some answers.

1.1

Crisis of American Political Legitimacy

WALTER DEAN BURNHAM

The American political system was organized and achieved its concrete behavioral reality under social, economic and international conditions which have ceased to exist in our time. The whole system is based upon several primordial elements, elements which may well be sine qua non for its survival in recognizable form. The first of these was a belief, revolutionary in its time and for many decades thereafter, in the inherent equality and dignity of the individual. Associated with this was a political machinery developed by the founders which explicitly denied that sovereign power existed anywhere within it in domestic affairs, while concentrating such sovereignty in the president so far as the country's relations with foreign powers were concerned. This denial of internal sovereignty is of course enshrined in two key elements of the Constitution: the separation of powers at the center and the centrifugal force of federalism.

Thirdly, the whole enterprise was based upon the development and maintenance of a very broad consensus within society on fundamentals involving the place of organized religion in the political system and the place of private initiative and the private sector generally in the political economy. Without such a consensus the cumbersome machinery would have collapsed; but that is another way of saying that sovereign power in the state develops historically in response to fundamental conflicts among sharply discrete social groups over control of society through politics. It represents the victory of one coalition of such groups over another and the positive use of state power to consolidate the control of the new group over the social system—for example, the bourgeoisie over pre-modern feudal and clerical elements.

In the American case, we find one spectacular example of this in the Civil War. And it is precisely here for a short season that we find the collapse of the Constitution and the development of sovereign power to an astonishing degree. The episode

Published by permission of Transaction, Inc. from Transaction, Vol. 10 # 1, Nov/Dec 1972, Copyright (©) 1972, from Transaction, Inc.

was temporary, though leaving some permanent residues, but it is also exceptionally instructive. Otherwise, however, the social consensus survived, changing in emphasis and shape as the society was transformed by industrialization. This consensus was essentially the ideology of liberal capitalism, coupled after the 1870s by an increasingly explicit racism which justified the reduction of the southern black to a limbo halfway between the slavery of old and genuine citizenship.

Sovereignty and Syndicalism

When we find ourselves in a political crisis, it is extraordinary to see how often older theorists of American politics—particularly those steeped in a juristic-institutional tradition—can illuminate the problem. An individualist, liberal-capitalist theory and practice of politics assumes by definition that the state, and above that the public, has no collective business to transact apart from the most marginal welfare and police-keeping functions. In turn this presupposes a socioeconomic system which is not dominated by collectivist concentrations of power. It also presupposes, far more than we have realized until recently, that American involvement with the outside world is episodic rather than permanent: a lack of external empire and the power structures which go with imperial world involvement.

In 1941 the late E. S. Corwin made precisely this point and coupled it with a warning for the future of American politics—and of constitutional liberty in this country, as that term had hitherto been understood. He identified two changes in the contexts of American politics which had arisen since 1929 and whose implications profoundly disturbed him. The first, of course, was the emergence of a permanent federal presence in the private sector necessitated by the collapse of free-market capitalism in the Great Depression. The second was the permanent mobilization of the United States in world politics—in a context of acute military threat.

Naturally, Corwin approached these issues from a juristic perspective which many today would describe as conservative if not reactionary. The same is even more true of the warnings which Herbert Hoover continually issued in the 1930s about the dangers of the kind of corporatist syndicalism which the New Deal was bringing into being. Yet in our own day such warnings may well be taken more and more seriously. While we cannot review all of these issues, we can give some indication of their relevance to the current crisis of political legitimacy which grips the United States.

We have argued that the American political system was set up according to a certain conception of liberty. which denied the normal existence of sovereign governmental power in domestic affairs. This implied the lack of need for permanent public regulation of or intervention into the private sector. Yet during industrialization this sector had elaborated one of the great collectivist organizations of all time—the business corporation; and the corporation became and remains the dominant form of social organization in the United States. It was not long after the turn of this century that the leaders of corporate capitalism discovered the uses of public authority to achieve some rationalization of their competitive activities and to avoid some of the more ruinous implications of truly free competition.

But the Great Depression which began in 1929 revealed that such marginal public-sector efforts were not enough even to protect the basic interests of entrepreneurs and management, not to mention those of the rest of society. So permanent public-sector involvement came with the New Deal but it came without any basic change in the political system. That system remained, as before, the kind of essentially non-sovereign collection of middle-class economic and political feudalities which it had been since the end of Reconstruction.

Public Interest Liberalism

The interaction between this archaic political system and an overwhelming demand, which it could not resist without courting social and political revolution, produced the hybrid phenomenon known as "interest-group liberalism." This in turn promptly received an ideological support base from political scientists and others who celebrated the virtues of pluralism and veto groups in the political process and of incremental change in policy outputs. Yet there were two significant problems in this rewriting of Locke, this recasting of atomistic individualism from the level of the individual to the level of the group. The first was that such a huge proportion of the American people were not actually included in the new groupist system. They belonged to no groups with political leverage, and—if not subject to outright disfranchisement and political persecution, as were the southern blacks—were excluded from the most elemental mode of participation, that is, voting.

Throughout the New Deal and down to the present time, these excluded people formed not less than two-fifths of the total adult population—concentrated, of course, at the bottom of the socioeconomic system. As the late E. E. Schattschneider pithily observed, "The flaw in the pluralist heaven is that the heavenly choir sings with a markedly upper-class accent." It is virtually impossible to overstate the importance of this steep class bias in our politics for the workings of interest-group liberalism since the New Deal.

The second major problem in interest-group liberalism was accurately pinpointed by Herbert Hoover, of all people. Such liberalism amounts to a kind of unresponsive syndicalism which can work oppression on individual human beings in several different ways. Such syndicalism rests upon the creation of very large-scale or "peak" organizations and ultimately upon power transactions between the top leadership of these organizations and the top leadership of Congress, executive agencies and independent regulatory commissions. Needless to say, the interests of the ordinary individual can and very often do get lost in this process at all levels—in the private-sector organizations themselves, in the interface transactions between peak groups and government, in the shaping of public policy and in the ordinary transactions between individual citizens and bureaucracies. This, of course, applies to individuals who are fortunate enough to be covered by the umbrellas provided by the corporation, the labor union or other group active in the pressure system.

How much more forcefully does it apply to the very large fraction of the population which is outside these groups.

"Power speaks to power;" if there is any part of the "old politics" which has generated more passionate opposition among Americans than any other, it is this. Such opposition is crystallized implicitly or explicitly around the belief that there is a common public interest which transcends group negotiations; that this interest is somehow grossly violated by the power game played by peak associations and top-level government people and that legislation is or of right ought to be the product of more than the temporary balance of power among these organized groups.

Pluralists either ignore or categorically deny the existence of such a public interest at home, though they find it easy enough to discover an American national interest abroad. But this rejection of the notion of a public interest reveals the true extent to which pluralism is bourgeois ideology—a logic of justification for an established order of things. The trouble with this line of argument is that it enshrines naked power relationships among group and political elites while arguing that these processes are beneficial because of social harmony. It is laissez-faire ideology writ large. But it is vulnerable when and to the extent that individuals come to disbelieve in this harmony; and in fact, the long-term workings of this syndicalism destroy, almost dialectically, public belief in the justness of political solutions and the legitimacy of government itself. At the "end of liberalism," as Theodore Lowi has precisely argued, is a felt lack of justice, of simple human equity in the political system.

It is no wonder that academic pluralism has been so hostile to the notion of a public interest. The existence of a public interest presupposes that there is collective business to transact at home. It necessarily presupposes a fundamental opposition to the theory and practice of corporate syndicalism. To the extent that such collective business is perceived to exist, a first and very long step has been taken toward the creation of a government which is responsible not merely to the leadership of private power concentrations but to the people of the United States. The struggle to create such a government is a basic ingredient in today's political turmoil. It will go on for the foreseeable future. Only such a government is likely in the long run to generate the moral authority necessary to function effectively without resort to armed force.

Military-Industrial Complex

Corwin was also apprehensive about the political implications of permanent mobilization of the United States in international politics. In his farewell address in 1961, President Eisenhower voiced a very similar concern when he warned against the acquisition of influence, sought or unsought, by the military-industrial complex. It is a pity that all of his successors have been so patently insensitive to this warning.

The reason for this worry is inherent in the American constitutional structure. It cannot be said often enought that the American political system is extremely archaic by comparative standards and that in foreign and military affairs it presupposes that the president will act very much like a seventeenth-century patriot king. Not only does sweepingly sovereign power exist so far as foreign and military affairs are concerned; in practice the power has been concentrated even beyond the Constitution's very broad grant in a very narrow executive elite.

Since World War II a well-known combination of factors—contextual (military threat from the Communist world), ideological (reflexive anti-communism) and economic (the possibility of large Keynesian public-sector expenditures without competition with private enterprise)—have contributed to the development of a colossal military and defense-related organizational structure. This structure ramifies throughout the political system. Four-fifths of all congressional districts now have defense installations or plants which are of more or less significance to the local economy. Perhaps one way to capture graphically the change which has occurred since Corwin wrote is to present the per capita expenditures on defense, space and military-assistance programs. In current dollars, these amounted to $4.19 per capita in 1935, $89.18 in 1950, $245.97 in 1960 and $387.75 in 1970. Even taking inflation into account, the burden of empire for the average American has grown enormously in the past generation.

The political implications of this immense proliferation in military activity and expenditure have been fundamental. In the first place, a vast new syndicalist complex has come into existence since the New Deal era. It is based squarely upon the top management of the leading industrial corporations, the political foreign-policy establishment around the president and in leading universities, the top Pentagon elite and the armed services and appropriations committees of Congress. It has been actively supported by another major element in the New Deal syndicalist coalition, the top leadership of organized labor—not only on grounds of international anti-communist ideology, but above all because where defense is, there are jobs also. Any effort to organize a domestic political movement calling for reallocation of our scarce resources and budget priorities must recognize the pervasiveness of this complex and the multitude of very large material and ideological interests which are permanently mobilized around it.

Granted the realities of international power configurations since World War II, it would be unrealistic to argue that defense and related burdens on American resources can be done away with or that they are not needed. But even if we cannot dismantle the military-industrial-academic complex if we would, the future of American domestic politics depends in a very real sense upon whether this immense set of power concentrations can be tamed and made politically accountable. This complex represents at its highest point of development the syndicalist interest-group liberalism which has dominated American politics. Perhaps the supreme example of the coercions which play upon the little man who is subject to power he cannot begin to control is the drafting of young men to fight in a war which was initiated entirely by the president and his narrow elite of military, civilian and academic advisers.

It is not possible to devote much time here to the Vietnam War. It has vastly accelerated the domestic political crisis in the United States and may even come to be viewed in retrospect as the most durably influential such experience since the Civil War itself. The decision to make war in Vietnam captures the essence of Corwin's worries about the operation of this political system under conditions of permanent imperial involvement in the outside world. It was an executive decision. It was made by a president who had campaigned a few months earlier on a pledge not to do so. The president so acted with the advice and consent not of the Senate but of a rarified elite of advisers who were accountable to no one but themselves and the chief executive. But it was also a decision which ordinary people had to pay for—in the case of 50,000 young men, with their lives. Naturally, the latter point, not less than the barbarously inhumane methods by which this war was and is being carried on, contributed immensely to the volcanic alienation of college youth and others in the late 1960s. But these considerations, however important, should not deflect our view from the core of the issue which the war has raised. This issue, baldly put, involves the ascendancy of a narrow executive-military elite in our politics and the absence of any organized institutional means for restraining the exercise of that power.

Constitutional Crisis

Lurking just beneath the once calm surface of American politics is a fundamental constitutional crisis, the gravest indeed since the Civil War a century ago. On the domestic scene the syndicalist politics of groups has produced in dialectical contradiction waves of antagonistic mobilizations and countermobilizations. The final product of the old politics of interest-group liberalism is the wavelike spread of acute relative deprivation feelings among more and more people. This is so not only because such a system "lacks justice" in Lowi's abstract sense, but because concretely it tends to operate only in response to organized pressures and protests. Action and reaction lead to ever wider senses of frustration and alienation; power groups proliferate at all levels; and the system jams in its practical operation while its very legitimacy suffers cumulative erosion. On the international front we find ourselves half-republic, half-empire; and one may doubt that this house divided can indefinitely survive divided any more successfully than did the house of which Lincoln spoke a century ago.

A number of revolutions have been unfolding during the past generation and pushing us toward and beyond the present political crisis. We have discussed the two most basic—the post-1929 revolution in political economy and the imperium revolution. But there have been others.

1) The demographic revolution. This involves the social and political effects of an enormous exchange of population since 1945; the urbanization of American blacks (and other groups such as Puerto Ricans and Chicanos) and the massive middle-class white flight from central cities to suburbs.

2) The civil-rights revolution and the political mobilization of the black and the poor, a revolution which, by destabilizing race relations and destroying the repressive compromise of 1877, has also effectively destroyed the old New Deal political coalition.

3) The combined education and media revolutions, themselves the product of increased economic affluence in American society. The education revolution has in a sense created the conditions, at least, for the emergence of a college-based class for itself among young people with common concerns and political values. But the

media revolution may prove at least as important. In a very curious way, it has permitted people who are physically separated but have common interests and problems to find one another. Moreover, it has drastically reduced the costs of political information and—even more subversively, from an official point of view—has permitted ordinary people to judge for themselves the falsity of official pronouncements about such basic events as the Vietnam War. The two revolutions together are producing a very large group of Americans who are well educated, who are politically committed and who are independent actors in the political arena.

4) Closely associated with both preceding revolutions—and the industrial affluence which underlies both—is a very far-reaching cultural revolution. One need not accept all of Charles Reich's pieties or naivetes in **The Greening of America** to realize that, among growing numbers of people—young and not so young—the traditional bonds and moral imperatives of such elemental social groupings as organized religion and the family, not to mention those of the old puritan work ethic, are rapidly dissolving. A worldwide crisis of authority is going on: as J. H. Plumb has pointed out, basic social institutions which in one form or another go back to the Neolithic era have suddenly become visibly fragile if not evanescent.

One primary feature of this cultural revolution is that—with all its bizarre and even repellent manifestations—an active search is going on for a new meaning in the lives of individuals. When old social myths and mazeways collapse, when they lose their coercive moral authority, predictably strange things happen to people in society. Group struggles and personal anxieties increase drastically. Some people move into politics with the kind of "Puritan saint" commitment of which Michael Walzer has written. Cults flourish, along with chiliastic and millenarian movements; "the end of the world" in one form or another seems remarkably close at hand to many. Ultimately, the quest is for revitalization: for some new set of social myths and routines which, because people come to believe in them, have the power to reintegrate this social chaos in some new and acceptable order.

Unhappily such conditions are not the stuff of which political pluralism or incremental bargaining in the policy process are made. They appear in fact to be essential ingredients of every truly revolutionary situation; and that is because, consciously or not, increasing numbers of people are searching for a reconstruction of themselves through a reconstruction of the social order itself. What they seek they will find, though not necessarily in the form that any individual might either foresee or desire a priori. At the same time, what makes revolutions what they are is the fact that this drive for revitalization, for political and social reconstruction, always encounters increasingly desperate resistance not only from established elites but from very broad masses of the population. Revolutions are virtually never matters of unanimous consent: the very revitalization which becomes psychically necessary to the person who supports the revolution becomes psychically intolerable to the person who cannot imagine his survival without his traditional beliefs.

Resolution of the Crisis

If all the foregoing has some relationship to today's reality, several propositions can be made about the near future of American politics:

The overall thrust of our revolutions, especially the last, is to rediscover the worth and dignity of the individual, be his social estate never so low. It is also to attack the fundamental legitimacy of political decisions based upon syndicalist bargains among elites and of the political processes by which such decisions are made.

The political thrust of these revolutions is aimed squarely against the coercive power of Big Organization, whether nominally public or nominally private. One very difficult question is the extent to which such attacks can proceed before they compromise or destroy the capacity of these organizations to perform their functions. In any case, the political organization of prisoners in jails, the emergence of storefront lawyers and many other signs of the times have come into being to give the little man the elemental leverage on his life that interest-group liberalism has denied him.

To the extent that the contemporary crisis in American politics is founded in a far-reaching if uneven collapse in traditionally held values, it can be resolved only through revitalizations of some sort. Whatever this revitalization turns out to be at the end, one thing is certain: it will not be liberal, for Lowi is quite right in claiming that liberalism has really come to an end.

Because of this, it seems increasingly certain that American political processes and structures will undergo profound transformation before the end of this century. It is possible that this change, when it occurs, will be revolutionary (or counter-revoltionary); it will in any case be sweeping in practical operation, even though the forms of the Constitution itself may not change very much. In view of the tremendous durability of this archaic political system, such a prediction seems rash, to say the least. But it is based upon certain basic propositions: first, that the system cannot operate without consensus on social fundamentals; second, that such consensus is now very rapidly disappearing; and third, that political involvement with both the value and operational problems of American society will of necessity create permanent sovereign political power resources in its national government. To the extent that the existing operation of American politics is based upon the denial of such sovereign power, it can hardly survive such a transition in recognizable form.

There is no reason to suppose with Charles Reich that the cultural revolution must succeed or that revitalization centered around its rediscovery of the individual's human, social and political needs must prevail. Indeed, it is very unlikely to prevail without political organizations which collectively concentrate the power of individuals and which will therefore articulate new needs in an organizationally familiar way. Every revolution has its counter-revolution, and counter-revolutions sometimes succeed.

The genius of American politics, as its past history abundantly demonstrates, has lain in the capacity of the system as a whole to undergo renewal and revitalization through critical realignments in the electorate and in the policy structure. Thus far the revolutionary thrust of the present-day changes we have discussed has been contained remarkably well through the existing instrumentalities of politics. But a trade-off is required sooner or later: at some point the old must yield at least partially to the new or resort to force, to breaking the system in the name of its preservation, and the preservation of the ascendancy of the old. If one thinks as a whole about all of the revolutions we have discussed, the most striking thing about them is that they point in increasingly polar-opposite directions. The older revolutions in political economy and world politics taken together point to a state with an explicitly clearly defined ruling class based upon an oligarchy of syndicalist elites and one whose leaders deal with revolutions aboard and discontent at home in an increasingly militarized, technocratic way.

The newer revolutions in media, education and culture have served to mobilize groups whose former passivity and non-participation have been essential preconditions for the smooth operation of the syndicalist welfare-warfare state. The Vietnam War somehow crystallizes for the newer America what has gone wrong with our national life under its bipartisan ruling class. It spells out for this newer America how far the syndicalist leadership of the old order has been prepared to drift away from the humane premises of the Republic in their pursuit of ideology, interest and, it may be, Empire. It is the dialectical polarization which our revolutions have generated, taken together in the same period of time, which has fueled the present crisis and which has eroded the legitimacy of the existing political order.

Now few sensible people seriously think that all the ills or dysfunctions of a social order undergoing such massive doses of change can be resolved by politics. But few would doubt either that politics is somehow integrally related to redefining the terms of conflict and compromise among major social forces. It seems to me that we have about reached the point in our national life where a clear breakthrough of the newer forces in American politics cannot be longer deferred without catastrophic intermediate-run consequences for the prospects of political freedom in the United States. Realignments have been the price which American politics pays for timely change which does not foreclose future options and which does not short-circuit the system into authoritarianism. A realignment is obviously due if not overdue: and this is clearly what the political struggles of 1968 and 1972 have been all about. If the old America, working through its entrenched syndicalist groups, can effectively choke off this peaceful revolutionary upsurge, I would regard the future of the Republic as very dim indeed.

Political forces such as those which are now on the move represent objective conflicts in society; these conflicts are long-term; and very broadly, they can be settled only by peaceful if rapid change, by violent revolution or by authoritarian reaction with clearly fascist overtones. The first alternative presupposes that the rot of syndicalism at home and of imperialism abroad has not gone so far that democratic revitalization has become excluded as a practical option. It presupposes that we have not yet crossed the point of no return on the march to the construction of the *Imperium Americanum*. This may seem to some an heroic assumption, but all the returns are not quite in yet. The second alternative is virtually certain to fail as such: but the danger is very real that newer America may be driven by desperation to violent collisions with the established political order if they cannot gain access to it peacefully. Such collisions would serve, in all probability, to speed up the processes involved in the third solution, one which carries out the implications of syndicalism and militarized foreign policy to their logical extreme. To the extent that manifest destiny dominates the political-economy and foreign-policy revolutions of our time—as an orthodox Marxist, for example, might well argue—it must candidly be said that this third option would clearly be the most likely one.

But this is to foreclose a future which has not yet occurred, in the name of a social and political determinism which cannot rest upon an adequate scientific basis. The precise point is that struggle is going on. This struggle is over peaceful penetration of democratic elements into an elite-controlled political system. But in a larger, perhaps almost mystical sense, the struggle is for the American soul. On its outcome, in my view, literally hangs the future of human freedom in United States.

1.2

What America Thinks of Itself

NEWSWEEK

With the nation fast approaching its 200th anniversary, disturbing majorities of Americans appear discontent with the quality of life in the U.S., distrustful of the men and institutions that shape it—and disconnected from the political process through which they might be able to change things. That is the unhappy message of a special public-opinion survey scheduled for release this week by a Senate subcommittee. Ironically, considering the survey's Congressional sponsorship, a staggering 71 per cent of those polled fault the Federal government for failing to improve conditions—or actually making them worse.

According to the 342-page study—made by polltaker Louis Harris for the Senate subcommittee on intergovernmental relations—the shadow of alienation now cuts across class, racial and regional lines. Fifty-five per cent of the 1,596 Americans surveyed last September felt that "people running the country don't really care what happens to you"—compared with only 26 percent who held that view in 1966. And 61 per cent in the new poll agreed with the proposition that "what you think doesn't count any more"—compared with 37 per cent seven years ago.

The impact of Watergate on the body politic was obvious, although the survey did not ask specifically about the break-in or related scandals. Among serious problems facing the country today a lack of integrity in government ranked second only to the nation's inflationary crunch. Three of every four Americans questioned agreed that "wire-tapping and spying under the excuse of national security is a serious threat to people's privacy." And a convincing 74 per cent majority agreed that "special interests get more from the government than the people do." Said a tobacco farmer in North Carolina: "The whole moral character of the country is going downhill, or we wouldn't have had a Watergate crisis. People in the top of government are power-hungry and they will do almost anything to get and keep their power . . . and that's downright corrupting."

The survey also shows a significant gap between the way ordinary citizens see

Copyright Newsweek, Inc. 1974, reprinted by permission.

the country's problems and the way those problems are viewed (or overlooked) by government officials. On the key question about the quality of life, for example, a solid 45 per cent plurality said that conditions had grown worse over the past ten years, compared with only 35 per cent who felt life had improved. Indeed, fully 53 per cent felt that there was "something deeply wrong in America today." By contrast, 61 per cent of the state and local officials polled independently by subcommittee staffers were confident that the quality of life was steadily improving. Leaders and led also disagreed about the extent of public disillusionment with government, the reasons for it and key steps by which confidence might eventually be restored.

There are some grounds for optimism. In their foreword to the study, subcommittee chairman Edmund S. Muskie and ranking Republican Edward J. Gurney note that "Ninety per cent of Americans—and a like percentage of state and local officials—are convinced that government can work effectively and well. Both share a faith in the ability of government, specifically the unpopular Federal establishment, to subordinate special influence to the general welfare and to bring in first-rate people whose first priorities will be 'helping the country' and 'caring about the people'." Moreover, Harris points out, although Americans by and large concede their lack of information about broad matters of politics and government, they also indicate a strong desire to obtain such knowledge—and to participate more widely and effectively in the democratic process.

Trailing

Still, the most dramatic results of the first opinion poll ever to be commissioned by Congress are undeniably negative. Public trust in the leaders of most American institutions—from major business concerns to organized religion to the U.S. military establishment—has fallen off significantly since 1966. And the White House trails the pack; no more than 19 per cent of those questioned expressed "a great deal of confidence" in the President and other leaders of the Federal executive branch. In only two cases has the standing of key institutions improved over seven years ago: television news, up from 25 per cent to 41 per cent, and the press generally, up from 29 per cent to 30 per cent. Interestingly, those two fared far less well in the survey of state and local leaders. Only 17 per cent of that group expressed a great deal of confidence in the people who control TV news today, and only 19 per cent felt confidence in the nation's press.

The notion that something is deeply wrong in America today is hardly the creation of any Eastern, liberal, youth-oriented establishment. In fact, the survey shows, the feeling is far stronger in the Midwest (54 per cent), South (55 per cent) and West (58 per cent) than it is back East (49 per cent). And it is more widely held among those between the ages of 30 and 49 (51 per cent) and those over 50 (62 per cent) than it is by younger adults (44 per cent). Predictably, the malaise is more prevalent at the lower end of the economic scale (63 per cent among those earning under $5,000) than at the top (47 per cent in the $15,000-plus group), and more serious for blacks (65 per cent) than whites (52 per cent). But it also sweeps majorities of executives (51 per cent), union members and white-collar workers (55 per cent each).

"If you could sit down and talk with the President," the survey asked, "what two or three things would you like to tell him?" The answers to that question illustrate the nature of public disenchantment. Nearly three out of every four respondents (74 per cent) were troubled by matters of honesty or integrity in government, volunteering that they would advise Mr. Nixon to "tell the truth about Watergate," "resign," "be honest," "Listen to the people more" and "get better advisers." Just over half of the sampling mentioned economic worries.

The crisis of confidence is clear—but the people and their leaders view it differently. While 70 per cent of the public said that "corrupt politicians" are a real problem for most citizens, no more than 48 per cent of local and state officials shared that opinion. While 61 per cent of the public feels that the "inability of government to solve problems" is a high priority concern, only 37 per cent of the leaders gave it that importance. More important, no more than a third of the public agreed that public officials "really care about people"—while a majority of leaders said they do. "America looks to the top of the governmental structure for inspiration and finds it missing," Harris concludes. "In that unhappy verdict is summed up the broad loss of confidence, the pervasive sense of discontent and the most serious reasons for concern about the future course of the American democracy."

Power

The public thinking was a good deal less clear in finding solutions to the country's problems. A clear plurality of those questioned (42 per cent) wanted power stripped from the Federal government and hefty majorities wanted power reallocated to the state and local levels—but, at the same time, 67 per cent agreed with the assertion that "It's about time we had a strong Federal government again to get this country moving." Harris, in partial explanation, suggests that " 'strong' may well be interpreted to reflect trustworthiness and sense of purpose, rather than added legal and programmatic authority."

The public is more sure about the kind of leaders the nation needs. Two-thirds (66 per cent) listed honesty as a prime qualification, followed by dedication to hard work (56 per cent), the desire to help people (51 per cent), intelligence (41 per cent) and courage (35 per cent). But there was another significant gap between leaders and led over the conditions that would permit better qualified public officials to work more effectively in the national interest. A substantial 71 per cent of the public agreed that "lots of problems connected with government could be solved if there weren't so much secrecy." Accordingly, a near majority (48 per cent) of ordinary citizens believe that government could be made to work better by "setting up tight checks by elected officials, the courts and citizen groups to watch closely over what government is doing." The alternative—"putting the right men in control of government and letting them run things with the best experts they can find"—drew only 40 per cent support.

Among the leaders, only 41 per cent saw government secrecy as a serious problem and the prescriptions were reversed. Fifty per cent advocated a freer hand and more trust for those in leadership roles, as against 39 per cent who felt the emphasis should be placed on a system of "tight checks" over government operations. "Actually," said one Midwestern governor, "both options are needed, but without vigilant citizens, even good leaders can lose sight of reality."

Involvement

Are Americans actually prepared to take on active roles as watchdogs or participants in the democratic process? The survey suggests not, although it found encouraging potential for growth in this area. But the current level of public knowledge about government and political affairs is fragmentary at best, and most Americans seem to have only the slightest personal involvement with the real workings of politics and government. Only 14 per cent of the sampling said they had campaigned for a Congressional candidate, and that figure is probably exaggerated. In that light, the sincerity of their expressed desire for more knowledge—and more participation—remains to be tested.

To its credit, the American public seems aware of its intelligence gap. Asked about being "up-to-date" on developments in the Federal government, 60 per cent confessed that they were not. Among those with the least education, 76 per cent felt inadequately informed in this area, as did 69 per cent of skilled laborers. In only three groups did majorities feel that they knew what was going on in Washington: the college-educated (56 per cent), those with incomes above $15,000 (54 per cent) and those who, because of past or present leadership roles in local organizations, are classified as active citizens in their communities (52 per cent).

To gauge public awareness of current affairs more objectively, the survey asked people if they could identify various government leaders—and then asked them to prove it. State governors, it developed, were easily the best known public officials. A healthy 91 per cent of all those questioned claimed to know who the governor of their state was—and 89 per cent actually did. Moreover, a 77 per cent majority correctly identified the governor's political party. A much smaller majority (64 per cent) said they could name at least one U.S. senator from their state—but only 59 per cent were correct, and only 53 per cent got the senator's party affiliation. As for their second senator, no more than 42 per cent of the public even claimed to know his name, and only 39 per cent really did.

Congressmen did scarcely better. Although 53 per cent of those questioned claimed to know the U.S. representative from their district, only 46 per cent could name him, and only 41 per cent were correct about his political affiliation. Asked to describe the composition of Congress as a whole, 62 per cent correctly said it was composed of the House of Representatives and the Senate. Twenty per cent thought Congress included the Supreme Court, 6 per cent said it consisted solely of the House, 4 per cent said just the Senate and 8 per cent had no idea whatsoever. In every category surveyed—regional, racial and economic—television news was the leading source of information on public affairs.

Nitty-Gritty

An accurate profile of citizen participation in politics and government is harder to draw, largely because of self-serving answers given by many citizens. Asked if they had voted in the 1972 Presidential election, for example, 73 per cent said yes—although actual voter turnout last year was just 55 per cent. Yet even with that kind of inflationary error, the degree of public involvement in the nitty-gritty of the democratic process is distressingly low.

On the most superficial level, 69 per cent of those questioned said they had signed at least one petition in their lives; 56 per cent reported voting on a school-bond issue—or "actively defending the action of a public official in private discussion." And 50 per cent said they had attended a speech or rally for a political candidate. But only 33 per cent claimed to have written to their local congressman or to have contributed to a political campaign.

And the fall-off was precipitous when it came to time-consuming actions with real impact: only 14 per cent said they had "campaigned or worked actively for a candidate for President"; 13 per cent had "visited or talked in person with their U.S. senator"; 11 per cent said they "picketed or took part in a street demonstration" (only 2 per cent reported participating in a demonstration where violence occurred).

Action

The Harris survey finds significant potential for citizen action in the future, however. Asked what actions they would take to change an unjust law or oust a corrupt politician, large majorities mentioned going to the polls (94 per cent), talking with friends (91 per cent), writing to congressmen (84 per cent) and to newspapers (65 per cent).

Perhaps more promising, in practical terms, were the hefty majorities who said they would pitch in through local groups they already belonged to (79 per cent) or join one of the new, hardworking citizen-action groups (72 per cent). Fully 49 per cent of the public agreed that such citizens' groups "are having more effect in getting government to get things done [than they did] five years ago." They cited the example of Martin Luther King's civil-rights marches and recent campaigns against industrial pollution. And then there was the black factory worker who praised the community lobbying effort that recently improved police protection in his Buffalo, N.Y., neighborhood. "I remember five years ago we tried to get a foot patrolman on this block," he said. "Nothing happened then, but now the police are coming by. They're cooperating."

1.3

Race, Revolution and Women

SHIRLEY CHISHOLM

Shirley Chisholm became the first black woman in the history of this country to be elected to the Congress of the United States, with her victory of November 1968. She represents the 12th District (Bedford-Stuyvesant), New York, and is a member of the House Committee for Veterans' Affairs.

◊

Everywhere we turn today we are confronted with a revolution of some kind. Slogans that range from "You've come a long way, baby" to "All power to the people" have become jaded chants that dribble from the mouths of jaded TV announcers.

There is an almost paranoid fear eating at the guts of all Americans. Black-White, Male-Female, Young-Old represent schisms between us. Racial Polarization, the Generation Gap and Virginia Slims are all brand names for products that may become lethal.

The Doomsday Criers are amongst us chanting their wares and bemoaning their fate. Vietnam and the Middle East are no longer powder kegs; they are instead sputtering fuses. The campuses and the ghettoes are eruptions of revolutionary acne.

The President circles the globe seemingly handing out carte-blanche military commitment credit cards and scientists in Houston dissect dusty rocks in search of other life-forms while humans starve to death—physically, mentally and spiritually—at home and abroad.

The author of *Soul On Ice,* Eldridge Cleaver, has become a soul on the run—an unwilling refugee from his heritage and his mission—a latter-day man without a country.

The King is dead and so are the Kennedy Princes of Politics—victims all of hot lead spit out by paranoia, collective guilt and their destructive handmaidens—hate and fear. Deaths purchased, some say, by modern-day robber barons immersed in the cement coffin of the status quo.

Reprinted by permission.

And here gather we, in this quiet retreat, to debate the possibility that there may be *no* future. Tomorrow we leave for our homes and our separate battlefields. What is it that we must find here that will sustain and strengthen us in the days, weeks and years ahead?

Communion, understanding, and agape certainly are on the list but there is one other I might point out—**Commitment.**

Most women in America have never had the opportunity to fully measure the extent of their own personal commitment to ending poverty, to ending racial discrimination, and to ending social and political injustice.

Many of us are old enough to remember the Second World War. In that war, women in many foreign countries learned first-hand what was necessary to maintain life under the most adverse conditions. While they were begging, stealing, fighting and even killing for bits and morsels of food to feed themselves and their families, we continued to enjoy a high standard of living, good jobs and a night's sleep uninterrupted by rifle and artillery fire.

I am not saying that any one of us escaped unscathed by the war and its surrounding horror. But I am saying that the flames in which our steel was forged was not hot enough, cruel enough, or close enough to produce an exceptionally high quality steel.

Today we are perched on the precipice of internal holocaust that may well be only the trigger for the world-wide one. And perched there, many of us continue to give the easiest things to give—the most detachable extensions of ourselves—money and sympathy.

There are revolutions going on. It is true that some of them are false, designed to build the ego, cleverly camouflaged in order to sell a product that in the final analysis is harmful to the purchaser's health.

Some of them are revolts by people who are refusing to accept age-worn patterns of doing things and who are therefore carving new ways that are more satisfactory to their needs.

And finally some of them are revolutions in deadly earnest designed to strike off the shackles of oppressed people throughout the world.

Both the so-called Black Revolution and the Woman's Liberation Movements fall into the last two categories. Black people are in deadly earnest about freedom from oppression and women are refusing to accept traditional and stereotyped roles.

Because I am both black and a woman, I will make some comments and observations about both.

First, the Black Revolution is not solely black. I say that what Black people in America are doing, is participating in a world-wide rebellion that encompasses *all* aspects of human life.

When we talk about the Black Revolution, therefore, we immediately attempt to limit the goals of the black man, attempt to strip black revolutionaries of the right to be idealistic, attempt to strip the black man of the right to feel that what he wants is not just freedom for himself, but a totally new, totally free world.

When we separate the so-called Black Revolution in America from the other revolutions—in literature, in the church, in the arts, in education and throughout the world—we attempt to maintain our own peculiar form of slavery.

People and Politics: The Prevailing Issues

One of the most noted and most quoted black revolutionaries in this country was Malcolm X. While Malcolm was on a trip through the Holy Land he sent back a letter that read in part:

> You may be shocked by these words coming from me, but I have always been a man who tries to face facts and to accept the reality of life as new experiences and knowledge unfold it. The experiences of this might have taught me much and each hour in the Holy Land opens my eyes even more . . . I have eaten from the same plate with people whose eyes are the bluest of blue, whose hair was the blondest of blond, and whose skin was the whitest of white . . . and I felt the same sincerity in the words and deeds of these 'white' Muslims that I felt among the African Muslims of Nigeria, Sudan and Ghana.

As Eldridge Cleaver so aptly pointed out, there were many blacks who were outraged and felt that Malcolm had betrayed them with that statement. It may very well have been Malcolm's signature on his own death warrant, but the point that I want you to bear in mind is that it is exactly that type of personal courage and integrity that marks the true revolutionary.

Malcolm X was certainly aware that as an established black leader who had consistently, constantly and continually assailed the "white devil" here at home, he was jeopardizing his position. But I think that Malcolm also knew, instinctively, what a Roman slave Epictetus had in mind when he said: "No man is free until he is master of his own mind."

White women, must realize that black people in America are not yet free and know that they are not yet free. That is true also for a great number of dark-skinned people throughout the world. But I do not find it astonishing that there are so many people who are aware that they are not yet free. What I do find astonishing is that so many of the nonhomogenous grouping that we call "white western" think of themselves as free. The master does not escape slavery simply because he thinks of himself as free—as the master. Neither do the brother and sister of the master escape slavery when they stand idly by and watch their brother enslave their brother. The master is inseparably bound to the slaves and so is white America inseparably bound to black America.

A few months ago while testifying before the Office of Federal Contract Compliance, I noted that anti-feminism, like every form of discrimination, is destructive both to those who perpetrate it and its victims; that males, with their anti-feminism, maim both themselves and their women. Bear in mind that that is also true in terms of black and white race relations.

No one in America has escaped the wounds imposed by racism and anti-feminism. In *Soul On Ice* Eldridge Cleaver pointed out in great detail how the stereotypes were supposed to work. Whether his insight is correct or not, it bears closer examination.

Speaking of the white woman in the passage "The Primeval Mitosis," Cleaver describes her stereotype thusly, ". . . she is required to possess and project an image that is in sharp contrast to his (the white man), so that the effeminate image of her man can still, by virtue of the sharp contrast in the degrees of feminity, be perceived as masculine. Therefore she becomes "ultrafeminine."

Isn't this an essential part of what the Women's Liberation Movements are all about? Women, especially in the upper classes, have been expected to be nothing more than dangling, decorative ornaments—non-thinking and virtually non-functional.

In other places in the passage, Cleaver describes the other stereotypes that white western society has accepted in the place of reality. He states that the black male is expected to supply the society with its source of brute power through his role as the "supermasculine menial"—all body and no brain.

The white male has assigned himself the role of the "omnipotent administrator" all brain and no body, because that could be seen as the clearly superior role. The black female was assigned the role of "subfeminine" or Amazon.

What the roles and the strange interplay between them have meant to America, Cleaver goes on to point out quite well. There is only one thing that I want to point out. Because of the bizarre aspects of the roles and the strange influence that non-traditional contact between them has on the general society, blacks and whites, males and females must operate almost independently of each other in order to escape from the quicksands of psychological slavery. Each—black male and black female—white female and white male must escape first from his or her own historical traps before they can be truly effective in helping others to free themselves.

The goal must clearly be freedom—integration is not yet feasible as a goal. It is not feasible because integration depends on mutual concepts of freedom and equality.

Cleaver stripped from some of our eyes for all time, the wool that we tried so desperately to hold over them.

Black women and white women have been for the most part, the opposite sides of the same coin, as have been black men and white men. Our society has always required that those coins come up head and head or tails and tails for all kinds of spurious reasoning. But no matter what the reasoning, it is part of the reason why white women are not now and never have been truly accepted working in the ghetto.

One of the questions that I am most often asked by white women these days is "What can we do?"

In many ways it is a strange question—strange because the phrase: "to help you people" is only implied. It is strange because of the implied assumption that they are free to help and strange because of the implied assumption that they are in a position to help.

I have responded to that question in many ways, pointing out the political arena, education and many other things. But I have always left only the implication of the real answer, the one thing that they not only might do—the only thing that they must do.

Today I must state it. Free yourselves! And in order to do that you must first free yourselves of the assumption that you are now free.

I have pointed out time and time again that the harshest discrimination that I have encountered *in the political arena* is anti-feminism—from both males and brain-washed "Uncle Tom" females.

When I first announced for the United States Congress last year, both males and females advised me, as they had when I ran for the New York Assembly, to go back to teaching, a woman's vocation, and leave politics to men.

I did not go back then and I will not go back as long as there exists a need to change the politics of this country.

Like the colleagues that I had in Albany, many of my fellow members in the House treat me with a deference that is patronizing.

On May 20 of this year I introduced legislation concerning the equal employment opportunities of women. At that time I pointed out that there were three and one-half million more women than men in America but that women held only two percent of the managerial positions; that no women sit on the AFL-CIO Council or the Supreme Court; that only two women had ever held Cabinet rank and that there were at that time only two women of ambassadorial rank in the diplomatic corps. In the Congress there were only ten representatives and only one senator. I stated then as I do now that this situation is outrageous.

I would like to quote an excerpt from the speech that I made on the Floor that day

> It is true that part of the problem has been that women have not been aggressive in demanding their rights. This was also true of the black population for many years. They submitted to oppression and even cooperated with it. Women have done the same thing. But now there is an awareness of this situation, particularly among the younger segment of the population.
>
> As in the field of equal rights for blacks, Spanish-Americans, Indians and other groups, laws will not change such deep-seated problems overnight. They can be used to provide protection for those who are most abused, and begin the process of evolutionary change by compelling the insensitive majority to re-examine its unconscious attitudes.

Women in this country must become revolutionaries. We must refuse to accept the old—the traditional roles and stereotypes.

Because of the present situation the tactics for black women must be slightly different than the tactics for white women but the goal can be the same.

The tactics of revolution used by the white liberal community must be, as they will be, slightly different than the tactics used by the black ghetto community but the goal can be the same.

The goal, though, must be more than political freedom. It must be more than economic freedom. It must be total freedom to build a world-wide society predicated on the positive values of all human life.

It must be freedom from the waste and ravages of all natural resources including human resources.

Women must do more than sacrifice husbands and sons in the present Social Revolution. They must also sacrifice themselves. And for many women, black and white, those who will call first for that sacrifice will be their own sons—their own husbands.

We must start in our own homes, our own schools and our own churches. This does not mean talk about integrated schools, churches or marriage when the kind of integration one is talking about is black with white.

We must work for—fight for—the integration of male and female—human and human. Franz Fanon pointed out in *Black Skins—White Masks* that the anti-Semitic was eventually the anti-Negro. I want to point out that both are eventually the Anti-Feminist. Furthermore I want to point out that all discrimination is eventually the same thing—anti-humanism.

Our task will not be easy. It will be hard—but it must be done. Perhaps the greatest power for social change, for a successful Social Revolution, lies in our hands. But it is not an unlimited power nor is it an invincible power. The use of power will always cause a reaction, therefore we must use our power well and we must use it wisely. Godspeed our success.

1.4

Good Things About America

U.S. NEWS AND WORLD REPORT
Through the Eyes of New Citizens

At a time when most Americans are beset by doubts or dismay at the state of the nation, one group of U.S. citizens still sees the country's weaknesses as relatively unimportant in comparison with its strengths.

These people are the more than 6.3 million immigrants, from virtually all countries of the world, who have come to the United States in the past 20 years, either to flee oppression or simply to better their chances in life.

To get an idea of how these Americans typically view their adopted land in a troubled time, staff members of "U.S. News & World Report" probed the reactions of four persons who have become naturalized citizens in recent years.

Over all, as these new Americans see things—

The U.S. is still a nation that offers unparalleled freedom—not only in politics but in social mobility, economic advancement and personal life.

They like the sheer size of America, its wide choice of careers and places to live, its readiness to assimilate foreigners, and the feeling of belonging to a society established to serve and protect the individual.

Immigrants do have complaints about the U.S., too.

They tend to believe that America is too permissive toward criminals and dissenters. Some miss the more-leisurely pace of life or the security offered by rigid conventions or social structures they left behind them.

Yet these Americans are inclinec to discount somewhat the turmoil over Watergate, inflation and shortages as being exaggerated in light of conditions elsewhere. In their view, the U.S. is still a nation that lives up to its historic pledge of liberty, justice and the pursuit of happiness for all.

Reprinted from 'U.S. News and World Report', April 1, 1974. Copyright 1974 U.S. News and World Report, Inc.

Readings

"In America, An Individual Has Value"

LOS ANGELES

Had he remained in South Korea, Norrie S. Yuh says, he probably could have taken over his family's prosperous dairy business and enjoyed special status as a son of the Government's former Minister of Reconstruction.

Instead, he completed his education in the United States and Switzerland, became a U.S. citizen and at the age of 33 has worked his way up to the ownership of a travel agency and a small export-import firm in Los Angeles.

Why did he give up a privileged role in Korea for an uncertain future here? He replies:

"It's not because the money is here—I could make a living back there—the thing is that here people speak freely."

In Korea, Mr. Yuh says, a prominent person could get in trouble just for speaking to a member of a political party opposing the regime. By his account, news media are censored or controlled by the Government, people must register to move from one city to another and businessmen have to bribe officials to get the many licenses and permits they need.

"I know when I call Korea, all calls are taped," Mr. Yuh says. "I have even been called on by two men from Korean intelligence who played back a tape of a telephone conversation I had with my mother, and they wanted me to explain the meaning of some remarks we made."

But in America, he believes, "there is complete freedom." He adds, "Maybe some people abuse that freedom, but even if you do abuse it, you're left alone as long as you don't break the law."

As an example of what he considers abusing freedom, Mr. Yuh cites the calls for the impeachment of President Nixon so soon after his overwhelming re-election.

"The business of immorality is overpublicized," he says. "This kind of situation you find in other countries—maybe worse than here—but they don't talk about it."

Mr. Yuh also enjoys the social liberties that Americans often take for granted.

"My father wanted me to marry a certain person whom I had never met," he says. "But here I married the girl I wanted—my secretary. If that sort of thing happened in Korea, everyone would talk. It was a marriage not properly arranged."

Mr. Yuh thinks America's racial problems are no worse than mutual antagonism between Koreans and Japanese living in each other's countries. He says:

"There are prejudices in every country. But this country has the least discrimination against minorities. I strongly believe that I was more discriminated against in Switzerland than over here."

Mr. Yuh feels he has equal opportunity, and prefers that to being part of a privileged class. "In this country, you get what you work for," he maintains. "I don't think that is valid in any other country. Unless you have good connections or influence, you probably will not succeed. If I make it here, the credit comes to me. There, no matter what I did, I would still be only the son of Mr. Şo-and-so."

What it all boils down to, Mr. Yuh says, is this:

"In America, an individual has value. He is recognized as a human being, equal to any other. There is respect for the value of one person."

"Life is More Exciting Here"

NEW KENSINGTON, Pa.

After more than 16 years in this country, Francesca Mognini early this year was sworn in as a U.S. citizen in Pittsburgh, Pa., 20 miles from her suburban home.

"Now I become an American," she said as she sat on a courtroom bench, waiting for the ceremony to begin. "But already I have been living like an American."

For Mrs. Mognini, 50, and her husband Cassio, 57, "living like an American" has been much like their life in Italy. Here, as in Italy, Mr. Mognini has tried to ply his trade as a shoemaker, then turned to construction labor. In both countries, Mrs. Mognini has gone to work whenever her husband was laid off, and at present she supplements the family income by working as a seamstress in her home.

"If Cassio was still working construction in Italy, we could make a living," says Mrs. Mognini. "But we could never own a house or a car. Only rich people have those things, because it's a small country and there isn't too much work."

During their first few years in the U.S., the Mogninis had to support two school-age children on $2,000 a year or less. But now Mr. Mognini brings home at least $200 a week when he is working steadily. Last year, they paid off the small frame house that they bought shortly after they arrived and have been renovating ever since.

"The real-estate lady and the man at the bank were so nice to us, even though we didn't have any money," says Mrs. Mognini. "They said because we were hard-working people we could have the house. In Italy, you have to know somebody to own property."

But they also met a fast-talking salesman a short time later who pressured them into buying $1,200 worth of faulty aluminum siding for their home. They got a lawyer who won an out-of-court settlement.

"Some people try to cheat you in every country," says Mr. Mognini. "Here, at least the lawyer could do something about it."

The Mogninis are sending their 23-year-old son to drafting school and paying tuition for their 30-year-old married daughter to become a trained beautician.

"In Italy," says Mrs. Mognini, "most children have to drop out of school and work because their families need money."

Mrs. Mognini also enjoys the more relaxed atmosphere in American homes. "In

Italy, if my husband tells me to do something, I have to do it to keep the peace," she says. "Here I do it because I like to. And if I tell him I want to go dancing, I go."

A little democracy sometimes causes friction in the family, she says, but in this country "husbands and wives understand each other better—when we're working together and making decisions together, it makes us better friends."

Mrs. Mognini says she likes the variety and the livelier pace in America, although she adds that "life is more exciting here, but there's more worrying, too."

She says she has never run into ethnic discrimination.

"My son-in-law is Polish," she says. "We have all kinds of friends—Hungarian, Irish—and we all get along fine. The only people who call us 'Dago' are our Italian friends, and it's just for fun."

"Here You Can Be Almost Anything"

WASHINGTON, D.C.

Marcelo R. Fernandez is a Cuban refugee who believes the great American ideal of freedom is already a reality in many ways.

"I don't mean just political freedom," he says. "I mean the freedom to choose."

Mr. Fernandez, 35, fled Cuba via the Brazilian Embassy in 1961, immediately after the abortive invasion at the Bay of Pigs. He says he was one of many Cubans who had stockpiled arms and awaited word to help the invaders, "but the word never came."

An economist by training, he has been a citizen since 1967 and works as an assistant to the superintendent of schools in Washington, D.C.

Says Mr. Fernandez:

"If I had stayed in Cuba and co-operated with the Government, I might have ended up in the same sort of position I'm in now. Or I could have kept on resisting and been shot."

This immigrant relishes the wide variety of careers offered in America.

"In many countries, there are only six or seven professions you can go into," he says. "Here, you can be almost anything, if you're able to do the work." He recalls:

"My father was a very successful man in Cuba, and because I was his son I had to conform to other people's ideas. Here, I am myself."

Having lived through the turmoil of revolution in Cuba, Mr. Fernandez is particularly impressed by America's political resilience. He observes:

"Look at the young people who used to be rioting. Now we have given them the vote, and they have a greater stake in society. In many countries, when one class or group gets upset, they just rise up and start their own repressive system."

Mr. Fernandez went to a park across the street from the White House the day

President John F. Kennedy was shot, "because it looked like the Government had fallen, and I wanted to see how the people would react." What he saw was this:

"People were going to church to pray. They were very sad, but no one was worried that things were going to collapse. In Latin America, everyone would have run home, because there would be a revolution."

Mr. Fernandez says the healing of rifts created by civil disturbances in the past decade shows "a great capability for love and compassion." By comparison, he maintains, "Latin Americans carry grudges and call it pride, but really it's compensation for their weaknesses."

Mr. Fernandez has also found Americans "very tolerant of foreigners," citing the quick reconciliation with Japanese Americans after World War II and the acceptance of German-born Henry Kissinger as Secretary of State.

"Once I criticized a taxi driver in Spain," he says, "and he told me to go back where I belonged if I didn't like his driving. Here, my accent is more noticeable, but people never say things like that to me."

Such tolerance is a sign that "Americans are becoming more mature and less arrogant," Mr. Fernandez thinks. "Since the difficulties in Vietnam and at home, we no longer act like we have all the answers for the rest of the world."

Watergate, he feels, will point up the nation's strength in the long run.

"Everyone knows these things happen at least as much in other countries," he says. "But we are able to get them out in the open in this country and perhaps keep them from happening again."

America's main drawback? Mr. Fernandez believes the pressures of the nation's economic competition produce excellence but are dehumanizing in some ways. Again, he recalls a recent trip to Spain:

"I went to visit a cousin I hadn't seen in 20 years, and he embraced me and kissed me. I remembered how an American friend of mine went to the airport to meet his son—who had been in Vietnam—and they just shook hands.

"I'm afraid, 10 or 15 years from now, I'll act like that toward my daughter."

Still, Mr. Fernandez would rather live in America than anywhere else in the world.

"For me, it's better to choose the way I want to live. I like the excitement of our wide-open, changing society."

"What I Like is the Freedom"

NEW YORK CITY

When the Yugoslavian Government confiscated his family's farmland and factories in 1947, Paul Konstantinovic began searching for two things that Americans often take for granted: political freedom and the right to own his own business.

On his seventh try, he escaped from Yugoslavia in 1958, only to spend seven frustrating years in France.

Now, after eight years in America, this 41-year-old refugee is a U.S. citizen and proud owner of an auto-repair shop in New York City.

Despite some grumbles about the attitudes of his fellow Americans, he declares, "I'm living a much better life here in every way." He says:

"I would never be able to be a manager or an independent businessman in Yugoslavia. I would always be working for someone else, because I am not a Communist."

Even in France, immigrants were barred from owning a business, he says. And he adds: "If you were a foreigner living in Nice, you couldn't get a permit to go and work in Paris."

Mr. Konstantinovic says of America:

"What I like is the freedom. You are free to do any type of business you can work at. And you can move about freely. There are no problems."

Recalling the discrimination he encountered as a foreigner in France, this refugee-turned-businessman says:

"When I hire people, I don't mind where someone comes from. In the U.S., people don't ask what race or religion you are or what your nationality is. They ask you, 'What do you know how to do?'"

Three years ago, Mr. Konstantinovic bought as an investment a $6,500 country house on Long Island, which he has fixed up until it is worth $36,000. Some day he would like to move out of the big city, but in the meantime he gets satisfaction out of working—frequently a 12-hour day—to provide little luxuries such as a recent $200 trip to Ohio for his son.

Even the basics of American life were luxuries for him once.

"In America, we can have meat two or three times a day," he says. "In Europe, we'd have it on Sundays and maybe three times during the week."

Despite his own long hours, he feels most Americans are too businesslike.

"In Europe, we talked more of cultural affairs," he says. "We also discussed vacations. Here, it's only business, business, business!"

Mr. Konstantinovic, whose apartment has been burglarized, is concerned, too, about lawlessness, strikes, racial troubles and the welfare situation. He warns:

"If the turmoil does not stop, people will want a strong man. Hitler, Mussolini and Napoleon came into power that way."

Although he feels the nation may be too permissive, he is optimistic:

"America is still an enterprising country. All the troubles we have here will settle down."

Study Questions

1. Identify some of the components of American ideology. How do these components operate today? Do you believe that they are still relevant?

2. Is there such a thing as a typical American? Describe him in terms of socioeconomic group, political beliefs, race, color, and creed. What conclusions can you draw?

3. Discuss the problems that develop between a sacred and secular so-

ciety. Are these problems irreconcilable? Identify sacred values in your home. How do they contrast with secular values? How do these views influence attitudes on democracy, morality, and ethics?

4. Do you agree that there is something decidedly wrong with American society? Are there any good things about it? How do these attitudes affect the working of the political system?

5. Is power the real motivator of the American political system?

6. Is America a melting pot or are we deceiving ourselves in thinking that American society accepts everyone equally and makes Americans out of them? What impact does this have on the American political system?

7. Is there something inherently wrong in our society when people must demand Power to the People, Chicano Power, Black Power, Indian Power, Latino Power?

8. Since you are just beginning the study of the American political system, what questions do you believe should be asked about the system? What is it that you think you ought to know about your own political system?

Bibliography

de Tocqueville, Alexis. *Democracy in America*. Edited by J. P. Mayer. Garden City, N.Y.: Doubleday, Anchor Books, 1969.

Graham, Hugh Davis, and Gurr, Ted Robert. *Violence in America* (A report Submitted to the National Commission on the Causes and Prevention of Violence). New York: Bantam Books, 1969.

Harward, Donald W., ed. *Crisis in Confidence: The Impact of Watergate*. Boston: Little, Brown and Co., 1974.

Lipset, Seymour Martin. *Political Man*. Garden City, N.Y.: Doubleday, Anchor Books, 1963.

McGinniss, Joe. *The Selling of the President 1968*. New York. Trident Press, 1969.

Moyers, Bill. *Listening to America*. New York: Dell Publishing, 1972.

Reich, Charles A. *The Greening of America*. New York: Bantam Books, 1971.

Schlesinger, Arthur M., Jr. *The Crisis of Confidence*. New York: Bantam Books, 1969.

Skinner, B. F. *Beyond Freedom and Dignity*. New York: Bantam/Vintage Books, 1971.

Wattenberg, Ben J., and Scammon, Richard M. *This U.S.A*. Garden City, N.Y.: Doubleday, 1965.

CHAPTER 2
Politics, Power, and the Political System

Before beginning the serious study of any subject, it is necessary to develop an understanding of the most important concepts and terms that will be used in the study. This is particularly true in the study of politics and political systems. All of us have been exposed to political language for a number of years and we take it for granted that we know the meaning of such words as politics, power, and political systems. Yet, if we look closely at the meanings of these words we find at best, surface understanding. It is on this assumption that we begin the study of the American political system.

The Meaning of Politics

The concept of *politics* usually creates negative images in the popular mind; it is usually thought of as a synonym for "wheeling and dealing." Yet no single phrase can give a true definition of politics, for it encompasses a wide range of human activity and is deeply embedded in the social environment. As Aristotle noted, "Man is by nature a political animal." Yet, politics does mean several specific things. It means conflict, ranging from simple disagreement to violence and even war. Karl von Clausewitz, a Prussian general and writer on military matters, wrote in the early nineteenth century, "War is the highest form of diplomacy." Conflicts arise because people (and nations) disagree over values, their meaning, and how to achieve them. Politics also means resolution of conflicts. This resolution can be achieved through discussion, that is, by developing a consensus, or in a number of other ways, including the use of force.

We should keep in mind that such definitions of politics are only the beginning. To understand fully the ramifications of conflict, one must undertake serious studies of the nature of human relationships, social systems, value systems, nations, and states—to mention but a few areas. Similarly, to understand the resolution of conflict, one must study the nature of governing institutions and the characteristics of society. Obviously such scholarship is beyond an introductory study of the American political system.

The Political System

Not many years ago, writers used the terms nation, state or government in discussing politics. Recently, however, the phrase *political system* has been used instead. This phrase suggests a broader scope, encompassing not only government but the dynamics of a system—the informal institutions (parties and groups), political processes, ideology, and individual political behavior. Additionally, the concept of system, borrowed from the hard sciences, denotes a concern for relationships between parts and suggests a living entity; thus it gives a much more relevant and realistic perspective in the study of politics and government. In such a concept, government is part of the political system and consists of those offices involved in enforcing the rules that operate the system.

The concept of political system becomes somewhat more complicated because we must include the meaning of politics and of system. In general terms, *system* suggests an interdependence of parts, a beginning and end. For example, the human body can be conceived of as a system; its parts are interdependent, and there are specific functions associated with it. We can apply the same kind of approach to a political system. All its parts are interdependent; change taking place in any one particular part has an effect on all others.

Political Community

Clearly an introductory textbook on American government is not the place for analytical discussions of sophisticated and complex social science phenomena. Yet, we ought to appreciate the complexity of politics and its place in our society. Using the initial discussion of the political system as a basis, let us briefly explore the notion of community and its relationship to the political system and politics. A political community is one in which certain basic values are shared by a great majority of people—shared strongly enough to allow the establishment of a political system. This political system operates on a base of shared values which identify its methods and procedures, that is, the "rules of the game."

All members of the community are also members of the political system, whether they like it or not. There are a number of other systems also operating within the community, e.g., social, economic, religious. However, what makes the political system unique is that it alone has the authority to make legitimate decisions affecting everyone and can use legitimate physical force to insure that people abide by its decisions. The purpose of the political system is to perpetuate the values shared by the community. It must resolve conflicts that arise between members of the community, and between the state and the community; and in doing so, it must provide some satisfaction to the mass of people in achieving their expectations.

Values and Perceptions

Thus, at the base of the community and political system are values. Values in this context means those things that are not only desirable, but essential for the proper functioning of the political system. The American people consider democracy a core value. That is, the political system must operate for the people and by the people. The great majority of Americans share this value strongly enough to support, maintain, and operate our political system. This does not mean that all agree on the interpretations of democracy, yet most agree that it must be a core value. There are other values that form the democratic ideology, or group of ideas and attitudes associated with the American political system. We will discuss the meaning of American ideology later. Suffice it to say here that ideology is the foundation of any political system; every community has an ideology upon which its political system rests. The ideology is the basis for establishing procedures and operational codes by which the political system operates to achieve the core values. Some scholars prefer to say that a political system must operate according to the rules of the game of the community from which the system evolves.

Only if the system operates legally will it be considered legitimate by the people. The way people perceive their political system forms the basis of legitimacy.

People act on what they perceive, whether it be in terms of the political system or in day-to-day living. "Beauty is in the eye of the beholder." In politics, people have mental images of the way the world should be and the way it is, and each person acts according to the way he sees it. The pictures in people's minds determine their political behavior and their ultimate assessment of the political system.

Our perceptions come from our total life experiences. The way in which we were brought up by our parents, religious experiences, friends and neighbors, education, etc.—all of these add to and shape the way we view the world around us.

Perceptions are to a person what blinders are to the horse. They provide a direction and point of view in assessing the environment and determining the breadth of that view. Thus, an individual with narrow perceptions is likely to be more rigid, dogmatic, and less tolerant in his political attitudes. (One should not necessarily assume that higher education will create broader perception; increased education can sometimes narrow perceptions.) In any case, the nature of the perceptions held by individuals is the basis upon which the rules of the game and the strength of the political system develop. In more technical or intellectual terms, what we have been talking about is *ideology*.

Ideology

Ideology means more than this, however. As noted earlier, it is the very basis for the existence of a political community and for the operation of the political system. We know that values are essential goals to be served by the political system, while perceptions are the way individuals view the political system and these values. Ideology incorporates both values and perceptions, while adding another dimension: action.

Ideology can therefore be defined as a function of three elements. First, it provides a picture of the world as it is perceived; second, it identifies the world as it ought to be (values); third, it provides a form of action to change the world from what it is to what it ought to be. For ideology to remain relevant and provide the necessary legitimacy for the political system, there must be expectations of a reasonable opportunity to change the existing world to what it ought to be. If the relevancy of the ideology is diminished by changing perceptions and inability to achieve values, it will necessarily diminish the legitimacy of the existing political system. The system then must readjust or adapt itself to regain and maintain the legitimacy of the ideology and to remain stable and solvent. In this sense, the operation of the political system and the meaning of ideology are closely interrelated.

As time passes values may change. As one faces new experiences and learns to deal with them, as one becomes more educated, perceptions may broaden or acquire a different perspective. These in turn provide a different interpretation regarding values and thus lay the groundwork for a revised or modified ideology. It can be said that the more dynamic the society, the more receptive it will be to changing values and perceptions and the more apt to establish an ideology that accepts change as a fundamental part of the value system. There is, however, some risk regarding changing perceptions and the ability of the political system to perform adequately to fulfill expectations. As one scholar of the American urban phenomenon has observed:

> ... improvements in performance, great as they have been have not kept pace with rising expectations. In other words although things have been getting better absolutely, they have been getting worse relative to what we think they should be. And this is because, as a people, we seem to act on the advice of the old jingle:
>
> > Good, better, best
> > Never let it rest
> > Until your good is better
> > And your better best.[1]

Briefly then, politics means a conflict over values and the means of resolving the conflicts. The concept of political system includes the idea that governmental and political processes arise out of the need to identify those conflicts and to apply the proper measures to solve them. All of this is done within the ideology of society.

The Meaning of Power

Power determines the way conflicts are resolved. The concept of power conjures up evil connotations in the minds of many. Yet power is inherent in all relationships and is a neutral instrument. It is not power per se that is essential, but the manner in which it is used.

The concept of power is an elusive one; few scholars agree on its specific meaning. In an introductory study of political systems, the focus on power provides a single essential theme that is a prime characteristic of all governments and politics. We must recognize, however, that power is difficult to measure. It operates sometimes in subtle ways and sometimes in quite visible fashion. It may be used in a number of ways on a number of people or events, with a varying degree of impact. Although power operates in multidimensional and complex forms, for our purposes it is sufficient to recognize that it exists in any political system. It is power that gets things done. Without it, there is little likelihood that any group or individual can make any impact on politics.

While power exists in substance, it is difficult to identify in form. Most people recognize power when it is used overtly—when they see it used, they can appreciate its impact—but few can really outline its boundaries or describe its specific form. In simplest terms, power means the ability to get another person to do what you want. To accomplish this, you can use a variety of methods, from bribes to outright threats—even a punch in the nose. Groups, institutions, and governments employ similar means, although in more sophisticated form. Thus, regardless of the complexities that the term power suggests, it is a useful and realistic concept.

One of the first uses of the concept of power in the study of governmental relationships was at the international level. In a noted study of international politics by Hans Morgenthau, *Politics Among Nations,* power is identified as the key purpose behind the relationships of states. According to Morgenthau, in international relations each state seeks to better its power position over other states. It is presumed that all policy and interest is based on this motivating factor.[2]

In applying the power concept to domestic politics, we find a number of similarities with the international arena, although with some qualifications. The formal and informal relationships between governmental institutions, decision makers, and groups in society, as well as individuals, are determined and influenced by power. The amount of power applied and the ultimate power outcome of these relationships determine the priority of values basic to the political system and the manner of resolving conflicts.

Consensus and Coercion

Power and influence will be used synonymously in this book to include a whole range of mechanisms from persuasion and bargaining to coercion and the use of physical force. Similarly, this concept will be used with regard to formal and informal institutions, groups, decision makers and individuals in our society.

In a broad sense, power has two faces, coercive and consensual. They are interconnected and interdependent. It is difficult to conceive of coercive power without appreciating consensual power. For example, during the period of student unrest, the demonstrations were attempts to force the government to stop the war in Vietnam. The government's response in such incidents as Kent State and Jackson State University could be described as the use of coercive power to halt the students' activities. An example of the effect of consensual power is President Johnson's decision not to run for a second term in 1968. There was growing dissatisfaction in the nation with the manner in which the government was conducting the war. The consensus was that President Johnson was not very popular and did not have a very good chance of being re-elected. Consequently, he did not run for the presidency, and we can say his decision was influenced by consensual power.

In a democratic society we would expect power to be based primarily on consensus, with the need for physical coercion rare. On the other hand, in a totalitarian system we assume that the use of physical coercion is a dominant feature, since the basis of such a system is total control of individuals and social groups. If a democratic system resorts increasingly to physical coercion, it is well on its way to undermining the democratic nature of the system and society. However, we must not forget that part of consensus develops out of the recognition that the political system does have a coercive capability. Similarly, even in a totalitarian system there must be some kind of consensus, even if only among the ruling elite. The relationship between coercive and consensual power is clearer when viewed in terms of totalitarian and democratic systems, as shown below.

The Power Scale as an Indicator of Types of Political Systems

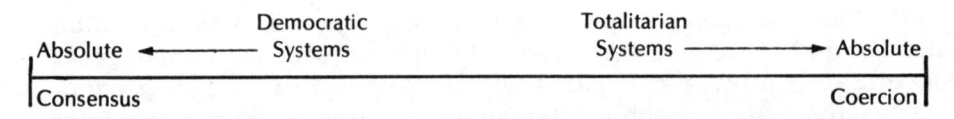

Absolute	← Democratic Systems	Totalitarian Systems →	Absolute
Consensus			Coercion

Thus we assume that in democratic systems, power is based primarily on consensus while in totalitarian systems, it rests mainly on the coercive power of the state. No state power rests totally on either coercion or consensus, however, but rather on a combination of both.

Power and Its Problems

One of the basic problems in any political system is that power is easily misused. The boundaries of power are obscure in a democratic system, which is replete with negotiations, bargaining, compromise, discussions, debate, shifting power alignments, and a variety of power holders. Thus each power holder is tempted to seek the limits of his power, restrained only by public reaction, other power holders, or his own conscience. This can easily lead to an environment in which power holders are enticed to seek more power for its own sake. As Lord Acton observed; "Power begot power." Nevertheless in our system of democracy there are countervailing forces: a free press, the opportunity for public scrutiny, the moral ingredient of democratic ideology, and the diffusion and decentralization of power.

Political Actors

Power holders in our society include a variety of individuals, institutions, and groups. Some achieve power by virtue of their wealth and ability to influence decision makers. Others achieve power because of their official position in government. Still others develop a power base because of their business interests or organizational associations. Yet, the most basic means of attaining power is through the ballot box, via election to some position, whether it be city alderman or president of the United States.

Power holders in society can be conceived of as political actors. We use this term to suggest that the political system consists of instruments, power bases, and processes upon which the power holder *acts* to achieve certain purposes. Political actors, therefore, are institutions, groups, and individuals who wield power to affect the political system. They determine how the system operates and how conflicts are resolved, and they set the limits and restraints on power.

All political actors are not struggling for power with the same intensity and scope over every issue. Where the issues are not of great concern, only a few participants will be involved in the power equation; as the issues become broader, they touch a great number of participants. The participants and the kinds of roles they play are likely to change depending on the issues involved. Regardless of who is involved in the power equation, the system is maintained by satisfied political actors, even though they may not achieve their goals in the power struggle. This satisfaction comes from the realization that within the system they can play the power game and will have continuing opportunities to achieve their goals.

In this context political actors include the following:

Decision makers: those persons who hold official positions within the political system high enough on the responsibility scale to make important decisions regarding the values, resources, and operations of the system

Groups: those interest groups whose main operational environment is or can be the political process, and which are organized specifically for political participation, e.g., political parties, Common Cause, labor unions

Institutions: formal or informal bodies that are primarily involved in implementing policy and whose character has some impact on the political system, e.g., informal structures that develop in relationships between various institutions such as the legislative branch, judiciary, and the bureaucracy

Political influentials: those persons who do not have official positions in the political system, but by virtue of their status and resources can have important impact on the operation of the political system, e.g., millionaire W. Clement Stone, contributor of large sums of money to the Republican party

Individuals: Very little can normally be accomplished by individuals working by themselves to influence the political system, although there are some exceptions. However, in times of crisis or when major issues arise, individuals become important as part of a national constituency or "public" that can be appealed to as the basis for legitimacy of certain policies. Elected officials also desire to maintain the proper image with the people. It is through such indirect linkages that individuals have an impact on the political system. The collective term "people" does perhaps have some substance but very little specific identity. It covers all sections of the country, all ethnic groups, all socioeconomic levels, and a multitude of political attitudes.

Political actors do not operate in isolated compartments; their boundary lines are not sharply drawn. Indeed, in a number of cases, they are inexplicably involved with one another. Nevertheless, it is useful to consider them in these categories because it helps make the study of the American political system manageable and comprehensible.

Some political actors who are in a position to exercise power and accept responsibility avoid both. They prefer to enjoy the trappings of office or the social status and the privileges that go with it rather than exercise power.

Former Secretary of State Dean Rusk, commenting on this type of political actor, stated:

> The processes of government have sometimes been described as a struggle for power among those holding public office. I am convinced that this is true only in a certain formal and bureaucratic sense, having

Politics, Power and the Political System

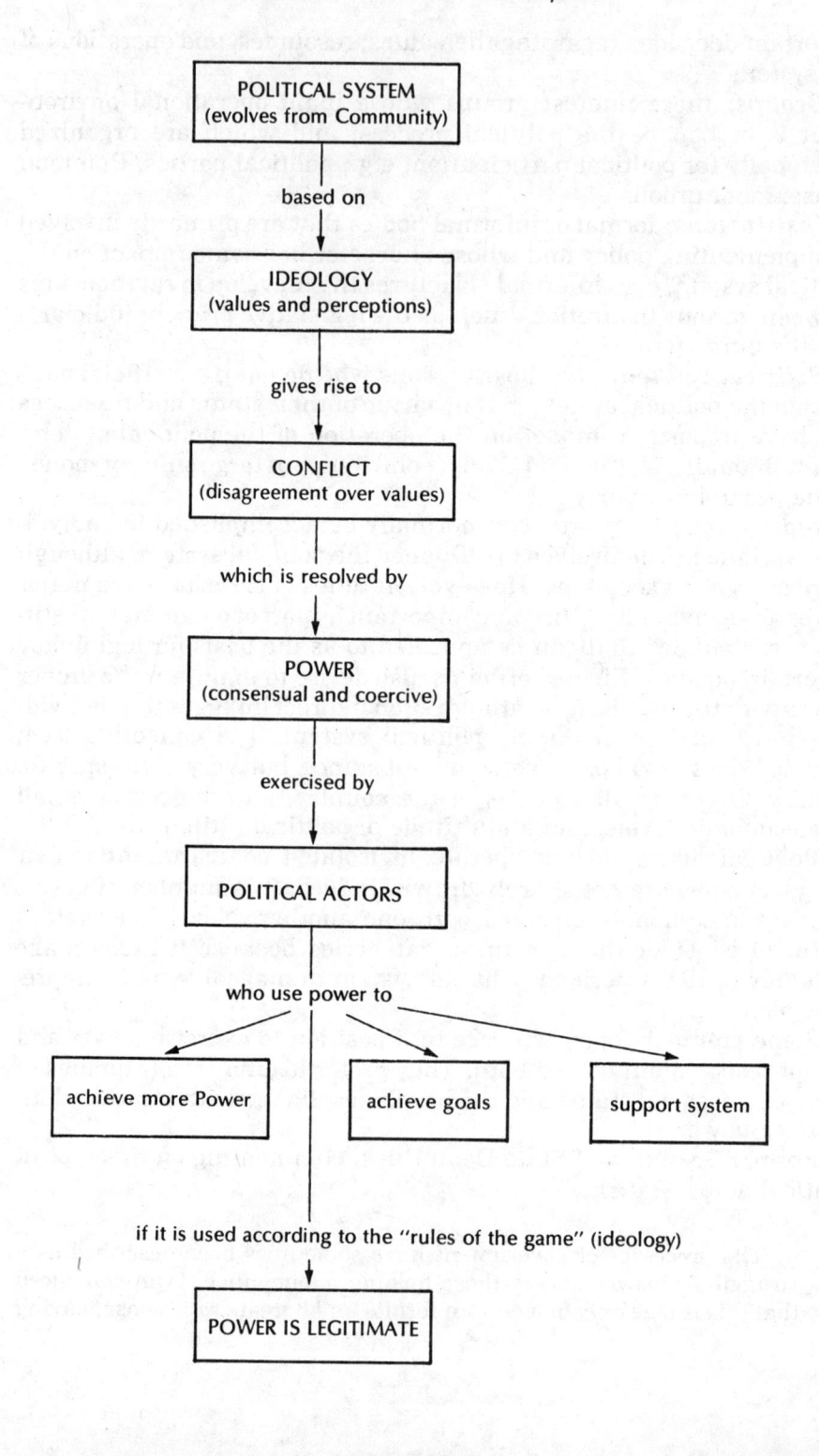

```
┌──────────────────────────┐
│    POLITICAL SYSTEM      │
│  (evolves from Community)│
└────────────┬─────────────┘
             │ based on
             ▼
┌──────────────────────────┐
│        IDEOLOGY          │
│  (values and perceptions)│
└────────────┬─────────────┘
             │ gives rise to
             ▼
┌──────────────────────────┐
│        CONFLICT          │
│ (disagreement over values)│
└────────────┬─────────────┘
             │ which is resolved by
             ▼
┌──────────────────────────┐
│          POWER           │
│ (consensual and coercive)│
└────────────┬─────────────┘
             │ exercised by
             ▼
┌──────────────────────────┐
│    POLITICAL ACTORS      │
└────────────┬─────────────┘
             │ who use power to
   ┌─────────┼──────────┐
   ▼         ▼          ▼
┌────────┐┌────────┐┌─────────┐
│achieve ││achieve ││ support │
│more    ││ goals  ││ system  │
│Power   ││        ││         │
└────────┘└───┬────┘└─────────┘
              │ if it is used according to the "rules of the game" (ideology)
              ▼
      ┌──────────────────┐
      │POWER IS LEGITIMATE│
      └──────────────────┘
```

to do with appropriations, job descriptions, trappings of prestige, water bottles and things of that sort. There is another struggle of far more consequence, the effort to diffuse or avoid responsibility. *Power gravitates to those who are willing to make decisions and live with the results,* simply because there are so many who readily yield to the intrepid few who take their duties seriously.[3]

Power Relationships

Let us review the concepts we have discussed in this chapter by studying the diagram of politics, power, and the political system. The relationships depicted are of necessity oversimplified, but the diagram is useful in placing these concepts in a clearer perspective. (See opposite page.)

In studying any political system, students must realize that there are a variety of approaches and a number of variables. No one particular approach is completely satisfactory. On the other hand, there are some common features of all political systems, which have been discussed in this chapter. We have focused on the power theme, because we believe it to be an essential element in all political systems. More important, this approach provides a link between the myths and realities of the American political process. Combining the power theme with the concept of political actors, we will be able to portray the American political system in a dynamic and realistic way.

Notes

1. Edward C. Banfield, *The Unheavenly City; The Nature and Future of Our Urban Crisis* (Boston: Little, Brown, 1970), p. 19.
2. Hans J. Morgenthau, *Politics Among Nations: The Struggle for Power and Peace*, 5th ed. (New York: Alfred A. Knopf, 1973).
3. As quoted in Roger Hilsman, *The Politics of Policy Making in Defense and Foreign Affairs* (New York: Harper and Row, 1971), p. 152. Italics added.

Selected Readings

As we have suggested in this chapter, there are a number of ways that one may study political systems. We have combined a systems approach with the power concept. Some familiarity must be developed with political concepts and their relationships with one another. We feel that the stress on the power concept provides a realistic perspective through which the student can develop a meaningful framework for understanding the American political system.

The readings in this chapter are selections from some of the most noted scholars on politics and power. The brief selections should provide an added dimension to the concepts developed in the chapter.

The first selection, by Robert Dahl, distinguishes between power, influence, and authority. He points out the various influences placed by one actor upon another in order to accomplish a specific goal. Dahl briefly examines the condition under which actors are influenced and directed in a particular course of action.

R. M. MacIver, in the second selection, discusses the meaning of power, expanding on the points made by Dahl. According to MacIver, "power is multi-form" and simply means the "capacity to control the behavior of others." He observes that power is inherent in all social relationships and that government power is only one aspect of it—but it is supreme.

The last selection, by Hans Morgenthau, is written from the perspective of international relations, but is particularly relevant here. He argues that "International politics, like all politics is a struggle for power." Morgenthau distinguishes political power from other forms, stating that political power refers to "man's control over the minds and actions of other men." He also discusses the meaning of legitimate and illegitimate power. His characterization of power, its meaning and political perspective are equally applicable to domestic politics.

The student will find these readings useful in understanding the general nature of power. However, the question that remains unanswered is: How can power be measured?

2.1

Influence, Power, Authority, Coercion

ROBERT A. DAHL

Obviously a person is likely to do something if he expects that he will be better off all around if he does it; and he is likely to avoid doing something if he expects that he will be worse off all around if he does it.

This elementary axiom will help us to distinguish certain varieties of influence that have very different significance for us, such as authority and coercion. Imagine a continuum that represents various degrees of value for something that B regards as important—for example, his honor, wealth, prestige, popularity, or health. Assume that a move to the left means that B will be worse off—he will suffer a loss in, say, his wealth; a move to the right means that he will be better off.[1] Thus if A wants to induce B to do something he would not otherwise do, A may promise to make him better off than he would otherwise be ($100 reward if he does), threaten to make him worse off ($100 fine if he doesn't), or both ($100 reward if he does, $100 fine if he doesn't).

Now let us assume that in the absence of any attempt by A to influence B, B would be located at the center of the continuum at O:

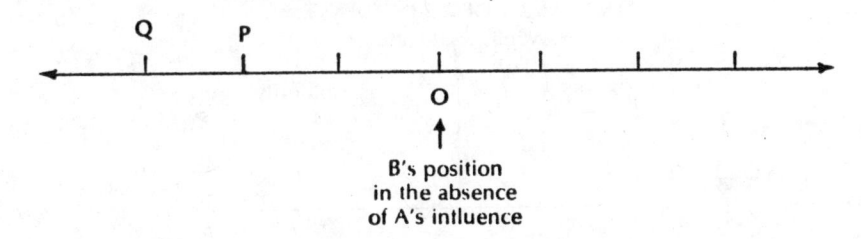

```
   Q     P
───┼──┼──┼──┼──┼──┼──┼──┼──▶
            O
            ↑
        B's position
        in the absence
        of A's influence
```

The concept of *influence*, one might say, includes the whole continuum; it runs all the way from the one extreme to the other and includes all possible combinations.

Robert A. Dahl, *Modern Political Analysis*, 2d ed., © 1970, pp. 32-34. Reprinted by permission of Prentice-Hall, Inc., Englewood Cliffs, New Jersey.

Power, on the other hand, is often defined as a special case of influence involving severe *losses* for noncompliance. If A confronts B with the prospect of shifting from O to P unless he complies with A's wishes, then A is attempting to exercise *power* over B.[2]

Exactly what constitutes a "severe" loss or deprivation is, to be sure, somewhat arbitrary. No doubt what a person regards as severe varies a good deal with his experiences, culture, bodily conditions, and so on. Nonetheless, probably among all peoples exile, imprisonment, and death would be considered severe punishments. Therefore whoever can visit penalities like these on people is bound to be important in any society. Indeed, the State is distinguishable from other political systems only to the extent that it successfully upholds the claim to the exclusive right to determine the conditions under which certain kinds of severe penalties, those involving serious physical pain, constraint, punishment, or death, may be legitimately employed.

A particularly ominous kind of power involves *only* the prospect of great loss. Suppose that A confronts B with the alternative "Your money or your life!" In general terms, B must choose between something bad (P) or something very much worse (Q). If B hands over his wallet, as he probably will, he may say later, "I had no choice." In one sense, of course, B does have a choice; but he has no reasonable or satisfactory choice. Hence he considers himself *coerced. Coercion,* then, is a form of power that exists whenever A compels B to comply by confronting him *only* with alternatives involving severe deprivation. The ultimate case of coercion is taking B's life.

An interesting question arises at once. Suppose that A, the Government, commands B: "Pay your income taxes or go to jail." Supposed further that B is a law-abiding citizen who believes in paying his income taxes. In one sense, B will be worse off if he pays his taxes; and certainly he will be worse off if he goes to jail. Even so, he quite willingly pays his taxes. Shall we now say that B is *coerced?*

FIGURE 5 Some dimensions of influence.

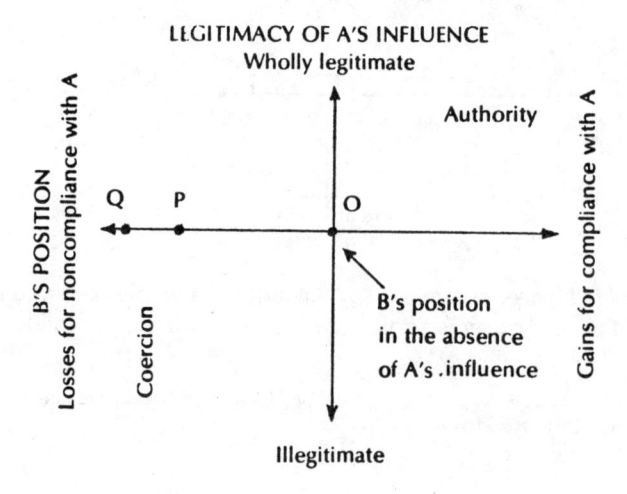

To answer this question, let us imagine a second dimension. At one end of this continuum are all the commands or requests by A which B feels has a perfect right to ask of him, and which he has a complete obligation to accept. Influence or power of this kind is often said to be *legitimate*. At the other end of the continuum are all the commands or requests by A which B feels A has absolutely no right to ask him to obey, which he has no obligation to obey, and which, perhaps, he actually has an obligation to resist. Influence or power of this kind is often said to be *illegitimate*. Legitimate power or influence is generally called *authority*.

Let us now combine the two dimensions of influence and legitimacy, as in Figure 5. The shaded segment at the top of Figure 5 is the area of meaning included in the term "authority." To return now to the question about coercion, shall we say that the upper left-hand corner of Figure 5 refers to power that is both legitimate and coercive? To do so would, I think, run so counter to the usual meaning of our language as to be confusing. It seems wise, then, to restrict the meaning of coercion to the shaded area at the lower left of the figure. In this sense, coercion implies *illegitimate* power involving *only* the prospect of great loss.

It is easy to see, then, why political philosophers have generally regarded coercion as an evil—not necessarily an evil that can be avoided, but surely an evil that ought to be minimized. It is also easy to see why access to the power of the State is fought over so fiercely. For whoever controls the State inevitably has access to coercion. What is more, those who control the State rarely forgo entirely the use of some degree of coercion.

Finally, it is now easy to see why the analysis of power is so full of pitfalls. Here are some common errors that the preceding discussion should help one to detect and avoid:

1. Failing to distinguish clearly between participating in a decision, influencing a decision, and being affected by the consequences of a decision.
2. Failing to identify the scope within which an actor is said to be influential.
3. Failing to distingusih different degrees of power—for example, by equating the proposition that power is distributed unequally in a political system with the proposition that the system is ruled by a ruling class.
4. Confusing an actor's past or present power with his potential power, particularly by assuming that the greater the political resources an actor has access to, the greater his power must be.
5. Equating an actor's expected future power with his potential power, particularly by ignoring differences in incentives and skills.
6. Forgetting that an actor's reputation for influence is only a resource, and therefore may be a bad predictor of potential influence, particularly if he lacks other resources or the skills and incentives to use his resources.
7. Ignoring the possibility that if A has potential power, B may too. If A attempts to use his resources, B may too. Thus the costs of A's exercising power may escalate. Knowing this in advance, A may decide that the game isn't worth the candle. Consequently: don't think only about A's resources and forget about B's.

The discussion also suggests the following injunctions to the student of politics:

1. Remember that the concept of influence covers an enormous variety of relationships. The less care you take in specifying exactly what you have in mind, the greater the ambiguity in your analysis.

2. When you try to estimate the relative influence of different actors, look for information that will enable you to use as many measures as possible.
3. Adapt your comparison to the kind of information available.
4. Be specific. A paradigm for any comparison of power might be: "____ is more influential than ____ with respect to ____ as measured by ____ and ____."
5. Be constantly aware of what you had to leave out of your analysis. In later chapters, we may violate every injunction except this one.

NOTES

1. Many other terms to describe this kind of situation can be used interchangeably. Becoming better off is equivalent to gains, rewards, benefits, advantages, inducements, positive incentives, indulgences. Becoming worse off is equivalent to losses, penalities, disadvantages, negative incentives, deprivations, sanctions.

2. This accords with the definition of Harold D. Lasswell and Abraham Kaplan, in *Power and Society* (New Haven: Yale University Press, 1950): "A *decision* is a policy involving severe sanctions (deprivations)- . . . *power* is participation in the making of decisions. . . . It is the threat of sanctions which differentiates power from influence in general. Power is a special case of the exercise of influence: it is the process of affecting policies of others with the help of (actual or threatened) severe deprivations for non-conformity with the policies intended." Lasswell cites as comparable Locke's use of the term in the *Two Treatises of Government:* "Political Power, then, I take to be a right of making laws, with penalties of death, and consequently all less penalties" (pp. 74-76).

2.2

The Nature of Social Power

R. M. MacIVER

Power is multi-form. By social power we mean the capacity to control the behavior of others either directly by fiat or indirectly by the manipulation of available means. Property and status are thus sources of power. But there are various other sources. The office a man holds gives him a certain amount of power, apart from the status attaching to it or the particular prestige of the office-holder. This is the power of bureaucracy. Akin to it is the power of any specialist, who can take advantage of his function or technique to control to his liking the actions of other men. There is also the ampler power accruing to the leadership of any organization, varying with the kind of organization and its extent. In the modern world managerial and executive functions constitute one of the primary sources of power. Now that all interests are organized these posts of power are vastly more numerous and multifarious than formerly. Social groups and classes that once were nearly powerless, servants and not masters of men, such as farmers and industrial workers, have through organization gained for themselves new economic power of far-reaching significance; but even more phenomenal is the power that thus falls into the hands of the men who head and often dominate these organizations. The leader of a great trade union organization can now, under favorable conditions, dictate to president or king, and may finally elevate himself to the highest position in the land.

Similarly, throughout the economic structure, no matter whether it be established on capitalist or on socialist lines, there is a hierarchy of power leading up from the corporals to the captains and the generals of industry. In the modern world this power attaches far more to the management than to the ownership of property, and this fact tends to create a certain resemblance between the power structure of capitalism and that of socialism. It is true that the managers of capitalistic enterprise, of railroads and telephone systems and public utility chains and steel corporations and many other great businesses are themselves men of means and are themselves greatly interested in the profits reaped by their corporations. But their economic

R. M. MacIver, *The Web of Government*, Revised Edition, 1965, pp. 66-68 and 71-72. Reprinted with permission of Macmillan Publishing, Inc. © R. M. MacIver, 1965.

reward comes primarily from the salaries they draw and has usually no relation to the number of shares they own. The property stake of the directors of a modern corporation may be quite insignificant compared with the dominion they enjoy over it. The possessor of a few shares of stock may control the fate and fortune of a corporation capitalized at twenty million shares. Parallel with this industrial domination there runs a system of financial domination, exercised by banks, trust companies, insurance companies, and so forth. The power of this "money trust" is in various ways linked up with that of industrial corporations, though sometimes it gains supremacy over the latter. To complete this brief picture of economic power we must include the ramifying combines and trusts, the inter-locking directorates, and the numerous kinds of informal agreement that give the great entrepreneurs a massive control over the economy of nations. Beyond these stretch the portentous imperia of the cartels, each dividing the whole earth or large portions of it between its constituent members in order to control the supply and distribution of its particular product or products, to the greater profit of its constituents and for the greater dominion of its economic overlords.

When we turn to the fields of cultural activity we observe that here also power breeds and proliferates. In these fields also leadership and office give men control over the behavior of other men. This control is more selective in the sense that those who primarily respond to it are united not so much by a common territory or a common nationality as by a common faith, a common ideology, or a common mission. But it easily exceeds these limits. We have seen that from the earliest times the priest, the master of the lore, the mandarin, have disputed pre-eminence with the chief and the war-leader. In the advanced civilization of Egypt and in the feudal theocracy of the Middle Ages the priestly hierarchy was at times strong enough to command the secular authority. Under modern conditions the diversity of faiths has in many countries made this direct supremacy of the religious order no longer feasible, but even in these countries the organized church often remains a great power. It sometimes has also the advantage of being an international power. This advantage belongs in especial to the Roman Catholic Church.

Numerous other forms of cultural activity also generate power after their kind. Eminence in the creative arts carries a prestige that gives some weight to the opinions of the artist. Somewhat more impressive, though still rather transient and limited, is the power that springs from the popular acclaim of the successful actor, movie star, opera singer, novelist, columnist, and so forth. Publicity in our times is itself a kind of power, an asset that gives influence as well as social éclat to its possessor.

The agencies of publicity take higher rank in the power structure. Here we reach a source of power peculiarly modern, the control, through ownership or otherwise, of those media of communication that transmit news or promulgate opinion. We include here the motion picture industry, since it purveys news and since the films it produces inevitably are impregnated with some kind of doctrine or at least with some philosophy of life. We include the radio, though, owing to the technical conditions of broadcasting, government regulation and other considerations restrict tendencies to make this medium the organ of the particular doctrines or policies of the companies which own it—where the radio system is not state-administered.

Where democratic conditions prevail state administration is itself subject to similar restrictions. It is otherwise with the business of publishing, especially the publishing of newspapers and periodicals. Since news-gathering is a vast and costly enterprise and since the economics of newspaper publishing limits the number of major newspapers in any area to a very small group, the power of the press is concentrated in the hands of a few men. This power of the press is increased through the develpment of newspaper chains under one ownership, through the syndication of articles and features, and through the hook-up of newspapers with radio stations. The newspaper has another kind of power, in that it determines the degree of publicity to be assigned to the doings of persons and organizations, apart from the publicity of paid advertising. The importance of this power depends on the fact that publicity in modern society is not only a factor of prestige but also, for certain occupational categories and for many kinds of organization, a primary condition of success in their respective pursuits.

This brief conspectus shows us again what we have already noted, that social power inheres in all social relations and in all social organizations. The power of government is one aspect of power among many. It is formally supreme, in the sense that government alone has the ultimate right to use direct coercion. Formally it assigns limit and place to all other exercises of power. But this statement is barren if not supplemented by the further statement that government itself is a creature of society and is subject to the pulls and pressures of the other foci of power. What power the government wields and to what ends it directs this power depends on these other forces, on the manner in which they are operatively adjusted to one another in the struggle and clash, the convergence and divergence, of power-possessing interests. . . .

Having vindicated political power from the charge that it is merely the agent of another form of power we can now complete our survey by examining its distinctive character. We have noted that certain social attributes, themselves elements of power, such as status and property, have under historical conditions determined in what hands the authority of government shall reside and to what ends it shall be mainly directed. We have noted also that the bases of authority change with the changes in the society. We must now make it clear that, whatever its derivation, the power of government is different from the power which gains access to it. What status and property accomplish under the given conditions is to determine *who* shall hold the reins of political power, rather than *what* shall be the essential functions of that power. For under all conditions political power is the final regulatory control of the social order. The character of that order is to some extent, but only to a quite minor extent except in the rare convulsions of revolution, modified by the will of the particular government in office. To a vastly greater extent government does not create the social order that it sustains. Hence the power of government is entirely different in kind from the powers that may at any time determine who shall govern.

Political power has a mission and an authority to which no other can lay claim. It alone is the organ of a whole community. It alone requires and demands the obedience of all who live within its territory, without regard to faith or class or race. It alone has determinate geographical frontiers. This eminent difference does not signify, as many have pretended, that the state, the realm of government, is the same thing as the social order itself. It does not signify that all other social organizations are merely parts of the inclusive political organization. It does not signify that citizenship comprises the whole duty of man or sums up all his relationships. This assumption of Hegelian and totalitarian dogma has never been in accord with social realities. What it does signify is that the state supervises the fundamental order of society, that whatever ordinances are deemed necessary to sustain that order, so that some system of justice prevails and so that the disputes and dividing interests of men are adjusted without recourse to violence and in accordance with an established code, fall within the competence of government. Political power is then the power requisite to accomplish these ends.

The ends of political power do not require that it be absolute but they do require that it be superior with respect to whatever it may ordain, subject only to constitutional limitations, and they do require that it alone have in the last resort the right of coercion and alone be invested with the force necessary to ensure coercion. These requirements are formally satisfied in all states except in times of revolution. The formal superiority of government does not imply that the laws of and decrees of government express the particular will of the particular "man or assembly of men" who enact or proclaim them. Behind the monarch stands the adviser or the clique, the favorite, the strong man, or even the mistress. Behind the senate and the assembly stand the strong interests and the pressure groups. Behind them all there stands the ultimate court of public opinion, never wholly to be ignored, however inert and however acquiescent it may remain for long periods under certain social conditions. In short, all the components of social power impinge on government, diverting its formal superiority to the service of their own ends. Since these ends are in conflict one with another there is nearly always struggle and often division of counsel within the governing body itself. . . .

2.3

What Is Political Power?

HANS MORGENTHAU

As Means to the Nation's Ends

International politics, like all politics, is a struggle for power. Whatever the ultimate aims of international politics, power is always the immediate aim. Statesmen and peoples may ultimately seek freedom, security, prosperity, of power itself. They may define their goals in terms of a religious, philosophic, economic, or social ideal. They may hope that this ideal will materialize through its own inner force, through divine intervention, or through the natural development of human affairs. They may also try to further its realization through nonpolitical means, such as technical cooperation with other nations or international organizations. But whenever they strive to realize their goal by means of international politics, they do so by striving for power. The Crusaders wanted to free the holy places from domination by the Infidels; Woodrow Wilson wanted to make the world safe for democracy; the Nazis wanted to open Eastern Europe to German colonization, to dominate Europe, and to conquer the world. Since they all chose power to achieve these ends, they were actors on the scene of international politics . . .[2]

Its Nature

When we speak of power in the context of this book, we have in mind not man's power over nature, or over an artistic medium, such as language, speech, sound, or color, or over the means of production or consumption, or over himself in the sense of self-control. When we speak of power, we mean man's control over the minds and actions of other men. By political power we refer to the mutual relations of control among the holders of public authority and between the latter and the people at large.

From *Politics Among Nations: The Struggle for Power and Peace,* Fifth Edition, by Hans J. Morgenthau. Copyright 1948, 1954, © 1960, 1967, 1972 by Alfred A. Knopf, Inc. Reprinted by permission of the publisher.

Political power is a psychological relation between those who exercise it and those over whom it is exercised. It gives the former control over certain actions of the latter through the impact which the former exert on the latter's minds. That impact derives from three sources: the expectation of benefits, the fear of disadvantages, the respect or love for men or institutions. It may be exerted through orders, threats, the authority or charisma of a man or of an office, or a combination of any of these. . . .

Finally, legitimate power, that is, power whose exercise is morally or legally justified, must be distinguished from illegitimate power. Power exercised with moral or legal authority must be distinguished from naked power. The power of the police officer who searches me by virtue of a search warrant is qualitatively different from the power of a robber who performs the same action by virtue of his holding a gun. The distinction is not only philosophically valid but also relevant for the conduct of foreign policy. Legitimate power, which can invoke a moral or legal justification for its exercise, is likely to be more effective than equivalent illegitimate power, which cannot be so justified. That is to say, legitimate power has a better chance to influence the will of its objects than equivalent illegitimate power. Power exercised in self-defense or in the name of the United Nations has a better chance to succeed than equivalent power exercised by an "aggressor" nation or in violation of international law. Political ideologies, as we shall see, serve the purpose of endowing foreign policies with the appearance of legitimacy.

While it is generally recognized that the interplay of the expectation of benefits, the fear of disadvantages, and the respect or love for men or institutions, in ever changing combinations, forms the basis of all domestic politics, the importance of these factors for international politics is less obvious, but no less real. There has been a tendency to reduce political power to the actual application of force or at least to equate it with successful threats of force and with persuasion, to the neglect of charisma. That neglect, as we shall see,[3] accounts in good measure for the neglect of prestige as an independent element in international politics. Yet without taking into account the charisma of a man, such as Napoleon or Hitler, or of an institution, such as the Soviet Government or the United Nations, evoking trust and love through which the wills of men submit themselves to the will of such a man or institution, it is impossible to understand certain phenomena of international politics which have been particularly prominent in modern times.

The importance which charismatic leadership and the response to it as love of the subject for the leader has for international politics is clearly revealed in a letter which John Durie, Scottish Presbyterian and worker for Protestant unity, wrote in 1632 to the British Ambassador Thomas Roe, explaining the decline of the power of Gustavus Adolphus of Sweden, then fighting for the Protestant cause in Germany:

> The increase of his authority is the ground of his abode; and love is the ground of his authority; it must be through love; for it cannot be through power; for his power is not in his own subjects but in strangers; not in his money, but in theirs; not in their good will, but in mere necessity as things stand now betwixt him and them; therefore if the necessity be not so urgent as it is; or if any other means be shown by God (who is able to do as much by another man as by him) to avoid this necessity; the money and the power and the assistance which it yieldeth unto him will fall from him and so his authority is lost, and his abode will be no longer: for the Love which was at first is gone . . .[4]

The President of the United States exerts political power over the executive branch of the government so long as his orders are obeyed by the members of that branch. The leader of the party has political power so long as he is able to mold the actions of the members of the party according to his will. We refer to the political power of an industrialist, labor leader, or lobbyist in so far as his preferences influence the actions of public officials. The United States exerts political power over Puerto Rico so long as the laws of the United States are observed by the citizens of that island. When we speak of the political power of the United States in Central America, we have in mind the conformity of the actions of Central American governments with the wishes of the government of the United States.[5] Thus the statement that A has or wants political power over B signifies always that A is able, or wants to be able, to control certain actions of B through influencing B's mind. . . .

Regardless of particular social conditions, the decisive argument against the opinion that the struggle for power on the international scene is a mere historic accident must be derived from the nature of domestic politics. The essence of international politics is identical with its domestic counterpart. Both domestic and international politics are a struggle for power, modified only by the different conditions under which this struggle takes place in the domestic and in the international spheres.

The tendency to dominate, in particular, is an element of all human associations, from the family through fraternal and professional associations and local political organizations, to the state. On the family level, the typical conflict between the mother-in-law and her child's spouse is in its essense a struggle for power, the defense of an established power position against the attempt to establish a new one. As such it foreshadows the conflict on the international scene between the policies of the status quo and the policies of imperialism. Social clubs, fraternities, faculties, and business organizations are scenes of continuous struggles for power between groups that either want to keep what power they already have or seek to attain greater power. Competitive contests between business enterprises as well as labor disputes between employers and employees are frequently fought not only, and sometimes not even primarily, for economic advantages, but for influence over each other and over others; that is, for power. Finally, the whole political life of a nation, particularly of a democratic nation, from the local to the national level, is a continuous struggle for power. In periodic elections, in voting in legislative assemblies, in lawsuits before courts, in administrative decisions and executive measures—in all these activities men try to maintain or to establish their power over other men. The processes by which legislative, judicial, executive, and administrative decisions are reached are subject to pressures and counterpressures by "pressure groups" trying to defend and expand their positions of power. As one of the Dead Sea scrolls puts it:

> What nation likes to be oppressed by a stronger power? Or who wants his property plundered unjustly? Yet, is there a single nation that has not oppressed its neighbour? Or where in the world will you find a people that has not plundered the property of another? Where indeed?

"Of the gods we know," to quote Thucydides, "and of men we believe, that it is necessary law of their nature that they rule wherever they can."[6] Or, as Tolstoy put it:" . . . the very process of dominating another's will was in itself a pleasure, a habit, and a necessity to Dólokhov."[7]

And in the words of John of Salisbury:

> Though it is not given to all men to seize princely or royal power, yet the man who is wholly untainted by tyranny is rare or nonexistent. In common speech the tyrantis one who oppresses a whole people by a rulership based on force; and yet it is not over a people as a whole that a man can play the tyrant, but he can do so if he will even in the meanest station. For if not over the whole boey of the people, still each man will lord it as far as his power extends.[8]

In view of this ubiquity of the struggle for power in all social relations and on all levels of social organization, is it surprising that international politics is of necessity power politics? And would it not be rather surprising if the struggle for power were but an accidental and ephemeral attribute of international politics when it is a permanent and necessary element of all branches of domestic politics?

NOTES

1. The concept of political power poses one of the most difficult and controversial problems of political science. The value of any concept used in political science is determined by its ability to explain a maximum of the phenomena that are conventionally considered to belong to a certain sphere of political activity. Thus the coverage of a concept of political power, to be useful for the understanding of international politics, must be broader than the coverage of one adopted to operate in the field of municipal politics. The political means employed in the latter are much more narrowly circumscribed than are those employed in international politics.

2. For some significant remarks on power in relation to international politics, see Lionel Robbins, *The Economic Causes of War* (London: Jonathan Cape, 1939), pp. 63 ff.

3. See Chapter 6.

4. Gunnar Westin, *Negotiations About Church Unity*, 1628-1634 (Upsala: Almquist and Wiksells, 1932), p. 208. The spelling has been modernized.

5. The examples in the text illustrate also the distinction between political power as mere social fact, as in the case of the lobbyist, and political power in the sense of legitimate authority; i.e., of the President of the United States. Both the President of the United States and the lobbyist exercise political power, however different its source and nature may be.

6. Thucydides, Book V, § 105.

7. Leo Tolstoy, *War and Peace*, Book Eight, Chapter XI.

8. John of Salisbury, *Policraticus*, translated by John Dickinson (New York: Alfred A. Knopf, 1927), Vol. VII, p. 17.

Study Questions

1. In your own words, define *politics, political system,* and *political community.* How does the concept "rules of the game" relate to *political community*?

2. Why is ideology important to the understanding of politics? Do you have an ideology? If so, what are some of its main elements? Does every political system need an ideology? Why?

3. Discuss and relate the concept of power to politics and political systems.

Point out some examples of power in day-to-day relationships in which you are involved.

4. Discuss the problems of power in a democratic system. All democratic systems operate on a consensual basis. Is this true or false? If it is false, then how can a democracy really be a democracy if it must use coercion?

5. Power holders are political actors. Is this a contradiction in the operation of the American democratic system? Who and what are political actors? Why are they called actors?

6. When is power legitimate? Does this mean that all political systems must be democratic if their power is to be called legitimate?

7. Explain the power model used in this book. Does this appear to be a valid approach for the study of the American political system? Other political systems?

Bibliography

Books

Almond, Gabriel A., and Powell, G. Bingham, Jr. *Comparative Politics: A Developmental Approach.* Boston: Little, Brown and Co., 1966.

Cassinelli, C. W. *The Politics of Freedom: An Analysis of the Modern Democratic State.* Seattle: University of Washington Press, 1961.

Charlesworth, James C., ed. *Contemporary Political Analysis.* New York: The Free Press, 1967.

Cohen, Carl. *Democracy.* Athens, Ga.: University of Georgia Press, 1971.

de Tocqueville, Alexis. *Democracy in America.* Garden City, N.Y.: Doubleday. 1969.

Easton, David. *A Framework for Political Analysis.* Englewood Cliffs, N.J.: Prentice-Hall, 1965.

Hass, Michael, and Kariel, Henry S., eds. *Approaches to the Study of Political Science.* Scranton, Pa.: Chandler Publishing Co., 1970.

Lippmann, Walter. *The Public Philosophy.* Boston: Little, Brown and Co., 1955.

Mills, C. Wright. *The Power Elite.* New York: Oxford University Press, 1956.

Sargent, Lyman T. *Contemporary Political Ideologies.* Homewood, Ill.: The Dorsey Press, 1969.

Wiseman, H. V. *Political Systems: Some Sociological Approaches.* New York: Praeger Publishers, 1966.

Articles

Deutsch, Karl W., and Rieselbach, Leroy M. "Recent Trends in Political Theory and Political Philosophy," *The Annals of the American Academy of Political and Social Science,* Vol. 360 (July 1965), pp. 139–162.

Easton, David. "Approach to the Analysis of Political Systems," *World Politics,* Vol. 9, No. 3 (1957), pp. 383–400.

CHAPTER 3
The Constitution: Basis for Power

The American bicentennial celebration not only commemorates two hundred years of American history, but also recognizes the success of the Constitution, written almost two hundred years ago. Although the Constitution has been amended, reinterpreted, and criticized many times, the basic grant of power to the political system remains essentially the same.

From rather simple beginnings, the American nation has developed into a powerful industrial democracy under the same basic document. It is this peculiarity that makes study of the American political system difficult for many Americans and almost incomprehensible to foreigners. Even the most astute observer, for example, would have difficulty in explaining the relationships between the national government and each of the individual states under our system of federalism. Our system of judicial review is unique. The concept of separation of powers and checks and balances is likewise a unique feature of the American system. And most important of all, the concern with individual rights and freedoms is well established in our political system. These principles developed out of the particular conditions the American nation faced in the late eighteenth century and form the basis of our political system.

The Constitutional Convention

The framers in 1787 were faced with a number of important issues. First, they were aware of the weaknesses in the Articles of Confederation. A government with a strong central executive that could take positive measures in emergencies was needed. The Hamiltonians, in particular, did not want another government in which the central authority had to go begging to the states for money and men to fight a war. Second, the framers were concerned about the tyranny that could develop from power granted to a strong central government. They wanted to insure that one part of the government could not control other parts. They spoke in terms of a balanced government, one in which there existed powers to restrict any attempt by one branch to gain control over others. Third, the framers desired a constitutional government that could exercise limited power—only that power expressly given to it by the people. Admittedly, there were many disagreements, selfish sectional interests, and conflicts over economic issues at the Constitutional Convention. Yet, nearly all of the delegates agreed on the basic issues.

> That there should be a federal system, with sovereignty somehow divided between the states and central government, was accepted by all but one or two of them. Republican government drawing its authority from the people and eventually responsible to them, was also a universal assumption. A measure of democracy followed inevitably from this principle, for even the most aristocratic delegates agreed that the ordinary citizen should share in the process of selecting those who were to make and execute the laws. All also agreed, however, that no group within society, no matter how numerous should have unrestricted authority . . .[1]

The fifty-five delegates to the Convention were men of property and wealth, representing a wide range of political views, and the average age was about forty. The initial purpose of the Convention was not to write a new constitution, but to revise the Articles of Confederation. Yet the delegates understood the need to establish a working national government.

Their activities did not receive unanimous support. From the very beginning there was controversy regarding the Convention itself. Patrick Henry, who did not attend, stated, "I smelt a rat." For various reasons, other noted figures in the struggle for independence, including John Adams, Samuel Adams, John Hancock, Thomas Paine, and Thomas Jefferson were not present. Most Americans look back at the Constitutional Convention and the document it created as a work of heroes, almost divinely ordained. Actually, during the Convention and the subsequent period of ratification, there were a number of opponents. While Thomas Jefferson and others might consider the framers' work a masterpiece of political genius, others would say,

> These lawyers and men of learning, and monied men that talk so finely, and gloss over matters so smoothly, to make us poor illiterate people swallow down the pill, expect to get in the Congress themselves ... get all the power ... and then they will swallow up us little fellows, ... just as the whale swallowed up Jonah.[2]

The framers were not theoreticians, but practical men representing distinguished families and the elite of American society. They were bankers, lawyers, merchants, and congressmen. Their views on government were grounded in the practicalities of the day. They knew of the theories of Montesquieu, Locke, and Mill, but they also were aware of the needs of a new nation faced with immediate problems of unity and control.

Compromises

What emerged from the Convention was a short compromise document, providing specific grants of power, while leaving many things unsaid. Certain features were incorporated to protect the government against the irrational action of the masses, e.g., the electoral college, indirect election of senators, and the difficult amendment process. The document attempted to protect against authoritarian control while providing for an effective central government and maintaining maximum freedom for the people and individual states. Provision was made for the direct involvement of the people in choosing their government representatives. Aside from political compromises, the framers had to compromise with various interests represented at the Philadelphia gathering.

One of the most notable debates was that associated with the nature of the national legislature and the representation of the states. Small states and those favoring some form of confederation supported the New Jersey plan, which provided for a one-house legislative body, similar to the Confederation, with equality of state representation. This plan would provide for a strong national government, but one that would not be dominated by large wealthy states. On the other hand, the Virginia plan provided for a two-house legislature, the first branch to be elected by the people and the second to be chosen from persons nominated by the state legislatures. Representation of a state in both houses was to be based on the state's financial contributions and size of the population. Obviously, this plan would be highly advantageous to the large wealthy states.

What eventually evolved was the "Connecticut Compromise," which provided for a bicameral legislature with one house representing the people and the other, the states—the system still in use.

The Changing Constitution

Since the Constitutional Convention, the United States has grown into a powerful industrialized democracy. We have had to cope with many complex social, economic, and political issues that the founding fathers could not have foreseen. This has resulted in a number of amendments to the Constitution, many judicial interpretations, and continually changing constitutional practices.

For example, the growth and development of a strong political party system has worked against the separation of powers and federal structure. When the president, Congress, and many state executives come from the same political party, the tendency may be to act in concert rather than to limit or restrain power.

Similarly, the rise of the presidency to a dominating position in our political system may have circumvented some of the countervailing power concepts envisioned by the founding fathers. The establishment of a large and efficient bureaucracy, which remains outside of the electoral process, cuts across constitutional and party lines. These and other factors must be considered as qualifications to the original concepts of the framers.

However, the Constitution should not be viewed as a rigid answer to all men for all times. It was not intended to provide answers for all problems. What the founding fathers intended was a document capable of establishing a stable democratic government, which would still be flexible enough to respond to changing times and demands.

Constitutional Principles

What ultimately evolved was a document based on four fundamental principles: federalism, separation of powers and checks and balances, limited government, and judicial supremacy. Each of these has been interpreted over the past two hundred years in response to the requirements of the particular age. Nevertheless, the substance remains as the framers had envisioned. These principles established the

Constitutional Principles

basis, limits, and constraints on power to be exercised by the political actors within the political system. Moreover, they embodied the core values of the American ideology. Let us now turn our attention to the study of these principles.

Federalism

Political systems can be organized in one of three ways: federal, unitary, or confederation. In a federal system, power from the people is delegated to two political systems, i.e., the central authority and the states. Each authority has autonomous powers in its own sphere. Certain powers are shared while others are exclusive.

In a unitary system, powers are delegated by the people solely to the central authority, which may itself delegate some of its power to subordinate government units. For example, the state system within the United States is based on a unitary system: The states establish local governments and delegate varying degrees of authority to them. Similarly, in England, Parliament is supreme over all other governmental units.

In a confederation, such as the American Confederation of 1775, power of the people is given to the states, which in turn may delegate certain powers to a central authority. The central authority does not

Three basic political systems.

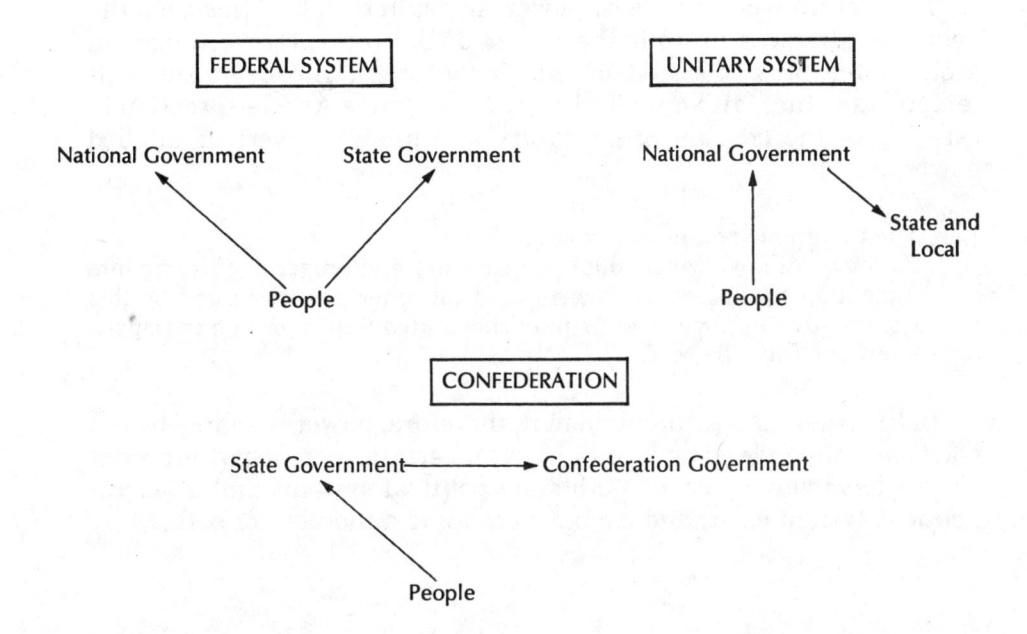

FEDERAL SYSTEM

National Government ← People → State Government

UNITARY SYSTEM

People → National Government → State and Local

CONFEDERATION

State Government → Confederation Government
↑
People

derive its power directly from the people; the states are clearly superior to the central authority. The power patterns in each of these systems becomes clearer when viewed as a schematic.

The Constitution establishes a federal system in the United States by creating two political systems with authority divided between them. Paragraph 2 of Article VI explicitly provides for national supremacy or, more pointedly, constitutional supremacy:

> This Constitution, and the laws of the United States which shall be made in pursuance thereof; and all treaties made, or which shall be made under the authority of the United States, shall be the supreme law of the land; and the judges in every State shall be bound thereby, any thing in the Constitution or laws of any State to the contrary notwithstanding.

Thus, although a federal system is established, it is clearly one in which the national government shall prevail when there is conflict between the laws of the state and the national government.

The Tenth Amendment to the Constitution provides another element of federalism:

> The powers not delegated to the United States by the Constitution, nor prohibited by it to the States, are reserved to the States respectively, or to the people.

This doctrine of "reserved" powers or "states' rights" has been the basis for attempts to limit the power of the federal government in areas not expressly stated in the Constitution. However, such attempts have met with only limited success, since Article I, section 8, establishes the concept of necessary and proper powers or implied powers:

> The Congress shall have power:
> To make all laws which shall be necessary and proper in carrying into Execution the foregoing Powers, and all other powers vested by this Constitution in the Government of the United States, or in any Department or Officer thereof.

In the American political system, therefore, power is shared by the states and the federal government, with certain specific powers exercised exclusively by each. Both state political systems and a federal political system exist, and each American is a member of both.

Separation of Powers and Checks and Balances

In addition to allocating power to the states and the national government, the Constitution distributes power among the various branches of government. Concerned over the possibility of tyranny, the framers established a balanced government, in which each of the branches would share a degree of power with one another. Article I states that "All legislative powers herein granted shall be vested in a Congress of the United States, which shall consist of a Senate and House of Representatives." Article II states that "The executive power shall be vested in a President of the United States of America." Finally, Article III gives power to the judiciary. "The judicial power of the United States shall be vested in one Supreme Court, and in such inferior Courts as the Congress may from time to time ordain and establish."

While these articles appear to provide exclusive powers to each of the three branches of government, in reality there are provisions in the Constitution for the sharing or checking of power. For example, the president takes part in the legislative process by his power to call special sessions of Congress, veto bills, and decide aspects of policy directly affecting the legislative process. Congress becomes involved in the executive branch by its power to approve ambassadorial appointments and hold hearings on many aspects of the executive office, as well as by its power in financial matters and impeachment. The judiciary, by virtue of its power to invalidate legislation and rule on the extent of executive power, provides a check on the powers of the other branches. An example was the Supreme Court's 8 to 0 ruling in July 1974, that President Nixon could not refuse to turn over tapes in his possession to the special Watergate prosecutor, effectively establishing some limits to the concept of executive privilege.

These are not the only shared powers. As a matter of fact, beyond the legal provisions, there are many informal means by which the power of the branches can be checked. The web of personal relationships and the exercise of power by individuals in each of the branches through the use of mass media, personal contacts, and "behind the door" pressures in many cases provide substantial sharing of power between the various branches. For example, President Lyndon Johnson enjoyed close friendships with many of the senior senators who were important sources of power in proposing and supporting legislative programs. He was able to go beyond the formalities of executive-legislative relationships to take advantage of his friendship with key members of the Senate. On the other hand, the lack of such close relationships can isolate a president and diminish his influence on the legislative process. This was apparent during the last days of the Nixon administration. Cut off from enduring relationships with senior congressmen, and operating within a staff system which was inclined to protect him from the "outside," Richard Nixon was increasingly isolated in office, and his power was thus diminished.

The concept of shared powers and exclusive powers, therefore, has a legal connotation as well as an informal one. The overall relationships are illustrated in the following:

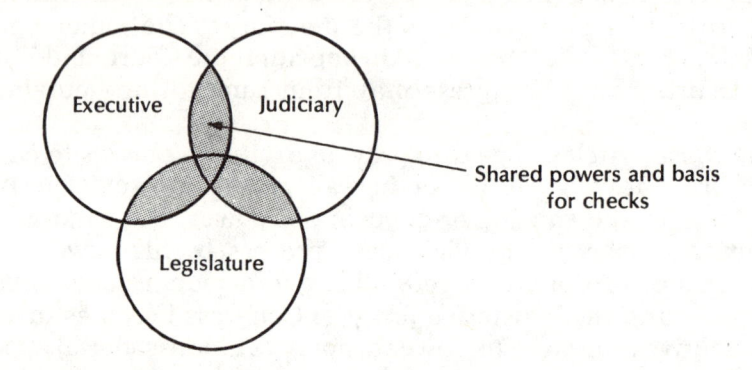

Executive — Judiciary — Legislature: Shared powers and basis for checks

Limited Government

The concept of constitutionalism and limited government go hand-in-hand. A constitution both authorizes and limits the scope of government power. It is the instrument by which boundaries are established for the power of government; it embodies the principles of governmental authority, the philosophy of the political system, and the rules of public debate regarding the aims of government and restraints on the exercise of power. Thus, government can never be an ultimate authority unto itself, but is limited by the grants of power it receives from the people. The basis for popular sovereignty—the idea that the ultimate authority rests with the people—lies in the concept of limited government. Limited government can be partially achieved from the checks and balances system, the federal structure, or the decentralized and diffused power characteristic of a pluralistic system.

Pluralism rests on the concept that American society is made up of a variety of ethnic, economic, religious, and cultural groups that are reflected in heterogeneous institutions and organizations, each having some element of power. Moreover, it is assumed that the political institutions of the country, in order to remain legitimate, must reflect society; they do not have to reflect it perfectly but they must contain elements of the social organization and interests. Thus, each of these groups and institutions tends to counterbalance the others. Pluralism in the United States has also been at the root of the concept of "participatory democracy" in which each group expects some "piece" of the power pie. Indeed, this very expectation has been responsible for the proliferation of organized groups.

Judicial Supremacy

The concept of judicial supremacy is one of the most important characteristics of the American system. It is based on the idea that the judiciary is the final authority in interpreting the meaning of the Constitution. The highest court in the land, the Supreme Court, thus becomes the final authority in any constitutional or legal conflict.

Judicial supremacy is not explicitly granted in the Constitution, however. Article III, section 2 states: "The judicial Power shall extend to all Cases, in Law and Equity, arising under this Constitution, the Laws of the United States, and Treaties made, or which shall be made, under their authority..." It was the famous case of *Marbury* v. *Madison* (1803), which clearly established the principle of judicial supremacy. Chief Justice John Marshall held that the Supreme Court had the power to invalidate federal laws when they conflicted with the Constitution. This does not mean that the Supreme Court is supreme over all other branches as such, only that it has the authority of judicial review. The Supreme Court is indeed supreme when it comes to interpreting the Constitution and reviewing the constitutionality of other branches of government. All political actors in the system are legally bound by the decisions of the Court.

Democratic Ideology

In the American political system, the concept of democracy is the context within which the four constitutional principles operate. It is presumed that the four principles are the most effective way to achieve the goals of democracy. But what are the goals of democracy? How are they to be achieved? Indeed, what is meant by democratic ideology? In this section we will explore these questions in detail.

The constitutional principles, the Bill of Rights (the first ten amendments), and some of the later amendments, for instance, the Fourteenth, encompass the essential features of a democratic government. Limited government provides the basis, while a number of other features protect the individual from invasion of his rights. To properly understand the operation of the political system, one must have some idea not only of the power vested in the Constitution, but also of how this power is to be exercised and for what purpose. Fundamentally, power is to be exercised according to constitutional principles in order to foster the goals of democracy. Therefore, the ends of government are important, but so also are the means. That is, to achieve peace, one is not supposed to kill all those who disagree. In the name of freedom of speech, one cannot scream "Fire" in a crowded theater when there is no fire.

The American political system rests on a set of core values based on the concept of "democracy." We will speak more of the meaning of democracy later. At the very least democracy implies the political importance of the individual and accountability of those in power. As long as there is a high degree of commitment to these core political values by the society, the political system is likely to remain relatively strong and effective. There are a number of other political values that are not necessarily core values and which can be used as a basis for compromise or negotiations. Obviously, if everyone in a political system agreed at all times on the values, their meaning and implementation, there would be no conflict, hence no politics. This is the ideal and no political system has yet reached, or will ever reach, this state.

Although the concept of democratic ideology is basic to the American political system, many persons, scholars and students alike, have difficulty in identifying its specific elements. The problem arises not only because of varying perceptions, but also depends upon the perspective from which the definition of democracy is approached. In simple terms, if one is an idealist the concept of democratic ideology is tied in closely with the Declaration of Independence, the Constitution and the Bill of Rights. Moreover, the nature of man is viewed as being basically "good" and capable of the highest moral behavior. The realist, on the other hand, would probably accept the Declaration of Independence, the Constitution and the Bill of Rights as the working basis for democracy, but he would claim that these idealistic documents do not and cannot realistically reflect human nature and the workings of political systems. He would stress the idea that there is no such thing as a democracy that works perfectly, and that democratic ideology should be based on the reasonably adequate operation of a political system striving to achieve the best for the most. Needless to say, the idealist and the realist have been arguing since the time of Socrates and there is no end in sight.

Democratic Premises

The meaning of democracy arises primarily from a way of making decisions. In other words, democracy is a form of decision making based on several basic premises. One premise assumes that the machinery of the political system includes: (1) a regularized system of periodic elections, which in turn gives rise to representative government; (2) public access to facts upon which to base political decisions; (3) the basic right of the people to criticize the operations of the political system; (4) the right of the people to participate in all aspects of the political system and to organize for political purposes; (5) majority rule, with basic safeguards for minorities; and (6) equal voting power for all people, as individuals.

Another premise upon which democratic ideology rests is the group of basic values, including: the legal equality of human beings; stress on the individual, or individual worth; the supremacy of the people over their officials, and ultimate responsibility and accountability of elected officials to the people; the derivation of authority from the people; and maximum freedom and dignity of the individual in order to foster all other democratic values. This does not mean unrestrained freedom, but freedom consistent with maintaining a relatively balanced and stable society.

The final premise is that a certain type of social environment must exist if the democratic machinery and values are to operate. Democracy cannot be established in the political sphere unless the rest of society is in harmony with democratic ideology. In short, certain social and economic conditions must exist to further democratic practices and values. There must be reasonable opportunity for social mobility, or advancement from a lower social group to a higher one. Similarly, there must be reasonable opportunity within the system for individuals to acquire a share in the economic wealth. The political system must provide opportunities for individuals to better themselves politically, socially, and economically if in fact, democratic machinery and values are to operate. Since the late 1960s the social premise of democracy within the American political system has been particularly susceptible to criticism. Unemployment and poverty have been particularly acute among black Americans. Similarly, Spanish-speaking and Indian Americans have been vocal in their criticisms regarding social and economic opportunities. Having noted this, however, we ought also to note the observation of de Tocqueville, that "The advantage of democracy does not consist, therefore, as has sometimes been asserted, in favoring prosperity to all, but simply in contributing to the well-being of the greatest number."[3]

How to Achieve Democracy

If we are to have democracy then, all three of these premises must be at least reasonably operational. None of them will work perfectly in any system, no matter how democratic, but the people must perceive that the political system is at least based on all three premises.

As suggested earlier, ideology is supposed to provide some plan of action to change the existing world into something that ought to be. A democratic ideology is likely to have many such routes, whereas a totalitarian system is likely to have one specific route. Therefore, most totalitarian systems are preoccupied with the relevance of their ideology and can provide a coherent explanation, while democratic systems have difficulty explaining theirs. For example, democratic countries include the United States, England, Sweden, Canada, France, Japan, and Norway, to mention a few; in each country democracy has a different meaning, while operating with a different political system. Yet in Communist countries, there is an ideological cohesion based on the strong central party structure and dominance of the state over the individual. Moreover, in such authoritarian countries, the ideology spells out programs to be achieved and goals to be accomplished in specific terms.

Democratic ideology does not presuppose a party system; it does not require two, three, or more, parties. Indeed, one can argue that democracy does not require any particular form of government as long as the three premises are the basis for establishing the government and the political system is actively and effectively acting on these three premises.

Ideology always has a Utopian element or ideal, which can motivate people to strive to reach it. For an ideology to remain relevant, it must never be without the Utopian "impossible dream." If people actually perceive that they have reached the goal, then the political system is faced with the end of ideology, and in essence, the end of the rationale behind the political system, tantamount to the end of the system itself.

Democratic ideology expects much of human beings. Man is expected to be "involved" in the political system and view issues and conflicts in a reasonable and rational way. Only in such circumstances can a democratic political system be made to work. Yet there is a basic dilemma. Should men be forced to be democratic? Can a democratic political system operate in an atmosphere of apathy and noninvolvement?

Another basic problem for any democratic system that attempts to provide the greatest good for the greatest number is the nature of the individual's role. If we accept the concept of pluralistic politics, that all groups should have a channel into the political system, then we must recognize that the individual has little impact on the power equation, unless he is a political actor with power by virtue of status, prestige, or wealth. In the drive to develop a highly representative and responsive political system, the individual somehow has become politically diminished. The diminished role of the individual can lead to a number of dangerous tendencies in a democratic system: arrogance of power of a few irresponsible bureaucrats, subsystems that perpetuate selfish interests above national interests, increasing restriction of individual rights and liberties, and the distortion of the democratic quality of the social environment. How then can the involvement of the people be stimulated while the stability of the system is maintained? The answers are difficult to find, but are the essence of democracy.

Political Actors, The Constitution, and Democracy

We have discussed the fundamental constitutional principles and democratic ideology; we must now turn to the connecting link between principles, ideology and the people. The manner and spirit in which these principles are implemented in the day-to-day operations as well as long-range considerations of the political system depend on the political actors because they translate constitutional principles into political reality. For example, regardless of the principles embodied in limited government and the rights of all individuals, it required the actions of Congress and the President, as political actors, to legislate and execute the Civil Rights Act of 1964; among other things, that Act insured equal voting rights for blacks by prohibiting discrimination in voter registration procedures and standards. It was the active exercise of power by the House of Representatives, as reflected in the House Judiciary Committee, that checked the power of the presidential office following the Watergate affair. Similarly, it was the Supreme Court, in the case of *Brown* v. *Board of Education, et al.* in 1954, that abolished the "separate but equal" doctrine of education that for years had kept black and white students segregated in separate schools. The unrelenting pressure of labor union organizations in the early twentieth century was chiefly responsible for achieving the necessary legislation for recognition of workers' rights. In recent times, the women's liberation movement and civil rights groups have been instrumental in changing not only legislation but attitudes and ideas about the concept of democratic ideology. These are examples of political actors operating on the political system and exercising power to achieve certain goals. The list is endless.

As already stated, our approach in this book focuses on power: its acquisition, maintenance, and use. We will analyze several useful models and examine the links between the major political actors, the institutions of the political system, and the role of individuals, calling attention to psychological motivations at the base of political operations. We must, however, recognize that there are weaknesses to this type of approach. Perhaps the major problem is that the study of power does not readily lend itself to data analysis or empirical testing. It is difficult, for example, to measure the influence of one person upon another or of a decision maker upon an institution. Similarly, it is very difficult to assess or identify the power relationships between any two political actors that are important to the operation of the political system. Another weakness is that power may not explain all of the most important considerations in the political system. Having noted these problems, let us look more closely at the meaning of this power approach.

The political actor can be assessed in the following terms:
1) What is his perception of the office and his role?
2) From where does his power arise? Has he received his office or grant of power as the result of elections, or appointment, or as a result of positions and relationships with other political actors and institutions?
3) In what way do institutions, both formal and informal, and other political actors both restrain and provide the basis for expansion of power?
4) What are the dimensions and scope of the physical attributes of power? Is the actor in a position to distribute wealth, status, or other resources?
5) For what purposes is the power used?
6) What role does the actor play in the political system? What are the functions and purposes of his position in the political system?
7) What is the legal basis of his power and the legal interpretations of his power?

8) What is the dimension of his responsibility and accountability?
9) What is the degree of susceptibility to the power of other actors?

These questions do not apply with equal intensity or scope to all political actors, but they establish the boundaries within which we will assess the actors and the political system. Moreover, the questions can be used whether the political actor is an institution, such as Congress; a group, such as a labor union; an individual, such as the president; or an informal institution, such as a political party.

The relationships among political actors, constitutional principles, and democratic ideology can be shown in a diagram that reflects the model to be used in this book.

The Power Model (Simplified)

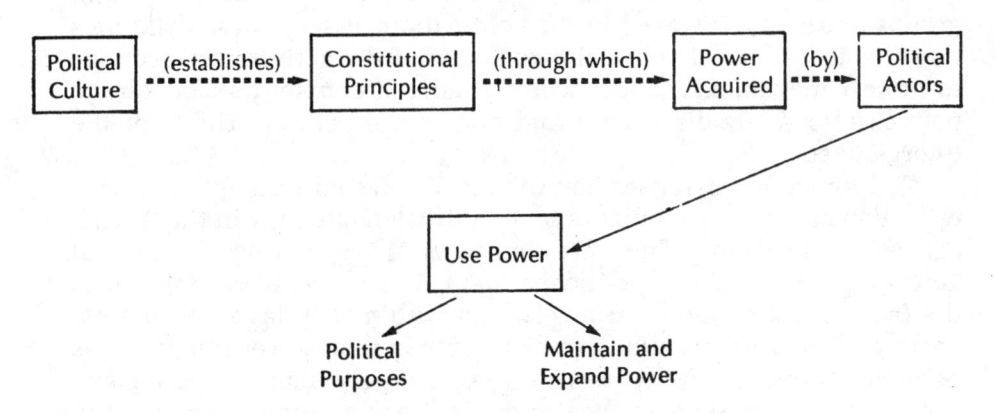

Political Culture —(establishes)→ Constitutional Principles —(through which)→ Power Acquired —(by)→ Political Actors → Use Power → Political Purposes / Maintain and Expand Power

The American Political System: An Overview

How does the power model apply to the American political system in general? American politics has long been regarded as pluralistic. Power is considered to be divided among various groups, individuals, and institutions within the political system. Theoretically, the American political system is multicentered, open, and responsive to all elements of American society. It is thought that no one group is strong enough to gain complete and absolute power. But there are countervailing powers not only for groups but also at various levels of governmental institutions. There is no unified monolithic power structure behind the making of national policy; rather a policy evolves and emerges through a variety of processes including bargaining, coalition building, and compromise, not only among the groups concerned but among decision makers and institutions. Most scholars would categorize the American political system as brokerage politics, assuring that various contending groups resolve their differences to their mutual satisfaction and with virtually no harm to the public interest.

In arguing the pluralistic concept of democratic government, Robert Dahl of Yale University states, "the existence of multiple centers of power, none of which is wholly sovereign, will help (may indeed be necessary) to tame power, to secure the consent of all, and to settle conflicts peacefully . . ."[4] Indeed, one can argue that these "multiple centers of power" are the basic safeguards in American politics, in which there is a strong desire to get a piece of the "pie." The attempts to get their share involve groups and individuals in the processes of the political system; this generates a host of policy decisions, which in turn generate new conditions and stimulate other groups to become involved in the political processes. These dynamics have led to a range of political involvement from activism in elections to protest movements. Some would argue, of course, that brokerage politics effectively disregards and denies the political rights of the unorganized.

The apparent disregard for the rights of some groups is also a reflection of the decentralization and diffusion of power in the American political system. There are a number of ways in which political actors can influence the political system. There are layers of power at the federal, state, and local levels, and within each layer there are a variety of institutions that exercise the power of government. Thus political actors can apply pressure on local politicians, state legislatures, and congressmen; they may also seek influence among city aldermen, local courts, and various city bureaucrats. In any case, such a system gives rise to a variety of political actors, seeking coalitions and alliances among themselves in order to bring power to bear at appropriate levels (or layers) of government. In sum, the American political system and its method of resolving conflicts is determined primarily by the power of shifting coalitions. The character and composition of these coalitions change depending on the issues and the stakes involved.

These concepts do not provide the complete picture of the way our political system operates. Obviously there are always some political actors who are dissatisfied with policy and the working of the political system at specific times and on specific issues. Why then doesn't the political system collapse? As long as the core political values are abided by, and as long as some expectation and opportunity remains, the political system continues to enjoy legitimacy and can function relatively stably and effectively. Although all political actors are not involved at all times in conflict or in making policy decisions, they implicitly and explicitly support the way the political system functions and are relatively satisfied with its operations. Similarly, those political actors who do not win in the power struggle at any particular time will normally accept the decision, knowing that they have the opportunity to win in the future. Again this rests on the assumption that the core values are being protected and the rules of the game are being followed properly by all involved.

The continual working of the political system depends partly upon its ability to offer access to power to unorganized and dissatisfied groups. A system such as ours, based on democratic values, cannot continue to exist for any length of time with a permanently dissatisfied group. Hence there is a continuing need to make the system responsive to all major groups, to insure that priorities and resources are shifted if necessary, and to change dissatisfaction to satisfaction and support. Otherwise dissatisfied groups may assume that the only remaining alternative is violence. In the final analysis, the political system will be termed legitimate only as long as there is a consensus that there is a reasonable opportunity for everyone to achieve his values within the system.

In order to maintain its legitimacy, stability, and solvency, the political system of the United States must use the power inherent in institutions and major political actors to fulfill at least minimum expectations, maintain a balance between contending groups, and insure that the system remains open and responsive to all. In the following chapters we will investigate how this is attempted in the American political system.

NOTES

1. John A. Garraty, *The American Nation: A History of the United States* (New York: Harper and Row, 1966), p. 147.

2. Richard A. Watson, *Promise and Performance of American Democracy* (New York: John Wiley, 1972), p. 33.

3. J. P. Mayer (ed.), *Alexis de Tocqueville in America* (New York: Anchor Books, 1969), Translated by George Lawrence, p. 233.

4. Robert A. Dahl, *Pluralistic Democracy in the United States: Conflict and Consent* (Chicago: Rand McNally & Co., 1967), p. 24.

Selected Readings

There are many studies available on the constitutional history of the United States. They are written from different perspectives, ranging from economic interpretation to a purely legalistic approach. The document adopted on September 17, 1787, and ratified on March 4, 1789, remains the basic and supreme law of the land. It establishes the general basis of power for our political system and identifies the underlying purpose and meaning of democratic ideology in the American system.

The first selection in this chapter is a letter from James Madison to Thomas Jefferson shortly after the adoption of the Constitution. In it Madison discusses the results of the Convention and provides an insight into his views. He focuses specifically on the problems of presidential–congressional relationships, distribution of power between the federal and state governments, the need to accommodate various interests, and the existing rivalries between small and large states.

The second selection, by Kevin Phillips, focuses on similar issues in modern America. Calling the present system obsolete, Phillips argues that the power of the president is insufficient to deal with a myriad of modern problems. He argues that the system of checks and balances and separation of powers is a hindrance rather than a help to the democratic processes. Note that this selection was written prior to the Watergate revelations in 1973. In any case, it appears that many of the arguments that were being debated in 1787 are still relevant today.

3.1

Letter To Thomas Jefferson
From James Madison

Dear Sir

New York Octr. 24. 1787.

My two last, though written for the two last Packets, have unluckily been delayed till this conveyance. The first of them was sent from Philada. to Commodore Jones in consequence of information that he was certainly to go by the packet then about to sail. Being detained here by his business with Congress, and being unwilling to put the letter into the mail without my approbation, which could not be obtained in time, he detained the letter also. The second was sent from Philada. to Col. Carrington, with a view that it might go by the last packet at all events in case Commodore Jones should meet with further detention here. By ill luck he was out of Town, and did not return till it was too late to make use of the opportunity. Neither of the letters were indeed of much consequence at the time and are still less so now. I let them go forward nevertheless as they may mention some circumstances not at present in my recollection, and as they will prevent a chasm on my part of our correspondence which I have so many motives to cherish by an exact punctuality.

Your favor of June 20. has been already acknowledged. The last packet from France brought me that of August 2d. I have received also by the Mary Capt. Howland the three Boxes for W. H. B. F. and myself. The two first have been duly forwarded. The contents of the last are a valuable addition to former literary remittances and lay me under additional obligations, which I shall always feel more strongly than I express. The articles included for Congress have been delivered and those for the two Universities and for General Washington have been forwarded, as have been the various letters for your friends in Virginia and elsewhere. The parcel of rice referred to in your letter to the Delegates of S. Carolina has met with some accident. No account whatever can be gathered concerning it. It probably was not shipped from France. Ubbo's book I find was not omitted as you seem to have apprehended. The charge for it however is, which I must beg you to supply. The

The Papers of Thomas Jefferson, Volume 12, 7 August 1787 to 31 March 1788. (Princeton, N. J.: Princeton University Press, 1955), pp. 270–282 and 284–285.

duplicate volume of the Encyclopedie, I left in Virginia, and it is uncertain when I shall have an opportunity of returning it. Your Spanish duplicates will I fear be hardly vendible. I shall make a trial wherever a chance presents itself. A few days ago I received your favor of the 15 of Augst. via L'Orient and Boston. The letters inclosed along with it were immediately sent on to Virga.

You will herewith receive the result of the Convention, which continued its session till the 17th of September. I take the liberty of making some observations on the subject which will help to make up a letter, if they should answer no other purpose.

It appeared to the sincere and unanimous wish of the Convention to cherish and preserve the Union of the States. No proposition was made, no suggestion was thrown out in favor of a partition of the Empire into two or more Confederacies.

It was generally agreed that the objects of the Union could not be secured by any system founded on the principle of a confederation of sovereign States. A voluntary observance of the federal law by all the members could never be hoped for. A compulsive one could evidently never be reduced to practice, and if it could, involved equal calamities to the innocent and the guilty, the necessity of a military force both obnoxious and dangerous, and in general, a scene resembling much more a civil war, than the administration of a regular Government.

Hence was embraced the alternative of a government which instead of operating, on the States, should operate without their intervention on the individuals composing them: and hence the change in the principle and proportion of representation.

This ground-work being laid, the great objects which presented themselves were 1. to unite a proper energy in the Executive and a proper stability in the Legislative departments, with the essential characters of Republican Government. 2. To draw a line of demarkation which would give to the Geneal Government every power requisite for general purposes, and leave to the States every power which might be most beneficially administered by them. 3. To provide for the different interests of different parts of the Union. 4. To adjust the clashing pretensions of the large and small States. Each of these objects was pregnant with difficulties. The whole of them together formed a task more difficult than can be well conceived by those who were not concerned in the execution of it. Adding to these considerations the natural diversity of human opinions on all new and complicated subjects, it is impossible to consider the degree of concord which ultimately prevailed as less than a miracle.

The first of these objects as it respects the Executive, was peculiarly embarrassing. On the question whether it should consist of a single person, or a plurality of co-ordinate members, on the mode of appointment, on the duration in office, on the degree of power, on the re-eligibility, tedious and reiterated discussions took place. The plurality of co-ordinate members had finally but few advocates. Governour Randolph was at the head of them. The modes of appointment proposed were various, as by the people at large—by electors chosen by the people—by the Executives of the States—by the Congress, some preferring a joint ballot of the two Houses—some a separate concurrent ballot allowing to each a negative on the other house—some a nomination of several candidates by one House, out of whom a choice should be made by the other. Several other modifications were started. The expedient at length adopted seemed to give pretty general satisfaction to the members. As to the duration in office, a few would have preferred a tenure during good behaviour—a considerable number would have done so in case an easy and effectual removal by impeachment could be settled. It was much agitated whether a long term, seven years for example, with a subsequent and perpetual ineligibility, or a short term with a capacity to be re-elected, should be fixed. In favor of the first opinion were urged the danger of a gradual degeneracy of re-elections from time to time, into first a life and then a hereditary tenure, and the favorable effect of an incapacity to be reappointed, on the independent exercise of the Executive authority. On the other side it was contended that the prospect of necessary degradation would discourage the most dignified characters from aspiring to the office, would take away the principal motive to the faithful discharge of its duties. The hope of being rewarded with a reappointment, would stimulate ambition to violent efforts for holding over the constitutional term, and instead of producing an independent administration, and a firmer defence of the constitutional rights of the department, would render the officer more indifferent to the importance of a place which he would soon be obliged to quit for ever, and more ready to yield to the incroachments of the Legislature of which he might again be a member.—The questions concerning the degree of power turned chiefly on the appointment to offices, and the controul on the Legislature. An *absolute* appointment to all offices—to some offices—to no offices, formed the scale of opinions on the first point. On the second, some contended for an absolute negative, as the only possible mean of reducing to practice, the theory of a free government which forbids a mixture of the Legislative and Executive powers. Others would be content with a revisionary power to be overruled by three fourths of both Houses. It was warmly urged that the judiciary department should be associated in the revision. The idea of some was that a separate revision should be given to the two departments—that if either objected two thirds; if both three fourths, should be necessary to overrule.

In forming the Senate, the great anchor of the Government, the questions as they came within the first object turned mostly on the mode of appointment, and the duration of it. The different modes proposed were, 1. by the House of Representatives, 2. by the Executive, 3. by electors chosen by the people for the purpose, 4. by the State Legislatures. On the point of duration, the propositions descended from good behavior to four years, through the intermediate terms of nine, seven, six and five years. The election of the other branch was first determined to be triennial, and afterwards reduced to biennial.

The second object, the due partition of power, between the General and local Governments, was perhaps of all, the most nice and difficult. A few contended for an entire abolition of the States; Some for indefinite power of Legislation in the Congress, with a negative on the laws of the States, some for such a power without a negative, some for a limited power of legislation, with such a negative: the majority finally for a limited power without the negative. The question with regard to the Negative underwent repeated discussions, and was finally rejected by a bare majority. As I formerly intimated to you my opinion in favor of this ingredient, I will take this occasion of explaining myself on the subject. [Such a check on the States appears to me necessary 1. to prevent encroachments on the General authority, 2. to prevent instability and injustice in the legislation of the States.

1. Without such a check in the whole over the parts, our system involves the evil of imperia in imperio. If a compleat supremacy some where is not necessary in every

Society, a controuling power at least is so, by which the general authority may be defended against encroachments of the subordinate authorities, and by which the latter may be restrained from encroachments on each other. If the supremacy of the British Parliament is not necessary as has been contended, for the harmony of that Empire, it is evident I think that without the royal negative or some equivalent controul, the unity of the system would be destroyed. The want of some such provision seems to have been mortal to the antient Confederacies, and to be the disease of the modern. Of the Lycian Confederacy little is known. That of the Amphyctions is well known to have been rendered of little use whilst it lasted, and in the end to have been destroyed by the predominance of the local over the federal authority. The same observation may be made, on the authority of Polybius, with regard to the Achæan League. The Helvetic System scarcely amounts to a confederacy and is distinguished by too many peculiarities to be a ground of comparison. The case of the United Netherlands is in point. The authority of a Statholder, the influence of a standing army, the common interest in the conquered possessions, the pressure of surrounding danger, the guarantee of foreign powers, are not sufficient to secure the authority and interests of the generality, against the antifederal tendency of the provincial sovereignties. The German Empire is another example. A Hereditary chief with vast independent resources of wealth and power, a federal Diet, with ample parchment authority, a regular Judiciary establishment, the influence of the neighbourhood of great and formidable Nations, have been found unable either to maintain the subordination of the members, or to prevent their mutual contests and encroachments. Still more to the purpose is our own experience both during the war and since the peace. Encroachments of the States on the general authority, sacrifices of national to local interests, interferences of the measures of different States, form a great part of the history of our political system. It may be said that the new Constitution is founded on different principles, and will have a different operation. I admit the difference to be material. It presents the aspect rather of a feudal system of republics, if such a phrase may be used, than of a Confederacy of independent States. And what has been the progress and event of the feudal Constitutions? In all of them a continual struggle between the head and the inferior members, until a final victory has been gained in some instances by one, in others, by the other of them. In one respect indeed there is a remarkable variance between the two cases. In the feudal system the sovereign, though limited, was independent; and having no particular sympathy of interests with the great Barons, his ambition had as full play as theirs in the mutual projects of usurpation. In the American Constitution The general authority will be derived entirely from the subordinate authorities. The Senate will represent the States in their political capacity, the other House will represent the people of the States in their individual capacity. The former will be accountable to their constituents at moderate, the latter at short periods. The President also derives his appointment from the States, and is periodically accountable to them. This dependence of the General, on the local authorities seems effectually to guard the latter against any dangerous encroachments of the former: Whilst the latter within their respective limits, will be continually sensible of the abridgment of their power, and be stimulated by ambition to resume the surrendered portion of it. We find the representatives of counties and corporations in the Legislatures of the States, much more disposed to sacrifice the aggregate interest, and even authority, to the local views of their Constituents, than the latter to the former. I mean not by these remarks to insinuate that an esprit de corps will not exist in the national Government, that opportunities may not occur of extending its jurisdiction in some points. I mean only that the danger of encroachments is much greater from the other side, and that the impossibility of dividing powers of legislation, in such a manner, as to be free from different constructions by different interests, or even from ambiguity in the judgment of the impartial, requires some such expedient as I contend for. Many illustrations might be given of this impossibility. How long has it taken to fix, and how imperfectly is yet fixed the legislative power of corporations, though that power is subordinate in the most compleat manner? The line of distinction between the power of regulating trade and that of drawing revenue from it, which was once considered as the barrier of our liberties, was found on fair discussion, to be absolutely undefinable. No distinction seems to be more obvious than that between spiritual and temporal matters. Yet wherever they have been made objects of Legislation, they have clashed and contended with each other, till one or the other has gained the supremacy. Even the boundaries between the Executive, Legislative and Judiciary powers, though in general so strongly marked in themselves, consist in many instances of mere shades of difference. It may be said that the Judicial authority under our new system will keep the States within their proper limits, and supply the place of a negative on their laws. The answer is that it is more convenient to prevent the passage of a law, than to declare it void after it is passed; that this will be particularly the case where the law aggrieves individuals, who may be unable to support an appeal against a State to the supreme Judiciary, that a State which would violate the Legislative rights of the Union, would not be very ready to obey a Judicial decree in support of them, and that a recurrence to force, which in the event of disobedience would be necessary, is an evil which the new Constitution meant to exclude as far as possible.

   2. A Constitutional negative on the laws of the States seems equally necessary to secure individuals against encroachments on their rights. The mutability of the laws of the States is found to be a serious evil. The injustice of them has been so frequent and so flagrant as to alarm the most stedfast friends of Republicanism. I am persuaded I do not err in saying that the evils issuing from these sources contributed more to that uneasiness which produced the Convention, and prepared the public mind for a general reform, than those which accrued to our national character and interest from the inadequacy of the Confederation to its immediate objects. A reform therefore which does not make provision for private rights, must be materially defective. The restraints against paper emissions, and violations of contracts are not sufficient. Supposing them to be effectual as far as they go, they are short of the mark. Injustice may be effected by such an infinitude of legislative expedients, that where the disposition exists it can only be controuled by some provision which reaches all cases whatsoever. The partial provision made, supposes the disposition which will evade it. It may be asked how private rights will be more secure under the Guardianship of the General Government than under the State Governments, since they are both founded on the republican principle which refers

the ultimate decision to the will of the majority, and are distinguished rather by the extent within which they will operate, than by any material difference in their structure. A full discussion of this question would, if I mistake not, unfold the true principles of Republican Government, and prove in contradiction to the concurrent opinions of theoretical writers, that this form of Government, in order to effect its purposes must operate not within a small but an extensive sphere. I will state some of the ideas which have occurred to me on this subject. Those who contend for a simple Democracy, or a pure republic, actuated by the sense of the majority, and operating within narrow limits, assume or suppose a case which is altogether fictitious. They found their reasoning on the idea, that the people composing the Society enjoy not only an equality of political rights; but that they have all precisely the same interests and the same feelings in every respect. Were this in reality the case, their reasoning would be conclusive. The interest of the majority would be that of the minority also; the decisions could only turn on mere opinion concerning the good of the whole of which the major voice would be the safest criterion; and within a small sphere, this voice could be most easily collected and the public affairs most accurately managed. We know however that no Society ever did or can consist of so homogeneous a mass of Citizens. In the savage State indeed, an approach is made towards it; but in that state little or no Government is necessary. In all civilized Societies, distinctions are various and unavoidable. A distinction of property results from that very protection which a free Government gives to unequal faculties of acquiring it. There will be rich and poor; creditors and debtors; a landed interest, a monied interest, a mercantile interest, a manufacturing interest. These classes may again be subdivided according to the different productions of different situations and soils, and according to different branches of commerce and of manufactures. In addition to these natural distinctions, artificial ones will be founded on accidental differences in political, religious and other opinions, or an attachment to the persons of leading individuals. However erroneous or ridiculous these grounds of dissention and faction may appear to the enlightened Statesman, or the benevolent philosopher, the bulk of mankind who are neither Statesmen nor Philosophers, will continue to view them in a different light. It remains then to be enquired whether a majority having any common interest, or feeling any common passion, will find sufficient motives to restrain them from oppressing the minority. An individual is never allowed to be a judge or even a witness in his own cause. If two individuals are under the biass of interest or enmity against a third, the rights of the latter could never be safely referred to the majority of the three. Will two thousand individuals be less apt to oppress one thousand, or two hundred thousand, one hundred thousand? Three motives only can restrain in such cases. 1. A prudent regard to private or partial good, as essentially involved in the general and permanent good of the whole. This ought no doubt to be sufficient of itself. Experience however shews that it has little effect on individuals, and perhaps still less on a collection of individuals, and least of all on a majority with the public authority in their hands. If the former are ready to forget that honesty is the best policy; the last do more. They often proceed on the converse of the maxim: that whatever is politic is honest. 2. Respect for character. This motive is not found sufficient to restrain individuals from injustice, and loses its efficacy in proportion to the number which is to divide the praise or the blame. Besides as it has reference to public opinion, which is that of the majority, the standard is fixed by those whose conduct is to be measured by it. 3. Religion. The inefficacy of this restraint on individuals is well known. The conduct of every popular assembly, acting on oath, the strongest of religious ties, shews that individuals join without remorse in acts against which their consciences would revolt, if proposed to them separately in their closets. When Indeed Religion is kindled into enthusiasm, its force like that of other passions is increased by the sympathy of a multitude. But enthusiasm is only a temporary state of Religion, and whilst it lasts will hardly be seen with pleasure at the helm. Even in its coolest state, it has been much oftener a motive to oppression than a restraint from it. If then there must be different interests and parties in Society; and a majority when united by a common interest or passion can not be restrained from oppressing the minority, what remedy can be found in a republican Government, where the majority must ultimately decide, but that of giving such an extent to its sphere, that no common interest or passion will be likely to unite a majority of the whole number in an unjust pursuit. In a large Society, the people are broken into so many interests and parties, that a common sentiment is less likely to be felt, and the requisite concert less likely to be formed, by a majority of the whole. The same security seems requisite for the civil as for the religious rights of individuals. If the same sect form a majority and have the power, other sects will be sure to be depressed. Divide et impera, the reprobated axiom of tyranny, is under certain qualifications, the only policy, by which a republic can be administered on just principles. It must be observed however that this doctrine can only hold within a sphere of a mean extent. As in too small a sphere oppressive combinations may be too easily formed against the weaker party; so in too extensive a one a defensive concert may be rendered too difficult against the oppression of those entrusted with the administration. The great desideratum in Government is, so to modify the sovereignty as that it may be sufficiently neutral between different parts of the Society to controul one part from invading the rights of another, and at the same time sufficiently controuled itself, from setting up an interest adverse to that of the entire Society. In absolute monarchies, the Prince may be tolerably neutral towards different classes of his subjects, but may sacrifice the happiness of all to his personal ambition or avarice. In small republics, the sovereign will is controuled from such a sacrifice of the entire Society, but it is not sufficiently neutral towards the parts composing it. In the extended Republic of the United States, the General Government would hold a pretty even balance between the parties of particular States, and be at the same time sufficiently restrained by its dependence on the community, from betraying its general interests.]

Begging pardon for this immoderate digression, I return to the third object abovementioned, the adjustment of the different interests of different parts of the Continent. Some contended for an unlimited power over trade including exports as well as imports, and over slaves as well as other imports; some for such a power, provided the concurrence of two thirds of both Houses were required; some for such a qualification of the power, with an exemption of exports and slaves, others for an exemption of exports only. The result is seen in the Constitution. S. Carolina and Georgia were inflexible on the point of the slaves.

The remaining object, created more embarrassment, and a greater alarm for the issue of the Convention than all the rest put together. The little States insisted on retaining their equality in both branches, unless a compleat abolition of the State Governments should take place; and made an equality in the Senate a sine qua non. The large States on the other hand urged that as the new Government was to be drawn principally from the people immediately and was to operate directly on them, not on the States; and consequently as the States would lose that importance which is now proportioned to the importance of their voluntary compliances with the requisitions of Congress, it was necessary that the representation in both Houses should be in proportion to their size. It ended in the compromise which you will see, but very much to the dissatisfaction of several members from the large States.

It will not escape you that three names only from Virginia are subscribed to the Act. Mr. Wythe did not return after the death of his lady. Docr. MClurg left the Convention some time before the adjournment. The Governour and Col. Mason refused to be parties to it. Mr. Gerry was the only other member who refused. The objections of the Govr. turn principally on the latitude of the general powers, and on the connection established between the President and the Senate. He wished that the plan should be proposed to the States with liberty to them to suggest alterations which should all be referred to another general Convention to be incorporated into the plan as far as might be judged expedient. He was not inveterate in his opposition, and grounded his refusal to subscribe pretty much on his unwillingness to commit himself so as not to be at liberty to be governed by further lights on the subject. Col. Mason left Philada. in an exceeding ill humour indeed. A number of little circumstances arising in part from the impatience which prevailed towards the close of the business, conspired to whet his acrimony. He returned to Virginia with a fixed disposition to prevent the adoption of the plan if possible. He considers the want of a Bill of Rights as a fatal objection. His other objections are to the substitution of the Senate in place of an Executive Council and to the powers vested in that body—to the powers of the Judiciary—to the vice President being made President of the Senate—to the smallness of the number of Representatives—to the restriction on the States with regard to ex post facto laws—and most of all probably to the power of regulating trade, by a majority only of each House. He has some other lesser objections. Being now under the necessity of justifying his refusal to sign, he will of course, muster every possible one. His conduct has given great umbrage to the County of Fairfax, and particularly to the Town of Alexandria. He is already instructed to promote in the Assembly the calling a Convention, and will probably be either not deputed to the Convention, or be tied up by express instructions. He did not object in general to the powers vested in the National Government, so much as to the modification. In some respects he admitted that some further powers could have improved the system. He acknowledged in particular that a negative on the State laws, and the appointment of the State Executives ought to be ingredients; but supposed that the public mind would not now bear them and that experience would hereafter produce these amendments.

The final reception which will be given by the people at large to this proposed System can not yet be decided. The Legislature of N. Hampshire was sitting when it reached that State and was well pleased with it. As far as the sense of the people there has been expressed, it is equally favorable. Boston is warm and almost unanimous in embracing it. The impression on the country is not yet known. No symptoms of disapprobation have appeared. The Legislature of that State is now sitting, through which the sense of the people at large will soon be promulged with tolerable certainty. The paper money faction in Rh. Island is hostile. The other party zealously attached to it. Its passage through Connecticut is likely to be very smooth and easy. There seems to be less agitation in this state than any where. The discussion of the subject seems confined to the newspapers. The principal characters are known to be friendly. The Governour's party which has hitherto been the popular and most numerous one, is supposed to be on the opposite side; but considerable reserve is practiced, of which he sets the example. N. Jersey takes the affirmative side of course. Meetings of the people are declaring their approbation, and instructing their representatives. Penna. will be divided. The City of Philada., the Republican party, the Quakers, and most of the Germans espouse the Constitution. Some of the Constitutional leaders, backed by the western Country will oppose. An unlucky ferment on the subject in their assembly just before its late adjournment has irritated both sides, particularly the opposition, and by redoubling the exertions of that party may render the event doubtful. The voice of Maryland I understand from pretty good authority, is, as far as it has been declared, strongly in favor of the Constitution. Mr. Chase is an enemy, but the Town of Baltimore which he now represents, is warmly attached to it, and will shackle him as far as they can. Mr. Paca will probably be, as usually, in the politics of Chase. My information from Virginia is as yet extremely imperfect. I have a letter from Genl. Washington which speaks favorably of the impression within a circle of some extent, and another from Chancellor Pendleton which expresses his full acceptance of the plan, and the popularity of it in his district. I am told also that Innis and Marshall are patrons of it. In the opposite scale are Mr. James Mercer, Mr. R. H. Lee, Docr. Lee and their connections of course, Mr. M. Page according to Report, and most of the Judges and Bar of the general Court. The part which Mr. Henry will take is unknown here. Much will depend on it. I had taken it for granted from a variety of circumstances that he would be in the opposition, and still think that will be the case. There are reports however which favor a contrary supposition. From the States South of Virginia nothing has been heard. As the deputation from S. Carolina consisted of some of its weightiest characters, who have returned unanimously zealous in favor of the Constitution, it is probable that State will readily embrace it. It is not less probable, that N. Carolina will follow the example unless that of Virginia should counterbalance it. Upon the whole, although, the public mind will not be fully known, nor finally settled for a considerable time, appearances at present augur a more prompt, and general adoption of the plan than could have been well expected.

When the plan came before Congress for their sanction, a very serious report was made by R. H. Lee and Mr. Dane from Masts. to embarrass it. It was first contended that Congress could not properly give any positive countenance to a measure which had for its object the subversion of the Constitution under which they acted. This ground of attack failing, the former gentleman urged the expediency of sending out the plan with amendments, and proposed a number of them corresponding with the objections of Col. Mason. This experiment had still less effect. In order however to obtain unanimity it was necessary to couch the resolution in very moderate terms. . . .

With the most affectionate attachment I remain Dear Sr. Your obed friend & servant,

Js. Madison Jr.

3.2

Our Obsolete System

KEVIN P. PHILLIPS

The current debate about power in Washington—who's losing it and who's abusing it—is not helped by exaggerated Congressional cries of Caesarism, abridged prerogatives and autocracy that make Richard Nixon sound almost like King George III. Such pronouncements smack less of realistic political analysis than warmed-over eighteenth-century theory.

If we have a constitutional crisis, it's largely the opposite of the one identified by Congress. The "separation of powers" concept—which lives on so vigilantly in the name of Sen. Sam Ervin's subcommittee—may in fact be obsolete: an eighteenth-century theory turned late twentieth-century malfunction that is beginning to cause dangerous trouble. For too long, we have taken our system of checks and balances and separate powers for granted as an institutional "genius of American politics."

How, then, should we look at the problem? My proposal—still a hesitant one—is a second U.S. constitutional convention during our 1976 bicentennial year. In the era of megabudget government, archaic constitutional provisions are causing more of a destructive warp of power than a constructive separation.

Misperception

To begin with, "separation of powers" must be rated as one of the best-dignified mistakes of the eighteenth century. Our constitutional architects took the concept from a number of sources, but especially "The Spirit of Laws" conceived by French Baron Montesquieu in 1748. A great admirer of England, Montesquieu saw the benign secret of English politics as the separation of powers between the executive (the king), the legislative (Parliament) and the judiciary (the House of Lords). Fusion of executive and legislative power, he thought, would lead to tyranny. Alas, Montes-

Copyright Newsweek, Inc., 1974, reprinted by permission.

quieu *misperceived* the English system: its genius lay in the fusion of powers between the parliamentary legislature and the cabinet executive (which was displacing the king). So much for history; unfortunately, our Constitution freezes Montesquieu's mistake in legal concrete.

Several banana and betel-nut republics have imitated us, but the United States has the only clear "separation of powers" among the entire spectrum of Anglo-European democracies. With the partial exception of Finland, none has seen fit to adopt the system that Capital Hill finds so institutionally compelling. From Iceland to Australia, Anglo-European democracies are parliamentary systems with a *fusion* of legislative and executive branches. Citizens vote for legislators of the party or parties they wish to form the cabinet executive. Within this fused structure, meaningful twentieth-century decision-making has invariably passed to the executive.

Congress's separate power is an obstacle to modern policymaking. For example, no foreign system parallels the authorization and appropriations process of the U.S. House and Senate. Britain and other parliamentary regimes have budget procedures wherein the Treasury and Cabinet draw up requests that are routinely (and in toto) endorsed by the supporting legislative majority. Bluntly put, Congress has taken its "separate power" and institutionalized it into several hundred committees, subcommittees, special committees and joint committees. One has to go back to the Ottoman Empire for a similar array of pompous, uncoordinated satrapies.

A special inertia flows from Congress's empire of committees and subcommittees, pork barrels, personal policy dukedoms, huge personal staffs and so forth, all by-products of our unique separation of powers. Typical congressmen and senators tend to fill these local pork barrels, avoiding locally unpopular issues and Presidential candidates (only about half of the House Democrats openly backed George McGovern by name). Better equipped than Parliament members to survive ideological vicissitudes, only a dozen or so incumbents now lose every two years. Most vacancies open up through retirement or death.

Despite gathering reform, Congress only slowly reflects national political change. Party patterns tend to lag. Right now, for example, the South is solidly Republican on the Presidential level, but still largely conservative Democrat in Congress. Were this a parliamentary regime, Prime Minister Nixon would head a Republican-Dixiecrat ministry with a working legislative majority. As it is, conservative Southern legislative votes support a liberal Democratic leadership structure hostile to the Administration.

To marshal executive-branch power on behalf of his "New American Revolution," President Nixon is necessarily trying to end-run not only Congress but the bureaucratic structure built up under the Democrats from 1933 to 1966. Federal management is being centralized in the White House under the aegis of a "supercabient," efficiency experts and advertising men. Under our "separation of powers," Presidential aides have "executive privilege" not to testify before Congress. The result: an unprecedented, unreachable elite managerial cadre in the office of the President.

As for our all-too-separate Federal judiciary, I cannot think of another Anglo-European nation where the courts can substitute their judgment for that of the popularly elected bodies in such fields as biomedicine (abortion), sociology (busing) and politics (legislative apportionment). What modern logic gives this authority to a *court?*

In sum, we may have reached a point where separation of powers is doing more harm than good by distorting the logical evolution of technology-era government. Perhaps this can all be resolved by a realignment that will put Republicans and Southern Democrats in one party, thus ending the executive-legislative anomaly that underlies a good part of the present crisis.

Deeper Problem

But it seems to me that the problem runs deeper. First, our "separate power" centers are uniquely responsive to interest groups. Second, Congress, with its rubber-chicken circuitry and local-ombudsman mentality, is not a prime gathering place for the nation's leaders. Third, the White House structure is essentially a cadre of managers and propagandists; it lacks a leavening of politicians and thinkers. Fourth, more than political realignment is necessary to resolve the question of the Federal judicial role.

Might not the answer lie in a *fusion of powers* tying Congress and the executive together, eliminating checks and balances and creating a new system? In a parliamentary regime, our present sort of paralysis would be impossible. Budgeting and spending would be coordinated. Interest groups and lobbies would lose access. Congress would open up to more talent. So would the executive branch. Obligatory interaction with party legislators—to say nothing of parliamentary queston periods —would curb the growth of a secretive White House managerial elite.

Several states have already called for a constitutional convention to prohibit busing. While I realize it is well-nigh blasphemous to doubt our Founding Fathers, perhaps we ought to consider a constitutional convention that could undertake a fundamental re-examination of separation of powers.

Study Questions

1. It has been said that the U.S. Constitution is a compromise document. Do you agree with this? What kinds of conflicts arose during the Constitutional Convention regarding distribution of power between states and between branches of government? Are these conflicts relevant to twentieth-century America?
2. Has the Constitution changed over the past 200 years? Explain.
3. Identify and discuss the basic constitutional principles. Are these principles still relevant today? Examine a current political issue in terms of the principles established in the Constitution.
4. What is the meaning of democracy? Does democracy require a two-party system or a two-house legislature? In your own words, explain the meaning of legitimacy in terms of democratic ideology. Do the majority of people in America agree on the meaning of American democracy?
5. Explain the relationships between power, political actors, and the Constitution. In what way can the Constitution be considered a basis for power? Can it be considered a basis for limiting power?
6. It has been said by some that the Constitution, written over two centuries ago, is an outdated document. Indeed, some argue that the time has come for a new constitution and that another constitutional convention ought to be called for this purpose. If this took place, and you were a member of the convention, what changes, if any, would you strive for? Explain.

Bibliography

Books

Bonham, Barbara. *To Secure the Blessings of Liberty: the Story of our Constitution.* New York: Hawthorn Books, Inc., 1970.
Cooke, Jacob E., ed. *The Federalist.* Middletown, Conn.: Wesleyan University Press, 1961.
Dewey, Donald O. Union and Liberty: *A Documentary History of American Constitutionalism.* New York: McGraw-Hill Book Co., 1969.
Ford, Paul Leichester, ed. *Essays on the Constitution of the United States.* New York: Burt Franklin, 1970 (originally published in 1892).
Ford, Paul Leichester, ed. *Pamphlets on the Constitution of the United States.* New York: Da Capo Press, 1968 (originally published in 1888).
Kenyon, Cecelia M., ed. *The Antifederalists.* Indianapolis: The Bobbs-Merrill Co., Inc., 1966.
Madison, James. *Notes of Debates in the Federal Convention of 1787.* Athens, Ohio: Ohio University Press, 1966.
Magrath, C. Peter. *Constitutionalism and Politics: Conflict and Consensus.* Glenview, Ill.: Scott, Foresman and Company, 1968.

Peltason, J. W. *Corwin and Peltason's Understanding the Constitution*. 6th ed. Hinsdale, Ill.: Dryden Press, 1973.

Pritchett, C. Herman. *The American Constitution*. 2d ed. New York: McGraw-Hill Book Co., 1968.

Schlechter, Alan H. *Contemporary Constitutional Issues*. New York: McGraw-Hill Book Co., 1972.

Articles

Donahoe, Bernard, and Smelser, Marshal. "The Congressional Power to Raise Armies: the Constitutional and Ratifying Conventions, 1787-1788." *The Review of Politics*, Vol. 33, No. 2, April 1971, pp. 202-211.

Gazell, James A. "One Man, One Vote: Its Long Germination." *Western Political Quarterly*, Vol. 23, No. 3 (September 1970), pp. 445-462.

Marks, Frederick W., III. "Foreign Affairs: A Winning Issue in the Campaign for Ratification of the United States Constitution." *Political Science Quarterly*, Vol. 86, No. 3 (September 1971), pp. 444-469.

CHAPTER 4
The Presidency: The Burden and the Glory

Throughout American history, the presidency has held a unique position in the political system. Revered by some as a kingly office, challenged by others as dictatorial, and supported by many as the epitome of popular government, the presidency has evolved into a monarchial, dictatorial, and democratic office. This apparent contradiction is the basis for the never-ending debate on the presidency.

In his recent study of the presidency Emmet John Hughes clearly identifies the contradictions. He writes:

> ... any President finds himself commanded to perform an almost interminable series of conjuring acts to control the ceaseless contradictions of Presidential life. He must proudly cherish and profess political principles—yet sometimes pursue his greater purposes unslowed by lesser scruples. He must summon his people to be with him—yet stand above, not squat beside them. He must question his own wisdom and judgment—but not too severely... He must be aggressive without being contentious, decisive without being arrogant, and compassionate without being confused... He must be pragmatic, calculating, and earthbound—and still know when to spurn the arithmetic of expediency for the act of brave imagination, the sublime gamble with no hope other than the boldness of vision.[1]

One can only marvel at how this office has evolved. The delegates to the Constitutional Convention, faced with the dilemma of choosing between a weak executive and the possibility of aristocratic government, found it necessary to release a statement to the Pennsylvania

Herald in August 1787 saying: "Tho' we cannot, affirmatively, tell you what we are doing; we can, negatively tell you what we are not doing —we never once thought of a king."

A weak executive had rendered the Confederation formed in 1777 powerless in dealing with the individual states. The delegates were convinced that they would have to strengthen the office of the executive, but not to the degree that they would be guilty of establishing an "American royalty." The office that emerged was based on the delegates' desires for a strong executive, and on their perceptions of George Washington. Washington, esteemed as the architect of the military victory that had won independence, and admired and trusted for his fairness, honesty, and integrity, was the unanimous choice to be the first president. While Washington helped to establish the majesty of the new executive office, the framers of the Constitution also helped define the limits of his responsibility.

The concept of a single president was by no means unanimous. Many delegates favored a multiple executive branch. Some thought the president should be chosen by Congress rather than by the people. What resulted was the basic structure of the presidency as we know it: a president heading one of three separate branches of government and elected independently every four years. The procedures for separation of powers and checks and balances written into the Constitution were designed to curb the authority of the president.[2] In time the growth of the federal system, the rise of political parties, and the impact of the press and other mass media were to expand both the power of the chief executive and the restraints upon the use of that power.

Upon assuming the office of president, Washington commented that the feeling was not unlike "a culprit who is going to the place of his execution." Other presidents have had similar feelings on assuming office: William Howard Taft thought it "the loneliest place in the world"; Harry Truman declared that "being a President is like riding a tiger. A man has to keep riding or be swallowed"; and Warren Harding referred to the White House as "a prison."

While every man who has held the office has, at one time or another, commented on its enormous demands, some chief executives have used the power of the presidency to its fullest and in many cases endeavored to expand that power. The presidencies of George Washington, Andrew Jackson, Abraham Lincoln, Theodore Roosevelt, Woodrow Wilson, and Franklin Roosevelt are referred to as "strong" or "expansionist" periods for the office. Beginning with Andrew Jackson, who provided the ingredients for what scholars label the "modern" presidency, presidents have used the modern methods of "going to the people" to gather support for their programs. Jackson rationalized his view of the office by stating that "Each public officer who takes an oath to support the Constitution swears that he will support it as he understands it, and not as it is understood by others." The growth of the power of the presidency has accelerated in the twentieth century to the point where Arthur Schlesinger has referred to it as "The Imperial Presidency."[3] In the next section of this chapter we shall discuss the ways in which the presidency became so powerful and assess the impact that President Nixon's resignation may have on the office.

An Overview of the Presidency

President Harry S. Truman, commenting on the office, said "To be a good President I fear a man can't be his own mentor. He can't live the Sermon on the Mount. He must be a Machiavelli, Louis XI of France, Caesar, Borgia . . . a liar, double-crosser . . . a hero and a what-not to be successful. So I probably won't be, thanks to God. But I'm having a lot of fun trying the opposite approach. Maybe it will win."[4]

The presidency is a special creation and invention of the American political system. There is no other executive in the world that has developed into such a unique, pervasive, and powerful office. It is paradoxical that although it was fashioned by men who had a deep mistrust of executive power, the office has become the apex of national politics and the only single office with which most Americans can identify.

The President serves as the symbol of American prosperity and decline. He is visible and acts as a lightning rod for the praise and criticism of the electorate. He has the power to order a worldwide alert of the armed forces but he is unable to fire a bureaucrat like J. Edgar Hoover, the late director of the FBI. He can submit programs to Congress but he cannot allocate money for these programs. As Harry S. Truman put it, in discussing the problems Eisenhower would have in adjusting to the office, "He'll sit here" (tapping his desk), "and he'll say, 'Do this! Do that!' And nothing will happen. Poor Ike, it won't be a bit like the army. He'll find it very frustrating!"[5]

It is not surprising that there is so much disagreement among scholars and serious students regarding the limits of the office and its influence on the American political system. Most scholars would agree on the more clearly identifiable roles and functions of the presidency. Nevertheless, how these roles are to be performed, the extent to which the incumbent can expand these roles, and the constitutional and practical restrictions on the office, remain matters of study and serious debate.

Presidential Models

Students of government must understand not only the political basis of the office and its tremendous potential for power, but also its constitutional basis. Some scholars suggest that the presidency can best be understood by examining its role in domestic affairs rather than in international affairs. It is suggested that in international matters the President has almost unlimited powers, while in domestic affairs his power is considerably limited by constitutional safeguards, the role of the bureaucracy, and Congress. In the final analysis, then, students of American government are faced with a variety of considerations and a number of models in the study of the presidency.

Studies of the American presidency have attempted to provide some focus by developing models and identifying specific functions of the office.[6] For example, some scholars regard the President as primarily a manager of the bureaucracy, and a legislative leader; he establishes priorities and goals for the nation, and subsequently uses his office to shape the bureaucracy and the legislative program to reach these goals.

Those who accept this model of presidential management also suggest that it is a personalized presidency in which key positions in the bureaucracy, the cabinet, and throughout the federal structure are filled by the "President's men." Incumbents, therefore, are assessed with respect to their ability to manage the bureaucracy and the extent to which they can succeed in achieving legislative goals. Implied in this concept, of course, is that the incumbent must be an "active" president.

Some would place the extent of power of the presidency on one end of the spectrum and call him an absolute monarch with all the trappings of divine majesty. Indeed, a number would suggest that the presidency is the most powerful office in the world limited only by the perceptions and personality of the incumbent. On the other end of the continuum, some scholars suggest that the President is almost a pawn of entrenched bureaucrats; that he can in fact produce no change while in office, and that he is bound by existing procedures, policies, and constitutional safeguards against making any dramatic changes. There are a variety of concepts of the presidency between these two positions.

Active and Passive Presidents

The demands of a mature industrial democracy make it highly unlikely that anyone can occupy the presidency without a set of positive programs that are promoted vigorously. The office has grown in power over the past thirty years and it appears unlikely that a newly elected president would not use all of these powers. Indeed, the very existence of these powers has a significant impact on other political actors, whether or not they are actually used. Passive presidents like Buchanan, Harding, Coolidge, and in some respects Eisenhower, are probably relics of the past. President Gerald Ford, for example, immediately upon taking office was faced with grave economic and international issues. Only an "active" president would be able to deal with these issues.

The active president is defined as one who uses all the powers he has to promote his programs. He is not constrained by the explicit powers given him in the Constitution and will, when necessary, use the implied powers to expand his influence. Another concept that recent presidents have called upon is that of "executive privilege." President Nixon relied heavily on the theory that certain activities of the White House could not be investigated because they fell within the area of privileged activities. The subsequent Watergate investigations proved him wrong, and probably served to erode the concept of executive privilege.

Traditional Models

The more traditional models of the presidency rest on historical assessments. The so-called Buchanan model takes its name from a president who viewed the office as primarily an administrative arm of Congress. In this concept, the president is limited to the powers expressly enumerated in Article II of the Constitution. In essence, this seems to be the kind of role envisioned by the authors of the Constitution. President Buchanan considered himself a custodian and remained aloof from political conflict. In 1860 he even denied that he had the power to use force to prevent the secession of the southern states.

The Lincoln model of the presidency grew out of President Abraham Lincoln's actions during the Civil War. In his exercise of presidential power, Lincoln "made clear that to meet the challenge of a major emergency, the barriers against omnipotent government established by the Constitution must often be transcended." Furthermore, he established the concept that the presidency "must always be the dominant organ of crisis government. Only the President can satisfy the crisis demand for unity, action and leadership for he is the sole representative of all the people and the only agency capable of responding quickly and decisively." Indeed, it was Lincoln's presidency that clearly established the concept that the President is the first politician in the land, and that he is the major source of political goals and the leader of public opinion.

The Eisenhower model of the presidency borrows something from both the Buchanan and the Lincoln models. Although standing aloof from party politics and party battles, President Eisenhower felt that his veto power of legislative bills was the key to the presidential office. From this he took the position that he would advise the nation, negate ill-advised legislation and ill-advised policies and, in this sense, be the chief broker of the political system.

Many scholars use the detailed criteria of these three models or some variation of them, to assess the effectiveness of various presidents. For example, most would agree that Presidents Woodrow Wilson, Theodore Roosevelt, Franklin Delano Roosevelt, Harry Truman, and John F. Kennedy would fit the model of the Lincoln presidency. On the other hand, Presidents such as Taft, Harding, Coolidge, and Hoover would fit the Buchanan model. The Eisenhower model, relatively recent, has not been applied to any administration since President Eisenhower's. One could suggest that President Lyndon Johnson, though actually fitting the Lincoln model of the presidency, attempted to project the image of an Eisenhower administration. In light of the complexities and ramifications of the Watergate affair and the resignation of President Richard M. Nixon, it is difficult to categorize the Nixon presidency—at least at this stage of history. The problem of critical assessment becomes more difficult if one recognizes that the foreign policy of the Nixon administration introduced a flexibility and pragmatism not generally characteristic of American foreign policy. Until the disclosures of the Watergate incident, President Nixon seemed to have adopted the Lincoln style while attempting to project an Eisenhower image—similar to that of Johnson's technique.

Regardless of what future historians may say about Lyndon Johnson or Richard Nixon, each has contributed an additional dimension to the concept of the presidency. Johnson, in reaffirming and expanding the concept of the presidency as a people's office, stated, "The source of the President's authority is the people. He is not simply responsible to an immediate electorate either. The President always has to think of America as a continuing community. He has to prepare for the future." Nixon, reaffirming the national character of the office, stated, "The first responsibility of leadership is to gain mastery over events, and to shape the future in the image of our hopes. He must lead. The President has a duty to decide, but the people have a right to know why. The President is the only official who represents every American rich and poor. The Presidency is a place where priorities are set and goals determined." Only time will tell how Watergate will reflect on the credibility of these concepts.

In a recent assessment of presidential character, James David Barber identifies four basic character patterns: active-positive; active-negative; passive-positive; and passive-negative. He suggests that each type is characterized by certain personality traits.

> Active-positive Presidents want most to achieve results. Active-negatives aim to get and keep power. Passive-positives are after love. Passive-negatives emphasize civic virtue. The relation of activity to enjoyment in a President thus tends to outline a cluster of characteristics, to set apart the adapted from the compulsive, compliant, and withdrawn types.[7]

It is interesting to note that Barber places both Lyndon Johnson and Richard Nixon in the active-negative categories, while placing Dwight Eisenhower in the passive-negative group. Barber's approach in studying the man in the White House appears to be particularly useful in assessing the nature of power and power seekers in the presidency. For example, the author assesses the Nixon approach in these terms: "Nixon has within him a very strong drive for personal power—especially independent power—that pushes him away from reliance on anyone else and pulls him toward stubborn insistence on showing everyone that he can win out on his own."[8] Incidentally, this was written before the Watergate affair.

The Presidential Personality

A number of studies also separate the character of the office from that of the man occupying it in an attempt to point out the impact of personalities. One can argue that the growth of the office has been stimulated not only by the complexity and industrialization of American society, but also by the perceptions of office held by incumbents. Each brings with him his own views of the office, and each adds or perhaps subtracts something from it.

The importance of the personality of the president has grown as the technological skills and impact of the media have developed. It is now important, for example, what the President thinks of women's liberation, how long his children's hair is, and how he treats the family dog.

Perceptions of the presidential personality are affected by an off-the-cuff statement or by business reverses of a member of his family. A president who radiates youth, health, and an optimistic air enjoys a certain advantage. It was striking to note the reception that "warm, open, and friendly" President Gerald Ford received upon replacing a president noted for his secretiveness and insularity.

The growth of the mass media, particularly since the end of World War II, has given additional dimensions to the concept of the presidency. As Richard Nixon found out during the 1960 presidential campaign, television exposure can have a significant influence on the public and its assessment of the candidates. On September 26, October 7, 13, and 21, John F. Kennedy and Vice-President Richard M. Nixon met in the first nationally televised live debates between presidential candidates. These debates have been widely credited with Kennedy's victory in the following election.

> Vice President Richard Nixon was better known than Kennedy at the beginning of the 1960 campaign. And the question has often been raised as to why he agreed to the debates in the first place. Nixon was to write later, "Looking at the problem from a purely political standpoint, Kennedy had much more to gain from joint appearances than I did. Had I refused the challenge, I would have opened myself to the charge that I was afraid to defend the Administration's and my own record."[9]

It also seems that Nixon was not fearful of Kennedy's political ability.

> Nixon also had reason for self-confidence. He had launched his political career in 1946 by out-debating an able congressman. His "Checkers" speech in 1952, defending his private political fund, was generally regarded as the most skillful use of television in the campaign that sent him to the Vice Presidency. His impromptu "kitchen debate" with Chairman Khrushchev in Moscow had measurably improved his ratings in the polls.[10]

When the candidates met in Chicago for the first debate Nixon was only recently recovered from a stay in the hospital for an infected knee. He looked pale and had lost weight; to make matters worse, his heavy beard, a favorite target of political cartoonists, was not very well covered by an application of Lazy Shave powder. Kennedy, as was to become his style, looked tan and fit. Theodore White described the scene:

> Probably no picture in American politics tells a better story . . . than that famous shot of the camera on the Vice President as he half slouched, his "Lazy Shave" powder faintly streaked with sweat, his eyes exaggerated hollows of blackness, his jaw, jowls, and face drooping with strain.[11]

Most observers would agree that the results of the television debates between Richard Nixon and John F. Kennedy during the 1960 campaign provided a very important boost to John F. Kennedy's candidacy. An important work on this is Joe McGinness' *The Selling of the President, 1968*. The fact that a candidate for President can be packaged and sold to the American people, using Madison Avenue techniques, disturbs a number of scholars and libertarians.[12] They feel that this practice negates the very concept of individual participation in democracy. Nevertheless, the use of mass media is important not only in winning election to the presidency, but in carrying out the role as top politician of the country.

The President must not only build the proper image, but maintain that image with respect to his constituency, to members of Congress, and to the world. The major tool for this are the mass media, which can be used to reinforce his programs, denounce his critics, and give him an advantage over members of Congress and challengers to his position. The President is constantly in the limelight. Whatever he does is news. Whatever is his is also news, his family as well as his friends. Because of the nature of his office, the President dominates the attention of the media and of the people. No other political actor can hope to compete with him. A shrewd incumbent, therefore, can use the mass media not only to shape public opinion but to influence the constituency and in turn influence Congress. His overall personal appearance and the character he projects on the television screen become important ingredients of the office.

The individual's impact on the office was clearly demonstrated when Gerald Ford became President. His informal style, outgoing personality, and perceived integrity and honesty immediately affected the Washington environment and those around him. The mass media conveyed the mood to the country. Coming on the heels of the dreary and tension-filled final days of the Nixon administration and the Watergate imbroglio, the new open administration of President Ford was received like a breath of fresh air by most Americans. Indeed, Mike Mansfield, the leader of the Democratic majority in the Senate seemed to say it for the country, "The sun is shining again." As one weekly magazine noted:

But the manner of his coming felt as cool and cleansing to a soiled Capital as a freshening Lake Michigan breeze. Ford's young Presidency was open where Nixon's was insular, straight where Nixon's was devious, plain where Nixon's was imperial, and above all cheery where Nixon's had gone sullen under its long seige.[13]

The virtual euphoria dissipated quickly, however, as President Ford made a historic announcement on September 8, 1974, pardoning former President Nixon "for all offenses against the United States which he, Richard Nixon has committed or may have committed or taken part in during the period from January 20, 1969 through August 9, 1974." Democratic party leaders were outraged while Republicans felt that it was the proper thing to do. President Ford granted the pardon in the hopes of finally bringing the Watergate affair to an end, while saving the former President from additional burdens of indictments and possible prosecution. Whether the pardon would in the long run salve the Watergate wounds was difficult to predict, but at the time, arguments were raised regarding not only the legality but also the propriety of President Ford's action.

Presidential Roles

In describing the role of the President, Harry S. Truman stated:

> I am frequently asked how much a President depends upon advice and directions from his Cabinet or staff or military leaders or advisers. I always point out that it is absolutely essential for a President to have information and advice. But he does not take directions, because it is the President's responsibility alone to give directions.[14]

This certainly is one of the roles of the President but he has many more to fill in the performance of his office. The President is required to be above the normal vices of other mortals; he is the moral leader of the country; he is the symbol of the American people abroad; he is peacemaker and commander in chief; he is a diplomat and chief legislator.

In his celebrated account of the presidency, Clinton Rossiter lists the roles of the President:[15]
1) Chief of state, he is ceremonial head of government and represents the American nation.
2) Chief executive—The President rules and runs the government.
3) Commander in chief—The nation's armed forces take their orders directly from the President.

4) Chief diplomat—The President's position in foreign affairs is paramount.
5) Chief legislator—The President plays a key role in determining legislative programs.

The following additional functions have evolved:
1) Chief of party—The President has the absolute right and duty to be leader of his party, through which he has reached the highest office.
2) Voice of the people—The President serves as a spokesman for the people, and a formulator and expounder of public opinion.
3) Protector of the peace—Americans expect the President to take the key role in times of crisis.
4) Manager of prosperity—The President is expected to use his powers to maintain stable economic conditions.
5) World leader—The President's constituency is much broader than the United States—it stretches out to foreign shores. What America does or doesn't do has significant impact on world conditions and the environment in other countries.

Rossiter's categories are the basis for our own assessment of the presidential roles.

Chief of State

The President is chief of state. He is today, as he has always been, the ceremonial head of the government of the United States. He usually takes part in a range of activities from meeting diplomats to dedicating monuments in the name of the United States.

Chief Executive

The President is also chief executive. He is directed by the Constitution to "take care that the laws be faithfully executed." He is the chief bureaucrat, and it is his responsibility to insure that the federal bureaucracy operates efficiently and in accordance with the laws of the land. He heads a federal establishment with a combined payroll of $51 billion.

The President receives $200,000 per year plus $50,000 in expenses (both taxable) and $40,000 in travel expenses (tax-free). After retirement he receives $60,000 per year. The Constitution requires that he be thirty-five years of age, a natural-born citizen, and fourteen years a resident of the United States.

Beneath the President in the executive branch are the eleven cabinet departments, and more than fifty-two major independent

THE EXECUTIVE BRANCH OF GOVERNMENT

(Numbers in parentheses indicate approximate number of employees in each agency - excluding military)

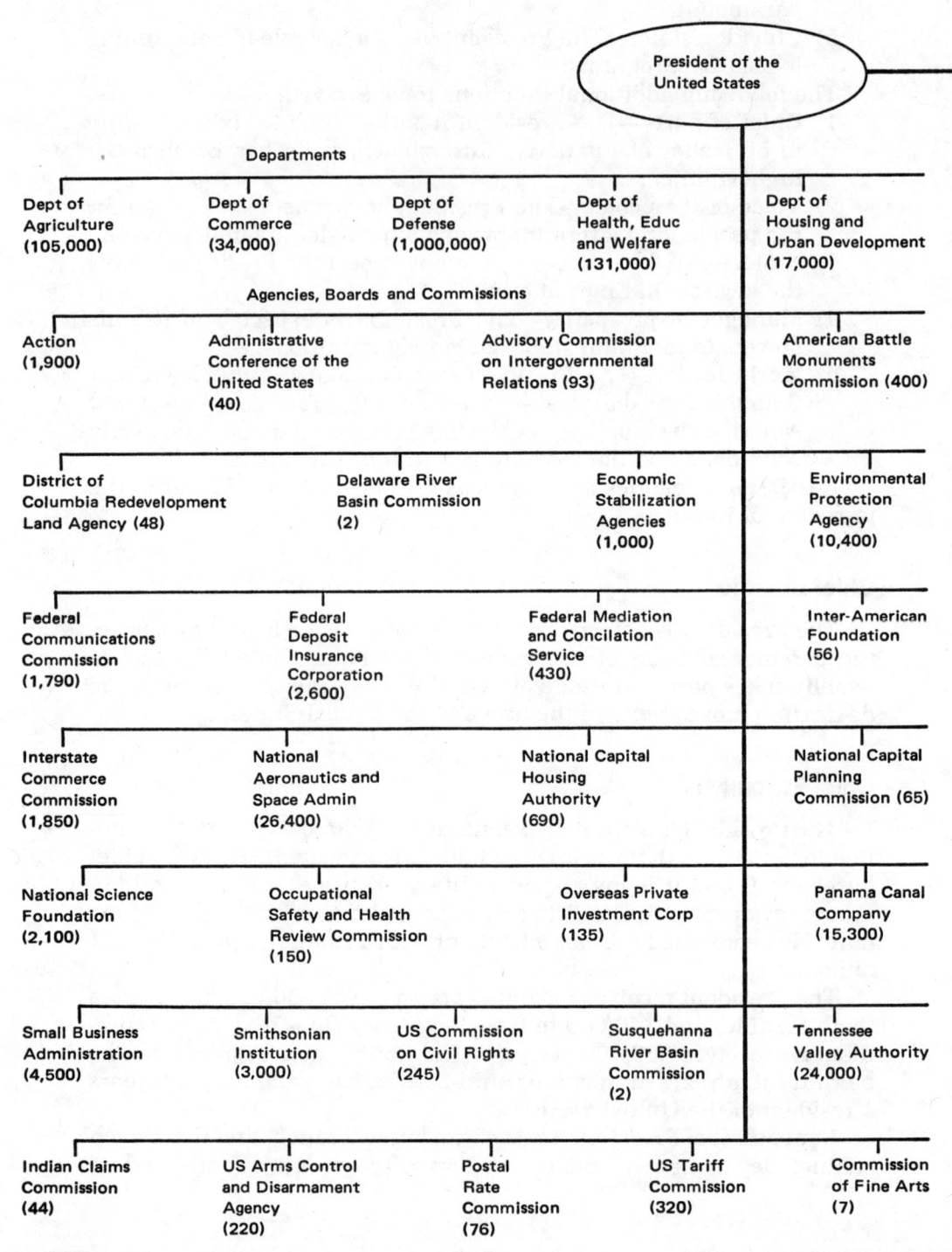

President of the United States

Departments

Dept of Agriculture (105,000)	Dept of Commerce (34,000)	Dept of Defense (1,000,000)	Dept of Health, Educ and Welfare (131,000)	Dept of Housing and Urban Development (17,000)

Agencies, Boards and Commissions

Action (1,900)	Administrative Conference of the United States (40)		Advisory Commission on Intergovernmental Relations (93)	American Battle Monuments Commission (400)
District of Columbia Redevelopment Land Agency (48)	Delaware River Basin Commission (2)		Economic Stabilization Agencies (1,000)	Environmental Protection Agency (10,400)
Federal Communications Commission (1,790)	Federal Deposit Insurance Corporation (2,600)		Federal Mediation and Conciliation Service (430)	Inter-American Foundation (56)
Interstate Commerce Commission (1,850)	National Aeronautics and Space Admin (26,400)		National Capital Housing Authority (690)	National Capital Planning Commission (65)
National Science Foundation (2,100)	Occupational Safety and Health Review Commission (150)		Overseas Private Investment Corp (135)	Panama Canal Company (15,300)
Small Business Administration (4,500)	Smithsonian Institution (3,000)	US Commission on Civil Rights (245)	Susquehanna River Basin Commission (2)	Tennessee Valley Authority (24,000)
Indian Claims Commission (44)	US Arms Control and Disarmament Agency (220)	Postal Rate Commission (76)	US Tariff Commission (320)	Commission of Fine Arts (7)

120

Source: Adapted from "Organization of Federal Executive Departments and Agencies, (Chart), as of January 1, 1974 (Washington, D.C.: US Government Printing Office)

Executive Office of the President

White House Office	Council on International Economic Policy	Office of the Special Representative for Trade Negotiations
Executive Residence	Domestic Council	Office of Telecommunications Policy Prevention
Office of Management and Budget	Central Intelligence Agency	Special Action Office for Drug Abuse Prevention
Council of Economic Advisors	National Security Council	Special Assistant to the President Federal Energy Office
Council on Environmental Quality	Office of Economic Opportunity	

Dept of Interior (68,000)	Dept of Justice (48,000)	Dept of Labor (13,000)	Dept of State (23,000)	Dept of Transportation (69,000)	Dept of Treasury (110,000)
American Revolution Bicentennial Admin (95)	Appalachian Regional Commission (9)	Atomic Energy Commission (7,600)	Civil Aeronautics Board (690)	Cabinet Committee On Opportunities for Spanish Speaking People (45)	Consumer Product Safety Commission (690)
Equal Employment Opportunity Commission (1,800)	Federal Maritime Commission (290)	Federal Reserve System (1,280)	Foreign Claims Settlement Commission (47)	Export-Import Bank (400)	Farm Credit Administration (210)
National Mediation Board (100)	Federal Home Loan Bank Board (1,280)	Federal Power Commission (1,230)	Federal Trade Commission (1,560)	General Services Administration (37,400)	National Transportation Safety Board (270)
National Council on Indian Opportunity (15)	National Credit Union Administration (500)		National Foundation of the Arts and Humanities (1,300)		National Labor Relations Board (2,450)
Renegotiation Board (195)	Railroad Retirement Board (1,690)		Selective Service System (3,800)		Securities and Exchange Commission (1,700)
US Civil Service Commission (7,150)	US Postal Service (720,800)		US Information Agency (9,000)		Veterans Administration (197,150)

agencies, boards, and commissions. President Truman, reflecting on his position as head of the country's largest bureaucracy said, "I sit here all day trying to persuade people to do the things they ought to have sense enough to do without my persuading them. . . . That's all the powers of the President amount to." The Constitution does not give the President the right to fire government employees, but a Supreme Court decision has established that he may fire his appointees.

Eventually all the major decisions arrive at the President's desk. He must make the necessary decision based on the information his staff gives him, his own understanding of the problem, and the impact that his decision will have on all his other roles. When he was President Harry Truman kept a small four-word sign on his desk. The sign read: "The Buck Stops Here."

Commander in Chief

The President is commander in chief of the Army and Navy of the United States and of the militia of the several states when called into the actual service of the United States, under the provision of the Constitution. Whether in peace or in war, he is the supreme commander of the armed forces and thus is a living symbol of the supremacy of the civil over military authority. Recently, as a result of the conduct of the war in Southeast Asia, Congress moved to limit the President's warmaking power. Soon after the Vietnam peace settlement a bill was passed, over President Nixon's veto, that provided:

1. Within 48 hours of committing armed forces to combat abroad, the President must report to Congress in writing, explaining the circumstances and scope of his action.
2. Use of American forces in combat would have to end in 60 days unless Congress authorized a longer period, but the deadline could be extended for another 30 days if the President certified that the time was necessary for the safe withdrawal of the forces.
3. Within the 60 or 90 day period, Congress could order an immediate withdrawal of American forces by adopting a concurrent resolution—which is not subject to a presidential veto.[16]

Some members of Congress felt the new measures simply gave the President the power to wage 60-day wars but, no matter the interpretation, it was apparent that Congress had seized the moment to attempt to reassert congressional authority over the combat use of American military power. Nevertheless, the President's constitutional power to command the armed forces of the United States has rarely been questioned. The President can, if he so desires, control military operations in the field. President Abraham Lincoln on many occasions during the American Civil War went into the field. President John Kennedy exercised strict control over movements of ships during the Cuban Blockade in 1963. The important point is that the President is the commander of a military instrument that has an impact throughout the world as well as within the borders of the United States. With a budget of about $85 billion in 1975, the armed forces also influences the economy of the country. All of this adds to the power of the presidential office.

Chief Diplomat

The President is chief diplomat. The Supreme Court has made it clear that although authority in the field of foreign relations is shared constitutionally among three branches of government, the President, the Congress, and the Supreme Court, it is the President who is paramount and can alone represent the United States in international relations. Because the State Department, the CIA and the Armed Forces report directly to the President, he usually has more information about foreign affairs than Congress does. The result is the generally accepted theory that the President makes foreign policy.

Chief Legislator

The President has become the chief legislator, although no such provision is made in the Constitution. Congress has a wealth of strong and talented men, but the complexity of the problems they are asked to solve by people who assume that all problems are solvable has made external leadership a requisite for effective operation. Because the office is occupied by a single man, and because there are a number of constitutional and practical factors involved, the presidency is looked to for legislative leadership. Although presidential involvement was not originally anticipated by the framers of the Constitution, it soon became apparent that some active role was necessary in order to carry out active programs. Thus, even during the first years of Washington's tenure, there was an inclination for presidential concern in the legislative process. Since the days of Franklin Roosevelt's New Deal (1933), the President has been deeply involved in legislation.

Chief Politician

There are at least two roles of the presidency that began with the administration of Thomas Jefferson. The first of these is as chief of party. The President by virtue of his office is the most prominent member of his party and the focal point of party politics on the national level. His fortunes with the electorate are also the fortunes of the party. What he does or doesn't do while in office reflects on the party as a whole. Moreover, he becomes the dominant force in projecting the image of the party to the American people. The second extra-constitutional role, so to speak, is that of chief politician. Given all the people that the President must deal with—members of his own party, members of Congress, the bureaucracy, foreign diplomats, and the public as a whole—he must develop a political awareness and astuteness to maintain the power and influence of his office and to fulfill all of his other functions and roles effectively. This role also presupposes his ability to develop and maintain a consensus for his style of leadership. In essence, he must establish a political authority to allow him the moral leadership of the American political system.

Each of these roles can be further characterized as primarily a political, legal, or symbolic act depending on the purpose of the role. Thus the President's role as Party Chief is obviously a political act, yet it is also symbolic, i.e., symbolizes the party and the party program.

One can argue that there are no clear distinctions among the various roles of the President. He does not necessarily act politically at one time, legally at another, and symbolically at still another. Rather there are elements of all of these in virtually every official and unofficial act of the President. In almost all cases one or another act is more pronounced. For example, President Ford's 1974 meeting with the Secretary General of the Communist Party of the Soviet Union, was initially as Chief of State. Nevertheless, no one can put aside the fact that President Ford was present in the Soviet Union as the Chief Executive of the United States and Chief Diplomat.

Regardless of how intelligently the roles of the President are delineated, however, justice cannot be done to the complexities and multidimensional nature of the office. We are not trying here to provide a detailed assessment of these roles. Our purpose is to develop in the student an appreciation of the complexities and imponderables inherent in the presidential office. This will hopefully lead to a realistic and manageable basis for studying the presidency, since such role distinctions form the wellspring of presidential performance.

Limits on Executive Power

Role Conflict

What makes it difficult for the President is that these roles may be contradictory. The need to perform a particular role or roles in any given situation may diminish his power and influence in other roles. For example, President Nixon's concern and power with his role as chief diplomat may have diminished his role as chief legislator. The need to balance the power and influence of these various roles places tremendous burdens upon even the most energetic individual. The demands of each of the roles are physically exhausting and mentally exasperating and it is a difficult task to maximize the power and influence inherent in each of these roles. Nevertheless the man who is to succeed is one who can judiciously balance the roles while maximizing the power and influence of his office.

Depending on the issues he is dealing with, the President is faced with a variety of limitations which differ in scope and effectiveness. His major areas of concern involve the international arena, the domestic community, and the local communities. In each of these areas he must deal with a different constituency, a different set of government officials, a different decision-making process, and a different cause-and-effect impact of his decisions and policies. For example, there is a different power equation and constituency when dealing with the international community rather than with the domestic community.

Public Opinion

The President is affected by the force of public opinion. One of the most powerful weapons in the hands of the President is a so-called mandate from the American people. Lyndon Johnson received such a mandate in the 1964 elections, and it ultimately led to the vast number of legislative programs dealing with the "Great Society." In this same sense, Richard Nixon may well have received a mandate to bring the Vietnam War to an end on his terms as a result of the 1972 elections. (In 1972, President Nixon received 62 per cent and Senator George McGovern 37 per cent.)

On the other hand, a President who is elected on a small plurality, such as President Nixon in 1968, and attempts to use this as a springboard for a vast legislative program, is likely to be viewed with suspicion by Congress and the people at large. Lyndon Johnson's decision not to run in 1968 may very well have been based on the public's vast disapproval of his performance on the Vietnam War issue.

Similarly public approval can provide a presidential weapon to overcome Congressional obstacles. A President, therefore, is quite concerned about his image and about the use of the mass media to project this image to the American people. Image-making is an important factor in generating public approval for even the most rational and relevant policies.

Congressional Approval

Congressional checks on presidential power have become a major issue as a result of the policies associated with the Vietnam War. Congress is a jealous governmental body, sensitive to presidential encroachments on its prerogatives. More important, most congressmen are suspicious of aggrandizement of power by a single individual. Because of the ultimate need of congressional approval, or at the minimum, indifference, the President is limited in the extent to which he can make changes in policy. Furthermore, Congress has always assumed that it is representative of the public will and does not hesitate to use its prerogative in checking presidential power. Since Congress is made up of a number of political leaders, each having his own power base and representing various interests, the President is always faced with competing and conflicting interests which ultimately limit his ability to exploit the executive prerogative.

Judicial Approval

The Supreme Court often acts to limit the power of the executive. Based on the accepted concept of judicial review and supremacy with respect to constitutional interpretation, the Court can declare an executive program unconstitutional. For example, during Franklin Delano Roosevelt's first term, the Supreme Court declared unconstitutional the National Industrial Recovery Act, a major part of the New Deal program designed to reduce unemployment.

Over the past three decades the Supreme Court has generally supported the expansion of executive power, particularly with respect to implementing civil rights policies. Indeed, since the *McCulloch* v. *Maryland* decision in 1819, ruling that the national government had implied and inherent powers to make all laws necessary and proper to carry out its enumerated powers, the general trend has been toward expansion of the power of the national government, and with it the power of the executive.

The President and Bureaucracy

The federal bureaucracy is the instrument through which the President hopes to put his policies into effect. Because of the vastness of the bureaucracy and the manifold problems and issues that must be faced, the President must depend on a host of people to assist him. Consequently, many decisions are made throughout the bureaucracy which have the effect of shaping policy, without specific knowledge or control by the President. Part of this problem is the relatively small span of control that can be exercised by any one individual. This span normally is limited to about a dozen or so people. The President depends on subordinates, who in turn depend on other subordinates, and so on down the line, building a vast bureaucracy. As a consequence, the amount of personal control that the President can exercise is limited, as is the amount of information that he receives.

The nature of the bureaucratic structure, however, inherently resists any important change in policies and techniques. The complexity and vastness of the bureaucracy, combined with its tendency to follow accepted practices, result in a practical limitation on how far the President can go in actually implementing policies. The President may make a variety of pronouncements on policies, but they become meaningful only when accepted philosophically and procedurally by the bureaucracy. Bureaucrats detest changes in procedures that have already been mastered and they resist changes in intellectual processes and working accommodations. Security, comfort, and success become associated with the efficiency of the existing structure and its operating procedures.

When Franklin Delano Roosevelt was Secretary of the Navy, he became so infuriated by his inability to get the Navy bureaucracy to move that he compared it to a feather bed. He complained that "To change anything in the Navy is like punching a feather bed. You punch it with your right and you punch it with your left until you are finally exhausted, and then you find the damn bed just as it was before you started punching."[17] President Kennedy's disenchantment with the bureaucratic rigidity of the Department of State led him to seek more imaginative and innovative foreign policy initiatives elsewhere, including advice from his brother, Robert Kennedy, the Attorney General.

The President and Change

Both past policies and traditional expectations temper the incumbent's ability to make radical shifts in direction of policies or behavior.

Since one of the President's functions is to provide a cohesiveness, stability and legitimacy to government, he must move carefully in office so as not to destroy the credibility of national institutions and the effectiveness of policies. Much of the stability, for example, stems from smooth transition and continuity of operations—in the eyes of many Americans as well as in the eyes of foreigners. The President who expects to make vast changes must do so either in perceived crisis situations or by judicious use of power, image making and persuasion.

Power in the Presidency

We return again to the question: how do we study the American presidency? Although there is no single explanation or model of the presidency, we nevertheless suggest an approach which provides a useful beginning and is essential to grasping the realities of the office.

One of the most realistic ways to study the presidency is to examine first the context within which the office operates, keeping in mind that it is inherently an office of power. One mark of an incumbent's effectiveness is his ability to use appropriate forms of power inherent in the office at the most important moment of conflict. The other mark is the efficiency with which he uses his power to perform the functions of office while steadfastly projecting the image of the just, moral and competent national leader.

There are four major ingredients which shape the context in which this power is exercised:
1) Personality—the basis for image-making.
2) The incumbent's views of the office—its functions and influence in the American political system.
3) The domestic environment—including the mood of the people, temper of the times, character of the bureaucracy, political attitudes of Congress, strength of Congress vis-à-vis the presidency, and the nature of the consensus on major issues.
4) International environment—including perceptions and response to crisis, extent of lasting American commitments, demands and requirements of allies, and techniques and procedures (diplomatic or military) required to achieve policy goals.

Let us look briefly at each of the major ingredients.

Personality

In one sense the President must appear to be all things to most men. He must project the image of a cool, calm leader who is his own man. Moreover, he should project a sense of humor, charm, and friendliness, without losing the image of a leader.

Basically, the President must project himself as an equal with most other Americans—to be sure, first among equals. Being a good family man with an attractive, though not too attractive, wife, at least two children, and a pet, helps to project the proper image and ultimately gain acceptance by the American people.

As for pets, Franklin Delano Roosevelt's dog, Fala, was well known to most Americans at the time. John F. Kennedy had Pushinka, daughter of a Soviet space dog, and Lyndon Johnson had his beagles, named Him and Her. President Nixon had an Irish setter named King Timahoe in 1973, but even more famous was his pet of an earlier day, a cocker spaniel named Checkers. As Vice-Presidential candidate in 1952, Nixon appeared on television to respond to his critics' allegations that he had accepted contributions while senator. He disclaimed wrongdoing, made his net worth public, and said the only gift he had accepted was the dog, Checkers. "The kids love the dog and regardless of what they [Nixon's critics] say about it, we're going to keep it."

It is obvious that we are unrealistic in our expectations that the President be a super human being—wise and prudent, a philosopher-king. It seems that the office has become the embodiment of what the framers of the Constitution felt was "monarchial sentiment."

The Incumbent's View of the Office

Most incumbents come to the office with some ideas of what it should be, its role and function, and how he, as an individual, will proceed as President. This view includes some ideas as to the policies and programs that need to be initiated as well as the techniques and procedures to be used to insure passage of his legislative program. The incumbent's perceptions as to his ability and the power and limits of the office are significant in shaping the character and nature of his administration.

The Domestic Environment

This is one of the most difficult elements to delineate. Nevertheless, there are signs and indicators as to the temper of the times and the mood of the people. A good politician will feel the "pulse" of public opinion and identify the kind of policies and programs needed to respond to the public mood. For example, at the beginning of his first administration, President Nixon was aware, as were most politicians, that Vietnam was a key issue and the public's mood was for peace—

almost a frantic desire for peace. He therefore directed his program primarily toward Vietnamization and withdrawal to reduce American casualties, and thus ease public concern.

Other elements of the domestic environment include the bureaucracy, attitudes of Congress, congressional-executive relationships, and the nature of consensus on major issues. All of these variables influence what the President can or cannot do with respect to his programs. In many cases they actually determine what kinds of programs will be presented to the country and how powerful the President will be vis-à-vis other governing institutions in implementing his policies.

The International Environment

Past foreign policy as well as the current and future national interests of the United States provide the context within which the President must operate in the international sphere.

The Vietnam involvement, for example, began with President Eisenhower's administration, was inherited by President Kennedy, escalated to a deeper involvement under President Johnson, and was passed on to President Nixon. Similarly, the commitments made to Europe during the Truman administration remain part of the general policy of the United States.

Nevertheless, the President can take a number of initiatives in foreign affairs with little in the way of checks and balances from other institutions—particularly in times of crisis.

At the same time, it is the President who is ultimately responsible for judiciously balancing domestic priorities, public support, and foreign policy initiatives. He must keep in mind the international constituency with whom he must deal in a manner similar to his domestic constituency. The President's view of the national interest of the United States does much to shape the scope and type of foreign involvement.

President Nixon in his first administration took a number of foreign policy initiatives which not only disarmed his critics and caused concern among some allies, but generally began a new era in the international environment. Visiting China and the Soviet Union, concluding the SALT agreement (Strategic Arms Limitation Talks) and withdrawing from Vietnam were foreign policy initiatives which developed from his decision to reshape the international environment in what he perceived to be the best interests of the United States. To reiterate, the executive and his individual perceptions of the office and the international environment are the foundations of these initiatives.

Summary

Our approach in studying the presidency is to focus on the power of the office as it is used to perform the major roles (political, legal, symbolic) within the context of the presidential world (personality, incumbent's view of the office, the domestic and international environment). It should be remembered that presidential power does have its limitations and that Presidents are rarely free agents when it comes to effecting new policies or changing policies which they have inherited.

The presidency, then, is a political mixture whose unique flavor cannot be accounted for simply by listing its ingredients. It is a whole greater than and different from the sum of its parts, an office whose power and prestige are something more than the sum total of all its functions. In this sense, the President must be a jack-of-all-trades. However, he must be master of at least one—balancing conflicting demands on his office while judiciously applying power not only to solve conflicts and meet these demands, but to shape the political system in the direction that he deems necessary. As Lyndon B. Johnson so succinctly stated in his book, *The Vantage Point,* "I used the power of the President proudly, and I used every ounce of it I had." He adds:

> No one can experience with the President of the United States the glory and agony of his office. No one can share the majestic view from his pinnacle of power. No one can share the burden of his decisions or the scope of his duties. A Cabinet officer, no matter how broad his mandate, has a limited responsibility. A Senator, no matter how varied his interests, has a limited constituency. But the President represents all the people and must face up to all the problems. He must be responsible, as he sees it, for the welfare of every citizen and must be sensitive to the will of every group. He cannot pick and choose his issues. They all come with the job. So his experience is unique among his fellow Americans.[18]

This lofty view must be conditioned by the realities of the office. For example, Rossiter writes of Thomas Corcoran, a Washington lawyer during the Franklin Delano Roosevelt administration,

For the next five years Corcoran was a White House agent-without-portfolio, working directly under FDR and authorized to act in his name. Every President needs a resident bastard, a pragmatist capable of working in the lower sewers of politics and government, if necessary, to move things along. Corcoran once described his role: "There isn't enough time to explain everything to everyone, to cajole everyone, to persuade everyone, to make everyone see why it has to be done one way rather than another. If a President tried to do this, he would have no time left for anything else. So he must deceive, misrepresent, leave false impressions even, sometimes, lie—and trust to charm and loyalty, and the result to make up for it. . . A great man cannot be a good man."[19]

Although the practicalities of gaining and maintaining power in the office of the President may develop according to Corcoran's concept, the implications of Watergate may prove the dangers inherent in such a perspective.

The resignation of Richard Nixon from the presidency on August 9, 1974 in the wake of the Watergate affair is likely to leave indelible marks on the office and its relationship with other political actors. Moreover, the mass media coverage of the various hearings on Watergate gave the public deep insights into the presidential office, insights which had not previously been available. Regardless of the ultimate impact, Nixon's resignation and the Watergate affair have probably influenced the people's perception of the presidency. The office probably will appear to be less overpowering, the men who occupy it less majestic and awesome, and the people will probably harbor a lingering suspicion that the President may be, after all, just another politician.

In the long run, however, we feel that the President can be as big a man as he wishes—limited only by his own conscience. As Rossiter observed:

> He will feel few checks upon his power if he uses that power as he should. This may well be the final definition of the strong and successful President: the one who knows just how far he can go in the direction he wants to go. If he cannot judge the limits of his power, he cannot call upon its strength. If he cannot sense the possible, he will exhaust himself attempting the impossible. The power of the Presidency moves as a mighty host only *with* the grain of liberty and morality.[20]

NOTES

1. Emmet John Hughes, *The Living Presidency* (Baltimore, Md.: Penguin Books, 1973), pp. 74-75.
2. Carl Van Doren, *The Great Rehearsal* (New York: Viking Press, 1948), pp. 145-146.

Notes

3. Arthur Schlesinger, Jr., *The Imperial Presidency* (Boston: Houghton Mifflin Co., 1973).
4. Margaret Truman, *Harry S. Truman* (New York: Pocket Books, 1974), p. 349.
5. Ibid., p. 603.
6. Richard E. Neustadt, *Presidential Power* (New York: Wiley, 1960), p. 9.
7. James David Barber, *The Presidential Character, Predicting Performance in The White House* (New York: Prentice-Hall, 1972), pp. 12-13.
8. James David Barber, "Passive-Positive to Active-Negative: The Style and Character of Presidents," in *Inside the System,* Charles Peters and John Rothchild (eds.) (New York: Praeger, 1973), 2d ed., p. 75.
9. Richard M. Nixon, *Six Crises* (Garden City, N.Y.: Doubleday, 1962), p. 323.
10. Theodore C. Sorenson, *Kennedy* (New York: Bantam Books, 1966), p. 221.
11. Theodore H. White, *The Making of the President 1960* (New York: Atheneum, 1961), p. 289.
12. Joe McGinniss, *The Selling of the President, 1968* (New York: Trident, 1969).
13. "The Sun is Shining Again," *Newsweek,* August 26, 1974, p. 16.
14. Harry S. Truman, *Mr. Citizen* (New York: Bernard Geiss Associates, 1960), p. 265.
15. Clinton Rossiter, *The American Presidency,* 2d ed. (New York: Mentor Books, 1960), pp. 13-37.
16. See for example, *Congressional Quarterly Weekly Report,* Vol. XXXI, No. 45, November 10, 1973, pp. 2985, 2986.
17. Marriner S. Eccles, *Beckoning Frontiers* (New York: Knopf, 1951), p. 336.
18. Lyndon Baines Johnson, *The Vantage Point* (New York: Holt, Rinehart and Winston, 1971), from the Preface.
19. Joseph C. Goulden, *The Superlawyers* (New York: Dell Publishing Company, 1973), p. 159.
20. Rossiter, p. 69.

Selected Readings

There has always been a gap between what the American people expect of their President and his ability to perform. This is particularly true in regard to scholarly assessment of the President's office and the President as a man. In the first reading, Thomas E. Cronin clearly distinguishes the gap between perceptions and expectations of the President and his capability. He concludes that "The more we learn about the processes of government, the more it becomes apparent that presidents are rarely free agents when it comes to effecting new policies—or dismantling policies which they have inherited."

The next two readings are from *Time* magazine and outline the Watergate affair and the resignation of Richard Nixon from the presidency. These readings clearly illustrate the glory of the presidency and more clearly, the burden of the office. Coming in on a massive vote in 1972, Richard Nixon inherited all of the glories of the office. On the heels of a rather amateurish "break-in," he felt the burdens of the office, which ultimately led to his resignation.

The reading by Cronin and the selections from *Time* magazine should provide you with some insights into the nature of the presidential office and how the President is torn between the demands of the office and his own human limitations.

4.1

Our Textbook President

THOMAS E. CRONIN

Franklin D. Roosevelt personally rescued the nation from the depths of the great Depression. Roosevelt, together with Harry Truman, brought World War II to a proud conclusion. Courageous Truman personally committed us to resist communist aggression around the globe. General Eisenhower pledged that as president he would "go to Korea" and end that war—and he did. These are prevailing idealized images that most American students read and remember. For convenience, if not for simplicity, textbooks divide our past into the "Wilson years," the "Hoover depression," the "Roosevelt revolution," the "Eisenhower period" and so forth.

Presidents are expected to perform as purposeful activists, who know what they want to accomplish and relish the challenges of the office. The student learns that the presidency is "the great engine of democracy," the "American people's one authentic trumpet," "the central instrument of democracy," and "probably the most important governmental institution in the world." With the New Deal presidency in mind the textbook portrait states that presidents must instruct the nation as national teacher and guide the nation as national preacher. Presidents should be decidedly in favor of expanding the federal government's role in order to cope with increasing nationwide demands for social justice and a prosperous economy. The performances of Harding, Coolidge, and Hoover, lumped together as largely similar, are rejected as antique. The Eisenhower record of retiring reluctance elicits more ambiguous appraisal; after brief tribute to him as a wonderful man and a superior military leader, he gets categorized as an amateur who lacked both a sense of direction and a progressive and positive conception of the presidential role. What is needed, most texts imply, is a man with foresight to anticipate the future and the personal strength to unite us, to steel our moral will, to move the country forward, and to make the country governable. The vision, and perhaps the illusion, is that, if only we can identify and elect *the right man*, our loftiest aspirations can and will be accomplished.

Reprinted with permission from *The Washington Monthly*. Copyright by The Washington Monthly Co., 1028 Connecticut Ave., N.W., Washington, D.C. 20036.

With little variation, the college text includes two chapters on the presidency. Invariably, these stress that the contemporary presidency is growing dramatically larger in size, gaining measurably more responsibilities (often referred to as more hats) and greater resources. Students read that more authority and policy discretion devolve to the president during war and crises; and since our country is now engaged in sustained international conflict and acute domestic problems, presidents are constantly becoming more powerful. One text points out that "as the world grows smaller, he will grow bigger."

Then, too, writers tend to underline the vast resources available for presidential decision-making—the array of experts, including White House strategic support staffs, intelligence systems, the National Security Council, the Cabinet, an Office of Science and Technology, the Council of Economic Advisers, and countless high-powered study commissions. To the student, it must appear that a president must have just about all the inside information and sage advice possible for human comprehension. A casual reading of the chapters on the presidency fosters the belief that contemporary presidents can both make and shape public policy and can see to it that these policies *work as intended*. Textbooks encourage the belief that the "president knows best" and that his advisory and information systems are unparalleled in history. The capacity of the presidency for systematic thinking and planning is similarly described as awesome and powerfully suited to the challenges of the day.

Clinton Rossiter wrote one of the most lucid venerations of the chief executive. In the *American Presidency*, he views the office as a priceless American invention which has not only worked extremely well but is also a symbol of our continuity and destiny as a people:

> Few nations have solved so simply and yet grandly the problem of finding and maintaining an office or state that embodies their majesty and reflects their character. . . .
> There is virtually no limit to what the President can do if he does it for democratic ends and by democratic means. . . .
> He is, rather, a kind of magnificent lion who can roam widely and do great deeds so long as he does not try to break loose from his broad reservation. . . .
> He reigns, but he also rules; he symbolizes the people, but he also runs their government. . . .

Recently written or revised government textbooks emphasize the importance of personal attributes, and there is little doubt that dwelling on the president's personal qualities helps to capture the attention of student learners. Not surprisingly, this personalization of the presidency also is reflected in a great deal of campaign rhetoric. Presidential candidates go to a considerable length to stress how personally courageous and virtuous a president must be. Nelson Rockefeller's (1968) litany of necessary qualities is as exaggerated as anyone else's:

> The modern Presidency of the United States, as distinct from the traditional concepts of our highest office, is bound up with the survival not only of freedom but of mankind. . . . The President is the unifying force in our lives. . . .
> The President must possess a wide range of abilities: to lead, to persuade, to inspire trust, to attract men of talent, to unite. These abilities must reflect a wide range of characteristics: courage, vision, integrity, intelligence, sense of responsibility, sense of

history, sense of humor, warmth, openness, personality, tenacity, energy, determination, drive, perspicacity, idealism, thirst for information, penchant for fact, presence of conscience, comprehension of people and enjoyment of life—plus all the other, nobler virtues ascribed to George Washington under God.

The Lion's Transformation

The personalized presidency is also a central feature of contemporary political journalism, and no journalist does more to embellish this perspective than Theodore White. His "Making of the President" series not only enjoys frequent university use but additionally serves as presidency textbooks for millions of adults who savor his "insider" explanations of presidential election campaigns.

White's unidimensional concentration on the presidential candidates, their styles, and personalities promotes a benevolent if not reverential orientation toward the American presidency. His narrative histories of American political campaigns have an uncanny way of uplifting and seducing the reader to watch and wait an election's outcome with intense concern—even though the books are published almost a year after the event. His style ferments great expectations and a heightened sense of reverence for the eventual victor. At first there are seven or eight competing hopefuls, then four or five, penultimately narrowed down to two or three nationally legitimized candidates and finally—there remains just one man. Clearly the victor in such a drawn-out and thoroughly patriotic ritual deserves our deepest respect and approval. White subtly succeeds in purifying the victorious candidate: in what must be a classic metamorphosis at the root of the textbook presidency image, the men who assume the presidency seem physically (and implicitly almost spiritually) to undergo an alteration of personal traits.

On JFK's first days in the White House, 1961:

> It was as if there were an echo, here on another level, in the quiet Oval Office, of all the speeches he had made in all the squares and supermarkets of the country. . . . He had won this office and this power by promising such movement to the American people. Now he had to keep the promise. He seemed very little changed in movement or in gracefulness from the candidate—only his eyes had changed—very dark now, very grave, markedly more sunken and lined at the corners than those of the candidate.

On Richard Nixon soon after his ascendancy, 1969:

> He seemed, as he waved me into the Oval Office, suddenly on first glance a more stocky man than I had known on the campaign rounds. There was a minute of adjustment as he waved me to a sofa in the barren office, poured coffee, put me at ease; then, watching him, I realized that he was not stockier, but, on the contrary, slimmer. What was different was the movement of the body, the sound of the voice, the manner of speaking—for he was calm as I had never seen him before, as if peace had settled on him. In the past, Nixon's restless body had been in constant movement as he rose, walked about, hitched a leg over the arm of a chair or gestured sharply with his hands. Now he was in repose; and the repose was in his speech also—more slow, studied, with none of the gearslippages of name or reference which used to come when he was weary; his hands still moved as he spoke, but the fingers spread gracefully, not punchily, or sharply as they used to.

What, then, constitutes the recent textbook version of the American presidency? As always, any facile generalization of such a hydra-like institution is susceptible to oversimplification, but, on balance, more consensus than contention characterizes literature on the American presidency. Four summary statements may be singled out without doing great violence to the text literature. Two of these accentuate a dimension of presidential omnipotence, and two others emphasize an expectation of moralistic-benevolence. Taken together, this admixture of legend and reality comprise the textbook presidency of the last 15 years.

Omnipotence

1. The president is the strategic catalyst in the American political system and the central figure in the international system as well.
2. Only the president is or can be the genuine architect of United States public policy, and only he, by attacking problems frontally and aggressively and interpreting his power expansively, can be the engine of change to move this nation forward.

Moralistic-Benevolence

3. The president must be the nation's personal and moral leader; by symbolizing the past and future greatness of America and radiating inspirational confidence, a president can pull the nation together while directing us toward the fulfillment of the American Dream.
4. If, and only if, the right man is placed in the White House, all will be well, and, somehow, whoever is in the White House is the right man.

The "Selling of a Textbook"

Radio, television, and the emergence of the United States as a strategic nuclear power have converged to make the presidency a job of far greater prominence than it was in the days of Coolidge and before. While this is readily understood, there are other factors which contribute to runaway inflation in the attributed capabilities of White House leadership.

A first explanation for the textbook presidency is derived from the basic human tendency toward belief in great men. Most people grow up with the expectation that someone somewhere can and will cope with the major crises of the present and future. Since the New Deal, most Americans have grown accustomed to expect their president to serve this role. Who, if not the president, is going to prevent the communists from burying us, pollution from choking us, crime and conflict from destroying our cities, moral degradation from slipping into our neighborhood theaters? Within the complexity of political life today the president provides a visible national symbol to which we can attach our hopes. Something akin to presidential cults exists in the United States today just as hero-worship, gerontocracy reverence, and other forms of authority-fixation have flourished in most, if not all, larger societies. Portraits of Washington, Lincoln, the Roosevelts, and Kennedy paper many a classroom wall alongside of the American flag. While deification is presumably discouraged, something similar is a common side product during the early years of schooling.

On all but two occasions during the past 17 years, the president of this nation has won the Most Admired Man contest conducted annually by the Gallup polls. The exceptions in 1967 and 1968 saw President Johnson lose out to former President Eisenhower. Mentioning this pattern of popular response to a recent conversation partner, I was informed that "If they were not the most admired men in the country they wouldn't have been elected president!" And his response is, I believe, a widely respected point of view in America. On the one hand we are always looking for reassurance that things will work out satisfactorily. On the other hand we admire the dramatic actions of men in high places who are willing to take action, willing to cope with the exigencies of crisis and perplexity. Political scientist Murray Edelman writes quite lucidly about this problem:

> And what symbol can be more reassuring than the incumbent of a high position who knows what to do and is willing to act, especially when others are bewildered and alone? Because such a symbol is so intensely sought, it will predictably be found in the person of any incumbent whose actions *can* be interpreted as beneficent.

A second explanation of recent textbook orthodoxy is unmistakenly related to the commercial and political values of most text writers. Market considerations are hard to ignore and several text authors unabashedly cite commercial remuneration as a major incentive. The "selling of a textbook" may not be unrelated to a book's function and ideological orientation.

Most textbook authors are motivated by the goal of training "good" citizens just as much as by the goal of instructing people about the realities of the highly competitive and often cruel world of national party and policy politics. But the training of citizens often seems to require a glossy, harmonious picture of national politics, which inspires loyalty but conflicts with reality. When this occurs, as one text writer told me, "the author almost invariably emphasizes citizen training, usually at the expense of instruction."

Building the Great Cathedral

A Franklin Roosevelt halo-effect characterizes most of the recent treatments of the presidency. Writers during the 1950s and well into the '60s were children or young adults during the Depression years. Not infrequently, they became enlisted in one way or another in executive branch service to help fight or manage World War II. These times were unusual in many ways—including an extraordinary amount of attention paid to the way in which President Roosevelt employed the powers of the presidency. Moreover, in the arena of national and international leadership, FDR upstaged all comers as he magnified the personal role and heroic style of a confident, competent leader in the context of tumultuous times. The mantle of world leadership was passing to the U.S., beginning what some writers refer to as the American Era. Understandably these developments, especially the dramaturgy of the New Deal presidency, affected soon-to-be written interpretations as well as popular images of the presidency.

A final reason for the textbook presidency lies in the very nature of the American political and electoral system. We elect a president by a small margin, but after election he is supposed to speak for *all* the people. Textbook and school norms suggest that one can vigorously question a presidential candidate, but after the election it is one's duty to unite behind the winner. It is as though the new president were the pilot of an aircraft with all of us as passengers, whether we like it or not. Hence, we all have a stake in his success.

To be sure, this institution of ritualistic unification serves a need: it absorbs much of the discontinuity and tension promoted in our often hectic and combative electoral campaigns. Then there is the typical first-year grace period in which serious criticism is generally considered off limits. This presidential honeymoon is characterized by an elaborate press build-up in which it appears as though we are trying to transform and elevate the quite mortal candidate into a textbook president.

Other methodological factors also contribute to idealized versions of presidential leadership. Overreliance on case studies of presidential behavior in relatively unique crises is part of the problem. Textbook compartmentalization of problems and institutions is yet another. Both the student and the average citizen may quite reasonably get the impression that national policy is almost entirely the product of a president and a few of his intimates, or alternately of a few select national officials along with the president's consent. Only the presidents can slay the dragons of crisis. And only Lincoln, the Roosevelts, Wilson, or men of that caliber can seize the chalice of opportunity, create the vision, and rally the American public around that vision. The end result may leave the student quite confused, if not ignorant, about the complex transactions, interrelationships, and ambiguities that more correctly characterize most national policy developments.

In all probability we pay a price, however unwittingly, for the way we have over-idealized the presidency. Although this price is difficult to calculate, I shall suggest some of the probable consequences of the textbook presidency—beginning with the dangers of our unwarranted expectations of the president's power and of his capacities as a spiritual reservoir.

Most Americans now believe, along with Theodore and Franklin Roosevelt's celebrated assertions, that the presidency is a "bully pulpit" and preeminently a place for moral leadership. Few of our citizenry wince at James Reston's observation that "the White House is the pulpit of the nation and the president is its chaplain." British Prime Minister Harold Macmillan, on the other hand, could quip, "If people want a sense of purpose, they should get it from their archbishops."

We are accustomed to regarding our "sense of purpose" and pious presidential pronouncements as nearly one and the same. Accordingly, Richard Nixon invoked God five times in his presidential inaugural and talked often of spirit and the nation's destiny: "To a crisis of the spirit, we need an answer of the spirit. . . . We can build a great cathedral of the spirit. . . . We have endured a long night of the American spirit. But as our eyes catch the dimness of the first rays of dawn, let us not curse the remaining dark, let us gather the light. . . . Our destiny offers not the cup of despair, but the chalice of opportunity."

But the trappings of religiosity, while temporarily ennobling the presidential personage, may run the risk of triggering unanticipated and undesirable consequences. Some presidents apparently feel the need to justify a particular strategy on the grounds that it is the moral and righteous course of action. But this moral emphasis can become elevated to overblown courses of behavior. For example, Wilson's attempts to help set up the League of Nations became imbued with a highly moralistic fervor, but the moral environment that generated the commitment was allowed to expand, as Wilson's own role as the nation's preacher expanded, until there was virtually no room for a political negotiator, a non-moralist Wilson to transform the idea into a reality. Perhaps Herbert Hoover's apolitical moral and ideological commitment to rugged individualism similarly inhibited alternative approaches in response to the Depression. Similarly, President Johnson's drumming up of moral and patriotic support for our Vietnam commitment probably weakened his subsequent efforts at negotiations in the languishing days of his Administration.

Part of the problem is related to the way campaigns are conducted and to the intensive hard sell—or at least "oversell"—seemingly demanded of candidates. Necessarily adopting the language of promise and sloganism, candidates and their publicists frequently pledge that they will accomplish objectives that are either near impossible or unlikely. Recall the early declaratory intentions of the War on Poverty, Model Cities, the Alliance for Progress, the war on behalf of safe streets, and an ambitious Nixon promise to underwrite "black capitalism."

The Cost of Elevation

The textbook presidency image may also influence the quality of civic participation. The moral-leader-to-layman relationship is quite often viewed as a one-way street. If the president is our national chaplain, how do we cultivate a democratic citizenry that is active and not passive, that may, on selective occasions, responsibly dispute this national moral eminence? Having been nurtured in the belief that presidents are not only benevolent but also personally powerful enough to end war, depression, and corruption, it is difficult for most average citizens to disagree strongly with their president, no matter what the circumstances. Students are instructed that it is proper to state one's differences in a letter to congressmen or even to the White House. But beyond these rather limited resources, the citizen-student is left alone and without a sense of personal efficacy. Due to the almost assured deference and relative lack of opposition, American presidents can expect at least a five-to-one favorable ratio in national opinion poll responses about their handling of the presidency.

Most popular is the choice of quietly (if not silently) rallying around the president and offering him permissive support, hoping by such action to strengthen his and the nation's resolve against whatever real or apparent challenges confront the nation. Another pattern of behavior, that of apathy and indifference, is selected by sober citizens who feel secure in the belief that "presidents know best." Thus, a president can usually take it for granted that when major difficulties are faced, most Americans will support and trust him, at least for a while, often tendering him even increased support. It is difficult sometimes for Americans to differentiate between loyalty to president and loyalty to nation. As a result, presidential public support comes not only from those who feel the president is right, but is measurably inflated by those who, regardless of policy or situation, render support to their president merely because he is their president, or because he is the only president they have.

Few people are inclined to protest the actions of their president, but for those selecting to dissent, the textbook wisdom seems to encourage a direct personal confrontation with the president. If he alone is so powerful and independent, it appears logical to march on the White House and, if necessary, "break" or "dump" the president in order to change policy. But this may be one of the least economical strategies, for, as we have seen, breaking or changing presidents does not ensure any major shift in the execution of national policies.

The point here is that on both sides of the presidential popularity equation his importance is inflated beyond reasonable bounds. On one side, there is a nearly blind faith that the president embodies national virtue and that any detractor must be an effete snob or a nervous nellie. On the other side, the president becomes the cause of all personal maladies, the originator of poverty and racism, inventor of the establishment, and the party responsible for a choleric national disposition.

If the textbook presidency image has costs for the quality of citizen relationships with the presidency, so also it can affect the way presidents conceive of themselves and their job. To be sure, the reverence and loyalty rendered to a new president are a rich resource and no doubt are somewhat commensurate with tough responsibilities that come along with the job. But, at the same time, an overly indulgent citizenry can psychologically distort the personal perspective and sense of balance. Former presidential press secretary George Reedy's acrimonious criticisms of the monarchical trappings of the contemporary White House deserve attention:

> The atmosphere of the White House is calculated to instill in any man a sense of destiny. He literally walks in the footsteps of hallowed figures—Jefferson, of Jackson, of Lincoln. . . . From the moment he enters the halls he is made aware that he has become enshrined in a pantheon of semi-divine mortals who have shaken the world, and that he has taken from their hands the heritage of American dreams and aspirations.
> Unfortunately for him, divinity is a better basis for inspiration than it is for government.

The quality of advice, intelligence, and critical evaluation necessary to balanced presidential decision-making can also be adversely affected by too respectful an attitude toward the chief executive. If presidents become unduly protected or insulated, and if White House aides and Cabinet members tender appreciation and deference in exchange for status and accommodation, then the president's decision-making ability is clearly harmed.

The relatively sustained 15-year ascendancy of the textbook presidency's idealized image of presidential leadership may be coming to an end. The general American public probably still believes in a version of the New Deal presidency caricature, but the near monopoly of this view is under challenge from a growing list of critiques of liberal presidential government. We are currently witnessing an apparent recrudescence of an interpretation of the presidency, which holds that no one national political leader can galvanize our political system toward the easy accomplishment of sustained policy change or altruistic goals.

Toward Revision

Contemporary policy studies suggest that the more we learn about presidential policy performance, the more it appears that presidents (in both domestic and foreign policy) only rarely accomplish policy "outcomes" that can be credited as distinct personal achievements. More realistically, the presidency serves as a broker for a few party priorities and as a strategically situated and important participant among vast numbers of policy entrepreneurs and policy-bearing bureaucrats. More often than not a president's personal policy views are essentially moderate and only vaguely refined. When in office, however, he finds himself constantly surrounded by people who have "high-energy" interest and investments in specific policy options. Both the president and these elites, however, are in turn surrounded by what Scammon and Wattenberg call the real majority—the large majority of American voters in the center.

In a sample of recent in-depth interviews with 30 White House staffers who served Presidents Kennedy and Johnson, I found that a majority of these presidential advisers feel that the president exercises selective or relatively little power over policy matters. There are some who say that "he [the president] has a lot of influence on those problems he is willing to spend time on," but more responded that "he has far less than people think he has, he is far more constrained than popularly thought." In fact, many even express the somewhat restrained and almost anti-textbook presidency view that presidents can accomplish a limited number of projects and hence should carefully measure their requests and energies. Emphasizing this point were the following two respondents:

> I think the White House under Johnson was excessively activist—there was an impulsive need to do something about everything RIGHT NOW! There was always the feeling [given by the president] that we should fix this and fix that and do it now! Overall I think it went too far—there are definite costs and liabilities in that type of excessive aggressive activism....

And a second staffer:

> Except in times of emergencies, presidents cannot get much accomplished.... In some areas a president can have a psychological influence, a psychological effect on the nation, for example by speaking out on crime concerns. And in an eight-year period a

president can start a shift of the budget and of the political system, but it takes a lot of pressure and a lot of time. Basically, the thing to remember is that a presidential intention takes a very long time to get implemented.

On balance, of course, it is true that under certain circumstances a president can ignite the nuclear destruction of a substantial portion of the world or commit U.S. troops into internationally troubled crisis zones. But the American president is in no better position to control Bolivian instability, Chilean Marxism, or Vietcong penetration into Cambodia than he can make the stock market rise or medical costs decline. It is misleading to infer from a president's capacity to drop an A-bomb that he is similarly powerful in most other international or domestic policy areas. The more we learn about the processes of government, the more it becomes apparent that presidents are rarely free agents when it comes to effecting new policies—or dismantling policies which they have inherited.

4.2

Time For Healing

TIME

It was over. At last, after so many months of poisonous suspicion, a kind of undeclared civil war that finally engaged all three branches of the American Government, the ordeal had ended. As the *Spirit of '76* in one last errand arced across central Missouri carrying Richard Nixon to his retirement, Gerald Rudolph Ford stood in the East Room of the White House, placed his hand upon his eldest son's Bible, and repeated the presidential oath "to preserve, protect and defend the Constitution of the United States." By the time the 37th President of the U.S. arrived at the Pacific, the 38th President had taken command of a new Administration.

It was the first time in American history that a President had resigned his office. The precedent was melancholy, but it was hardly traumatic. All of the damage had been done before in the seemingly interminable spectacle of high officials marched through courtrooms, in the recitation of burglaries, crooked campaign contributions and bribes, enemies lists, powers abused, subpoenas ignored—above all, in the ugly but mesmerizing suspense as the investigations drew closer and closer to the Oval Office. Now the dominant emotion was one of sheer relief.

A few of Nixon's last supporters still summoned up bitterness. Not a few Americans cracked open bottles of champagne for the event. Mostly, the nation was massively grateful to have it ended. As Ford said at his swearing-in, "Our long national nightmare is over." By his leaving, Nixon seemed at last to redeem the 1968 pledge he took from a girl holding up a campaign sign in Ohio: BRING US TOGETHER. The resignation brought at least the unity of hope for a fresh beginning, and with Ford, the hope for a new style of presidential leadership. After the long, obsessional preoccupation with Watergate and its claustrophobic underground works, most Americans felt last week as if they were emerging for the first time in a long while into the upper air.

The denouement was jarring in its swift resolution and therefore a bit surreal. Nearly 800 days after the Watergate break-in, 289 days after the Saturday Night Massacre, 97 days after the White House transcripts were released, twelve days after

Reprinted by permission from *Time*, The Weekly Newsmagazine; Copyright Time, Inc.

the Supreme Court voted, 8 to 0, that the President must surrender 64 more tapes, five days after the House Judiciary Committee voted out articles of impeachment, Nixon's defenses finally vanished. On Monday he issued the June 23, 1972 transcript that amounted to a confession to obstruction of justice and to lying to the American people and his own defense counsel. With that his clock had run out.

His Healthy Practical Effects

His nationally televised resignation speech was a peculiar performance. In some ways, it sounded like a State of the Union address, a familiar recitation of his achievements in office. He admitted no guilt, only casually did he mention mistakes made "in the best interests of the nation." Yet in a way, he smoothed the process of transition by sounding, rather eerily, as if his resignation was, after all, a sort of parliamentary setback—no great dislocation. If some expected a bitter, angry valedictory, Nixon was controlled and ultimately conciliatory. Nixon once said that the test of a people is the way it handles the transition of power, and last week—in his resignation speech if not in his mawkish, self-pitying White House goodbye—he deserved credit at least for helping to bring off the transition with dignity in what must have been the most painful moment of his life.

Apart from its stimulating effect on American morale, Nixon's departure will have some healthy practical effects. Had he insisted upon a long Senate trial, lasting into the fall, the Republican Party might have faced disastrous results in the November elections—losses so great that they might temporarily have disabled the two-party system. As it is, Republicans have a new opportunity to fight their opponents on equal ground, out of the shadow of Watergate.

A President who is not preoccupied with his own survival will be able to deal with much-neglected items of national business. The problems, of course, are extremely grave, and will not yield simply to candor and good will. The most urgent is inflation. Although Ford will not be a hyperactive President with a governmental solution for every problem, he will at least provide direction for reforms long overdue. The nation's foreign policy, despite Henry Kissinger's guidance, has also suffered from the suspense over Nixon's fate: the leadership crisis substantially reduced the chances for major agreements during Nixon's trip to Russia and if continued much longer, might have caused dangerous instability in the major-power relationships. With Ford securely in office, the conduct of foreign policy should resume the high level of competence Nixon and Kissinger established several years ago.

A Triumph for the System

Nixon virtually ignored his Cabinet. Ford promises to restore its power and influence. Most important, the Administration should be able to develop once again a coherent legislative policy. The leftover Nixon legislative program is a shambles. There is no energy policy. Attempts at a foreign trade bill, welfare reform and land-use legislation have bogged down. In what promises to be a protracted honeymoon period, and the President undistracted by scandal, such programs can presumably be pushed forward again.

Nixon's resignation leaves a residue of unanswered questions, some of them with long-range historical reverberations. What of Nixon's legal future? Should he be prosecuted? What becomes of the White House tapes and documents that may contain the full story of Watergate? Should Nixon have stayed to allow the constitutional process to play itself out to a crushing bipartisan vote of conviction in the Senate? No doubt a kind of selective memory will set in among hard-core Nixon supporters, a feeling that the case was never clearly judged, that Nixon martyred himself for the good of the nation. But the case against Nixon was so clear that most of his supporters had deserted him before he quit; he was in effect *judged* by his own friends and allies in the Congress. It should be sufficiently obvious to history that Nixon was not driven from office but resigned because he was guilty of, at least, obstruction of justice, and his cause was hopeless. Some diehards, of course, will always believe that the offense was not really serious anyway—and other Presidents have behaved badly too.

Did Nixon's departure weaken the presidency? Will future Presidents have to operate with one wary eye on the polls and the opposition in Congress, not to mention the press, because the precedent now exists that a President can be overthrown? On the contrary: it was Nixon himself who foreshortened the constitutional process out of a realization that the case against him was overwhelming. By resigning, he conceded the inevitability of impeachment and conviction. Anyone who argues that Nixon was hounded unjustly from office has a quarrel not with Nixon's enemies but with the U.S. Constitution, for the Constitution would have done the work that Nixon chose to do himself.

The departure of Nixon was, above all, an extraordinary triumph of the American system. The nation is not wrong to permit itself some self-congratulation on that. Just after he had sworn in the new President, Chief Justice Warren Burger grabbed the hand of Senator Hugh Scott, the Government colleague nearest to him. "Hugh," said Burger, "it worked. Thank God, it worked." He meant the system.

There were, of course, useful accidents of fate and generous helpings of blind luck. A night watchman named Frank Wills came upon the Watergate burglars one night when they taped some door locks with an almost ostentatious incompetence. The system was fortunate that Judge John Sirica pursued the case. And above all that Richard Nixon was surreptitiously taping his own conversations, and that he somehow never thought, or considered it necessary, or perhaps just did not dare, to heave all the tapes into the White House incinerator after their existence became known. Had it not been for the tapes, Richard Nixon would quite possibly have remained in the White House until January 1977. (Still, much of his misconduct could have been inferred.) No presidency in the nation's history has ever been so well documented, and it is safe to predict that none will be again.

But it was, at last, Richard Nixon who destroyed his own presidency. In his farewell speech to his staff, he counseled his audience never to be petty and never to hate those who hate them, because such hatred can destroy. Yet his White House, as revealed in the transcripts, was saturated with pettiness and hatred, a siege mentality, Us against Them. It was an unhappy and self-defeating spirit in which to govern a democracy.

In a curious way, Gerald Ford comes to the presidency under a kind of grace precisely because he was not elected to the office. No one would propose such a succession as a model for a representative democracy, but it has its refreshing advantages just now. It is frightening to contemplate the prospect if Spiro Agnew or John Connally, Nixon's first choice to succeed Agnew, had been sworn in last week. But Ford promises a new and welcome style in the White House, an openness and candor harking back perhaps to Truman or to the more amiable qualities of Eisenhower. The office, surely, will be shorn of some of the pretentious Caesarism that has been growing for 40 years, of its imperial paraphernalia and edgy hauteur.

Nixon is gone—not a martyred figure as he may believe, but tragic at least in his fall from a great height. He is gone because, with all its luck in this case, the American system, the Congress and the Judiciary, with the eventual overwhelming support of public opinion, slowly and carefully excised him from the body politic. If there is a certain "the-king-is-dead-long-live-the-king" spirit in the American mood, the nation feels also that it deserves something better in its leadership, and is going to get it.

The Decline and Fall

TIME

The inadequate term Watergate has come to encompass all the wrongdoing of which Richard Nixon and other members of his Administration stand accused—and in many cases convicted—including the politicization of federal agencies, misuse of federal funds for private purposes, attempted bribery by milk producers, misprision of felony, subornation of perjury, obstruction of justice. This catalogue of crimes and misdeeds did not begin with the break-in at the Democratic National Committee headquarters, but were it not for that bungled burglary and the subsequent cover-up, most or all of the offenses might have gone unnoticed and unpunished. Why the President allowed himself to become entrapped in the web of events that followed the crime is a puzzle. Indeed, there is a great deal about Watergate that will only be sorted out after much time has passed. But much is already known. Here is a recapitulation of the critical events that destroyed Nixon's presidency.

I The Break-In

Planning for the Watergate operation begins in January 1972. In his office, Attorney General John Mitchell, along with Presidential Counsel John Dean and Acting Director of the Committee for the Re-Election of the President (C.R.P.) Jeb Stuart Magruder, listens as G. Gordon Liddy, general counsel to C.R.P., spells out a $1 million intelligence plan: electronic surveillance, abduction of radical leaders, muggings, the use of call girls to obtain information from leading Democrats. According to Magruder, Mitchell tells Liddy to come up with something more "realistic." On March 30, Mitchell, now director of C.R.P., meets with Magruder to

Reprinted by permission from *Time*, The Weekly Newsmagazine; Copyright Time, Inc.

discuss a $250,000 proposal. Magruder later says that Mitchell approved the plan; Fred LaRue, a special assistant to Mitchell who was present at the meeting, says it was tabled for future discussion; Mitchell denies ever giving his approval. Two crucial questions remain: Who gave final O.K. for the burglary? What were they seeking that would justify so bizarre a crime?

An intelligence-gathering operation is set into motion. Checks worth $89,000, illegal corporate contributions, are laundered through a Mexican bank and transmitted to Bernard Barker, who deposits them in his Miami bank. He also deposits a $25,000 check given to C.R.P. by Kenneth Dahlberg, Republican finance chairman in the Midwest. This money will help uncover the C.R.P. involvement in Watergate.

Liddy takes charge of the operation, aided by former CIA Agent E. Howard Hunt and C.R.P. Security Coordinator James McCord. Several Cuban refugees are recruited: Barker, Eugenio Martinez, Virgilio Gonzalez and Frank Sturgis. The stage is set.

After two botched attempts, the burglars on May 27 get into the D.N.C. offices. McCord places wiretaps on the phones of Democratic National Chairman Lawrence O'Brien and Executive Director of Democratic State Chairmen R. Spencer Oliver Jr. Soon transcripts of Oliver's conversations are being passed to Magruder and through him to Mitchell. As Magruder later testifies, Mitchell orders Liddy to get better information.

Another break-in is arranged for June 17. But shortly after 1 a.m., Private Security Guard Frank Wills spots a door in the Watergate with its lock taped open. He summons the police, who catch McCord, Barker, Sturgis, Gonzalez and Martinez in the D.N.C. The police confiscate surveillance equipment and find 32 sequentially numbered $100 bills, which Barker has withdrawn from the $89,000 in Miami.

II The Cover-Up Begins

Two days after the arrest, White House Press Secretary Ronald Ziegler dismisses the affair as "a third-rate burglary attempt," adding that "certain elements may try to stretch this beyond what it is." But others are less blasé. Within hours of the break-in, FBI agents find Hunt's name in the address books of Barker and Martinez. Administration officials are also worried because Hunt and Liddy were involved in another secret operation, the White House plumbers, set up in mid-1971 to stop security leaks and investigate other sensitive security matters.

The cover-up begins. On June 20, Dean cleans out Hunt's safe, discovering files on the Pentagon papers case and a forged diplomatic cable that implicates the Kennedy Administration in the assassination in 1963 of South Vietnamese President Ngo Dinh Diem. Dean later testifies that Nixon's chief domestic adviser John Ehrlichman subsequently tells him to "deep six" a briefcase full of surveillance equipment and other evidence.

On June 23, Nixon orders Haldeman to have the CIA block the FBI's investigation into the source of Watergate funding. That day Haldeman and Ehrlichman meet with CIA Director Richard Helms and Deputy Director Vernon Walters. Helms says that no CIA operations will be endangered by the FBI probe. Haldeman insists that it is the

"President's wish" that Walters ask the FBI not to pursue the investigation into Mexico. A tape transcript of a conversation with Haldeman (released last week in the move that finally forces Nixon's resignation) shows that Nixon hopes to hide White House and C.R.P. involvement in the break-in by getting the CIA to limit the FBI's activities. Nixon's personal attorney Herbert Kalmbach gets $75,000 from Maurice Stans, chairman of the Finance Committee to Re-Elect the President—the first of more than $400,000 distributed to the Watergate defendants and their lawyers.

The cover-up holds through the summer. On Aug. 29, Nixon tells a news conference that Dean has conducted a thorough investigation and "I can say categorically that . . . no one in the White House staff, no one in this Administration, presently employed, was involved in this very bizarre incident." Dean never made such an investigation, according to his testimony months later. On Sept. 15, in a recorded Oval Office conversation, Nixon congratulates Dean: "The way you, you've handled it, it seems to me, has been very skillful, because you—putting your fingers in the dikes every time that leaks have sprung here and sprung there."

On Nov. 7, Nixon and Vice President Spiro Agnew are re-elected by a landslide. Watergate is all but forgotten. Early the next year, as the Watergate trial of the five burglars plus Liddy and Hunt gets under way with Judge John J. Sirica presiding, there is no hint that anybody else will be implicated. On Jan. 11, Hunt pleads guilty to all counts against him, and four days later the four Cuban Americans follow suit. Despite pressure from Sirica to get the burglars to tell the whole story, Hunt tells reporters that no "higher-ups" are involved.

III Cracks in the Stonewall

Still, there have already been some damaging disclosures. The Washington *Post*, relying partly on a still secret source known to outsiders as "Deep Throat," reports that Dahlberg's $25,000 check found its way into Barker's bank account, and that Watergate was part of a massive program of political sabotage. TIME discloses that Donald Segretti had been hired by White House Aides Dwight Chapin and Gordon Strachan and paid out of C.R.P. funds by Kalmbach to sabotage the Democratic presidential campaign.

Sirica, meanwhile, continues to push aggressively for the truth. On Feb. 2 he says he is "not satisfied" that the trial disclosed the full story. On Feb. 7, the Senate votes 77-0 to establish a select committee to investigate Watergate. Sam Ervin is named its chairman the next day.

Within a few weeks, the engineers of the cover-up begin to lose control. On Feb. 28, the Senate Judiciary Committee begins hearings on L. Patrick Gray's confirmation as FBI director. Gray discloses that he gave Dean FBI reports on the Watergate and that Chapin and Kalmbach have been involved in Republican espionage activities. These revelations precipitate a frantic scramble in the White House.

March 13: Nixon learns that Gordon Strachan has reportedly lied to federal investigators. The President explicitly rejects "the hang-out road," the White House term for full disclosure. March 17: Nixon later tells Ziegler that on this day, he has ordered Dean "to cut off any disclosures that might implicate him in Watergate."

Worried that Magruder could implicate Haldeman in the affair, Nixon says: "We've got to cut that back. That ought to be cut out." March 21: Talking about Hunt's demands for money, the President says: "For Christ's sake, get it!"

At this point, Sirica's efforts pay off. On March 23 he reads the court a letter from McCord charging that perjury has been committed in the Watergate trial and that defendants have been pressured to remain silent. Pouring on the pressure, Sirica gives Hunt and the Cubans harsh provisional sentences of up to 40 years in an effort to make them talk.

IV The Gathering Storm

Maintaining a "stonewall" policy on Nixon's instructions, Ehrlichman on March 28 informs Attorney General Richard Kleindienst that nobody in the White House had prior knowledge of the burglary. Two days later he has Ziegler tell the press that "no one in the White House had any involvement or prior knowledge of the Watergate event."

But on April 13, Magruder tells U.S. attorneys that he perjured himself during the burglars' trial. He implicates Dean and Mitchell in Watergate crimes. On April 15, according to his testimony, Dean tells Nixon that he has been cooperating with the U.S. attorneys.

On April 15, prosecutors tell Nixon that Haldeman, Ehrlichman, Dean and other White House officials are implicated in the cover-up. Faced with the evidence against his top aides, knowing that Dean and Magruder are talking and concerned that the upcoming Senate hearings will cast even more suspicion on the White House, Nixon makes the first of a series of strategic retreats.

April 30: He announces the resignations of Haldeman and Ehrlichman, calling them "two of the finest public servants it has been my privilege to know," and of Dean and Kleindienst. Nixon grants the new Attorney General the authority to appoint a special prosecutor.

May 18: Attorney General-Designate Elliot Richardson names Archibald Cox to the promised new position. In the days following, McCord tells his story to the nationally televised Senate Watergate committee hearings, which open May 17. Faced with a flood of revelations, Nixon issues a statement admitting that there was a cover-up within the White House, though he denies participating in it. Nixon says that after the break-in he had restricted certain aspects of the investigation on the grounds of "national security."

Nixon's speech is designed to end suspicions of his own involvement, but the televised Senate hearings provide a flood of incriminating new revelations. From June 25 to 29, Dean tells the committee that Nixon knew about aspects of the cover-up as early as Sept. 15, 1972. Equally embarrassing: Dean discloses White House efforts to hound political "enemies."

The White House retaliates on June 27 by calling Dean the "mastermind" of the cover-up and Mitchell his "patron." But the President's position is weakened by the release the same day of the "enemies lists" by the Senate committee.

152   *The Presidency: The Burden and the Glory*

V The Telltale Tapes

A far more devastating blow comes on July 16. Former White House Aide Alexander Butterfield tells the Watergate committee that Nixon secretly taped his own conversations.

Why Nixon allowed his participation in the cover-up to be recorded is one of the affair's greatest mysteries. Cox and Ervin request that Nixon turn over key tapes. On July 23, he rejects the requests on the ground of Executive privilege. Ervin and Cox issue subpoenas.

On Aug. 15, the President maintains: "Not only was I unaware of any cover-up. I was unaware there was anything to cover up." Earlier, Ehrlichman and Haldeman tell the Senate committee that Dean was responsible for the cover-up, and that they and the President are innocent. Aug. 22: Nixon terms Watergate "water under the bridge." But on Aug. 29, Sirica orders that he turn over tapes of the nine conversations subpoenaed by Cox.

Meanwhile other developments further tarnish the image of the White House.

"... And Liddy spake unto Magruder, and Magruder telleth Mitchell, and Mitchell saith unto Dean, and Dean informeth Ehrlichman, and Ehrlichman conveyeth it unto Haldeman, and Haldeman ..."

Reproduced by permission from the Chicago Sun-Times. Cartoon by Jack Burck, Chicago Sun-Times, June 27, 1973, p. 43

In early September, a Los Angeles grand jury indicts Ehrlichman, Liddy and Plumbers Co-Directors Egil Krogh and David Young in connection with the break-in at the office of the psychiatrist of Daniel Ellsberg, the man who claimed to have given the Pentagon papers to the press. Oct. 12: Nixon nominates Gerald Ford as the new Vice President. On the same day, the U.S. court of appeals rules that Nixon must turn the subpoenaed tapes over to Judge Sirica. A week later the President publicly offers a compromise: he will issue summaries of the tapes that will be checked by Senator John Stennis for accuracy. Cox rejects this. Cox is already probing other embarrassing situations, including the mysterious disposition of a $100,000 contribution from Howard Hughes to Nixon Pal Charles ("Bebe") Rebozo. The following evening, in the "Saturday Night Massacre," Nixon fires Cox; Richardson and his deputy, William Ruckelshaus, resign. There follows what White House Chief of Staff Alexander Haig calls "a fire storm" of protest, leading to calls from TIME (in its first editorial in 50 years), the New York Times, the Detroit News and National Review for the President's resignation.

Angered by Cox's dismissal, Democratic House leaders agree to have the Judiciary Committee begin an investigation into impeaching the President. On Oct. 23, Nixon agrees to hand over the subpoenaed tapes. Three days later he promises that there will be a new special prosecutor with "total cooperation from the Executive Branch."

Texas Lawyer Leon Jaworski is appointed to the post on Nov. 1, in the midst of new disclosures. The day before, Presidential Lawyer J. Fred Buzhardt revealed that two of the subpoenaed conversations did not exist on tape. Three weeks later, the White House discloses that there is an 18½-minute buzz obliterating a crucial taped discussion between Haldeman and the President on June 20, 1972; Jan. 15: electronics experts report that the gap was the result of at least five separate erasures.

March 1: the Watergate grand jury indicts seven former Nixon aides or re-election officials—Mitchell, Haldeman, Ehrlichman, Strachan, former Special Counsel to the President Charles Colson, former Political Coordinator for Nixon's Re-Election Committee Robert C. Mardian, Washington Attorney Kenneth W. Parkinson —for conspiring to obstruct justice. In a secret report to Sirica, Nixon is named an unindicted co-conspirator in the case. Jaworski on April 18 subpoenas 64 more taped conversations for use in the Watergate prosecution. April 11: the Judiciary Committee subpoenas 42 conversations.

On April 30, one year after the departure of his top aides and his announcement that he would appoint a special Watergate prosecutor, the President says he is making public edited transcripts of certain subpoenaed conversations. Republican Senator Hugh Scott declares that they reveal "deplorable, disgusting, shabby and immoral performances." Worse for the President, the 1,254 pages of conversation seem to corroborate some of Dean's allegations: that Nixon was aware of aspects of the coverup before March 21; that he seems to have wanted to pay hush money to Hunt.

VI The Final Debacle

On May 9, the Judiciary Committee begins its inquiry into Nixon's conduct in office. Over the next two months, 19 volumes of evidence are accumulated. During that time, several top Nixon aides either plead guilty or are convicted of crimes: Kleindienst on May 16, Colson June 3, Ehrlichman July 12.

July 24: the Supreme Court rules 8-0 that Nixon must turn over the tapes subpoenaed by Jaworski, rejecting Nixon's claim of.absolute Executive privilege. On the 27th, the Judiciary Committee votes 27-11 to recommend the impeachment of Nixon for obstruction of justice. Two more articles are passed in the next three days.

On Aug. 5, in the most sensational revelation of the entire two years of Watergate, Nixon admits that by June 23, 1972, six days after the break-in, he did indeed know of the involvement of C.R.P. and White House officials and tried to cover it up. The apparent reason for his admission: pressure from Presidential Counsel James St. Clair, who is stunned by the contents of the July 23 tape and strongly suggests that he will resign unless the President makes his statement. Whether Nixon had prior knowledge of the break-in or the intelligence-gathering plan is still unanswered, but the Aug. 5 revelation gives the lie to all his past assertions that he was not involved in the cover-up. In the wake of Nixon's disclosures, all the Republicans on the Judiciary Committee who voted against impeachment say they will change their votes when the issue comes before the full House. Republican Senators say that Nixon has almost no chance of acquittal.

Faced with impeachment and conviction, Nixon goes before a nationwide TV audience and announces that he is resigning.

Study Questions

1. Survey members of your class, friends, or neighbors for the purpose of assessing their concept of a "good" President. In so doing, develop a simple questionnaire which effectively identifies the criteria for an effective presidency. How does President Nixon compare with Lyndon Johnson and John F. Kennedy? How do these Presidents compare to the discussions by the various authors contained in the readings?

2. "The President is at liberty both in law and conscience to be as big a man as he can." What does this mean? Do you agree with the statement? How do you think various groups of American people would respond to this statement?

3. Identify and analyze the various arguments presented on different "models" of the presidency. In light of the problems of the 1970s do you believe that all Presidents must be a Lincoln model? How would a Buchanan or Eisenhower model fare? What other models of the presidency might be valid?

4. In what ways is the study of the presidency a complex and difficult undertaking? Are there simpler, yet useful ways of studying the presidency?

5. Assume that you are a member of a top level policy group in the Democratic party. You are preparing for the presidential campaign two to four years from now. What kind of man would you desire to run for President? Are there any Democrats who now fill the bill? Why do you believe your criteria would bring success to the party and the man? Discuss the same questions

as a member of the top policy group in the Republican party. Would the search focus on the same kind of individual?

6. It has been said that the President is a monarch who surrounds himself with "yes-men" since his main concern is loyal subordinates who are committed to him and who will carry out his policy unquestioningly. What are the advantages and disadvantages of this type of presidency? Are there any modern examples? Can a President operate efficiently if he has a number of subordinates who oppose him and question his policies?

7. In what ways did the Watergate issue affect the presidential office? Relate this to the concept of power in the American political system.

8. It has been suggested that a President must often engage in deception and misrepresentation in order to meet the many demands of his office. Do you agree with this argument? Explain your reasons.

9. What evidence would you marshal to support the contention that the presidency has grown more powerful through the course of history? Do you think this has been good or bad for the country?

10. State the various limitations on the power of the President. Which ones do you regard as being the most important constraints? Why is the office a burden and a glory?

Bibliography

Books

Barber, James David. *The Presidential Character*. Englewood Cliffs, New Jersey: Prentice-Hall, 1972.

Cochran, Bert. *Harry Truman and the Crisis Presidency*. New York: Funk and Wagnalls, 1973.

Corwin, Edward S. *The President: Office and Powers*. 4th ed. New York: New York University Press, 1968.

Hirschfield, Robert S., ed. *The Power of the Presidency*. New York: Atherton Press, 1968.

Hughes, Emmet John. *The Living Presidency*. Baltimore, Maryland: Penguin Books, 1974.

Johnson, Lyndon B. *The Vantage Point*. New York: Holt, Rinehart and Winston, 1971.

Koenig, Louis W. *The Chief Executive*. New York: Harcourt, Brace Jovanovich, 1968. Revised edition.

Lash, Joseph P. *Eleanor and Franklin*. New York: Signet Books, 1971.

McGinniss, Joe. *The Selling of the President, 1968*. New York: Trident, 1969.

Neustadt, Richard E. *Presidential Power: The Politics of Leadership*. New York: John Wiley, 1960.

Polsby, Nelson, ed. *The Modern Presidency*. New York: Random House, 1973.

Rossiter, Clinton. *The American Presidency*. New York: Mentor Books, 1960. Revised edition.

Reedy, George E. *The Twilight of the Presidency.* New York: World Publishing Company, 1970.
Schlesinger, Arthur, Jr. *The Imperial Presidency.* Boston: Houghton Mifflin, 1973.
Sorenson, Theodore. *Kennedy.* New York: Harper and Row, 1965.
Truman, Margaret. *Harry S. Truman.* New York: William Morrow, 1973.

Articles

Barber, James David. "Passive-Positive to Active-Negative: The Style and Character of Presidents." Charles Peters and John Rothchild, eds. *Inside the System.* New York: Praeger, 1973.
Burns, James MacGregor. "Seat of Glory, Cockpit of Raw Conflict." Life, July 5, 1968.
Cronin, Thomas E. "Our Textbook President." *Washington Monthly,* Vol. 2 (October, 1970).
Commager, Henry Steele. "The Misuse of Power: The Disease is the Psychology of the Cold War." *The New Republic,* April 17, 1971.
Wildavsky, Aaron. "The Two Presidencies." *Transaction,* December, 1966.

CHAPTER 5
The Presidency in Domestic Politics

Presidential power is centralized in one office and in one man. Nevertheless, there are some fundamental differences between the President's power in domestic and foreign affairs. According to one observer, the President is a helpless giant when it comes to domestic affairs. As a matter of fact,

> When a president turns from foreign affairs to domestic affairs he slips down the rabbit hole and through the door at the bottom leading to his own daffy wonderland of Cheshire advisors and twiddle-de-dum-twiddle-de-dee cabinet members. It is a setting in which a president can stand up and grandly proclaim, "I shall not ask simply for more new programs in the old framework, but to change the framework itself," into a new American revolution—a peaceful revolution in which power was turned back to the people and then when he has finished speaking and looks around at the impact of the speech he sees nothing changed: only bureaucratic dormice still sleeping in their teacups and mad Congressmen still moving from chair to chair. Logic has no impact here nor persuasion nor craftiness.[1]

The President, it would seem, has his power limited at every turn in domestic affairs while on the foreign scene he seems to have the widest discretion, with minimum interference from the other branches of government. This is not to suggest, however, that presidential power is lacking in the domestic sphere. Perhaps we ought to view the presidential power as if it were on a continuum, with power in domestic affairs at one end and power in foreign affairs at the other.

At the domestic affairs end of the continuum we would see a variety of countervailing powers which tend to counterbalance and constrain presidential power with varying degrees of intensity. At the foreign affairs end, however, there are few such powers except for those which are brought to bear by foreign nations. In between these two extremes are a variety of power equations, with presidential power increasing as one moves towards the foreign affairs end, and diminishing as one moves towards the domestic affairs end of the continuum. Both the legislative and judicial branches of government have historically held this view of presidential power. For example, in the Watergate hearings of 1973 a number of legislators observed that a president had no right to get involved in wiretapping and political espionage in domestic affairs, but foreign affairs were another matter. As the continuum shows, however, there is an inseparable link between domestic and foreign affairs. At the very least, there must be a strong domestic base for the success of any foreign policy.

**Presidential Power
in Domestic and Foreign Spheres**

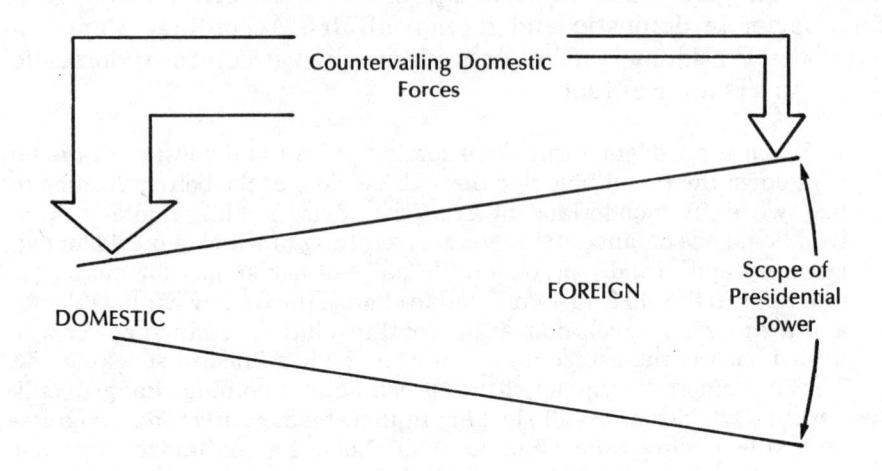

Vietnam and the Presidency

The war in Vietnam dramatically illustrated the dual nature of the presidency in regard to domestic and foreign affairs. In domestic policy, the President must enlist the support of Congress and other political actors who exercise important power; in foreign policy, he exercises much greater power, but at least must convince a majority of Americans of the viability of his program. While political actors do exist who can exercise countervailing power with respect to foreign policy, they are much less united and have less power than those found in domestic matters. As we shall see, the President is able to implement many foreign policy programs without congressional or popular support.

During the Vietnam War, President Eisenhower and later Kennedy, Johnson, and Nixon spoke of the "American commitment" and the importance of "national security." The United States was originally drawn into it because of the withdrawal of the French from Indochina. The initial involvement, begun under President Eisenhower in 1954, expanded, inevitably (as some would suggest), into involvement of over 500,000 American troops by 1968.

The rationale for our involvement was based on the concept of national security, but more specifically on the U. S. view that the war was an example of armed aggression by one country against another. Under the Southeast Asian Treaty Organization (SEATO) commitment, the United States was thought to be obligated to come to the defense of South Vietnam. Another consideration was the belief that the "invasion" of South Vietnam by the North Vietnamese was part of a worldwide Communist conspiracy to take over the world.

Although initially the rationale was not seriously questioned by many, this changed after 1965, when large numbers of American troops entered combat in South Vietnam. By 1967, the American people were seriously challenging the administration's prosecution of the war. The seriousness of the criticism and the level of opposition rose with each increase in the number of American troops operating in South Vietnam and each increase in casualties.

The involvement of the United States in the Vietnam War was virtually an act of the President and his advisors and the subsequent decisions regarding the prosecution of the war also rested with the executive office. Such decisions included the commitment of 500,000 men to South Vietnam, the bombing of North Vietnam, the invasion of Cambodia, the mining and blockading of North Vietnamese harbors, the use of new weapons and technology, and finally, the withdrawal of American troops and Vietnamization of the war. In spite of increased opposition to the war and critical outbursts by congressmen, lawyers, doctors, priests, individual Americans, and military men, Congress continued to appropriate the necessary funds to continue the war and the Supreme Court sidestepped the issue of the war's constitutionality.

Although the Vietnam War was viewed with increasing alarm by many Americans after 1965, people continued to support the administration. They did so partly because of the President's tremendous authority and out of respect for his office, but more specifically because they thought that each new presidential decision would finally end the war. Indeed, after each dramatic move by the President, his popularity rose.

Public Approval of Vietnam Actions

Action	Favoring Proposed Action	Favoring Action Already Taken
Invade Cambodia	28%	50%
Bombing Halt	40	64
Rate of Troop Withdrawal	30*	56+

*Favored withdrawal at the then current rate
+Favored rate after President's speech on November 2, 1969
Source: After Mark V. Nadel, "Public Policy and Public Opinion," in Robert Weissberg and Mark V. Nadel (eds.), *American Democracy: Theory and Reality* (New York: Wiley, 1972), p. 539.

Nevertheless, in the end, the high level of opposition to the war, demonstrations in the streets, campus rioting, and political party disaffection, forced President Johnson to decline to run for the office in 1968.

President Richard Nixon came to office in 1969 on a program of "Peace in Vietnam," knowing that the people were disenchanted with the war and President Johnson's prosecution of it. Lengthy negotiations resulted in an agreement for gradual withdrawal of virtually all American troops from Vietnam, and by the opening days of Nixon's second term a peace pact was signed. Originally identified as a strong opponent of communism, President Nixon did a complete turnabout in his foreign policy, eventually leading to a policy of detente.

The lesson to be learned from this is that, although the President has a great deal of power in foreign affairs, the articulation of domestic criticism and the rise of organized groups to challenge his policy can prove to be a formidable countervailing power. We should also note how the President can engage in dramatic policy initiatives with the support of a majority of the American people because of his ability to mobilize their opinions.

In the past few years the role of presidential power in foreign affairs has increasingly been under attack. This has led to demands of greater participation in foreign policy by Congress as well as the people. Such demands for democratization of the foreign policy process, stemming from the Vietnam experience as well as from the disclosures of the Watergate affair, are likely to reduce the President's latitude in foreign and defense policies. An even more critical eye will probably be cast on his domestic power as well. Not only will Congress exert more pressure and create a more effective opposing force, but the people are likely to be more politically sensitive and suspicious of foreign and defense decision-making processes as well as domestic policies.

As suggested earlier, although the individual has little impact on the total political system, the emerging sentiment and attitudes of individuals provide a broad, basic concept of the rules of the game. The moral and ethical content of presidential policies and behavior are likely to take on a more meaningful dimension in both domestic and foreign affairs. Particularly in his domestic role, the President is likely to be the object of much more vigorous scrutiny as to expected political behavior.

The Presidential Mandate

There are three basic ingredients which provide the initial grant of power to any President. The first is based on the realities of winning the presidential office. Regardless of the number of votes received or, to put it another way, regardless of the number of people who did not vote for him, he still remains President of all the people. Hence, his power stems partly from the fact that his constituency is all of the people in the country. Secondly, he receives a legal grant of power from Article II, Section 1 of the Constitution, which states: "The Executive power shall be vested in a President of the United States of America." Thirdly, with the grant of power from the people and the legal base of power, there arises a vast range of powers that are accorded the presidential office by virtue of tradition, the expectations of people, and the informal grants of power.

In domestic politics, however, the President is faced with the problem of developing a consensus for his political style and policies, not only from his election constituency (the national constituency) but from Congress, the bureaucracy, his own staff, and an array of special interest groups.

In these circumstances, the first indicator of the extent of presidential power is the election results. A President who receives a large majority of the votes may be considered to have a "mandate" to carry out his legislative program. For example, in the elections of 1964, President Johnson received over 61 per cent of the popular vote as compared to 38 per cent for Barry Goldwater. Many legislators felt that Lyndon Johnson, therefore, had a clear mandate to carry out his civil rights legislative program. Similarly, in 1972, the incumbent, Richard Nixon, received 61 per cent of the vote as compared to Senator McGovern's 38 per cent; many legislators felt that President Nixon, therefore, had a clear mandate to carry out his Vietnamization policy and pursue law and order policies at home. It is presumed that such clear majorities provide the President much more freedom of action and greater influence with Congress when it comes to passing legislative programs. As some are quick to point out, however, this clear majority can quickly disappear if the President does not show reasonable progress in solving the problems of the country.

Very few problems in foreign affairs other than wars can arouse public sensitivity as much as problems of employment, law and order, and inflation do. At the height of the Senate Watergate hearings in the summer of 1973, Leonid Brezhnev, First Secretary of the Communist party of the Soviet Union, met with President Nixon in a historic summit meeting. The importance of the meeting was quickly overshadowed by the Watergate hearings. Moreover, during both the hearings and the summit meeting, polls indicated that the primary concern of the majority of people was with the high cost of living and inflation.

Who Affects the President

Political actors are sensitive to the public's perception of presidential competence and style of politics. Presidential constituencies are also influenced by the public's image of the presidential style. Earlier, we suggested that constituencies refer to those political actors who are very likely to be of special importance to the maintenance, expansion, or diminution of power of the power holder in question. We do not include the public as a whole here because it can be moved only in times of great crisis. Here we use the term constituencies to refer to those who are politically aware of the impact of power holders on constituency interests. For example, those exercising power in the area of veterans' affairs have an existing constituency of the American Legion, Veterans of Foreign Wars, and Retired Servicemen's Associations. The public at large can become a constituency with respect to veterans' affairs when and if the issue takes on major

Who Affects the President 163

national importance, and is perceived as such by the public. The diagram gives a clearer picture of the relationships among the public, constituencies, political actors, and the President.

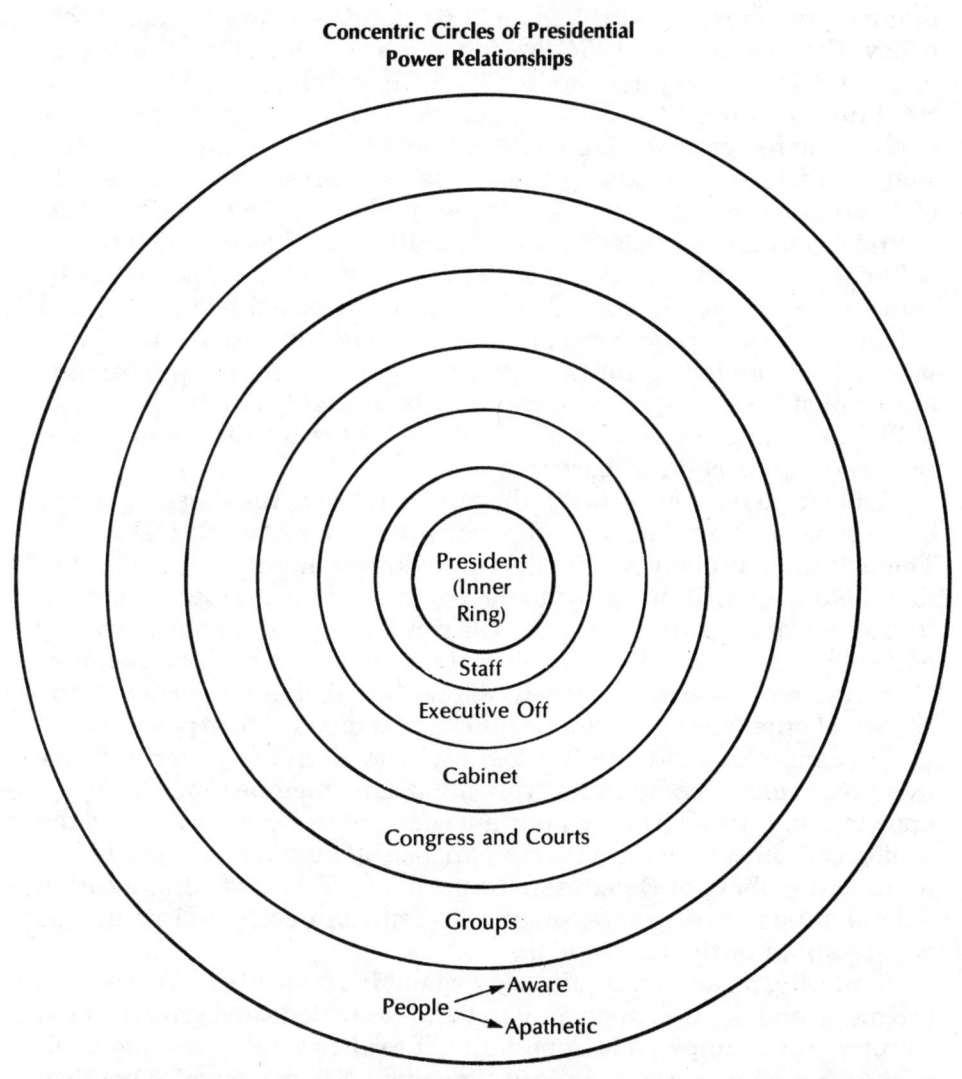

Concentric Circles of Presidential Power Relationships

- President (Inner Ring)
- Staff
- Executive Off
- Cabinet
- Congress and Courts
- Groups
- People → Aware / Apathetic

In reality, the relationships pictured here are not as clear nor consistently circular. Indeed, most of the relationships are much more complex and intertwined. Individuals or groups in any of the circles may be privileged to be within the inner ring of the Presidency, depending on their personality or characteristics and of course the desires of the President himself.

Generally, as one moves closer to the President, the political awareness and political participation increase. Indeed, when one moves into the circle of political actors, numerous powers can be set in motion. It is conceivable that issues of national crisis will motivate all the circles to become politically involved, either increasing or diminishing presidential power. In addition, the President has the ability to manipulate interest groups and mobilize political actors to support his policy. For example, in 1964 President Johnson was instrumental in procuring from Congress the Tonkin Gulf Resolution, which authorized him to "take all necessary measures to repel any armed attack against the forces of the United States and to prevent further aggression." This resolution passed the House of Representatives by a vote of 466-0 and the Senate by 88-2. Initially, this provided the President with the consensus needed to develop unity and cohesion among other political actors with respect to his Vietnam policy. Press releases, statements by officials, control of the instruments of foreign policy and defense, and the recognition of the President as the center of the policy process, all tended to unite many political actors and subdue any criticism of Vietnam policy. It was only later that President Johnson's ability to maintain the momentum of his Vietnam policy diminished, thus ending his political career.

Aside from his concern with the public at large, the President must be responsive to a number of other constituencies and political actors. The astute incumbent will deliberately keep channels open to all of them. Not only will this provide the communications system required to use power effectively, but it will reinforce presidential power by association and contact with political actors and important members of the system. In essence, it will allow the President to draw on the powers of other political actors, while broadening his own power base.

For example, an astute President will do all in his power to maintain close and friendly links with important members of Congress, knowing that his legislative programs depend to a great extent on the senior committee chairmen. He can use a number of techniques: inviting members of Congress to a presidential breakfast, allocating federal funds to a congressman's favorite project, or praising the congressman in the mass media.

Similarly, he can maintain and expand his power base by creating programs and policies appealing to various sections and groups in the country. For example, it is important not to alienate the working man, or the farmers as a group. Indeed, President Nixon's favorite political base was the "silent majority." An astute President, of course, makes every attempt to appeal to all important segments of society, without alienating any.

By the same token, important congressmen, bureaucrats, and leaders of special interest groups seek presidential approval not only for reinforcement of their own positions, but also to gain some influence on the presidential office. It is here that vast amounts of money can be allocated to various sections of the country. It is here that the power of the federal government resides, and it is the President who symbolizes the American nation. What better way can other political actors find to show their importance and gain prestige, than in their association with the center of national power?

The power acquired by the President through the constituencies must be nurtured. How well this is accomplished depends on the competence of the President to build his image, on the style of his leadership, and on his relationships with other political actors—in other words, how well he can succeed in enhancing his power. By actively seeking and maintaining links with important segments of society and other political actors, the President can expand his own power. But all of this is dependent on how he fills the office of the President.

In a perceptive assessment of the United States involvement in Vietnam, David Halberstam, a Pulitzer prize winning journalist, provides some insight into the meaning of constituency. In the following excerpt, he describes the strained relationships that existed between Adlai Stevenson and John Kennedy during the 1960 campaign, the staffing of the Kennedy cabinet, and the struggle for supporters.

> . . . Kennedy wanted to be his own Secretary of State, and above all, he did not want a Secretary who already had a constituency worthy of a President, rather he wanted Stevenson's constituency, both here and abroad. Kennedy knew that he could not really perform as a President until he had taken Stevenson's people away from him. This he proceeded to do with stunning quickness, depending more on style and grace than policies; nonetheless, when Stevenson died in 1965, a year and a half after Kennedy, he seemed a forlorn and forgotten figure, humiliated by his final years; his people mourned the loss of Kennedy more than of Stevenson. It would only be later, as the full tragedy of the Vietnam war unfolded and a Stevenson disciple named Eugene McCarthy challenged Johnson, as humanist values seemed to be resurgent and regenerative against the rationalist values, and the liberal community looked back to see where it had gone wrong, that Stevenson would regain his constituency. Posthumously.[2]

The nurturing of the power of the President can also be reinforced by the kind of programs and policies he introduces. These considerations are circular in impact. The relative effectiveness of such programs and policies will not only nurture his power among the constituencies, but in turn will create a more receptive environment for additional programs and policies. In this instance, the observation that "power begets power," is appropriate.

However, any specific programs and policies may well create dissatisfaction among one or a number of constituencies, and thus develop opposing forces to the exercise of presidential domestic power. It is difficult for any President to be able to maintain a strong consensus among all of the domestic constituencies for any length of time. Normally, after the initial period in office he is faced with constant struggles with Congress, his own bureaucracy, special interest groups and sometimes the judiciary, regarding not only his legislative programs, but also the conduct of his office. His various roles may conflict with one another. At the same time, each constituency may perceive him in a different role. For example, members of his party may consistently view him as the party chief while the great mass of people may assess him in terms of his role as chief of state. Such divergent perspectives can create a number of problems in presidential image-making and in developing consensus. It is a difficult task, even for the most seasoned politician and expert administrator, to insure that these various roles do not contradict each other, and at the same time to perpetuate presidential power.

The President is at the pinnacle of the American political system. Therefore, many people feel that he has and should have the most power to guide and lead the American political process, but only if he demonstrates an ability to fulfill those expectations and develop the supporting relationships previously discussed. Each incumbent, by virtue of his own views and personality, shapes the office; at the same time he is also shaped by it. There is no one set way to become a successful President. At the very least, however, the basic considerations of power relationships must be understood, appreciated and utilized in order to succeed.

The Presidential Constituencies

Let us now turn our attention to a more specific analysis of some of the major constituencies associated with presidential power. Each of the following constituencies has two sides. They can add to the power of the President, either by agreement with his programs and policies or by inability to act in opposition; or they can diminish his power by acting as a cohesive opposition force. The direction they take depends on the President's ability in acquiring, maintaining and using power.

Congress

Historically, presidential-congressional relationships have been the most important in determining the scope of presidential power and the relative success or failure of presidential programs and policies. Most congressmen and senators, particularly those who have been in office for a number of years, dislike any suggestion that Congress is subordinate to the President in any way. Acknowledging the fact that the President is the chief legislator, they nevertheless point out that Congress provides the barometer of public opinion and is the institution in which the final legislative power rests. In this respect, each member of Congress has his own constituency and in many instances is a political power unto himself. Yet, it is rare indeed that Congress can mobilize its own forces and public opinion to effectively check the power of the President. It is one thing for each individual member to develop a power base, and another for Congress to be able to develop a cohesive and effective power base as an institution. Only in instances such as the Watergate affair, can the country be so moved and the Congress so united, that an effective check on presidential power can be achieved.

Members of Congress are not necessarily dependent upon the President or the national party in elections, but rather their own political astuteness and political organization within their own states or districts. Indeed, the issues confronting their own constituencies do not necessarily correspond to the issues concerning the presidency as far as elections are concerned.

Within Congress itself there are a number of power systems in operation, which we will discuss in more detail in the chapter on Congress. Briefly, however, seniority and the committee system provide the real power base. Therefore, a small handful of congressmen can do much to obstruct any presidential program.

Furthermore, each member of Congress is a political actor in his own right. In a sense, everything that the President attempts to do at the national level, congressmen attempt to do in their own smaller spheres of activity. More often than not, there is a clash between their roles. Congressmen, for example, are sensitive to their prerogatives in the legislative field, particularly in matters of finances. The President's request for budgetary support for his many programs involves, in most cases, vigorous defense of his programs. Congressmen are aware of their primary role in the legislative field and resent any tangential role in this area. Yet it is the President who is the center of power and the policy process, and he can easily usurp the congressional role. Hence, there are frequently struggles between Congress and the President regarding money allocations and the role each institution should play in the process.

The skills and knowledge of most congressmen are greatest in domestic affairs. Their constituencies tend to have a domestic perspective rather than a foreign affairs outlook, and congressmen tend to be much closer to the domestic issues on a day-to-day basis than the President. Moreover, many powerful interest groups concerned with domestic issues and interests focus much of their activity on members of Congress. The American Farm Bureau Federation, for example, has lobbyists who keep in close touch with congressmen from rural states, and it is unlikely that congressmen would defy one of the most powerful interests in their states. The Tobacco Institute operates in a similar manner with respect to representatives from those states with an important tobacco crop. Such activities are not limited to congressmen from these areas, but extends to general lobbying to maintain federal subsidies on their crops, and insure protection from foreign products, and from increased tax rates. Such groups, as well as labor unions, are focused primarily on domestic economic policies and the fiscal policy of the government. Their interest in foreign affairs is marginal, although in recent years the state of the international economy has become an increasing concern.

Congressional power to pass laws and allocate funds provides essential elements for presidential programs and policies and hence, represents a key ingredient in the dimensions of presidential power. The President whose party is in control of Congress is not necessarily assured of success. Local issues and political gamesmanship make Congress more complex than a simple Democratic-Republican division. A variety of political relationships and issue orientations can frustrate presidential programs even if the President's party is in power.

Within the major parties there are regional interests which tend to divide the party from within. Thus, the Democratic party has within it a Southern group and a Northern group, while the Republican party has a Western and Midwestern element, and an Eastern group. The Southern Democrats are conservative in their domestic politics, as are the Republicans from the Western and Midwestern regions. On the other hand, the Democrats and Republicans from the large Northern cities and from the Eastern seaboard tend to be more liberal in their politics. Thus, a Democratic President from the East is likely to find greater support for his policies from liberals of both parties than from the Democratic party as a whole. This phenomenon is observed in an important work by James MacGregor Burns, who argues that there are essentially four parties in the United States: a Democratic presidential party, a Republican presidential party, a Democratic congressional party, and a Republican congressional party. The presidential parties come from the Northern establishment, while the congressional parties come from the South, West, and Midwest.[3] We will discuss political parties in a later chapter, but it is important to note here that a President cannot necessarily expect total support from his own party in Congress. John F. Kennedy, for example, was continually attempting to gain support for his programs from the Southern Democrats, but he rarely succeeded in doing so. His support, which came primarily from the liberals of both parties, was not enough in most cases to overcome the conservative coalition of both parties.

A President who is to further his own power position must have a deep understanding of the political processes and power systems within Congress. Through personal persuasion, distribution of favors, negotiation (deals), and coercion, he attempts to enhance his power and succeed in his programs and policies. Regardless of party, most congressmen desire national exposure in their relationship with the President to enhance their own prestige and power and strengthen their political base.

The Watergate affair provided a clear exception to this observation. Once public hearings by the special Senate Select Committee on Watergate (the Ervin committee) began, President Nixon's involvement became increasingly accepted by many Americans. Thus, most congressmen, regardless of party affiliation, felt it politically prudent not to be closely associated with the President. Upon completion of the House Judiciary Committee hearings in July, 1974, the President's isolation from Congress was even more clearly demonstrated. Republican members of Congress were fearful lest they be connected with the Watergate affair and lose all chance for reelection. Hence, the President was virtually shunned in the last days of his administration.

Generally, however, there are few congressmen who are not influenced by the President's personal attention. For example, President Johnson flattered a number of congressmen by personal telephone calls to them asking for their help in a number of issues. Even the most hardened opposition congressmen found it difficult to resist his overpowering personality and his personal attention to congressional matters. There are few congressmen who are not flattered by having their picture taken with the President of the United States and flashed across the country. Similarly, most congressmen are honored if invited to an intimate breakfast or lunch with the President.

The President is also in a position to do a number of favors for individual congressmen. His power of appointment and his authority to initiate programs and dispense financial resources can have a great impact on congressional constituencies. The appointment of a prominent member of a congressman's constituency to a federal position can have a great impact on the congressman's standing. Through the judicious use of such techniques, the President can create a number of informal obligations on the part of congressmen, who then may feel disposed to support the President on a number of issues.

Through his legislative liaison staff the President is constantly negotiating to determine the extent of his power in Congress and to identify those areas that require additional effort. Through such negotiations key members of Congress can also determine the presidential view on various legislative programs. Political compromise leads to the formulation and enactment of legislation which is mutually beneficial to the presidential power structure and Congress as well as other constituencies.

Perhaps the least effective method of furthering presidential power is through the use of coercion. Presidential threats not to implement policies stemming from congressional legislation may provoke counterthreats in Congress in regard to passing presidential legislation and budgetary bills. Similarly, attempts by the President to disregard senatorial courtesy with respect to federal appointments may cause congressional reaction in both the legislative process and appointment procedures. It is not unusual, for example, for Congress to hold up presidential appointments, whether civilian or military, until due regard is given to congressional desires and interests. The President is likely to accomplish more through his consensual powers, by persuasion, negotiations, and favors, than through the use of coercion or so-called political "arm-twisting."

The size of Congress (535 members), the laborious legislative process, and the complexity of the issues are the primary reasons that Congress generally limits itself to broad legislative enactments and allows the executive to interpret and implement the laws. This provides additional power to the President, since it gives him a range within which he can make decisions normally reserved to the legislature, e.g., tariffs, export/import regulations, fiscal policy. As a matter of fact, the President's State of the Union address and his annual budget message are implicit legislative programs which determine,

The Presidential Constituencies 171

for all practical purposes, the programs of the nation. Congress, operating as a vast committee, could not hope to provide the nation with the unified and cohesive leadership it gets from the President.

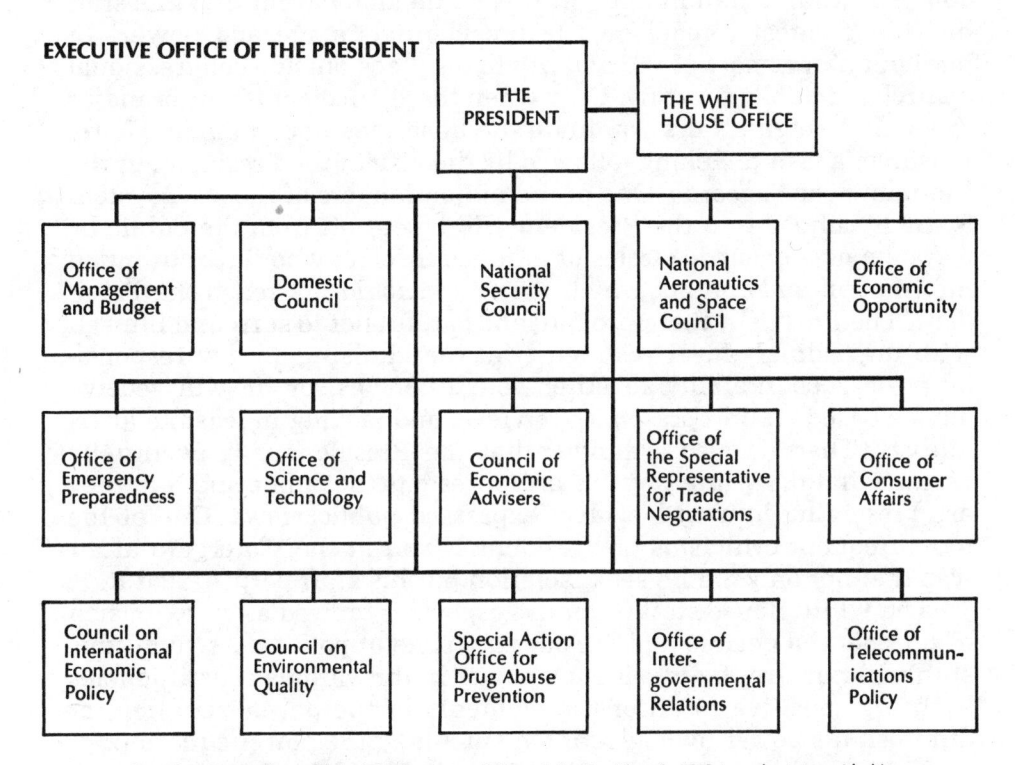

EXECUTIVE OFFICE OF THE PRESIDENT

- THE PRESIDENT
- THE WHITE HOUSE OFFICE
- Office of Management and Budget
- Domestic Council
- National Security Council
- National Aeronautics and Space Council
- Office of Economic Opportunity
- Office of Emergency Preparedness
- Office of Science and Technology
- Council of Economic Advisers
- Office of the Special Representative for Trade Negotiations
- Office of Consumer Affairs
- Council on International Economic Policy
- Council on Environmental Quality
- Special Action Office for Drug Abuse Prevention
- Office of Intergovernmental Relations
- Office of Telecommunications Policy

President Roosevelt established the Executive Office of the President in 1939 in order to provide him assistants that he could personally control and direct in carrying out Executive policy. Since that time it has grown significantly to what it is today.
*The White House Office or the White House Staff as it is often called, is the President's personal staff. They are directly and personally responsible to him and can be appointed or dismissed at the President's pleasure. Normally, the staff numbers from 15-20 persons (not including secretaries) including such positions as Press Secretary, and Special Assistant on National Security Affairs.

The White House Staff

Operating within the Executive Office is the White House staff. Considered the President's own staff, it exercises perhaps the strongest influence on his policies. This staff and its functions vary according to the needs and desires and personality of the incumbent. The range of tasks of members of the White House staff is as varied and broad as the President's own responsibilities. The Watergate hearings gave the public some indication of the complexities and variety of tasks associated with the President's staff.

The functioning of the White House staff is much more visible in domestic affairs than in foreign. It is on the home front that this staff has the greatest impact on the presidential image and power. In foreign affairs, most of the activity takes place outside congressional control and public scrutiny. Only when there are clear issues or major crises do foreign affairs dominate the headlines, for example, Henry Kissinger's visit to Peking followed by the visit of the President, or the Vietnam peace accords. One of the major dangers of the staff system is the likelihood that the President will be cut off from the public by a system of concentric circles of inner counselors who filter out much information and contact which they feel should not reach the President. The President therefore must be careful not to surround himself with unyieldingly loyal yes-men who would disregard any responsibility or accountability to other constituencies, or he will receive advice based on unrepresentative views and lacking in feasible alternatives. There is also a danger that the President may eventually assume that the White House staff represents the public and that they are presenting him with widely expressed public views. One of the most frequent criticisms of President Nixon in the Watergate affair was that not only did he seek isolation but his staff perpetuated it.

The White House staff in many respects is viewed as an extension of presidential desires and presidential style of politics. As such, this staff can nurture the President's power in the various constituencies by being sensitive to all of the elements in the power equation, or diminish his power by neglecting elements in the power equation.

This was demonstrated in the involvement of the President's staff in Watergate. Acting imprudently, disregarding the need to use the presidential instruments of power properly, and insensitive to the limits of power, members of Nixon's staff persisted in using extralegal means to repress critics. In the long run, this so diminished presidential power that it led to Nixon's resignation. One can argue, of course, that the staff members were following the dictates of the President, yet one cannot help but wonder why there were no resignations in protest before the actual Watergate incident. Why didn't members of the President's staff make it clear that involvement in such activities was detrimental to the image and power of the presidency? On the other hand, the actions of President Nixon's advisor and chief of staff, Alexander Haig, during the last days of the administration may have been a mark of statesmanship. Sensitive to the significance of the President's involvement in Watergate and recognizing the complete loss of congressional support, Haig provided direct channels to the President for Republican congressional leaders so they could make him aware of the disastrous political consequences of continuing in office.

The power and role of the White House staff has come under increasing criticism, as indicated by the following comment:

> The strangest and most questionable feature of the government of the United States is the President's political family. The President, after his election, appoints a band of personal aides and advisers . . . The electorate has no say in this. Yet some of the President's personal minions have greater power de facto than any officer of the United States government who has been appointed by constitutionally established procedures.[4]

It is interesting to note that one of the major recommendations for the incoming Ford administration in August, 1974, was that the power of the staff should be reduced and that of the Cabinet increased.

The Presidential Cabinet

The President's Cabinet consists of the secretaries of the eleven executive departments. These include the following: State; Treasury; Defense; Justice; Interior; Agriculture; Commerce; Labor; Health, Education and Welfare; Housing and Urban Development; and Transportation. (See Appendix for Organization of the Government of the United States.) These departments comprise the greatest part of the federal bureaucracy and have a primary function of administering the policies, programs and laws as directed by the President of the United States. In general, the Cabinet members (heads of departments) have at least two primary functions: as individuals they serve as heads of the departments, and collectively they serve as advisers to the President.

The Cabinet system was instituted by George Washington, who viewed the Cabinet chiefly as advisers to discuss governmental problems. It was not until the twentieth century that the Cabinet as an institution was officially recognized and legalized.

Since the establishment of the White House staff, however, the usefulness of the Cabinet as an advisory body has diminished considerably. Nevertheless, it does play a part in the presidential power equation. Cabinet members are not necessarily chosen for their administrative competence. In a number of instances, the President selects them in order to repay political debts or perhaps to provide representation to different factions in the party. Certain Cabinet members are chosen for their ability to work well with Congress. In all cases, however, Cabinet members themselves represent certain constituencies. The President must be sure that the persons he selects are acceptable to the constituencies primarily concerned with the particular department. For example, it would be politically unwise to select a Secretary of Labor who was basically an anti-labor businessman and whose political views conflicted with those of the country's powerful labor unions. Presidents, of course, have made some selections for purely personal reasons—a desire to select individuals who are personally compatible and whom he knows well. In any case, the makeup of the Cabinet and its acceptance by various constituencies can extend the presidential power. Each Cabinet member in turn may develop into a political actor in his own right and, through his own power base, reinforce that of the President. On the other hand, the images and actions of Cabinet members can diminish presidential power as well as develop a focus for opposition to presidential policies. Here again, presidential-congressional relationships come into play, since all Cabinet members must be approved by the Senate. Finally, in order to develop the broadest impact of presidential power, there must be some consensus among the Cabinet members regarding presidential programs and policies.

The Federal Government[5]

Aside from the armed services, the federal bureaucracy consists of approximately three million civilian employees. The members of the bureaucracy perform a variety of activities and engage in a variety of programs that cover every aspect of life, whether individual, group or institutional. There is no citizen whose life is not touched in some way by the federal government. At the head of this vast, complex bureaucratic structure stands the President of the United States. Theoretically, he is the chief bureaucrat. Although the bureaucracy has been criticized for its vastness, complexity and sluggishness, it is nevertheless clear that it operates the federal system.

The competence of the bureaucracy, in the main, determines how well the government operates. It has a two-fold impact on presidential power. The fact that the President, as chief bureaucrat, theoretically heads this vast bureaucracy, gives him an organizational structure that commands most of the nation's resources and affects every aspect of the nation's political, social and economic life. Therefore it is presumed that this instrument can further presidential power, with little possibility of limitation by countervailing forces.

On the other hand, the bureaucracy itself contains power systems on top of power systems on top of power sub-systems which may or may not operate in accord with presidential desires. Every bureaucratic organization, every department, division, and section, has its own constituency and power equation. As a result, there are numerous power plays at various levels and within the various departments of the bureaucracy. Furthermore, Congress, Cabinet members, special interest groups, and other constituencies have influence upon the bureaucracy, which in many instances tends to reflect political conflicts within these various constituencies. This very complexity and political struggle create a number of limitations to the exercise of presidential power. In addition, each of the many decision-makers within the bureaucratic structure tends to interpret presidential decisions and guidelines according to his own perspective and within his own power equation, in order to maintain and enhance his own power base. Conflicts are not uncommon among bureaucrats and between bureaucrats and the President over implementation of programs and policy. If such conflicts and diminished consensus within the bureaucracy become frequent, they can weaken the President's power and his ability to accomplish the goals of his administration.

> A shadow "opposition government" exists within the bureaucracy, staff attorneys and assistant division chiefs and deputy administrators, a Civil Service old-boys'-club, ever ready to whisper information embarrassing to an administration with which it disagrees. Politics, mischief, altruism—the motive really isn't important. Every administration lives with the knowledge it can be clobbered by a brick thrown from its own backyard.[6]

In other words, within any particular administration, there are those who are inclined to criticize the administration's policy. Some do this by leaking embarrassing items to the press, others do it by sending out press releases or holding press conferences.

Regulatory Commissions

An independent regulatory commission is an organization headed by a committee and concerned principally with regulating some essential private economic activity. For example, the Interstate Commerce Commission is concerned primarily with regulating the railroads and trucking industry; the Federal Power Commission regulates electric power and the natural gas industry. These commissions occupy a unique position in the American political system. Congress establishes them to make necessary decisions in areas of the economy which it feels are too complex to tackle itself. The courts generally have also felt incapable of mastering the complex technical matters with which the commissions deal; therefore, quasi-judicial powers have been granted to the various commissions. The fact that these commissions receive their grant of power from Congress makes them relatively exempt from presidential influence. The President cannot remove the commissioners from office except for specific cause. Yet, the commissions make decisions in areas which are important to the total domestic program and policies of the President.

Although these commissions have been relatively isolated from congressional, judicial and presidential control, they are highly susceptible to the power of special interest groups representing the major industries they are supposed to regulate. Acting as quasi-judicial, quasi-executive, and quasi-legislative administrative bodies, the commissions have their own special constituencies and power bases. The major industries that form the constituencies control many of the activities of the commissions. This in turn provides a power base from which the industries can support or obstruct presidential programs and policies and hence have an impact on presidential power.

The Interstate Commerce Commission was organized in 1887 primarily to protect farmers from the abuses of the railroad industry. The Act to Regulate Commerce created the ICC and gave it jurisdiction over railroads. In later years legislation strengthened its hand in dealing with rates and punitive action. Shortly after World War I, the ICC began to promote railroad interests and indeed became a champion of railroads, on the assumption that the economic health of the nation depended on a healthy railroad industry. The argument has been advanced, and rightly so, that "Once the need to regulate the industry disappears, the political pressure that led to the creation of the commission also fades away. The agency then has to cast about for new sources of support. Turning to the industry that it regulates is only natural."[7] This can lead to the agency's being too relaxed in its control of an industry. In defiance of President Kennedy's antitrust attempts in 1963-64, for example, the ICC allowed the Sante Fe Railroad to acquire control of the Western Pacific.

There are a number of examples of loose controls on industry with respect to not only the ICC but virtually all regulatory agencies. The rise of consumer protection agencies in the 1960s has developed an awareness on the part of the public and other government agencies of the need for representation of consumer interests in the political system. This new phenomenon is beginning to develop a countervailing power to the independent regulatory agencies, and some consumer agencies are now seriously involved in trying to regulate industry. The Food and Drug Administration is an example. After sporadic efforts to regulate the food industry in past years, the FDA recently took a strong stand against the use of cyclamates as an artificial sweetener in soft drinks and other products. As a result of this stand, a multi-million dollar business collapsed. In 1974, Abbott Laboratories, the major manufacturer of cyclamates, failed in its efforts to have the FDA decision reversed.

Most observers of the American political system, however, agree that the independent regulatory commissions tend to favor their own particular constituency, i.e., the industries they serve. Recently, a columnist for the *Chicago Daily News,* Carl Rowan, observed

> Too often . . . government agencies have become protectors, and advocates of the people and organizations they are supposed to regulate, rather than of the public.
> As a result there is a glaring need for someone inside government to look out for the average guy's health, safety and pocketbook—in matters like airline rates, gasoline prices, deceptive advertising, drug or school bus regulations.[8]

The independent regulatory commissions are discussed in further detail in Chapter 11 on the bureaucracy.

Special Interests

Many scholars feel that a prime characteristic of the American political system is the nature of special interest groups that have important political roles. Such groups arise out of the desire to further their own particular interests, in the areas of industry, labor, education, religion, etc. Most people belong to one or more interest groups which are directly or indirectly associated with the political system.

The attitudes and perceptions of these politically influential groups can do much to enhance or diminish presidential power. All Presidents, for example, must walk a wary line between the interests of the National Association of Manufacturers and the Chambers of Commerce and those of the AFL-CIO and other labor organizations. If the incumbent can balance the demands of these two major interests he has done much in furthering his own power base. On the other hand, the variety of interest groups in this country makes it very difficult for any one political leader to develop and maintain a consensus for his programs and policies for any length of time.

In most cases, the President must decide on which interest groups are the most important in furthering his power so that his efforts will not be dissipated. By concentrating his efforts on the most significant interest groups, it is likely that presidential power will be better served. This does not necessarily mean that other interest groups are given short shrift; rather it means that their interests are given lesser priority and lesser resources of the presidential office. Indeed, in some cases, such interest groups may be treated with "benign neglect." The term actually "came from an 1839 report on Canada by the British Earl of Durham . . . describing Canada as having grown more competent and capable of governing herself 'through the many years of benign neglect' by Britain and recommended full self-government."[9] This term was publicized in 1970 when Daniel Patrick Moynihan, counselor to President Nixon, used it in recommending a policy for the Nixon administration regarding racial issues. In a memo to the President, Moynihan stated ". . . the time may have come when the issue of race could benefit from a period of 'benign neglect.'" The memorandum further recommended that the Nixon administration avoid favoring extremists of either race. Recognizing that Negroes had made "extraordinary progress," Moynihan urged that attention be given to the problems of Indians, Mexican-Americans, and Puerto Ricans. He felt that the Negro problem has been "too much talked about" and "too much taken over to hysterics, paranoids, and hoodlums on all sides." Although attempts were made by the Nixon administration to solve problems of welfare and poverty associated with the black population, little impact was made in terms of perceived progress by the black minority. There was an underlying antagonism between the black population and the Nixon administration that no amount of welfare payments or guaranteed income levels could resolve. In addition, there was an increasing feeling among middle-class white citizens that somehow the administration was favoring non-whites at their expense. It was in such a context that Moynihan recommended a low profile or "benign neglect," in dealing with racial issues.

The Presidential Veto

There are a number of powers given to the President by the Constitution which in their aggregate are formidable in circumscribing Congress. In addition to the power to call Congress into special session, to report to the Senate and the House on the State of the Union, and to recommend national programs, the President has the power to veto legislation. This alone is an important legislative weapon. The threat of presidential veto may be enough to prevent Congress from passing a particular piece of legislation. To over-ride the veto requires two-thirds vote of Congress. Thus a successful veto, with all of its accompanying publicity, tends to diminish the power of Congress in the eyes of the people. Rather than expose Congress to this possibility, many congressmen are reluctant to support legislation that is likely to be vetoed by the President. Moreover, the President's threat of veto provides a "cue" to many congressmen sympathetic to the President or to the presidential party—indicating to them the presidential sentiment on a piece of legislation.

Obviously, when Congress is unified on a particular bill, i.e., there is a decisive commitment by many to support legislation, it does not fear a presidential veto. Indeed, in such circumstances, it is the President who must be wary of vetoing a bill because of the possibility of over-riding it by Congress. This would tend to diminish presidential power vis-à-vis Congress. Equally important, Congress may enact a stronger bill (one that is less desirable) in reaction to the veto.

The Economy and Presidential Power

The economy of the United States is based on a free enterprise system which assumes that the free play of market forces, i.e., supply and demand, is the best system and conducive to a democratic government. However, since the great depression of the 1930s, most observers have accepted the idea that the government must play a forceful role in the economy to insure that everyone has some economic benefits from the system. The major arguments have occurred over how much power the government should exercise and how economic policy should be pursued. What has evolved is a mixed economic system in which there are large areas of government control mixed with private enterprise.

The problems of the American economy became particularly acute in 1973, when the oil-producing nations in the Middle East decided to use oil as a foreign policy weapon. By instituting an oil embargo on Western countries, including the United States, they caused severe economic stress. The resulting shortage deepened economic problems in the United States. The prices of oil products skyrocketed, while oil companies achieved record-breaking profits. Unemployment rose, inflation increased, and the cost of living rose sharply. Major economic groups in the country, as well as the general public, looked to the President to correct the economic situation.

Some idea of the inflationary spiral can be seen in the following table:

Item	1948	1958	1968	1974	Per Cent Change 1948-1974
House	$47,409.00	$59,558.00	$72,840.00	$100,000.00	+110.9%
Family Size Chevrolet	1,255.00	2,081.00	2,656.00	4,119.00	+228.2%
Pair of Blue Jeans	3.45	3.75	5.29	11.25	+226.1%
Year's Tuition at Harvard	455.00	1,250.00	2,000.00	3,400.00	+647.3%
Hospital Cost per in-patient day	13.09	28.17	61.38	114.90	+777.8%
Pound of Round Steak	.90	1.04	1.14	1.81	+100.1%
Pound of Chicken	.61	.46	.39	.55	−9%
Phone Call, New York to Topeka, Kansas (day rate)	1.90	1.80	1.40	1.25	−34.2%

From *The New York Times*, August 25, 1974, Section 4, page 2.

The people's concern over inflation and unemployment was reflected in the Democratic victories in the 1974 congressional elections. Clearly the voters were unhappy with what they perceived as Republican mismanagement of the economy. Although the Democratic party had controlled Congress for over twenty years, the voters apparently blamed the Republican President for the nation's economic problems.

One of President Ford's first priorities after taking office was an attempt to correct "stagflation," i.e., a combination of high prices and low productivity. High level economic conferences were held in Washington in September 1974, with the President and top labor leaders, businessmen and economists in attendance. No clear-cut policy emerged, but the public was made aware of the crucial issues involved. Some people argued that wage and price controls should be instituted by the President. Others argued that indirect methods, such as control over interest rates and profit margins, would be sufficient. Still others preferred a combination including higher taxation.[10] In any case, all looked to the President to provide economic leadership. What the economy did or did not do would ultimately be placed at his doorstep.

In reality though no one individual or agency can control the economy. There are a number of forces and a variety of people, agencies, industries, and governments involved, with varying degrees of power and a diversity of interests. Thus, business groups may use their economic power to influence legislators to vote for better business tax advantages; labor unions may use their strike power to gain better wages; consumers may organize a boycott of certain products; individual government agencies may be overprotective of their interests, e.g., the Department of Labor regarding labor, or the Department of Commerce regarding stimulation of industry. All of these provide pressures on government policy-making that prevent cohesive and unified policy. Indeed, the very nature of the economic system defies government regulatory direction.

The President does not have control over all the agencies that influence the economy. The regulatory agencies are virtually independent of his control and may view the economy in quite different terms than he does. Similarly, many private industries and businesses have direct influence on the state of the economy. The steel industry, by increasing the price of steel per ton, can affect the price of major goods such as automobiles, and ultimately the entire economic picture. Yet the President, except in major crises, can do no more than use the indirect powers of his office to restrain price increases. Establishment of wage and price controls is always a difficult step, because the American ideology militates against such dire government economic intervention. Besides, such controls do not always bring the desired effect, and may even exacerbate economic problems by reducing productivity.

Congress has much to say about the expenditures and agencies of government involved in economic ventures. The issues of welfare, social security, tax policies are all critical ones which no President can approach without congressional involvement and support. In addition, the expenditures by the Department of Defense ($85 billion in 1974), which have a major impact on the economy, are influenced by Congress, and the same holds true for the expenditures of many other Departments, for example, Health, Education and Welfare or the Department of Housing and Urban Development.

Yet with all these restraints, the President still commands a major role in the economy. Not only does he have direct control over vast expenditures, but he has a bureaucracy, and a legal basis for his economic involvement. There is little question that presidential power is a major, if not the crucial, element in determining the state of the economy. What is wrong or what is right with the economy is generally viewed as a direct result of presidential policy, as demonstrated by the results of the 1974 congressional elections, when the voters blamed the presidential party for economic ills.

The reaction of the voters to the Watergate affair, but more importantly to the problems of inflation and unemployment were clearly reflected in the November, 1974 elections. Suspicious of Republican leadership and tired of the deteriorating state of the economy, the voters elected a predominantly Democratic 94th Congress. For only the fifth time in a century, one party was able to acquire more than two-thirds of the seats in the House of Representatives. Moreover, only nine times since 1900 had a party been able to control 61 seats in the Senate.[11]

Comparing the 93rd Congress to the 94th gives a clear indication of the extent of Democratic control.[12]

	93rd Congress	94th Congress
Senate		
Democrats	58	61
Republicans	42	39
House		
Democrats	248	291
Republicans	187	144

Combining the control of Congress with that of a number of state legislatures and governorships won by the Democrats, it was clearly an impressive victory for the Democratic party at both national and state levels.

Presidential programs were obviously going to be difficult to pursue in the 94th Congress. It was also clear that President Ford's attempt to influence the election in favor of those persons supporting his program had not succeeded. In the final analysis, it appeared that the 94th Congress would be in a position to challenge presidential power and even to restore congressional power in many areas such as defense spending and foreign affairs.

The long-range implications were for some restoration of congressional prestige and a continuing suspicion of presidential intentions.

Only in 1976 will the voters have a chance to express their choices not only in terms of a new Congress but a new President. Meanwhile the 1974 elections made it clear to the President's party that in instances of mismanagement or perceived mismanagement, the people can and do act.

The Vice President

Very little has been said of the Vice President's role in domestic affairs and his power relationship to the President. This is a deliberate omission because he does what the President desires. Until very recently, the office of Vice President was viewed as politically inconsequential and powerless. In an interesting study of the Vice President's role in history, one author quotes a number of American political leaders and their views on the Vice Presidency.

> John Adams: "My country has in its wisdom contrived for me the most insignificant office that ever the invention of a man contrived or his imagination conceived."
> John Nance Garner: "The vice-presidency isn't worth a pitcher of warm spit."
> Harry Truman: "Look at all the Vice Presidents in history. Where are they? They were about as useful as a cow's fifth teat."[13]

There have been a number of events since, however, which have strengthened the position of the Vice President, at least in terms of potential power. The heart attacks of President Eisenhower, the assassination of President Kennedy, and the resignation of President Nixon, have raised serious doubts about the relatively indifferent procedures for selecting a Vice President. The presidency of Gerald Ford rested on his appointment as Vice President after the resignation of Vice President Spiro Agnew in 1973. Thus, Gerald Ford moved into both the second and first political offices in the land through appointment rather than election. His appointment to the vice presidency and his succession to the presidency were based on the Twenty-fifth Amendment, ratified in 1965. The amendment states in part:

> In case of the removal of the President from office or of his death or resignation, the Vice President shall become President.
> Whenever there is a vacancy in the office of the Vice President, the President shall nominate a Vice President who shall take office upon confirmation by a majority vote of both Houses of Congress.

The administrations of President Nixon and Ford have set a mark in history. For the first time, this nation has seen the resignation of a Vice President (Spiro Agnew in 1973), the resignation of a President (Richard Nixon in 1974) two appointments of Vice President (Ford in 1973 and Rockefeller in 1974) and the succession of a Vice President to the presidency (Ford in 1974), all within a matter of 18 months. And for the first time in American history, the President and the Vice President have gained office without being elected by the people.

As events in recent years have shown, the Vice President is within a "heartbeat" away from becoming President. A number of scholars and politicians now ask "should we not be as careful in selecting the Vice President as we are in selecting the President?"

Summary

In sum, the President comes to office with an initial grant of power based primarily on the election constituency and legal authority. The nature of this initial grant of power, in many respects, depends on the kinds of mandates received during the election and the expectations with which he comes to office. From this base the aggrandizement or diminution of power rests primarily on his leadership ability and style of politics in dealing with other political actors and constituencies. The problem in domestic affairs is a difficult one because there are many centers of power. The domestic political environment gives rise to a number of effective opposing power centers with the potential to limit and challenge presidential power.

Nevertheless, we must remember that the President is the head of a vast bureaucracy and intelligence service. More than any other politician the President embodies the "nation." As an institution the presidency has tremendous power vis-à-vis other institutions in the political system. If the President is an astute politician, and a sympathetic, responsive and intelligent leader, it is difficult to conceive of sufficient resistance to deter his policies—aside from the very important one of "the people" every four years.

NOTES

1. Robert Sherrill, *Why They Call It Politics* (New York: Harcourt, Brace, Jovanovich, 1972), p. 66.
2. David Halberstam, *The Best and the Brightest* (New York: Random House, 1969), p. 29.

Notes

3. James MacGregor Burns, *The Deadlock of Democracy: Four Party Politics in America* (Englewood Cliffs, N.J.: Prentice-Hall, 1963).

4. As quoted in the *Alabama Journal*, July 19, 1973, p. 4.

5. See Appendix F for a schematic of the federal government.

6. Joseph C. Goulden, *The Superlawyers* (New York: Dell Publishing Co., 1973), p. 228.

7. Peter Woll and Robert Binstock, *America's Political System* (New York: Random House, 1972), p. 375.

8. Carl Rowan, "Consumer Effort Lost Its Zip?" *Chicago Daily News*, September 10, 1974, p. 10.

9. *The New York Times*, March 1, 1970, pp 1 and 69.

10. Julius Duscha, "Economists at the White House—Telling it Like it is," *The New York Times*, Section 3, pp. 1 and 7, September 8, 1974.

11. *The New York Times*, November 7, 1974, p. 30.

12. R.W. Apple, Jr., "National Vote Pattern: A Sweep if not a G.O.P. Debacle," *The New York Times*, November 7, 1974, p. 34.

13. Donald Young, *American Roulette: The History and Dilemma of the Vice Presidency* (New York: Holt, Rinehart and Winston, 1972), p. 5.

Selected Readings

Since the Watergate affair, many people have been concerned about the extent of presidential power in domestic affairs; the results of the 1974 election partly reflected this concern. However, there are a number of causes for the growth of presidential power—Watergate is but one manifestation of this.

Richard E. Neustadt, in the following selection, argues that "Presidential powers are substantially unchanged, what has changed is a set of inhibitions on their use." According to him, it is the view of the office held by the incumbent that shapes the extent of presidential power. The Watergate affair may have a silver lining according to Neustadt, for by illuminating the extent of presidential power it may lead other institutions to establish some effective opposing power. He identifies Congress, the party, and the Cabinet as external constraints, and the President's schedule, press conferences, and staff system as internal constraints. Neustadt argues that even after Watergate the informal restraints—those imposed by Congress, the Cabinet, and the party remain negligible, at least until the political system adjusts to the repercussions of Watergate. In the meantime, the internal constraints will remain the basis for countervailing power to the President. As Neustadt states ". . . the man's methods alone define the sense of prudence he may call to the support of his own sense of propriety. All is subjective, turning on him as it was ultimately with Nixon."

5.1

The Constraining of the President

RICHARD E. NEUSTADT

The White House was once—and will be again—a great place for a young man to work. I did it myself and have never been sorry. Fate was kind and my age was right: It was Harry Truman's White House, and I worked for Charlie Murphy—Charles S. Murphy, to give him his due. He was the President's Special Counsel, successor to Clark Clifford in that post and one of Truman's senior aides. Working for Murphy and with him for the President was a fine experience, as unlike Egil Krogh's or Gordon Strachan's as day from night. A story illustrates what made it so, and the story is a starting point for looking at the Presidency now, by light of Watergate.

In December, 1950, at the wrenching turn of the Korean war, amidst Chinese attack, American retreat, renewed inflation, fears of World War III, Truman met at the White House with the Congressional leaders of both parties. Their meeting in the Cabinet room was largely symbolic, underlining events; it was an occasion for briefings, not actions. Soon after it broke up, a White House usher came to Murphy's office with a memorandum found under the Cabinet table. This was a document of several pages addressed by the staff of the Senate Minority Policy Committee to Senators Robert A. Taft and Kenneth S. Wherry, the Republican leaders. Some of his assistants were with Murphy at the time, and we fell upon it with whoops of joy. As I recall, one of us read it aloud. It dealt with the contingency (which had not arisen) that the President might use that meeting to seek pledges of bipartisan support for the Administration's future conduct of the war. This, the memorandum argued, ought to be resisted at all costs. By Easter recess the war could have taken such a turn that Republicans might wish to accuse Truman of treason, and they should be free to do so. The term "treason" fired in me and my associates an outrage we wanted the world to share. With the loyalty of subalterns, more royalist than the king, we cried, "Get it copied . . . show it to the President . . . leak it to the press!" Murphy smiled at us, took the memorandum from us, sealed it in an envelope, summoned a messenger and sent it by hand to Senator Taft. End of story.

From *The New York Times Magazine*, October 14, 1973. © 1973 by The New York Times Company. Reprinted by permission.

Murphy's conduct showed propriety—indeed, for me defines it—so that much recent White House staff behavior simply shocks me. His conduct also showed prudence. He worked in a White House where seniors had constant incentive to contain themselves and restrain the young.

The Presidency as we know it now took shape in Franklin Roosevelt's time, the product of Depression, war, the radio and Presidential personality. Truman inherited and consolidated. In terms of personnel, both military and civilian, the Federal Government during his later years was roughly the same size as it is now. (The great growth of the civilian public service since has been at state and local levels.) In constitutional and statutory terms, the Presidency's formal powers then were much what they are now. Like President Nixon, Truman fought undeclared war, imposed price controls, presided over a great turn in foreign policy, sought changes in domestic policy and championed "executive privilege." But if, in these respects and others, Presidential powers are substantially unchanged, what has changed is a set of inhibitions on their use.

Formal powers stay about the same, but their conversion into actual power—into making something happen—takes place with less restraint than formerly. If the Nixon regime felt itself under siege in 1971, so did Truman's in 1951. Yet there were no do-it-yourself White House horrors. Had propriety not barred them, prudence would have done so.

Almost surely, Watergate's effect upon the Presidency will be to prop up old incentives for restraint, restoring White House prudence to something like its former state. Such a prop is artificial and cannot last forever, but it should hold good for years to come. Score one for Watergate! In that perspective it is not a tragedy—far from it.

So the modern Presidency's past and prospects are bound up with the questions: What was prudence made of? What became of those ingredients? And on what terms does Watergate restore them?

A generation ago, our system's formal checks and balances were strongly reinforced by an array of informal constraints on White House conduct. Some were external, imposed on the White House, equally affecting President and staff. Others were internal, products of his operating style, affecting the staff more than him. External constraints reflected his dependence upon men whom he could not control for work he wanted done. Such men were found in many places, but let me single out three: the Congress, the party and the Cabinet. As for internal constraints I shall single out another three: his schedule, press conferences, and the staff system.

The Congress

Those men on whom the President depended were his "colleagues" in the quite specific sense that while he needed them, their power did not stem wholly from his. To need is to heed, or at least to listen. Truman had one such set of colleagues on Capitol Hill: the Speaker of the House, the House and Senate floor leaders and the committee chairmen. As the modern Presidency emerged before and during World War II, it was assumed that those posts would go to men of the same party as the

President. So it had been for all but four years since the turn of the century. So it remained in Truman's time for six years out of eight. Under F.D.R. and Truman this assumption was built into Governmental practice, not least at the White House where it moderated tones of voice, promoted consultation and preserved respect, at least for working purposes. Speaker Sam Rayburn and the floor leaders met Truman every week. They were colleagues together: At Rayburn's wish they met alone, no staff—and no recordings.

While all the posts of power on the Hill were manned by men who shared the President's party label, Truman could not do what he did in 1948 and in effect run against Congress, lambasting it for a "do-nothing" record he himself had forced on it by seeking bills he lacked the votes to pass. But that was the 80th Congress, elected two years earlier with Republican majorities in both Houses. Truman could not turn as sharply on an institution led by Rayburn. Nor would he have wanted to. Nor could his staff. Family quarrels were of a different quality than conflict with the rival clan.

And even as he rose to the attack in 1948, Truman carefully walled off from party battle what he took to be the cardinal field of foreign relations, including European policy, and especially the Marshall Plan. Under the aegis of Senator Arthur H. Vandenberg, the Congressional Republicans did likewise. For limited purposes, the Truman-Vandenberg connection linked the White House to Republican leaders as closely as ever to Democrats.

In 1954, Truman's successor General Eisenhower faced the reverse situation when the Democrats regained control of both houses of Congress. He then faced it continuously for six years. Eisenhower was a national hero, consciously so, and only lately become a Republican. He joined Rayburn and the latter's protégé, the new Senate Leader Lyndon Johnson, in a loose but comfortable connection. Over a wide range of issues this served much as Truman's with Vandenberg.

What Truman had for two years and Eisenhower for six, Nixon now has had for more than four, with no prospect of change: Congress organized by the other party. But Nixon, despite intermittent caution in his first term, seems not to have wanted special connections of the sort his predecessors threw across the party breach between themselves and Congress. And after his triumphant re-election, he immediately tried a reverse twist on Truman's warfare with the 80th Congress. Truman had made demands that Congress would not meet, and cried "do-nothing"; now Nixon made budget cuts that Congress would oppose, and readied taunts of "fiscal irresponsibility." In such a game the negative makes for even less restraint than the affirmative. Truman wanted the program he requested but lacked votes and did not get it. Nixon no doubt wants to keep the cuts he made, and wields the veto. Until scandal overtook him I think he was winning hands down—and he is not defeated yet. In all events, little remains of a once-strong constraint.

The Party

Twenty years ago, both parties were what they had been since Andrew Jackson's time: confederal associations of state parties grouped together for the sake of Presidential nominations and campaigns. The state parties, in turn, consisted of some relatively standard parts: city machines, court-house gangs, interest-group leaders, elective office-holders, big contributors. Stitching them all together nationally every fourth year was a task for party regulars assembled in convention. Barons strongly based in interest groups or regions or machines collectively had power to decide, or at least veto, and their number at a given time was never very large. Perhaps 50 or 100 men—buttressed, of course, by aides and friends and clients—were crucial to each party's nomination and campaign, crucial in convention and in canvassing and funding. And they were a known circle, shifting over time but usually quite easy to identify at any moment.

As with Congress, Truman was linked in stable fashion to the party leaders by a common interest: the Presidential succession. Such a relationship constrains one politician's staff in dealing with another politician, and even more so when, as was usually the case with Truman, he needed more help than he could give. Gallup Poll approval of his conduct fell to 32 per cent in 1946 and then as low as 23 per cent in 1951, eight points below Nixon's low last August. Not coincidentally, in 1946 Truman was requested by the Democratic National Committee *not* to campaign for Congress. In 1948 the railroads withdrew credit and his famous whistle-stop tour almost stopped for lack of funds. In 1952 Gov. Adlai Stevenson of Illinois persistently evaded his embrace, insisted on a draft, refused a White House build-up. The party barons out in states and cities may have liked the President and felt some kinship for him, but few if any were prepared to die for him, and none, so far as I know, were content to work through staff in lieu of him. Like Rayburn, they preferred to deal, and to be known to deal, and to be known to deal directly. In Truman's situation their preferences mattered a lot.

As organizations our two national parties have never been twins. But insofar as both shared features of the sort I have described, both are now changed almost beyond recognition. TV and jet aircraft, primaries and ticket-splitting join with education, affluence and population shifts to outmode old customs and weaken old fiefdoms. We have left the age of barons and entered the age of candidates. Its hallmarks are management by private firms, exposure through the tube, funding by direct-mail drives as well as fat-cats and canvassing by zealous volunteers.

For the Republican party nationally, 1964 exposed the passing of the old regime; for Democrats the year was 1972. Nixon in a sense is our first President to deal with party ties wholly in terms of the new conditions. Watergate sheds light on how his White House dealt. What is shows is an inordinate concern for raising money, coupled with a campaign organization run by White House aides. The Committee for the Re-election of the President was wholly independent of the Republican National Committee; it remained in existence after the campaign. Perhaps coincidentally, the White House planned that after the election those aides and others should fan out all over town, taking up sub-Cabinet posts or civil service supergrades in every major agency. Much of this actually happened last winter; it was the most determined such effort by any Administration in memory.

Why grab so much money? Why carry on C.R.P.? Why scatter subalterns all over the place? Likelier than not the answer lies in sheer momentum, in doing what comes naturally (and to excess, as was typical of the Nixon staff). But possibly they are related. It is conceivable these three developments were part of a scheme for dominating not only the Administration, but also the Republican succession. In an age of candidates, could White-House controlled bank accounts combined with White-House controlled agencies provide a substitute for defunct party baronies? As hopefuls crowded the primaries in 1976, could these assets have given the power of decision or veto to the White House staff? In any event, the setting does not make for much constraint!

The Cabinet

Truman's Cabinet officers were his appointees, for the most part, but rarely his creatures. Some of them (not many) had party standing of their own, linked to a faction of those old-style barons. Some bureau chiefs (a lot) had the equivalent in links to leading Congressmen and vital interest-groups. Everyone, regardless of his standing, owed a duty to the statutory programs he administered, and so to the Congressional committees that controlled their life blood: laws and funds. Since the "Compromise of 1789"—when Congress took the power to create departments, leaving the Presidents the discretion to dismiss department heads—it had been recognized in practice, if not always in words, that "executive" agencies of all sorts were subordinate at once to President *and* Congress, a triangular relationship that left them with two masters who could frequently be played off against each other. J. Edgar Hoover's practice of this art in 1971 seems newsworthy today but would have seemed the norm for any self-respecting bureau chief in 1951 or earlier, the period when Hoover perfected his technique.

So it was in Truman's time, and so with variations it appears to have remained. But the variations are important. They suggest that Nixon's White House up to now has rarely felt the full constraint shared mastership used to impose. That Nixon's aides thought otherwise—as their extraordinary memoranda show—hints at either ignorance or paranoia.

Viewed from a distance, two changes stand out. As of, say, 1970 compared with 1950, most Cabinet officers seem less important to the President, while bureau chiefs appear less certain of Congressional support against the President, or anyway less likely to invoke it. The latter change reflects what may have been a passing phase—much of Washington heeds the dictum "never hit a man unless he's down," and Nixon, like Truman before him, has become vulnerable. Or maybe it reflects a downward shift of levels for Congressional support deep into program management, and well below the bureau chiefs, almost out of sight. And possibly the change is greater than it would be if party ties helped connect committees to agencies. But if this change is hard to pin down, the Cabinet change is not.

The low estate of most contemporary Cabinet posts reflects reduced White House dependence on departments as well as increased dependence of departments on each other. Twenty years ago the President relied on Cabinet members for a great deal of the staff work now performed inside the White House. President Eisenhower was the first to pull into the White House the detailed work of lobbying with Congress for Administration bills; Truman had mostly kept it out. And the hiring and firing of agency officials below Cabinet rank is now centralized as never before. Whatever its purpose—partisan or managerial or both—the fanning out of

Nixon aides last winter into agencies reflects unprecedented White House planning and initiative in lower level appointments. Initiative once rested mostly with department heads; they usually won their contests with the White House staff. (It has been only a dozen years since Kennedy's Defense Secretary rejected out of hand a White House proposal for Secretary of the Navy, none other than Franklin Delano Roosevelt Jr.)

In Truman's years, moreover, a department head could look down at his bureaus, out to their clients and up to subcommittees on the Hill without having to think hourly about other departments. A bailiwick was still a bailiwick. For many department heads this is no longer true. I once worked closely with the head of the housing agency that preceded HUD. I do not recall that he gave a thought to the Federal Security Agency, the forerunner of H.E.W. But there was then no Model Cities Program.

Since President Johnson got his chance to put through Congress a whole generation's worth of Democratic programs—many stemming from Truman proposals stalled since the nineteen-forties—new endeavors have entangled departmental jurisdictions in such a web of overlapping statutes, funding, staffs and clientele that no one moves without involving others, often painfully. I gather it is even hard to stand still on one's own. In dealing with the consequences, bureaus are important, and so are Presidential staffs; the bureaus can operate, albeit on a narrow front, while the staffs can coordinate, at least in terms of budgets. Department heads are often poorly placed to do either. Their positions often are at once too lofty and too low.

Johnson once wanted super-managers to rationalize his programs as they built them up. Nixon called for super-managers to rationalize those programs down, and build up revenue-sharing. From either standpoint, Cabinet posts seemed cramped in White House eyes. In addition, the incumbents were cramped for time. New programs conferred on most departments new relationships with more Congressional committees than before. These Cabinet members still were in position to testify. So they did, over and over. It took a lot of time. But it added little to their weight at the White House. And Ehrlichman condescended.

Down the drain went still another set of Presidential colleagues—and constraints.

The Schedule

As for internal constraints on Truman's Presidency, the first derived from his operating style. He was accessible beyond contemporary belief. Following Roosevelt's peace-time practice and a long Presidential tradition, H.S.T. stood ready to see any member of Congress, granting 15 minute interviews to anyone who asked, if possible within 24 hours of the asking. The same rule held for Cabinet and sub-Cabinet officers, heads of lesser agencies and governors of states—these among others. His days were chopped up into 15-minute segments, morning and afternoon. He managed to include not only those who wanted to see him but also those he wished to see. He was available to staff early and late. And he met weekly, in addition, with the legislative leaders, the Cabinet, the National Security Council and the press—all this on top of ceremonies and aside from reading, late into the night.

Those 15-minute interviews, on the callers' business, at their option, took a large amount of time—no mean constraint—and also follow-up, which constrained his staff all the more, as Truman, like Roosevelt before him, usually met his callers alone. Inefficiencies resulted, and waste motion. But at the same time, this President was personally exposed, day in and out, to what a lot of people wanted from him; he learned what they cared about, believed, hoped and feared. And constraining or not, I think Truman liked the flow. He found in it large compensations.

Eisenhower, by contrast, chafed under it, found it intolerable, channeled off all he could to his aides. Until his heart attack in 1955, members of Congress complained, and so did Cabinet members and others. Afterwards, acceptance set in. Before President Kennedy took office he was warned (to his discomfort) that he would be pressed to resume Truman's custom. But this did not occur. Washington had accepted the Eisenhower custom. Kennedy and Johnson were as free as had been Nixon to receive or put off whom they chose. Their choices were very different from his. But their freedom to make them eased his choice of relative isolation.

The Press

Twenty years ago, another internal constraint derived from White House press relations, above all from the press conference as a regular weekly undertaking. These were no longer the intimate affairs of Roosevelt's time, with reporters crowded compatibly into the Oval Office; by Truman's second term they had become big-scale affairs in larger quarters, less educative for the correspondents, less fun for the President. But they still served many other functions, communications functions *within* Government, connecting our peculiarly separated branches, as well as informing the public. Regular press conferences gave the White House staff a chance to put the President on record unmistakably with Congressmen or bureaucrats or interest groups or partisans who could not be convinced at secondhand. They gave those others chances to check up on the assertions of the staff. They gave the President himself a chance to reinforce or override the claims made in his name by staff and everybody else. They gave him, finally, opportunities to puncture myths and gossip.

Truman did not always turn these chances to his own account. Sometimes he backed into unintended promises, disclosures or embarrassments. Thus press conferences constrained him. But I think they constrained others more, not the least his staff. At any rate, whatever pain they caused, those regular press conferences offered all concerned, the President included, compensations not obtainable from any other source. This we found out after Johnson impaired them by irregularity, still more after Nixon virtually shut them down. By Johnson's time, of course, press conferences had come to be live television shows. He reacted against the risks to his own image and his programs inherent in exposure through an entertainment medium, where many things besides words are conveyed to many publics viewing as a passive audience. Endowed with different style and temperament, Kennedy had faced those risks with relish. Not Johnson, and not Nixon. Seeking to safeguard their public relations, these Presidents backed out of regular press conferences; in the process—inadvertently perhaps—they impaired their internal communications.

The Staff

The last constraint I want to mention arose from Truman's staff system, which as its central feature made him his own chief of staff. He chaired the morning staff meeting; he parceled out assignments; he watched the White House budget; he approved new staff positions. He dealt directly, one by one, with all but junior aides; he allowed few of these, kept an eye on them and made sure that in meetings they saw a lot of him. He was immersed in detail, and it all took time. Thereby he was constrained. His aides, though, were also constrained—by him.

In this and other respects Truman followed rather closely, although not very consciously, the pattern F.D.R. had brought to Presidential staffing in his second term. Roosevelt's pattern had four features; he clung to them consistently, and so did Truman. First, the President, and only the President, was the chief of staff. Second, there was a sharp distinction between "personal" and "institutional" staff. The latter worked in such places as the Budget Bureau, with a mandate to think always of the Presidential office apart from personal politics. The former, the White House staff per se, would think about the President's personal interests, while he could weigh both views and choose between them. Third, personal staff meant only those who helped the President to do what was required of him day by day, manning his schedule, drafting his speeches, guarding his signature, nursing the press corps or, during the war, dealing with Stalin and Churchill. "This is the White House calling" was to mean the President himself or someone reliably in touch with him. Roosevelt cared devoutly for the symbolism of that house. All other aides were "institutional," to be kept out of there and off that phone. He overlapped staff duties, reached out to departments, pored over newspapers, probed his visitors and quizzed his wife. Not only was he chief of his own staff, he also was his own director of intelligence on happenings in his Administration. Except when they embarrassed him, he looked upon press leaks as adding to his sources.

The Rooseveltian pattern has had a curious history over the years. It evolved under Truman and then was abandoned by Eisenhower. The General could not abide it and thought it wrong in principle. Rather than immersion he sought freedom from detail and built a bigger staff than Truman's to relieve him of it. He made someone else his chief of staff, and created a swirl of secretariats to serve committees of Cabinet members. In reaction, Kennedy scrapped most of that and consciously restored the Rooseveltian arrangement, adapting as he went but following all its features. Johnson adapted further, but with less care as he grew more and more immersed in his war. Nixon evolved a different pattern that somewhat resembled Eisenhower's, but with a marked change in its means for tackling policy. Committee secretariats became substantive staffs, with initiative and discretion independent of Cabinet members. A much larger White House staff resulted. Seeking freedom for himself, Nixon left its management to others.

Thus in the more than 30 years since the White House staff became a major feature of our Government, we have alternated between two contrasting patterns for its composition and control. Numbers tell part of the story. In 1952, civilian aides with some substantive part in public business numbered 20. In 1962 the number was the same. In 1972 it seems to have been somewhere between 50 and 75 (depending on how one counts the third-level assistants). Moreover, the alternation follows party lines; the contrasting patterns have almost become matters of party philosophy. At least they are matters of party experience, handed down through the political generations from old cadres to the young. When a Haldeman eloquently testifies on the philosophy of Nixon's system, Democrats scoff. Republicans did likewise at the lack of system in Roosevelt's arrangements, to say nothing of Kennedy's. It naturally is harder now for Democrats than for Republicans to think Nixon could genuinely, if wishfully, not know—and then be cramped in finding out about—the cover-up of Watergate. Students of the Eisenhower Presidency are less skeptical.

A staff system that liberates the President to think frees staff men from his watchful eye. The price he pays for liberty comes in the coin of power. So we have seen with Nixon since last March. This always worried Roosevelt.

It is a matter of coincidence, I think, that even as the old constraints of prudence slackened, the White House staff fell under the control of senior aides so lacking in propriety as those we saw this summer on our television screens. Men like these are the opposite of Truman's Counsel, Murphy. Not everyone who ever served in the White House met his standard. But few if any ever fell so far below it as those Nixon aides. Men of their extraordinary impropriety have not been found there before, at least not in such numbers. Their like might not have been there under Nixon, or not so many of them, had he won the Presidency eight years earlier, succeeding Eisenhower. Even in 1969 they did not have the place all to themselves, but had to share it for a while with seniors of a different sort, men who were old hands at governing, experienced downtown and tempered by long contact with the Hill. Murphy's sensitivities owed much to the flavor of Congress—especially the Senate (where he himself had been a legislative counsel) and most especially the Senate of the old Southern ascendancy, exemplified by Senator Richard Russell. (In 1951, Russell's masterful performance in the chair of the MacArthur hearings caused the General to fade away, no harm to the Republic, and set a high standard for Senator Ervin.) But in Nixon's White House those most respectful of the Hill's old flavor did not long survive a contest with the masters of new-style campaigning. Zealous for their chief, the winners packed the place with second and third-level men of their own mind, magnified his wishes by their own means and wound up blighting the bright prospect of his second term.

Excess now has bred its own corrective. Watergate puts new life into old constraints, or more precisely, it assures a set of temporary substitutes. If the White House is forced into continuous give-and-take, this after all is what the Constitution intended. If the give-and-take sometimes degenerates into sheer nastiness, that will reflect the way it all began, in White House zealousness. Near-term results are predictable. If he wants, Nixon can have a limited connection with the Congressional leaders, though at a higher price than formerly. Where he does not, stand-offs will ensue, with each side using assured powers to harass the other. Budget cuts and vetoes will be countered by withheld appropriations or rejected confirmations. Bargains will be struck, *ad hoc*, on relatively even terms, a process hardly conceivable six months ago. At the same time there will be fresh support by subcommittees for pet programs, and vice versa, no matter what the White House says or wants. Caught in between, department heads will drift toward their subordinates regardless of the White House, or subsist increasingly in lame-duck isolation. Some Cabinet officers will probably emerge as major figures in their own right. And while the President himself cannot now be expected to change operating styles, the senior aides now near him, and particularly those inflicted on him, should be quite able to do so in the direction of caution. Their accessibility compensates a little for his isolation.

If these predictions are borne out, the three-and-one-half years remaining for this President—assuming, as I do, that he fills out his term—will be neither easy nor tidy; in domestic terms they will produce more noise and less redirection than he wanted, and in foreign terms they will produce less movement than he hoped. But he would have faced some shortfall even if Watergate had not happened. The failure of Phase Three to keep down prices, and the failure of bombing in Cambodia to bring "peace," assured that opposition would revive on the Hill and in the press.

The modern Presidency is a sturdy vehicle. Hardship and untidiness are frequently its lot. But at worst a President retains his formal powers. These put him at the center of the legislative process, the administrative process, national politics, foreign relations; combined they make him central to the news. Accordingly, so long as he has time ahead, there will be men in every part of Washington who are mindful of his wishes because they in their own jobs have need of him in his. Until his last appointment, his last budget, his last veto, his last summit, he cannot sink to insignifance in Government; his office will uphold him. As for changes in the office of the sort now being argued both in Congress and the courts—limiting impoundment, or his use of force abroad, or claims to executive privilege—each dents the Presidency at an outer edge, narrowing discretion, reducing flexibility, but strikes no vital spot. What is vital to the office is that combination: processes, politics, peace and the news. Within our Government the combination is unique, and so confers unique advantages. These remain.

(The Nixon proposal for a single six-year Presidential term is in a different category. It would change the Presidency's central core, to my mind, for the worse. We now have, in effect, an eight-year term subject at midpoint to an opposition audit reviewed by the electorate and then a vote of confidence without which he retires. The required re-election at midterm is one of the most democratic features of the office and adds to its legitimacy in a system of popular sovereignty. Removal of this feature to protect us from its possible corruption is a frivolous proposal for a President to make, especially when his regime has been the most corrupt. Nixon, I hope, was not serious.)

The Supreme Court last interfered with Presidential powers in 1952 when Truman was denied authority to seize the nation's steel mills. But the Court managed not to say it never could be done again in any circumstances. On the contrary, the artful spread of concurring opinions left the future relatively open. The Presidency is limited only a little. This is the likeliest outcome again when current issues reach the highest Court. The net result may be to make some future Presidents work harder, under more restrictions, conciliating more, and forcing issues less than Nixon chose to do in his first term—or Truman at the time of the steel seizures. The presidency won't be flattened by that!

To write of Truman is to recall the trouble and the pain associated with his Presidency: the pain of the Korean war and those interminable truce talks; the pain of domestic reforms deferred, of foreign developments blighted; the pain of MacArthur, and McCarthy; the China charges; the corruption charges; the list goes on and on. But where is that pain now? The young know nothing of it; the old have long since put it out of mind. A few of us would gladly show our scars, but we have no viewers except for historians, and not even many of them. Truman never captivated the campuses. And so I predict it will be with our current trouble. At the same time, though, short-term results have a way of shedding light on problems for the more distant future.

If the value of Watergate is great as a temporary renewer of old constraints, it is not unqualified. We now are in a period of antipolitical politics, with journalists and politicians playing to their own sense of successive, cumulative, public disillusionments. Watergate feeds the mood. When such a period descended on us in the early fifties we got Eisenhower for President, the hero-above-politics. Since we lack heroes nowadays, the next time could be worse. Moreover, the renewed constraints on Nixon cannot last forever. Watergate's effects will wear off over time, perhaps by his successor's second term (taking us no farther than 1984). As this occurs the weakened state of old constraints will be exposed once more: the parties gone beyond recall, the Congress mortgaged to ticket-splitting, the Cabinet frayed by overlapping jurisdictions, the dependence of all the rest on the President's own style.

But separated powers still define our system, so new colleagues, bringing new constraints, may replace the old, and some of the old may revive. What happens in our parties is especially important. We may face perpetual disarray, a dire prospect. But renewal is by no means inconceivable. For instance, big-state governors, linked to professional managers and money, may revive party baronies in the guise of perpetual candidacies. Reagan and Rockefeller may be precursors. As part of the same vision, or perhaps quite separately, cadres of volunteers funded by direct-mail drives may come into existence state by state to man elective party posts and staff campaigns, substituting, in relatively stable fashion, for old-style machines. "Favorite sons" may come to have renewed significance. The national convention may again become the place for interstate negotiations (especially if the TV networks cut back live coverage). A President, like others, then negotiates again.

If national parties revive, this makes it the more likely that Congress and the White House will some day be run again by men with the same party label. A President then will welcome back old colleagues. As for executive operations, residual price and wage controls—an incomes policy with some sort of club in the closet—may well join revenue sharing and resource regulation as likely long-term features of the Federal scene. White House attention may be focused on them in the future, along with defense and diplomacy. If so, no matter what becomes of traditional Cabinet posts, the President will gain new executive colleagues: corporation officials, union leaders, governors, mayors.

Even the traditional executive positions may again turn more collegial from a President's standpoint than most of them were six months ago. Much depends upon the evolution of relationships with Congress. Senator Walter F. Mondale recently has urged, as one of several new checks on the White House, a televised Senate question-period for Cabinet officers. This is an old proposal, but with the new addition of television, no small matter. Such appearances would distance Cabinet members from the President and so make them more important to him, in the very act of making them perform independently. But television is not without risk. While distancing them, it might also diminish them—and the Senate along with them—especially if viewers were to compare Senate sessions with, say, the press conferences of a J.F.K. The tube is a two-edged sword, thus, so is Mondale's scheme. But it suggests how readily the future may be open to some changes in the status of traditional Cabinet posts.

In short, I think it possible that 20 years from now constraints upon a President will be at least as strong as 20 years ago. While we wait for the emergence of new colleagues or a welcome-back to old, we have little to depend on by way of these informal checks and balances, except constraints of the other sort, those of operating style. Then the man's methods alone define the sense of prudence he may call to the support of his own sense of propriety. All is subjective, turning on him, much as it was until lately with Nixon.

But for a while Watergate supervenes. Nixon's successor, I predict, will not be tarred by it. Indeed he probably will be its beneficiary, winning as a "Mr. Clean." Almost surely he will pledge to make himself accessible and to rein in his staff. So did Nixon five years ago, but the next President will have more need to be serious about it, and more reason, and he may well possess a temperament more suited to the task. Voters, I suspect, will shun secretive types. God willing, they will welcome humor. At worst we should get prudence with a pretense of propriety. At best we will get the genuine article.

Study Questions

1. Cite recent examples where the President has had wider discretionary powers in the realm of foreign affairs than in domestic affairs. How much additional power did Congress bestow on President Nixon in the areas of wage and price controls and fuel conservation? What motivated Congress to do so?

2. Did Presidents Johnson and Nixon seek to make maximum use of their election triumphs in 1964 and 1972 respectively in trying to get thier policies implemented by Congress? Were they successful? Why or why not?

3. Give examples where departments in the federal bureaucracy have helped to block the President's program. Give arguments both pro and con for extending the President's personal control over the bureaucracy.

4. List the various sources of presidential influence or power in the President's relations with Congress. Are they adequate in terms of a President getting most of his programs through Congress? Rate the performances of Presidents Kennedy, Johnson and Nixon in terms of effectively using the

power resources at their disposal to get most of what they wanted from Congress.

5. What are the strong points and weaknesses of the presidency and Congress as governmental institutions capable of taking actions required to meet the nation's domestic needs?

6. Some political scientists have argued that we are living in a period of essentially "presidential government" in the United States, where the presidency is the dominant branch. Would you agree with this assessment in terms of domestic affairs? Are there any additional powers that you think the President should be granted in domestic affairs?

7. Describe the present structure and operations of the Executive Office of the President. Evaluate the strengths and weaknesses of the White House staff system. What improvements would you suggest in terms of the White House staff's operations?

8. Could the vice presidency be made more important in terms of domestic affairs? Would a stronger vice presidency correspondingly weaken the powers of the presidency? If so, would this be desirable in terms of the overall strength of the federal government?

Bibliography*

Books

Bernstein, Carl and Woodward, Bob. *All the President's Men.* New York: Simon and Schuster, 1974.

Burns, James MacGregor. "The Central Decision Makers," *Presidential Government: The Crucible of Leadership.* Boston: Houghton Mifflin Company, 1973, Chapter IV.

Cronin, Thomas E. and Greenberg, Sanford D., eds. *The Presidential Advisory System.* New York: Harper and Row, 1969.

de Grazia, Alfred. "The Myth of the President." *Republic in Crisis.* New York: Federal Legal Publications, Inc., 1965, Chapter V.

James, Dorothy Buckton. "Prometheus Bound?" *The Contemporary Presidency.* New York: Western Publishing Company, Inc., 1969. A Pegasus original.

Johnson, Donald Bruce and Walker, Jack L., eds. *The Dynamics of the American Presidency.* New York: John Wiley and Sons, Inc.,1964, Sections VII, VIII and IX.

White, Theodore. *The Making of the President 1972.* New York: Atheneum, 1972.

Young, Donald. *American Roulette: The History and Dilemma of the Vice Presidency.* New York: Holt, Rinehart and Winston, 1972.

Articles

Thomas, Norman C. and Baade, Hans W. eds. "The Institutionalized Presidency." *Law and Contemporary Problems,* Vol. 35, No 3 (Summer, 1970): 427-625.

Thomas, Norman C. and Baade, Hans W., eds. "The Institutionalized Presi- Formulation: The Task Force Device." *Public Administration Review,* Vol. XXIX (September/October, 1969): 459-470.

Zentner, Joseph L. "Presidential Transitions and the Perpetuation of Programs: The Johnson-Nixon Experience." The *Western Political Quarterly,* Vol. XXV, No. 1 (March, 1972): 5-15.

*Many of the items listed in the bibliography for Chapter IV are relevant here. Therefore, such items will not be repeated. The list of references included are those particularly relevant to the presidency in domestic affairs and not included previously.

CHAPTER 6
The Presidency in Foreign Affairs

One of President Harry S. Truman's most publicized remarks on the presidency is "The buck stops here." Nowhere is the statement more true than in respect to the President's role in foreign policy. In contrast to the domestic environment, the President is faced with few limiting powers in the conduct of foreign policy. Whatever happens or doesn't happen in foreign affairs is directly associated with the President. He gets the credit when policy is a success and gets the blame when policy fails. More than any other institution and more than any other individual, the President symbolizes the United States in foreign affairs. Aided by a vast array of institutions, the President has legal as well as political authority and is ultimately responsible for the conduct of foreign affairs.

Constitutional Provisions

Article II, Section 2 of the Constitution provides the President with specific grants of power both as commander in chief and chief diplomat. Thus he commands the two major instruments in the conduct of foreign affairs, i.e., the Department of State and the Department of Defense. Obviously, there are other instruments of the federal government that are involved in foreign affairs but they are tangential to the foreign policy process. (For example, the Department of Agriculture has a direct concern with respect to wheat sales to the Soviet Union and the exportation and importation of food products.) The general policy direction and decisions are primarily in the hands of the President, who usually operates through the Department of State.

Even more important than the specific legal grants of power, however, are the judicial interpretations and practices arising out of the requirements of government and the political system. For example, the Supreme Court explains the inherent and exclusive powers of the federal government in foreign affairs in the case of *United States v. Curtiss-Wright Export Corporation* (1936).

> It results that the investment of the federal government with the powers of external sovereignty did not depend upon the affirmative grants of the Constitution. The powers to declare and wage war, to conclude peace, to make treaties, to maintain diplomatic relations with other sovereignties, if they had never been mentioned in the Constitution, would have been vested in the federal government as necessary concomitants of nationality. . . . As a member of the family of nations, the right and power of the United States in that field are equal to the right and power of the other members of the international family. Otherwise, the United States is not completely sovereign.

Treaties and Executive Agreements

Two of the major procedures in dealing with foreign countries are treaties and executive agreements. Although treaties are specifically noted in the Constitution, executive agreements are not; yet this kind of agreement has become one of the President's most powerful instruments in dealing with other nations.

Article II, Section 2 of the Constitution states: "He shall have power by and with the advice and consent of the Senate to make treaties provided two-thirds of the Senators present concur." Thus the treaty-making power of the President is directly tied to the Senate, which has a clear check in this field.

This was clearly demonstrated after World War I when President Woodrow Wilson attempted to commit the United States to the League of Nations. President Wilson was committed to the creation of a League of Nations to ensure the preservation of peace and the right of self-determination of all nations. During the elections of 1918 he appealed for Democratic majorities in both the House and Senate in order to have congressional support in his postwar negotiations. However, the appeal failed. Not only did the electorate return Republican majorities in both houses of Congress, but also his appeal appeared to downgrade the Republican effort in the war and therefore offended Republican party leaders. Thus the stage was set for a Republican-controlled Senate to strike back at the Democratic President.

Returning from Paris, President Wilson presented to the Senate the treaty with the League of Nations that he had negotiated. It was referred to the Senate Foreign Relations Committee under the chairmanship of Republican Senator Henry Cabot Lodge. From July 1919 until January 1920, it was assessed and debated; it was reported out of committee with a number of reservations attached to it by Senator Lodge. Finally submitted to a vote it failed to get the necessary two-thirds majority (the vote was 49 yes to 35 no).

Wilson was uncompromising in demanding approval of the treaty as he had originally negotiated it, but Senator Lodge, equally unyielding, demanded revisions to protect the United States. According to one noted historian:

> Thus the Treaty, with the revamped Lodge reservations, received the votes of a majority of the senators but of fewer than two-thirds of those present. Twenty-one Democrats broke away from administration dictation and voted for ratification. Had only seven of the remaining twenty-three done likewise, the Treaty would have been approved 56 to 28. Such a result however, would hardly have changed history, for the ill and stubborn President would almost certainly have refused to ratify the Treaty with the reservations that he had repeatedly denounced as nullification. In any event, the Treaty was dead.[1]

This lesson in the problems of treaty-making was not lost on Presidents following Woodrow Wilson. Most of them resort primarily to executive agreements in conducting foreign policy. Indeed, over the past twenty years, there have been more than 2,000 executive agreements concluded and fewer than 300 treaties. There are limits, of course, to the scope of executive agreements. In areas of danger, and crucial national security commitments, where the public voice is likely to be well articulated and discussions and debates motivated in Congress, the President will probably resort to treaties. For example, it would be virtually impossible for the President to commit the United States to an organization such as the United Nations with all of the future involvements this implies, without having the treaty approved by the United States Senate. On the other hand when an immediate or rapid response is required, an executive agreement is likely to be used rather than a treaty, which involves the relatively long and tedious process of approval by two-thirds of the Senate.

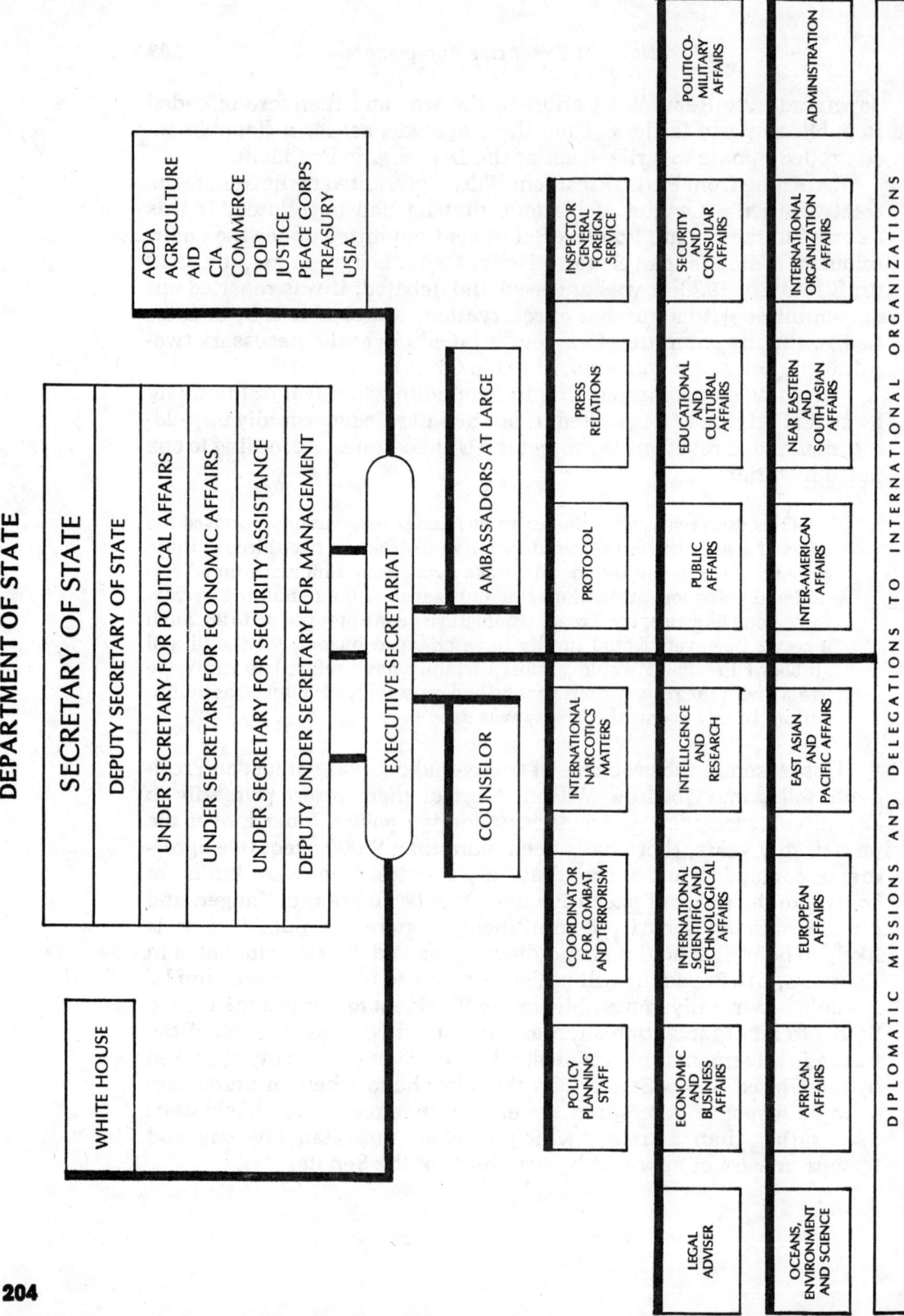

DEPARTMENT OF STATE

SECRETARY OF STATE

- DEPUTY SECRETARY OF STATE
- UNDER SECRETARY FOR POLITICAL AFFAIRS
- UNDER SECRETARY FOR ECONOMIC AFFAIRS
- UNDER SECRETARY FOR SECURITY ASSISTANCE
- DEPUTY UNDER SECRETARY FOR MANAGEMENT

WHITE HOUSE

ACDA
AGRICULTURE
AID
CIA
COMMERCE
DOD
JUSTICE
PEACE CORPS
TREASURY
USIA

EXECUTIVE SECRETARIAT

- AMBASSADORS AT LARGE
- COUNSELOR

- PRESS RELATIONS
- PROTOCOL
- INTERNATIONAL NARCOTICS MATTERS
- COORDINATOR FOR COMBAT AND TERRORISM
- POLICY PLANNING STAFF

- INSPECTOR GENERAL FOREIGN SERVICE
- EDUCATIONAL AND CULTURAL AFFAIRS
- PUBLIC AFFAIRS
- INTELLIGENCE AND RESEARCH
- INTERNATIONAL SCIENTIFIC AND TECHNOLOGICAL AFFAIRS
- ECONOMIC AND BUSINESS AFFAIRS
- LEGAL ADVISER

- POLITICO-MILITARY AFFAIRS
- SECURITY AND CONSULAR AFFAIRS
- NEAR EASTERN AND SOUTH ASIAN AFFAIRS
- INTER-AMERICAN AFFAIRS
- EAST ASIAN AND PACIFIC AFFAIRS
- EUROPEAN AFFAIRS
- AFRICAN AFFAIRS
- OCEANS, ENVIRONMENT AND SCIENCE

- ADMINISTRATION
- INTERNATIONAL ORGANIZATION AFFAIRS

DIPLOMATIC MISSIONS AND DELEGATIONS TO INTERNATIONAL ORGANIZATIONS

Source: U.S. Department of State

The Department of State

It is clear that the President as a single individual cannot personally look after the day-to-day operations in foreign relations nor personally deal with many short-range policy considerations. This is the primary function of the Department of State headed by the Secretary of State, who is the President's chief Cabinet adviser on foreign policy and coordinator of the major instrument of foreign policy.

The diplomatic corps, which forms an integral part of the Department of State, is controlled by the President through the Secretary of State. Therefore, in every country of the world with which the United States has diplomatic relations, there is a personal representative of the President—an ambassador who controls a staff for the prime purpose of representing the United States and the President. It is through this structure that the President gets a wealth of information regarding not only the internal dynamics of these countries but their policies and attitudes toward the United States.

The Department of State is a complex administrative structure headed by the Secretary of State. He is the personal choice of the President and serves only at the discretion of the President. The Secretary of State ranks first among the Cabinet members. This was clearly demonstrated when President Nixon resigned. He sent his letter of resignation to the highest ranking Cabinet officer, Secretary of State Henry A. Kissinger.

The relationship between the President and his Secretary of State is a very personal one. The character, personality and competence of the Secretary of State have a great impact on the total power exercised by the President in foreign affairs. As an extension of presidential power, the Secretary of State can expand this power by his political astuteness and ability to deal with foreign nations.

Secretary of State Kissinger's involvement in bringing about a Mideast Peace in 1973, for example, added considerably to the prestige and power of the Nixon administration (albeit short-lived because of Watergate). On the other hand, the secret and perhaps questionable involvement of Secretary of State Kissinger and the Central Intelligence Agency in the affairs of Chile and the overthrow of its president, Salvador Allende during 1970-73, diminished the prestige of the Secretary of State and the administration. Perhaps as important, the revelation of these activities also brought into question the foreign policy posture of the Ford administration in 1974.

In any case, there is a close link which makes the fortunes of the

Secretary of State almost indistinguishable from those of the President. Dean Acheson, former Secretary of State, succinctly identified that relationship, stating:

> While the security of the country demands that considerations of foreign policy shall dominate the more parochial interest of finance or of military strategy and tactics, final decision and synthesis lie not in any of them, but in the presidency. To give the Secretary legal authority in these far flung fields would be to usurp the presidential office. But the best, even a good operation of government requires that the Secretary be able to advise about the most important of these matters from the point of their incidence on our foreign problems and policies. It requires too, that his advice be given great and respectful consideration. Unless the Secretary has the President's most intimate and abiding confidence and respect, he is only a diplomatic bureaucrat. He must not merely persuade the President but press him with all the means at his command to use the Presidential influence, authority, and where available, command to resolve national policy in accordance with the scale of values just mentioned.[2]

Although the Department of State is the key foreign affairs organization, there are a number of semiautonomous organizations that are loosely associated but act quite independently of the Department. These include the Agency for International Development, the Peace Corps, the United States Information Agency, and the Arms Control and Disarmament Agency. These four agencies have their own funds to dispense for their overseas operations, and in a number of instances, the agency heads have direct access to the President, bypassing the Secretary of State. As such, they can be considered additional organizations through which the President can direct foreign policy.

The Department of Defense

What has been said of the relationship between the Secretary of State and the President is also generally true of the Secretary of Defense and the President. The President, as commander in chief, commands the entire military establishment. His primary assistant in this matter is the Secretary of Defense. It is through him that the President has absolute control of all of the nation's military forces. Here again, the President cannot be involved in day-to-day operations of the military, in all aspects of weapons development, or in all considerations of force postures. Nevertheless it is with presidential authority that all of these things are done. The principle of civilian control

DEPARTMENT OF DEFENSE

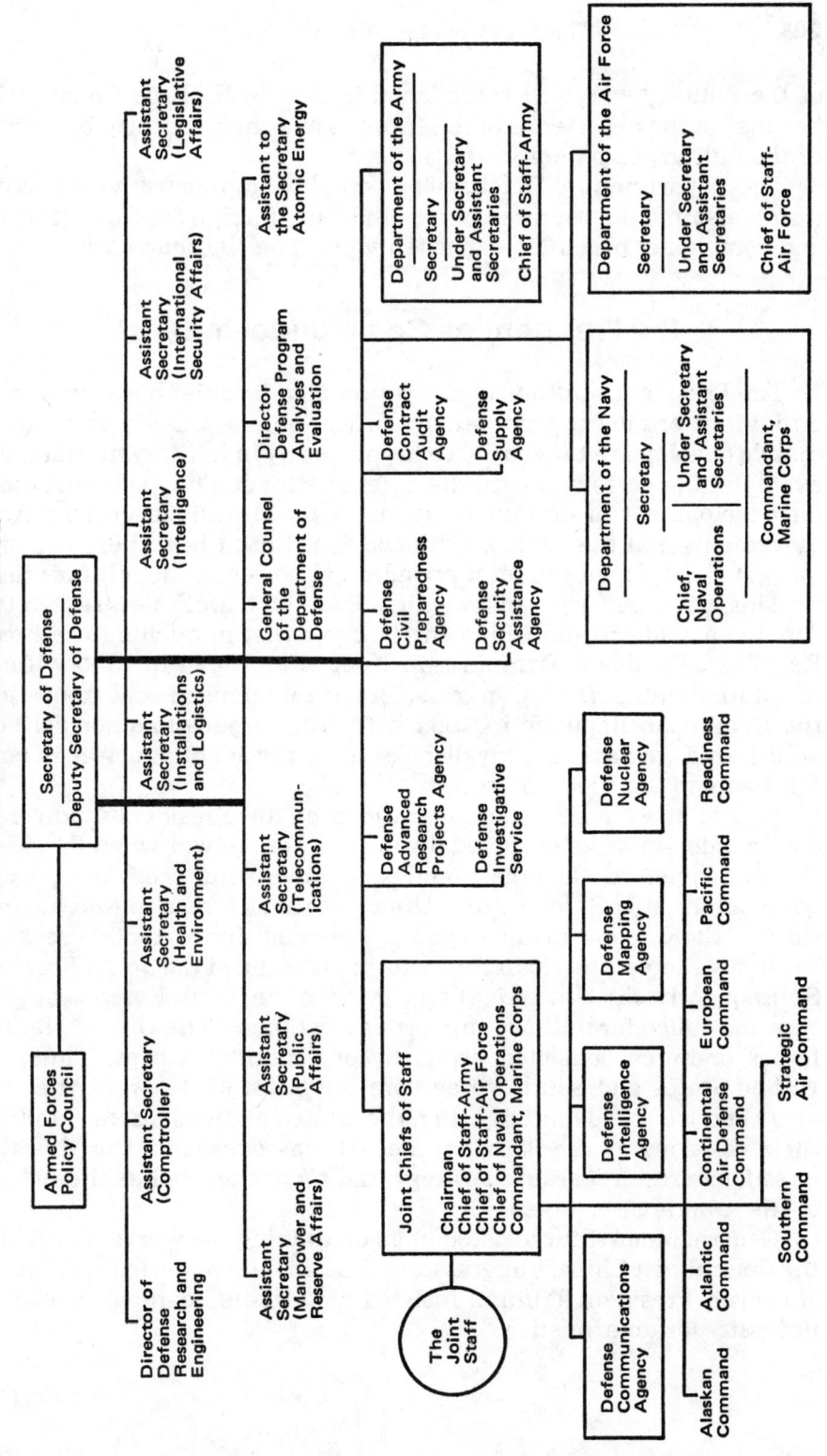

Source: Adapted from U.S. Government Organization Manual, 1974-75

Secretary of Defense
Deputy Secretary of Defense

- Armed Forces Policy Council

- Director of Defense Research and Engineering
- Assistant Secretary (Comptroller)
- Assistant Secretary (Health and Environment)
- Assistant Secretary (Intelligence)
- Assistant Secretary (Installations and Logistics)
- Assistant Secretary (International Security Affairs)
- Assistant Secretary (Legislative Affairs)

- Assistant Secretary (Manpower and Reserve Affairs)
- Assistant Secretary (Public Affairs)
- Assistant Secretary (Telecommunications)
- General Counsel of the Department of Defense
- Director Defense Program Analyses and Evaluation
- Assistant to the Secretary Atomic Energy

- Defense Advanced Research Projects Agency
- Defense Investigative Service
- Defense Civil Preparedness Agency
- Defense Security Assistance Agency
- Defense Contract Audit Agency
- Defense Supply Agency

Department of the Army
- Secretary
- Under Secretary and Assistant Secretaries
- Chief of Staff-Army

Department of the Navy
- Secretary
- Under Secretary and Assistant Secretaries
- Chief, Naval Operations
- Commandant, Marine Corps

Department of the Air Force
- Secretary
- Under Secretary and Assistant Secretaries
- Chief of Staff-Air Force

Joint Chiefs of Staff
- Chairman
- Chief of Staff-Army
- Chief of Staff-Air Force
- Chief of Naval Operations
- Commandant, Marine Corps

The Joint Staff

- Defense Communications Agency
- Defense Intelligence Agency
- Defense Mapping Agency
- Defense Nuclear Agency

- Alaskan Command
- Atlantic Command
- Continental Air Defense Command
- European Command
- Pacific Command
- Readiness Command
- Southern Command
- Strategic Air Command

of the military was well established in Article II of the Constitution because of the experience of the framers and their concern for the role of the military in a democratic society.

The Department of Defense is a complex administrative structure which also has its representatives in many foreign lands. The scope and complexity become clear when viewed on the schematic.

The President as Commander-in-Chief

The President's authority as commander-in-chief has virtually no limitations or checks from other political actors. Clearly any checks that do develop are tangential to his authority in military matters. For example, Congress can trim the defense budget, deny appropriations for development of certain weapons or for support of certain troop movements and has done so on occasion. But at best these are only marginal checks on the total presidential power in the military field.

This has been true historically. President McKinley sent 5,000 American soldiers into China in 1900 to assist in quelling the Boxer Rebellion; President Truman sent troops into Korea in 1950 without any authorization from Congress; President Johnson sent troops into the Dominican Republic in 1965 without reference to other political actors; and we have already discussed the presidential power in commitments to the Vietnamese war.

One of the clearest demonstrations of the President's power as commander-in-chief occurred during the Korean war when President Truman removed General Douglas A. MacArthur from his post as commander of U.S. forces and United Nations forces in Korea. After the North Koreans invaded South Korea in June, 1950, President Truman ordered American troops to go to the aid of the South Koreans. Subsequently, the United Nations branded the North Koreans aggressors and called for military support against them. The United Nations forces in Korea consisted primarily of American troops. Thus, the United States and South Korea bore the brunt of the war. After two years of retreat and hard fighting, the United Nations forces stabilized their positions at the 38th parallel. It was subsequent to this that questions arose regarding strategy and tactics as well as the politics of the American involvement.

General MacArthur insisted upon continuing the war and crushing the Communist Chinese aggressors who had intervened in the fighting. However, President Truman insisted on a limited campaign and the necessity for an armistice.

Contrary to all instructions by the President, who was supported by members of the United Nations and the Joint Chiefs of Staff of the United States, MacArthur issued a statement which said in part, "The enemy, therefore, must by now be painfully aware that a decision of the United Nations to depart from its tolerant effort to contain the war to the area of Korea, through an expansion of our military operations to its coastal areas and interior bases, would doom Red China to the risk of imminent military collapse."[3]

The Chinese, the United States and the United Nations were all surprised by this obvious threat to the very existence of the Chinese mainland. To President Truman this was the last straw in a series of political battles with MacArthur concerning the conduct of the Korean war. In an official statement to the White House press corps, President Truman stated:

> With deep regret, I have concluded that the General of the Army, Douglas MacArthur is unable to give his wholehearted support to the policies of the United States government and of the United Nations in manners pertaining to his official duties. In view of the specific responsibility which has been entrusted to me by the United Nations, I have decided that I must make a change of command in the far east. I have, therefore, relieved General MacArthur of his commands and have designated Lt. Gen. Mathew B. Ridgway as his successor.[4]

There were tremendous public and congressional outcries against the seemingly arbitrary decision of President Truman to remove a highly successful and popular general. Nevertheless, when the initial emotions passed and people objectively assessed the decision of President Truman, he was applauded for his actions. Indeed in his memoirs, General Ridgway concluded:

> President Truman's decision should act as a powerful safeguard against the time in some great future crisis when perhaps others may similarly be tempted to challenge the right of the President and his advisers to exercise the powers the Constitution grants them in the formulation of foreign policy.[5]

The National Security Council

The third organization directly involved as an extension of presidential power into the foreign policy field is the National Security Council. It was established by the National Security Act of 1947 for the purpose of advising the President on the integration and coordination of foreign, military, and domestic policies so as to achieve national security goals. It differs from the Departments of State and Defense in that it is a part of the executive office, directly under the control of the President, and generally free from congressional inquiry. However, as a staff agency with no command lines or organizations to implement its will, it usually must work through other agencies, such as the Department of Defense.

ORGANIZATION OF THE NATIONAL SECURITY COUNCIL

Chairman of the NSC – President of the United States
In his absence, the Vice President

    Secretary of State
    Secretary of Defense
    Director, Office of Emergency Preparedness
    Chairman, Joint Chiefs of Staff
    Director, Central Intelligence Agency

The President may ask any other individual to attend the Council meeting if he so desires. Indeed the President may use the National Security Council in any way he wishes. For example, President Eisenhower used to have formal meetings with the Council every week, whereas President Kennedy rarely used the organization.

The Central Intelligence Agency

The last major organization that assists the President in wielding power in foreign affairs is the Central Intelligence Agency. Although there is not much public knowledge on how the Central Intelligence Agency works nor on its expenditures, we do know that it is involved in intelligence gathering and in many cases intelligence operations overseas. All of its information is funneled to the President through the National Security Council. It, too, is a vast and complex organization. Its director is appointed by the President and selected according to criteria similar to those used for senior cabinet officers. However, it is presumed that the director of the CIA is not a political office holder but one who can serve succeeding administrations as well. He normally continues to serve as long as he can function effectively and efficiently in office.

Other Agencies and Individuals

Aside from these agencies, there are particular individuals and staffs which constitute informal, yet important instruments in presidential conduct and control of foreign affairs. On the White House staff, the President's special assistant for national security is a key member of the foreign policy elite. Henry Kissinger held this position in the Nixon administration until 1972, when he became Secretary of State, still retaining his position as special assistant. He continued in both capacities under President Ford. Other special assistants and aides play similar roles, although they do not have the power exercised by the special assistant. The Office of Management and Budget also plays a role in foreign policy by its involvement in coordination, programming and policy. It is a key instrument for the President in developing a systematic plan for the conduct of foreign affairs.

The following U.S. Agencies have resident personnel overseas:

American Battle Monuments Commission
Agency for International Development
Agriculture Department
Atomic Energy Commission
Bureau of Narcotics and Dangerous Drugs
Central Intelligence Agency
Commerce Department
Customs Department
Defense Department
Environmental Science Services Administration
Export-Import Bank
Federal Aviation Administration
Federal Bureau of Investigation
Foreign Agriculture Service
General Services Administration
Health, Education and Welfare Department
Housing and Urban Development Department
Immigration and Naturalization Service
Interior Department
Internal Revenue Service
Justice Department
Labor Department
Maritime Administration
National Aeronautics and
National Science Foundation
Peace Corps
Public Health Service
Smithsonian Institution
State Department
Tennessee Valley Authority
Transportation Department
Treasury Department
United States Information Agency
United States Travel Service
Veterans Administration

Adapted from *The New York Times*, January 18, 1971.

Other lesser agencies are also involved. Although we will not discuss them here, for they have specialized roles, it is useful to mention them: the National Aeronautics and Space Council, the Office of Emergency Preparedness, the Office of Science and Technology, the Office of Special Representative for Trade Negotiations, and the Council of Economic Advisors. All of these are agencies within the executive office and report directly to the President. They all become involved in foreign affairs now and then in varying degrees.

Clearly the President has a vast array of organizations working directly for him, extending his power to all areas of the world and to all sectors of the political system. These agencies place vast resources and manpower at the President's disposal. With these instruments and his legal authority, the President exercises a vast amount of power, relatively unchecked, in the foreign area.

Our purpose here, however, is not to discuss the complexities of the administrative structure. We have pointed out the major organizational structures primarily to show the instruments which the President commands to carry out his power in foreign affairs. It is equally important to note that there are few political actors in our system with sufficient countervailing powers to affect this vast organization, or to counter the legal and exclusive powers of the President in foreign relations. This must, of course, be qualified by the fact that in the final analysis, the President must explain, rationalize, and defend his foreign policy in the eyes of the American people.

Political Aspects of Presidential Power

To this point we have been discussing primarily the President's legal power and the power that develops from his organizational control. Let us briefly turn to the other aspects of power that evolve from his role as chief foreign policymaker and the commander-in-chief. There is a distinctly *political aspect* to this power. Not only is the President responsible for coordinating the activities of all of the vast numbers in this organizational structure, but he must become involved in developing the necessary legislation, appropriations and public support for those programs directly associated with foreign policy.

This raises the issue of constituencies with which the President must deal in his foreign policy sphere. There is a domestic constituency to whom he is ultimately responsible for his actions in foreign policy. There is also the congressional constituency, in which he must develop some support for appropriations for foreign initiatives and to maintain the effectiveness of the military institution. And thirdly, the President has an overseas constituency. That constituency is made up of allies, and countries that look to the United States for military or economic help, as well as those countries that may consider the United States an enemy. The President also has a constituency made up of the press, which can become a countervailing power in the foreign policy field. This was well demonstrated during the Vietnam war; it was the press that first began to question not only the role of American troops in Vietnam, but also the tactical operations with respect to the South Vietnamese and the Vietcong.

In foreign policy the President must be acutely aware of the impact his statements and his effectiveness in policy have on these various constituencies. He obviously can attempt to use his power to persuade, to mobilize public opinion, and to develop consensus in all of these constituencies regarding the correctness of his policies. For example, when President Ford, upon taking office, announced that Kissinger would remain Secretary of State in his administration at least for the foreseeable future, it was taken as a distinct signal to allies and others that U.S. foreign policy initiatives established under President Nixon would continue. President Ford was announcing the continuity of these policies not only to the overseas constituency but also to his domestic constituency.

Symbolic Role

Another aspect of the President's power is based on the symbolic roles given to him as President of the United States. Whatever the President says, whatever he does and wherever he goes, he represents the United States. Indeed he symbolizes the country and it is presumed that he can mobilize all of the resources of the United States to carry out foreign policy goals. Some scholars would say that the President is not only the chief executive of the political system but the monarch of the political system, with the trappings of king inherently combined with those of chief executive.

Thus we can see that the President has the legal base, the organizational instruments, and the political role, and symbolizes the United States in the foreign policy field. The combination of all of these various roles and their inherent power gives him virtually unlimited scope in what he can do in the name of the United States in the foreign policy field.

Countervailing Power

There are, of course, certain countervailing powers to presidential authority. But in contrast to checks and balances in the domestic sphere these limitations in many cases, are ineffective. The ultimate countervailing power is the attitude and opinions of the American people. As we have suggested, the attitude of the American people to the U. S. involvement in the Vietnam War was the direct cause of President Johnson's refusal to run in 1968, and led to the Vietnamization policy and withdrawal of troops from Vietnam. In viewing other political actors, one can identify some potential for checking presidential power. Congress can conduct hearings to assess and study foreign policy. It can withhold appropriations; it can question the rationale behind foreign policy; it can assess military posture. But in the long run, Congress has very little power in terms of its legal and political base, its symbolic or its organizational structure, to compete with the President. All of the vast informational sources on foreign policy and the major institutions that carry out foreign policy are directly under the control of the President. Congress has no institutions or sources that can compete with them. What makes it even more difficult for other political actors to check his power is the fact that the President can mobilize a vast number of resources to persuade the public, to articulate policy goals, and to mobilize his constituencies in support of particular policies.

Informal Checks

Informal limiting powers are inherent in the bureaucracy, which by its very character has its own interests, motivations and policies. In the vast bureaucratic maze, presidential policies and power can become diffused and obscured—simply through bureaucratic inertia and resistance. We will discuss this further in the chapter on bureaucracy.

There are also a number of special interest groups that have an impact on foreign policy decisions. Such groups include the Council of Foreign Relations, the RAND Corporation, the Brookings Institution, government commissions, and individuals in the academic community. Some scholars consider these groups and individuals as part of a foreign policy elite whose influence is more important than that of Congress or the American people. Such groups can develop alternative policy positions, criticize the President, and influence the people through the mass media. By virtue of their recognized competence in the field of foreign affairs and their linkages to the academic and business world, such groups can provide some resistance and checks to presidential power.

Other Limitations on Presidential Power

There are certain subtle limitations to the President's power, which few people understand. Any President who takes office is faced with a number of ongoing commitments made by previous Presidents. For example, the United States is directly involved in the North Atlantic Treaty Organization (NATO). It has a primary role and commitment to the United Nations, the Organization of American States (OAS), and a number of other regional and international organizations. Moreover, the United States has agreements and treaties with a number of countries that range from defense to economics. The President is thus committed to a vast array of arrangements and agreements made by previous Presidents for the United States. He could abrogate these only under the most dire circumstances.

Moreover, the United States is also committed to act in certain accepted ways in the international field and in accordance with democratic ideology. This presupposes that the United States will not become a military aggressor; will defend the rights of smaller nations; will adhere to the principles of international law; and will not act in an arbitrary unprincipled fashion.

The combination of previous commitments, need for policy continuity, and tradition of American actions in foreign policy provides a boundary beyond which a President dare not venture. And finally, of course, there is the problem of developing consensus among political actors within the Department of State, the Department of Defense, the National Security Council and the CIA. These various institutions have their own power structures and within them are political actors, each struggling to insure that a particular perception of foreign policy is accepted and acted upon. Thus, while the President's power and resources give him virtually unlimited powers they can also be the basis for checking of his power.

Roger Hilsman, Assistant Secretary of State for Far Eastern affairs under President Kennedy, observing this phenomenon, stated:

> The power of the President in sum is vast, but it is not so much the power to command as the power to lead, to persuade, bargain and maneuver in the building of a consensus. It is this central fact that

President Truman had in mind when he chuckled over the difficulties he foresaw for President Eisenhower. It was also this central fact that Kennedy had in mind when he spoke of the inner club and their trials and tribulations in attempting to keep the government together and all different participants on board. And it was this central fact that Neustadt had in mind when he spoke of the half observed realities of presidents in sneakers, stirrups in hand, trying to induce so many different power holders to go along.[6]

The President's great powers in the field of foreign affairs do not necessarily lead to great policies. It requires an astute knowledge of politics and a deep understanding of foreign nations to be able to balance conflicting interests, satisfy competing constituencies, and protect the national security of the United States. With all of the instruments, resources, legal, political and symbolic power in hand, the President still must integrate these into a coherent policy. In so doing, he has virtually a free hand, limited only by a public that is aroused with difficulty, and a Congress that has limited countervailing powers.

In viewing the problems of the presidency in foreign affairs, Dean Acheson observes:

> The capacity for decision, however, does not produce, of itself wise decisions. For that a President needs a better eye and more intuition and coordination than the best batters in the major leagues. If his score is not far better than theirs he will be rated a failure... A President is not merely coping with the deliveries of others. He is called upon to influence and move to some degree his own country and the world around it to a purpose that he envisions... If he tries to do it all himself—to "be his own Secretary of State" or Defense, as the phrase goes—he will soon become too exhausted and immersed in manure and weed-killer to direct anything wisely.[7]

Notes

1. Julius Pratt, *A History of United States Foreign Policy* (Englewood Cliffs, N.J.: Prentice-Hall, 1960) p. 521.
2. Dean Acheson, "The President and the Secretary of State" in *The Secretary of State* (Englewood Cliffs, N.J.: Prentice-Hall, 1960), pp. 40-41.
3. Margaret Truman, *Harry S. Truman* (New York: William Morrow, 1973), p. 559.
4. *Ibid.*, pp. 562-563.
5. As quoted in Margaret Truman, pp. 565-566.
6. Roger Hilsman, *The Politics of Policy Making in Defense and Foreign Affairs* (New York: Harper and Row, 1971), p. 31.
7. Dean Acheson, *Present at the Creation* (New York: W. W. Norton & Co. Inc., 1969), pp. 928-929.

Selected Readings

Although there are a number of ways that a President can be checked in exercising his power in the domestic field, most scholars agree that there are few such restraints on presidential power in foreign affairs. He can call upon a vast bureaucracy, intelligence service, military establishment, and other resources to carry out foreign policy with little reference to Congress, the judiciary, or the people.

It is this fact that is addressed by Henry Steele Commager in the selection for this chapter. Commager decries the "unlimited power of the Executive in foreign relations," and argues that such power is not justified in "normal" times. In a brief historical overview, he points out examples of the unlimited use of executive power and the problems it can create. He is particularly concerned with executive agreements. Finally, he discusses what must be done to establish a balance of power between the President, Congress, the people, and foreign states. He concludes, "As we have greater power than any other nation, so we should display greater moderation in using it, greater humility in justifying it, and magnanimity in withholding it." Students will find here a reasoned argument for limiting the presidential power in foreign affairs. Interesting questions are raised by his analysis. How can Commager's suggestions about congressional checks actually be implemented? In what way can the executive withhold power for the sake of moderation and humility? Do people expect the President to act positively and forcefully in foreign policy? How does this differ, if at all, from attitudes on domestic policy?

6.1

The Misuse of Power

HENRY STEELE COMMAGER

In the historic steel seizure case of 1952 Justice Jackson said that, "what is at stake is the equilibrium of our constitutional system." Now, after 20 years marked by repeated, and almost routine, invasions by the executive of the war-making powers assigned by the Constitution to Congress, we can see that more is at stake even than the constitutional principle of the separation of powers. At stake is the age-long effort of men to fix effective limits to government, the reconciliation of the claims of freedom and of security, the fateful issue of peace or war, an issue fateful not for the American people alone, nor alone for the stricken peoples of southeast Asia but for the entire world.

It is not sufficiently realized that the kind of military intervention we have witnessed in the past quarter century is, if not wholly unprecedented, clearly a departure from a long and deeply rooted tradition. Since the Neutrality Proclamation of 1793 that tradition has been one of nonintervention. Washington, and his cabinet, refused to intervene in the wars between France and her enemies even though the United States was far more deeply "committed" to come to the aid of France by the terms of the Treaty of Alliance of 1778, than she was to intervene in Vietnam by the terms of the SEATO Treaty. Notwithstanding almost universal sympathy for the peoples of Latin America who sought to throw off Spanish rule, we did not intervene militarily in that conflict. The ideas of "Manifest Destiny" and "Young America" dictated support to peoples everywhere struggling to throw off ancient tyrannies, but no President intervened militarily in the Greek struggle for independence from Turkey, the Italian uprisings against Austria, the Hungarian revoltion of 1848 or other internal revolutions of that fateful year, Garibaldi's fight for Italian independence, the many Irish uprisings against Britain, in Ireland and even in Canada—close to home, that—or even *mirabile dictu*, the ten-year war of the Cubans against their Spanish overlords from 1868–78. Nor, in more modern times, did Presidents see fit to intervene on behalf of Jewish victims of pogroms, Turkish genocide against

Reprinted by permission of *The New Republic*, © 1971 Harrison-Blaine of New Jersey, Inc.

Armenians, Franco's overthrow of the Loyalist regime in Spain. Whether such abstention was always wise is a question we need not raise here. The point here is that in none of these situations did the Executive think it proper, or legal, to use his powers as Commander-in-Chief or as chief organ of foreign relations to commit the United States to military intervention in distant lands. With the sole exception of McKinley's unnecessary participation in the Boxer Expedition, that concept of executive powers belongs to the past quarter century. And if it should be asked why the United States should refrain from intervention in the internal struggles of other nations, even when her sympathies are deeply involved and her interests enlisted, it is perhaps sufficient to say that few of us would be prepared to endorse a principle that would have justified the intervention of Britain and France in the American Civil War—on behalf of the Confederacy of course—and that in international law you cannot really have it both ways.

The unlimited power of the Executive in foreign relations is no longer justified as an emergency power, but asserted to be a normal and almost routine exercise of executive authority. Lincoln pushed his authority to the outward limits of what was constitutionally permissible, but confessed, with characteristic humility that the emergency required him to do what he did, and asked Congress to give retroactive sanction to his acts. No such humility characterizes what we may call The Johnson-Nixon Theory of Executive Authority. Thus President Johnson asserted that he did not need the authority of the Tonkin Gulf Resolution to justify his bombardment of North Vietnam, for he already had that: thus President Nixon's assistant attorney general asserted that the President's authority to invade Cambodia *"must* be conceded by even those who read executive authority narrowly" (June 16, 1970). Why must it be? Certainly not because of the persuasive character of the arguments advanced by this distinguished counsel, for that character is wanting.

The new commitments are not, as generally in the past, *ad hoc* and even fortuitous, but calculated and ideological. Thus we do not drop bombs on Vietnam or Laos because "American blood has been shed on American soil"—Polk's excuse. Nor does the President respond to an imperative like the attack on Fort Sumter or even to U-boat warfare. Nor do recent Presidents presume to act—like President Truman—in response to a United Nations decision. Now Presidents act to "contain communism" or to protect "vital interests" 9000 miles away, or to fulfill "commitments" that are never made clear and that other nations (pledged to them just as solemnly) do not think require military fulfillment (e.g. the SEATO "commitments" that bind Britain, France, Pakistan, etc.). And they do so by programs that are by their very nature open-ended and tenacious. Thus Secretary Rusk's assertion in 1966 that "no would-be aggressor should suppose that the absence of a defense treaty, congressional declaration, or United States military presence, grants immunity to aggression"; the key words, for our purposes, are "absence of treaty" and "absence of congressional declaration." For this left only the alternative of the application of the executive power, unilaterally in the international arena, unilaterally in the constitutional arena too.

As power corrupts, the possession of great power encourages and even creates conditions in which it seems imperative to use it, and the concentration of that power vastly increases the risks of misuse. We had one example of that as early as 1846: what began as a simple vindication of a boundary line ended up as a war in which we tore Mexico in two.

Now the original assumption of our Constitution framers, that Presidents could not engage in war on their own, was greatly strengthened by the elementary fact that they could not if they wanted to, because there were no armies or navies with which to war. At the time of the ratification of the Constitution the United States Army consisted of 719 officers and men. Our armed forces increased to some 20,000 by 1840, to 28,000 on the eve of The Civil War and to 38,000 by 1890. Even in 1915, with the world locked in mortal combat, the armed forces of the United States were less than 175,000. With the worst will, there was little that Presidents could do with these forces. Now we have a wholly new situation. Not only do we keep some three million men under arms at all times—since 1951 the number has rarely fallen below that—but we have the greatest and most formidable armaments that any nation ever commanded.

The problem is complicated by a new terminology: the obsolescence of older terms that once had clear legal meaning, and the emergence of new terms, some of them (like "combat" meaning only ground troops, or "protective reaction") designed to deceive. Thus it is conceded that the President has authority to "repel" attacks, but the term has been drained of meaning. When we launch or support invasions of Cambodia and Laos not to defeat the enemy or to conquer territory but to enable us to withdraw, anything can be called a protective reaction. Besides, it has become a truism that all wars are defensive. Hitler claimed that his assaults on Denmark and Norway were "defensive."

Even the constitutional concept of a declaration of war has been drained of meaning by the presidential interpretation of the Tonkin Bay Resolution. Thus in congressional testimony in 1967, it was formally asserted that that resolution, together with the SEATO treaty, constituted a "functional declaration of war"—thus combining an original contribution to international law with repeal of an important provision of the Constitution.

There is a final consideration of importance: the growing role of the Executive Agreement—a method for bypassing the requirements of treaty-making. Unknown to article II of the Constitution, this emerged early as a useful method of disposing of routine business that did not rise to the dignity of a treaty. Until very recent times it was customarily used only for such routine business as tariff agreements, postal conventions, patent arrangements and so forth, the great majority of which were negotiated in pursuance of congressional authorization. As late as 1930 the United States concluded 25 treaties and only nine executive agreements. But in 1968 it concluded 16 treaties and 266 executive agreements. As of January 1, 1969 the US had a total of 909 treaties and 3973 executive agreements. And while the great majority of these were still concerned with routine matters, a substantial number dealt with problems that in the past had been considered proper subjects of the treaty-making power.

In 1940 Attorney General Jackson spelled out the permissible and impermissible limits of the use of executive agreements in foreign affairs: "The President's power over foreign relations, while delicate, plenary and exclusive, is not unlimited. Some negotiations involve commitments as to the future which would carry an obligation to exercise powers vested in the congress. Such presidential arrangements are customarily submitted for ratification . . . of the Senate before the future legislative power of the country is committed."

And he made a distinction between what was proper and what was improper relevant to the current scene: "The transaction now proposed represents only an exchange with no statutory requirement for the embodiment thereof in any treaty and *involving no promises or undertakings* by the United States that might raise the question of the propriety of incorporation in a treaty." (Hackworth V, 407) It is superfluous to point out that the use of executive agreements in such areas as joint use of air bases and joint defense of them in Spain, repudiates these carefully drawn limitations. For these, and similar agreements, do "carry promises and undertakings of future action." They *are* properly the subject for treaties.

Great questions of constitutional law are great not because they are complicated legal or technical questions, but because they embody issues of high policy, of public good, of morality. We should therefore consider the problem of the presidential authority to make war not merely in the light of constitutional precedents, but in the light of wisdom and justice.

In 1967 Under Secretary of State Nicholas Katzenbach asserted that "history has surely vindicated the wisdom of the flexibility of the conduct of our foreign affairs." Two years later Senator McGee stated that, "the decision-making process may be reduced by events to a single day, or even hours. On more than one occasion the time allotted by crisis incidents to those who must make the decisions has been less than the time it would take to assemble a quorum of the Congress." Is that true? Have Presidents been well advised, in the light of history, to bypass Congress in using American armed forces overseas? Would consultation with the Congress, would even second-thoughts and delay, have made a difference detrimental to national, or world, interests? Was it really of vital importance that General Jackson pursue the Seminoles and hang Arbuthnot and Ambrister? Would the fate of Texas have been different had Polk consulted the Congress before launching a war? Had he done so he might have escaped the name that has clung to him through history— "Polk the Mendacious." Was it essential to bombard Greytown on the Mosquito coast in 1854—would we do that now? Grant himself learned what a mistake it was to send troops to the Dominican Republic in 1869, for a Senate, perhaps more strong minded than later Senates, refused to back him up or to allow him to go through with his plans for annexation. Was McKinley wise to commit 5000 troops to the invasion of China in 1900, and would we do this today in a comparable situation? Our commitment to the provisions of the constitution of the Organization of American States is perhaps sufficient commentary on the wisdom of our many military interventions in the Caribbean, and President Wilson's resort to an international conference—that rescued us from an ugly situation in Mexico—sufficient commentary on the wisdom of the Pershing expedition into Mexico. Would any President launch such an expedition today? In 1919 the hapless Jacob Abrams was sentenced to jail for 20 years for distributing leaflets criticizing the Archangel and

Siberian expeditions: at the time he had only the consolation of being the occasion for one of the greatest of all Justice Holmes's opinions. If he were living now he might have the dubious consolation of knowing that almost everyone agrees with his argument. We have paid a high price in the long-range enmity of the Russians for that particular folly. A strong case can be made out for FDR's destroyer bases exchange and for extending protection to Greenland and Iceland, but is it conceivable that the Congress would have denied him the right to carry through these programs?

If we turn to the many examples of presidential war-making in the past 20 years we are, I submit, impressed by the fact that in almost every instance the Congress was actually in session and available for consultation: the Korean intervention, the landing of troops in Lebanon, the Bay of Pigs, the occupation of the Dominican Republic by President Johnson, and the successive series of forays into Vietnam, Cambodia and Laos.

There is one further observation that may be instructive. Almost every instance of the use of presidential force in the past has been against small, backward, and distraught peoples. Call the role of the victims of presidential application of force in the past: Spanish Florida, Honduras, Santo Domingo, Nicaragua, Panama, Haiti, Guatemala, a China torn by civil war, a Mexico plagued by civil war, a Russia and a Vietnam likewise plagued. It is a sobering fact that Presidents do not thus rush in with the weapons of war to bring Britain, France, Italy, Russia, or Japan to heel. Would we have bombarded Southampton to collect a debt? Would we have sent an expedition into Rome to protect Americans against a threat from a fascist government? Would we have precipitated a war with Britain over a boundary dispute in Maine? Would we land marines in France if customs collectors did not behave themselves? Would we bomb Russia for years if shots were fired—without any hits—at an American vessel? And does it comport with the honor and dignity of a great nation to indulge its Chief Executive in one standard of conduct for the strong and another for the weak?

This record does not justify Mr. Katzenbach's rosy view of the use of presidential authority, nor is there a single instance that bears out Senator McGee's assertion that "on more than one occasion the time allotted by crisis . . . has been less than the time it would take to assemble a quorum of the Congress."

"Reason may mislead us, experience must be our guide," said James Madison at the constitutional convention. By "reason" he meant theory or doctrine. Experience must indeed be our guide, and on the basis of a century-and-three-quarters of experience, confirmed by a quarter century of intensive modern experience, we can say with some confidence that: with the exception of the Civil War—a special case—and perhaps of the Korean War where the President acted in conformity to the decision of the UN Security Council—there are no instances in our history where the use of war-making powers by the Executive without authority of Congress was clearly and incontrovertibly required by the nature of the emergency that the nation faced. On the contrary, in almost every instance the long-run interests of the nation would have been better promoted by consultation and delay. We can also say that great principles of government are not to be decided on the basis of the *argumen-*

tum ad horrendum—by conjuring up hypothetical dangers and insisting that the structure and operations of government must be based on the chance of these rather than on experience. It was to this kind of argument that Thomas Jefferson said, "Shake not your raw-head and bloody-bones at me."

It is possible to mitigate the dangers of the misuse of the executive power in the war-making arena? I think it is, and venture a few recommendations.

What Justice Jackson said in the steel seizure case is relevant now as then. "Power to legislate for emergencies belongs in the hands of Congress, but only Congress itself can prevent power from slipping through its fingers." That power has been slipping from the hands of Congress. That Congress has the power to reverse this trend should be clear. It can pass the Javits Bill designed to limit the use of armed forces in the absence of a declaration of war or affirmative authority from the Congress; this together with the Fulbright resolution on national commitments and the Cooper-Church amendment might provide an effective curb on presidential war-making.

I suggest also that the Senate meet the argument of emergency, hypothetical as it is, by creating a permanent committee, a quorum of whose members would remain permanently in Washington, with authority to require that the President consult with the Senate or the Congress before taking any action that might involve the nation in armed conflict. Such a committee could be counted on to respond to a genuine emergency just as promptly as would the President, and counted on, too, to present the case for caution.

The Senate should create a standing committee to consult with the President on all executive agreements, and with authority to designate those of sufficient importance to require submission to the Senate as treaties.

And finally, the Congress should reinvigorate the power of the purse, that power which, as James Madison said, "may be regarded as the most complete and effectual weapon with which any Constitution can arm the immediate representatives of the people." It should use with more particularity than in the past the power to limit the place and the manner of the introduction of American arms and armed forces.

The problems that confront us cannot be solved by debates over precedents, by appeals to constitutional probity, or by confronting presidential power with congressional. These may mitigate but will not resolve our crisis. For all of these gestures address themselves to symptoms rather than to the fundamental disease. That disease is the psychology of the cold war, our obsession with power, our assumption that the great problems that glare upon us so hideously from every corner of the horizon can be solved by force.

Abuse of power by Presidents is a reflection, and perhaps a consequence, of abuse of power by the American people and nation. For two decades now we have misused our prodigious power. We misused our economic power, not least in associating economic with military assistance, and in imposing economic sanctions against nations who did not see eye to eye with us about trade with our "enemies." We misused our political power by trying to force neutrals onto our side in the cold war by bringing pressure on the nations of Latin America to support our shortsighted policy of excluding China from the United Nations—surely the most egregious blunder in the history of modern diplomacy. We misused our political power by planting the CIA in some 60 countries to carry on what we chose to regard as national defense but what was in the eyes of its victims the work of subversion. We misused our military power in forcing our weapons on scores of nations, maintaining military alliances like NATO and SEATO and imposing our will upon these where we were able. We misused our international power by flouting the sovereign rights of neighboring countries like Cuba and Guatemala and the Dominican Republic and violating our obligations under the OAS treaty and the United Nations. And we are even now engaged in a monstrous misuse of power in waging war on a distant people that does not accept our ideology, or our determination of its future. Is it any wonder that against this almost lurid background, Presidents misuse their power?

As we have greater power than any other nation, so we should display greater moderation in using it, greater humility in justifying it, and greater magnanimity in withholding it. In the long run the abuse of the executive power cannot be divorced from the abuse of national power. If we subvert world order and threaten world peace, we must inevitably subvert and threaten our own political institutions first. This we are in the process of doing.

Study Questions

1. Do you believe that it is proper for the President to use executive agreements rather than treaties in conducting foreign relations? Why?

2. What is the relationship between the President, the Secretary of State and the Department of State? It has been said that the President is a prisoner of the Department of State in conducting foreign policy. Do you believe that this is true? In what way does the Department of State expand the President's power? In what way does the Department of State limit the President's power?

3. In what way does the Department of Defense expand and/or limit the power of the President? Has the President's power as commander-in-chief been firmly established? In your own studies, analyze the role played by General Alexander Haig, the Department of Defense, and the President during the crucial week in August, 1974 that culminated in Nixon's resignation from the presidency. What did this week indicate in terms of power of the President as commander-in-chief?

4. Examine the role that Congress plays in foreign policy. How does this compare with the powers of the President? Should Congress have additional power in foreign policy? Why?

5. Identify the instruments the President has to assist him in his foreign policy role. What is the National Security Council and what is its purpose?

6. Briefly discuss the political and symbolic aspects of presidential power in foreign policy.

7. What are the limits to presidential power in foreign affairs? Should the President have a relatively free hand to conduct foreign policy? Why?

Bibliography

This list does not include the many historical studies of Presidents, Secretaries of State, specific policy issues, or the insights available in various Presidential papers.

Acheson, Dean. *Present at the Creation*. New York: Signet Books, 1969.

Donovan, John C. *The Cold Warriors: A Policy-Making Elite*. Lexington, Mass.: D. C. Heath and Co., 1974.

Gilbert, John C., ed. *The New Era in American Foreign Policy*. New York: St. Martin's Press, 1973.

Halperin, Morton H. *Bureaucratic Politics and Foreign Policy*. Washington, D.C.: The Brookings Institution, 1974.

Hilsman, Roger, *The Politics of Policy Making in Defense and Foreign Affairs*. New York: Harper and Row, 1971.

Hilsman, Roger. *To Move a Nation*. New York: Delta Books, 1967.

Johnson, Richard A. *The Administration of United States Foreign Policy*. Austin: University of Texas Press, 1971.

Kennedy, Robert F. *Thirteen Days*. New York: Signet Books, 1964.

McNamara, Robert S. *The Essence of Security*. New York: Harper and Row, 1968.

Nash, Henry T. *American Foreign Policy: Response to a Sense of Threat*. Homewood, Ill.: The Dorsey Press, 1973.

Radway, Laurence. I. *Foreign Policy and National Defense*. Glenview, Ill: Scott, Foresman and Co., 1969.

Stupak, Ronald J. *The Shaping of Foreign Policy: The Role of the Secretary of State as Seen by Dean Acheson*. New York: The Odyssey Press, 1967.

CHAPTER 7
Congressmen and Their Constituents: Representing the People

Legislatures stand at the heart of a representative system of government. It is their representative character that makes them authoritative and legitimate, empowering them to act for the whole body politic. It is because of their representative character that citizens of a democracy accept the decisions of legislators as authoritative. It is therefore appropriate that we begin the study of our legislature, Congress, with an examination of its representative character—the social background of its members, their representational role perceptions, and their relation to their constituents.

The Composition of Congress

The population of Congress is not a true reflection of the population in the general public. In the 93rd Congress (1973-74), the average age of the members of the House of Representatives was fifty-one and the average age of senators was fifty-five. Only a few persons become congressmen while they are young, say in their thirties, although the constitutional age requirement is only twenty-five for the House and thirty for the Senate. Partly due to lack of resources, the youth in the general population are not at all represented. Congress is mostly an organization of men. At present (1974) there are no women senators and only seventeen of the 435 members of the House of Representatives are women. If women were represented in accordance with their proportion in the population, they would constitute a majority in

Congress. And furthermore, Congress underrepresents the minorities: there are no Chicano congressmen, and only sixteen black members of Congress (fifteen in the House and one in the Senate). If the blacks were represented in accordance with their proportion in the population, there would be sixty-one in Congress, with about a fifth of that number in the Senate.

Other aspects in which the composition of Congress differs from that of the general population are religion, education, and occupation. In the 93rd Congress (1973-74), there were 379 Protestants compared with 116 Catholics and 14 Jews. Legislators belonging to Protestant denominations made up 71 percent of the membership of Congress, although Protestants constitute only 55 percent of national church membership. Catholics and Jews, with about 41 percent of the church membership held only 24 percent of congressional seats.

Most congressmen have college degrees, but most members of the general public do not. The professions predominate and wage earners are scarce in Congress. In the 93rd Congress, 54 percent were lawyers, 33 percent were active in business or banking, 13 percent were teachers, 9 percent farmers, and 5 percent journalists.

Of what significance is this demographic imbalance? The answer perhaps depends upon the observer's point of view. It can of course be argued that a congressman does not have to be a blue-collar worker to represent the interests of labor; there are other ways (via interest groups, etc.) through which communication links can be established between the representative and the represented. On the other hand, those elements that are excluded from the system are not only alienated, but are also denied a fair share of the national product.

Take, for example, the case of blacks. Although there are only a handful of black congressmen, there are many white members of Congress who have large numbers of black voters in their constituencies, so that the claims of the blacks have not gone entirely unrepresented. Still it is evident that policy outcomes have been less than equitable: the blacks continue to face discrimination and deprivation. There has been, for instance, little improvement in the relative income position of blacks since World War II. In 1947, the median income of white Americans was $2520 and the median nonwhite income $1363—a gap of $1147. By 1969, this income gap had more than doubled, to $2773, with the white median income of $6765 and the nonwhite income $3992. From another point of view, over a twenty-two year period nonwhite income relative to white income showed only an insignificant increase, from 54 percent to 58 percent.

The unrepresentative character of Congress in respect to women may have had similar consequences. They too have suffered from institutional discrimination and social coercion, for example, in the labor market. The recent emergence of the women's movement is in part the result of such discrimination.

While the consequences of underrepresentation of Catholics and Jews are perhaps insignificant as political issues in the United States rarely split voters along religious lines, the upper-class nature of Congress does tend to bias its policy preferences. This tendency is, of course, curbed to a degree by a politician's need for votes. Nevertheless, social and economic policies have not been really geared to the needs of the lower-income groups. Some observers argue that this is partly a reflection of lack of political organization and resources on the part of such groups—that is to say they are unable to influence the policies of the administration. So it would seem that those whose interests are not represented, who are denied a share in political power, are also denied a fair share of the nation's resources and advantages.

Representational Styles

The problem of representation is central to all discussions of the behavior of legislators. What is a congressman, as a representative of the people, supposed to do? Should he carry out the will of his constituents or should he exercise his independent judgment on their behalf? One view holds that a representative should faithfully mirror the wishes of his constituents in his legislative conduct and advance the interests of those who put him in office. A rival theory holds that while the wishes and opinions of the constituents should be respected and given due consideration, the representative is not obligated to follow the will or whims of his constituents slavishly. He should, in fact, exercise his own mature judgment in determining what is best for his people. This second view has been forcefully presented by Edmund Burke, an eighteenth-century English essayist and member of the House of Commons. In a speech to his constituents, he said:

> Certainly, Gentlemen, it ought to be the happiness and glory of a representative to live in the strictest union, the closest correspondence, and the most unreserved communication with his contituents. Their wishes ought to have great weight with him; their opinions high respect; their business unremitted attention. . . . But his unbiased opinion, his mature judgment, his enlightened conscience, he ought not to sacrifice to you,

to any man, or to any set of men living. These he does not derive from your pleasure, —no, nor from the law and the Constitution. They are a trust from Providence, for the abuse of which he is deeply answerable. Your representative owes you, not his industry only, but his judgment; and he betrays, instead of serving you, if he sacrifices it to your opinion.[1]

Broadly, therefore, a representative can perceive his representational role either as that of a delegate or a trustee. He can also combine these roles in some fashion. These three types of representational styles may be described as follows:

Trustee

The representative considers himself a free agent. He will act in Congress according to his own judgment based on an assessment of the facts in each case. He will act in accordance with what he considers to be the best interests of his constituents or the nation. He will follow his own principles, convictions or conscience.

Delegate

The representative thinks of his job in terms of reflecting his constituency's opinion. He votes in Congress in accordance with his perceptions of what his constituents want, whether he himself likes that or not. He does what the people want, not what he wants. When he does not know what the people want, he may even consult them for instructions.

Politico

(combined-type): The representative wears both hats. Sometimes he is a trustee, acting in terms of what he thinks is best for his people; at other times, he acts as a delegate, merely conveying his constituency's wishes.

Role Choice

How are members of the U. S. Congress distributed among these three role perceptions? How do they view their representative role? To find out, Professor Roger Davidson conducted interviews with a sample of eighty-seven members of the House of Representatives. Their replies were distributed as follows:

**Representational Role Perceptions
of House Members**

Role Style	Percent
Trustee	28
Politico	46
Delegate	23
Unclassified	3
(N=87)	100

Source: Roger Davidson, *The Role of the Congressman* (New York: Pegasus, 1969), p. 117.

The response indicates the politico role perception as the dominant one, being named by nearly half of the members of the sample. Its popularity is probably due to its flexibility in allowing the congressman to choose his role according to circumstances.

The nature of the electoral district is an important influence on role choice. Thus Davidson found that the trustees came disproportionately from electorally safe districts, whereas the delegates tended to come from competitive or marginal districts. The table below indicates the relation between the congressmen's role choices and the type of districts they represented:

**Relation between Representational Role Choice
and District Type**

Role Chosen	District Type	
	Marginal	Safe
Trustee	19%	35%
Politico	37	54
Delegate	44	11
	(N=32)	(N=52)

Source: Adapted from Roger Davidson, *op. cit.*, p. 128.

Local v. National Orientation

It has been observed that congressmen are very parochial, tending to assign local interests primacy over the interests of the nation. Senior congressmen usually advise freshmen to "vote the district," and many legislators do. Thus, for example, legislators from farming areas support agricultural subsidies and those from oil-producing districts support legislation allowing oil depletion tax allowances. It appears from the way congressmen behave that localism does dominate their policy orientations. This inference is supported by empirical evidence provided by Roger Davidson. He found that local interests are put first by a large plurality of members. As the table below indicates, district orientation was mentioned most frequently by the members of the House of Representatives (42 percent). Still about half (28 percent plus 23 percent) of the House membership is also attuned to some larger constituency, which is surprising in view of the fact that they have been elected to the House by votes in their own district only.

Areal Role Orientations

Areal Focus	Percent
Nation	28
Nation-district	23
District	42
Unclassified	8
	(N=87)

Source: Adapted from Roger Davidson, *The Role of the Congressman* (New York: Pegasus, 1969), p. 122.

As might be expected, those congressmen who have national orientation tend to be drawn largely from electorally safe districts, whereas localists come from marginal districts:

Areal Role Orientation and District Type

Areal Focus	District Type Marginal	Safe
Nation	19%	34%
Nation-district	28	29
District	53	38
	(N=32)	(N=53)

Source: Adapted from Roger Davidson, *op. cit.*, p. 128.

In summary, the analysis of representational styles indicates that most congressmen do not want to be mere agents of the voters. They think of themselves sometimes as trustees elected by their constituents to exercise mature judgment or enlightened conscience on behalf of the people and sometimes as delegates elected to transmit the will of the majority of their constituents. It also appears that congressmen for the most part tend to be district-oriented, viewing most policy issues in a local rather than a national frame of reference. In other words, they appear to assign considerable weight to the interests of their constituents in their evaluation of public policy matters. One congressman summed it up:

> We have much leeway in voting, but we can't go against the district too often . . . On really important issues, I always vote my conviction regardless of the pressures which are put upon me. On less important votes, politics may be followed on an expedient basis. I think members have to decide where they are going to make their stand and at what point the issue isn't too important. Sometimes it is easier to follow what your district wants you to do.[2]

Communication With Constituents

The original and legal definition of the term "constituency" is "set of individuals who have the legal right to vote for a legislative representative upon reaching the age of competence [recently set at eighteen]. The legal right to vote is established by the individual's place of legal residence within the boundaries of an areally defined legislative district." However, a more realistic and up-to-date definition of the term might be "the subset of voters who supported the representative in the last election."[3] This small subset includes friends, relatives, colleagues, and those who would most benefit from the specific representative's election (e.g., active party workers, city or local employees of the government, special interest groups and individuals). Most often, the constituency of an elected representative consists mainly of members of his party, plus a few members of opposing parties for whom he has special appeal; therefore little diversity in their views would be expected. The representative, his constituents, and his political party will have a somewhat homogenous policy view that might be different from the policy views of members of other parties in the area or state. Voters supporting him for his policy positions are less likely to vary in their views than a full set of constituents in the area.

Therefore, although popular opinion on issues may fluctuate, the subset constituency's views will remain generally the same. In addition, the representative will have greater contact with this subset of constituents, both during and after the election, and will learn their views better and more precisely than the views of the full set of constituents in the area. Hence the elected legislator may well be representing only a fragment of the total constituency in Congress.[4]

According to this view, the subset constituency is very well represented indeed, because the legislator knows both the persons and their party affiliations and policy opinions. What about the original meaning of the term constituency, though? What of the full set of constituents who do not belong to his party, who may not agree with his stands on various issues, who may not even know what his opinions on various issues are? Here we can see a major problem in the relations between congressmen and their constituents. Who is represented? What are the duties of the congressman to his constituents? A congressman's duties can be summed up as being twofold: the function of representation and the function of service. The former function implies representing the district and the latter function implies representing the individual constituent.

Representing the District

Representing the district means, among other things, expressing the opinions of constituents in a legislative body. How well does the average congressman fulfill this function?

The problem here is one of identifying those opinions. Most congressmen are uncertain as to what their constituents' wishes are with regard to most of the issues that come before Congress. There are few indices of public sentiment available to a congressman. He can, of course, look to election results, but these are often difficult to interpret. Most people vote not just on the basis of issues, but for a variety of reasons which are impossible to untangle. Besides, on many issues that are of no particular interest to them constituents simply have no opinion. Donald Stokes and Warren Miller provide evidence on the ignorance of voters. According to their article, voters' knowledge is limited as to public issues, the identity of their congressman, the policy stands of individual congressmen, and even the identity of the majority party in Congress.[5] Such widespread voter ignorance makes it almost impossible for the congressman to interpret any electoral mandate.

The congressman can, of course, turn to his constituency mail to find out what his district's opinion is on an issue. Such mail, however, rarely reflects opinion in his district; it is often deliberately "inspired" by an interest group trying to influence him on a particular issue, and therefore an unreliable indicator of what the constituents really want.

Because of this mandate uncertainty and voter ignorance, the congressman is left with ample leeway in his policy behavior and can adopt any policy stance. Of course, there are some issues on which constituency opinion is so clear that a congressman needs no indicators to tell him what the constituents want. On such issues, he may have no option but to vote the district's preference, acting as a mere agent. According to Miller and Stokes, the views of congressmen are most congruent with their districts concerning issues of civil rights, and least congruent concerning matters of foreign policy.[6] Most legislative questions however, do not deal with major issues like civil rights. When the constituents have no opinion or are divided in opinion, the congressman must follow his own personal judgment or act in accordance with his own inclination. His personal preferences also assume importance on issues on which constituency opinion is still unformed; here he leads public opinion rather than follows it.

Representing the Individual Constituent

In representing his district, a congressman expresses the policy demands of his constituents. But in serving the needs of individual constituents, he is engaged in nonpolicy matters, or casework. Casework involves the processing of numerous requests that stream in from thousands of constituents. Some requests are made in person, but most come in the mail or through phone calls. They relate to a variety of services and the congressman tries to help whenever he can. The following are some of the major categories:

1. Many constituents simply seek information about federal programs or federal regulations or government research. This is easily supplied by the congressmen or their staffs, usually by turning to the federal agencies involved. These agencies are only too happy to oblige congressmen because it costs them little but earns them great dividends in the form of legislative goodwill.

2. Constituents may seek redress from governmental action or inaction. A widowed mother may have stopped receiving her monthly child support checks from the Veterans Administration. A pensioner may have lost his social security check. A handicapped father may be interested in favorable discharge of his son from military service or an assignment near home. A young man may want his congressman to speed up action on his

application for a federal loan. These and other specific cases require a great deal of time and attention, requiring a congressman to intercede on behalf of his constituents. Congressmen usually have on their staffs persons who are experienced in handling such casework. Information must be requested from the agency involved regarding the status of the pending matter; a telephone call or a letter from the congressman is likely to expedite action. Several agencies have procedures to deal promptly with matters in which congressmen express concern. According to one source, some thirty-five federal agencies and three military services have liaison offices to help congressmen.[7] But congressmen do not always intercede with the federal agencies on behalf of their constituents. They use their influence judiciously as too-frequent use would result in decreasing returns. Moreover, a congressman's influence does not span all the federal agencies; he is likely to be most effective in areas where his committees have jurisdiction.

3. Individual constituents may be interested in employment with the federal government. A congressman can be of assistance by supplying information on application procedures, or by contacting the Civil Service Commission or other agency to request reconsideration of an unfavorable decision. Congressmen also recommend appointments to the various service academies. Each congressman is allotted a quota of five positions at each of the three major academies, the Military, the Naval, and the Air Force Academy. They also have a hand in filling a few Capitol Hill posts—doormen and pages. Until 1970, when President Nixon removed those positions from the patronage process, congressmen had some influence in filling positions of postmaster and of rural carrier. They can also appoint their own staff members and where feasible they favor people from their home district.

4. Civic, business, labor and other groups often call their congressman's attention to the need for federal offices, military installations, or public works projects in their district. Such projects insure influx of federal money into the district and constitute a means of employment for constituents and profit for some business groups. When an incumbent congressman campaigns for reelection, he reminds the voters how he has successfully endeavored to bring money into the district to ensure the security and prosperity of its residents.

5. Many tourists and groups of constituents (high school classes, service club members, etc.) visit the capital and call on their

congressmen for assistance in obtaining visitors' gallery passes to the House or Senate, hotel accommodations or other sightseeing arrangements. Much of this drop-in tourist work is handled by the staff, but at times a congressman will himself want to meet, greet and be photographed with certain visitors such as a graduating high school class from his home town.

Thus, the services which congressmen render to their constituents are many and varied. A member of the House of Representatives once remarked:

> A Congressman has become an expanded messenger boy, an employment agency, getter-out of the Navy, and Marines, a wardheeler, a woundheeler, troubleshooter, law explainer, bill finder, issue translator, resolution interpreter, controversy-oil-pourer, glad hand extender, business promoter, veterans' affairs adjuster, ex-serviceman's champion, watchdog for the underdog, sympathizer for the upper dog, kisser of babies, recoverer of lost baggage, soberer of delegates, adjuster of traffic violators and voters straying into the toils of the law, binder-up of broken hearts, financial wet nurse, a good "samaritan," contributor to good causes, cornerstone layer, public building and bridge dedicator and ship christener.[8]

Average Work Loads by Function

Function	Congressman Hours per week	%	Congressman's Staff Hours per week	%
Legislative	38.0	64.6	30.8	14.3
Constituency Service	16.3	27.6	53.5	24.7
Correspondence (mixed constituency service, education)			88.6	40.8
Education and Publicity	4.6	7.8	22.4	10.3
Other			21.4	9.9
	58.9	100.0	216.7	100.0

Source: John S. Saloma, *Congress and the New Politics* (Boston: Little, Brown & Co., 1969), pp. 184–185.

These varied services to the constituents, of course, consume a substantial amount of a congressman's time. According to one source, several congressmen devote 90 percent of their time to casework or errands for the constituents.[9] This figure is perhaps exaggerated. A recent study of 150 congressmen's work loads shows that only about a fourth of their workweek is devoted to serving their constituents while two-thirds of their time is devoted to legislative business. The same study also shows, however, that the congressmen's staff members spend more than half of their time rendering constituent services.

The data in the table clearly indicate that no matter how much time a congressman personally spends serving his constituents and looking after their interests, his staff is usually busy most of the time answering mail and handling constituents' problems. All in all, congressmen devote a substantial part of their resources to running errands for their constituents.

Quite obviously, then, a congressman regards the service function as an important part of his job. He feels that voters couldn't care less how he votes on legislative measures; what they are really concerned about is what he does for the district. Gerald Ford, then a congressman, advised a freshman colleague in 1963: ". . . you will find that your constituents will evaluate your merit or lack of it, based on how well or badly you handle the cases which they submit to you. I won't pass judgment on whether this is right or wrong. I am simply saying that as a matter of fact, this is true."[10] This feeling is perhaps justified. As already mentioned the voters are largely unaware of the issues or the specific votes of their legislators. They probably have only a general impression of a certain congressman, and they vote according to whether that impression is good or bad. Service to constituents is one way of building the image that the congressman really cares for his people.

Critics allege that the service function is detrimental to the congressman's ability to legislate because he must spend so much time performing these tasks. Moreover, since these grievances are handled individually they rarely come to the official attention of Congress even if they have a general import. Thus Walter Gellhorn complains:

> . . .casework tends to go no further than the case at hand, leaving untouched the problems that generated it. Ordinarily, investigation is superficial. Implications, if not altogether unperceived, are in any event likely to be ignored. So long as the present case has an appropriately happy outcome, tomorrow's case is left to its own devices; anyway, it may involve some other congressman's constituent. Always pressed for time and almost always untrained generalists in a world of trained specialists, congressmen pass on to other things—and so do the administrators.[11]

Finally, critics point out, some administrators resent congressional interference. Such intervention short-circuits the normal, systematic, administrative processes by "going to the top" or using friendly contacts.

While there is an element of truth in these criticisms, it appears to us that the advantages outweigh the disadvantages. The service function keeps the congressman in touch with the problems of his constituents. It informs him about the laws that need revision and agencies that would benefit from reorganization. It enables him to exercise a measure of control over the slow and sometimes arbitrary behavior of bureaucrats. In a sense, it enables Congress to fulfill its constitutional responsibility of overseeing the executive branch. Checking with the administrative agencies about citizens' complaints is not necessarily interference; it is also a way of rectifying arbitrary official acts or delays, of ensuring responsiveness, and of humanizing the anonymous, hardened bureaucratic processes.

Serving constituents is just another way of representing the interests of people, which is the essence of representative democracy, which is America. The representatives, by serving as middlemen between the constituents and the federal administrators, help to bridge the political distance that divides the ordinary citizens from their rulers.

NOTES

1. Edmund Burke, *Speech to the Electors of Bristol, November 3, 1774* Bobbs-Merrill reprint #PS 366, p. 95.
2. A congressman quoted anonymously in Charles L. Clapp, *The Congressman* (Washington, D.C.: The Brookings Institute, 1963).
3. Agage R. Clausen, *How Congressmen Decide: A Policy Focus* (New York, St. Martin's Press, 1973), p. 126.
4. Ibid., pp. 126–127.
5. Donald Stokes and Warren E. Miller, "Party Government and the Saliency" *Public Opinion Quarterly* 26 (Winter, 1962), pp. 532-46.
6. Warren Miller and Donald Stokes, "Constituency Influence in Congress," *American Political Science Review* 57 (1963), pp. 45-56.
7. Donald Tacheron and Morris Udall, *The Job of Congressman* (Indianapolis: Bobbs-Merrill, 1970), p. 68.
8. Luther Patrick, "What is a Congressman?" reprinted in *Daily Congressional Record*, 88th Congress, 1st session, May 13, 1963, p. A 2978; cited in John Saloma, *Congress and the New Politics* (Boston: Little, Brown & Co., 1969), p. 190.
9. Charles Clapp, *The Congressman* (Washington, D.C.: The Brookings Institute, 1963), p. 54.
10. Tacheron and Udall, p. 66.
11. Walter Gellhorn, *When Americans Complain: Governmental Grievance Procedures* (Cambridge, Mass.: Harvard University Press, 1966), p. 76.

Selected Readings

Congressmen have bases of power which differ from each other and from the constituencies of the President. To maintain these bases of power and to ensure reelection, members of Congress must not only respond to their individual constituencies, but also to their colleagues, and to the institution of Congress. Few people know what congressmen do on a day-to-day basis. Yet such knowledge is essential to an understanding of the role of Congress, the various pressures involved, and the nature of the environment in which congressmen must work.

In a particularly interesting article, Senator James L. Buckley of New York provides insights into these areas. He assesses the various organizational mechanisms at work in the Senate, focusing particularly on the committee system. He notes the great power wielded by the committee chairman and the committee staff and recommends that the seniority system be abolished. Noting the enormous amount of business, Senator Buckley suggests some procedural changes that might be useful to ease the work load. He looks at the way senators vote and concludes that the Senate is always ten to fifteen years behind the mood of the American people. This he attributes to the relatively long term of six years and the need for senators to protect their "flanks"—i.e. minimize future political controversy or embarrassment. Senator Buckley points out a number of procedures through which senators can have some impact on the legislative process. Regardless of all the problems with the Senate, he concludes "It is a place where many of the major decisions affecting the shape of our times are made; a place where even the least of its members may have a hand in making them."

7.1

On Becoming A United States Senator

JAMES L. BUCKLEY

On January 22, 1971, Jacob Javits, pursuant to custom, escorted me down the center aisle of the United States Senate Chamber. Vice President Agnew swore me in, and I was handed a pen with which I entered my name on the books of the Senate. I then walked a few steps to my desk on the Republican side of the aisle. I had become the Junior Senator from the State of New York. Or, as senatorial courtesy puts it, the distinguished and honorable Senator from the great State of New York.

Rarely has anyone, distinguished and honorable—or otherwise—entered the United States Senate so innocent of the mechanisms of a legislative body or of the impact of politics on the legislative process. Prior to my election I had never held public office or participated in any organized political effort other than the third-party mayoral and senatorial campaigns of the brothers Buckley.

Shortly after my election Clif White, my campaign manager and guide into the political world, organized a private dinner with a few of the senior Republican senators so that I might acquire a better feel for the life I was about to enter. I had hoped to get specific advice on how to go about the job of being an effective senator. What I got instead were affable assurances to the effect that anyone capable of winning election to the Senate would find no difficulty in getting along once in it. This was all, in its own way, reassuring; but I did not emerge from that dinner with the mother lode of hard, practical information that would help me thread my way through the complexities of the senatorial life.

The first formal business for a senator-elect is the meeting with the Sergeant at Arms and the Secretary of the Senate, who give you the basic housekeeping instructions, take from you sample signatures for franking privileges, and explain insurance and retirement benefits, as well as such perquisites as the right to a District of Columbia license plate, numbered according to one's rank in the Senate pecking order—plus one, Number One being reserved for the Vice President. (My rank was 99 because I had no prior service as a congressman or governor, which

From the *National Review*, February 2, 1973. Reprinted by permission.

adds into the calculation of seniority. I beat out Lawton Chiles of Florida because New York has the larger population.) At that meeting I was presented with three books: *The Rules and Manual of the United States Senate;* an exegesis thereof by the chief parliamentarian, Dr. Floyd Riddick; and the *Congressional Directory* for the second session of the prior Congress. I determined to spend the next few weeks mastering the parliamentary rules, but was soon bogged down in their intricacy. I would learn to my relief that the Senate operates in a reasonably free and tolerant manner, and that much of its business is conducted not so much by the rule book as by continuing recourse to unanimous-consent agreements. Those who do know the rule book, however, are equipped, at critical moments, to take the parliamentary advantage.

New senators learn that they are expected to carry the principal burden of presiding over the Senate. For someone like me, who had never presided over any function, nor even scanned *Robert's Rules of Order,* the prospect seemed ominous. It isn't all that difficult, however, because sitting immediately in front of the Chair is one of the three parliamentarians, who whispers up the appropriate instruction. The most difficult task is to learn the identity of eighty or ninety brand new faces, together with state of origin, so that one can recognize the Senator from So-and-so without any excessive or obvious fumbling.

During this orientation period, I introduced myself to the Senate Republican leadership—to Minority Leader Hugh Scott, Minority Whip Bob Griffin, Chairman Gordon Allott of the Republican Policy Committee, and Chairman Margaret Chase Smith of the Republican Conference.

An important call was at the office of Senator Wallace Bennett, Chairman of the Republican Committee on Committees, in order to learn how committee assignments were made, and to register my preferences. The process is in fact mechanical. Once the minority vacancies on the various committees become known, the Republican members of the incoming class line up in order of seniority, and take their pick. Each senator is appointed to two major committees, and often to one or more minor ones. My own initial assignments were to Public Works, Space, and the District of Columbia.

The Committee Shuffle

It was in committee work that I first came to appreciate the enormous volume of business that courses through the Congress, and its implications. It is not unusual to find meetings or hearings involving as many as three committees or subcommittees of which one is a member scheduled for the same time, each involving business of some importance. One either spreads himself thin by putting in token appearances at each, or devotes himself to one meeting, relying on an overworked staff member to keep abreast of what is going on in the other two. I have yet to be convinced that there isn't somewhere in the bowels of the Capitol a computer programed to arrange as many conflicting appointments as possible.

The committee system constitutes a delegation of responsibility for legislative work in designated areas. It should not be assumed, however, that a given committee will be representative of the Senate as a whole. Senators naturally tend to gravitate to those committees that interest them most or whose work is most important to their particular constituencies, and a committee can become as "mission-oriented" as an executive agency. Given the broad range of viewpoints represented on each side of the aisle, the requirement that each committee have a majority and minority membership roughly comparable to that of the Senate as a whole is no guarantee that it will reflect the political spectrum in any other sense. Thus committee reports are too often "selling documents" that do not provide other senators with the kind of balanced information needed to help them reach a reasonably educated opinion regarding a particular bill's merits.

It isn't long—especially if controversial and complex legislation is being worked on—before a newcomer senses the enormous influence wielded by committee staffs. These are usually heavily loaded in favor of the majority party, in terms both of outlook and of availability to committee members. Time and again after new points are raised in committee, the staff will disappear to return the next day with what is often a significantly new or considerably refocused bit of legislation.

It can be extraordinarily difficult for committee members, even those particularly concerned with the legislation in question, to keep up with what is happening to it. There simply isn't time for a member to rethink and reconsider every interlocking provision of a complex bill each time a substantive change is made—hence the heavy reliance on staff. Furthermore, committees often work under enormous time pressures to report out particular pieces of legislation by certain deadlines which at times are set not so much by the natural rhythm of the legislative process as by political considerations.

Thus major legislation is often rushed through committee, reported out on the floor of the Senate, and put to a vote with few senators fully understanding it. It must be understood that it is virtually impossible for a senator to keep up with most—let alone all—of the significant legislation being considered by committees other than his own. I do not refer to legislation that grabs the headlines and occasions national debate: A senator has to examine such legislation in some detail if only to answer his mail and reply to reporters' questions. It is, after all, by his positions on conspicuous legislation that he establishes his political identity.

Most of the bills considered by the Senate are relatively inconspicuous—though by no means unimportant. They may involve new programs that will have an enormous impact on American society, on the states, or on the economy; programs that in time may grow into multibillion-dollar commitments. Yet many of these bills will be enacted with little real examination by most of the senators who will have to vote yea or nay on them, and with less than adequate comprehension of what the bill involves.

The average senator simply does not have sufficient legislative help to get a proper analysis of every bill that issues from the legislative mill. Too many bills are called to a vote before the ink has dried on the explanatory report. Thus, all too often a senator's vote is based simply on a summary description of the bill (which can be totally inadequate), plus whispered conversations with colleagues who may or may not have detailed information as to the content—all in the fifteen-minute period allowed for voting after the bells ring to summon him to the floor.

Technically speaking, any senator can insure that adequate time is allowed for debate of any bill. He can simply register his refusal to agree to a unanimous-consent agreement limiting the time allotted for debate. This presupposes, however, that he has had enough advance warning of the particular mischief at hand to record a timely objection to any agreement to which he is not a party. It also presupposes that he will be able to educate and energize a sufficient number of his all-too-preoccupied colleagues to assure himself of sufficient floor support to make the effort worthwhile.

I recall two cases in my own experience—although there are, unfortunately, many more—that dramatize the pressures under which the Senate operates.

In early 1971, Governor Daniel Evans of Washington suggested the need for legislation to cope with economic disasters similar to existing legislation designed to cope with natural disasters. The law he proposed would be narrow in its focus, providing relief on a short-term, emergency basis to help communities ride out sudden economic catastrophes.

Two bills incorporating this approach were introduced, and hearings on them were held by the Public Works Committee. Several months later the Committee met in executive session to consider the legislation as revised by staff after the hearings. To the astonishment of at least some, the draft bill differed in fundamental respects from both of the measures that had been introduced. The basic concept had shifted from bringing maximum effort to bear on specific emergency situations, to an amorphous bill that would also cover areas of chronic unemployment or chronically low economic activity for which there already existed thirty or forty other federal programs. The definition of areas which could be made subject to the legislation was such that even a neighborhood could qualify for the most exotic kinds of federal help.

Nevertheless, this basically new legislation was approved in a single day by the full committee, and reported out. The legislation was then rushed to the floor of the Senate, debated before a largely empty chamber, and put to a vote—all within a day or two of the time printed copies of the bill and of the accompanying committee report had become available to senators. This legislation opened up a whole new area of federal intervention; it carried no price tag; and it was approved by senators only a few of whom had any grasp of its scope.

The second example concerned a new program of a truly sweeping nature, enacted by an overwhelming majority of senators, many of whom I am convinced had little understanding of the real issues involved. Just before the August recess in 1971, the Committee on Labor and Public Welfare reported out a measure innocuously titled "A Bill To Extend the Equal Employment Opportunity Act 1968 and Other Purposes." The "other purposes" turned out to be the inauguration of a comprehensive federal program for "child development" services designed ultimately to embrace a very large proportion of pre-school-age children regardless of financial need. Whereas in its first year the new program would cost a mere $100 million (chickenfeed these days), the Committee report placed the figure for the second year at $2 billion—an amount significantly greater than the projected cost of all the rest of the OEO's activities. Furthermore, the report stated that the cost of the child-development program would double every two years thereafter for some time hence. Secretary Elliot Richardson, then of the Department of Health, Education, and Welfare, estimated that the annual cost of the new program would come to $20 billion before the end of the decade.

Thanks to an interested housewife who had followed the progress of the bill in committee, my office was alerted to its implications. Because of the recess, we had time to examine its horrors and I was in a position to argue on the basis of expert opinion against the child-development section. (The bill had been scheduled as the first order of business on the day Congress returned, and was voted on in the Senate the next day, "other purposes" and all.)

Senators who had happened to be on the floor to hear the debate would have learned that there was substantial controversy among professionals over the child-development section, a fact they would not have discovered from reading the report. They would have learned that a number of experts in the field questioned the need for such a vast undertaking, and, in fact, warned that permanent harm could be done to younger children placed in the impersonal "warehouse" environment of the kind of day-care facility that was apt to result from the legislation. They would have learned also that the expert opinion heard in committee was entirely one-sided, and that even among the experts who favored the program, one had remarked that its far-reaching provisions would revolutionize the concept of the family in American life.

Unfortunately, almost no one besides the sponsors of the bill and the two or three senators arguing for the elimination or modification of the child-development section were on hand to hear the debate. Thus when the time came to vote, most senators voted aye on the assumption that nothing significant was involved in the bill beyond a simple two-year extension of existing OEO programs. (This bill, incidentally, was later vetoed.)

This rush of business with little or no time allowed for legislative pause, thought, or deliberation brings to mind another aspect of the Senate's current way of conducting its affairs. I speak of the phenomenon of the amendment—printed or unprinted—offered from the floor with little or no notice, which can cover the range from purely technical corrections of statutory language to the most far-reaching changes in the legislation under consideration.

There is usually little check on the scope of amendments that can be offered from the floor, and no opportunity for the relevant committees and their staffs to study them so that some measure of expert analysis can be brought to bear in arguing their merits for the benefit of the Senate—always assuming other senators are on hand to hear the debate. Thus all too often, especially when the Senate is operating under unanimous agreements severely limiting the time for debate on amendments, they are apt to be adopted or rejected on the basis of their emotional or political appeal. So it was with the floor amendments that last October added $4 billion, or more than 27 percent, to the cost of the Welfare-Social Security bill reported out by the Senate Finance Committee, with the amendments that added, in one day's time last June, almost $2 billion to the HEW-Labor appropriations bill. Surely there is a better way in which to conduct the nation's vital legislative business short of the highly restrictive rules that obtain in the House.

Too Much Business

All of which brings me to certain observations about the Senate today.

At the root of most of the problems of the Senate is the enormous expansion of federal activities in recent years. A recent study by the Association of the Bar of the City of New York found that the workload of members of Congress had doubled every five years over the past several decades. The Congress, like the Federal Government itself, is simply trying to handle more business than it can digest. The results too often are waste, conflicts, inconsistencies, and superficiality.

Once upon a time Congress was in session only six or seven months a year. There is every reason to believe that during these months there was time and opportunity to think, to study, to argue, and to come to educated conclusions. As the volume of work increased, the Congress was able to cope by extending the length of its sessions. But now, as a result of the explosion of federal activity resulting from the War on Poverty and other programs of the 1960s, it is conceded that Congress is in session essentially on a year-round basis.

One consequence of these increasing demands on senators' time is that it can no longer be said of the Senate that it is a club, exclusive or otherwise. Members once were able to spend unhurried time together, to get to know one another and develop a sense of fraternity while working toward common goals in a highly civil environment. I do not mean to suggest that all of this has disappeared. Real friendships and a sense of belonging do develop, but the sense of community which must once have existed has certainly been dissipated by the preoccupations that tend to keep senators concentrating on their own separate concerns except as their work requires them to come together. It is difficult, in fact, to come to know members of the opposition party who do not happen to serve on one's committees.

Whether the situation can be changed, only time and a differently constituted Congress will tell. But even assuming that the volume of business can be held at present levels, there remains the fact that each senator has only so many hours per day to devote to his job. A senator must be able not only to bring effective judgment to bear on his legislative duties, but also to maintain contact with his own constituency so as to find out what are the real problems people are faced with, and what are the real effects of the legislation he has helped enact.

All of this, in turn, takes adequate staff and office space. Mundane as this may seem, one quickly finds that staffing and space can become important factors in determining just how good a job he is going to be able to do.

A new senator from a state like New York quickly learns that the Senate places great emphasis on the equal sovereign dignity of each individual state; which is a polite way of saying that when it comes to allocating rooms and funds, senators from the larger states invariably feel short-changed. It should be kept in mind that the volume of work that must be handled by a senator's office depends largely on the size of his constituency. I speak of handling mail and constituent problems (the so-called case work), which have been increasing at an enormous rate as the Federal Government has become more and more intrusive into its citizens' lives.

Case work involves such things as immigration problems, chasing down Social Security checks, helping municipalities process their applications for this or that program, helping businesses thread their way through red tape—you name it. Whereas the office workload of a senator from New York may not be sixty times as heavy as that of a senator from Alaska, it certainly involves significantly more than two or three times the volume of work. Yet when I entered the Senate in 1971, the smallest number of rooms assigned to any senator was five and the largest (California and New York), seven. As I started out with a staff of 35 and needed one room for myself, this created a degree of congestion. In like manner, my allowance for hiring staff was less than twice the allowance for the smallest state. It is of course true that each senator bears an equal legislative responsibility and needs equal facilities to keep track of legislative matters and to help him do his individual and committee work. But this doesn't explain the disparity (or lack thereof) in space and staff allowances. In my own case, for example, staff members directly involved in legislative matters are less than one-fifth of the total.

Easing the Workload

Committee problems, time problems, space problems . . . it would seem from my description that a senator's lot is not entirely a happy one. There are, of course, compensations, not the least of which is the pervasive air of civility and mutual respect with which the business of the Senate is conducted. But even the extraordinary civility and respect that are the hallmark of the institution cannot overcome organizational and structural complexities that make a difficult job even more difficult.

What, if anything, can be done about the ever-increasing workload that is at the heart of the Senate's problems? I am not so romantic as to believe that we can dismantle the Departments of HEW and HUD in the immediate future and return most of their functions to the states and localities. Therefore another approach to restructuring the work and the flow of business in the Senate must be considered if senators are to be able to use their scarce time more effectively, and if they are to bring a maximum degree of thought to bear on legislation.

One useful approach might be to place as much of the legislative business of the Congress as possible on a two-year cycle. One year might be devoted to debate and action on bills reported out of committees the prior year, and to the holding of public hearings to assemble information for committee consideration in the succeeding year. (Ideally, both of these activities, which are of a very public nature and which tend to attract headlines, would be scheduled in non-election years so that the participants would not needlessly be distracted from the business at hand. There are, however, technical difficulties with this.) The alternate years would then be available for detailed consideration in executive session of new legislative proposals without arbitrary deadlines requiring hurried, patchwork approaches to important bills, and for the important work of legislative oversight.

A system that would require committees to report out legislation one year, and to have that legislation considered on the floor the next, would allow ample time for special-interest groups, for the public at large, and for members of individual senatorial staffs to digest what it is that the senator will be asked to vote upon when the legislation reaches the floor. It would also provide a period within which amendments could be introduced sufficiently in advance of debate to enable the members of the relevant committees to study them and to give the Senate as a whole the benefit of their expert assessment.

Whether the appropriation process could also be placed on a biennial basis, do not know; and of course, any fundamental reordering of business would have to make special provision for the handling of emergencies. But if the work of the Senate could be organized in some such manner—and I see no reason why it is necessary to enact routine legislation every year instead of every other year—then the conflicts between committee hearings and executive sessions could be eliminated or greatly reduced, the members of the Senate would have time to participate more fully in floor debate, and it ought to be possible—at least every other year—to adjourn the Congress early enough to provide senators with a greater opportunity to return to their states to listen and to observe.

In this connection, I believe the Congress should schedule more "free" time for its members—at least a week each month—for consecutive thought, for planning, for study, for travel, for meaningful contact with their constituents. All of this is necessary if a senator or representative is to bring the best that is in him to bear on his work as a legislator. This would also help with the problem of absenteeism, as senators would be able to schedule their out-of-town engagements during these periodic recesses.

No discussion of possible changes in the way the Senate goes about its business would be complete without further mention of the committees.

As I have already pointed out, although the Senate relies heavily on its committee system for the conduct of its business, there is no assurance that the membership of a committee will reflect the views of the Senate as a whole. Thus it will very often happen that legislation that is highly controversial in nature will be reported out unanimously, or with appended minority views that are more concerned with details of the legislation than with its basic merit. This means that in too many cases the report which accompanies a new bill is not nearly as informative as it ought to be, and fails to alert the Senate as a whole to its controversial features.

This is especially true of committees that have a tradition of trying to iron out all differences of opinion within the committee so that legislation may be reported out unanimously. This practice has a certain utility in that it results in a genuine effort within the committee to reach reasonable compromises among conflicting views. Yet I wonder if the interests of the Senate are necessarily best served by this drive to consensus; for it encourages a sense of commitment to the end product which inhibits any public expression of misgivings by individual committee members. Thus the Senate is apt to be deprived of the candid insights of those senators who are best informed about the weaknesses of the legislation in question.

It might be desirable to require that every committee report outline as objectively as possible the principal arguments for *and* against each new legislative proposal, even when the bill is in fact unanimously supported by the entire committee. I also feel that whenever a member of a committee has strong reservations about any feature of a proposed bill, he has an obligation to the Senate to spell them out in a minority view printed in the committee report.

One recommendation I will not make is that the seniority system be abolished. This does not mean that I find it in all respects to my liking, or that I will not support (as I did) such serious proposals for restricting its application as the one recently offered by Senator Howard Baker (and adopted by the Senate Republican Conference) which affects the selection of a committee's ranking member. Rather it means that I find greater potential problems with the alternatives thus far advanced. An often overlooked fact is that the seniority system was introduced some years ago as a reform measure to minimize politicking and power plays within the Congress. The system as it operates within the Senate today is reasonably benign; and I, as a most junior senator, have not found myself unduly abused by it. There are far more important targets, it seems to me, for a reformer's zeal.

The Balance Wheel

I have often been asked whether I find work in the Senate frustrating, and whether I have found any surprises. I have not found the work frustrating because I had few illusions as to what a very junior member of the minority party could accomplish on his own. Nor have I experienced any really major surprises, although I was not at all prepared for the enormous demands that would be made on my time, seven days a week, or for my loss of anonymity (the unsurprising result of six hundred or so thousand well-deployed dollars on television advertising during my campaign, reinforced by periodic meetings with the press since election).

Early on, I was struck by the number of extracurricular demands on a senator's time, especially one who lives as close to millions of constituents as does a senator from New York: invitations to speak which for one good reason or another cannot be declined, ceremonial visits, people with problems whom one must see and cannot refer to staff, people in the Federal Government to get to know, and so on. The day begins to be splintered into all kinds of pieces, even before the business of legislative work begins.

One thing that in my innocence I had not anticipated was the intensely political atmosphere that prevails within the Senate, the great impact of purely political considerations on specific actions taken by individual senators. It may well be, of course, that mine was an unusual introduction to the institution, as at least a half-dozen of my colleagues were beginning to jockey for position in the presidential race within months after I had been sworn in. This had an inevitable influence on how they orchestrated their performance in the Senate. Also there was the fact that the Senate was controlled by one party and the White House by the other; and as the presidential elections approached, the political atmosphere palpably intensified.

But these unusual considerations notwithstanding, I early learned that many senators tend to cast their votes with a view toward minimizing future political controversy or embarrassment. When a senator's vote is clearly not critical to the fate of a bill, it is often deployed for future political convenience on the grounds that it "wouldn't count anyway." Thus the Senate will often cast a lopsided vote on questions on which public opinion and the real opinion within the Senate is much more evenly divided.

This protecting of political flanks seems harmless enough, but it vitiates what I have discovered to be the important educational function of the Senate. If citizens see that members of the Senate have voted overwhelmingly in favor of this or that piece of legislation, many not entirely certain of their own ground may decide that they have in fact been wrong or backward or insensitive. Yet if on such issues each member of the Senate had voted his true convictions, the breakdown might have been, say, 55 to 45 instead of 70 to 30. I can't help but wonder to what extent this form of political expediency may affect the public's perception of the issues.

There may be another reason why the opinion of the Senate—even when accurately recorded—is very often at odds with what I, at least, take to be the current mood of the American people. Without having researched the point, I suspect that the Senate incorporates a cultural lag of ten or fifteen years; that it is out of phase by a period approximately equivalent to the average tenure of its membership.

A decade or so ago, the Senate was considered by some to be a backward, conservative body whose Republican-Southern Democrat coalition lay athwart progress and the will of the people. Others viewed it as a necessary brake on the rasher impulses of the House of Representatives. Today the situation is quite the reverse. The liberals in the Senate are clearly in the majority, and they do not reflect the growing public skepticism over federal initiatives; and today, for example, it is the House which tends to blow the whistle on the excessive spending approved by the Senate.

There is a reason for this cultural lag, if it indeed exists. A member of the House of Representatives is up for election every two years and studies the views of his constituency with particular care. Also, because each member of the House represents a relatively compact area, his constituency tends to be more homogeneous than a senator's and there is less of an impulse to cater to the fringe groups within it. A member of the Senate, on the other hand, represents an entire state incorporating a multitude of conflicting claims and interests. For better or worse (I suspect the latter) a senator tends to pay a disproportionate amount of attention to the loudest voices, to editorial writers and commentators, to the pressure groups. Furthermore, once in office, he tends to stay there. Thus a senator may be less sensitive than a representative to basic shifts in the underlying mood of the electorate as a whole.

I make this comment by way of observation and not of criticism. The Founding Fathers intended, after all, that the Senate be a balance wheel which would moderate the impulses of the moment. This function it in fact performs, even though at any point of time those who believe the current impulses are the correct ones may tend to impatience. The Senate, however, is not an institution to which the impatient should gravitate. It has its own pace; and, under the present rules, it takes a little maturing on the vine of seniority to be in a position to have a large impact on the body politic.

It would be inaccurate, however, and unfair to the institution to suggest that the newest members are without the power to do more than register their 1 per cent of the Senate's total vote. The ancient tradition that stated that freshman senators were to be seen and not heard has disappeared. Somewhat to my surprise, on my initial rounds I was encouraged by the most senior members to speak out when I felt I had learned the ropes and had something to say—which was not, I hasten to say, an invitation to be brash.

In point of fact, I soon learned that there are a number of ways in which even Number 99 can make his imprint on the law of the land. If he is willing to do the necessary homework on a bill before his committee, if he attends meetings, if he presents arguments for or against specific provisions, he does have a chance to mold its final form. I have found that my own views will be given as careful a hearing as those of any other member of the committees on which I have served; again the essential courtesy of the Senate comes to the fore. It is also possible, by submitting appropriate amendments, to shape legislation after it has reached the floor.

It will also occasionally be the lot of a senator to come across an idea of such universal appeal that it will whisk through the legislative process in record time —witness two bills I introduced involving certain benefits for prisoners of war and those missing in action in Indochina. Each immediately attracted more than sixty co-sponsors, and each has since been signed into law.

Finally, there are the educational opportunities—and hence, responsibilities —which the Senate opens up to the newest of senators. These had not occurred to me when I first decided to run for office, but it did not take long for me to appreciate the skill with which some of the more liberal members were utilizing their office to reach the public. They would schedule time on the Senate floor, often in tandem, to deliver themselves of learned or impassioned speeches to an empty chamber. Their wisdom might be wasted on the Senate air, but the exercise enabled them to alert the press that Senator So-and-so would deliver remarks on such-and-such a topic at the scheduled time. Copies of the speech would be distributed, and the gist of the senator's argument and points he wished to make would become part of the nation's informational bloodstream. I also noted that conservative-minded senators were generally not so alert in this regard.

Whether utilized or not, the opportunity does exist for a senator to present his views on the important issues with some reasonable assurance that they will not be totally lost. Only by exploiting these opportunities for public education can he expect to help the electorate become more adequately informed on the basic issues. This in turn bears on the legislative process because, in the last analysis, public opinion dictates the outside limits of the options available to the Congress. By joining in the public debate and articulating the arguments in support of his own positions, a new senator—even one labeled "Conservative-Republican"—can contribute to the educational process which ultimately finds its reflection in national policy.

Snuff and Civility

These, then, are the random impressions of the United States Senate by one of its newest members: It is a deliberative body in which there is too little time to deliberate. It is a place where a senator is entitled to free haircuts (although he is expected to tip the barber a dollar) in a barbershop which keeps a shaving mug with his name on it. It is a place where on each desk there is a little inkwell, a wooden pen with steel nibs, and a glass bottle filled with sand with which to blot writing, and where on either side of the presiding officer's desk is a spittoon and a box of snuff.

Yet it is also a place where the rules of civility are still observed, and the rights and independence of each individual still respected. It is a place where many of the major decisions affecting the shape of our times are made; a place where even the least of its members may have a hand in making them.

It is, all in all, a good place to be.

Study Questions

1. Whom does the congressman represent? If you were elected congressman of your district, what kind of constituency would you represent? What kind of "representative role" would you pursue? Why?

2. Define "constituency" in terms of congressional electoral behavior. What problems does a congressman have in communicating with his constituents?

3. How many "constituencies" does a congressman have? To which one does he owe his responsibility?

4. A congressman need not worry about the service function of his job—his staff can take care of this, allowing the congressman maximum time for meaningful legislative work. After all, legislation is a key issue with the voters. Comment on these statements.

5. Construct a voting profile of your senator and congressman (i.e., votes on key issues). Do you believe that they are representing their constituencies in a reasonable way? Why?

6. On what kind of platform would you campaign as senator in your state? As a member of the House of Representatives? Explain.

7. As a voter, what is the best way to communicate with your congressmen and get them to respond to your grievances or opinions? What impact do you have as an individual voter?

Bibliography

Books:

Berman, Daniel M. *In Congress Assembled.* Toronto, Canada: The Macmillan Company, 1969, Chapters 1-3 and 6-7.

Clausen, Aage R. *How Congressmen Decide: A Policy Focus.* New York: St. Martin's Press, 1973.
Davidson, Roger H. *The Role of the Congressman.* New York: Pegasus, 1969.
Dexter, Lewis Anthony. *The Sociology and Politics of Congress.* Chicago: Rand McNally and Co., 1969.
Green, Mark J., Fallows, James M., and Zwick, David R., *Who Runs Congress?* (Ralph Nader Congress Project) New York: Bantam Books, Inc., 1972.
Harris, Joseph P. *Congress and the Legislative Process.* 2d ed. New York: McGraw-Hill Book Company, 1972; Chapter 2: "The Member of Congress and his World."
Hartke, Vance. *You and Your Senator.* New York: Coward-McCann, Inc., 1970.
Hinkley, Barbara. *Stability and Change in Congress.* New York: Harper & Row, Publishers, 1971; Chapter 3: "Representational Roles."
Huitt, Ralph K., and Peabody, Robert L. *Congress: Two Decades of Analysis.* New York: Harper & Row, Publishers, 1969; Part II, Chapter 4: "The Outsider in the Senate: An Alternative Role."
Matthews, Donald R. *U.S. Senators and Their World.* New York: W. W. Norton & Company, Inc., 1973.
Peabody, Robert L., and Polsby, Nelson W., eds. *New Perspectives on the House of Representatives,* 2d ed. Chicago: Rand McNally & Company, 1969; Part I.
Ripley, Randall B. *Power in the Senate.* New York: St. Martin's Press, 1969.

Articles:

Deckard, Barbara. "State Party Delegations in the U.S. House of Representatives—A Comparative Study of Group Cohesion." *The Journal of Politics,* Vol. 34, No. 1 (February, 1972), pp. 199-222.
"Tulips to Politics—The World of Congressmen's Aides." *U.S. News and World Report,* Vol. 77, No. 1 (July, 1974), p. 28.

CHAPTER 8
Authority, Leadership and Policy-Making in Congress

Leadership in the United States Congress is a very delicate balance between influence and democracy. In one sense, the individual member of Congress is independent of leadership or centers of power because the legitimacy of his office depends on his constituency, not on his fellow congressmen. There are few effective sanctions that can be imposed upon him in his own district or state as long as he retains constituency support. His colleagues in Congress can, to a certain extent, punish his insubordination or maverick tendencies, but as long as his constituents believe him solicitous of their welfare, such punishment will not seriously affect his chances for reelection. Because of this one might expect leadership to be so far decentralized as to be ineffective. However, this is not the case at all.

Leadership in Congress is very much evident and very important in policy-making decisions. Basically, this is because the individual member of Congress can accomplish nothing alone. He is almost completely dependent upon others to get things done, whether for his district, state, or the nation as a whole. Every bill needs many supporters, and this means that there is a constant interplay of accommodation and compromise. Leadership is necessary to see that this process is carried out as smoothly as possible.

There are two distinct types of leaders in Congress: the elective or the party leaders, that is those with formal positions of leadership within the parties, and the seniority leaders, such as usually act as committee chairmen. Both types of leaders provide a measure of control and direction to the otherwise decentralized and divided nature of business in Congress.

Party leaders are able to provide organization because Congress is structured on party lines and because all congressmen have a stake in their party. If the party is unsuccessful and loses control of Congress, all legislators of that party suffer, including those from safe districts, who must lose committee chairmanships. Also the party members, as a result of their long association and socialization, do develop a certain sense of party loyalty and camaraderie.

The party leaders have some formal powers that they can use against dissident members, as we shall see later. More important than formal powers however, are the informal powers that result from expertise and personal charm. These assets are more useful and effective than formal powers in influencing colleagues. Influence in the context of equality and non-hierarchy depends on the respect the leaders can command from their colleagues. Such respect results from a leader's awareness of his fellow members' needs and aspirations, his knowledge of the rules, and his skill and personality. Party organization is needed more in the House than in the Senate, because of the larger membership. As a result, the House leaders tend to be stronger vis-à-vis their colleagues than Senate leaders.

The Republican and Democratic party organizations, in both houses of Congress are very similar. They consist of (1) the party caucus, or the conference, as the Republicans call it, of all members of the party; (2) the party leaders—the Speaker, the majority and minority leaders; (3) the whips—a chief whip and assistant whips in each party; and (4) the respective party Committees on Committees. In the House, the Rules Committee may also be regarded as an instrument of the majority party.

Party Leadership in the House

The *Speaker* is the principal party leader in the House. Although formally chosen by the whole House of Representatives, he is in fact picked by the party that commands a majority in the House. Once in office, the Speaker acts openly as party leader and is expected to use his position to support his party's program. His formal powers, though not as great as in the past, are still important. He can grant or withhold recognition to those who wish to speak. He settles parliamentary disputes (with the help of a specialist in procedure); he appoints members of select and conference committees (but not standing committees); he refers bills to committee, and, in general, directs the business on the House floor.

Next to the Speaker, the most important party leader in the House is the *majority floor leader*. Like the Speaker, he is chosen by the majority party caucus, but unlike the Speaker, he is an officer only of his party and not of the House proper. The majority leader, along with the Speaker, helps plan party strategy, confers with other party leaders and key committee members, and keeps in touch with party members. He also has the power to appoint members of the Policy Committee to help him in the task of scheduling legislation. The power of scheduling, if used discreetly, can decide the fate of a bill. Bills that reach the floor late have a smaller chance of being voted upon; in addition, the Senate will probably have little time to act on the bill in the same session. Bills that do not pass both houses before the next congressional election (which is never far off as it comes every two years) must be re-introduced in the next Congress. Scheduling or timing is, therefore, important.

The *minority floor leader* plays a role similar to that of the majority leader; each is engaged in winning support for his party's position on an issue. But the minority leader has little influence on the House timetable, because his party is not in power. He is his party's prospective Speaker; he will step into the Speakership when his party gains a majority in the House. Although a minority party is always at a disadvantage when it comes to legislative power, a President of a minority party can use the veto effectively to offset the majority's power, as Eisenhower did in his later years of office.

Next, we come the the *party whips*. They are two-way channels of communication. They inform the leadership of the views and voting intentions of members of the party, and pass down information as to the position of the leadership on legislative issues before Congress. The whips exert mild pressure to support the leadership, and try to insure maximum attendance on the floor when critical votes are imminent. The whip is in a potential power position because of his information resources.

Backing up the party leaders in the House are the two *Committees on Committees*. They assign members to the various standing committees of the House, where substantive policies are shaped. Naturally, each congressman wants to be on the most powerful committees, particularly those whose work affects his district or constituency.

Although technically one of the twenty standing committees of the House, the *Rules Committee* is in a class by itself. It derives its power from its function as a traffic director. It must sort the important legislation from the relatively unimportant and set rules for discussion and priority time (how long a bill should be debated and what floor amendments should be allowed). In view of the crowded calendars of the House, this procedure was established to regulate the flow of business. In practice the procedure benefits the majority. The Rules Committee sets time and terms of floor debate not on the basis of a bill's overall importance, but rather on one of two criteria: (1) Whether the proposed bill is a good public policy or not; and (2) whether it has a chance, in the judgment of party leaders, of passing. Sometimes the committee members exercise their own judgment on the merits of legislation, but quite often they act on the policy of the party leadership. As the present chairman of the Rules Committee, Ray J. Madden (D-Indiana), says: "We go along with the leadership just like the Rules Committee should, but when bills come along that look like they're going to be upset on the floor, we hold them up until some more work can be done on them." The Rules Committee can thus promote a bill, or bargain to get the type of bill it wants by refusing to grant it a rule (i.e., prescribe procedure for its consideration) until it is modified, or hold it up until the time is favorable or unfavorable for passage, depending on the committee's own inclinations. The committee also controls the process of amendments from the floor; it can permit or prevent an amendment unwelcome to the bill's sponsors. The Rules Committee thus occupies a pivotal position in the congressional power structure.

Party Leadership in the Senate

Two important positions in the Senate are those of the *president* and the *president pro tempore*. The president of the Senate is the Vice President of the United States. Despite his position, he has much less control over the Senate than the Speaker has over the House. He is not a member of the Senate and he can vote only in case of a tie. He is supposed to recognize members in the order in which they rise. The president pro tempore in reality is chosen by the majority party and presides in the absence of the Vice President. He may have personal influence but he has no control over the business of the Senate. Such power resides elsewhere or is controlled by Senate rules.

The source of leverage in the Senate is the *majority floor leader*. Unlike the majority leader in the House, he does not have to share his authority with a powerful officer like the Speaker, or a Rules Committee. However, he is restricted by the strong-willed individuals of the Senate, and he must contend with the only slightly less influential minority party leader. Both the majority and minority leaders, in consultation with other Senate members, set the order of business in the Senate but they have no power to control the debate; the Senate allows virtually unlimited debate.

As a result of decentralized leadership in the Senate, the power of a majority floor leader varies greatly, depending on the individual. For example, Lyndon Johnson was an aggressive and dominating leader; he had, according to popular reports, great influence. The present majority leader, Mike Mansfield, is more passive and is reported to be less directly influential on fellow members. This does not necessarily mean that Mansfield's leadership produces fewer victories for his party than Johnson did. In fact, the data bear out the reverse: Mansfield scores better both on party cohesion and party unity.

Johnson's and Mansfield's Senate Majority Leadership: A Comparison

	\multicolumn{4}{c}{Congresses}
	85th	86th	87th	88th
	LJ	LJ	MM	MM
1. Democratic victories on "party line" roll call votes	50%	70%	96%	84%
2. Index of party cohesion	26	41	40	45

Source: John Stewart, "Two Strategies of Leadership: Johnson and Mansfield" in Nelson Polsby (ed.), *Congressional Behavior* (New York: Random House, 1971), pp. 85–86.

The reason for this apparent contradiction is that party unity and victories do not depend on a majority leader's personal influence alone; there are other factors involved. For example, Johnson held the position under a Republican minority President whereas Mansfield served under a Democratic (majority party) President until 1969.

The *whips* in the Senate perform functions similar to those of whips in the House. They check voting intentions of their party's rank and file, and they inform them of the party's position on issues; they try to round up supporters of party line when important votes are taken. A whip's effectiveness in his job depends on his awareness of what's happening in and around the legislative chamber, and his capacity to anticipate the approximate time when a vote might be taken so that he can call the party faithfuls to the floor. If he puts out the call much in advance of voting time, the members may assemble, wait for a while, and then disperse. So timing is crucial.

Like the House, the Senate also has two *Committees on Commit-*

tees. They perform the same functions as their House counterparts—distributing the available committee assignments among the party members to seventeen standing committees in the Senate.

Of course, when we talk about party leaders in Congress, we ought to be clear about what we mean by the term *leaders*. Congressional party leaders are not leaders in the sense that brigadiers are leaders of their battalions. They have no formal powers to command allegiance of fellow partisans. They do, of course, have some favors and advantages which they can bestow on party faithfuls and withhold from frequent mavericks. Thus, for instance, they can facilitate assignment of a congressman to a desirable committee; they can help a congressman with his voters by providing support for a project which his constituents desire or stand to benefit from; they have a voice in the allocation of office space, which can vary in size and quality; they control appointments to various blue-ribbon fact-finding overseas commissions that are set up from time to time. There are also intrinsic rewards that flow from being close to leaders. Still, all these inducements do not guarantee the congressional party leaders the allegiance of fellow partisans. As already stated, the leaders' personality and personal skills are more important in acquiring influence and power than are their formal positions of leadership.

The Committee System

The heart and center of the legislative process lies in the committees. These committees were set up to handle the enormous volume of bills and resolutions introduced in each legislative session of Congress. There are four types of committees:
1. *Standing committees* are permanent units established by the rules of each house; they continue from one session to the next. The House of Representatives has twenty and the Senate seventeen such committees, and there are some 250 subcommittees. The standing committees are by far the most important, for they do the main work of shaping legislation.
2. *Select committees* are special or ad hoc units established for a specific purpose such as an investigation (e.g., the Senate Watergate Committee). After submitting their report, these committees are dissolved.
3. *Joint committees* are composed of legislators from both chambers (e.g., Joint Committee on Atomic Energy).
4. *Conference committees* are a special type of joint committee. Their members are appointed by the presiding officers of the

House and Senate. Their function is to iron out differences over legislative proposals which have passed through both houses in different versions. These committees are of crucial importance since the fate of many legislative proposals depends on what happens here.

While all the standing committees of Congress have authority and expertise in their own policy areas, not all of them are equally prestigious or of equal concern to a congressman. It is important for an individual congressman to be assigned to a committee which is concerned with a subject of importance to his district and of interest to him. The committee assignments are made by seniority by each party's Committee on Committees. Until recently, House Democrats empowered Democratic members of the Ways and Means Committee to act as their Committee on Committees, making an already influential committee a controlling force in an otherwise decentralized system. Following Chairman Mills' widely-publicized scandal with stripper Fanne Fox, House Democrats, in 1975, transferred the power of making committee assignments to the Democratic Steering Committee, subject to the approval of the party caucus.

The Committee Chairmen:
The Seniority Rule and Their Power

Under the unwritten rule of seniority, chairmanships of standing committees are awarded to majority party members with the longest continuous service on the committee, and chairmanships of special committees are awarded according to length of service in the chamber itself. The senior member of the minority party serves as vice chairman. This rule is not found in the rule books of either house, but has long been accepted by most congressmen as the simplest and usually fairest way to choose heads of committees.

The chairmen have almost dictatorial power within their committees. They decide what bills will be discussed at what time in the calendar year, and place bills they do not like at the bottom of the list. They decide which members will study what questions, and how much money will be allotted to do the work. They set times of meetings, and if they do not want certain members there, they can conveniently forget to inform them of the time and place. Moreover, because they are usually on good terms with other committee heads, they may get legislation in another committee speeded up or slowed down. They may do this to reward or to discipline one of their own committee members for his cooperation or lack of it. In short, committee chairmen dominate committee procedure.

"Unwieldy? You call that unwieldy?"
Michael Witte Time Magazine © Time Inc.

The seniority, and therefore the power, of a committee chairman is linked to his home district, which is usually a safe one. If he has no major competition from rivals, and is continually reelected, he can move up from the ranks of relatively powerless junior congressmen to the ranks of the extremely powerful senior members of Congress, with positions on important standing committees. "The few members who reach the ultimate goal, chairmanship of a standing committee, do so by virtue of sheer endurance, and by being reelected and reelected by their constituents."[1] Thus, the key makers of national policy in Congress are locally chosen and locally responsible.

The seniority rule puts a premium on careful cultivation of the district. It bestows the most influence in Congress on those constituencies that are politically stable or even stagnant—where party competition is low, where a particular interest group or city or rural machine predominates. It stacks the cards against areas where the two parties are more evenly matched, where interest in politics is high, and competition between groups keen—those areas most likely to reflect quickly and typically the political tides that sweep the nation. The seniority system has given Southern Democrats, who meet little political competition in their districts, a disproportionate amount of power in Congress. In 1973, for example, eight of seventeen Senate standing committees and seven of twenty-one House standing committees were chaired by Southern Democrats.

If a man is elected by a very large majority in his district or state, therefore, the other members of Congress will tend to be deferential to him, thinking of him as a potential committee chairman who will one day be able to dispose favors himself. Current committee chairmen will try to get him on their committees, gain his friendship, and shape his thinking so he will support their policies and continue them after their own retirement. Members of his own age group will also try to gain his friendship; if they should fail to be reelected, he can help them. Also, after a few consecutive elections, he will be one of the "old men" looked to for leadership by freshman members. If he is continually reelected by large majorities, his colleagues will think he must be picking the right sides of the issues as far as the voters are concerned; they will listen to his opinions if for no other reason than to be on the side that will give them the desired popularity at home.

The unfortunate result of the seniority system is that most key congressional committees end up with stereotypes: older members, older chairmen, conservative Republicans or conservative Southern Democrats, often with the same general viewpoints, interests and values. They are closed-in pockets of power that can very easily shut off outside influences. This is dangerous in a fast-changing world. Seniority can also promote mediocre congressmen to top positions of power and prestige.

Sometimes seniority produces chairmen of key committees who are out of sympathy with the objectives of their party and its presidential leadership. Thus a President devoted to foreign aid might find an old-style isolationist as chairman of the House Foreign Affairs Committee. Seniority can make party responsibility and discipline difficult.

The system, however, does provide the legislators with two main advantages. It provides an objective and impartial alternative to the bitter feuding that might otherwise occur over committee assignments and chairmanships; it acts as a buffer against the executive branch or pressure groups that might try to get particular legislators assigned to committees they are anxious to stack.

Although it cannot be called a breakdown of the seniority system, the 94th Congress that met in January, 1975 has certainly struck at the exclusiveness of this custom. The House Ways and Means Committee was shorn of its formidable power to make or break members by controlling their committee assignments, and this responsibility was transferred to the 2-year old Democratic Steering and Policy Committee of the House. The Steering Committee of the Democratic congressmen did not recommend the re-appointment of certain mighty committee chairmen and some of the old hands who were recommended by the committee were voted out by the caucus of all Democratic House members, for example, the now deposed chairmen, Edward Hebert of Armed Services, and W.R. Poage of the Agricultural Committee. Behind this buffeting of the age-old seniority rule are the 75 new freshmen Democrats in the 94th Congress who came to Washington in the 1974 Democratic landslide and who seem to be in no mood to simply sit in congressional committees, nod, and say "Amen, Charlie!" They expect themselves to be heard and not merely seen—a mood which is indicative of the times in which we live. From now on the chairmen of the myriad congressional committees will have to be more responsive to their committee members. This seems to portend a series of power conflicts between the traditional powerholders and the young members. It also may mean some new relationships between congressional committees, the executive, the bureaucracy, and interest groups.

Congressional Committees as Wielders of Power in Congress

Immediately following the initial reading of a bill before Congress it is sent to a standing committee under whose jurisdiction it seems to fall. The committee jurisdictions occasionally overlap; this increases the discretion of party leaders in assigning bills to committees thought to be favorable or unfavorable to a particular proposal. From then on, the concerned committee is free to act upon it the way it wants to; it may or may not report the bill for House or Senate consideration. Most bills are simply pigeonholed by the committees. The committee can speed a bill through, that is, send it back to Congress for a quick vote, or, it can sit on a bill until late in the session. There is one remedy available to congressmen, from these delaying tactics, namely, the discharge procedure. Simply stated, the discharge procedure forces a bill to be brought to the floor for action by discharging the standing committee from further consideration of it. However, in order to discharge a committee of a bill, a majority of the total membership of that house must sign a petition. This procedure is a difficult one because challenges to one committee represent a threat to other committees of which other congressmen are members. Hence, congressmen shy away from the use of the discharge rule. For example, Professor James Robinson reports that out of more than two hundred discharge petitions filed between 1937 and 1960, only twenty-two received enough signatures to go on the calendar; fourteen of these bills were passed by the House, but only two become law.[2]

The committees thus determine what happens in Congress by their ability to determine proposed legislation. Committees can kill a bill by failing to act on it. If they do present it to the floor, they determine the form that will be considered by the House or Senate, and can exercise great control on the floor decision. Clearly then, committees are little legislatures with big powers in themselves. As Woodrow Wilson observed in 1885, "Congress in session is Congress on public exhibition, while Congress in its committee-rooms is Congress at work."[3] The two houses largely sit to sanction the conclusions of their committees.

Woodrow Wilson also noted two facts so obvious and familiar that their deep significance and profound effect are often missed. One fact is that the number of the committees and subcommittees is legion. The second fact is that these committees are bipartisan in composition, with the two parties represented in proportion to their total strength on the respective chamber. They are not working instruments of the majority party. The committees have become the instruments for resolution of conflicting policy views because of their bipartisan composition, their expertise in handling complex legislation, their domination of the legislative process, and the relationships of their members with constituents and key interest groups.[4]

The leaders of the House and Senate are in fact the chairmen of the standing committees, and there are as many of them as there are subjects of legislation. These chairmen do not constitute a cooperative body; each committee goes its own way, at its own pace. The Speaker is "a great party chief" but at bottom, the committees and the chairmen, because of their experience and seniority, shape, control and present legislation.

The bipartisan composition of the committees also has its consequences. Wilson observed that it is the representation of both parties on the committees that makes party responsibility indistinct and organized party action almost impossible. If the committees were composed entirely of majority party members, committee reports would be taken to represent the views of the party in power. The work of the committees makes it possible for a great many bills to be passed by bipartisan majorities in both the House and the Senate. This helps Congress run more smoothly and effectively, because such bills are passed not along strict party lines, but with basic consensus.

The 94th Congress

As a result of the 1974 congressional elections, the Democrats regained the initiative in domestic politics. The 94th Congress attempted to liberalize procedural rules. In the House, some power of the chairmen of the standing committees has been transferred to the numerical majority in the Democratic caucus. Conduct of committee business must now be palatable to that majority. In the Senate, under a new rule, it will take 3/5ths rather than 2/3rds of those voting to stop a filibuster. Filibuster will now be harder to practice and it may become harder to block progressive legislation. However, in view of the continuing strength of the traditional powers, the liberals and moderates will probably find it difficult to bring about significant changes.

In any case, the initiative rested with the Democrats. They were placed in a position where blame could not be shifted to the presidency. As Senator Walter F. Mondale (Democrat from Minnesota) stated a day after the election, "Now the heat is on us." With 291 Democrats in the House as opposed to 248 in the 93rd Congress and 61 in the Senate as opposed to the previous 58, it was clear that the Democrats had the numbers to do important things in the 94th Congress, including developing a coalition that could block presidential power.

Patterns of Policy-Making

Nature of Power in Congress and Policy-Making

From the above discussion, it is evident that power in Congress is diffused and fragmented. However, some coherence and direction to legislative business is provided by congressional parties and the congressional committees.

Since it is difficult to pin down any single center of leadership in Congress, the arena of leadership will vary with the type of issue in question. On party matters, leadership will repose in party leaders and its style will be patrimonial, stemming from personality and commitment to the party as the base of legitimacy.

Regional or local distributive policies follow a somewhat different pattern. This is the sphere of logrolling, where small groups band together and trade votes to help each other get bills passed. Leadership, therefore, is very decentralized and shifting.

Some issues are very technical or specialized; leadership in such instances belongs almost entirely to the realm of expertise. The relevant committee and individual members who have the necessary knowledge of the underlying facts and probable consequences will emerge as the accepted leaders on such issues. Once a committee has reached a position, it is usually accepted by the majority of members.

Often debate on the floor is perfunctory because members recognize that all of the relevant aspects have already been debated in committee by the experts in the field.

On major or controversial issues, which usually concern redistributive policies, leadership is found in an interplay of the President, the relevant Cabinet member, the party leadership in Congress, the responsible committees, and even individual members who have either a strong stake in the results or an authoritative competence in the subject. This conflictive type of politics invokes the full range of the various centers of power and leadership.

Congress versus the President

Commentators agree that over the years the power of Congress has diminished. Today it no longer effectively checks the President. It no longer is the originator of domestic programs; it does not have its own list of national priorities but merely reacts to the legislative measures recommended by the President. In foreign affairs, it has almost completely surrendered its role to the President. Whereas Congress once determined, item by item, how much money the government should spend and for what purpose, today it rarely alters the administration's budget by more than five percent. Although it has responsibility for appropriating funds, the President himself can impound them, as Nixon did with some eleven billion dollars in water-pollution control and highway money.

But while it is true that the power of Congress has diminished, it is also true that the President is not the master of all he surveys. Much of the congressional session may be taken up by the President's legislative programs, but he does not monopolize the legislative agenda, nor can he legislate without Congress. Congress may have little power in foreign policy decision making but it still must be called upon to legitimize or support the President's decisions. And while Congress may have lost the initiative in policy formulation, it still retains the crucial function of oversight, which is an important component of the policy-making process.

Legislative Oversight or
Congressional Control of Administration

By enacting laws and authorizing programs, Congress hopes to realize certain policy goals, but the goals cannot be achieved until the programs are funded and implemented. This implementation of programs and spending of money appropriated by Congress is, however, the function of the executive branch. Policy outcome depends as much on the implementation of legislation as on its enactment, but congressional intentions and executive implementation rarely correspond exactly. This divergence is partly due to the fact that the pressures exerted on Congress are not the same as those exerted on the executive branch. Different special interest groups have different degrees of access to the two branches of government, and they try to influence policy outcome by applying pressures where they can.

Congressmen, as representatives of taxpayers, are naturally interested in watching and controlling the executive agencies. This function of supervising and controlling, which is inherent in the congressional power to legislate new programs and create new agencies, is often known as legislative oversight of administration. There are basically seven ways in which the oversight function is performed by Congress:

1. Individual congressmen, as already noted, constantly interact with administrative agencies in response to the demands of their constituents who have problems with those agencies. This oversight procedure is, however, ad hoc and sporadic in manner. It is not a formal and systematic method of reviewing and evaluating the performance or efficiency of executive agencies.
2. The various congressional committees acquire great expertise in the policy areas under their respective jurisdictions. This expertise equips committee members to evaluate the effects of authorized programs against intended goals. To arrive at such assessments, the committees often hold hearings or embark upon investigations, which constitute a common means of congressional control of the executive. This method can be used to discipline a recalcitrant administrator by keeping him on Capitol Hill five days a week, thus using up all his time, or (rarely) by launching an inquiry into an administrator's role.
3. Government agencies need funds every year to carry on their activities and must therefore make annual requests to Congress for appropriations. This enables the Appropriations Committees of Congress to review the work of the administrative agencies and to decide whether to continue, curtail or abolish any of the programs or agencies.
4. From time to time, Congress appoints ad hoc committees to inquire into selected government activities; an example of this was the Senate Watergate Committee.
5. The Government Operations Committees of Congress have the

formal authority to investigate any government activity, but they usually do so only when a substantive committee fails to act.
6. The Senate has the authority to confirm or reject presidential appointments of certain high-ranking officials of the federal government. This share in the appointive power gives it a measure of influence over bureaucratic policy-making. In addition, both houses of Congress are involved in confirming vice presidential appointments, in accordance with the Twenty-fifth Amendment.
7. Finally, there is the seldom-used process of impeachment.

In conclusion, we may point out that government policy-making involves battles not only among special interests, and between those interests and the government branches, but also among the government branches, particularly between the executive branch and Congress. Over the years, Congress has lost the initiative in policy-making to the executive. It is in the President's office that programs originate today, and Congress merely reacts to proposals presented to it by the President. But Congress still retains the function of oversight, which may involve as much policy-making as legal action does. However, despite the variety of tools or techniques available, the investigative capacity of Congress does not seem adequate. This is due partly to lack of adequate staff and partly to the confusion surrounding the exercise of oversight responsibilities. The lack of congruence between congressional committee organization and the frequently changing organization of executive agencies contributes to this confusion. There are also difficulties inherent in arriving at objective assessments, due to lack of adequate evaluative yardsticks or standards. The Watergate events pointed out the crucial need for strengthening the surveillance function of Congress so that a checked and balanced system of government may be realized.

How a Bill becomes Law

Generally the odds are against a proposed bill becoming law. This is because the process is lengthy and complicated. There are numerous phases or steps involved, and defective or negative action at any step is fatal. The procedure furnishes more opportunities to the opponents, who may want to kill or delay a bill, than it does to those congressmen or interest groups who seek positive action. It also forces the proponents to compromise and yield at each of the multiple steps in the decision process.

While the course of a bill is full of obstacles and possibilities for untimely death, a simplified analysis of the general procedure by which a bill becomes law is presented below:

1. *Introduction:* A bill may be introduced by any member of the House or Senate in his respective house. Most legislation begins with similar proposals in both houses. This is because most bills are actually drafted by the executive branch, although they are formally introduced by congressmen.
2. *Referral of bills to committees:* After a bill is introduced, it is given the prefix "HR" in the House or "S" in the Senate, and a number that indicates the order of its introduction. It is then referred to an appropriate committee by the Speaker of the House or the presiding officer of the Senate. The Committee may:
   (a) pigeonhole or disregard the bill (in which case the bill dies)
   (b) hold public hearings
   (c) report the bill to the house favorably or unfavorably, with or without amendments
   There is a procedure (the discharge rule) by which a committee can be forced to report a bill to the house, but it is rarely used because of operational difficulty, as we explained previously.
3. *Floor Action:* When a committee reports a bill, it is placed on the calendar, to await consideration. If it is not considered before the end of the session, the bill dies. If it is called up for consideration, it is debated, amended, and then passed or rejected or recommitted. (A motion to recommit the bill to committee, if carried, usually means the bill is dead.)
   If a bill is passed, it is sent to the other house, which may:
   (a) pass it as submitted
   (b) reject it and advise the other house of its action
   (c) simply ignore the bill
   (d) refer it to a committee for study and attention
   (e) pass it but not in the same form as passed in the other chamber
4. *Conference Committees (or Conflict Resolution):* Since important bills almost always pass the two houses in differing versions, it is often necessary to seek a basis of agreement. The usual method of resolving differences between the two houses is for the presiding officer of each house to appoint members to

serve on a Conference Committee which endeavors to work out a compromise. The compromise bill which emerges could virtually amount to a new bill, although in theory the conferees are not allowed to write new legislation when reconciling the two versions.
5. *Back to Each House:* The report of the Conference Committee is then accepted or rejected as a whole by each house. The approval of the report is of course approval of the compromise bill worked out by the Conference Committee. If it is accepted by both houses, it is signed by the Speaker of the House and the presiding officer of the Senate and sent to the White House for presidential action.
6. *Presidential Action:*
   (a) The President may sign the bill, whereupon it becomes law.
   (b) If he does not sign it within ten days (Sundays excepted) following congressional approval, and Congress is in session, the bill becomes law.
   (c) If, however, Congress adjourns before the ten days expire, as sometimes happens because of the rush of legislation in the last days of a session, and the President has not signed the bill, the bill is dead. This procedure is called the pocket veto.
   (d) The President may return the bill to the house which originated it, without his signature but with a message giving reasons for his action. If no action is taken on the message by the chamber concerned, the bill is dead.
   (e) Finally, the President may veto the bill.
7. *Back to Congress* (maybe): Congress can override the President's veto and enact the bill, the objections of the President to the contrary notwithstanding. This requires a two-thirds vote of those present (who must form a quorum) in both the House and the Senate.

The intricacies and complexities of the legislative process test even the most committed and skilled congressman. Not only must he develop his knowledge of the legislative procedures and rules of order within the Congress, he must establish a wide web of personal relationships with his colleagues, interest groups, the presidential office, the bureaucracy, and his own constituency. At the same time the congressman must always be sensitive to the impact of the mass media and his image. How the congressman views his role in Congress will in many ways determine the kinds of relationships that will be established with the individuals and groups that have an influence on his office. How well the congressman can develop and maintain a working relationship with his colleagues will determine his effectiveness. Most important, his ability to balance his congressional obligations with those of his constituency will significantly affect his ability to win in the next election.

Legislative Flow of a Bill

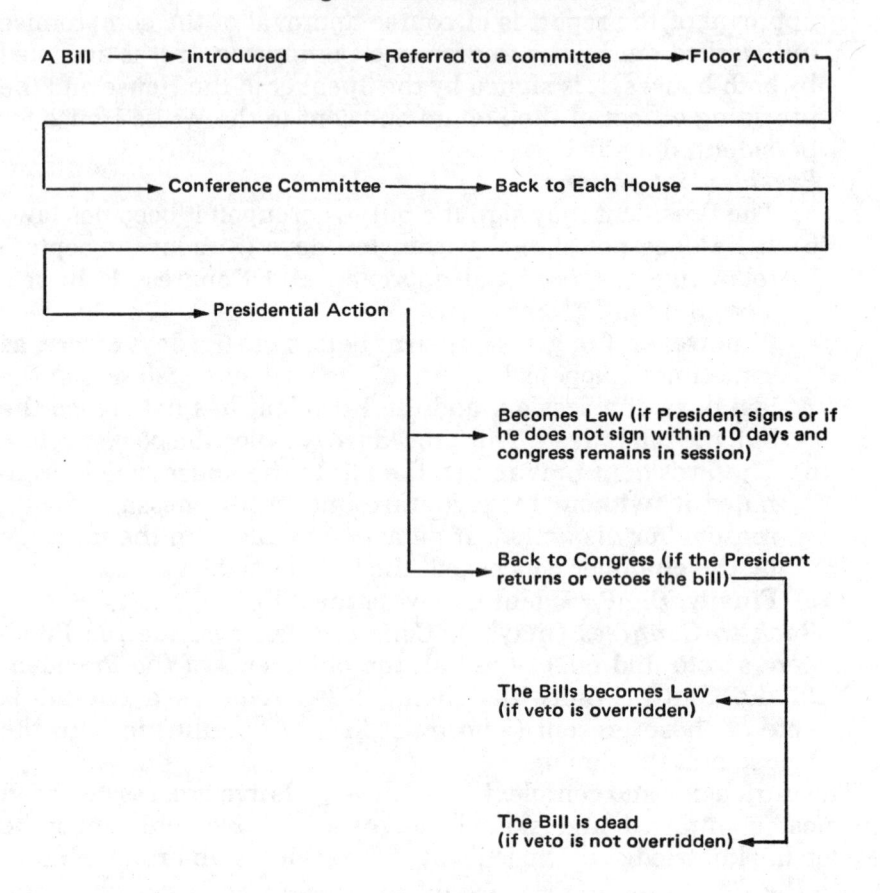

A Bill ⟶ introduced ⟶ Referred to a committee ⟶ Floor Action

⟶ Conference Committee ⟶ Back to Each House

⟶ Presidential Action

⟶ Becomes Law (if President signs or if he does not sign within 10 days and congress remains in session)

⟶ Back to Congress (if the President returns or vetoes the bill)

The Bills becomes Law (if veto is overridden)

The Bill is dead (if veto is not overridden)

NOTES

1. Richard Bolling, *House out of Order* (New York: E. P. Dutton & Co., 1967), p. 39.
2. James A. Robinson, *The House Rules Committee* (Indianapolis: Bobbs-Merrill, 1963), pp. 6, 33.
3. Woodrow Wilson, *Congressional Government* (New York: Meridian Books, 1956), p. 69.
4. William Morrow, *Congressional Committees* (New York: Scribner's Sons, 1969), p. 89

Selected Readings

One of the major criticisms of Congress is its failure to develop an effective counter to presidential programs. As a matter of fact, it is usually the President who takes the initiative in legislative programs. In most cases Congress becomes a reactive instrument rather than an initiating one. Some scholars also suggest that Congress is not a very good reactive instrument either. They would point to the many interests within the Congress and the concern to satisfy special constituencies or regional interests which militate against the development of a unified congressional front to counter the President—except in times of clear crisis, such as the Watergate affair. Elizabeth Drew, in the selection to this chapter is highly critical of Congress. Reviewing recent historical events, she argues that even when Congress did act on some important issues, it was only forced to do so by its own embarrassment or outside pressure. For example, she notes that Congress finally cut off the bombing in Cambodia—but this was done only after nine years of war. She notes however that "Because the Congress moves slowly and in strange ways, it is difficult to take its true measure at any given time." Nevertheless, there have been some reforms in the House. For example, the Democratic party members have agreed "to limit to one the number of committees or subcommittees a member may head." This allows more participation by junior members of Congress. Also, there is a continuing evaluation by congressional committees regarding congressional procedures. In the final analysis, however, Drew suggests that the inner conflicts of Congress, the character of the congressional constituency, and the slow, lumbering process of legislation give the institution a disadvantage in terms of the executive branch. The author concludes that lack of congressional responsiveness, citizen apathy, congressional self-interest, and general disgust with politicians coming out of Watergate may do much to undermine congressional power. The elections of 1974 provided large majorities for the Democrats in Congress. They have an opportunity to make some important changes. All one can do is wait and see what evolves out of the 94th Congress.

8.1

Why Congress Won't Fight

ELIZABETH DREW

"I think," said the Senator, summing up a conversation about attempts by the Congress to restore its powers, "we've made substantial headlines—I mean headway."

"Never again," said the Congressman, "will the Congress approve a Gulf of Tonkin resolution—I hope."

When the 93d Congress convened at the beginning of this year, many politicians were saying that the imbalance of power between the legislative and executive branches was such that we were facing a "constitutional crisis." To politicians, phrases like "constitutional crisis," and "the survival of our democratic system," like the deep tones on the organ, lend solemnity to the topic at hand.

But causes for their expressions of concern were apparent enough. The President was unilaterally terminating programs and impounding money. The "carpet bombing" of North Vietnam over the Christmas holidays was sufficiently contrary to the growing Congressional opposition to the war that it had been done while the lawmakers were out of town. Several lawmakers thought that the bombing lacked legal authority. Major policy-makers were refusing to appear before the Congress to explain their policies. The Attorney General, stretching the doctrine of "executive privilege" to unprecedented breadth, stated that the President could prevent anyone in the executive branch from appearing before, or releasing any documents to the Congress. The President did not trouble himself to make the traditional trip down Pennsylvania Avenue to deliver a State of the Union message, but instead sent it to the Capitol by messenger.

Enraged and embarrassed, aware that the President had turned them into walking cartoons, members of Congress made speeches about the need to restore the balance of power. There was also, it seemed, an unprecedented consensus on

From *The New York Times Magazine*, September 23, 1973. © 1973 by The New York Times Company. Reprinted by permission.

Capitol Hill that if the Congress was to meet the "crisis," it had to change its ways. And it commenced, with unaccustomed vigor, to do so.

Within three months, the dam holding back that collection of events known as "Watergate" had burst. It stood to reason that the President's troubles enhanced Congress's opportunity to restore itself as an effective branch of the Government. Moreover, "Watergate"—and the uses of power by the executive branch it revealed—underscored the necessity that it do so. But now there is evidence that "Watergate" has diminished Congress's zeal to restore itself. The President and the Congress are now in a name-calling match over who is responsible for how many bills that have or have not passed. But that is not the central issue. The central issue is whether or not we have a system of checks and balances. To the extent that the Congress was motivated at the beginning of the year by its own embarrassment, the embarrassment of the President has reduced its motivation. "There is," Senator Adlai Stevenson, Democrat of Illinois, said recently, "a new complacency because the President is weakened." "The heat's off," said Representative Les Aspin, Democrat of Wisconsin.

This should not, in fact be very surprising. It is not inconsistent with deeply ingrained Congressional habits. To understand how it does and does not work, a minimal grasp of the Congress's tribal culture is essential. The quality of ego that attracts most people into politics is not conducive to collective action once they succeed. Even when a consensus has formed that it is time to act, the burning question may be whose name is on the bill. The Senate's consideration of campaign spending reform legislation has been marked by senatorial jockeying for the lead position. Once elected, most politicians' primary ambition is to get re-elected. This requires, as they see it, playing it safe. The Congress does not like to take responsibility. It would prefer not to have to end a war, delay development of a weapon, raise taxes, or take on a President—except when it appears safe to do so. And after it has taken an important action, it usually wants to take a rest.

The Congress tends to deal in indirection, to avoid substantive questions. When it does vote on an important issue it is likely to obscure the question in baroque language and then put it in the form of a motion to table a motion to do something or other. The Congress's distaste for confrontation spills over into its language: It is not accidental that members of Congress refer to each other not by name, but as "the gentleman from Illinois," "the Senator from Nevada," or that the Senate and the House refer to the other body as "the other body." The quaint rituals, the disinclination to give offense do help to keep the Congress from flying apart.

They also have substantive consequences. The Congress's prophets are usually without honor. (Wayne Morse's obsessive opposition to the war was considered a bit embarrassing.) The talents of its more gifted members, those most in touch with contemporary questions, are often suppressed. Respect for territorial rights can have important effect. If John Stennis, Democrat of Mississippi, says that he is keeping an eye on the C.I.A., others won't. This reinforces the buddy system by which the Congress "oversees" so many executive branch functions. The overseers are cultivated by, befriend and often end up protecting the overseen. Outright confrontations between Congress and the executive branch, such as they are, are generally limited to the White House or Cabinet levels. At less lofty heights, there

276 *Authority, Leadership and Policy-Making in Congress*

is a rich proliferation of sweetheart contracts. The subcommittee chairman and the agency chief are often the best of friends (as political "friendships" go). The Congress's fraternal way of making decisions about its own procedures and structure can shape our destiny in rather important ways. When the Congress convened at the beginning of this year, only Philip Hart, Democrat of Michigan, had the temerity to object when his fellow Democrats bestowed the title of President pro tem, by virtue of his seniority, upon James Eastland, Democrat of Mississippi. The position is largely ceremonial, but it also places James Eastland third in line of succession to the Presidency.

Because the Congress moves slowly and in strange ways, it is difficult to take its true measure at any given time. The box score of bills passed is misleading. A seemingly minor, perhaps unnoticed, provision of a piece of legislation can have a major effect on national policy. Almost imperceptibly, forces can build that will, at some future point, have great impact.

If one is to accept Congress's self-advertisements, it has already taken major steps to redress the balance of power. Both the House and the Senate have passed bills designed to circumscribe the President's powers to wage war and impound funds. But as of now, both bills still have some hurdles to overcome. The House and the Senate have to reach compromises on important differences in both measures. If the President vetoes them, both chambers have to muster the votes of two-thirds of their members to override the veto—an uncertain prospect. Moreover, both measures could be seen as conferring some legitimacy on the President's unilateral right to go to war and impound money. They state certain circumstances under which he could do both, thus perhaps lending authority to Presidential actions that might otherwise be without authority. They could, in other words, amount to Congressional complicity in its own undoing. Like Huck Finn, the Congress might

The Exorcist

Cartoon by Joseph Fischetti, Courtesy of Publishers-Hall Syndicate
Chicago Daily News—Sat./Sun. Feb. 16/17 1974

be attending its own funeral, the differences being that Finn, at least, saw what was going on.

Congress did, to be sure, vote to cut off the bombing of Cambodia, a move that is presumed to have ended the war in Southeast Asia. It was an unprecedented action. But the degree of courage that can be attributed to this step depends upon one's view of the context in which it was taken. The war had lasted nine years. A peace agreement had been reached. The bombing of Cambodia, a "neutral" country, was without legal authority. American troops, whose protection had been cited to justify previous bombing, were home. When important members of Congress questioned Administration officials about the bombing, they were told that even if Congress denied funds for the bombing, it would be continued. The logical extension was that a President could bomb anywhere, any time, no matter what the Congress said. Even some of the fiercest old former hawks were disturbed at this notion. The termination date was, moreover, a compromise—a compromise with curious implications. Before the vote, there was no Congressional authorization for the bombing. As some see it, the Congress in effect sanctioned 92 days of illegal bombing of a country with whom we were not officially at war.

And there is another fact about the bombing cutoff that even some of its sponsors, in their jubilation and self-congratulation, seem to have missed. Through a last-minute piece of legislative legerdemain by opponents of the cutoff—by the removal of two words—its effect was rendered short-lived. The reports from Capitol Hill led the nation to believe that Congress had ended the war in Southeast Asia. In fact, it had ended it only until September 30. After that date the President may feel that he is free once more to bomb.

Whether even these actions would have been taken if the President had not been in a weakened condition is anybody's guess. Perhaps they would have. But the Congress does have a sort of animal instinct about changes in the flow of power. There was a time when Lyndon Johnson was extracting bill after bill from a complaisant Congress. Suddenly, he was defeated on a relatively minor measure in the House of Representatives. Johnson, who understood these things, turned to an aide and said, "Now the whale has shed some blood, and the sharks will move in." He was correct.

"What this institution needs," said Senator Stevenson, who has held some hearings on Congressional reform, "is power. Our wounds are self-inflicted. The weaknesses will come back to haunt us. I want a strong executive, but I also want to restore the system of checks and balances. We can't do that through a series of confrontations between Congress and the executive, where one kicks the other because it is crippled. The President did that to us, and now we are doing that to the President." The real question, then, is how the Congress is doing at other than playing "kick the President."

One example is indicative. The Congress was sufficiently disturbed at the President's impoundment of funds, and also its own vulnerability to charges of profligacy, that it set out to overhaul its methods of dealing with the Federal budget. The idea was to replace its haphazard method of funding the various Federal activities with a comprehensive approach. To avoid being labeled "spenders," the Congress would set a spending ceiling, and then consider the trade-offs of spending for different purposes within the Congressionally set limit. A joint Senate-House budget committee would be established to set the ceiling and allocate the priorities. It was an earnest move to reform, earnestly pushed by reformers within the Congress. Many believed that as Congressional budgeting became more "rational" in form, it would also change in substance. It was assumed that more money would be spent for domestic, as opposed to military, purposes, and some pointless subsidies would be dropped. On this, it seemed clear, reasonable people could agree.

But there was some miscalculation. The reformers had fashioned an instrument of enormous potential power. The senior members of the appropriating and taxing committees, not about to give up power, simply arranged that they would be in charge of the proposed joint committee. The liberals woke up one day and realized that they had been had, and sent their proposed reform back to the drawing boards. And a more informal attempt by Senate Democrats to draw up an alternative to the President's budget also foundered. Whenever a budget cut is proposed—in spending for anything from a weapon to school children's milk—the well-being of someone's constituency is threatened. Politicians are loath to gore their own oxen.

There have been, however, several reforms in the procedures by which Congress conducts its business, particularly in the House of Representatives. The impetus for change in the House began to make itself felt in 1971. That the House has done more than the Senate to modernize is attributed in part to the fact that it had more to do, in part to the passage of time, and in part to outside pressures for reform brought by such groups as Common Cause, the League of Women Voters, the antiwar and environmental movements and by Ralph Nader. In addition, an unusually large proportion of the most senior members of the House have succumbed in the past few years to mortality, fatigue or unaccustomed electoral challenges. The newest members of the House are not inclined to sit still for the "get-along, go-along" philosophy by which Sam Rayburn used to tame his flock. They are not content to wait, as their elders often did, some 10 or even 20 years to have a voice. House members' impatience is in almost direct proportion to their juniority. The chief beneficiaries of the pressures from the bottom and turnover at the top have been some middle-rank members who in an earlier era, say three years ago, would be frozen in a system of obeisance to their elders. The transformation has, however, stopped short of the miraculous. "This is still," said one House member, "the most enduring Oriental society in America."

But within the traditional frame of reference, there has been substantial change. Two years ago, House Democrats limited to one the number of committees or subcommittees a member may head. This has given more junior Democrats—such as John Culver of Iowa, Don Fraser of Minnesota, Lloyd Meeds of Washington—a chance to head subcommittees, and thus raise issues, hold hearings and play a major role in legislative debate. This year, the Democrats decided that committee chairmen must be approved by a caucus of House Democrats. This did not have the effect of dethroning any committee chairman, but House members maintain that the change makes a difference. Some chairmen did exhibit unease that there were any votes against them in the caucus, and it is hoped that this will discourage some of their more domineering ways.

Roll-call votes in the House are now electronically conducted, an innovation last

January that made the House as up-to-date in this respect as several state legislatures and the Parliament of India. (Reducing the time required for a roll-call vote from about 45 minutes to about 15 has also had the effect of interrupting more phone calls and lunches, and leaving Representatives more in the dark as to what they are dashing to the floor to decide. When, following a vote, one of the most thoughtful members of the House returned to his half-eaten hamburger in the House dining room one day, I asked him what the issue had been. "I don't know," he replied. "Something about limousines. Eddie Boland [Democrat of Massachusetts] was for it, so that's how I voted.") Teller votes, in which House members file down the aisle to cast a vote, must now be recorded, thus eliminating a time-honored method of camouflaging one's true position on a national issue. And it is now easier for members to offer amendments to bills under debate. Many Congressmen find this a mixed blessing, one which forces them to endure longer sessions and, worse, to take positions on issues they would just as soon avoid.

Several House members say that it is highly significant that there is now a commitee to study its committees. The basic arrangement of committee jurisdiction in the House has not been revised since 1946. At that time there were no urban, monetary or energy crises, among other things. In fact, compared to current times, there was hardly any Federal Government. The antiquated nature of the committee structure is evident in the response in both chambers to the energy crisis, currently all the rage on Capitol Hill. Several committees of the two houses have staked out jurisdiction over various pieces of the problem—mining, public works, antitrust, tax, trade and foreign policies—thus precluding the possibility of a coherent approach. Another basic problem in the committee structure, at least as difficult to resolve, arises from the fact that the committees are largely self-selected, skewing results of what they do and so what the full Congress usually does. Members from port cities anxious to protect domestic shipping and shipping subsidies, join the House Merchant Marine and Fisheries Committee, and do so. Members from areas that depend on military bases or contracts proceed, if they can, to the Armed Services Committees, and protect—as they were elected to—their constituents' interests.

The committee to study the committees is headed by Richard Bolling, Democrat of Missouri, a sophisticated student as well as member of the House. If Bolling succeeds in persuading the House to accept a more rational arrangement of committee jurisdiction—a process requiring extensive reallocations of power—he will have wrought one of the greatest miracles since the fishes and the loaves.

The recent changes in the processes and arrangements by which the House does its business have the effect of redistributing power from the committee chairmen to the leadership. (These transfers seem to be cyclical. When Speaker Joe Cannon was considered too powerful in the early nineteen-hundreds, power was transferred from the Speaker to the committee chairmen.) They give more scope to younger members, and make the politicians more accountable for their actions. "There has been," says Representative Tom Foley, Democrat of Washington, a "subtle and imperceptible change in the *Zeitgeist*. But frankly, I don't see the Congress yet really wanting to change its role from the passive one to the active one of being makers of policy. It has become accustomed to passivity. It still waits for 'the department' to come up with proposals. The basic reasons for this are tradition and convenience.

It's what most of the members have always known." I asked Aspin what the real purpose of the changes was. "I don't know," he replied. "We're making tactical adjustments without a strategy."

The Senate has not even done that much. While many of the most vital members of the House envy, and seek to join, their Senate counterparts, many of the most vital members of the Senate are less than delighted with their own lot. The heavy hand of seniority still dominates the Senate. It can affect the size of one's staff and the plenitude of one's office space. Early this year, Stevenson became chairman of a Senate Subcommittee on International Finance. The trade deficit was rising and the dollar value was dropping, but he still had to wage a floor fight in order to hire one professional subcommittee staff member. "The seniors," said one junior Senator, "don't see the necessity for more staff because they have more. They don't see the need to change the status quo because they are its architects." Seniority thus has an impact not just on the substance of the work that gets done, but on the authenticity of the democratic idea: It is not clear why some citizens should receive fewer benefits and services if they do not choose to return the same person to Congress, term after term, be he ever so senile.

It is symptomatic that it was not until 1971, and after several years of study, that the Senate equipped itself with microphones. (Perhaps the Senators kept each other inaudible for as long as possible by preference.) In this respect, it made itself as up-to-date as the House of Representatives. Not long ago, some Senators suggested that Senate offices be wired so that the Senators could attend to office business and still be informed as to what was happening on the Senate floor. But the proposal met with all manner of objections. As a trial compromise, someone sat in the gallery and typed notes on what was taking place, and the notes were sent to a few interested Senators' offices. The time-lag between the event and the informing of the Senators about it was approximately 20 minutes—just enough to prevent a Senator from rushing over to the floor to protest or participate in a decision. The project was abandoned. While the House voted earlier this year to hold its committee meetings in open session—a practice that some of its more important committees have already ceased to follow—the Senate decided against an open-meetings policy. Many of the most important decisions that the Congress makes are thus made in secret, and the politicians cannot be held accountable. (Several state legislatures now have open-meetings laws.)

Carl Albert, the Speaker of the House, and Mike Mansfield, the majority leader of the Senate, operate in similar styles: *laissez faire*, deferential. When they do take the lead from time to time, it is usually in response to strong pressures from within their ranks. Yet for all of the talk by both House and Senate Democrats about how they want strong leadership, the truth of the matter is that they don't. At least, not the strong leadership the Congress used to know. If the spirits of Lyndon Johnson and Sam Rayburn returned to reimpose the kind of order with which they ruled the Congress in the late nineteen-fifties, they would meet an unholy rebellion. Many of the politicians and much of the press and the reform-bent pressure groups would not tolerate the kind of passivity and inside game-playing that such leadership required. But it was that sort of leadership that enabled Johnson and Rayburn to go to the White House and negotiate as representatives of a co-equal branch. "If," says one House member, "we all toed the line and did what Carl Albert said, Carl Albert could go down there and negotiate with the President as an effective opponent. But who wants to do that?" Advocates of a "strong Congress" have tended to avoid that question. The Democratic majorities in both chambers are in fact more splintered than at any time in memory. The caucuses have caucuses. (House Democrats, who have a caucus, are divided in turn into a liberal caucus, a middle-of-the-road caucus, a Southern caucus, a rural caucus and a black caucus, which in turn is splintering into a black men's and a black women's caucus. There is also a bipartisan women's caucus.) If, then, there is no returning to the nineteen-fifties version of an "effective" Congress, the question is whether the Congress can find a new form of effectiveness.

In talking about what the Congress is not, it is important to keep in mind what it can be. There may be more than a little illusion behind some of the criticisms of Congress. Portrayals of the Congress as a lumbering institution seem to suggest that it could be otherwise. But it was not designed to, and it cannot behave as a brisk executive. It cannot perform as an analytic, systematic, apolitical "think tank," carefully judging the trade-offs in the decisions it faces, and the consequences of its choices. It cannot, without a blueprint from the executive, design a comprehensive program of government. The Congress has, moreover, a deeply unheroic streak. It cannot be expected to play Saint George and slay the dragon—though it might nibble one to death if it were not a very big dragon.

And in talking about what the Congress should be, some perspective is in order. An unbridled Congress could also be cause for concern. A bestirred, unrestrained Congress is capable of irresponsible action, of responding to the passions of the moment. A Congress cooperating with a President who is responding to the passions of the moment, and who may also have had the opportunity to effect a Supreme Court majority, could mean trouble. It was just that sort of not inconceivable situation that the constitutional checks and balances were designed to prevent. The Congress's sluggardly ways could, at some crucial moment, save us. Moreover, there is a kind of goose-gander principle at work here. Many of those who are now anxious to see the Congress act as a check on the executive sought to reduce the powers of the Congress when an executive of a different ideological persuasion—their own—was in power. There is reason to wonder whether they will be as concerned with checks and balances when their own kind return to power in the White House.

The Congress is a parliament, and there is a serious question whether contemporary issues lend themselves to parliamentary management. I put the question to various members of Congress. "No," said Representative Morris Udall, Democrat of Arizona, "a parliamentary system probably can't handle contemporary problems. But there isn't any better system." Representative Fraser is one of the few who will say the almost unsayable on Capitol Hill. "The role of the Congress," he argues, "should not be looked at as a classic, text-book 'third branch of Government,' sharing decisions. I don't think Congress has worked that way or will work that way. Congress provides a legitimization of decisions that flow from the Presidency. It's not a partnership."

"The nice people," said another Congressman, "write and say the Congress should take charge. No way it's going to take charge." There are, however, some things that the Congress can do. It can, on occasion, take an important step. But it usually needs a dance partner. If it is in the embrace of a strong executive (Lyndon Johnson) or an important and outraged segment of the citizenry (the civil rights or consumer movements) or a determined special interest (oil companies in search of an Alaska pipeline), it can move. Second, even when it does not act as a collective body, it can provide a platform from which individuals can speak to our condition, utter their prophecies, try to have an impact. It can offer a forum for a Fulbright, Mondale, Hart or Robert Taft Sr., for people who can step aside from the swirl of daily events and constituent claims, and think about what we are doing and where we are headed. Through well-timed and carefully considered hearings and speeches —avoiding the excesses that can make them dismissable as bores—individuals can catch the attention of their colleagues and the press, and affect the national dialogue. Individual members can change certain Government practices simply by throwing the spotlight on them. This requires neither legislation nor even hearings —just a flair for obtaining, and dramatizing, information. Third, the Congress can perform its role, as the founding fathers intended, as a check on the executive branch. It can see that the laws are carried out as intended. It can oversee.

Perhaps the Congress cannot run the Government, but it still can, and occasionally does, on its own initiative produce legislation. And there could be limits to what it will permit to go wrong. It could, if it chooses, intervene in the way the economy is being managed. It is not inconceivable that the Congress, without awaiting an Administration proposal, could reform or raise taxes. "It's the tough decisions that we are unable to make," says Fraser. "The fancy proposal for a joint budget committee just provides a mechanical substitute for making hard political decisions. All we need to do is, after we have made the appropriations decisions, make tax decisions accordingly, every year. It's very simple, but we lack the guts."

Congressional oversight of the executive is a function that is clearly within the grasp of the Congress. It does not call for collective action. It does not require heroism. It does not even demand determined nibbling at a dragon. It does demand an interest in doing the job, and in making the appropriate arrangements. But the Congress has a curious disinclination to do so.

Some recent events have shown what this can mean. It is reasonable to wonder where the Congress was when the Administration waged a secret war and established a secret police. Some senior members of Congress are said to have been informed about the fact of the secret bombing of Cambodia and Laos. These were members whom the Administration could trust not to raise questions, or voices. And even these members apparently did not know the extent of the bombing, since the records on that were falsified. One might ask whether the appropriate Congressional committees did not know, or did not care that intelligence-gathering and law-enforcement agencies were being put to political use. To the extent that such practices went on under previous administrations, the question becomes more urgent. One might also question whether we really had to run out of gasoline and beef and other food. If the executive branch did not know, or did not care, that these things were going to happen, could the Congress not have seen what was developing, and done something? The Congress apparently was not informed about Soviet food shortages, or "the wheat deal."

The Congress need not establish a Pentagon-on-the-Hill to rival the one across the Potomac. It need not replicate the Federal bureaucracy. It need only have the interest, and give itself the capacity, to ask the right questions. "The House of Representatives," said one of its members, "does not have the computer capacity of the State Bank of Kenosha, Wisconsin." The Senate has one computer that, in accordance with its priorities, it uses for sending newsletters. The Congress can call upon the Library of Congress for research and the General Accounting Office for investigations of some Government programs. But this amounts to something like attacking the Sixth Fleet with a rowboat. There is pending a proposal that the Congress establish an Office of Technology Assessment, so that it can gather its own information on such questions as how an SST or a nuclear power plant might affect the environment. The idea is to free the Congress from dependence for such information on Government agencies that may or may not supply it, in a form that may or may not represent the truth. But this proposal is now caught in the kind of web that the Congress, with its intriguing ways, can weave. It is hostage to a dispute between the Senate and the House over whether the West Front of the Capitol should be rebuilt. (The O.T.A. and the West Front issues are in the same bill. The House is pro new West Front; the Senate con). Moreover, some lawmakers soured on the proposal to know more about technology when they considered that the Joint Committee to develop such a capacity would be headed by Senator Edward Kennedy, Democrat of Massachusetts, who might, they worried, use it to enhance his political position.

The Congress's customary incapacity, and disinclination, to take on "the experts" are thus of its own making. The exceptions—the successful fights to limit the antiballistic missile and postpone the SST—were major efforts mounted by coalitions of opponents within and outside of the Congress, and *were* exceptions. The failures of oversight have been failures of will. The C.I.A. oversight committee, Senator Fulbright said to me earlier this year, "functioned as an umbrella to protect the C.I.A." Senator Stennis, its chairman, he added, "never called a meeting of that committee." "Now if there was anybody in the Senate who really undertook to understand the C.I.A.," said Fubright, "I don't know who it was." The complaisance of the overseers toward the overseen had come to be accepted practice. Now some of the politicians who had gone along with the practice—and had wars waged and agencies compromised under (presumably) unseeing eyes—are embarrassed. There is talk on Capitol Hill of a new determination to give Government agencies the gimlet eye. But these moods, we now know, can come and go.

Institutionalization of closer oversight would be more reassuring. There is pending in the Senate a very simple bill that could have important effects. It says that all Congressional committees should be kept fully informed by every Government agency in all matters pertaining to their jurisdiction, and that every agency shall answer every request for information. The bill has 40 co-sponsors. Its seemingly unexceptionable purpose could make it easier for politicians to know what is going on, when they care to. Some members of Congress who have tried to extract information from the executive have found themselves in long and often losing guerrilla warfare. But once the politicians obtain the information, they still have to want and figure out how to use it. There is no automatic correlation between more information and better legislative control.

It would also be helpful to get the foxes out of the hen-houses, or at least establish methods of warning us that they are there. It is not beyond the mind of man to design reporting systems that would let us know how a Congressman benefits from an agency he is supposed to supervise. Politicians' intercessions on behalf of favored constituents or contributors, need not be secret from the public, for whom the agencies supposedly work. It would also be healthy to spread the oversight duties around—by rotation or even duplication. This might break up the buddy system. In the "real world," no prudent person sends the same auditors around year after year. There is no reason to expect members of Congress, unlike other human beings, not to become comfortable with the familiar.

Aspin is one of the few members of Congress who has thought through a redefiniton of its role. He likens the Congress to a board of directors. A board of directors, he points out, does not try to manage, but if it wants to be other than a doormat there are things it can do. It can have a voice in major personnel decisions, consider major policy questions, keep itself informed and make occasional forays into detail. Aspin argues that the Congress's penchant for avoiding issues, its preference for dealing with procedures rather than substance, can be turned to advantage. The Congress, he argues, could impose procedural changes on the executive branch that would have major substantive effect. For example, Congress wrote into the National Environmental Protection Act a requirement that there be a statement on the impact on the environment of any Government-supported project. The provision has not worked perfectly, but it has made a substantial difference. This kind of change can transfer the burden of proof, insert other voices with other interests in the decision-making process, set up a system of clearances within the Government that offers more possibilities for fail-safe mechanisms, and institutionalize the requirement of certain kinds of information.

The danger of spending too much time on Capitol Hill (or, for that matter, perhaps, in Washington), is that one begins to see things within the frame of reference of Capitol Hill (or Washington). After the umpteenth conversation about the new system of voting for committee chairmen in the House, one can begin to think that it is pretty terrific, that it will make quite a difference. And it is a worthy reform. But within the frame of reference of what's going on in the country, the sum total of all of the actions and reforms on Capitol Hill so far this year is not yet cause for celebration.

Moreover, the Congress's limited attention span is cause for unease. "What makes them move up here," said one Senate aide, "is what makes news." The Congress can, given sufficient hue and cry, respond. The politicians are aware, moreover, that the public is not watching them with undiluted admiration. They have noticed that incumbency is not the safe perch it used to be. They fear a wave of antipolitics, which could sweep many of them from office. It is interesting to recall that until just over 60 years ago, Senators were chosen by state legislatures. When the public reaction to the corrupt results became sufficiently strong, the Congress, including the Senators who stood to lose, voted to change the system.

"Great outside pressures," said one Congressman, "produce great change." That may be our best hope. We have had a glimpse of what it can mean to have a Government of men, not laws. A top Presidential aide declared the Bill of Rights "eroded." The President claims the "inherent" right to take otherwise illegal measures against dangers, as he perceives them, to the "national security." His power is subject only, he says, to "the limitation of public opinion and of course Congressional and other pressures that may arise." Provided, of course, that the measures are known. The Congress has yet to devise methods of preventing the executive from arrogating authority that is above and beyond the law. It has as yet done almost nothing to prevent a "Watergate"—perhaps a more smoothly executed one—from happening again. At the same time, citizens are faced with a Government that, if one can speak of "public opinion," they find ever more expensive and less responsive. Things seem out of control. The result could be greater apathy, or acceptance of order—order in a form that could be drained of humanity and liberty.

The Congress is, or is supposed to be, the most responsive branch of Government we've got. The Supreme Court is remote, austere, guided by canonical doctrine. The executive branch can become arrogant and inaccessible. Congress is the accessible branch. It is sloppy, but it is also the only place where all of the interests can be represented. It is unheroic, but it also reads its mail. The Congress cannot be expected to change simply as a result of inner-generated pressures; there are strong countervailing, inner pressures against change. It would be the ultimate irony, if not tragedy, if the result of "Watergate" were greater apathy on the part of the public, disgust with the politicians to the point that it gave up on the Congress. The result could be even greater imbalance of power between Congress and the executive branch. And then when the politicians in their orotund fashion, talked of a "constitutional crisis" and their fears for "the survival of our democratic system," they would be right.

Study Questions

1. Congress has been described as the branch of the federal government whose powers have eroded the most over the years in the face of the growing influence of the presidency. Do you agree with this assessment, and if so, do you think this situation is healthy or not for our system of government? Why?

2. Describe the leadership structure in both houses of Congress. Contrast the difference in structure between the two houses.

3. Describe the role of congressional committees and the powers of committee chairmen. Detail the functions and powers of the Rules Committee in the House of Representatives.

4. What has been the impact of the seniority system on Congress?

What are the assets and weaknesses of the system? Would you advocate modifying the seniority system?

5. Describe the different types of congressional committees and the work they do.

6. In this chapter, power in Congress has been described as being dispersed and fragmented. What are the causes of this fragmentation and what are its consequences?

7. What structural reforms would you prescribe for Congress? What impact would you expect these reforms to have on Congress' performance, and on its position vis-à-vis the presidency within our constitutional system of checks and balances?

Bibliography

Books

Bailey, Stephen K. *Congress in the Seventies.* New York: St. Martin's Press, 1970.

Bolling, Richard. *House out of Order.* New York: E. P. Dutton & Co. Inc. 1965.

Clark, Joseph S., ed. *Congressional Reform: Problems and Prospects.* New York: Thomas Y. Cromwell Company, 1965.

Froman, Lewis A. Jr. *The Congressional Process: Strategies, Rules and Procedures.* Boston: Little, Brown & Co., 1967.

Harris, Joseph P. *Congress and the Legislative Process.* 2d ed. New York: McGraw-Hill Book Company, 1972.

Hinkley, Barbara. *The Seniority System in Congress.* Bloomington, Ind.: University Press, 1971.

Lees, John D. *The Committee System of the United States Congress.* New York: Humanities Press, 1967.

Moe, Ronald C., ed. *Congress and the President.* Pacific Palisades, Calif.: Goodyear Publishing Co. Inc. 1971.

Orfield, Gary. *Congressional Power: Congress and Social Change.* New York: Harcourt Brace Jovanovich, Inc. 1975.

Polsby, Nelson W. *Congress and the Presidency.* Englewood Cliffs, New Jersey: Prentice-Hall, Inc., 1971.

Rieselback, Leroy N., ed. *The Congressional System: Notes and Readings.* Belmont, California: Wadsworth Pub. Co. Inc., 1970.

Truman, David B., ed. *The Congress and America's Future.* 2d ed. Englewood Cliffs, New Jersey: Prentice-Hall, Inc., 1973.

Wolfinger, Raymond E. *Readings on Congress.* Englewood Cliffs, New Jersey: Prentice-Hall, Inc., 1971.

Vogler, David J. *The Politics of Congress.* Boston: Allyn and Bacon, Inc. 1974.

Articles

Davidson, Roger H., and Packer, Glenn R. "Positive Support for Political Institutions: The Case of Congress." *The Western Political Quarterly*, Vol. 25, No. 4 (Dec. 1972), pp. 600-612.

Vinyard, Dale. "The Congressional Committees on Small Business: Pattern of Legislative Committee-Executive Agency Relations." *The Western Political Quarterly*, Vol. 21, No. 3 (Sept. 1968), pp. 391-399.

CHAPTER 9
The Supreme Court and Society

In 1907, Chief Justice Charles Evans Hughes declared, "We are under a Constitution, but the Constitution is what the judges say it is." Few would argue with this observation today. In no other political system do judges of the highest court hold such a position of power as they do in the United States.

Article III of the Constitution states: "The Judicial power of the United States shall be vested in one Supreme Court and in such inferior courts as the Congress may from time to time ordain and establish." From this rather vague provision, the court has evolved into a virtually autonomous partner, equal to the executive and legislative branches. It has become the legitimate and supreme arbiter of constitutional disputes.

The American political system prides itself on being a system of laws. Under such a system, theoretically, all men are equal before the law. Laws are promulgated by the elected representatives of the people, expressing popular will and manifesting popular sovereignty. However, all of these laws must be in accord with the supreme law of the land, the Constitution. This very brief document set forth general principles but left much unsaid. It has thus provided a flexibility and relevancy for succeeding generations of Americans to deal with serious contemporary issues. Judicial interpretations and usage have developed a complex system of laws, all stemming from the basic document. In such a system of government, however, questions arise as to the legality of the laws passed and enforced in the name of the Constitution. Therefore, the Court as an institution is given primary responsibility for insuring that the system of laws is in keeping with the spirit of the Constitution.

It has also been said that laws are a reflection of basic values of the country. They reflect the legal and moral perceptions of society, hence providing criteria to judge its individual members and society as a whole. In this concept of government and politics, laws become the framework within which the political system operates. It would be difficult to conceive of a political system that did not have some system of laws and institutions for making and interpreting laws. The Supreme Court, therefore, is a key institution in the operation of the American political system.

Inside the Supreme Court

The Chief Justice's role and the relationship between the justices of the Court are best examined through a brief overview of the internal decision-making processes. It is in the actual operation of the Court, in the selection of cases to be heard and in the writing of decisions, that the student can recognize the complexity of the process and the difficulty in reaching a just and relevant decision.

Most Americans are familiar with the generalities of courtroom procedure. The mass media carry detailed information about prominent cases, and television dramas such as "Perry Mason," "The Defenders" and "Owen Marshall, Counsellor at Law" provide useful insights into the courtroom. Although they capture neither the specifics of court procedure nor the administrative practices involved in bringing a case to court, they do provide a surface familiarity. Many Americans serve as members of juries, and this is a useful learning experience regarding the judicial process.

Few citizens, however, have any understanding of what goes on in the Supreme Court. The seemingly mechanical decisions made by the Court cloak a highly fluid and politically stimulating decision-making process. The relationships between the justices of the Supreme Court and the verbal sparring and litigation that occur within the closed chambers of the Court epitomize the fluidity and political sensitivity of the total court system.

The Court normally is in session from October through June, listening to arguments for two weeks and then adjourning for two weeks to study the issues and write opinions. At least six justices must participate in each decision. Cases are decided by the majority and in the event of a tie, the decision of the lower court is sustained. During oral arguments, an attorney usually has one-half hour to make his case before the Court. Five minutes before his time expires, he is cautioned by a white light and when his time is up, a red light flashes. Contrary to procedures of lower courts, justices often interrupt the attorneys to question points of law or interject their own commentary. Additionally, justices see a great deal of information about the case beforehand because they have to decide whether the Supreme Court should hear it. The Court normally accepts a case if the justices feel that it is important enough to be considered by the highest court. There are, of course, many reasons why the Supreme Court may refuse to hear a case. The justices may feel that a satisfactory decision has already been rendered, or, at the other extreme, they may not wish to become involved in an extremely political case, particularly with respect to disagreement between various branches of government.

The justices meet in conference on Fridays during the months the Court is in session to discuss the vote on various cases and applications before the Court (writs of *certiorari*). These meetings are secret, presided over by the Chief Justice, who plays a very important role in the Court. He influences the selection of cases, chairs the conference, and assigns the writing of opinions to the justices.

Indeed, his selection of one justice or the other to write the opinions has significant influence, since such writing in essence lays down legal doctrine and moral and ethical values of the American political system. The political ideology of the justice writing the opinion can be important and it makes a difference whether he is a judicial activist or one who follows the concept of judicial self-restraint.

Decisions are made on a majority vote. Observers of the Court assess the relative unity or disagreement over issues according to the margin of the vote. Similarly, dissenting opinions have important influence in legal doctrine and moral and ethical values of society. In certain instances, dissenting opinions of yesterday may become legal doctrine today. The Court usually hands down its opinions each week on Monday—decision Monday—although at times this is also done on other days of the week.

The justice selected to write the Court's majority opinion has a difficult task. Normally he does considerable research and writes a draft, which he circulates for comment by the other justices. Throughout this process of writing, advising, and perhaps even redrafting the opinion, there is a great deal of exchange between the justices as well as additional study of the issues. At times this process can produce a change in the Court's opinion, since additional evidence can be uncovered causing a reassessment.

The process by which the Supreme Court selects cases, and arrives at a decision is a dynamic one. It is not bound by legal rigidity, but rather by common sense procedures and a serious attempt to weigh the moral and ethical values within society. In this respect, perhaps the most important part of the decision is the rationale upon which it is based. When these judicial opinions are made public they provide insight into the perceptions and the values upon which the political system rests. The Court therefore has power to influence not only political institutions, but relationships throughout society.

Role and Function of the Court

The role and function of the Supreme Court raises a number of issues regarding the operation of a democratic political system. President Franklin D. Roosevelt argued that "nine old men" should not be in a position to overrule representatives of the people. Some observers claim that the Supreme Court, rather than being just a court, is a political institution that has an impact on national policy. "To consider the Supreme Court of the United States as a legal institution is to underestimate its significance in the American political system. For it is also a political institution, an institution, that is to say, for arriving at decisions on controversial questions of national policy."[1]

Others argue that the Supreme Court becomes involved only in issues that are the direct result of court cases, whereas most political issues are resolved through legislative and executive channels; their decisions, even on controversial issues, are based on reasonable and rational arguments that are made public. Furthermore the Supreme Court justices are competent and committed men who are not under the influence of other political actors.

These two views are at the base of most of the arguments and disagreements among scholars, lawyers and judges regarding the role and function of the Supreme Court. Indeed, since the decision of the Court in *Marbury* v. *Madison,* the arguments about the Court have become familiar issues. As long as the Court remains the final decision-maker in matters of constitutionality and powers of other branches, it will continue to be a focal point of controversy.

The role of the courts in the modern American political system involves them deeply in national and local decision-making processes and in shaping the political environment. Indeed, over the past twenty years the Supreme Court has played an important role in shaping the public policy of the nation. This power stems from the Court's role in questions of constitutionality with respect not only to decisions of government, but to the rights and freedoms of individuals, to conflicts between national and state governments, and to the interpretation of powers for other branches of government. In fulfilling its role the Court implicitly provides guidelines as to the directions of national policy. This has been particularly true since the era of the New Deal in the 1930s.

During the depression years of the 1930s, more and more Americans expected their government to take positive action in the regulation of the economy and protection of individuals from business organizations. As a consequence, the government became involved in many sectors of society. Prior to this, it had been thought that a laissez-faire policy was best—that is, minimum interference by government. Government involvement in these areas raised a host of constitutional questions, some of which reached the Supreme Court. For example, in 1933, during the first year of the Roosevelt administration, the National Industrial Recovery Act was passed, guaranteeing the right of collective bargaining. It was declared unconstitutional by the Supreme Court two years later. Shortly thereafter, however, Congress passed the National Labor Relations Act (Wagner Act) based on the right of collective bargaining for all workers engaged in interstate commerce, and prohibiting unfair labor practices by employers. The constitutionality of this act was challenged and in a 5-4 decision, the Supreme Court held that the power of Congress over interstate commerce reached into labor relations, and that industrial strife was harmful to the national economy.

Beginning in early 1950, the government became further involved in political and social issues, leading to decisions by the Supreme Court which had far-reaching effects on society. Some of the most historic decisions came out of the Warren Court period. Chief Justice Earl Warren, appointed by President Eisenhower in 1953 remained in office until retirement in 1969. During the period of his leadership a number of important decisions were made, beginning with the *Brown v. Board of Education* (1954) school desegregation case. Since that time,

> ...the Court has declared Bible reading and all other religious exercises in public schools unconstitutional; it has ordered the reapportionment of the national House of Representatives, of both Houses of state legislatures, and of local government bodies on a one-man, one-vote basis; it has reformed numerous aspects of state and federal criminal procedure, significantly enhancing the rights of the accused, including juvenile offenders; it has laid down a whole set of new rules

governing the admissibility of confessions in evidence, and in effect, the conduct of police throughout the country toward persons arrested on suspicion of crime; and it has held that wiretapping and eavesdropping are subject to the Fourth Amendment's prohibition against unreasonable searches and seizures. The Court has also enlarged its own jurisdiction to hear cases challenging federal expenditures. . . . [it] has limited the power of state and federal governments. . .[2]

Whether or not one agrees with the decisions of the Warren Court, one must admit that this brief cataloging of its actions shows an active Court with many accomplishments.

Judicial Supremacy

Although it took ten years after the establishment of the Constitution to develop the doctrine of a powerful judiciary, the basis for it was laid in *The Federalist*. These essays published in pamphlet form in the late 1780s by Alexander Hamilton, James Madison and John Jay, urged ratification of the new Constitution. These papers are the historic rationale regarding the principles and interpretation of the Constitution. In number 78 Hamilton argued that the Constitution was supreme and that it provided the basic framework and powers for the government. It followed naturally, therefore, that no legislature could pass laws that were inconsistent with the Constitution. Furthermore, all elected officials as well as appointed officers of the government could operate only within the authority granted by the Constitution. Hamilton argued therefore, that the courts were responsible for the interpretation of the laws and the constitutionality of laws. If there was any question as to constitutionality then in the final analysis the Constitution must prevail, and the courts were to be the final interpreters of the Constitution. Of course, the Hamiltonians were chiefly concerned about the check that the judiciary would have on the so-called popular passions and the excesses of a democratic majority. The courts would act as a balance to insure government stability and continuity, because they would stand apart from control by the people or their representatives. However, during the first ten years of operation, the courts were relegated to a rather subordinate position in comparison to the other branches of government.

Marbury v. Madison

It was the landmark case of *Marbury* v. *Madison* (1803) that propelled the Supreme Court into prominence. Not only was the Court

"Do you ever have one of those days when everything seems un-Constitutional?"

The New Yorker, Dec. 30, 1974, p. 31.

thereby placed on an equal footing with the other branches of government but its superiority was established with respect to authority over constitutional disputes. Its importance is worthy of some additional study.

In the election of 1800 the Republicans, led by Jefferson, ousted President John Adams and the Federalists. On the eve of his departure, President Adams appointed a number of his friends to judicial posts. Marbury was one of these and received an appointment as justice of the peace for the District of Columbia. Madison, the new Secretary of State acting for President Jefferson, refused to follow through on the appointment, and Marbury appealed to the Supreme Court. The appeal was based on the Judiciary Act of 1789 which conferred upon the Court the right to issue writs of mandamus (judicial orders commanding officials to perform duties required by law). The dilemma for Chief Justice John Marshall and his associates was obvious. If the Court denied the writ, Federalist party friends would be angry and it would raise the question of legality of presidential orders. On the other hand, if the Court were to support Marbury, it would anger the new administration and invite reprisals; besides, the Court had no way of enforcing its orders against an antagonistic administration.

The Chief Justice, avoiding the major political issues, simply denied Marbury's petition on the premise that the portion of the Judiciary Act of 1789 upon which the petition was based was unconstitutional.

Marshall said that the act granting the Supreme Court the right to issue writs of mandamus was an illegal enlargement of the Court's original jurisdiction as spelled out in the Constitution. Therefore, Congress had acted unconstitutionally in this matter, and more important, the Court was the institution to make this judgment. This established the doctrine of judicial review and laid the foundation for the Court to become the final arbiter in matters of constitutionality.

Court Structure

The court structure in the United States political system is a complicated and complex one. We have already noted that the American political system consists of a national system and a state system. Each one of these has its own executive, legislature, bureaucracy, judiciary, and laws. In addition to the federal system which has as its pinnacle the Supreme Court, there is a state judicial system which has as its pinnacle the state supreme court. Theoretically, the state supreme court holds a position in the state structure similar to that held by the Supreme Court in the federal structure, but it is not as simple as that. The Supreme Court in certain cases has authority over the state judiciary in determining constitutionality. In this sense the Supreme Court straddles both national and state systems. For example, the constitutionality of state laws may be challenged through the state legal system. But in such cases, the state supreme court need not be the final authority. Decisions of state supreme courts can be appealed to the Supreme Court of the United States in cases where the constitutionality of state laws is questioned with respect to the federal Constitution. Similarly, in cases where the defendant's rights under the federal Constitution are questioned, the ruling of the state courts can be overturned by the U.S. Supreme Court.

In civil and criminal cases also, there is an overlapping jurisdiction between the state and federal judiciary. This complicates the proceedings, as a potential litigant often has a choice of courts. Furthermore, in matters of criminal law, it is conceivable that an individual may be prosecuted in both federal and state courts if, in fact, he has violated both sets of laws.

Powers of the Court

Although the power of judicial review is now inherent in the role of the Court, how it is used by the Court depends on a number of other considerations. Like all officials of government and political actors, the members of the Supreme Court are human. They see their positions on the Court according to their own perceptions and preconceived ideas on how the American political system should operate. The Court as an institution also has an impact on the individual judge. Since appointments to the Supreme Court are lifetime appointments, the judges are freed from the requirements of catering to political forces. Furthermore, sitting in the lofty chambers of the Supreme Court does create new perspectives and attitudes on issues of constitutionality and the workings of the political system.

Each of the justices, nevertheless, has his own particular perspective while at the same time developing a perspective on the role of the Court as an institution. Decisions of the Court are influenced by the attitudes and perceptions of individual judges and by their recognition of the necessity to maintain and consider the role of the Court as an institution. For example, the views of the Chief Justice and his discussions of cases in conference with the other justices have an influence on the outcome of the case. The Chief Justice speaks first, and is followed by the other justices according to seniority. The views expressed in judicial conference are carefully assessed by other and more junior justices. The dignity of the Court would be damaged and its power significantly diminished if individual justices complained publicly about Court decisions or the judgment of their colleagues. Minority opinions are expected, as are disagreements, but they must be expressed in judicial terms, with proper decorum, and based on reasonable perspectives.

Part of the power of the Court also stems from the expectations of other political actors as to the role of the Court and its decisions. A great deal of judicial power and enforcement rest on consensus within society regarding the role of the Supreme Court and the individual justices. In every case, the Court must depend on other branches of government to implement its orders. Political actors are likely to accept the Court's decisions enthusiastically when there is a consensus that these decisions are just and correct.

The Court's power can also be expanded or diminished as a consequence of the impact of judicial decisions on other institutions of government. As suggested above, enforcement of judicial decisions depends greatly on the acceptance of their legitimacy and consensus within the bureaucratic structure. Enforcement depends also on acceptance by elected officials and society as a whole. For example, although the Warren Court made a landmark decision in *Brown* v.

Board of Education of Topeka (1954), it required a virtual social revolution in the 1960s before its decision became part of public policy. The Court's decision alone could not eliminate racial segregation in American society, but it did make it clear that racial discrimination followed as a policy by any governmental institution was unconstitutional. The Court decided that segregation of races in public schools violated the equal protection clause of the Fourteenth Amendment, thus overruling the "separate but equal" doctrine that had been in effect since 1896. This finally led to the overturning of many segregation laws; it was left to the federal courts to determine proper implementation. This decision created tensions between national and state institutions, and was one of the major factors leading to civil rights demonstrations in the late 1950s and early 1960s.

Finally, the relationships within the judicial system can also add to or diminish the power of the Court. The judiciary is not a monolithic structure in which the robed hierarchy has absolute and unquestioned support. There is a continual struggle within the judiciary not only as to the role of judges, but as to interpretations of judicial decisions and their impact on society. More often than not there are violent dissenting opinions.

It is the interplay of these four factors that provides the power boundaries within which the Supreme Court operates. These boundaries may be quite broad, as they were during a period of the Warren Court in the 1950s and 1960s. During those years the Court took a direct lead in determining national policy, not only through its civil rights cases, but in matters of representation in the legislature (*Baker v. Carr*, 1962). On the other hand, in the post-Civil War period, the Court's conservatism and pro-industrial attitudes considerably diminished its vanguard role in society. In more recent years, the Burger Court, although reflecting a more conservative attitude than its predecessor, the Warren Court, has made a number of decisions considered to be liberal in viewpoint. For example, it has legalized abortion, outlawed capital punishment under existing laws, and held that the government could not engage in wiretapping of domestic groups without a court order.

Restraints and Limitations

There are a number of restraints on the power of the Court. Some of these have already been mentioned. The Court cannot act until an actual case occurs, i.e., a "proceeding." Policy cannot be initiated until the proper question has arisen. In some cases, it may take years for such issues to be resolved. Second, the Court does not have built-in machinery to enforce or supervise its judicial decisions. Therefore, it must rely primarily upon the executive branch as well as a vast array of local officers to enforce its decisions. Obviously, this presents a number of problems. It is conceivable that local officers executing the Court's decisions may interpret them differently and with varying degrees of enthusiasm. By the time the Court's decisions reach the lower rungs of the political system, they may be considerably diluted.

The members of the Supreme Court are not democratically elected; they are not held responsible to the electorate. Political decisions arising out of judicial interpretations are not controlled by other branches and are not necessarily accountable to popular will. Therefore, it is very difficult for the Court to develop popular support for its decisions or develop any kind of mandate for directing public policy. This is at the base of criticism of the workings of the Supreme Court. Chief Justice Earl Warren was the center of much criticism by groups in the South as a result of the *Brown* v. *Board of Education* decision. A number of groups called for his impeachment.

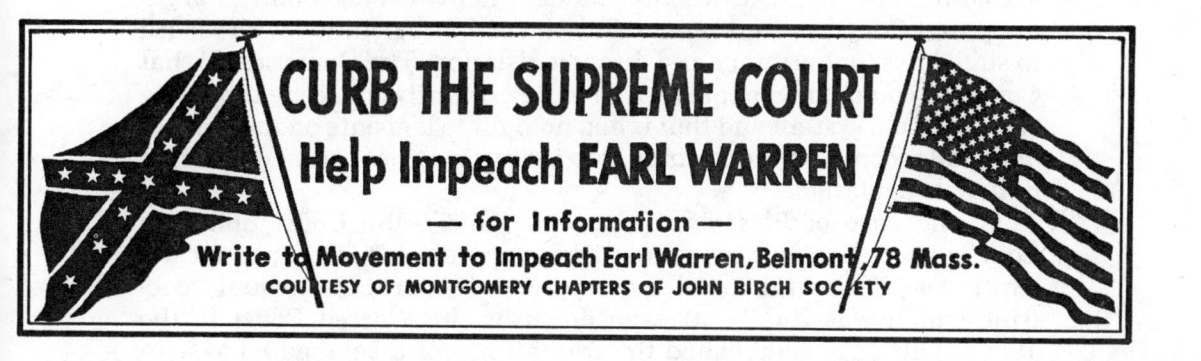

CURB THE SUPREME COURT
Help Impeach EARL WARREN
— for Information —
Write to Movement to Impeach Earl Warren, Belmont, 78 Mass.
COURTESY OF MONTGOMERY CHAPTERS OF JOHN BIRCH SOCIETY

The Court as Oracle

Because of all these factors, there are both implicit and explicit roles associated with members of the Court and the Court as an institution. At times, the Court plays the role of oracle, stressing its policy-making function as well as its role in identifying the meaning and direction of public morality. In this role the Court focuses primarily on the legal and moral requirement of the laws. For example, the legalization of abortion by the Burger Court raised a storm of controversy ranging from theological arguments and moral issues to those involving national policy. The decision made abortion legal, and also provided guidelines for the morality of the nation.

At other times, the Court may play the role of guardian of due process of law, stressing procedural safeguards for individual citizens. In this role, the Court is concerned with cruel and unusual punishment, unreasonable search and seizure, right to counsel, freedom from self-incrimination and the right to confront witnesses. While these roles overlap considerably, they provide a focus or perspective for both individual justices and the Court as a whole.

These perspectives can be more clearly appreciated by reference to several important cases. In its function as oracle, the Court ultimately led the way in civil rights doctrines. Beginning with the separate-but-equal concepts, the Court virtually dictated national policy by its decisions regarding equality in education. Let us look at this evolution in more detail.

In 1875, Congress passed a Civil Rights Act designed to prevent any form of discrimination against Negroes. This law was enacted on the assumption that Congress had power to pass laws to enforce the Fourteenth Amendment in both the federal and state political systems. The Supreme Court at that time, however, disagreed and declared the law unconstitutional. Its decision was based on the argument that Congress could enact only corrective legislation with regard to state laws, not primary and direct legislation. The Court stated that Congress could not enact laws that were primarily concerned with the state political system and that it had no right to legislate on the subject of equal accommodations since this matter was not in the domain of national regulation.

In the case of *Plessy* v. *Ferguson* (1896), the Court upheld a Louisiana statute requiring railroads to provide separate cars for the two races. This established the notorious "separate-but-equal" doctrine which was finally stricken down by the Warren Court in the 1950s. This case established the framework for a segregated system not only in public accommodations but in education.

Beginning in the 1930s, however, a series of cases slowly chipped away at the separate-but-equal concept. This culminated in the case of *Brown* v. *Board of Education of Topeka* (see above). In this landmark decision, the Warren Court concluded that separate-but-equal was essentially discrimination because segregated educational facilities provided inferior education.

The Court as Guardian

As guardian of due process of law, the Court has over the past generation focused on making the Fourteenth Amendment and the procedural safeguards established in the Bill of Rights applicable to states. In earlier years, these were considered primarily applicable to the federal political system and had no great impact on the state system. Therefore, there was much abuse in the states regarding procedural safeguards, due process of law, and equal protection of the law. The Court has sought to rectify these problems, not only with respect to overall social considerations but also with regard to the individual. Nowhere has this been more true than in protection of the individual who is accused of a crime.

For example, the decision in *Gideon* v. *Wainwright* (1963) established the principle that an accused individual who is too poor to hire a lawyer cannot be assured a fair trial unless counsel is provided. In the case of *Escobedo* v. *Illinois* (1964), the Supreme Court ruled that a suspect had the right to advice of counsel not only during a trial but also during police interrogation. It thus applied a stricter interpretation of the Bill of Rights—the presumption is that one is innocent until proven guilty and also that due process applies to a person who is criminally accused from the moment that he is accused.

Judicial Activism and Self-Restraint

The degree to which the Court performs its role as oracle or guardian is contingent upon its members' perceptions of their role with respect to the Constitution and political actors. They may perceive their role as one of *judicial activism* or of *judicial self-restraint*.

As judicial activist the Court plays a prominent political role and becomes a vanguard in areas of national policy, particularly when the other branches of government are reluctant or unable to come to grips with crucial issues, matters of constitutionality and individual rights and freedoms. In the absence of specific laws and in the face of hesitation by other institutions, the Supreme Court has sometimes become a political guiding force. Whether or not it does so, of course, depends on the considerations discussed earlier with respect to the boundaries of its power.

Judicial self-restraint is based on the concept that the Court is primarily a legal technician; therefore decisions are to be made primarily on the legal content that can be specifically traced to constitutional provisions. The executive and legislative branches are recognized as the primary institutions for determining national policy and social morality, in this view. Courts following the maxims of judicial self-restraint have been inclined to overlook certain legislative or executive actions by simply classifying them as political questions and thus refusing to deal with them judicially. Even though such legislative or executive actions may be unwise, unjust or questionable in terms of democratic institutions, they may still be considered constitutional by the Court. Furthermore, operating under this concept, the Court does not see itself as a check against the stupidity and emotionalism of government officials. Finally, judicial self-restraint is based on the premise that other institutions lead and the court follows.

Obviously, one cannot categorize the Court's role as one of judicial activism or judicial self-restraint. A realistic approach combines some elements of both. For example, under Chief Justice Morrison Waite, appointed by President Grant, under Chief Justice Melville Fuller, appointed by President Cleveland, and under Chief Justice Edward D. White, appointed by President Taft, the Court generally followed the idea of judicial self-restraint. On the other hand, the most pronounced example of judicial activism has been the Warren Court, which took the lead in desegregation and on the issue of one man-one vote representation. Many observers feel that since the appointment of Chief Justice Warren E. Burger by President Nixon in 1969 the Court has moved away from the activist role. It is still too early to know how far the Burger Court will move toward judicial self-restraint, but in recent pronouncements regarding criminal law, education, and pornography, it seems to have qualified some of the major decisions of the Warren Court.

Perspectives on the Functions of the Court

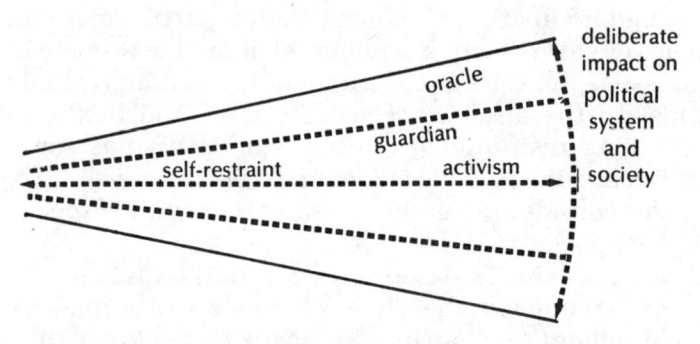

This diagram shows the relationship between the various perspectives regarding the Court's role in the system. It should not be construed necessarily as accurately showing the limits of the Court's ultimate impact, since it is conceivable that cases stemming out of the Guardian role could ultimately have a large impact on society. Similarly, inaction of the Court can also have a large impact on society. Nevertheless, the general result of the various perspectives are as shown, with an activist-oracle role providing the most likely deliberate large scale impact on the political system and society.

Major Periods of the Supreme Court

The extent and use of the Court's power has varied since its establishment. For purposes of a historical survey we can identify five major periods in the Supreme Court's history.

The Chief Justices

Chief Justice	Term	Appointed by
John Jay	1789-95	Washington
John Rutledge	1795	Washington
Oliver Ellsworth	1796-1800	Washington
John Marshall	1801-35	Adams
Roger B. Taney	1836-64	Jackson
Salmon P. Chase	1864-73	Lincoln
Morrison R. Waite	1874-1888	Grant
Melville W. Fuller	1888-1910	Cleveland
Edward D. White	1910-1921	Taft
William H. Taft	1921-30	Harding
Charles E. Hughes	1930-41	Hoover
Harlan F. Stone	1941-46	Roosevelt
Fred M. Vinson	1946-53	Truman
Earl Warren	1953-69	Eisenhower
Warren E. Burger	1969	Nixon

The Marshall Period

The first period begins with Chief Justice John Jay in 1789 and ends with Chief Justice John Marshall in 1835. For all practical purposes, we can call this the Marshall period. It was during the period of the Marshall Court that the Supreme Court evolved into a prominent national institution, establishing its role as the final interpreter of the Constitution. Moreover, it was during this period that the Court laid the foundation of national power. In addition to the landmark case of *Marbury* v. *Madison*, the Court made at least two other historic decisions.

In the case of *McCulloch* v. *Maryland* (1819), Chief Justice Marshall established the concept of necessary and proper powers for the national government. The state of Maryland had placed a tax upon the money issued by the Baltimore branch of the Second United States Bank. The bank refused to pay the tax. Two questions evolved: First, did the United States government have authority to charter such a bank? Second, did the state have the power to tax the bank, an institution of the United States government? The Court upheld the authority of the United States government to charter such a bank and denied the state's authority to tax a federal institution. In his argument Chief Justice Marshall stated, "concerning the scope of federal power, let the end be legitimate. Let it be within the scope of the Constitution and all means which are appropriate, which are plainly adopted to that end, which are not prohibited but consistent with the letter and spirit of the Constitution are constitutional." Explaining the Court's decision in the second question, Chief Justice Marshall stated that the power to tax involves the power to destroy and thus the state must not be in a position to destroy an instrument of the federal government. From this also developed the concept of intergovernmental tax immunity; that is, that neither the states nor the federal government could tax one another.

In the case of *Gibbons* v. *Ogden* (1824), the Supreme Court for the first time defined the meaning of interstate commerce and laid the basis for the regulation of this commerce by the national government. This decision provided extensive power which has been amplified considerably over the years. Congress had passed a law authorizing federal licensing of all vessels using coastal waters. Under this law Thomas Gibbons obtained a federal license to use the waters between New York and New Jersey. However, Aaron Ogden had been given an exclusive right by New York to use the state's waters. Upon Ogden's petition a New York court ordered Gibbons to stop operating his vessels between New York and New Jersey. Gibbons appealed to the Supreme Court. The Court "nullified a state grant giving an exclusive right to use navigable waters within a state. The Court held that congressional control over interstate commerce includes navigation. It was the first case involving the commerce clause and the powers of Congress to regulate interstate commerce were broadly interpreted by Chief Justice Marshall and the Court."[3]

Civil War, Reconstruction and Industrialization

The next period of the Court can be very broadly categorized as that of the Civil War, reconstruction, and industrialization. This extended from the appointment of Chief Justice Taney by President Jackson in 1836 through the end of Chief Justice William H. Taft's Court in 1930. During this period the Court generally exercised judicial self-restraint, following legal formulas which upheld economic laissez-faire and protected property interests.

The Court was chiefly concerned with guarding the free enterprise system and was conservative by today's standards. Although it was not completely hostile to federal power, it tended to construe the powers of federal government narrowly. For example, during this period the Court limited federal protection of civil rights, establishing the separate-but-equal doctrine which for all practical purposes permitted racial discrimination; provided a narrow construction of the commerce clause, thus preventing Congress from regulating large-scale industry; declared unconstitutional a number of federal laws such as child labor legislation, minimum wage and maximum hour laws and federal grants in aid to states for health benefits. One of the most historic cases of this era was the Dred Scott case (*Scott v. Sanford*, 1857). In this case the Court declared the Missouri Compromise of 1820 unconstitutional and that for all practical purposes even a free Negro was not a citizen. This decision was overruled by the fourteenth Amendment which was ratified in July of 1868. In the case of *Strauder v. West Virginia* (1880), the Court held that the fourteenth Amendment protected a Negro's right to trial by jury.

The Court was even more strict on the attempts by the states to control and regulate labor and business. Using the fourteenth Amendment as the constitutional basis, the Court struck down laws on regulation of private property (*Smyth v. Ames*) and declared that due process was a direct limitation on the enactment of certain laws. Furthermore, the Court held that freedom of contract was protected by the same clause and the state could not, therefore, pass laws infringing on contracts.

In the hysteria of the First World War, the Court reacted to the patriotism of the times by upholding the conviction of Schenck (*Schenck v. United States,* 1919), the General Secretary of the Socialist Party who was arrested and convicted under the Espionage Act of 1917 for mailing pamphlets to draftees urging them to oppose the draft since it violated the Constitution. In an important concept on freedom of speech Justice Holmes declared:

> ...the question in every case is whether the words used in such circumstances are of such a nature as to create a clear and present danger that they will bring about the substantive evils that Congress has a right to prevent.[4]

The Court's tendency toward judicial self-restraint and laissez-faire in social and economic matters continued into the post-World War I era. It ended with the crisis of the depression period of the 1930s.

The New Deal Period

The New Deal brought with it a more liberal nationalism and a desire for positive governmental action to remedy the ills of the depression. In his efforts to rebuild the economy, President Franklin D. Roosevelt was determined to overcome legal obstacles to economic regulation and expansion of presidential power.

This period began with Chief Justice Charles E. Hughes, appointed by President Hoover in 1930, and extended through the next Court, under Chief Justice Harlan F. Stone, ending in 1946. The first four years of the New Deal period placed the Court in a highly sensitive and controversial position. Perhaps at no other time in history has the Court been faced with so many controversial issues. These issues stemmed from the economic crisis in the United States and led to struggles within the Court itself between conservative and liberal justices. It is important to note that no vacancies occurred during this first four year period; the justices, holdovers from the Hoover administration, did not perceive the political environment or political actors in terms of the relative radicalism of President Roosevelt's administration. Many of the laws passed from 1933 to 1937 were declared unconstitutional, in an unprecedented number of 5-4 decisions. After his reelection in 1936, President Roosevelt was determined to change the composition of the Court and establish a Court more amenable to New Deal legislation. He failed in his attempt to enlarge the Court to fifteen by adding a number of justices. Nevertheless, by the end of 1937, because of resignation, retirement, or death, liberal justices were in the majority. By the middle of World War II seven of the nine Justices were Roosevelt appointees. A host of relatively revolutionary statutes were ultimately declared constitutional by the Courts. The Roosevelt-appointed Court clearly reversed many of the decisions of the previous one, and greatly broadened the powers of both the federal government and the states.

During World War II the Court upheld the constitutionality of the incarceration of citizens of Japanese descent as a measure of national security. Under Chief Justice Fred Vinson, appointed by President Truman in 1946, until the appointment of Chief Justice Earl Warren in 1953, the Court continued the expansion of national power that began to develop in World War II.

The Warren Court

The Warren Court period, from 1953 to 1969, was the most revolutionary in the modern Court's history. Operating according to the premises of judicial activism, the Court left hardly any area of the political system or society untouched. At times playing the role of oracle and at times of guardian of due process of law, the Warren Court in fact became the spearhead for much-needed political and social reform.

Beginning with *Brown* v. *Board of Education* (1954) in which it overturned the separate-but-equal doctrine, the Court established new concepts in the protection of individual rights and freedom with respect to social and moral considerations as well as criminal and civil law. Additionally, the Warren Court reversed the pro-government trend established by Chief Justice Fred Vinson, and focused primarily on protection of the individual. The landmark cases of *Gideon* v. *Wainwright* (1963) and *Escobedo* v. *Illinois* (1964) have already been discussed. In another historic case, *Baker* v. *Carr* (1962) the Supreme Court decided that matters of legislative reapportionment could be considered by the federal courts under the equal protection clause of the Fourteenth Amendment. As a result, the federal district court decision dismissing a suit against the apportionment law of Tennessee was reversed. This led the way for a number of decisions in which the Court required that districts in both houses of state legislatures and in the House of Representatives be apportioned on the basis of population. These decisions had a major impact on the makeup of the legislative bodies in the United States.

The Court was accused of being hostile to religion because of its decision in *Engle* v. *Vitale* (1962). In a New York school district, students started each school day with the prayer: "Almighty God, we acknowledge our dependence upon Thee and we beg Thy blessings upon us, our parents, our teachers and our country." Some parents challenged the use of prayer in the schools and the case reached the Supreme Court. The Court declared that the use of the prayer was unconstitutional under the First Amendment. The complexity of the issues surrounding religion and the state remain with us today; the question of government aid to parochial schools, for example, has still not been resolved.

There were other important decisions in which the Warren Court specifically endorsed the right of privacy and took a more tolerant attitude on determining the limits of obscenity. It took a liberal attitude also regarding the role of Communist party members in the political system. The cases noted here are illustrative of the trends and new directions established by the Warren Court, particularly in its definition of civil rights. In the words of a former Justice of the Supreme Court, Arthur J. Goldberg:

To me the major accomplishments of the Supreme Court during the 15 years in which Earl Warren was Chief Justice were the revolution in criminal justice both state and Federal; a translation of our society's proclaimed belief in equality into some measure of legal reality, and the beginning of the profound change in the mechanics of our political democracy.[5]

The Burger Court

The Burger Court began in 1969 with the appointment of Chief Justice Warren E. Burger by President Richard Nixon. There ensued a struggle between Congress and the President as to an appointment to a vacancy on the Supreme Court.

Justice Abe Fortas had resigned under heavy pressure because of alleged improprieties. He had been accused of receiving a legal fee, while serving on the Court, from a private foundation that had been convicted of violating a federal law. His resignation paved the way for the Haynsworth-Carswell-Blackmun episode. To fill the vacancy, President Nixon first chose Clement F. Haynsworth of South Carolina. Senate liberals protested the appointment of a man they believed to be an apparent prosegregationist. His nomination was defeated. G. Harrold Carswell of Florida was Nixon's next nominee; he was also rejected by the Senate. Finally Harry Blackmun, a Court of Appeals judge, was nominated and approved unanimously by the Senate. Blackmun was considered more of a liberal; he was not closely identified with the conservative Southern viewpoint associated with Haynsworth and Carswell.

The Burger Court—1974

Justice	Age	Appointed in
Warren E. Burger	66	1969 by Nixon
William H. Rehnquist	49	1971 by Nixon
William O. Douglas	75	1939 by Roosevelt
Lewis F. Powell, Jr.	66	1971 by Nixon
William J. Brennan, Jr.	67	1957 by Eisenhower
Potter Stewart	58	1959 by Eisenhower
Byron R. White	56	1962 by Kennedy
Thurgood Marshall	65	1967 by Johnson
Harry Andrew Blackmun	65	1970 by Nixon

Chief Justice Burger's leadership seemed to introduce a period of judicial self-restraint. Although the Burger Court up to this date has not swung the pendulum dramatically away from the trends of the

Warren Court, it has modified and qualified a number of the decisions stemming from the Warren period. For example, it has allowed individual communities to determine the meaning of obscenity locally (*Miller* v. *California*), paving the way for possible local actions against pornographic literature and movies. Additionally, the Burger Court has allowed a ten percent deviation with respect to representation and apportionment in the legislature, in effect modifying the *Baker* v. *Carr* ruling. However, as noted earlier, the Burger Court has also made a number of liberal decisions, e.g., legalization of abortion and extension of the right to counsel of poor defendants; it also declined to stop the publication of the Pentagon papers.

The Court and Democratic Society

In this brief overview of the Court, one can see that the political and social environment is an important determinant of its decisions. Moreover, it is clear that the Court's power over the other institutions of government is quite broad and its impact on the political system, society, and the economy can be of major importance. Finally, the personalities in the Court, particularly the Chief Justice, are important factors in the power and nature of the decisions. Strong Chief Justices inevitably dominate the Court and give it a broad and very visible impact on the politics of the country. Similarly, the composition of the Court—the attitudes of the individual justices—has significant influence on judicial decisions and perceptions regarding the proper role of the Court. To understand the full substance of the Supreme Court, students should study the philosophy and decisions of such renowned justices as Holmes, Cardozo, Frankfurter and Black, to name but a few.

The basic dilemma faced by a democratic society with respect to its laws is a need to reconcile stability with the need for change. Because of its flexibility, the Constitution has provided the basis for stability and also the basis for change. Through custom and usage, judicial interpretation, legislative acts, and constitutional amendment, the system of laws has remained relatively responsive and flexible.

However, this does bring with it some harsh criticisms as to the role of the courts. As mentioned at the beginning of this chapter critics question whether these nine men should be the moral and legal guide to society, or whether they should be in a position to make national policy. They point out that the justices are not elected or accountable—their political decisions are not under the control of popularly

The Supreme Court and Society

elected representatives nor of the popular will. For proponents of popular will, such power seems elitist and arrogant. Some suggest that the popularly elected legislature should be the final determinant of constitutionality, as it is in England where the laws of Parliament are supreme. Critics also point out the fact that in a number of cases, Presidents who have long departed still have an impact on national policy through their lifetime appointments of Supreme Court judges. Scholars still debate whether Supreme Court judges should serve for only ten years, or be liable to elections by popular vote. However, the American political system has built into it so much diffusion and decentralization, so many checks and balances, that Court decisions require the cooperation and consensus of various political actors within the system in order to be effective. If the Court gets too far ahead of the times, that is, goes beyond the political and social climate as perceived by the political actors, it will lose power and diminish its credibility. Its decisions would then have no real authority behind them.

What made the Warren Court exceptional in this respect was the support it received from its constituencies, the political actors. This support expanded its power and enabled it to make vanguard decisions. On a more moralistic plane, the Warren Court also served as a federal conscience by putting into practice some of the high pronouncements of equality and justice embodied in the Constitution. Although the Court's power stems from its legal role, the essence of its power is political in nature. If power is viewed as the ability of the Court to shape the political system, then this is primarily a perceived matter based on the character of other political actors and society as a whole —not on legal mechanics. Thus, in order for the Court to carry on the tradition established by John Marshall, judges must perceive the Court as a political as well as judicial institution.

NOTES

1. Robert A. Dahl, "Decision-Making in a Democracy: The Role of the Supreme Court as a National Policy-Maker," in Raymond E. Wolfinger, ed., *Readings in American Political Behavior* (Englewood Cliffs, N.J.: Prentice-Hall, 1966), p. 166.
2. Alexander M. Bickel, "Close of the Warren Era," *The New Republic*, July 12, 1969.
3. Jack C. Plano and Milton Greenberg, *The American Political Dictionary* (Hinsdale, Ill.: The Dryden Press, 1972), p. 317.
4. Hirabayashi v. United States, 320 U.S. 81 (1943).
5. Arthur J. Goldberg, "On The Supreme Court: I" *The New York Times*, April 12, 1971.

Selected Readings

As we have seen, only a small number of cases actually reach the Supreme Court. The process from lower court to the Supreme Court can be a lengthy and tedious one. Once the case does reach the highest level, the Court itself engages in an initial screening process. What the Court does review and what it refuses to review, in itself is an important indication of the direction of judicial thought. The types of cases the Court accepts are also indications of the perspective on the judicial role held by a majority of justices. The Warren Court, for example, was a most active one, addressing many thorny constitutional issues. In the first selection, Arthur J. Goldberg, a former justice of the Supreme Court, assesses the Warren Court and provides general insights into the role of the Supreme Court. Briefly reviewing some of the general principles of judicial review while criticizing certain Court actions, Goldberg praises the Warren Court and its handling of major constitutional issues. Arguing that the Court cannot solve all of the political and social ills of American society, he contends that it must nevertheless face the constitutional issues that arise from these ills. Goldberg believes that the Warren Court did just that—particularly in terms of civil rights. The second selection is a brief excerpt from *Gideon's Trumpet,* an excellent insight into the issue of rights in a criminal justice system. Anthony Lewis briefly reviews the concept of judicial review and notes that it has been repeatedly questioned throughout the Court's history. He notes that justices have frequently disagreed regarding the role the Court should play in defending rights under the First Amendment and in its judicial review of legislation and actions of other branches. In any case, Lewis argues that judicial review is an established principle of American democracy.

9.1

On the Supreme Court

ARTHUR J. GOLDBERG

I

To me, the major accomplishments of the Supreme Court during the fifteen years in which Earl Warren was Chief Justice were the revolution in criminal justice, both state and Federal; a translation of our society's proclaimed belief in equality into some measure of legal reality, and the beginning of a profound change in the mechanics of our political democracy.

Among all of the decisions in these three areas, many believe Brown vs. Board of Education to be the most significant decision of the Warren Court. In deciding Brown, the Court cut through the fiction surrounding the old "separate but equal" doctrine to the realities which had always been patently obvious to all who were willing to see: that "separate" could never be "equal" because its very genesis and its only purpose for being was to be invidiously discriminatory, to keep the black man in an inferior status.

Brown was not the first case in which the Court rejected legal fiction in favor of perceivable fact. There are criminal justice decisions of like import, but if belated, Brown was still more dramatic than the others.

In Brown and other cases, it appeared that the Warren Court was manifesting an impatience with legalisms, with dry and sterile dogma, and with virtually unfounded assumptions which served to insulate the law and the Constitution it serves from the hard world it is intended to affect.

The Supreme Court has recently spoken of courts in general as "palladiums of liberty" and as "citadels of justice." I profoundly believe that the Supreme Court is such a court, as well as many lower courts. But we cannot act on the assumption that all courts are or that many are perceived as such. To elements of our population the judicial system is viewed as anything but a "citadel of justice."

I do not refer to the view taken by those who style themselves revolutionary and who are blind to our constitutional commitment to the rule of law. I am describing the perceptions of some of the residents of our ghettos and barrios, of our urban

From *The New York Times*, April 12 and 13, 1971. © 1971 by the The New York Times Company. Reprinted by permission.

and rural poor, of the economically and socially deprived. These are people to whom the law may seem to be both a mystery and an oppression; they are people whose vaunted "day in court" may well consist of a few minutes—or even a few seconds—before an impatient judge in a dingy courtroom; people for whom a plea or verdict of guilty is an inevitable conclusion. Having spent six months or a year without bail in a city jail even before the trial, there is commitment perhaps to an antiquated prison to spend years in confined and destructive idleness.

How can we possibly expect those whose lives are directly or indirectly touched by such a system of justice to share our own deeply held views as to the integrity of our institutional legal process? And, to the extent that our own exhortations ring with commitment to the process and fail to take full measure of the failures of that system, how can we expect our words to be viewed as responsive or less than hypocritical?

Nine justices in Washington, of course, cannot build new courtrooms or prisons, eliminate solely by their own action congested court calendars, provide rehabilitative services for prisons, appoint needed new judges or educate old ones to meaningful understanding of the law or their role in it. But, if the Court cannot "solve" these problems, it is also true that it cannot avoid them. They will come to it in the form of constitutional claims concerning rights to speedy trial, to bail, or to treatment instead of simply a useless confinement after conviction.

There will be many such questions to come to the Court in one form or another. For it is true, as Professor Freund has pointed out, that we transform many of our most and important controversial social issues into legal ones. The future of our cities and their teeming population is one of our most pressing domestic problems and is overlaid with the burden of racial and economic decision. Inevitably, the Court will become involved. The Fifth Circuit has recently dealt in dramatic fashion with the misallocation of municipal services within the community. It found a constitutional violation in Shaw, Miss., where city authorities had provided white neighborhoods with lights and paved streets and left the black area to live with darkness and mud. The implications of this ruling are manifold and broad and the Court will be asked, I am sure, to treat of them sooner or later.

The Court has thus far refused to discuss the constitutionality of unequal public expenditures for education of children in poorer or richer areas. But the issue will rise again, I am sure, with respect not only to the number of dollar support per pupil, but with regard to disparities in the quality of education provided even when there is no great gap in spending. And there will be need to face the issue of so-called de facto segregation in schools or in housing.

Without at all purporting to prejudge the issues themselves, let me suggest finally that the judicial responses which purport to resolve legal and constitutional claims—either affirmatively or negatively—without considering the reality from which the claims spring and in which the claimants live cannot fit the requirements of a relevant justice.

It was one of the great virtues of the Warren Court that it brought to constitutional adjudication common-sense willingness to deal with the hard and often unpleasant facts of contemporary life.

II

Our system has now been operating with a Supreme Court exercising the great power of judicial review of the constitutionality of Federal and state legislation for almost two centuries. Yet during all that time the Court has never overruled precedent to any significant degree in order to facilitate a significant contraction of human liberties.

In arriving at this conclusion, I have excluded consideration of decisions being handed down during the current term of the Court. Since some have just been announced and others will come, it seems to me it will be more fruitful to test the validity of my statement after the term ends rather than in midstream.

To be sure, the Court has not been a perfect champion of civil liberties, nor have these rights undergone a continual and steady expansion. There have been periods in which the Court refused to recognize rights embodied in the Constitution. *Dred Scott* and *Plessy vs. Ferguson* are obvious examples.

But once fundamental rights have been recognized, there has never been a general reversal of direction by the Court, a going back against the trend of history.

Existence of this expectation of continued expansion is relevant to the Court's judgment in two ways. The first is that the Court can discount the fears voiced by critics that expansion of personal liberties will be met by enduring public resistance. As much as the defenders of the status quo may grumble or resent the change, they grow accustomed to the continued growth and, when the "newness" wears off, they come to accept the new status quo. Irrefutable examples here are the reapportionment decisions, long postponed and initially met with a flurry of attacks and criticism, but which went on to be "implemented quickly and with surprisingly little dislocation." It was this turnabout which earned reapportionment the sobriquet of the "success story of the Warren Court."

So this expectation of growth of civil liberties weakens the *stare decisis* arguments against overruling to permit expansion of constitutionally protected personal fundamental rights. On the other hand, expectation of continued growth and adaptation, which is the unique aspect of our constitutional development, counsels in the strongest possible terms against the contraction of liberties.

I think this lack of precedent for contraction explains the alarms in some quarters when it is suggested that some of the civil liberties decisions are to be reconsidered; and explains the belief of, say, Prof. Charles A. Reich that we are at "the brink of an authoritarian or police state." These are obvious overstatements; for confirmation of the fact that we are at present far from such dangers, we need only compare our system with some of the real totalitarian states that exist all too commonly abroad. Nevertheless, the overreaction is itself instructive. The cries of repression are the result, at least in part, of such a long-sustained expectation.

And cries of repression will not be the only result. As a sort of self-fulfilling prophecy, the overreaction of the concerned may induce in others the belief that the Court is sanctioning repression—inviting it and condoning it. The Court plays a most important role in expressing the essential morality inherent in the Constitution. It is the voice not only of what the Constitution commands but also of what it inspires. This responsibility counsels against contracting fundamental rights, since the signal to the nation—the moral message of a reversal of the trend—will be damaging. There is an enormous difference between not opening new frontiers of human liberty and closing ones formerly open.

Furthermore, no carefully worded opinion can lessen the momentousness of an unprecedented reversal of the trend of expanding constitutional rights. Nor can its effects be limited to a single civil right or single area of civil liberties. Any overruling acts as an admission that some right the Court had formerly called "fundamental" was not so fundamental after all; that admission will undermine the public belief that the other rights labelled fundamental in the past retain their status.

An interesting parallel exists with the power of legislature and executive in constitutional interpretation. They, under the constraints of the Constitution, rather than *stare decisis*, can expand but not contract the people's fundamental liberties. Or, as explained in *Katzenbach vs. Morgan*, they may enforce or expand existing rights, but they have "no power to restrict, abrogate, or dilute these guarantees."

This concept, history and tradition shows, applies to the constitutional decisions of the Supreme Court. It both justifies the overruling involved in the expansion of human liberties during the Warren years, and also counsels against the future overruling of the Warren's Court libertarian decisions.

9.2

From Gideon's Trumpet

ANTHONY LEWIS

We have come to take it for granted in this country that courts, especially the Supreme Court, have the power to review the actions of governors, legislators, even Presidents, and set them aside as unconstitutional. But this power of judicial review, as it is called, has been given to judges in few other countries—and nowhere, at any time, to the extent that our history has confided it in the Supreme Court. In the guise of legal questions there come to the Supreme Court many of the most fundamental and divisive issues of every era, issues which judges in other lands would never dream of having to decide.

The consequences are great for Court and country. For the justices power means responsibility, a responsibility the more weighty because the Supreme Court so often has the last word. Deciding cases is never easy, but a judge may sleep more soundly after sentencing a man to death—or invalidating a President's seizure of the nation's steel mills—if he knows there is an appeal to a higher court. Justices of the Supreme Court do not have that luxury.

"We are not final because we are infallible," Justice Jackson wrote, "but we are infallible only because we are final." Men who know their own fallibility may find it hard to bear the burden of final decision. A few months before the Supreme Court agreed to hear Gideon's case, Justice Charles Evans Whittaker retired after only five years on the Court explaining candidly that he found the strain of its work too great. He told friends that when he wrote an opinion, he felt as if he were carving his words into granite.

Other men may not be bothered by judicial power, may indeed revel in it. But the existence of power so great inevitably raises questions. Is it consistent with democracy to let nine men, appointed for life and directly answerable to no constituency, make ultimate decisions about the direction of our society? How free should a judge feel to set above the will of the people's elected representatives the principles that he finds in the Constitution? How does he find them, given the

Copyright © 1964 by Anthony Lewis. Reprinted by permission of Random House, Inc.

Constitution's vague words and the conflicting interpretations of them by judges of the past?

The very legitimacy of judicial review has been questioned repeatedly from the time the Supreme Court first held a federal statute unconstitutional, in *Marbury v. Madison* in 1803. The Jeffersonians accused John Marshall of usurpation. Liberals said the same of the Court in the 1930's, and revisionist historians of that day tried to prove that it really had not been given the power of judicial review. Today the epithets come from extremists of the right, disaffected by the Court's decisions on individual liberty and racial equality.

Scholarly opinion has long since dismissed the charge that judicial review was illicitly imported into our system by John Marshall or anyone else. The Constitution does not explicitly provide for its enforcement by the federal courts, but the text—including the grant of jurisdiction over cases arising under the Constitution—indicates that expectation. The records of the Philadelphia Convention of 1787 point the same way; at least a substantial number of the delegates assumed that the Supreme Court would pass on the constitutionality of state and federal acts that came before it in lawsuits. The delegates, in fact, considered a proposal to go further and have the Court share the President's veto power in a Council of Revision, but that suggestion was rejected on the ground that the Court already had a "sufficient check" by its power to declare laws unconstitutional. The very conception of a written constitution binding on governments as well as citizens, the great American contribution to political history, presupposed some institution to enforce the rules. Theoretically that could have been Congress, but the episodic and political nature of the legislative process would have made that choice doubtful. In fact we have lived for one hundred and seventy-five years with the Supreme Court as the final interpreter of our fundamental law, and our whole system of government is now built on that assumption. Justice Jackson, no starry-eyed admirer of judicial review, wrote in 1954: "The real strength of the position of the Court is probably in its indispensability to government under a written Constitution. It is difficult to see how the provisions of a one-hundred-and-fifty-year-old written document can have much vitality if there is not some permanent institution to translate them into current commands. . . ."

But if the issue of legitimacy is foreclosed, there remain very live questions of when and how the Supreme Court should exercise its great power to nullify what other branches of government have done. These questions have been the subject of a fierce and unending debate among commentators and among the justices themselves. The opposing positions can best be summarized in terms of the two uncommonly able and determined justices who led the debate for a generation, Felix Frankfurter and Hugo L. Black.

Justice Frankfurter's motto was "judicial self-restraint." He counseled judges to defer to Congress and the states, even where their actions seemed unwise; to be cautious in reading prohibitions into the Constitution; to respect history; to balance against the interest of the individual the interest of society. Justice Frankfurter warned that relying too much on judges to protect our freedoms sapped the strength of democracy by distracting attention from the political forum where unwise policies should be corrected. He felt the Court was often less equipped to deal with a problem than expert administrators or politicians closer to the public will. He was motivated also by a deep concern for the Supreme Court as an institution, a fear that it might destroy itself if it pressed its power too far. He and others remembered the 1930's, when a self-willed Court tried to stand against history by stopping urgent economic and social measures and thus brought itself to the brink of drastic reform —reform which it avoided only by a political change of course. Not that Justice Frankfurter never found state or federal action unconstitutional. His vote to invalidate school segregation, his concern for the freedom of commerce from state barriers, and his careful scrutiny of police behavior and of state assistance to religion all testify to his acceptance of the Court's role as enforcer of the Constitution. But right up to his retirement in 1962 his opinions preached judicial caution, self-examination and restraint. Since then his restraining role has been carried on by others, especially his friend Justice John Marshall Harlan, who in a notable speech in 1963 criticized what he called the "cosmic" view of the judicial function—the idea "that all deficiencies in our society which have failed of correction by other means should find a cure in the courts."

Justice Black, by contrast, has emphasized the duty of judges to preserve individual liberty, and has argued that excessive deference to other branches of government amounts to abdication of that responsibility. In the Black view, the framers of the Constitution made the decision to protect individuals from governmental repression, so a judge should not feel timid or self-conscious about doing so. Particularly obnoxious to Justice Black is the Frankfurter thesis that the Court must balance individual interests against the needs of government and uphold any reasonable governmental course of action. Justice Black argues that this weighing and balancing of what is reasonable leaves judges too much at large. He looks to history and finds definite rules in the Constitution—"absolutes," as he has called them. His favorite example is the First Amendment: "Congress shall make no law respecting an establishment of religion, or prohibiting the free exercise thereof; or abridging the freedom of speech, or of the press. . . ." To Justice Black, as he has put it, "no law means *no law.*" Thus he has gone much farther in finding violations of the First Amendment than almost any other justice, past or present. He has argued, in dissent, that no government has the power to censor obscenity. And he has repeatedly dissented from decisions upholding federal action against the Communist party and its members, decisions in which the majority found the injury to free speech outbalanced by the need of society to protect itself against an international conspiracy.

Study Questions

1. What arguments could you make that the U.S. Supreme Court is an equal branch of the federal government along with the presidency and the Congress? Can you think of any arguments that would imply that the Court is less powerful in our federal system than either of the other two branches?

Could you argue that the Court may be more powerful than the other two branches?

2. Since the judges of the Supreme Court are not elected by anyone, would you go along with the argument that the Court is an aristocratic element in our federal system? Why or why not? In recent years it has been argued by supporters that the Court is the people's safeguard of their liberty and freedom in the federal system. How would you evaluate this argument?

3. Despite the many controversies Supreme Court decisions have stirred up in the last couple of decades, do you think that for the most part, the Court has made decisions that were in accord with the opinions of most Americans? Or do you think the Court paved new directions which the majority of the American people needed time to catch up to?

4. Argue the relative merits of judicial activism and judicial self-restraint as approaches to the role of the Supreme Court. Do you think that either approach is more in tune with the intentions of the framers of the Constitution? Would either approach be more in tune with the temper and needs of contemporary American society?

5. Do you think selection of Supreme Court justices by the President, with confirmation by a majority of the Senate, for unlimited tenure, is a good procedure? Can you suggest some changes?

6. How would you evaluate the judicial decisions by the Warren Court? Do you think they went too far, or not far enough? Evaluate the impact on American society of the 1950s and 1960s of those decisions. Do you think their impact has been exaggerated?

7. Do you think the attitudes and personal philosophies of the individual justices should influence their decisions? Why or why not? Should the justices consider the needs of the country in their decisions, or are the needs of the country best served by a rigid interpretation of the laws?

8. Do you agree with the judgment of this book that the Supreme Court is a political as well as judicial institution, in terms of its ability to shape the American political system? Why or why not?

Bibliography

Books

Acheson, Patricia C. *The Supreme Court: American Judicial Heritage*. New York: Dodd, Mead & Company, 1961.

Bickel, Alexander M. *The Least Dangerous Branch: The Supreme Court at the Bar of Politics*. Indianapolis: The Bobbs-Merrill Co. Inc., 1962.

Hyneman, Charles S. *The Supreme Court on Trial*. New York: Atherton Press, 1963.

Lewis, Anthony. *Gideon's Trumpet*. New York: Alfred A. Knopf, Vintage Books, 1966.

Mason, Alpheus Thomas. *The Supreme Court: Palladium of Freedom.* Ann Arbor: The University of Michigan Press, 1962.
Mendelson, Wallace, ed. *The Supreme Court: Law and Discretion.* Indianapolis: The Bobbs-Merrill Company, Inc., 1967.
Murphy, Walter F. *Congress and the Court.* Chicago: The University of Chicago Press, 1962.
North, Arthur A. *The Supreme Court, Judicial Process and Judicial Politics.* New York: Appleton-Century-Crofts, 1964.
Schubert, Glendon A. *Constitutional Politics.* New York: Holt, Rinehart and Winston, Inc., 1960.
Shapiro, Martin. *Law and Politics in the Supreme Court.* New York: The Free Press of Glencoe, 1964.
Westin, Alan F., ed. *An Autobiography of the Supreme Court.* New York: The Macmillan Company, 1963.
Westin, Alan F., ed. *The Supreme Court: Views from Inside.* New York: W. W. Norton and Company, Inc., 1961.

Articles

Bender, Paul. "The Techniques of Subtle Erosion." *Harper's,* December 1972.
Beth, Loren P. "The Supreme Court Reconsidered: Opposition and Judicial Review in the United States." *Political Studies,* Vol. 16, No. 2 (June 1968), pp. 243-249.

CHAPTER **10**
Politics, Society and the Judicial System

The dominant position of law in our society has led to the evolution of a complex judicial bureaucracy and legal system. Simultaneously, it has caused the development of a highly influential and powerful legal profession.

In 1970, there were over 350,000 practicing lawyers in the United States, 35,000 of whom were employed by various agencies of the federal, state and local governments. It is interesting to note that in Washington, D.C. there are over 15,000 lawyers or 1 for each 49 District of Columbia residents, whereas in North Carolina there are 4,000 lawyers or 1 for each 1,164 residents.[1]

The use of law not only to solve individual and group conflicts, but as an instrument of political change, has also created a special constituency made up of lawyers, bureaucrats involved in administering the judicial system, judges, and a number of politicians. For all practical purposes, it is this special constituency that gives shape and substance to the judicial system. It serves both as a link between the people and the courts and as a special interest group overseeing the operation of the judicial system.

Power of the Judiciary

The power of the judiciary stems partly from the existence of this special constituency, and partly from the autonomous position of the judiciary. In the American political system, as noted earlier, an independent judiciary is considered to be an essential characteristic of democracy. This independence presupposes a judiciary that is relatively immune from political interference and public manipulation.

There is yet another basis for the power of the judiciary, which also provides a power base for the special constituency. This is best stated by the old adage that "knowledge is power." The complexity of the judicial process, and of the judicial structure, and the technicalities and intricacies of law cloak the entire legal system in relative obscurity from public scrutiny. Few laymen understand the essentials of the system; most are only spectators in a drama involving the special constituency and the formal judicial structure. For the people to gain access to the courts or to inject their power into the process, they must first have access to knowledge, which means dealing with members or institutions in the special constituency.

To appreciate the extent of judicial power and the role the judiciary plays, the student of American politics must go beyond the Supreme Court. Since most Americans deal with the lower courts, it is important to develop some understanding of that vast and complex court hierarchy, and the historical and philosophical bases, as well as the mechanics, of the judicial process.

Historical View of the Legal System

It is fair to say that the character of American law and the judicial process is bound up in the common law system. It may be useful to point out some of the historical antecedents, beginning with some general observations regarding the Western systems of law.

In the Western world there are two major legal systems: common law and Roman law. Roman law evolved from the Roman Empire dating from 450 B.C. In order to control the vast lands and diversified peoples, the Roman Empire evolved a rather detailed system of laws culminating in the Justinian Code in 533 A.D. Roman law recognized the rights of subjects (non-citizens) as well as citizens and spelled these out in detail. In most disputes, the codified laws governed. Over the years, other influences were incorporated, including a system of tribal law, a body of canon law developed by the church, and commercial and maritime laws which developed as cities grew and trade increased. Ultimately, all of these various facets were combined into the French Civil Code or Napoleonic Code of 1804, which still serves as the basis for the legal structure in France and other European countries. It is characterized primarily by codification—that is, the building up of a body of written rules on all known procedures. The primary role of judges is to examine the facts of the case to find the objective truth, even if it overshadows individual rights and safeguards. Thus, the role of judges includes a direct involvement in questioning witnesses and seeking evidence and in this sense, "seeking the truth." Litigation, legislation, and courtroom procedures in France, for example, revolve around these basic characteristics.

In most English-speaking countries, including the United States, the common law system prevails. It evolved from medieval feudal practices by which the Norman rulers of England attempted to centralize their power. Anglo-Saxon law, customary law, a multitude of local laws, and kingly edicts were consolidated. In attempting to broaden royal authority and in applying the king's law throughout the realm, English monarchs authorized inquests into the facts of any particular case according to the locality. Clergymen acted as judges, touring the countryside applying the king's law; thus the concept of the circuit rider (or circuit judge) developed. Since these judges had to visit outlying localities which had their own peculiar local laws and customs, attempts were made to combine and balance the requirements of the king's law with the peculiarities of local law. This led to a degree of flexibility with respect to the application of the king's law. From this evolved the concept of "common sense and reason" founded on Christian ethics.

As the English political system developed, other principles of common law evolved, including parliamentary supremacy, equity, and *stare decisis* ("let it stand") or following precedents. Precedent is the basis for most arguments in law:

> Legal disputes in the United States are fought out largely over the application of precedents in a particular controversy. A lawyer will try to convince the court that the precedents serve to prove his case. Judges, in turn, must decide between competing precedents in reaching a decision. If precedent appears to be unreasonable or unjust, a court may specifically overrule it and establish a new precedent.[2]

These principles, as well as others, formed the basis of the English judicial system. By the turn of the seventeenth century, there was a relatively sophisticated and systematic judicial structure in England, much of which found its way into the American colonies.

Among the major common law principles and procedures adopted in the American judicial system are the adversary process and the jury system. In the adversary process, it is assumed that truth will emerge as a result of the confrontation between the accuser and the accused, i.e., the adversaries. In this process, the judge and jury are assumed to be neutral arbiters of the conflict, each playing specific roles in the courtroom. The jury system, although not required for all trials, is based on the common law assumption that an accused has the right to be tried by a group of his own peers.

The promulgation of the Constitution and the establishment of a judiciary led to litigation, legislation and constitutional interpretations, adding some distinctly American concepts to the existing body of common law. While a relatively coherent system developed at the federal level, the states developed their own systems attuned to the peculiarities and needs of localities. It is at the state level that we encounter a diversity of court mechanics.

Although there are various types of law (e.g., maritime, commercial, and international), our concern here is primarily with constitutional, criminal and civil law. We have already touched upon constitutional law, which in the main involves interpretation and application of the Constitution, with the final decision in the hands of the Supreme Court. Civil law, on the other hand, involves conflicts between private parties in such matters as business relations, domestic relations, contracts, and accidents. The legal system provides the arena in which these disputes are settled. The government may be a party in civil suits, either as defendant or plaintiff. Criminal law involves criminal conduct by individuals; the government is the plaintiff against individuals, who are the defendants. In such circumstances, the government, representing the political system, prescribes the law, defines the crime, and imposes punishment on the defendant.

Dual Court System

One of the unique features of the American judiciary is the existence of a dual court system. This is a reflection of the federal system of government, with two political systems—national and state—each with its own judiciary and laws. Each is organized in a hierarchical fashion, with three main levels of courts: ordinary courts, intermediate, and final.

In the state system, trial courts (ordinary courts) include a variety of courts such as police, traffic, juvenile, probate, and justice of the peace. The intermediate state courts are appellate courts, or courts of

Dual Court System

Organization of the Courts

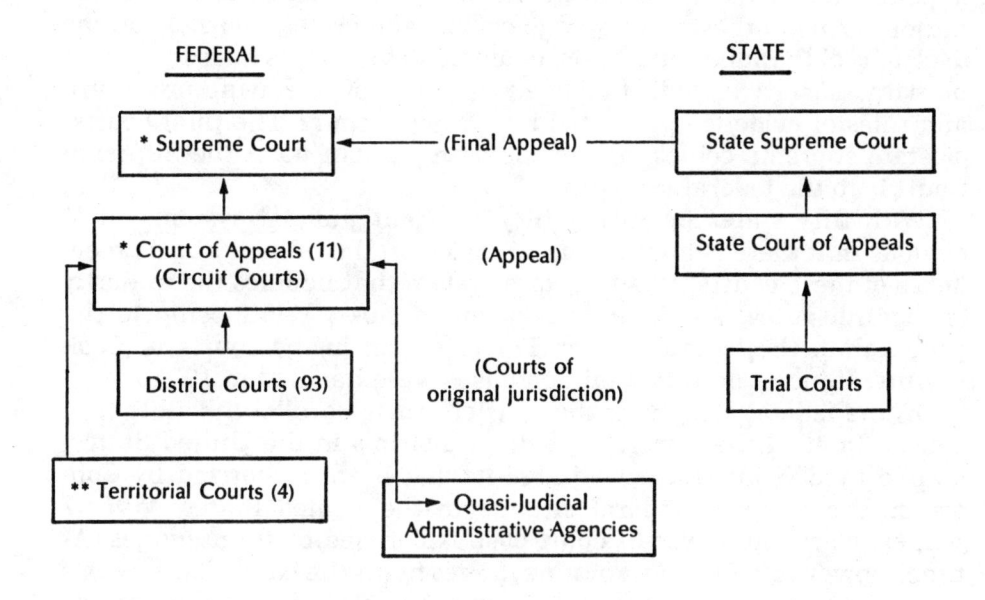

FEDERAL

- *Supreme Court ← (Final Appeal)
- *Court of Appeals (11) (Circuit Courts) — (Appeal)
- District Courts (93)
- **Territorial Courts (4)
- Quasi-Judicial Administrative Agencies

(Courts of original jurisdiction)

STATE

- State Supreme Court
- State Court of Appeals
- Trial Courts

SPECIAL JURISDICTION

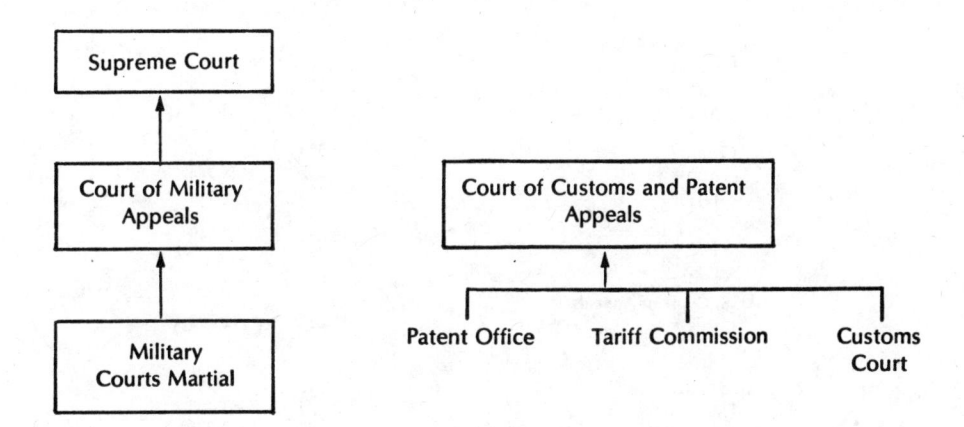

- Supreme Court
- Court of Military Appeals
- Military Courts Martial

- Court of Customs and Patent Appeals
  - Patent Office
  - Tariff Commission
  - Customs Court

* Multi-member courts, decisions reached by majority vote
** Puerto Rico, Virgin Islands, Panama Canal Zone, Guam

appeal, which review the work of those below them. Decisions are by majority rule in these three-judge courts, and are based solely on the decisions of the subordinate courts; no new evidence is introduced and no witnesses are called. It is solely a matter of reviewing procedure and rules of evidence presented in the lower court. The final courts, or state supreme courts, are to the state system what the Supreme Court is to the federal system.

With fifty states operating fifty different judicial systems, it is obvious that there is a tremendous variety in the numbers and procedures of these courts. It is the state system that handles the majority of legal disputes, and thus is in a much closer relationship to the people than the federal courts. For example, in the courts in Cook County, Illinois, close to 4 million cases were handled in 1971.

In the federal structure, the district courts parallel the state trial courts. In 1974 there were 93 federal districts in the United States, staffed by 385 judges, each judge having been authorized by Congress. There are 11 federal circuits in the United States with 97 judges. Normally a circuit court case is handled by three judges. At times however, a full court of nine judges hears the case. These courts act in the same capacity as state courts of appeal; they are not courts of original jurisdiction.

The table below shows that most of the litigation in the federal

		1970	1971
U. S. District Courts			
Civil trials		9,449	10,093
non-jury		6,078	6,600
jury		3,371	3,493
Criminal		6,583	7,456
non-jury		2,357	2,923
jury		4,226	4,533
	Total	16,032	17,549
U. S. Court of Appeals			
Cases		11,662	12,788
U. S. Supreme Court	Year	*1968*	*1969*
Filed		3,271	3,405
Disposed		3,117	3,379
Petitions denied or dismissed		2,586	2,880
Number of Cases		116	105
Written Opinions		99	88
Concurring Opinions		48	49
Dissenting Opinions		77	73
Separate Opinions		19	17

structure takes place in the lower courts, as is true in the state court system.

For example, when an individual commits a crime and crosses state boundaries, there is federal jurisdiction; while at the same time the actual crime, whether it is kidnapping or automobile theft, may also fall under the jurisdiction of the state in which it was perpetrated. Where he will be brought to trial depends largely on who makes the arrest. It is also possible that the accused will be prosecuted in both state and federal courts since theoretically he has committed two crimes.

In civil law similar problems of jurisdiction arise. For example, civil suits involving citizens of different states, where the amount at issue is more than $10,000, normally fall into the jurisdiction of the federal system. Yet the individuals involved in the dispute may choose to take the case to a state court. Obviously, in those cases where the federal government is involved or where federal laws are specifically violated, the federal system has exclusive jurisdiction. The federal courts also have jurisdiction in civil actions in which states are parties.

Jurisdiction of the Federal Courts

The jurisdiction of the federal courts is defined by Article 3 of the Constitution on the basis of subject matter and the parties involved. Subjects that can be brought before the federal courts include the following:
1. All cases in law and equity arising under the Constitution
2. All cases in law and equity arising under the laws of the United States
3. All cases in law and equity arising under treaties made under the authority of the United States
4. All cases of admiralty and maritime jurisdiction (the primary purpose here is to promote uniform regulations)

Article 3 of the Constitution also extends federal jurisdiction to the following parties involved:
1. Controversy to which the United States is a party
2. Controversy between two or more states
3. Controversies between the state and citizens of another state
4. Controversy between citizens of different states
5. Controversies between a state or the citizens thereof and foreign states, citizens or subjects
6. All cases affecting ambassadors, other public ministers and consuls.

Regardless of whether the state or federal courts apply the law, it is the U.S. Supreme Court that is the final appellate tribunal for both systems. For example, any decision of a state supreme court that may involve a federal question is subject to review by the U.S. Supreme Court.

In both the operation of the courts and the selection of judges, there is a difference between the state and federal methods, and differences among the various states. As noted earlier, trial courts at the state level include various types of courts each exercising a relative autonomy within its jurisdiction.

State Courts

Historically, the state judicial system has been very decentralized. There has been no central authority with responsibility for its operation. Once assigned, judges normally remain within their particular jurisdiction regardless of how efficiently they have run their courts. Furthermore, judges have usually not been responsible to a higher authority for their efficiency. There has been some movement towards a more efficient centralized system; large cities have set up unified municipal courts to replace the haphazard collections of various types of courts. Additionally, some states, beginning with New Jersey in 1948, have been moving toward a more integrated judicial system, in which all judges except those on the state supreme court work within one system and can be reassigned by the chief justice of the supreme court, depending on where court traffic is greatest.

For example, a 1964 amendment to the state constitution completely reorganized the Illinois courts. The twenty-one circuit courts within the state system are each administered by a chief judge elected by his fellow judges. This reorganization allowed all of the various types of ordinary courts to be consolidated and centralized within each circuit. But in general, improvements are still needed in the administration of state and municipal courts in order to eliminate delays and use judges more efficiently.

Selection of State Judges

Judges are elected or appointed in the various states. The argument still continues as to which is the best method. In most states, election is the chief method of choosing judges. The problem here is that voters really do not have a basis for making a choice between various judges, and they usually just follow the party label. Furthermore, judges who win their seats by election tend to feel obligated to their constituents; the question then arises as to how objectively they can perform their judicial function.

Some observers argue that appointment of state and local judges by governors or mayors avoids the pitfalls of electing judges. Here, however, there is still some concern that political influence and ideology may be the determining factors. Nevertheless, it is felt that responsible officials will be more inclined to select good judges since the selection reflects on them.

To avoid the pitfalls of both appointment and election of judges, some states have implemented a commission plan. Generally, a commission for the selection of judges includes the chief justice of the state supreme court, representatives of the state bar association, and perhaps one or two other persons appointed by the governor. This commission draws up a list of persons it considers qualified, and the governors and mayors appoint state and local judges from this list.

Appointment of Federal Judges

All federal judges are appointed by the President with Senate confirmation. The appointment of judges is perhaps more political in the federal system than in the state system. Each President generally appoints judges from his own party, thus making the positions vehicles for political patronage. For example, President Franklin Roosevelt appointed over 200 Democrats to judgeships and only 8 Republicans. President Kennedy appointed over 100 Democrats and only 11 Republicans. By the end of 1973, President Nixon had appointed over 195 Republican judges and 15 Democrats, not including the appointments to the Supreme Court. As with Supreme Court appointments, the President tends to choose not only a member of his own party, but also someone with the proper political attitudes. For example, a highly conservative Republican President is not likely to appoint a highly liberal Republican to the bench. Thus, federal judges generally reflect the President's political attitudes and, in a sense, are an extension of the presidential perception regarding the operation of the political system.

However, since federal judges have lifetime appointments, based on good behavior, they do have a high degree of political independence once appointed. Invariably the responsibilities of office and the relative isolation from political machinations after appointment, create an independence from the dictates normally associated with political appointees. Since judges in the federal system remain in office for life, there is always a mix in the judicial system of Republicans, Democrats, conservatives, liberals, advocates of judicial self restraint and those of judicial activism, oracles and guardians of due process. Therefore it is difficult to label the entire judiciary with any particular political ideology or political attitude.

One method that the party in power may use to increase control over the judiciary is the creation of new judicial posts. In order to accomplish this, however, the party must control not only Congress but also the presidency, and they would have to be in agreement regarding political ideology. Even if Congress approves the creation of new judicial posts, it is the President who actually appoints the judges. It is unlikely that Congress would agree to such enlargement of the judiciary without some understanding regarding the persons who would be named to such posts.

Administration of the System

The federal judiciary must deal with a number of administrative problems regarding supervision of judges and court congestion in a centralized system. In the federal system, however, the picture is much brighter than in the state systems. Each circuit has a judicial council, consisting of all the judges of the court of appeals, which supervises the work of the federal judges within that circuit. The judicial council assesses the court calendars and assigns or reassigns judges accordingly. The Chief Justice of the Supreme Court spends a considerable amount of time on administrative duties, presiding over the judicial conference of the United States. This conference consists of the chief judges of the circuit courts and one district judge from each circuit. The purpose of the conference is to assess the functioning of the federal judiciary and to make recommendations to Congress concerning the judiciary system. It can be reasonably argued that in such instances, judges form a special interest group applying their own power to influence the legislative branch.

From this discussion, we can readily appreciate some of the complexity, as well as the perplexity, of the American judicial system. Based on common law principles inherited from the English, the American judicial system has a national judiciary which exists side by side with fifty state judiciaries, each operating in its own unique fashion. Moreover, the judicial system is not simply a matter of making decisions in the courtroom—this is only a small part of the total process.

There is a large administrative bureaucracy to insure that cases are properly processed and brought to trial, witnesses called, and final disposition made. The role of the judges is not limited to courtroom practice, but also includes matters concerning judicial appointments, petitions to Congress, electioneering, political involvement, interest group activity, and a host of other questions normally associated with political actors.

Courtroom Practices and Processes: A Case Study

It is useful to highlight some of the most common courtroom practices and processes to point out the complexity of the system and to support our assertion that part of the power of the judiciary rests on the special knowledge associated with it and the special constituency.

Let us turn to a hypothetical case, bearing in mind that the outline and discussion here are necessarily brief and oversimplified.

An automobile driven by Ms. Jane Smith of Alabama jumps across a lawn and smashes into a home owned by John Doe in Missouri, causing considerable damage. John Doe calls the police, who cite Ms. Smith for reckless driving. John Doe could have gone to the police station and signed a complaint against Ms. Smith on the same charge. In any case, a court date is established for trial in a local (state) court at public expense. Ms. Smith is issued a warrant to appear at the court on the date specified. If appropriate, other witnesses can be subpoenaed to appear. Thus the criminal trial begins.

John Doe is concerned about damages to his house. Therefore, he must now institute a civil suit to recover the damages. Consulting with a lawyer, he finds that it might be best to settle out of court since the government does not pay court expenses in a civil suit. Parenthetically, unless John Doe already has a lawyer, the process of finding a suitable one can be quite perplexing. Many bar associations have legal counseling services which assist persons in need of legal advice, and also help to find lawyers for their particular problem. Jane Smith is determined to fight the civil suit, since she fears a large money claim may be placed against her. Moreover, she does not have adequate insurance.

John Doe's lawyer decides to sue in federal district court, since Jane Smith is from another state. Additionally, the lawyer has learned that Jane Smith owns property in her state which could be the basis for legal settlement. If the civil action were to be brought in a state court, any judgment awarded to John Doe would have to be reinstituted in Alabama, the state in which Jane Smith resides, in order to collect the award. Yet, if the civil suit were to be brought in Alabama initially, it would involve expense and inconvenience for John Doe because the out-of-state court is miles from his home.

The civil action begins by John Doe signing a complaint with the clerk of the federal district court. A summons is delivered to Jane Smith, who consults her own lawyer. Her lawyer must file an answer within twenty days. Subsequently, the trial date is set. A pretrial conference takes place in which the judge and the attorneys for the plaintiff (John Doe) and the defendant (Jane Smith) confer and attempt to settle out of court. An out-of-court settlement cannot be arrived at and the case goes to the federal district court. Either party may request a jury or waive these rights to save time and money.

Jane Smith requests a jury trial, thinking that she can get a more sympathetic hearing because she is pregnant and a mother of a 3-year old child. Moreover, she was returning home after caring for a sick grandmother when the accident occurred.

The court bureaucracy now goes through the arduous procedure of selecting a jury. This process is so burdensome that in most cases it not only embitters many persons who have been selected for jury duty, but it may well affect the outcome of the case.

The case comes to trial, although there are continuances (postponements). Each side proceeds to convince the jury of the correctness of its own case. In civil actions, the jury generally decides the outcome for one or the other parties based on the preponderance of evidence. If it decides for the plaintiff, he must take action to collect the award granted by the jury. This can be done by placing a lien on the defendant's property or garnisheeing her salary, or, the defendant may simply make mutually agreeable arrangements for paying the award.

The jury brings in a decision for the plaintiff. Jane Smith's lawyer feels, however, that the jury acted in a prejudicial fashion. He notes that the jury is made up of ten men and two women. Most of the men are bachelors and neither of the women is married. Citing the Fourteenth Amendment, Jane Smith's lawyer charges that she was denied due process of law and equal protection of the laws. On this basis, the case is appealed to the federal circuit court (court of appeals).

The circuit court cannot reexamine the facts tried by jury. It is limited to reviewing the court procedures, admissibility of evidence, and interpretation of the laws. It can then affirm, reverse, or remand the case (order another trial). The court finds by a 2-1 decision that Jane Smith has not been denied her rights under the Fourteenth Amendment to the Constitution, since there is no indication that the jury was necessarily prejudicial. Moreover, the court rules that the jury selection was made according to accepted procedures.

Not satisfied, Jane Smith's lawyer decides to take the case to the Supreme Court. As noted earlier, few cases go beyond the federal circuit court. The Supreme Court usually hears most of its cases through writs of *certiorari,* and these cases normally involve broad national principles rather than disputes over amounts of money or prison sentences. The Court decides to hear the case of Jane Smith, since at least four justices feel there is a significant question involved in terms of equality of sexes under the Fourteenth Amendment.

With respect to the case of *Doe* v. *Smith,* the Court in a 5-4 decision rules that the constitutional rights of the defendant were not violated as a result of the composition of the jury. The majority decision states in part that "the parties in any case before the courts in the United States are guaranteed the right to a fair trial and the judgment of his or her peers. Peers however, does not mean that each jury must have a specific number of certain types of individuals, but rather individual citizens regardless of class or sex who can reasonably decide the case impartially. Peer knows no sexual categorization, nor color, nor ethnic character. Moreover, the jury selection process was in accordance with just procedures. Affirmed."

The minority opinion however, states in part that "trial by peers must include consideration of the psychological aspect of peer. It is not simply a matter of physical characteristics, but of an understanding of the perceptions and beliefs of the individual. In this case, we find that the psychological justice for the defendant was violated since no one on the jury could possibly understand the meaning of motherhood and pregnancy and what effect this might have had on the defendant. Moreover, we find it difficult to accept the justice in a jury composition that neglects the basis of empathy with all parties in the case."

Although we have not gone into great detail in this hypothetical case, the complexities of the judicial process are clear. Not only are there complicated issues regarding administrative procedure within the judicial system, but there are important and intricate issues of law involved. Keep in mind that we have not described actual courtroom procedures or the work necessary outside the courtroom—not to mention the time and expense involved. Parenthetically, criminal proceedings may be even more involved although they follow similar patterns.

In retrospect, we can see that the major sources of judicial power and judicial procedures stem from the role of law within a democratic society, the authority and role of the Supreme Court, and the traditions emerging from common law. To this must be added the evolution of a special constituency and the fact that judges form an elite group of professionals, standing apart from society.

Legal Basis of Judicial Power

The realities of judicial power become clearer when we examine the instruments through which this power is exercised. The *decisions and opinions* of the courts are the most visible legal instruments available. Of course, these vary with each level of court. The appellate and supreme courts at both state and federal levels have a direct impact with their decisions and opinions. Even in lower courts, however, where jury trial is frequent, the judge has considerable influence on the outcome through his instructions to the jury and rulings on evidence. Opinions, both of the majority and minority in higher level courts, in many instances provide the basis for social and political change.

The *writ of habeas corpus* is a particularly effective instrument. It is a command from a judge to an official who has custody of a prisoner to bring that person before the court so that it may decide the legality of the detention. The writ of habeas corpus has become a major instrument for the protection of individual liberty.

The courts can also issue *injunctions*. This is a writ from the court enjoining or prohibiting certain persons from performing certain acts. The main purpose of the injunction is to prevent further aggravation of the injury. It must be shown by the person or party requesting an injunction that he has a major interest or right and that other remedies are inadequate.

The power of the judge to insure proper procedures in the courtroom and protect the nature of the court is embodied in the *contempt power*. The judge, when faced with disobedience or similar acts in his court, can immediately cite the party for contempt and sentence the perpetrator. It is an act that is direct and swift and in most instances, the party is faced with only one alternative—appeal to a higher court.

A final instrument of power is inherent in the very nature of the judiciary system and its relationship to other political institutions. The courts do not have the ability to enforce their decisions. That is left up to the other institutions of government, primarily the executive branch. Thus, a court decision can usually *marshal the executive forces to ensure enforcement* and move the instruments of the political system in a direction determined by the courts.

Moreover, it is assumed that a court decision is the best method to resolve differences peacefully. Consequently, the very decision of the court and the esteem of society for the judicial system constitute a basis of power.

As in most cases of power within our political system, the courts also have checks and countervailing powers that can be arrayed against them. Perhaps the clearest checks and counterbalances are the President and Congress. The very fact that the courts must depend upon other branches of government for support provides an effective counterbalance. It is the executive branch that must supply the physical force, while Congress has control of the allocations of money. The courts cannot compel Congress to spend money to support court-related activities or as a result of a court decision. Perhaps more important, Congress can propose constitutional amendments to reverse a decision of the court and can determine the jurisdiction as well as procedure of the federal court system—aside from the original jurisdiction specified in the Constitution. The entire lower federal court structure is basically a creation of Congress and there is no doubt that Congress has a wide range of discretion regarding the court's staffing procedures and jurisdiction.

Mass Media and the Courts

In any democratic society there are times when the freedom of the press comes into conflict with the judiciary process. While the mass media seek out news about important court cases or defendants, the courts must insure a fair trial while protecting the rights of the accused. The problem is particularly acute during the pretrial period when the mass media are likely to report information on the nature of a crime and the background of the accused. Thus before the case even comes to trial, the mass media may have had an influence on public opinion regarding the guilt or innocence of the accused. Moreover, during the trial there is a consistent problem regarding what can and cannot be reported to the public. Although reporters are allowed to cover trials, normally television, radio, and photography are prohibited. Moreover, reporters are usually cautioned about printing information that is likely to be prejudicial to the accused. Nevertheless, the influence of the mass media on the outcome of trials and in influencing public opinion on certain cases and defendants is well recognized.

The case of Dr. Sam Sheppard, convicted of murdering his wife in 1951 is an excellent example of the freedom of the press in conflict with the rights of the defendant and a fair trial. Prior to the trial there were "swarms of press men at city hall when Sheppard was brought there under arrest; and live broadcasting of a coroner's inquest . . ." During the trial, there was a "press table erected inside the bar of the court and extending the entire width of the room, within three feet of the jury box and so close to the counsel table that the defendant and his counsel could not consult without being overheard by reporters. . ."[3] There were continuous news stories regarding Sheppard and his crime. Editorials particularly in the Cleveland, Ohio newspapers clearly indicated their feeling about Sheppard. As most people expected, a verdict of guilty was brought in by the jury. After having spent 10 years in jail, Sheppard's case was reopened based on petitions by the defense attorney F. Lee Bailey. After hearing the case, the federal district judge ordered a new trial saying:

> If there was a trial by newspaper, this is a perfect example. And the most insidious violator was *The Cleveland Press* . . . Freedom of the press is truly one of the great freedoms we cherish; but it cannot be permitted to overshadow the rights of an individual to a fair trial.[4]

The state of Ohio appealed the decision to the U.S. Supreme Court which concluded that "the trial judge had improperly allowed the news media to inflame and prejudice the public."[5] It upheld the decision of the federal district court. Ironically, the retrial of Sheppard resulted in his exoneration. But the years in prison coupled with his embitterment made chaos out of his personal life. He died at the age of 46 from an overdose of pills.

In more recent times, the trial of the "Chicago Seven" and Watergate trial are illustrative of the role of the mass media in the judicial process. In the former, seven persons were accused of conspiracy in the August, 1968 riots and demonstrations in the city of Chicago during the Democratic Party National Convention. In a trial that lasted four and a half months, the jury found five of the seven guilty of rioting under the anti-rioting laws. The important part of the trial however was the treatment of the defendants—the contemptuous treatment by Judge Julius Hoffman and the harshness with which the defendants were treated in the courtroom. All of these details were newsworthy items covered in the Chicago newspapers and national dailies. Similarly TV coverage of the trial, although not from within the courtroom, was continuous. Moreover, the mass media coverage of the August demonstrations brought to the homes of millions of Americans the chaos and disorder that marked the convention. As one report noted:

Judge Hoffman's harsh terms imposed by the sequestering of the jury for four and a half months have received more attention than the fact that his original examination of prospective jurors raised no questions at all concerning possible bias from their prior exposure to press and TV coverage of the case.[6]

The Watergate conspiracy trial of five accused persons ended in December 1974 with four found guilty of covering up the scandal. In considering the mass of publicity on the whole Watergate affair, including the Senate hearings and the hearings of the House Judiciary Committee on TV, questions can be legitimately raised regarding the impartiality of jurors. The mass of publicity given to the Watergate affair undoubtedly had some impact on the jurors. The question is whether such publicity prejudiced prospective jurors with respect to their ability to objectively view the case.

These examples point out the many problems in trying to reconcile freedom of the press with a fair and just judicial process. There is no hard and fast rule in such circumstances. Each case must be weighed by both the mass media and those in the judicial process to provide a maximum of freedom of the press while balancing this with the right of the defendant to a fair and just trial. In any event, it is the Court that is charged with the responsibility to determine where the lines are drawn.

Limits to Judicial Power

The action of the special constituency can be an effective check on the judicial system. This constituency can publicize actions of the judicial system to influence public opinion and bring a great deal of pressure to bear upon the operation of the judicial system. Bar associations, for example, can make public pronouncements on the competence of judges, criticize court procedures, recommend judicial policy, etc. The prestigious bar associations, representing as they do a profession from which most judges are selected, have great influence on the minds of the public as well as on the judiciary.

Similarly, powerful interest groups can bring power to bear to influence the court. Since the court attempts to make decisions that are socially as well as judicially just, interest groups attempt to create a social climate to which judges must respond. By such actions, interest groups try to convince the courts of specific judicial needs of society. It seems clear that the activities of civil rights groups and the concomitant publicity and impact on society as a whole, was not unimportant in subsequent court decisions.

The individuality of the judges themselves creates counterbalancing power. Each judge has his own perceptions and attitudes on society and the role of the judiciary. The judicial system is, in many respects, a heterogeneous reflection of society, susceptible to a number of views. This tends to develop a hierarchy based on separate centers of judicial power—almost parallel to competing interest groups. Thus liberal views may conflict with conservative views which in turn may conflict with middle-of-the-road pragmatists. Similarly, judicial self-restraint may at times conflict with activist concepts of judicial function.

Finally, it should be recognized that judges are human beings and, like all human beings, they have human failings—bad judgments, dishonesty and incompetency. The power of the judiciary is directly related to the moral integrity and competency of the judges; such power is not an entrenched one, but is based on public esteem and perceptions. This is at best a fragile basis for power and must be continually nurtured.

The 1973 case of federal Judge Otto Kerner is instructive in this regard. Judge Kerner was the first federal judge in history to be convicted of federal offenses and subsequently sentenced to jail for his crimes. Kerner, along with a close associate, was convicted of fifteen counts of conspiracy, bribery, mail fraud, and tax evasion in a case involving $286,000 profit in racetrack stocks.

Changing the Court System

The courts in the United States face difficult problems in the immediate future. These problems stem not only from administrative procedures and the increase in criminal and civil suits, but also from the difficulties of insuring the principles of individual equality, freedom and rights, within the capability and continuity of the political system.

Administratively, observers agree that the court systems are clogged with cases. The problem is compounded by a number of archaic practices both within the courtroom and in the procedure for bringing cases to trial. There is also a question of legal justice. A great majority of criminal cases never go to trial. Most are resolved through bargaining between the defendants, counsel and plaintiff, or as is commonly known, plea bargaining. While the guilt or innocence of the

Changing the Court System

"Keep going men! I'm behind you all the way!"
Reprinted Courtesy of the Chicago Tribune
Chicago Tribune, February 5, 1975 section 2, p. 4.

accused person is not proven, the fact that agreement is made outside of the courtroom saves the government the time and expense of prosecution, while the attorneys can still collect their fees. Additionally, there are simply not enough judges to handle the volume of cases they must face each year. As a result, there is always a significant backlog as well as a high case load. Indeed, in a number of cities an accused may have to wait as long as a year from the time he is arrested until he actually comes to trial.

This also creates serious problems with respect to society's ability to protect itself. The inability to bring cases promptly to trial allows more time for criminals, released on bond, to commit other crimes. Additionally, a series of continuances has the same effect.

Crime in the United States, 1972

Crime Offenses	Estimated Number of Crimes	Rate per 100,000 Inhabitants
Total	5,891,900	2,829.5
Violent	828,150	397.7
Property	5,063,800	2,431.8
Murder	18,520	8.9
Forcible rape	46,430	22.3
Robbery	374,560	179.9
Aggravated assault	388,650	186.6
Burglary	2,345,000	1,126.1
Larceny $50 and over	1,837,800	882.6
Auto theft	881,000	423.1

Source: Adapted from *Crime in the United States,* Uniform Crime Reports—1972, Federal Bureau of Investigation (Washington, D.C.: U.S. Government Printing Office, 1973), p. 2.

Criminal Justice

The number of serious crimes and their handling by police add new dimensions to the problems of court administration. Problems of administration, backlog, and handling of criminal cases, raise many issues regarding the rights of the individual. In a number of important instances, these have led to Supreme Court decisions.

For example, in the case of *Gideon* v. *Wainwright* (1963), Justice Black, writing the opinion for a unanimous court, stated: "Reason and reflection require us to recognize that in our adversary system of criminal justice, any person hailed into court who is too poor to hire a lawyer cannot be assured a fair trial unless counsel is provided for him. The right of one charged with crime to counsel may not be deemed fundamental and essential to fair trials in some countries, but it is in ours." Since Gideon, when arrested and tried by lower courts, had been too poor to hire counsel, the Supreme Court in effect overturned the lower court decisions in Florida and established a landmark decision in criminal cases. In *Escobedo* v. *Illinois* (1964), the Court in a 5-4 decision extended the Gideon concept to include the right of an accused person to request counsel during the course of an interrogation. Thus, it became the right of the accused to have counsel

THE CRIMINAL JUSTICE TREADMILL

Half of all major crimes are never reported to police.

Of those which are, less than 25 percent are solved by arrests.

Half of these arrests result in dismissal of charges.

90 percent of the rest are resolved by a plea of guilty.

The fraction of cases that do go to trial represent less than 1 percent of all crimes committed.

About 25 percent of those convicted are sent to prison; the rest are released on probation.

Nearly everyone who goes to prison is eventually released.

Between half and two-thirds of those released are arrested and convicted again; they become repeat criminals known as recidivists.

—Adapted from *To Establish Justice, To Insure Domestic Tranquility*, Final Report of the National Commission on the Causes and Prevention of Violence.

from the very time he was arrested and to remain silent during interrogation. Not only did the Supreme Court become involved in an individual criminal case, but by elaborating on the concept of due process and the Sixth Amendment dealing with trial in criminal proceedings, it expounded on constitutional principles. The Court's impact is similar with respect to issues involving individual equality, freedom and rights and the individual's relationship to the political system.

The sentencing of a criminal and carrying out of the sentence is generally considered to be a part of the criminal justice system. This also includes prison management. As a number of observers have pointed out, many prisons in the United States need extensive modernization and efficient management. Over the past years, a number of riots have taken place within prisons, many in response to what inmates feel is a repressive and inhumane system resting on inadequate facilities and poor management. Moreover, the rehabilitation of prisoners has been remarkable for its lack of success. According to Ramsey Clark, at the end of 1970, there were 196,429 inmates in federal and state prisons. "The most important statistic on crime is the one which tells us that 80 percent of all felonies are committed by repeaters. Four-fifths of our major crimes are committed by people already known to the criminal justice system."[7]

Courts and Society

Court decisions such as *Brown* v. *Board of Education* deeply affect the individual's relationship to society and the political system. The overturning of the separate-but-equal doctrine has had a profound impact in broadening the scope of individual freedom and rights. Similarly, the Court's decision in *Baker* v. *Carr* not only expanded the idea of equal rights—that is, one man-one vote—but it changed the character of legislatures throughout the country. The great issues of freedom of speech, of the press, of religion, or to be more specific, the First Amendment freedoms, are continually before the courts.

As has been noted earlier, the Court need not abide by previous decisions; indeed it can expand such decisions, revise or lessen their impact. For example, in the case of *Miller* v. *California* (1973), the Burger Court returned to the local governments the authority to determine obscenity, on the basis of their own local social mores. This was a significant revision of the more liberal ruling by the Warren Court. This decision has caused serious problems in its application at the state level. In 1973 "a Georgia Court held that the film 'Carnal Knowledge' was obscene. The film, tho [sic] risque was widely accepted as a serious work. However, the Supreme Court ruled that no jury could find the film 'Carnal Knowledge' to be 'patently offensive' because among other things, the camera didn't focus on the bodies of the actors when ultimate sex acts were taking place."[8] Thus the Court became involved in determining what was or was not "patently offensive." This dilemma promises to create a number of constitutional issues in ensuing years.

All of these cases illustrate the Supreme Court's power in establishing ethical and social guidelines. They also illustrate the complicated and complex procedures that are associated with reinterpretations and revisions of the law, and how these reinforce the near-autonomous position of the courts. It can easily be seen how the characteristics of the judicial system perpetuate the special constituency and the power of the judiciary.

This brief commentary on the lower court hierarchy is not intended as a cataloging of landmark cases, nor as a systematic treatment of courtroom procedures and the judicial system. Rather, the intent has been to show how deeply the judiciary system is involved in the American political system and to demonstrate its potential impact on each citizen. The decisions of the court as the final arbiter in criminal, civil, and constitutional cases give it a power equal to, if not superior to, most other institutions of government. The courts, in the process of judicial decision-making, establish political, social, and ethical guidelines and set the directions for the future. In so doing, they contribute to the political environment and to the perceptions, attitudes and expectations of the members of the political system. In this role, the courts, of course, are susceptible to pressures from all other political actors as well as from within the judicial system itself. These forces influence the individual judge's perceptions and attitudes regarding not only his role but also the way the political system should operate. In light of the dual judicial system, the great number of judges, and the variety of political attitudes represented, the judiciary does not lend itself to a monolithic, legally rigid system. Indeed, such a system would be incompatible with the pluralistic adversary processes that are at the base of our political and judicial system.

We began this chapter by pointing out the relative autonomy that the courts enjoy: their power stems from their freedom from accountability to the electorate and their capacity to affect society and the political system. Historically, this has been the basis of an independent judiciary and a situation which fosters an impartial guardian of the Constitution. Obviously this must be qualified by the various channels of influence and political pressures exerted on the courts. This near-autonomy has led to a specialized judicial constituency, technical and complicated legal procedures, and an administrative maze which, combined with the constitutional authority, give the courts a unique base of power. Indeed few areas of our society are immune from judicial inquiry and judicial guidance. This leads to continual conflict between the judicial system and other political actors, as well as between the judiciary and the special constituency. The meaning of the law, how and to whom it is to be applied, and the resolution of such conflicts are not merely pro forma announcements based on documentary research. They embody political, social and economic judgments, articulated not only by the judges themselves, but by the special constituency and other political actors within our system.

Problems of Judicial Power

The major problem in such a judicial system is the propensity to respond to the greatest political power. That is, the judiciary and its decision-making process are likely to be more sensitive to the power of groups operating through the special constituency than to more generally articulated interests operating through the political system as a whole. Thus individual interests and those of less powerful groups are likely to be submerged by the interplay of power among special constituency groups. Indeed, large corporations, both public and private, have immense power to affect the judicial system.

Fortunately the courts have responded more or less adequately in balancing the needs of the political system with individual rights and freedoms. This has not been an easy balance however. It has generally required an assertion of individual power, the commitment of a number of political actors, and the integrity of members of the special judiciary constituency to maintain judicial responsiveness. The continuation of an independent judiciary and its ability to perform its proper role in the American system is contingent upon the quality of the judges, the morals and ethics of the special constituency, and the susceptibility of the judicial system to public scrutiny by the people and their representatives.

In the final analysis the judiciary's prime source of power rests on the nature of our democratic system which holds that conflict should be resolved peacefully. The institution to do this is the judiciary. This has become embedded in the heritage of America and is a basic tenet of American ideology. Alexis de Tocqueville made the succinct observation in 1835 that "Hardly any question arises in the United States that is not resolved sooner or later into a judicial question."[9] Combining this observation with that of Justice Hughes cited earlier that "We are under a Constitution, but the Constitution is what the judges say it is," one can readily understand the basis of judicial power.

NOTES

1. U.S. Bureau of the Census, *Statistical Abstract of the United States: 1972*, 83d ed. Washington, D.C., 1972, p. 159.
2. Jack C. Plano and Milton Greenberg, *The American Political Dictionary*, 3d ed. (Hinsdale, Ill.: The Dryden Press, Inc., 1972), p. 254.
3. Walter Berns, "The Constitution and a Responsible Press," in Henry H. Chor (ed), *The Mass Media and Modern Democracy* (Chicago: Rand McNally Publishing Co., 1973), p. 117.
4. F. Lee Bailey, *The Defense Never Rests* (New York: Signet Book, 1971), p. 93.
5. Berns, p. 118.
6. *Christian Century*, March 4, 1970, p. 260.
7. Ramsey Clark, *Crime in America* (New York: Simon and Schuster, 1970), p. 215.
8. *Chicago Tribune*, Sunday, August 4, 1974, Perspective, p. 3.
9. deTocqueville, p. 270.

Selected Readings

The readings that follow present a broad view of the procedures, organization, and problems within the judicial system. In the first reading, Jerome Frank, a former judge of the U.S. Court of Appeals, sharply criticizes the trial methods in the courtroom. He argues that lawyers' techniques and courtroom procedure tend to obscure the issues rather than clarify them. Not only are judges hampered in making legal decisions, but juries are manipulated by showmanship rather than facts. He concludes that "Our present trial method is thus the equivalent of throwing pepper in the eyes of a surgeon when he is performing an operation."

The final selection is comprised of a series of newspaper articles on the criminal court system in Chicago. Focusing on such matters as plea bargaining and continuances, the articles clearly show some of the major defects of the criminal justice system.

These readings should provide useful insights into the realities of the court system—realities that sometimes become obscured when discussing the role of the judiciary in our political system. It ought to be noted that the court systems discussed in these selections are those most likely to be encountered by the individual in his day-to-day living. These readings should also reinforce our observations regarding the complexity and at times perplexity of the American judicial system.

10.1

The "Fight" Theory Versus the "Truth" Theory

JEROME FRANK

When we say that present-day trial methods are "rational," presumably we mean this: The men who compose our trial courts, judges and juries, in each law-suit conduct an intelligent inquiry into all the practically available evidence, in order to ascertain as near as may be, the truth about the facts of that suit. That might be called the "investigatory" or "truth" method of trying cases. Such a method can yield no more than a guess, nevertheless an educated guess.

The success of such a method is conditioned by at least these two factors: (1) The judicial inquirers, trial judges or juries, may not obtain all the important evidence. (2) The judicial inquirers may not be competent to conduct such an inquiry. Let us, for the time being, assume that the second condition is met—i.e., that we have competent inquirers—and ask whether we so conduct trials as to satisfy the first condition, i.e., the procuring of all the practically available important evidence.

The answer to that question casts doubt on whether our trial courts do use the "investigatory" or "truth" method. Our mode of trials is commonly known as "contentious" or "adversary." It is based on what I would call the "fight" theory, a theory which derives from the origin of trials as substitutes for private out-of-court brawls.

Many lawyers maintain that the "fight" theory and the "truth" theory coincide. They think that the best way for a court to discover the facts in a suit is to have each side strive as hard as it can, in a keenly partisan spirit, to bring to the court's attention the evidence favorable to that side. Macaulay said that we obtain the fairest decision "when two men argue, as unfairly as possible, on opposite sides," for then "it is certain that no important consideration will altogether escape notice."

Unquestionably that view contains a core of good sense. The zealously partisan lawyers sometimes do bring into court evidence which, in a dispassionate inquiry, might be overlooked. Apart from the fact element of the case, the opposed lawyers

Courts on Trial: Myth and Reality in American Justice, published by Princeton University Press; Princeton Paperback, 1973 (copyright 1949 by Jerome Frank), pp. 80-85. Reprinted by permission of Princeton University Press.

also illuminate for the court niceties of the legal rules which the judge might otherwise not perceive. The "fight" theory, therefore, has invaluable qualities with which we cannot afford to dispense.

But frequently the partisanship of the opposing lawyers blocks the uncovering of vital evidence or leads to a presentation of vital testimony in a way that distorts it. I shall attempt to show you that we have allowed the fighting spirit to become dangerously excessive.

Newsweek, Feb. 11, 1974, p. 21.

This is perhaps most obvious in the handling of witnesses. Suppose a trial were fundamentally a truth-inquiry. Then, recognizing the inherent fallibilities of witnesses, we would do all we could to remove the causes of their errors when testifying. Recognizing also the importance of witnesses' demeanor as clues to their reliability, we would do our best to make sure that they testify in circumstances most conducive to a revealing observation of that demeanor by the trial judge or jury. In our contentious trial practice, we do almost the exact opposite.

No businessman, before deciding to build a new plant, no general before launching an attack, would think of obtaining information on which to base his judgment by putting his informants through the bewildering experience of witnesses at a trial. "The novelty of the situation," wrote a judge, "the agitation and hurry which accompanies it, the cajolery or intimidation to which the witness may be subjected, the want of questions calculated to excite those recollections which might clear up every difficulty, and the confusion of cross-examination . . . may give rise to important errors and omissions." "In the court they stand as strangers," wrote another judge of witnesses, "surrounded with unfamiliar circumstances giving rise to an embarrassment known only to themselves."

In a book by Henry Taft . . . we are told: "Counsel and court find it necessary through examination and instruction to induce a witness to abandon for an hour or two his habitual method of thought and expression, and conform to the rigid ceremonialism of court procedure. It is not strange that frequently truthful witnesses are . . . misunderstood, that they nervously react in such a way as to create the impression that they are either evading or intentionally falsifying. . . . An honest witness testifies on direct examination. He answers questions promptly and candidly and makes a good impression. On cross-examination, his attitude changes. He suspects that traps are being laid for him. He hesitates; he ponders the answer to a simple question; he seems to 'spar' for time by asking that questions be repeated; perhaps he protests that counsel is not fair; he may even appeal to the court for protection. Altogether the contrast with his attitude on direct examination is obvious; and he creates the impression that he is evading or withholding." Yet on testimony thus elicited courts every day reach decisions affecting the lives and fortunes of citizens.

What is the role of the lawyers in bringing the evidence before the trial court? . . . The lawyer considers it his duty to create a false impression, if he can, of any witness who gives such testimony. If such a witness happens to be timid, frightened by the unfamiliarity of courtroom ways, the lawyer, in his cross-examination, plays on that weakness, in order to confuse the witness and make it appear that he is concealing significant facts. Longenecker, in his book *Hints on the Trial of a Law Suit* . . . in writing of the "truthful, honest, over-cautious" witness, tells how "a skilful advocate by a rapid cross-examination may ruin the testimony of such a witness." The author does not even hint any disapproval of that accomplishment. Longenecker's and other similar books recommend that a lawyer try to prod an irritable but honest "adverse" witness into displaying his undesirable characteristics in their most unpleasant form, in order to discredit him with the judge or jury. . . . "And thus," adds Taft, "it may happen that not only is the value of his testimony lost, but the side which produces him suffers for seeking aid from such a source"—although, I would add, that may be the only source of evidence of a fact on which the decision will turn.

"An intimidating manner in putting questions," writes Wigmore, "may so coerce or disconcert the witness that his answers do not represent his actual knowledge on the subject. So also, questions which in form or subject cause embarrassment, shame or anger in the witness may unfairly lead him to such demeanor or utterances that the impression produced by his statements does not do justice to its real testimonial value." . . . Sir Frederick Eggleston recently said that . . . "the terrors of cross-examination are such that a party can often force a settlement by letting it be known that a certain . . . counsel has been retained."

The lawyer not only seeks to discredit adverse witnesses but also to hide the defects of witnesses who testify favorably to his client. If, when interviewing such a witness before trial, the lawyer notes that the witness has mannerisms, demeanor-traits, which might discredit him, the lawyer teaches him how to cover up those traits when testifying: He educates the irritable witness to conceal his irritability, the cocksure witness to subdue his cocksureness. In that way, the trial court is denied the benefit of observing the witness's actual normal demeanor, and thus prevented from sizing up the witness accurately.

Lawyers freely boast of their success with these tactics. They boast also of such devices as these: If an "adverse," honest witness, on cross-examination, makes seemingly inconsistent statements, the cross-examiner tries to keep the witness from explaining away the apparent inconsistencies. "When," writes Tracy, counseling trial lawyers, in a much-praised book, "by your cross-examination, you have caught the witness in an inconsistency, the next question that will immediately come to your lips is, 'Now, let's hear you explain.' Don't ask it, for he may explain and, if he does, your point will have been lost. If you have conducted your cross-examination properly (which includes interestingly), the jury will have seen the inconsistency and it will have made the proper impression on their minds. If, on redirect examination the witness does explain, the explanation will have come later in the case and at the request of the counsel who originally called the witness and the jury will be much more likely to look askance at the explanation than if it were made during your cross-examination." Tracy adds, "Be careful in your questions on cross-examination not to open a door that you have every reason to wish kept closed." That is, don't let in any reliable evidence, hurtful to your side, which would help the trial court to arrive at the truth.

"In cross-examination," writes Eggleston, "the main preoccupation of counsel is to avoid introducing evidence, or giving an opening to it, which will harm his case. The most painful thing for an experienced practitioner . . . is to hear a junior counsel laboriously bring out in cross-examination of a witness all the truth which the counsel who called him could not" bring out "and which it was the junior's duty as an advocate to conceal." A lawyer, if possible, will not ask a witness to testify who, on cross-examination, might testify to true facts helpful to his opponent.

Nor, usually, will a lawyer concede the existence of any facts if they are inimical to his client and he thinks they cannot be proved by his adversary. If, to the lawyer's knowledge, a witness has testified inaccurately but favorably to the lawyer's client, the lawyer will attempt to hinder cross-examination that would expose the inaccuracy. He puts in testimony which surprises his adversary who, caught unawares, has not time to seek out, interview, and summon witnesses who would rebut the surprise testimony. . . .

These, and other like techniques, you will find unashamedly described in the many manuals on trial tactics written by and for eminently reputable trial lawyers. The purpose of these tactics—often effective—is to prevent the trial judge or jury from correctly evaluating the trustworthiness of witnesses and to shut out evidence the trial court ought to receive in order to approximate the truth.

In short, the lawyer aims at victory, at winning in the fight, not at aiding the court to discover the facts. He does not want the trial court to reach a sound educated guess, if it is likely to be contrary to his client's interests. Our present trial method is thus the equivalent of throwing pepper in the eyes of a surgeon when he is performing an operation. . . .

10.2

Chaos in Our Courts

LOIS WILLE

Delayed Trials

It's 10 a.m. and the bailiff tells everyone to stand, the Honorable Judge Robert A. Meier is moving behind the bench and this courtroom is now in session.

First defendant: Salvatore Rosa, accused of armed robbery. He's not here.

Second defendant: Dan Harris, accused of attempted robbery. He's not here, either.

Third defendant: John Huff, accused of two armed robberies. Not here.

Ed Dolmant, 69, the Yellow Cab driver Huff is accused of robbing nearly two years ago, hurries up to the bench, flushed and trembling.

"Your Honor, I've lost eight days of work on this already. How many more years..."

Before he can say more, a bailiff hustles him away.

More names are called: Charges of rape, armed robbery, assault. Some defendants are here, but their attorneys are missing.

("Mr. Holt called, Your Honor," said the clerk. "He's on trial in another courtroom.")

("Mr. Stein's partner was here, Your Honor. He said Mr. Stein won't be back from California for two more weeks.")

Finally comes the case of Thomas Brown, and both he and his lawyers are in court.

"Your Honor," says the prosecuting attorney, "if we could pass on this one...." He explains that the man Brown is accused of robbing 15 months ago didn't show up today. And the policeman who investigated the case is appearing in another court.

Thus, begins a typical day in a criminal courtroom in Cook County, where last year 14,300 murders, rapes and armed robberies were committed—and only 471 persons were sentenced to prison for those crimes. That's about 3 per cent.

A series of articles on the Criminal Court System in the city of Chicago in the *Chicago Daily News*, April 19-23 (incl), 1973. Reprinted with permission from the *Chicago Daily News*.

And the other 97 per cent? What happened? In most of these lost cases, police were unable to arrest suspects. This is particularly true of armed robbery.

More often than you'd suspect, there is no arrest because the victim doesn't want to cooperate.

"Believe it or not, I was robbed in the hallway of our building two weeks after my husband was robbed in his cab," says Alberta Dolmant, Eds' wife.

"I told police, 'Don't ask me to go downtown and pick out suspects. I'm not going.' My husband's been robbed a couple of times, and it's always the same—case continued, case continued.

"Pretty soon nobody shows up anymore and the whole thing is dropped."

The average armed robbery case, for example, is continued 12 times before it is settled. Usually that means at least a year.

As their cases stretch on, defendants who are out on bond often get arrested again. And even people with long and brutal arrest records can sometimes get out on bond.

The most vivid recent example is Lester Harrison, 49, who was awaiting trial for a year-old attempted rape case when he was arrested and charged earlier this week for the murder of a young woman in Grant Park.

Lagging cases gradually whittle away at justice. Witnesses no longer show up, so the case has to be dropped. In a three-month study of armed robbery cases in Felony Court, the Chicago Crime Commission found that 473 were dropped for lack of prosecution, while only 350 were sent to the grand jury for indictment.

Or the defendant, if he's out on bond, may not show up. One day last week 3 of 15 defendants in Judge Meier's courtroom weren't there. Their bonds were forfeited, and arrest warrants issued.

The crime commission, in another study of Felony Court, found that in one week almost as many defendants failed to appear as were held to the grand jury.

Violent crime in Cook County, 1972

	Murder	Rape	Armed rob.
Cases considered valid by police	716	1,549	12,032
Arrests	1,032*	883	3,395
Persons indicted by grand jury	531	277	1,218
Sentenced to prison	81	71	319

*In many murders, groups of persons were arrested.

The reasons for continuances are endless.

"You hear a million and one," says Judge Kenneth R. Wendt, a big, white-haired, red-faced man who sputters and fumes about them in his courtroom more than most judges.

"The lawyers tell me, 'My star witness is sick,' or 'I need another psychiatric report.' If I force them to trial anyway, I'm opening the case to appeal. But most of the time, it's because the defense attorney is busy on another case."

He mentioned some of the busiest defense attorneys in town, adding: "Anybody who doesn't want to go to trial should hire one of them."

There is another reason for continuances, never mentioned in the courtroom. "Naturally, if an attorney hasn't been paid his fee—if I don't get my fee—I don't want to settle," says veteran defense attorney, Myron Feldman.

Plea Bargaining

On the night of July 18 a thin, wiry 22-year-old named Carl Davis was plunged into our Criminal Court system for the seventh time—and another round of barter-and-bargain began.

After seven arrests, a number of convictions and a few short jail terms, Davis still hasn't had a criminal trial.

But he's had a lot of "plea-bargainings"—secret, off-the-record haggling between opposing attorneys until they agree on a settlement.

Usually, this means a plea of "guilty" in return for a reduced charge and a light sentence. If the defendant agrees also, the case is almost always settled with a perfunctory appearance before a judge.

"Most of our serious criminal cases are disposed of like this, in the manner of a Moroccan market place," says Norval Morris, director of the University of Chicago's Center for Studies in Criminal Justice.

Here's how it works:

January, 1969: Davis is arrested for burglary. He says he didn't do it. Eventually, the felony charge of burglary is reduced to a minor offense called "criminal damage to property." Davis says he is guilty, and he is released on probation.

April, 1969: Davis is arrested for robbery. He says he didn't do it. Eventually, the charge of robbery is reduced to the lesser charge of theft. Davis says he is guilty, and he is sentenced to 60 days in Cook County Jail—the time he has spent awaiting trial. So he is released.

He is arrested twice in the next two years, but charges are dropped when witnesses fail to appear in court.

March, 1972: Davis is arrested for robbery. He says he didn't do it. He sits in jail nine months while his case is continued.

Eventually, in November, he says he is guilty. He is sentenced to one year in jail, including the nine months he already has spent there. He is released in February, 1973.

March, 1973: Davis is arrested for unlawful use of a weapon—he shot a handgun, police say, but luckily didn't hit anyone. He is released on bond.

July 18, 1973: Davis is arrested for aggravated assault. Police say he shot and wounded a man on the West Side. Now he's in County Jail again, awaiting trial again.

Except that he probably won't get a trial, but another plea-bargaining.

"I don't call this doing judicial work," complained Judge Kenneth R. Wendt after a court session that consisted of seven continuances and three cases settled by plea-bargaining.

"I was on the bench . . . what—15 minutes? It may look good on the record because I got rid of three cases, but I think the judicial process should be carried out in the courtroom, not the conference room."

But if cases weren't settled in conference rooms, it's likely the average criminal case in Cook County would take five or six years to settle instead of the current 9 or 10 months.

The county is so badly deficient in courtrooms, in criminal judges, in assistant state's attorneys and in public defenders that it couldn't possibly provide full-fledged trials for all the 21,000 persons arrested annually for felonies.

So 90 per cent of these cases are settled in pretrial hearings through plea-bargaining or through failure to prosecute because of inadequate evidence. Usually, that means witnesses don't show up. Only 2,100 of the 21,000 cases actually go to trial.

"We have roughly the same number of courtrooms for criminal trials—17 of them —that Detroit does," says Morton Friedman, chief of the state's attorney's criminal division. (Detroit's Wayne County has about half the population of Cook County.)

"That gives you some idea of how ludicrous the situation is. It's obscene."

One danger of plea-bargaining is that it usually results in specific sentences set by judges and lawyers, who may not be qualified to decide how long someone should stay in prison. Criminologists prefer indefinite sentences, with investigations by the Parole and Pardon Board to determine when the prisoner should be released.

There is another danger: An innocent person, weary of sitting in Cook County Jail while his case drags on, may plead guilty just to get out.

"It happens all the time," says Hans Mattick, criminologist at the University of Illinois Chicago Circle Campus and former assistant warden of County Jail.

State's Atty. Bernard Carey doesn't like plea-bargaining, either, and vows to pare it down—even though this means the current Criminal Court backlog of 2,300 cases will crawl higher. "The system looks to us to save it from being inundated by plea-bargaining," he says. "I don't like that role, and I refuse to play it."

Gun Court

The room is hot, noisy fans are whirring, a hundred persons sit packed together on benches and dozens more line the walls. Clerks at the front and the back call out names of defendants—because this is a double courtroom.

Shabby, chaotic Gun Court, jammed with 120 weapons cases a day, is so overloaded that it has two judges working at once.

One presides on the bench at the front of the room, and one presides in an oversized closet at the back of the room.

Lawyers and police and witnesses and defendants swarm in the middle, trying to hear their names called above the din.

A harassed public defender hurries from one end of the room to the other, trying cases in both places, squeezing in a few moments to talk to defendants she has never met before—but who are going on trial in minutes.

After hours on the bench without a break, Judge Charles J. Durham seems ready to collapse in the 85-degree heat.

Durham interrupts as a policeman explains how he happened to arrest so-and-so for not signaling a change in expressway lanes and found a handgun tucked into his belt.

"It's too hot to listen to all this," Durham says. "The man didn't do anything. He admitted he was armed."

Even Clare Hillyard, the public defender, looks surprised when Durham abruptly sustains her motion to suppress evidence, and the case is dropped.

But then Carl Piazza, the assistant state's attorney, sees in his mound of papers that this is the second time the man has been arrested for illegally carrying a weapon.

"Well, this is the last time," Durham says to the newly released defendant.

That's the way cases come and go in Gun Court—prosecutors and public defenders without time to study case files, charges thrown out because police didn't scrupulously follow search-and-seizure laws, and so much confusion that one defense attorney was halfway through his arguments when he realized he was talking about the wrong case.

Most of the 600 or 650 defendants who crowd into this room in Chicago Police Headquarters every week are charged with unlawful use of a weapon. What happened to them in one recent week is typical:

Six per cent didn't show up and were charged with bond forfeiture, 27 per cent had charges dropped for lack of adequate prosecution or improper police search, and 59 per cent had cases continued.

About 8 per cent were found guilty, and most of these got $45 or $90 fines. The charge, if it is treated as a misdemeanor, calls for a fine of up to $1,000 or up to one year in Cook County Jail.

Charges of unlawful use of a weapon also can be sent to the grand jury for felony indictments. But of 8,379 arrests last year, only 94 persons were indicted.

"That court represents what I consider a fraud on the public, an insult to police," says Peter Bensinger, executive director of the Chicago Crime Commission.

"The place is a zoo," says Morton Friedman, chief of the state's attorney's criminal division. "People are crawling up the walls. It's a pathetic waste of police manpower."

By 9:30 a.m., when court begins, 40 or 45 police are waiting to testify. Cases are not scheduled for specific times, so most of them wait and wait.

One recent day 31 were still sitting around at 1 p.m. The next day 20 were there at 1 p.m. And 23 the following day.

"I'm in court two or three days a week as a rule," says Patrolman Tom Prendergast of the Monroe District. "It can be for 15 minutes or for eight hours. Sometimes we sit until 2 or 3 in the afternoon, and then the case is continued and you blow your stack."

Policeman George Lucanti of the Grand Crossing District has been in Gun Court 18 times on one weapons case stretching back nearly two years.

"The defendant keeps saying his lawyer can't come, and the judge just keeps continuing it," he says.

For the public, failure to schedule cases and repeated continuances mean an enormous waste of police manpower, and of money, because police are paid for time spent in court.

In a study of Narcotics Court, which is as badly overloaded and chaotic as Gun Court, the Chicago Crime Commission found that 2,300 police waited there in one month without being called to testify.

"This translates on an annual basis to 13,000 police days lost and $700,000 in expenses," says Bensinger.

A Case in Point

Pharis Royster, 21, accused of rape, has been waiting for nearly 20 months to go on trial. He's angry.

"I'm on my fourth public defender now," he says. "Every time they change, it's continued some more.

"I was working at the post office but I got fired because of all the time in court, and because I couldn't get this thing settled."

The young woman he is accused of raping is just as angry.

"It's sickening," says her mother. "Every time we get subpenaed, we go down to court and it's postponed. Sometimes they call ahead and tell us it will be postponed, but not always.

"My daughter said to me, 'Mamma, I'm not going back next time.' But I keep pushing her. If everybody let things like this drop, nobody every would get put in prison."

Very few do get put in prison for rape in Cook County.

Last year, 3,268 rapes were reported to police, but only 1,358 were considered valid. In the others, women decided to drop charges or the police decided the charges were unfounded.

Arrests were made in 65 per cent of the "valid" cases, for a total of 883.

But only 71 men were sent to prison in 1972 for rape, slightly more than 5 per cent of the "valid" offenses.

One reason is that rape cases drag on exceptionally long in the courts. Even the sharpest recollections of the victims get blurred, and defendants can look quite different after a year or more.

James L. Cook, 30, of 7024 S. Clyde, has been indicted nine times in the last 18 months—eight times for rape and once for beating a woman. He was acquitted on one of the rape charges when the victim insisted the man who attacked her on March 20, 1972, had "a little fuzzy beard" and a small bald spot on the top of his head.

When the case finally came to trial 15 months later, the defense attorney pointed out that his client did not have a beard and no bald spot was visible at the top of his head. Judge Earl Strayhorn found him not guilty.

So far, Cook has been found not guilty on four of the rape charges. The woman who accused him in another of the "not guilty" verdicts is incensed over the questions put to her by Cook's lawyer.

"I'm alone, a single woman," she said. "The lawyer wanted to know, when was the last time prior to May 5—the day of the rape—that I had sexual relations? And the state's attorney who was supposed to be representing me never even objected.

"It was so embarrassing. Just a mock trial, really."

Cook, who is out on bond, will appear Sept. 24 before Judge Marvin Aspen in the Civic Center on four more rape charges.

The case of Pharis Royster, of 4446 S. University, is typical of the long delays in rape cases.

He was arrested on Feb. 2, 1971, for rape, but five months later the charge was dismissed for lack of adequate prosecution. Then on Jan. 18, 1972, police arrested him and accused him of forcing a young woman off an L train, pushing her into an alley at gunpoint and raping her. She picked him from a police mug book and lineup. He insists he was at his girlfriend's house at the time.

His bond is low—$2,000, which means he paid $200 to get out of jail. Royster has been in court 19 times since he was indicted in March, 1972.

Ten continuances were requested by various public defenders, three by the state's attorney and six by agreement of both attorneys.

At the last court date July 23, Asst. State's Atty. John DeRose told Judge Kenneth R. Wendt that Royster and another rape suspect assigned to Wendt both want jury trials, "and the public defender can't prepare both at once."

Cook County has 100 public defenders. They handle 60 per cent of the 6,300 criminal cases heard annually and 75 per cent of the 50,000 preliminary hearings and misdemeanors.

Another 26 defenders are authorized, but because starting salary is low—$11,070— it isn't easy to get them. Also, it takes two or three months to get an application approved by Chief Judge John S. Boyle's Circuit Court Committee on Help. "Between making application and getting hired, a lot of good people get other jobs," said an official of the public defender's office.

A major problem, too, is the critical shortage of assistant state's attorneys, courtrooms and Criminal Court judges in Cook County—less than half the per-person ratio in Los Angeles, Philadelphia and New York.

"When one case is being tried, there may be several others ready to go but no courtrooms available," says Morton Friedman, chief of the state's attorney's criminal division.

Wendt set an Aug. 28 court date for Pharis Royster, but DeRose wasn't too happy. "We've got another case scheduled for trial here that day," he said.

"I don't know," grumbled Wendt. "We've got two to go to trial, and probably none will go to trial."

Steps to Improvement

Small items such as microphones in courtrooms can help bring justice to our Criminal Courts, according to the experts. But what they want most of all is a speeded-up system.

"We need business efficiency in our courts," says Norval Morris, director of the University of Chicago's Center for Studies in Criminal Justice.

"We're faced with a lack of planning, a lack of adequate resources, a lack of discriminating the important from the unimportant.

"Really, what does it matter if gambling cases or prostitution cases go on forever, or never come to trial? But where people are threatened—rape, armed robbery— there, we must demand speed."

Morris and Peter Bensinger, executive director of the Chicago Crime Commission, have a number of ideas for a speed-up that would require little or no extra money. They include:

• Limit continuances

A limit already exists in Illinois law, but it is rarely followed. According to the state criminal code, continuances can be granted only if the prosecutor or the defense attorney is ill or on trial in another court—or if he has been unable to prepare his case for these reasons. Also, continuances can be granted if the defendant or key witnesses are incapacitated.

"Judges should start requiring affidavits to prove attorneys are busy in other courts, and what they are doing," Morris says. "We need strong, tough judges. You never hear them say, 'If you can't handle this case, don't you think you should pass it to somebody else?'"

Bensinger urges Criminal Court judges to follow the example of Federal Court judges, who have at times sent U.S. marshals to search out attorneys due for trial and haul them before the bench.

• Establish a separate Armed Robbery Court and a Rape Court

These stranger-against-stranger crimes present a grave threat to the public, and both are increasing in Cook County. And, with increasing frequency, persons who once were armed robbery or rape defendants turn up later as murder defendants.

"Continuances are more flagrant in armed robbery and rape," Bensinger says. "Specialized courtrooms would focus greater public attention on them. Now, our court calls are cluttered, with burglaries and thefts mixed with the violent crimes."

He also recommends a separate court to hear pre-trial motions, which also clutter the calls of trial judges.

• Stagger court calls

Cases should be scheduled at intervals, Bensinger suggests, such as 9:30 a.m., 11 a.m., and so on. Currently, everyone connected with a case is expected to be present when court starts at 9:30, even though the case may not be called until 2 p.m.

In particular, this results in an enormous waste of tax money in police salaries.

"If the lawyer isn't there at the scheduled time the judge could hold him in contempt." Bensinger says.

• Install microphones in front of the judge's bench

Some of the chaos in Criminal Courts is caused by cavernous, noisy and acoustically inferior courtrooms. In Gun Court, for example, waiting defendants frequently find at the end of a court session that they have been charged with bond forfeiture because they didn't hear their cases called.

The Cook County Board voted Monday to issue $7 million in bonds to renovate the old Criminal Court Building at 26th St. and California. This would include air-conditioning, new windows and new lighting.

Chief Judge John S. Boyle wants much more. He has asked for $33 million, half from the county and half from the federal government, to build an office structure next to the Criminal Court Building.

This would open enough space in the old building for 20 additional courtrooms, doubling the current number.

Boyle said he could get judges to fill the new rooms by transferring them from other divisions.

More courtrooms and more judges would do much to erase the Criminal Court backlog, now at 2,311 cases and climbing steadily. Cases ready for trial often are continued for months merely because no room, and no judge, are available. Cook County has about a third the number of criminal courtrooms and judges per 100,000 persons as New York, Los Angeles and Philadelphia.

It has about half the number of prosecutors per 100,000 persons as these other cities.

Bensinger also urges that judges examine a defendant's past records and psychiatric reports before setting bond. He would like more decisions based on open courtroom trials and fewer by off-the-record plea-bargaining sessions, more female police and court personnel in rape cases and a judicial ban on irrelevant and embarrassing "personal questioning" of rape victims by defense attorneys.

To help all this come about, he suggests that Boyle hire an administrative officer for the Criminal Courts, "somebody whose full-time job it is to see that calendars move."

Money for his salary would be available through federal grants to the Illinois Law Enforcement Commission.

"Our judges deserve a better environment and lower calendars," Bensinger says. "Our assistant state's attorneys and public defenders deserve smaller caseloads.

"Defendants, witnesses and police deserve speedier trials—and the public deserves the protection of a better criminal justice system."

Study Questions

1. What are the advantages and disadvantages of having a court system relatively immune to public pressures? Do you think this judicial independence is in line with democratic principles?

2. Discuss the characteristics of legal systems based on the Roman law. On the common law. Discuss the relative merits and weaknesses of the adversary system of justice. Does it seem adequate? What should be the proper roles of judges and juries in trial procedures?

3. Distinguish between criminal and civil law.

4. What do we mean when we say that we have a dual court system in

America? What is the difference between ordinary courts, intermediate courts and final courts?

5. State the relative merits and weaknesses of the cases for electing or appointing judges. Where judges are elected, do you think they should be listed on a party ballot or on a non-partisan ballot? Do you think that philosophical and partisan considerations should enter into a governor's or a President's thinking when making a judicial appointment?

6. What is the judicial conference of the United States? Who are its members? What are its functions?

7. Discuss the various problems that American courts face. What solutions do you think are possible?

8. Do you agree with the assertion that "the courts in the process of judicial decision-making establish political, social, and ethical guidelines and set the directions for the future?" If so, do you think this is desirable? Can you think of ways in which the courts' ability to set political, social, and ethical guidelines for society should be more limited than at present?

9. The power of the judiciary is partly based on its formal function within the political system. What is its formal function? What are other bases for the power of the judiciary? How would you assess the operation of the courts in your own locality?

10. In what way does the special constituency of the judicial system play an important role in the political system? Should this constituency have the power to influence and shape the judicial system? Do you agree with the concept of the special judicial constituency?

Bibliography

Books

Brennan, James T. *The Cost of the American Judicial System.* West Haven, Connecticut: Professional Library Press, 1966.

Bunn, Charles W. *Jurisdiction and Practice of the Courts of the United States.* St. Paul, Minn.: West Publishing Co., 1949.

Downie, Leonard Jr. *Justice Denied, The Case for Reform of the Courts.* New York: Praeger Publishers, 1971.

Mayers, Lewis. *The American Legal System.* rev. ed. New York: Harper & Row, Publishers, 1964.

Murphy, Walter F., and Pritchett, C. Herman, eds. *Courts, Judges and Politics: An Introduction to the Judicial Process.* New York: Random House, 1961.

Peltason, Jack W. *Federal Courts in the Political Process.* Garden City, New York: Doubleday & Company, Inc., 1955.

Schmandt, Henry J. *Courts in the American Political System.* Belmont, California: Dickenson Publishing Co. Inc., 1968.

Wellman, Francis L. *The Art of Cross-Examination*. New York: The Macmillan Company, 1924.
Wellman, Francis L. *Day in Court*. New York: The Macmillan Company, 1910.

Articles

Bloomstein, Morris J. "The American Jury System." *Current History*, June 1971.
Hughes, Graham. "Finding Fault and Fixing Blame: Rules, Principles and Legal Decisions." *Antioch Review*. Vol. 30 (Summer 1970), pp. 223-234.

CHAPTER 11
Bureaucracy and Bureaucrats: The Fourth Branch of Government

Most of us tend to associate bureaucracy with a modern and complex government. Yet it existed in rudimentary form even in the ancient empires in Egypt and Rome, as well as in Asia. It was only in the nineteenth century, however, that bureaucracy emerged as a modern institution with political power. In more recent times, bureaucracy has become so visible and so pervasive that it appears to touch upon all aspects of our lives and to be virtually a separate institution of government. Indeed, without it, it is unlikely that any large-scale administrative task could be accomplished or government function performed.

Bureaucracy can be defined in many ways. For many it has come to mean inefficiency, red tape, routine, and resistance to change. More objectively, however, it is an institutionalized way of organizing social and political behavior in order to further administrative efficiency. Bureaucracy is an organization established to perform large-scale administrative tasks, and no modern government could function without some form of it.

Who Are the Bureaucrats?

Many of the references to bureaucracy in this chapter are to those levels below the top management. The top management people, such as Cabinet officers, assistant secretaries, are political appointees who are generally appointed and removed by the President. Parenthetically, the top management is generally a "different breed" from the rest of the bureaucracy. Some people in this category may be politically powerful in their own right, even before assuming office; some move into public service directly from high-paying and important business positions. Most are highly educated and experienced administrators or politicians.

There is a vast bureaucratic structure below the top management level. Indeed, most bureaucrats fill nonexecutive white-collar and skilled blue-collar positions. There are about 2.5 million civilian federal employees; there were only about 800 in 1792, and 300,000 in 1900. The Department of Defense alone employs over 1 million civilians—the largest number in any one branch of the federal government. While we often think of Washington as the bureaucratic center, there are only slightly over 300,000 federally employed civilians located there. The vast majority, over 2 million, are employed throughout the 50 states. The average age of those employed in the federal government is slightly over 40, with about 43 per cent female; their average length of service is about 9.5 years. The employment figures for state and local governments overshadow those of the federal government. There are over 10 million persons employed in state and local governments with a payroll that exceeds $8 billion a year. Combining all the figures for federal, state, and local governments, we find that about 13 million persons are employed by governments within the United States (not including the military). This is out of a total of about 80 million employed in the United States.[1]

Bureaucracy and Policy Implementation

Once a law is passed or directive issued by the President most people assume that a goal has been reached or a policy established. However, nothing really happens until basic provisions, rules and regulations are devised and used in administering the laws and directives. It is the bureaucracy that links the passage of laws and the pronouncements of directives to the day-to-day lives of the people. In the main, it is the bureaucracy that assesses and applies the spirit of the laws in the daily operation of the government. It is for this reason that the bureaucracy is such an important and powerful institution in our political system.

As one expert has observed: "The basic issues of federal organization and administration relate to power: who shall control it and to what ends?"[2] Here is what Henry Kissinger, Secretary of State under the Nixon and Ford administrations had to say about the power of the bureaucracy:

> When I first started advising at high levels of the government in the early days of the Kennedy Administration, I had the illusion that all I had to do was walk into the President's office, convince him I was right, and he would then naturally do what I had recommended. There were a number of things wrong with this view . . . There is only so much that even a President can do against the wishes of the bureaucracy, not because the bureaucracy would deliberately sabotage him, but because every difficult issue is a closed one. The easy decisions are made at subordinate levels. A closed issue is characterized by the fact that the pros and cons seem fairly evenly divided and/or because the execution really depends on certain nuances of application. Unless you can get the willing support of your subordinates, simply giving an order does not get very far.[3]

At best, laws and policy pronouncements provide only general guidelines. The bureaucracy or the individual bureaucrat is thus given a wide range of discretionary power regarding the interpretation and application of rules. Not only does the bureaucrat interpret and give substance to laws and policies, but he can in a sense make decisions, identifying individuals and groups to which these are applicable. Moreover, he has a degree of discretion, allowing him to apply the letter of the laws with varying degrees of impact. This then is the first element of bureaucratic power—the opportunity to exercise choice and discretion in administering policy. From this stem a number of other related characteristics that reinforce and expand the power of the individual bureaucrat and of the bureaucratic institution. Bureaucrats are a major factor in the policy process—they initiate policy proposals, have a voice in considering various alternatives, and have a significant impact on the final policy and its implementation.

Knowledge and Power

It is more than likely that individual officeholders in the administrative structure have developed a particular expertise or skill in their assignments. Additionally, they have probably developed the political and social astuteness to operate in a highly complex institution. This expertise, both in the technicalities of their jobs and in their relationships within the institution, provides a source of power in dealing with the public and with elected government officials. It is unlikely that either the public or the elected officials have the information and access needed to properly assess the inner workings of the bureaucracy. Hence, there is a quasi-confidentiality that nurtures the power in the bureaucracy. In discussing this important characteristic, one scholar observes that:

> Every bureaucracy seeks to increase the superiority of the professionally informed by keeping their knowledge and intentions secret. Bureaucratic administration always tends to be an administration of "secret sessions": in so far as it can, it hides its knowledge and action from criticism . . . The absolute monarch is powerless opposite the superior knowledge of the bureaucratic expert. . .[4]

Indeed there are some who argue that modern government is virtually run by the bureaucrat because no politician can master its complexities. One observer claims: "There is no government today that can still claim control of its bureaucracy and of its various agencies. Government agencies are all becoming autonomous, ends in themselves, and directed by their own desire for power, their own rationale, their own narrow vision rather than by national policy."[5]

President Franklin Roosevelt, aware of the danger of becoming a prisoner of his own bureaucracy, made it a point to receive information from a variety of sources. He did not depend solely on official memoranda or briefings. Not only did the President take time to read a variety of newspapers daily, but he made it a point to talk to many people about all sorts of issues and policies confronting the government. Indeed, President Roosevelt would summon officers of various departments for consultation without notifying the appropriate department head. In this way, he would solicit views that had not been filtered or approved by his closest associates. According to one author, "Roosevelt was, for a President, extraordinarily accessible. Almost a hundred persons could get through to him by telephone without stating their business to a secretary; and government officials with anything serious on their minds had little difficulty in getting appointments."[6]

Other Bases of Power

The bureaucracy develops an entrenched interest in protecting itself and its individual members from outside interference and regulation. Bureaucratic procedure, areas of responsibility, and internal social relationships are viewed as the exclusive domain of the bureaucracy. This fosters autonomy and the self-regulating capacity in which the bureaucrats tend to determine values, rules and regulations by which individual bureaucrats must operate. Thus the bureaucracy acquires a formidable institutional power in dealing with other political actors.

The governmental bureaucracy is vested with authority by law. Aside from cloaking bureaucratic activities with legality, this provides the initial grant of power to the highest bureaucrat from whom power flows to subordinates, right down to the file clerks in a local office.

Most members of the bureaucracy retain their offices by virtue of tenure or seniority. In accordance with civil service regulations, officeholders cannot be dismissed after a certain period in office unless they are convicted of malfeasance, incompetence, or criminal or immoral acts. Mediocrity is an insufficient cause for firing the bureaucrat. Even the highest political appointees and elected political officials have limited leverage in dealing with this situation. In this sense bureaucratic power is enhanced by virtue of tenure.

On the other hand, no bureaucracy can exist without support from its clientele. To further its power and to protect its domain, the bureaucracy tends to solicit support from congressmen and congressional committees and subcommittees as well as interest groups. It is probably this characteristic that prevents the bureaucracy from becoming a totally autonomous, dictatorial system. In order to maintain and expand its power, the bureaucracy must adapt itself to the pluralistic and decentralized system in our society. Thus, disagreements, conflicts, and varying political views and styles are likely to be reflected within the bureaucratic structure.

Yet if the bureaucracy can succeed in developing support from particular interest groups as well as from Congress, it enhances its power to deal with other political actors. For example, the Departments of Agriculture, Labor, and Commerce realistically represent the special concerns and interests of the farmer, the laborer, and the businessman respectively. Special interests represented by such organizations as the American Farm Bureau Federation and the National Rural Elected Cooperative Association have a direct channel to the Department of Agriculture. Similarly, the AFL-CIO closely watches the activities of the Labor Department, as a number of business organizations watch the Department of Commerce. This close association between particular bureaucratic departments and their clientele leads to criticism: Some critics claim that this association provides interest groups with a direct official link, and thus leverage and influence, with the decision-making bodies of government.

Such a view is at the root of charges against the "military-industrial complex." Some observers argue that certain defense-related industries, in order to insure high profits, maintain a direct link with the military establishment since the military is interested in acquiring the most sophisticated and technologically advanced weaponry, regardless of cost. This informal alliance perpetuates high defense budgets.

According to another observer:

> The bureaucracy is recognized by all interested groups as a major channel of representation to such an extent that Congress rightly feels the competition of a rival . . . Agencies and bureaus more or less perforce are in the business of building, maintaining, and increasing their political support. They lead and in large part are led by the diverse groups whose influence sustains them.[7]

There are numerous examples of close links between interest groups and the federal bureaucracy. One of the clearest is the relationship between the Federal Power Commission (an independent agency), the Federal Energy Office (part of the Executive Office), and oil interests.[8] Important members of the oil industry and men holding large oil stocks are found in the Federal Power Commission and the Federal Energy Office as well as in most U.S. government departments and agencies dealing with oil or natural gas. According to one newspaper report, "Nineteen officials of the Federal Power Commission, or their families, owned stock in such firms as Exxon, Texaco, Union Oil, Standard Oil of Indiana, Tenneco, and Atlantic Richfield." The report also noted that "an assistant administrator-designate of the Federal Energy Administration, was an Exxon Corporation executive who received a $90,000 'termination' bonus from the company before going to work for the FEA." Moreover, an inquiry from Congressman Benjamin S. Rosenthal, Democrat from New York, resulted in identifying "102 former oil people serving in the Federal Energy Office, most of them in the upper grades."

There are similar linkages throughout the bureaucracy. Whether all such linkages mean an outright conflict of interest is difficult to ascertain. Nevertheless, continuing and consistent linkages create suspicion and concern.

It seems clear that such linkages create a common interest to perpetuate and implement policies favorable to oil and natural gas companies. It is difficult for the President and other agencies of government to develop policies and carry them out without the active involvement of the Federal Power Commission and the Federal Energy Office. In such situations, one can reasonably ask, in whose interest is policy made?

In a pointed observation, Francis E. Rourke states "In its most developed form the relationship between an interest group and an administrative agency is so close that it is difficult to know where the group leaves off and the agency begins."[9]

The Fourth Branch of Government

Bureaucracies have become a fourth branch of government. This stems partly from the characteristics we have already discussed and partly from the ambiguity of responsibility within the bureaucracy. Bureaucratic agencies come into existence by virtue of legislation by Congress, which places them under control of the executive. Inherently this creates congressional-executive conflict over the boundaries of bureaucratic responsibilities and their management. It creates a vast gray area, where there are no clear-cut responsibilities regarding issues of control and management. Bureaucrats are prone to exploit this ambiguity in order to provide the bureaucracy with greater flexibility and a greater base of power.

In reviewing the major characteristics of the bureaucracy, we can see its tremendous potential and actual power as an institution. The dangers are obvious. The bureaucracy is not accountable to the public at large. It is in a position to regulate itself as an autonomous institution. There is ambiguity of responsibility regarding its control. The entrenched institutional interests of the bureaucracy threaten any political system which prides itself on responsiveness to, and control by, the people.

In the American system, the power of the bureaucracy has been limited and controlled primarily by the pluralistic nature of politics which is reflected in the bureaucratic structure. Thus, the tendency for a monolithic structure to develop has been counterbalanced by a general diffusion and decentralization of power. Moreover, the prerogatives of various political actors are jealously guarded, creating additional countervailing forces to the expansion and exercise of bureaucratic power.

It should be noted here that bureaucracies exist in practically every economic enterprise and administrative agency, both public and private. Some are large; others are small. They are concerned with economics, research, education and a host of other activities. Indeed, bureaucracies are not only a dominant administrative institution in our society, but a dominant form of social organization. Our concern here is with public bureaucracy and public administration, and we will focus on these primarily at the national level, although a vast number of bureaucracies exist also at state and local levels.

Institutional Characteristics

The internal character of the bureaucracy has an important effect upon its ability to exercise power in the political system. Although we have alluded to some of these characteristics already, there is a need to develop a better understanding of the internal workings of bureaucracy.

Aside from the fact that bureaucracies are established to serve particular administrative purposes, they have three basic characteristics. These are:
1. Internal operations are based on specific rules and regulations. Bureaucracies tend to routinize all of their procedures, not only with respect to internal operations but also in their formal and informal relationships with the public.
2. Bureaucracies reflect a hierarchical structure and formal organization, identifying relationships and authority between all positions. Each position has a specified number of subordinates and a superior. Moreover, each position has specially assigned duties and specialized tasks, all interrelated to the total task of the bureaucracy. On an organizational chart this is likely to present an impressive picture of bureaucratic clarity and a neat organizational pattern; however, the true workings of the bureaucracy vary from the neat hierarchical pattern, as we will discuss later.
3. Bureaucracies operate impersonally. That is, personal idiosyncrasies, attitudes, and desires are generally not part of the bureaucracy's day-to-day operation with its clientele. Deviations from established rules and regulations or from the chain of command (internal organizational structure) are frowned upon and indeed generally prohibited. It is this impersonality and red tape that leads to the frustrating experiences that many people have when dealing with the bureaucracy; they often hear replies like "I'm sorry, we cannot give you special consideration." The capability of the individual member of the bureaucracy is measured in terms of his capacity to perform his specific job assignments according to rules and regulations.

These procedures and techniques in many cases produce a dull,

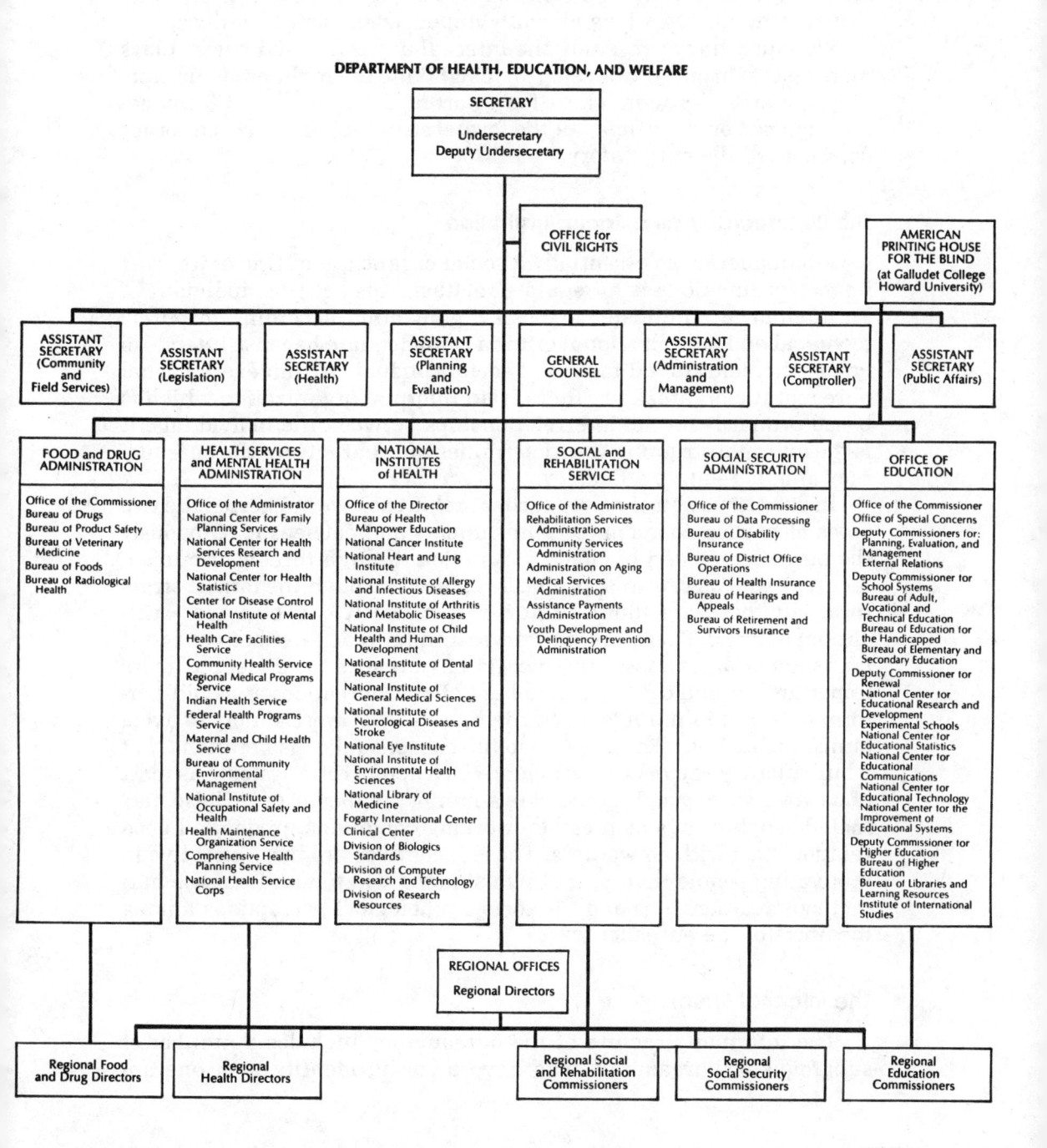

Institutional Characteristics

DEPARTMENT OF HEALTH, EDUCATION, AND WELFARE

- SECRETARY
  - Undersecretary
  - Deputy Undersecretary

- OFFICE for CIVIL RIGHTS
- AMERICAN PRINTING HOUSE FOR THE BLIND (at Galludet College Howard University)

Assistant Secretaries and Offices:
- ASSISTANT SECRETARY (Community and Field Services)
- ASSISTANT SECRETARY (Legislation)
- ASSISTANT SECRETARY (Health)
- ASSISTANT SECRETARY (Planning and Evaluation)
- GENERAL COUNSEL
- ASSISTANT SECRETARY (Administration and Management)
- ASSISTANT SECRETARY (Comptroller)
- ASSISTANT SECRETARY (Public Affairs)

FOOD and DRUG ADMINISTRATION
- Office of the Commissioner
- Bureau of Drugs
- Bureau of Product Safety
- Bureau of Veterinary Medicine
- Bureau of Foods
- Bureau of Radiological Health

HEALTH SERVICES and MENTAL HEALTH ADMINISTRATION
- Office of the Administrator
- National Center for Family Planning Services
- National Center for Health Services Research and Development
- National Center for Health Statistics
- Center for Disease Control
- National Institute of Mental Health
- Health Care Facilities Service
- Community Health Service
- Regional Medical Programs Service
- Indian Health Service
- Federal Health Programs Service
- Maternal and Child Health Service
- Bureau of Community Environmental Management
- National Institute of Occupational Safety and Health
- Health Maintenance Organization Service
- Comprehensive Health Planning Service
- National Health Service Corps

NATIONAL INSTITUTES of HEALTH
- Office of the Director
- Bureau of Health Manpower Education
- National Cancer Institute
- National Heart and Lung Institute
- National Institute of Allergy and Infectious Diseases
- National Institute of Arthritis and Metabolic Diseases
- National Institute of Child Health and Human Development
- National Institute of Dental Research
- National Institute of General Medical Sciences
- National Institute of Neurological Diseases and Stroke
- National Eye Institute
- National Institute of Environmental Health Sciences
- National Library of Medicine
- Fogarty International Center
- Clinical Center
- Division of Biologics Standards
- Division of Computer Research and Technology
- Division of Research Resources

SOCIAL and REHABILITATION SERVICE
- Office of the Administrator
- Rehabilitation Services Administration
- Community Services Administration
- Administration on Aging
- Medical Services Administration
- Assistance Payments Administration
- Youth Development and Delinquency Prevention Administration

SOCIAL SECURITY ADMINISTRATION
- Office of the Commissioner
- Bureau of Data Processing
- Bureau of Disability Insurance
- Bureau of District Office Operations
- Bureau of Health Insurance
- Bureau of Hearings and Appeals
- Bureau of Retirement and Survivors Insurance

OFFICE OF EDUCATION
- Office of the Commissioner
- Office of Special Concerns
- Deputy Commissioners for: Planning, Evaluation, and Management; External Relations
- Deputy Commissioner for School Systems
  - Bureau of Adult, Vocational and Technical Education
  - Bureau of Education for the Handicapped
  - Bureau of Elementary and Secondary Education
- Deputy Commissioner for Renewal
  - National Center for Educational Research and Development
  - Experimental Schools
  - National Center for Educational Statistics
  - National Center for Educational Communications
  - National Center for Educational Technology
  - National Center for the Improvement of Educational Systems
- Deputy Commissioner for Higher Education
  - Bureau of Higher Education
  - Bureau of Libraries and Learning Resources
  - Institute of International Studies

REGIONAL OFFICES — Regional Directors

- Regional Food and Drug Directors
- Regional Health Directors
- Regional Social and Rehabilitation Commissioners
- Regional Social Security Commissioners
- Regional Education Commissioners

unresponsive organization, striving for administrative efficiency for efficiency's sake alone, entrenched in the political system, and protected from outsiders by a virtually impenetrable veil of authority.

We must, however, study the internal dynamics and power plays more closely in order to develop an insight into the realities of bureaucracy. An organizational chart for a part of the government bureaucracy appears on page 369, but the formal structure of any bureaucracy does not tell the entire story.

The Bureaucracy as a Social Institution

A bureaucracy is essentially a social organization. One of its most important functions is to regulate relationships between individuals. To attempt to administer a social organization according to purely technical and organizational criteria is inadequate because it tends to ignore the nonrational factors of social conduct. Within every formal bureaucratic organization there is an informal organization which is based primarily on the interrelationships between the individuals; it is the informal structure that determines the character of the bureaucracy and its relative efficiency.

In our discussion of power earlier in this book we suggested the two faces of power: coercion (or punishment) and consensus. Obviously the bureaucracy can be made to function through threats of punishment, as well as rewards, primarily focused through the formal structure, but there are limits to how responsive it can be under such circumstances. There are certain restraints on the effectiveness of punishment since most bureaucrats have tenure in office, but more important psychologically, members of the bureaucracy would perform only at minimum levels if their motivation were simply to avoid punishment. It is primarily due to the consensual considerations that a bureaucracy can operate efficiently in a democratic system. As most of us are aware, people respond to a number of incentives. These may include such things as prestige, working conditions, pride, and good relationships with co-workers. These incentives are more effective in motivating people than fear of punishment. They stem from the harmonious relationships and the sociopsychological perceptions among members of the bureaucracy.

The Informal Structure

The informal structure of the bureaucracy includes a number of subgroups of bureaucrats who have a strong identity with one another. Normally, they are closely associated in a particular office or project, and develop strong feelings of identity and defensiveness as a group. These subgroups provide the individual bureaucrat with social and behavioral guidelines regarding his job and his sense of importance. Members of these subgroups share excellent communications, a sense of unity, mutual protectiveness, respect, and even affection. Belonging to such a group generally creates a sense of satisfaction and contentment with the job and the bureaucratic structure. It is the relationship between these groups, the hierarchy, and the entire organizational structure that makes up the informal structure.

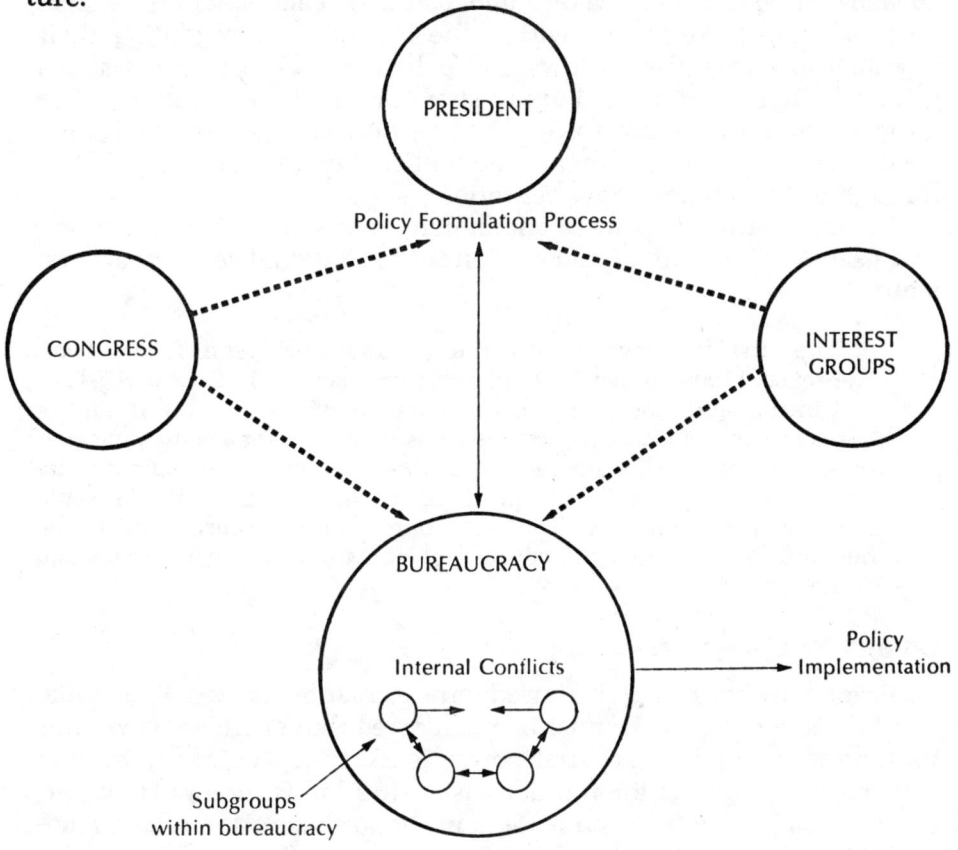

Policy directives by the President are refined and reinterprted within the bureaucracy by the various subgroups. Additionally, congressional power is exerted on the bureaucracy, as is power of interest groups, to attempt to direct it in the way deemed best for congressional or group interests. In the final outcome, policy implementation takes shape as a result of the continuing power interplay between these political actors.

Need for Consensus

For the bureaucracy to respond and perform effectively, these informal groups or subgroups must view the general operations in favorable terms. Decision-makers and politicians therefore must appeal to this informal structure for the proper response to policies and decisions. As we have already suggested, the bureaucracy does not necessarily interpret or implement decisions as intended by the top level decision-makers. A basic ingredient of bureaucratic power is its role in administering and interpreting the general guidelines developed by these decision-makers and political leaders. These leaders must develop a consensus within the bureaucracy regarding their intended interpretation of laws and policies. Such consensus stems primarily from the informal group structure. If the majority of these informal groups are convinced of the propriety of these laws and of the need for administering them, the entire bureaucracy will follow through on the proper implementation.

In commenting on this phenomenon, Henry Kissinger, after several years as President Nixon's assistant for national security affairs, stated:

> The outsider believes a Presidential order is consistently followed out. Nonsense. I have to spend considerable time seeing that it is carried out and in the spirit the President intended. Inevitably, in the nature of bureaucracy, departments become pressure groups for a point of view. If the President decides against them, they are convinced some evil influence worked on the President: if only he knew all the facts, he would have decided their way. The nightmare of the modern state is the hugeness of bureaucracy, and the problem is how to get coherence and design in it.[10]

Criteria for Efficiency

Practically speaking, the bureaucracy must be treated almost like a public constituency. It must be recognized that coercive power has its limitations and consensual power is likely to achieve more and develop a legitimacy for the actions of the bureaucracy. However, conflicts may arise between leaders in the formal structure and leaders in the informal structure. Therefore the most efficient bureaucracy is one in which the same individuals are leaders in both structures. Let us examine this consideration.

An individual appointed to head a particular bureau can exercise his legal authority to dispense awards or punishment to insure compliance with rules, regulations and directives. But the efficiency of the bureau and the attitude of its members is likely to develop primarily as a result of the bureau head's relationship with certain informal group leaders. Moreover, he is likely to be judged by his personality, style of operation, and relationship with his subordinates. Among the subgroups in the bureau, there may be an informal grouping of six or seven section chiefs. If one of them is generally recognized as a particularly outstanding leader, the whole group takes its cue from his attitudes and perceptions. If the director of the bureau is perceptive he will be able to identify the group leader. He will then either adjust his style of operation to insure compliance by the leader or he will try to shift the loyalty of the group away from the section leader and to himself. In order for the bureau to respond effectively to directives, its head must ensure consensus rather than coercive compliance, and this can usually be done by developing a working relationship and consensus with the group leader. These are the kinds of relationships that exist throughout any bureaucracy; they develop a web of complicated and complex informal relationships between most of its members.

In the final analysis, the top level decision-makers and political officials must be aware that people, particularly in a democratic society, have a mixed attitude towards authority. Certainly orders of superiors are generally accepted, but there are limits to this acceptance. Much depends on the manner in which authority is exercised and the relationships between administrator and employees. These relationships and attitudes towards authority are primarily the end result of informal group perceptions and attitudes. Few people perform in their jobs in a way to jeopardize their informal group membership. This is particularly true in a public bureaucracy where much depends on tenure, rules and regulations, and group cohesiveness.

On the other hand, major administrative tasks cannot be dealt with solely within the informal structure. If one were to disregard the formal organizational structure, i.e., rules and regulations, hierarchical relationships, and other criteria that we have discussed, it would probably create chaos. If the informal structure alone were dominant, the total bureaucratic system would become ineffective because the formal lines of authority would be unclear and the whole systematic concept of administrative efficiency would be greatly diluted. Still, to disregard the informal associations would severely limit the ability of the bureaucracy to operate properly.

Need for Balance

The obvious solution is to develop a harmonious balance between these two structures. Indeed, the most effective and efficient bureaucracy is one in which the gap between the formal and informal leadership and structure is narrow. In order for supervisory levels in the bureaucracy to perform well they must be responsive to both structures, because it is through both structures that the necessary information is received and the essential administration and implementation achieved. For the proper functioning and interpretation of laws and policy, it is necessary to develop a consensus from the highest to the lowest level of bureaucracy. It is this interplay between the formal and informal structures that has a significant influence on the total power of the bureaucracy. Where there is consensus and harmonious balance between formal and informal structures, the bureaucracy is likely to be significantly more powerful in its relationship to other political actors. On the other hand, if there is conflict and disagreement between formal and informal structures, the bureaucracy will become weakened and exposed to manipulations of outside political actors.

For an illustration, one need only look back to the presidency of Franklin Delano Roosevelt, who attempted to bypass the formal structures of the bureaucracy by deliberately and personally contacting second and third level bureaucrats for information and discussion of policies. This tended to subvert the formal structure while creating a pattern of unpredictability of the formal hierarchy; it also created tensions within the informal structures. By so doing President Roosevelt hoped to keep the power of the bureaucracy manageable and minimal, and thus more susceptible to direction by the executive.

Resistance to Change

Recognizing the fact that a bureaucracy is made up of a variety of subsystems and subgroups, we should keep in mind that such groups provide the character of the organization and support entrenched and accepted relationships and patterns. These groups are likely to resist any attempt at significantly changing operations. There is security and predictability in accepted procedures. Any change in these procedures is likely to cause changes in relationships and to create an environment which these informal groups find themselves unable to control, thus leading to frustration and insecurity. Therefore, most groups as well as individual bureaucrats are likely to accept and rigidly follow routine for routine's sake as a way of reinforcing their present positions and maintaining predictable relationships. Moreover, the older the bureaucracy and the longer the informal group structures have existed, the more likely it is to resist any change.

Procedures and relationships become institutionalized and tend to revolve around entrenched interests. As Drucker has stated: "Being by design a protective institution, it [government] is not good at innovation. It cannot really abandon anything. The moment government undertakes anything it becomes entrenched and permanent."[11]

This is not to suggest, however, that informal group relationships do not change. Obviously, if persons are transferred out and new ones are transferred in, some adjustment of these relationships must take place. Indeed, for new bureaucrats to perform properly, they must be accepted by the informal groups. New leaders of informal groups arise while others fade away.

Because of the tendency of bureaucracies to favor security and predictability, they usually lack imagination, resist innovation, and follow a rather rigid status quo philosophy. Indeed, only the most newly established bureaucracy can generally play an innovative type of role, and only the most efficient and persevering nonpolitical type of individual can hope to put a real dent in bureaucratic procedure. For example, Robert S. McNamara brought with him to the position of Secretary of Defense an intense dislike of bureaucratic inertia. Injecting a new perspective and a degree of innovation and imagination, McNamara introduced new insights into the bureaucratic procedures of the Department of Defense. However, even here, it took a number of years before these innovations gained minimum acceptance.

Types of Government Bureaucracies

There are a number of types of bureaucracies within the federal structure. Initially the bureaucracy consisted of a small group of people directly controlled by the executive and organized into the Departments of War, State and Treasury, but over the years it has expanded tremendously in a number of directions.

The first type of federal bureaucracy is the presidential bureaucracy, consisting of the White House Office and the Executive Office as shown in the following chart. Appointments to this bureaucracy are controlled by the President, with little involvement from other branches of government. This bureaucracy, the President's own, generally consists of individuals with a special commitment and loyalty to the President; they are the President's personal staff.

The second type of bureaucracy at the federal level is that associated with each of the executive departments. This bureaucracy pub-

THE EXECUTIVE BRANCH OF THE U.S. GOVERNMENT

THE PRESIDENT

WHITE HOUSE OFFICE

EXECUTIVE OFFICE OF THE PRESIDENT

Office of Management and Budget
Council of Economic Advisers
National Aeronautics and Space Council
National Security Council
Office of Economic Opportunity
Office of Emergency Preparedness
Office of Science and Technology
Office of the Special Representative for Trade Negotiations
Council on International Economic Policy
Office of Consumer Affairs
Office of Intergovernmental Relations
Council on Environmental Quality
Domestic Council
Office of Telecommunications Policy
Special Action Office for Drug Abuse Prevention

- DEPARTMENT OF STATE
- DEPARTMENT OF THE TREASURY
- DEPARTMENT OF DEFENSE
- DEPARTMENT OF JUSTICE
- DEPARTMENT OF THE INTERIOR
- DEPARTMENT OF AGRICULTURE
- DEPARTMENT OF COMMERCE
- DEPARTMENT OF LABOR
- DEPARTMENT OF HEALTH, EDUCATION, AND WELFARE
- DEPARTMENT OF HOUSING AND URBAN DEVELOPMENT
- DEPARTMENT OF TRANSPORTATION

INDEPENDENT OFFICES AND ESTABLISHMENTS

Administrative Conference of the U.S.
Atomic Energy Commission
Civil Aeronautics Board
District of Columbia
Economic Stabilization Agencies
Environmental Protection Agency
Export-Import Bank of the U.S.
Farm Credit Administration
Federal Communications Commission
Federal Deposit Insurance Corporation
Federal Home Loan Bank Board
Federal Maritime Commission
Federal Mediation and Conciliation Service
Federal Power Commission
Federal Reserve System, Board of Governors of the
Federal Trade Commission
General Services Administration
Interstate Commerce Commission
National Aeronautics and Space Administration
National Foundation on the Arts and the Humanities
National Labor Relations Board
National Mediation Board
National Science Foundation
Railroad Retirement Board
Securities and Exchange Commission
Selective Service System
Small Business Administration
Smithsonian Institution
Tennessee Valley Authority
U.S. Civil Service Commission
U.S. Information Agency
U.S. Postal Service
U.S. Tariff Commission
Veterans Administration

licly links the decisions and policies made at the highest level with the people. It is this bureaucracy that has the greatest numbers and the most pervasive structure of all the federal bureaucracies. Theoretically, it is controlled by the Cabinet members appointed by the President, but because of its vastness and the importance of its functions, it is subject to tremendous political pressures from other political actors. It is improbable that one man could control the day-to-day operations of this complex bureaucracy.

A third type of bureaucracy is that composed of administrators and staff associated with congressmen. Its main functions include linking the individual congressman with his constituency, establishing communications with other political actors, maintaining the proper congressional image, and in general, ensuring that the congressman and his constituents get a fair share of the resources.

The fourth type of federal bureaucracy is the independent regulatory commission. Each commission is under the direction of a board of commissioners that functions independently, outside the power of the executive. They are responsible for establishing regulations or standards with respect to certain operations in the private sector of the economy. The President cannot remove any of the commissioners although they perform functions crucial to executive control of policy. These independent regulatory commissions actually perform executive, quasi-legislative and quasi-judicial functions, in establishing rules and regulations, executing them, and punishing offenders. These commissions include the Interstate Commerce Commission, established in 1887; the National Labor Relations Board, established in 1935; the Federal Trade Commission, established in 1951; the Federal Communications Commission, established in 1934; and the Civil Aeronautics Board, established in 1938. There is little question of the necessity for such independent regulatory commissions, in view of the need for some type of government regulation of the vast range of economic activity in America. Each of these commissions has its own autonomous bureaucratic structure and each seems to be particularly responsive to interest group activities. Thus, this type of bureaucracy appears to serve a particular clientele, with little possibility of direction and supervision at the presidential level.

The Bureaucracy, Congress and Interest Groups

The bureaucracy, congressional committees, and interest groups, may become partners in tripartite alliances of power which can frus-

CIVIL AERONAUTICS BOARD

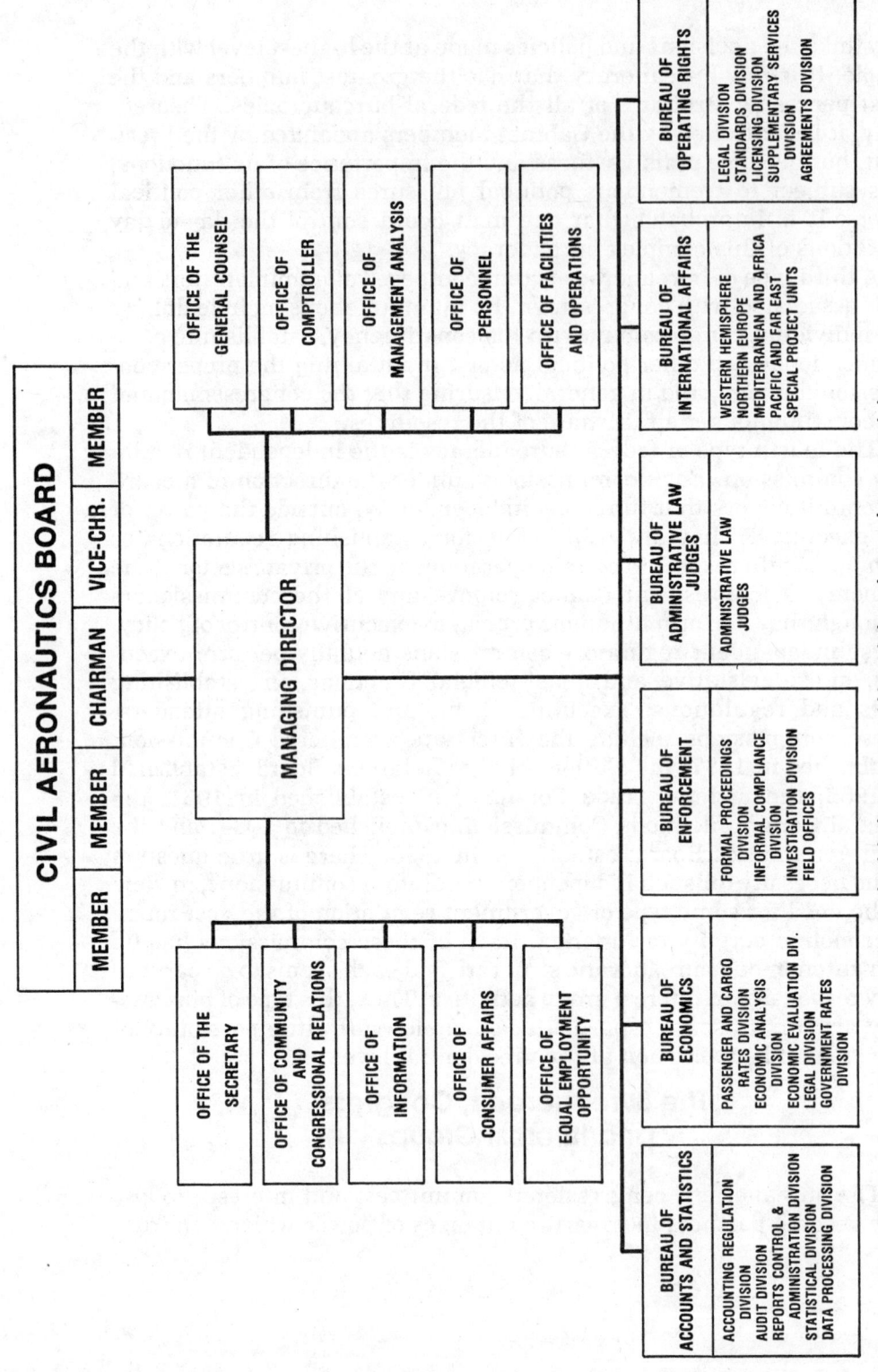

MEMBER	MEMBER	CHAIRMAN	VICE-CHR.	MEMBER

MANAGING DIRECTOR

Staff Offices (reporting to Managing Director):
- OFFICE OF THE GENERAL COUNSEL
- OFFICE OF COMPTROLLER
- OFFICE OF MANAGEMENT ANALYSIS
- OFFICE OF PERSONNEL
- OFFICE OF FACILITIES AND OPERATIONS
- OFFICE OF THE SECRETARY
- OFFICE OF COMMUNITY AND CONGRESSIONAL RELATIONS
- OFFICE OF INFORMATION
- OFFICE OF CONSUMER AFFAIRS
- OFFICE OF EQUAL EMPLOYMENT OPPORTUNITY

BUREAU OF ACCOUNTS AND STATISTICS
- ACCOUNTING REGULATION DIVISION
- AUDIT DIVISION
- REPORTS CONTROL & ADMINISTRATION DIVISION
- STATISTICAL DIVISION
- DATA PROCESSING DIVISION

BUREAU OF ECONOMICS
- PASSENGER AND CARGO RATES DIVISION
- ECONOMIC ANALYSIS DIVISION
- ECONOMIC EVALUATION DIV.
- LEGAL DIVISION
- GOVERNMENT RATES DIVISION

BUREAU OF ENFORCEMENT
- FORMAL PROCEEDINGS DIVISION
- INFORMAL COMPLIANCE DIVISION
- INVESTIGATION DIVISION
- FIELD OFFICES

BUREAU OF ADMINISTRATIVE LAW JUDGES
- ADMINISTRATIVE LAW JUDGES

BUREAU OF INTERNATIONAL AFFAIRS
- WESTERN HEMISPHERE
- NORTHERN EUROPE
- MEDITERRANEAN AND AFRICA
- PACIFIC AND FAR EAST
- SPECIAL PROJECT UNITS

BUREAU OF OPERATING RIGHTS
- LEGAL DIVISION
- STANDARDS DIVISION
- LICENSING DIVISION
- SUPPLEMENTARY SERVICES DIVISION
- AGREEMENTS DIVISION

An example of the bureaucracy within an independent regulatory commission trate attempts to override bureaucratic interests. When the three partners are in agreement regarding policy, they reinforce each other's powers, collaborating to protect their respective interests—epitomizing quid-pro-quo political gamesmanship. If the President or other political actors are to influence and manage the bureaucracy, they must prevent the coalescence of this "iron triangle." Commenting on the issues of Nixon's first term, Theodore White notes;

> Political Scientists identify in Washington examples of what they call an "Iron Triangle"—an interlocking three-way association between a well-financed lobby (whether it be mining, education, highways, oil or other areas), the Congressional committee or subcommittee that makes laws on such subjects, and the bureaucracy in Washington which applies these laws. When these three—the committee, the lobby and the bureaucracy—in any given area all agree, and wash each other's hands with influence, information and favors, they are almost impervious to any executive or outside pressures. Within their jurisdictions, they control national power.[12]

Internal Conflicts

Given the various structures of bureaucracy at the federal level, and the vast number of state and local bureaucracies with their own particular power bases, we can see that the term bureaucracy certainly does not mean a monolithic structure in our system of government. Indeed, one can argue that bureaucracies act similarly to interest groups, in certain instances providing opposition to other bureaucracies, in other instances joining together to perform some particular task.

At the federal level alone, significant conflicts arise from the operation of the four bureaucracies we have just discussed; indeed conflict arises within each of the individual bureaucracies. For example, most Americans are familiar with the kinds of conflict that arose between the Departments of State and of Defense over the prosecution of the Vietnam war. More recently, serious conflicts have developed between the Department of Agriculture and the Department of State regarding soybean and wheat deals with the Soviet Union.

Although bureaucracies do have a degree of autonomy which can frustrate the proper execution of government and its supervision at the highest policy level, they are themselves susceptible to the political pressures and power plays of other political actors. In this sense, as we have tried to demonstrate in this chapter, power within bureaucracy can be diffuse and decentralized, reflecting the diverse political characteristics of our system. This does not necessarily result in a high degree of efficiency. On the other hand, there is an argument in favor of such power diffusion, decentralization and susceptibility to political pressure. In a democracy, it is perhaps more important to have the bureaucracy susceptible to such power plays and internal informal groups than to achieve the high degree of efficiency which presupposes isolation from public pressures. The role of the bureaucracy in our system certainly seems to indicate that it has the power to perform as a fourth branch of government. To ensure that these operations are effective and stay within the rules of the game, it is necessary to have strong political leadership, as well as a strong sense of bureaucratic accountability to the people. The bureaucracy must remain open and responsive to the political pressures within the system. There is no greater danger to a democratic system than a bureaucracy shrouded in a cocoon of expertise, isolated from the public, and wielding power without responsibility—a state within a state.

Problems in a Democracy

The problems of bureaucracy have been with us since the earliest years of our government. Bureaucratic control has changed and expanded over the years, paralleling the expansion of federal power and the proliferation of agencies. During the initial years of our government, both the Federalists and the Jeffersonians assumed that the administration would be conducted primarily by the wealthy. There was a marked change in philosophy during the administration of Andrew Jackson, who rationalized the spoils system or political patronage as a method of giving the average person his due in a democratic society, and not necessarily as a sign of favoritism. This system of political patronage quickly became a basic underpinning for national administration as well as state and local systems. Under the administration of President Lincoln and the demands of the Civil War, the bureaucracy was strengthened and broadened. Vast abuses arose with respect to appointments until 1883 when a Civil Service Reform Act was passed. Political appointments were allowed only at the most senior decision-making levels, while most positions were placed under civil service rules and regulations, generally isolating them from political patronage. Although most of the abuses have been eliminated from the federal civil service, much political patronage remains at state and local levels.

The federal bureaucracy has had a stormy past. Beginning with an elitist concept of administration it has grown into an institution whose control is essential for the operation of the political system and whose internal character is replete with political struggles and power conflicts. In the history of its growth, the bureaucracy has been racked with corruption and graft, power aggrandizement, and political infighting. It has been characterized on one hand as a refuge of lackluster personalities and inept administrators and on the other as an institution representing the highest ideals of public service. Somewhere between these views lies the truth. In any case, there is much to be said for the view that America is a bureaucratic state, since nothing of importance can be accomplished without the existence and cooperation of the bureaucracy.

NOTES

1. These figures extracted from the *Statistical Abstract of the United States, 1972.*
2. Harold Seidman, *Politics, Position, and Power: The Dynamics of Federal Organization* (New York: Oxford University Press, 1970), p. 27.
3. Henry A. Kissinger, "Bureaucracy and Policymaking: The Effect of Insiders and Outsiders on the Policy Process," in Morton H. Halperin and Arnold Kanter (eds.), *Readings in American Foreign Policy: A Bureaucratic Perspective* (Boston: Little, Brown and Co., 1973), p. 86.
4. Max Weber, "Essay on Bureaucracy," in Francis E. Rourke (ed.), *Bureaucratic Power in National Politics* (Boston: Little, Brown and Co., 1972), pp. 61-62.
5. Peter F. Drucker, *The Age of Discontinuity* (New York: Harper and Row, 1969), p. 220.
6. Arthur M. Schlesinger, Jr., *The Coming of the New Deal* (Boston: Houghton Mifflin Co., 1959), p. 522.
7. Norton E. Long, "Power and Administration" in Rourke, pp. 8-9.
8. The quotes and discussion in this section is taken from "How Big Oil Primes Bureaucracy," *Chicago Tribune*, Perspective/Business, Section 2, November 17, 1974, p. 1.
9. Francis E. Rourke, *Bureaucracy, Politics, and Public Policy* (Boston: Little, Brown and Co., 1969), p. 15.
10. As quoted in Morton H. Halperin, *Bureaucratic Politics and Foreign Policy* (Washington, D.C.: The Brookings Institution, 1974), p. 245.
11. Drucker, p. 266.
12. Theodore H. White, *The Making of the President 1972* (New York: Bantam, 1973), pp. 71-72.

Selected Readings

For better or for worse, American people come into contact with government bureaucracy almost every day of their lives. What the bureaucracy does or does not do provides the images of government in the minds of most Americans. Bureaucracy is here to stay. The problem in a democratic society is to insure that the bureaucracies work for the people, respond to the people, and understand their responsibility in the pursuit of democracy.

The selection by Dumont is a scathing critique of the existing government bureaucracy. In order to achieve some social change, the author claims that there is a need for bureaucratic guerrilla warfare—the need to develop a sense of purpose for the benefit of the people rather than organizational stability. Dumont argues that bureaucrats are more concerned with organizational character than with program goals or purposes. Indeed, he argues that there are five principles to the bureaucracy. These range from the first principle of "maintain your tenure," or be sure you have a secure job, to "keep the boss from getting embarrassed" and lastly "maintain a stable and well-circumscribed constituency." What is required is to employ those who are not bound by such organizational behavior, but who are committed to social change and an effective and responsive bureaucracy. Only in this way can the bureaucracy be made to respond to social change and people's interests.

The second reading "Backstabbing, Inc.," focuses on business bureaucracies and office politics. Peter Chew writes that in order to get ahead in business, one must engage in office politics. He quotes a mid-level executive who says, "In our company it's not who you know but what you've got on who you know that counts." The article makes clear that informal structures and political relationships within any bureaucracy may be more important than formal structures or legal relationships. The author candidly describes the character of office politics and concludes that contacts and webs of personal relationships are the key to success in business. The assessment of business bureaucracy and office politics is generally true for government bureaucracy. To properly deal with such bureaucracies, the average citizen must understand the nature of office politics and the organizational behavior of entrenched bureaucrats. The key question is how to make the bureaucracy responsive and responsible to the electorate. One can easily argue that the government bureaucracy places responsibility to the electorate very low in its scale of priorities. Indeed, organizational loyalty and commitment to the boss above all else, seem to be the major characteristics.

11.1

Down the Bureaucracy

MATTHEW P. DUMONT

There has been a certain tension among the people of our federal city lately. I am not talking about the black population of the district, which becomes visible to the rest of the world only when its rage boils over. I am referring to the public servants who ooze across the Maryland and Virginia lines each day to manipulate the machinery of government.

It has never been a particularly gleeful population, but in the last year or so it has developed a kind of mass involutional melancholia, a peculiar mixture of depression, anxiety and senescence.

As in similarly depressed communities, the young, the healthy and those with good job prospects have tended to migrate. Among those who have departed are a large proportion of that scarce supply of idealistic and pragmatic people who try to work for social change "within the system." They are leaving because they feel unwanted and ineffectual. Let me describe what they are turning their backs on.

Washington is a malaria swamp covered over with buildings of neofascist design and ringed with military bases.

Do you remember Rastignac shaking his fist at Paris from Goriot's grave site? Washington is a city made for fists to be shaken at. Shaken at, not bloodied on. Federal buildings are especially constructed to be impervious to blood. You can rush headlong into a marble balustrade smearing brains and blood and bile three yards wide. But as the lady does on television, with a smile and a few whisks of a damp cloth, the wonderful material will come up as clean and white and sparkling as before.

Some people have tried burning themselves into the concrete. That doesn't work either.

And, as you might have guessed, all that urine on the Pentagon was gone within minutes after the armies of the night retreated.

No, you may, individually or en masse, descend upon the Federal Triangle. You

Published by permission of Transaction, Inc. from Trans-action, Vol. 7 #12, October 1970, Copyright © 1970, from Transaction, Inc.

may try to impale and exsanguinate yourselves, flay, crucify and castrate yourselves. You may scream shrill cries or sing "Alice's Restaurant" or chant "Om," but it won't help. The buildings were made to last forever and to forever remain shining and white, the summer sun glaring off their walls, stunning the passersby.

Inside, one might spend eternity hearing the sounds of his own footsteps in the corridors of these buildings and never see his sun-cast shadow. If you took all the corridors in all of the federal buildings in Washington and laid them end to end, and inclined one end slightly and started a billiard ball rolling down, by the time it reached the lower end, the ball would have attained such a velocity that it would hurtle on through space while approaching an infinite mass and thereby destroy the universe. This is not likely to happen because such coordination is unheard of among federal agencies. But we will get to that later.

Off the corridors are offices and conference rooms. (There is also a core of mail chutes, telephone lines, elevator shafts, sewer pipes, trash cans and black people, but these are all invisible.) The offices have desks—wooden ones for important people and steel ones for unimportant people. (Otherwise, the distinction is impossible to make unless you could monitor their telephone calls to each other and determine the relative hierarchy depending on whose secretary manages to keep the other party waiting before putting her boss on.)

The offices also contain file cabinets that are filled with paper. The paper is mainly memos—the way people in the federal government communicate to one another. When communication is not necessary, memos "for the record" are written and filed. It has been estimated that the approximate cost in labor and supplies for the typing of a memo is 36¢. The cost in professional time for its preparation is incalculable.

The conference rooms are for conferences. A conference is for the purpose of sharing information among a group of federal officials who have already been apprised of the information to be shared, individually, by memo. Coffee and cigarettes are consumed. By prior arrangement, each participant is, in turn, interrupted by his secretary for an urgent phone call. After the conference additional memos are exchanged.

But let me describe the people who work in the federal government because some mythology must be laid to rest.

They are good people, which is to say that they are no less good than anyone else, which is to say that we are all pretty much cut from the same material and most of it is pretty rotten. I do not wish to be cavalier about the problem of evil, but I will ask you to accept as a premise for this thesis that the differences between the "best of us" and the "worst of us" are no greater than the differences *within* each of us at varying times.

I have been and will be more sober and precise about this issue in other writings, but what I am attempting to convey is a conviction that the great evils of mankind, the genocides and holy wars, the monstrous exploitations and negligences and injustices of societies have less to do with the malice of individuals than with unexamined and unquestioned institutional practices.

I am talking about the Eichmannism—a syndrome wherein individual motives, consciences or goals become irrelevant in the context of organizational behaviors. This can be seen in pure culture in the federal government. There are a host of written rules for behavior for the federal civil servants, but these are rarely salient. It is the unwritten rules, tacit but ever present, subtle but overwhelming, unarticulated but commanding, that determine the behavior of the men and women who buzz out their lives in the spaces defined by the United States government.

These rules are few in number. Rule number one is to *maintain your tenure*. This is at the same time the most significant and the easiest rule to abide by. If you desire to keep a job for several decades and retire from it with an adequate pension, and if you have the capacity to appear at once occupied and inconspicuous, then you can be satisfied as a "fed."

Appearing occupied means walking briskly at all times. It means looking down at your desk rather than up into the distance when thinking. It means always having papers in your hands. Above all, it means, when asked how things are, responding "very hectic" rather than "terrific" or "lousy."

Being inconspicuous means that your competence in appearing occupied should be expressed quietly and without affect. The most intolerable behavior in a civil servant is psychotic behavior. Being psychotic in the federal government is looking people directly in the eye for a moment too long. It is walking around on a weekday without a tie. It is kissing a girl in an elevator. (It doesn't matter whether she is a wife, mistress, secretary or daughter.) It is writing a memo that is excessively detailed, or refusing to write memos. It is laughing too loud or too long at a conference. It is taking a clandestine gulp of wine in a locker room rather than ordering two martinis over lunch. (This explains why there are more suspensions for alcoholism among lower level workers than higher level ones.)

In short, there is no more sensitive indicator of deviant behavior than personnel records of the federal government.

This does not mean that federal officials never vary their behavior. Currently, for example, it is modish to sport sideburns and a moustache. The specter of thousands of civil servants looking like Che Guevara may seem exciting, but it has no more significance than cuffless trousers.

You may or may not wish to follow the fashions, but do not initiate them. In general, follow a golden mean of behavior, that is, do what most people seem to be doing. Do it quietly. And if you are not sure how to behave, take annual leave.

The second rule of behavior in the government, and clearly related to the sustenance of your own tenure, is to *keep the boss from getting embarrassed*. That is the single, most important standard of competence for a federal official. The man who runs interference effectively, who can anticipate and obviate impertinent, urgent or obvious demands from the boss's boss, or from the press, or from the public, or from Congress, will be treasured and rewarded. This is so pervasive a desideratum in a civil servant that the distinction between line and staff activities becomes thin and artificial in the face of it. Your primary function in the hierarchy (after the protection of your own tenure) is the protection of your superior's tenure rather than the fulfillment of assigned responsibilities. (Obvious exceptions to this rule are J. Edgar Hoover and certain elements in the Department of Defense, who, like physicians and priests, respond to a higher authority.)

The third unwritten rule of federal behavior is to *make sure that all appropriated funds are spent by the end of the fiscal year*. Much of the paper that stuffs the orifices of executive desks has to do with justifications for requests for more money. For money to be returned after such justifications are approved is to imply that the requester, his supervisor and Congress itself were improvident in their demands on the taxpayer's money. It would be like a bum asking for a handout for a cup of coffee. A passerby offers a quarter and the bum returns 15¢ saying, "Coffee is only a dime, schmuck."

Contract hustlers, who abound in Washington, know that their halcyon days are in late spring when agencies are frequently panicked at the realization that they have not exhausted their operating funds and may be in the black by the fiscal year's end. Agencies that administer grant-in-aid programs celebrate end-of-fiscal-year parties with Dionysian abandon when instead of having a surplus of funds they cannot pay all of their obligations.

The only effective way to evaluate a federal program is the rapidity with which money is spent. Federal agencies, no less than purveyors of situation comedies, cigarettes and medical care, are dominated by a marketplace mentality which assumes that you have a good product if the demand exceeds the supply.

The fourth unwritten rule of behavior in government is to *keep the program alive*. It is not appropriate to question the original purposes of the program. Nor is it appropriate to ask if the program has any consonance with its original purposes. It is certainly not appropriate to assume that its purposes have been served. It is only appropriate to assume that once a program has been legislated, funded and staffed, it must endure. An unstated and probably unconscious blessing of immortality is bestowed upon the titles that clutter organizational charts in federal agencies.

Congress, with its control of funds, is perceived as a nurturant breast with a supply of vital fluids that may at any time run dry and thus starve the program to death. Such a matter must be looked upon with intense ambivalence, a state of mind associated with schizophrenia in the hostile-dependent offspring. And, indeed, Congress is perceived by federal executives with a mixture of adulation and rage and, indeed, federal programming is schizophrenic. Like the schizophrenic, federal programs have the capacity to assume pseudomorphic identities, having the outline and form of order and direction and vitality but actually being flat, autistic and encrusted with inorganic matter. Like the schizophrenic, federal programs develop a primitive narcissism that is independent of feedback from the environment other than the provision of life-sustaining funds.

Even programs that are conceived with some imagination as relatively bold and aggressive attempts to institutionalize change, such as Model Cities or Comprehensive Community Mental Health Centers or Community Action Programs, become so preoccupied with survival that compromises in the face of real or imagined criticism from Congress very quickly blunt whatever cutting edges the program may have had.

The fifth and final unwritten rule of federal behavior is to *maintain a stable and well-circumscribed constituency*. With so great a concern for survival in the government, it is necessary to have friends outside of it. One's equity within an agency and a program's equity in Congress are a function of equity with vested interests outside. The most visible and articulate vestedness is best to cultivate. Every agency and every department knows this, as does every successful executive. The constituency not only represents survival credits but has the quality of a significant reference group. The values, purposes and rewards of the federal agent must mesh with those of his program's constituents.

It is easy to see how this works between the Defense Department and the military-industrial complex; between Agriculture and the large, industrialized farming interests; between Labor and the unions; between Commerce and big business. It is obvious that the regulatory commissions of government have a friendly, symbiotic relationship with the organizations they were meant to monitor. It is less clear, however, that the good guys in government, the liberals who run the "social programs," have their exclusive constituents as well. The constituents of welfare programs are not welfare recipients, but social workers. The constituents of educational programs are not students, but educators. The constituents of health programs are the providers of health care, not their consumers. The mental health programs of the government are sensitive to the perturbations of mental health professionals and social scientists, not so much to the walking wounded.

In the latter case, for example, to suggest that nonprofessionals should have something to say about the expenditure of millions of research, training and service dollars is to threaten a constituency. And a threatened one is an unfriendly one, which is not good for the program in Congress or for the job possibilities of the executive in the marketplace. As long as the constituency is stable and circumscribed, credits can be counted.

These, then, are the rules of behavior for functionaries in the federal bureaucracy. If they sound familiar, they should. They are not by any means unique to this system. With minor alterations, they serve as the uncodified code of conduct in any organization. They are what sustained every archbureaucrat from Pilate to Eichmann. They explain in large part why the United States government is such a swollen beast, incapable of responding to the unmet needs of so many people.

But only in part. One other feature of the Washington scene must be described before we can say we know enough of it to elaborate a strategy of assault. This has to do with power.

There is a lot of nonsense about power in the government. One sees a black Chrysler with a vinyl top speeding by. A liveried chauffeur, determined and grim, operates the vehicle. In the rear, a gooseneck, high-intensity lamp arched over his shoulder, sits a man studying the *Washington Post*. One is tempted to say, "There goes a man of power."

It is a vain temptation. Power in the government does not reside within gray eminences in black Chryslers. It is a soft, pluralistic business shared by a large number of middle managers. Organizational charts in federal agencies read as if there is a rigid line of authority and control from the top down. It would appear that the secretary of each department with his designated assistants and deputies would control the behavior of the entire establishment. In fact, there is a huge permanent government that watches with covert bemusement as the political appointees at the top come and go, attempting in their turn to control the behavior of the agencies "responsible to them."

This does not mean that there is not a good deal of respect and deference paid by middle managers to their superiors. But, as in many organizations, this deference can have an empty and superficial quality to it that amounts to mockery. In most hospitals, for example, it is not the doctors who determine what happens to patients, but nurses. Nurses may appear as subordinate to physicians as slaves to their masters, but as soon as the doctor has left the ward the nurse does what she wants to do anyway.

Similarly, in federal agencies, it is the great army of middlemanagers that controls the show. There is not even the built-in accountability of a dead patient for the boss to see.

Power in the government resides less in position and funds than it does in information, which is the medium of exchange. The flow of information is controlled not at the top, but at the middle. There is very little horizontal flow between agencies because of the constant competition for funds, and all vertical flow must be mediated by the GS 14 to GS 17 bureaucrats who make up the permanent government.

This concentration of power in the middle, controlled by masses of managers who subscribe to the unwritten code of behavior described above, is the reason why the national government is essentially unresponsive. It does not respond to the top or the bottom; it does not respond to ideology. It is a great, indestructible mollusk that absorbs kicks and taunts and seductions and does nothing but grow.

But it's worse than that. The government is righteous. The people who man the bastions of the executive branch (like the rest of us) have the capacity to invest their jobs with their personal identities. Because it is theirs, their function must be defended. Their roles become, in the language of psychiatry, ego-syntonic. Their sense of personal integrity, their consciences, their self-esteem begin to grow into the positions they hold. It is as if their very identities partake of the same definition as their organizationally defined function.

Can you imagine trying to fight a revolution against a huge, righteous marshmallow? Even if you had enough troops not to be suffocated by it, the best you can hope for is to eat it. And, as you all know, you become what you eat. And that is the point. For a revolution to be meaningful it must take into account the nature of organizational life. It must assume that the ideologically pure and the ideologically impure are subject to the same Eichmannesque forces. If a revolution harbors the illusion that a reign of terror will purify a bureaucracy of scoundrels and exploiters, it will fail. It matters little whether bureaucrats are Royalist or Republican, Czarist or Bolshevik, Conservative or Liberal, or what have you. It is the built-in forces of life in a bureaucracy that result in the bureaucracy being so indifferent to suffering and aspiration.

Does this mean that radical change is not possible? No. It means that intelligence and planning must be used, as well as rhetoric, songs, threats, uniforms and all the other trappings of a "movement." The intelligence and planning might orient themselves around a concept of nonalienated revolution that relies on a strategy of guerrilla administration.

This is not meant to be an exclusive strategy. Social change, radical and otherwise, has to be a pluralistic phenomenon. It needs to allow for foxes as well as hedgehogs. This represents one attempt, then, to approach the Great White Marshmallow in such a way that victories are neither impossible nor terrible.

Assuming that power in the federal government is controlled by a vast cadre of middle managers who are essentially homeostatic, and assuming the softness and purposelessness of the system in which they operate, it is conceivable that a critical mass of change agents working within that system may be effective in achieving increasingly significant ad hoc successes.

This requires a group of people who are prepared to work as civil servants but who have little or no concern with the five unwritten rules of behavior of such service. Specifically, their investment in their own jobs carries a very limited liability. The ultimate sanction, being fired, is no sanction at all. Either because they command credentials which will afford them the security they need wherever they work or because they emerge from a generation that has not been tainted by the depression and so have fewer security needs, they are not afraid of being fired.

While they may like the boss, and one may hope they do, they do not see themselves as primarily concerned with saving him from embarrassment.

Spending the program money by the end of the fiscal year and the related rule—keeping the program alive—are significant to them only insofar as the program's purposes mesh with their social consciences, and then only insofar as the program is demonstrating some fealty to those purposes.

Most important, however, is that this critical mass of change agents *not* abide by the rule of maintaining a stable and circumscribed constituency. This is at the same time a liberating principle of behavior and a major strategy of change. It is precisely by broadening the base of the constituencies of federal programs that they will become more responsible to the needs of more people.

This network of communication and collaboration shares as its purpose the frustration of the bureaucracy. But it is the homeostatic, self-serving and elitist aspects of bureaucratic life that are to be frustrated. And this can only be accomplished through the creative tension that emerges from a constant appreciation of unmet needs.

The network of change agents represents a built-in amplifier of those needs either because the agents are, themselves, among the poor, the colored and the young or because they are advocates of them.

It is not critical that the guerrilla administrators who compromise this network be in a position to command funds or program directions. They must simply have access to information, which, you recall, is the medium of exchange in government.

This network, in order to avoid the same traps as the bureaucracy it is meant to frustrate, should never become solidified or rigidified in structure and function. It may have the form of a floating crap game whose location and participation are fluid and changing, but whose purposes and activities are constant. The contacts should remain informal, nonhierarchical and task-oriented. The tasks chosen should be finite, specific, salient and feasible. The makeup of each task force is an ad hoc, self-selected clustering of individuals whose skills or location or access to information suggests their roles. This network of change agents becomes a reference group, but not a brotherhood. There need not be a preoccupation with loyalty, cordiality or steadfastness. They do not even have to be friendly.

This is a rather dry and unromantic strategy of social change. It does not stir one's heart or glands. Where is the image of Parnell pulling his cap low on his forehead as he points his gallant band to the General Post Office? Or Lenin approaching the borders of a trembling Russia in a sealed train? Or Fidel or Che? Or Spartacus, or Mao? Where are the clasped hands and the eyes squinting into a distant line of troops? Where are the songs, the flags, the legends? Where is the courage? Where is the glory?

Such a revolutionary force has nothing of the triumphal arch in it. Nor has it anything of the gallows. It lives without the hope of victory or the fear of defeat. It will yearn for saints and despair of scoundrels, but it will see as its eternal mission the subversion of those systems that force both saints and scoundrels into a common, faceless repression of the human spirit.

11.2

Backstabbing, Inc.

PETER CHEW

"In our company it's not who you know but what you've got on who you know that counts." Thus a mid-level executive for a major corporation reflects his distaste for a phenomenon that management experts say is increasing in recession-threatened U.S. business: "office politics." Surveys indicate that impatience with organizational politics is part of a larger dissatisfaction with life in the American corporation these days.

A Research Institute of America study says: "Today, when business can least afford a dissipation of effort, 'office politics' is on the rise within many companies. As a menace to individuals and organizations alike, it deserves more concentrated study than anyone has given it. The price of office politics is tremendous, both to management and the individual. That it has been encouraged by our present business structure of group management may be conceded. . . ."

Princeton University historian Richard Huber believes the words "contacts" and "know who" have all but replaced "merit" and "know how" among those scrambling on the corporate ladder.

Auren Uris, author of 20 books on business management, says: "There is indeed a corporate tradition in which not the deserving but the faithful win the spoils. This is the seamy side of business, where justice doesn't always triumph, but power always does."

The Life Extension Institute, which provides health services to U.S. industry, says the principal cause of tension among business executives is personality conflict associated with office politics and competition.

Dale Tarnowieski, who conducted a recent American Management Association survey of changing executive attitudes toward traditional concepts of "success," says, "Frustration and dissidence in supervisory and middle management in particu-

From *The National Observer*, January 26, 1974. Reprinted with permission from The National Observer, Copyright Dow Jones & Company, Inc. 1974.

lar are being traced more and more frequently to the effects of 'politics' at the policy-making level of the organization."

Among Tarnowieski's findings in a survey of nearly 3,000 U.S. businessmen—the largest survey in American Management's history—were these:

"Fifty-two per cent of all respondents—including 58 per cent of all middle managers, 69 per cent of all supervisory-level managers, and 71 per cent of all technical employes in managerial positions—believe that advancement and promotion . . . are most often based on 'a largely subjective and arbitrary decision on the part of corporate superiors in the position to decide who gets promoted and who doesn't.'

"Eighty-eight per cent of all respondents say that 'a dynamic personality and the ability to sell yourself and your ideas' is more of an attribute to the manager on the move today than is 'a reputation for honesty, or firm adherence to principles.'

"Eighty-two per cent of all respondents believe that 'pleasing the boss' is the critical factor in determining 'promotability' in today's organizational environment."

On the broader question of life in the executive suite, only about one-half of those responding "believe that the organizations for which they currently work provide them, or are likely ever to provide them, adequate opportunities to realize their job- and career-related goals." Finally, says Tarnowieski, "An alarming 40 per cent of all surveyed middle managers and 52 per cent of the reporting supervisory managers say they find their work, at best, unsatisfying."

Psychoanalyst Franz Alexander has written: "The analyst sees his patients—physicians, lawyers, engineers, bankers, advertising men—engaged in a marathon race, their eager faces distorted by strain, their eyes focused not upon their goal but upon each other with a mixture of hate, envy, and admiration. They would like to stop but dare not."

Roger M. D'Aprix, a Xerox Corp. executive and author of a penetrating work entitled *Struggle for Identity: The Silent Revolution Against Corporate Conformity*, says:

"The idealized goal has always been made clear to the individual: He is supposed to scale his pyramid to the limits of his energy and talent. But in actuality, the game has never been that simple because, as with other human relationships, there are undefined boundaries and subtleties which the individual must discover for himself. Talent and performance are usually essential, but in themselves they are not always adequate. Sadly for those who throw themselves unreservedly into the race to the top and who measure their self-esteem only according to its outcome, the results can be devastating."

Schools Ignore the Subject

D'Aprix and other students of the organization man agree that office politics is a fact of life, and that it's sometimes more dangerous to stay totally aloof from the fray than it is to get into the front lines. "To ignore the existence of company politics, when others in an organization are dedicating much of their time to it, can be as impractical as assuming that the right-of-way is always an assurance of safety in traffic," says the Research Institute of America study, *Coping With Office Politics*.

Yet office politics is a subject all but ignored in the nation's great business schools. Alan N. Schoonmaker, a prominent executive counselor and faculty member at Carnegie-Mellon University in Pittsburgh, marvels that candidates for advanced degrees are taught "the principles of marketing, finance, corporate planning, communication, and supervision," while such a critical subject as organization politics is treated as though it didn't exist.

Most professors of management, says Schoonmaker in a recent issue of the publication MBA, "have assumed that the only way to succeed is to do one's job well, that virtue is always rewarded, and sin is always punished. But the most casual examination of organizations should convince you that job performance and career advancement are not perfectly correlated. Some men do advance on merit, but others do not. Some men do their jobs superbly but do not get ahead, while others contribute little but are highly rewarded."

An Unavoidable Factor

Schoonmaker says "company politics" should be considered in its more general sense as "distribution of power." In this sense, then, "it becomes obvious that politics is unavoidable. Since power exists in every group or organization, politics must necessarily exist in every firm. You can therefore get away from politics only by becoming a hermit. As long as you live and work in groups and in organizations, politics will influence your career—whether you like it or not."

Auren Uris says there are two basic factors that give rise to such politics: genuine policy disagreements, and the career ambitions of higher executives.

"Let's say your company is producing chemical sprays that are destructive to the environment. One group within the company wants to modify production, or drop some of the lines, even if it costs the company money. The other group says: 'Well, the hell with it. We're in business to show a profit for ourselves, and for our stockholders. This ecology business is a lot of crap.' And so a power play begins within the company. People choose sides."

An individual might line up behind Executive A because he genuinely likes A's policy and thinks A will be the best man, says Uris. "Or it may be on a more acquisitive basis: 'He's the guy who can do the most for me.' Or, 'He always liked me, and he's the guy who, if appointed president, will see that I become a division manager or whatever, whereas Executive B doesn't like me and, if he gets in, I'm finished.'"

'Negative Reward'

In this little game, says Uris, one's *immediate* boss is critically important. You can agree with the course of action that he intends to take, and say, "I'm with you 100 per cent in this, boss." Or you can disagree with him—"in which case you better damn well keep it a secret, because you're susceptible to 'negative reward,' as we Skinnerians say."

The man who chooses incorrectly often faces unpleasant consequences: He's forced out of the company, fired outright, or eased into a dead-end job.

"In some situations, the man who refuses to play politics gets a kind of respect from both sides. It doesn't adversely affect his situation. He is the kind of man who knows his own ability and is confident of his worth to his company. He doesn't have to get himself involved in this political game to reinforce or secure his position. No matter who ends up on top in the power struggle, his situation remains secure because of what he has on the ball." The neutralist of course should not expect plums from the eventual winner, Uris adds.

In uncertain times such as these, politicking invariably increases markedly, says Uris. "Not to be liked by a key man has immediate and very serious implications for a guy's future in the company, and his peace of mind. This is borne out by the fact that whenever there are recessions, it's the middle managers who are always bounced out of an organization."

A Serious Message

In recent months several clever satirical books on office politics have been published, including Uris' *How to Win Your Boss's Love, Approval—and Job,* written in collaboration with Jack Tarrant; *The Radovic Rule: How to Manage the Boss,* by Igor Radovic; and *Bravely, Bravely in Business: 32 Ground Rules for Personal Survival and Success in Your Job—Any Job,* by Richard R. Connaroe.

While humorous, the message of all these books is serious: Before you can come to terms with corporate life, or life in any big organization such as the Government, a university, armed service, or whatever, you must become a serious student of office politics.

Suggests Uris: "In every company there's an 'informal organization' on the upper levels with power centers that are often at variance with what the company organization chart suggests. Try to figure out what's going on inside this informal organization. Who are the big guns? Who are the little guns? Who's opposed to whom? Who's on top now? Who may be on top tomorrow?

"Consider your own personal interests. Do you want to get in the game or don't you? If so, where do you pack clout? Or is any move you make likely to result in doubtful gains?

"Remember that your immediate boss is the key to your own role. Obviously his situation has implications for what you can or can't do.

"Finally, take heart. Office politics are never forever. There's always change at the top—new turns in the wheel—developed by political activity."

Robert N. McMurry, who heads the McMurry Co., Chicago-based management psychologists, is a man of extraordinary bluntness who attributes office politics to the type of people who, he feels, are drawn to corporations—especially big corporations—to begin with.

"People don't like to hear this sort of thing, but I'd say 75 per cent of corporation employes, including a lot of presidents and vice presidents, are very anxious, fearful people by nature, fundamentally insecure. Much of the internal conflict that takes place grows out of people's reactions to what they perceive as threats to their security.

"Many of the longest-service employes are the most frustrated, the most hostile. Many stay with one company not out of loyalty but because they lack the courage to quit and try something new. One of the biggest problems is the incapacity of many executives to tolerate strong subordinates. I can't tell you the number of companies I've seen composed of cringing wretches."

McMurry draws a depressing stereotype of a middle-range executive in today's corporation—"55 and frightened":

"Let's say I've gotten where I am because of seniority. I've kept my nose clean. I haven't antagonized anybody. I'm 100 per cent conformist. I've not thought any dangerous thoughts. Nor have I gone in for innovation—innovations have a way of going sour. So, at age 55, I'm vice president in charge of something or other.

How Bosses Handle 'Comers'

"I'm not really on top of my job any more; things have accelerated so, the job is running me. About all I can hope for is that no one will discover how basically incompetent I am.

"I'm assigned an assistant. He's a real young ball of fire, a real barn burner. He immediately becomes a threat to me. Now, 90 per cent of the jobs in industry are of such a nature that there's no objective measure of competence. My evaluation is the only criterion my superiors can go on. How do I cope?

"I can damn him with faint praise, see that he gets no promotions, and that he does get unpleasant assignments. I can make it obvious that he doesn't have a future. So he leaves. I am much happier with people who are not as good as me, who are docile, submissive, conformist."

Roger D'Aprix takes a less gloomy—though no less realistic—view.

"The dilemma for the individual is this: How does he make his peace within an organization? I believe you can be your own man—and for the sake of your sanity, you must.

"If my analysis is correct, then the individual is in a very tough psychological and philosophical bind in most companies. Specifically, he must answer the terribly difficult question of who he is and what he wants. And, further, he must relate that to a company abstraction difficult to define or understand. Then he must construct some sort of loyalty to people in power, people he rarely knows firsthand, people whose motives he can only guess at. And having done all this, he must be prepared to face an unrequited love affair because abstractions can't love back, and because people in power usually have other problems to deal with."

Study Questions

1. Summarize the functions of the federal bureaucracy. Would you classify the bureaucracy as constituting our fourth branch of government? Why or why not?

2. Based upon your reading of this chapter and your general knowledge, would you say that the bureaucracy is in accord with our democratic form of government? Why or why not?

3. It has been asserted that particular bureaus, congressional committees, and interest groups can, if they are in accord, determine public policy in their respective areas, impervious to outside pressures. Are there any advantages in such an arrangement? What are its disadvantages?

4. Much of the bureaucracy in the executive departments, as well as the various independent regulatory commissions, is more or less beyond the direct control of the President and other high executive branch decision-makers. What are the advantages and disadvantages inherent in this situation?

5. Most federal bureaucrats are covered by the Civil Service Act. Has this been a satisfactory mode of selecting employees for the federal bureaucracy? Would our system of government be better off if more bureaucratic jobs were removed from civil service and made appointable by the President and/or members of the Cabinet?

6. What are three basic characteristics of bureaucracies, as set forth in this chapter? What are the advantages and disadvantages of each of these three main characteristics in terms of their impact on the functioning of government?

7. Discuss the impact of informal subgroups and subsystems on the operations of the bureaucracy.

Bibliography

Books

Berkley, George E. *The Administrative Revolution: Notes on the Passing of Organization Man.* Englewood Cliffs, N.J.: Prentice-Hall, Inc., 1971.

Blau, Peter M. *The Dynamics of Bureaucracy,* rev. ed. Chicago: The University of Chicago Press, 1966.

Cohen, Harry. *The Demonics of Bureaucracy: Problems of Change in a Government Agency.* Ames, Iowa: The Iowa State University Press, 1965.

Downs, Anthony. *Inside Bureaucracy.* Boston: Little, Brown and Company, 1967.

Gawthrop, Louis C. *Bureaucratic Behavior in the Executive Branch.* New York: The Free Press, 1969.

Merton, Robert K., Gray, Alisa P., Hockey, Barbara, and Selvin, Hanan C., eds. *Reader in Bureaucracy.* New York: The Free Press, 1952.

Millett, John D. *Organization for the Public Service.* Princeton, N.J.: D. Van Nostrand Company, Inc., 1966.

Mosher, Frederick C., ed. *Governmental Reorganization: Cases and Commentary.* Syracuse, New York: The Inter-University Case Program, Inc., 1967.

Rourke, Francis E., ed. *Bureaucratic Power in National Politics*, 2d ed. Boston: Little, Brown and Company, 1972.

Articles

Fainstein, Norman I., and Fainstein, Susan S. "Innovation in Urban Bureaucracies." *American Behavioral Scientist*, Vol. 15, No. 4 (March/April, 1972), pp. 511-530.

"Federal Agencies Under Fire." *U.S. News and World Report*, November 9, 1970.

Meyer, Marshall W. "Expertness and the Span of Control." *American Sociological Review*, Vol. 33, No. 6 (December, 1968), pp. 944-951.

CHAPTER 12
Political Parties — Power to the Bosses

George Washington denounced political parties as "potent engines by which cunning, ambitious, and unprincipled men will be enabled to subvert the power of the people." Yet in a short number of years, political parties emerged and became a major ingredient in the U.S. political system. Political parties are generally in continuous competition in a democratic political system, attempting to acquire enough power vis-à-vis each other to gain control over the government. In authoritarian systems, on the other hand, political parties not only control government and destroy competing parties, but become a primary instrument of control over the people. Indeed, in modern times virtually all political systems are studied in terms of the role of political parties.

The Role of Political Parties

There are many types of parties, reflecting political attitudes from the extreme left through the extreme right. For parties to be even minimally successful they must in some way reflect attitudes within the social system. Our first point then is that a political party is an organized group of people who share certain values and a desire to control or influence public policy. Or, as a well known political scientist has written,

> Political parties constitute a basic element of democratic institutional apparatus. They perform an essential function in the management of succession to power, as well as in the process of obtaining popular consent to the course of public policy. They amass sufficient support to

buttress the authority of governments; or, on the contrary, they attract or organize discontent and dissatisfaction sufficient to oust the government.[1]

The primary purpose of political parties is to gain sufficient power to control government. In democratic societies this is done primarily through winning elections. In simple terms, it is a group that wants power to run the government; in order to do this it must have organization, leadership, resources, and programs.

There are a number of other roles that the political party performs that are valuable to the functioning of the political system. It provides a link between the masses of people and the government, beyond that provided by the representative assemblies. Similarly, it provides a link between decision-makers and their constituents. It provides a structural system for political actors with common attitudes to develop a base of power to win elections and influence government. It provides an organization for recruiting people to run as candidates. Political parties also shape public opinion and suggest alternative policies. They either govern or provide opposition to those governing.

Parties and Power

The power of political parties stems from four fundamental factors: leadership, organization, resources, and programs (political philosophy). Obviously, these factors are interrelated and the weakness of the party in any one of these areas has an impact on the ability of the party in other areas. The ideal, of course, is to be strong enough in all areas to win sufficient votes to acquire power in major national institutions. Let us examine each of these factors briefly.

Party Leadership

Party leadership can be divided usefully into two major categories: the flag bearers and the cadre. The flag bearers are those party leaders who provide the visible links between the party, its followers and other political actors. These are the people who publicly defend the party program and provide criticism of other parties or of government policy. They are the party's image-makers. Ideally, they are good party regulars who do not lean to any extreme political philosophy, at least in the public perception. Additionally, they should have experience and exposure in public office, an attractive personality, and intelligence. They should be able to give forceful direction to the party, and attract others to it.

The party cadre is the nucleus of professional party organizers. These people are rarely in the public eye; nor do they generally run for public office. They perform most of the major administrative and organizational chores upon which party success rests. In the broadest sense, the cadre includes those officers from the very lowest level, such as precinct captains and party committeemen, to the very highest, the chairman of the national party. In more cases than not, party success in any particular election rests on the competence of the party cadre. At the very least, such people are expected to be loyal to the party, to commit themselves to its programs, and to have administrative and organizational experience. Any successful political party normally has a balance between the ability of the flag bearers and the cadre. It is the harmonious working of these two elements that provides the basis for successful party operations.

Party Organization

When we speak of political party organization we obviously include some of the things already referred to under party leadership. Party organization must at a minimum provide channels by which the lowest element of the party can develop meaningful links with the major decision-makers both at state and national levels. The organization must be so structured as to allow maximum diversity at the local levels while fostering maximum unity at both state and national levels. Some accommodation must be made between these two apparently diverse threads if there is going to be party success. In any case, the major concern of the organization is to operate more efficiently than other party organizations. As we will discuss later, a highly structured, rigid, efficient party organization is unlikely in a democratic society. In democratic systems, political party organization must be highly pluralistic and open in order to succeed; hence the organizations tend to reflect a more or less anarchic and unstructured system. Nevertheless, party organization requires at the minimum a structure around which the party can systematically recruit people for campaigns, provide party literature, attract resources, and allocate to loyalists resources that are gained from party victories.

Party Resources

Party resources include financial support, access to manpower, access to jobs (patronage), and combinations of these. As we all know, it takes large amounts of money to run campaigns even at the local level. Money is needed to sponsor rallies, print and distribute literature, buy television and radio time, and for a multitude of other activities. The more important the office, the more money is likely to be required. It has been estimated that to nominate and elect all federal, state, and local officials it cost $175 million in 1960, $200 million in 1964, $300 million in 1968, and $400 million in 1972. The expenditure in television and radio broadcasting alone runs into the millions as illustrated by the following chart:

Expenditures for Political Broadcasts for Elections in Radio and Television in Millions of Dollars:

General Elections

	1960	1964	1966	1968	1970	1972
Total	14	25	20	40	33	65

Note: The years 1966 and 1970 were off-year i.e., non-presidential elections. Adapted from the *Statistical Abstract of the United States, 1972*.

Party resources also include the amount and quality of manpower available to do all of the mundane tasks in running a successful party organization. People are needed to mail announcements, ring doorbells, staff party headquarters, answer telephones, and provide the core of visible party support. During major elections the ability of the party to expand its manpower resources is most important. The party's access to jobs, particularly those associated with government, is an important element of resources. To put it in other terms, political patronage still plays an important role in enriching party resources. Used to reward party loyalists as well as to entice others, patronage can be a powerful instrument not only in entrenching the party's power but in diminishing the opposition's. For example, it has been estimated that the Democratic party in Chicago, in any given election, with minimum effort can turn out 250,000 votes simply by its patronage hold over jobs and those affected by city hall jobs. This is not an unimportant consideration particularly in elections at the local level.[2]

Party Program

It seems evident that political parties whose programs and political pronouncements are generally in the center of political philosophy are more likely to win elections. The 1964 and 1972 elections demonstrated that any party that adopts a stance that is perceived as either left or right of so-called mainstream politics will not win elections. In 1964, Senator Barry Goldwater, who was perceived by many Americans as projecting the extreme right-of-center view, was soundly defeated by Lyndon B. Johnson. In 1972, Senator George McGovern, running on a Democratic party platform that was perceived to be an extreme left-of-center view, was soundly defeated by the incumbent Richard Nixon. It would generally seem that parties, whether they be at the local, state or national level, fare best when they adopt programs which do not appear too revolutionary in either direction. Philosophically speaking, for parties to be successful they must not get too far ahead of, or too far behind, the general values of society.

Summary—Party Power

In sum, the power of the political party stems primarily from the ability of its flag bearers and cadre to develop and operate an organization with sufficient financial backing and power and influence, while pursuing a policy that can attract competent people as candidates. Moreover, all of these elements must be harmoniously combined to develop enough election support to win major political offices. Once in power, resources must be allocated, with respect to both money and position, to entrench the party and maintain its hold on its constituency to insure election success. At the same time, the party in power must resolve conflicts and develop policy in accordance with perspectives that remain imbedded in the mainstream political philosophy. No political party can do all of these things with complete success at all times. Opposition parties attempt to develop their power structure in order to depose the party in power; they are also quick to take advantage of governmental mistakes and embarrassments to diminish the image of the party in power. This continual interplay and conflict between those in power and those out of power provide the essence of party politics in our society. It is perhaps a basic feature of the American party system that no party has been able to remain in power indefinitely. Indeed this may well be the salvation of the party system in the United States. The concept of one party in power and one opposing has become imbedded in our democratic philosophy, and hence most Americans tend to accept the idea that a two-party system is the basis for democracy.

Because of the need to appeal to a great mass of voters, the two main parties have been accused of being almost identical in goals and ambitions. As Clinton Rossiter put it,

> In some important respects there is and can be no real difference between the Democrats and the Republicans, because the unwritten

laws of American politics demand that the parties overlap substantially in principle, policy, character, appeal, and purpose—or cease to be parties with any hope of winning a national election.[3]

Development of the Party System

Although the framers of the Constitution provided for the regular election of the President and Congress, nothing was mentioned about political parties. The reason was simple: they did not exist. Washington was chosen by acclaim and the members of the first Congress managed their own campaigns without the aid of party affiliations. It was only later that the members began to coalesce around the personalities and viewpoints of Alexander Hamilton and Thomas Jefferson, and the evolution of political parties began.

First Party System—
Federalists and Republicans

Alexander Hamilton, Washington's Secretary of the Treasury, organized the Federalists, the first national political party in the United States. The Federalists were proponents of a strong central government; they represented the shipping and building interests as well as the banking and commercial classes. Thomas Jefferson's supporters were known as Republicans or Democratic-Republicans. They were primarily small farmers, debtors, Southern planters, and frontiersmen. To broaden his base Jefferson struck an alliance with Aaron Burr and his political organization, which dominated New York City. In the partnership of rural America and the cities the original Democratic-Republican party was formed. The base of power for the modern Democrats has remained essentially the same.

Second Party System—
The Republican Party

When Jefferson was elected President in 1800, the Federalists began their long slide toward oblivion. By the end of the second decade of the 1800s the Federalist party virtually died, leaving the Republicans in control of almost a one-party government, ushering in a second party system. This period has been mistakenly called the era of good feelings because of the seeming absence of competitive party politics. However, there were significant struggles within the Republican party, sectional and ideological squabbles as well as serious conflicts over who would succeed President Monroe as the head of the party. In 1824, John Quincy Adams won the presidency, not on the basis of popular vote, but by election in the House of Representatives. He and Henry Clay had formed a coalition of their factions within the Republican party, and their supporters in the House voted for Adams. The President-elect immediately appointed Clay as Secretary of State. This was, however, the last gasp of the Republican party. In 1828, Andrew Jackson was elected President of the United States as a member of the Democratic party.

Third Party System— The Jacksonian Era—Democrats and Whigs

The Jacksonian era saw the development of a third party system which ran generally until the beginning of the Civil War. By the time of Jackson's election in 1828, there were thirty states and a broad male suffrage. The delegate convention, equivalent to our national party conventions, had become the most common method of nominating presidential candidates. Additionally, presidential electors were now elected by direct popular vote in most states. It became apparent that party organization and party roots had to be developed at local levels to win elections. Party structure was transformed from a primarily elite type leadership to one resting on popularly based leaders and popularly based politics—both epitomized by Andrew Jackson. The Jacksonian era ushered in the first populist politics and adminstration, and shifted the base of some of the political power to lower levels and grass roots organizations.

The shift in the political base, the inability of the Federalist party to broaden its base, and the divisions within the Republic party all set the stage for party reorganization and Jacksonian style politics. The original parties in our country sought power in the elite and wealthy classes; the Jacksonians represented the growing agrarian and urban base in American politics. During the Jacksonian era the party structure generally began at the grass roots level and consisted of a coalition of local and state leaders.

The Jacksonians, consisting primarily of anti-Adams Republicans, formed the Democratic party during the election campaign of 1828. In 1834, anti-Jackson factions formed the Whig party. The Federalist and Republican parties had disappeared. The Democratic and Whig parties were primarily pragmatic in approach, that is, non-ideological. Basically, they were decentralized parties, consisting of coalitions of local interests. The power had clearly shifted from the highest levels of government to local political leaders.

Fourth Party System— Democrats and Republicans

Because of the issue of slavery and the economic conflicts between North and South, the Whig/Democratic party system gave way to a fourth type of system around the 1860s. There reemerged a Jeffersonian type of political view contrasted to those of the commercial and economic interests of the North and Northeast. Due to emotionalism over the slavery issue, the fragile coalitions within the Democratic and Whig parties finally broke up. The bitter struggles that evolved destroyed the spirit of compromise and led to a restructuring of the party system with a focus on regional interests rather than broad national coalitions.

The Republican party emerged in 1856 as a new party with Jefferson as its symbol. The party platform rested on a slave-free society and free land in the West; it generally appealed to laborers and the common man in the North and West. At the same time, the reconstituted Democratic party now included some of the old Whig party stalwarts as well as Democratic loyalists; also its platform rested partly on the Jeffersonian approach, stressing agricultural interests primarily rooted in the South. Hence, the Democratic party developed a strong appeal in the Southern slave states, while the Republican party had a strong appeal to the more urbanized northern and industrial economy. This party structure and general philosophy continued on into 1970 with, however, some important realignments and readjustments over the years.

Following the Civil War, for example, the United States went through what has been called an economic revolution. Great centers of financial power and wealth developed in the Northeast and Midwest. There was a tremendous upsurge in population as immigrants from Europe flooded into the country. It was the Republican party that came increasingly to reflect the financial power and wealth of the more conservative and moneyed interests. At the same time the Democratic party stressed the appeal to the common man. It had greater receptivity among the masses of immigrants and lower class people residing in the urban areas, while still maintaining a solid base in the South and mid-Atlantic states—a heritage of the Civil War.

The impact of the depression of the 1930s restructured the party system along the lines as we generally know them today. The urban industrial workers aligned themselves with the Southerners in the Democratic party as a reaction against industrialists and financial interests which had control of the Republican party. By 1932, the Republican party was associated with big business interests and conservative coalitions in the Midwest and West, losing its hold on most large urban areas.

Fifth Party System?

After the 1968 presidential elections, there was some indication that a fifth type of party system might emerge, based on populist politics and a shift in composition of the two major parties. Moreover, the concept of the solid South perpetually supporting the conservative wing of the Democratic party appeared to be eroding as major Southern cities became more like large urban areas of the North. Also, civil rights groups had left a heritage of participatory democracy, providing examples for ethnic minorities and other group action-oriented politics. It appeared that the 1970s would bring with it a new style of politics that did not depend on the worn-out rhetoric of the Democratic or Republican parties. The Watergate affair and the resignations of Vice President Agnew and President Nixon, combined with grave economic problems, seemed to portend new political alignments. It appeared that by the mid-1970s, the old guard in both parties would fade away and a new politics with new faces would emerge.

Yet, as the results of the congressional elections of 1974 became clear, little seemed changed in the nature of party politics. What emerged was a victory for Democratic party incumbents and a defeat for many Republican incumbents. A fifth type of party system would have to wait for another time.

The 1974 Elections: Politics as Usual?

The 1974 congressional elections appeared to restore the Democratic party coalition among workers, professional people, and various regions in the country—a coalition that had brought victory in the past. It was difficult, however, to develop a national pattern from the election results, other than broad issues such as Watergate and the economy; many of the local races were based on local issues and personalities. Nevertheless, the Democratic party gained an impressive, if not extraordinary, victory in 1974. Whereas in previous off-year elections, about twenty or twenty-five House seats would be lost by the presidential party, in 1974 the Republicans lost forty. Similarly, the

Democrats won twenty-seven of the thirty-five gubernatorial races. Yet most observers were cautious in claiming permanent shifts in voting strength for the Democratic party; they felt that the vote was a negative vote against the Republicans and not necessarily a positive one for the Democrats.

In any case, the Democratic party gained access to many governorships and won large majorities in both houses of Congress. Based on this political power, much could be accomplished over the next two years to entrench Democratic incumbents. On the other hand, the Republican party was faced with a major reorganization task, not only at the national level, but also in the state and local political arenas. For both Republicans and Democrats, the real struggles would be between the various wings of their own parties, rather than with the opposition party. Liberal and moderate Democrats appeared ready to challenge the conservative Democrats for control of many congressional committees and of the party itself. Due to the fact that many liberal Republicans were able to maintain their seats, the Republican party began to rethink its strategy for 1976. For example, liberal Republican Senator Jacob Javits was reelected in New York, even though that state voted overwhelmingly for the Democratic gubernatorial candidate. However, there was no clear pattern for either party.

For both Republicans and Democrats, the reaction of the American people appeared to be primarily pragmatic and not necessarily based on any ideology or party orientation. The voters reacted to the issue of Watergate, the economy, and mismanagement in government. It appeared that many felt the Democratic party was the lesser of two evils —hardly a base to develop a strong party front for 1976. Regardless of the voting patterns, little seemed to change for either major party. There appeared to be much demand for party reform, but party tradition, procedures, and bases of power resisted major change after the 1974 elections.

As Senator Eugene McCarthy viewed the parties, "neither major party is what it ought to be and Americans might ease their misery if they put them both out of business. But thanks to tradition and the new campaign finance law, the elephant and the jackass are probably with us forever."[4] Several days after the November election, a political journalist wrote:

> So in the next few days, there will be a lot of voices raised in the name of national party reform. This does not mean there will be any reform or that either Democrats or Republicans will finally be able to tell you what they stand for. What it does mean is that both parties will make a lot of noise trying to convince the disinterested that they will be doing things differently in the future, and that indeed, they do stand for something.[5]

Two-Party System and the Third Party

Throughout the history of party development in the United States, one can identify the two-party phenomenon. Certainly there have been third parties, but in the main, to capture national office there is a need to get beyond the sectional interests or parochial issues generally represented by third parties.

> A salient characteristic of the American party system is its dual form. During most of our history power has alternated between two major parties. Although minor parties have arisen from time to time and exerted influence on governmental policy, the two major parties have been the only serious contenders for the Presidency.[6]

Nevertheless, third parties have played important roles not only in the development of our own political party system, but in publicizing important issues. For example, a number of policies that the Socialist party of Norman Thomas advocated in the 1930s were generally absorbed by the Democratic party and later by the Republican party as legitimate policies. The Socialist party provided a catalyst for a number of welfare issues that are now part and parcel of our major party programs, including Social Security.

Characteristics of Political Parties

As we have suggested, the modern U.S. party system has its roots in the competition between the Hamiltonians and Jeffersonians. In looking back over the history of our political party systems, as well as the current situation, we find a number of important characteristics. The first, as we have stressed, is the concept of the two-party system. Throughout most of our history, organizations have focused on two candidates in two general party structures. As Rossiter notes:

> Out of the conflict of Democrats and Whigs emerged the American political system—complete with such features as two major parties, a sprinkle of third parties, national nominating conventions, state and local bosses, patronage, popular campaigning, and the Presidency as the focus of politics.[7]

A decentralized party structure which emerged from the Jacksonian era is another major characteristic of our modern party system. Each political party has a large number of power centers; no one of these centers controls a majority of members. Indeed the very substance of the party rests at state and local levels. The parties at a national level are in essence confederations of state and local parties.

This leads to another major characteristic of our party system—lack of discipline and low cohesion. Since many of the party leaders have their own political power base resting on a local or state constituency, it is difficult for a national party to discipline those members who oppose the national leadership. Indeed the success of the national party rests primarily on the willingness of the state and local party leaders to support it. Additionally, there is a low percentage of party-line voting in Congress. This again is primarily due to the fact that congressmen are political leaders in their own right; they have their own power bases, which are not necessarily dependent upon the national party. Therefore, on a given issue only about 30 percent are likely to follow party lines in Congress, whereas in the British House of Commons, 95 percent usually follow strict party lines.

Another related characteristic is ideological similarity and issue conflict. This simply means that both the Republican and Democratic parties, if they are to have any chance of success at the polls, must attempt to remain in the mainstream political center to appeal to a broad mass of people. Avoiding extreme political orientation, both parties generally attempt to appeal to the same groups of people. Despite similarity in ideological orientation, there is party competitiveness and party conflict. These, however, are primarily over specific issues rather than ideology. For example, there has always been major disagreement between the two major parties concerning economic policy and welfare issues. Similarly, there have been disagreements over international trade and foreign policy. But these differences really relate to the manner of doing things and are not essentially disagreements on principle.

Although both parties attempt to gather their support from the political mainstream, they still differ in general party following. Democrats and Republicans draw from all strata of society, but can nevertheless be identified by the consistent and heavy support normally received from certain groups. The Democrats generally receive support, for example, from Catholics, blacks, and other ethnic minorities, as well as labor. The Republicans, on the other hand, normally are supported by Protestants, middle-class and upper-class groups, and business interests. In a sense, this following tends to reflect a historical division that reaches back into the Jeffersonian era. These are only generalizations, however, and do not always apply. Pressures created by the candidate's personality and the particular issues involved may, in the short run, override party sympathy. This was generally the case with the elections of 1964, when many Republicans either did not vote or switched their votes to the Democratic party in reaction to Republican Barry Goldwater's personality and platform. The same generalization can be made of the 1972 elections in which many Democrats did not vote or switched votes to the Republican party as a result of Democrat George McGovern's personality and platform.

Each of the major parties is also characterized by its having lasted for over a century. The Democratic party can be traced back to Andrew Jackson in the 1830s while the Republicans go back to 1856. In this respect, most people acquire party loyalties early in life and these loyalties are normally passed on from generation to generation. Therefore, barring any great national calamity affecting political life, parties tend to base their support on a long line of loyalists.

Nevertheless there is some fluctuation in party support. Disagreement with party pronouncements or candidates can create strong cross-pressures even among staunch party loyalists. This may lead to apathy and disinterest in party elections or even outright disaffection, albeit temporary. This was clearly reflected in the 1964 presidential elections, when the perceived extremist image of Goldwater's philosophy drove many Republicans into the arms of the Democrats, leading to a landslide victory for Lyndon Johnson. The same could be said of the 1972 elections in which the perceived left wing extremism of George McGovern drove many Democrats into the arms of the Republicans. Therefore the characteristic of durability has to be reconciled with that of fluctuations in party support. This is closely related to the idea that electoral success still stems from maintaining a center position with respect to political attitudes.

Parties and Federalism

The political system itself imposes limitations and restraints on the kinds of party systems that may develop. Since we operate under a dual political system, parties are conditioned by both state and national systems. Although they attempt to cut across these systems, their decentralization and diffuseness are perpetuated in the federal structure. The pluralistic tendency within our political system is also reflected in the nature of the political parties. Indeed, if the parties are to appeal to a broad segment of the American public they must not only include a number of diverse geographic areas and people, but they must make serious attempts at reconciling these diversities. It would be difficult for a rigid ideological party to exist under such circumstances.

Party Organization

Not only is this diversity reflected in the various interests in the party, but it is also reflected in the party composition itself. In general organizational terms, the two major parties can be divided into three elements: party organization; party in government; and the party in the electorate. The party organization is probably the backbone of any party structure. Theoretically, it consists of the hierarchy beginning at the lowest grass roots level extending to and through the national government. The lowest level party unit is normally the *precinct* which is the basic unit of electoral administration and includes an average of several hundred voters. In larger cities, the next level is *ward* or *district* controlled by a leader whose jurisdiction may compose several precincts. At this level the leadership is normally in the hands of precinct captains or committeemen who are the lowest level of party organization.

At the next level are *county committees*. They are major units in the party machinery and their chairmen may be local political potentates of considerable importance. These county committees are most commonly composed of the party's precinct captains, committeemen, township committeemen or party functionaries. For example, in Cook County, Illinois, the chairman of the Democratic county committee is Richard J. Daley, Mayor of the city of Chicago. The Democratic county committee is an important organizational structure.

At the next level are the *state committees*, not necessarily subordinate to national organs. They range in size and composition depending on the state. The chairman of the state committee is normally selected by members who are chairmen and vice chairmen of each of the county committees.

In certain states party committees are chosen in party primary elections. Both the county committees and the state committees are deeply involved in patronage and other rewards of party loyalty.

Most people are more familiar with the *national party committees* since they are the committees associated with electing candidates to the presidency. The chairman of the national committee is usually selected by the incumbent of the presidential office, or by members of the national committee when the party does not control the presidential office. The national committee is composed of two or three persons from each state. Its role includes fund-raising and performing as a personal staff of the candidate or of the President. Applicants for patronage jobs are normally cleared with the office of the national chairman. The national committee also engages in large-scale propaganda activities and at times functions as party spokesman.

In the 1972 presidential campaign there were tremendous internal struggles, particularly in the Democratic party, regarding the composition of the national party committees. The left wing faction of the Democratic party felt that, in order to reassert its role as the people's party, it should include representation from all elements in society on its national committee. The focus of the left wing effort was on the national committee because it is here that platforms are developed and influence is brought to bear on national candidates. They felt that the Democratic party was becoming too cautious and conservatively oriented. The McGovern supporters did indeed grasp control of the party—with disastrous results in the 1972 campaign.

Party National Conventions and Campaign Organizations

One of the most visible and important functions of the party is to elect a candidate for presidential office. This is done in national party conventions, which have been used since 1832. Each of the major parties usually has from 1200 to 3000 voting delegates. The delegates are elected by state parties, either by the state convention or primary system. At a national convention meeting every four years, each party sounds the roll call of states. Each state delegation has an opportunity to nominate its candidate. The balloting follows with a roll call of the states and each delegation casts its votes for the candidate of its choice. The candidate who receives a majority wins the party's presidential nomination. In a number of instances, many roll calls are taken before one candidate receives a majority.

For months prior to the convention, anywhere from two to two dozen candidates may have been active in campaigning, (unless the party is committed to the incumbent). This includes entering various state party presidential primaries to develop strength and demonstrate vote-getting potential. These primaries can have an important impact on the outcome of the party nominating convention. For example, in 1960 John Kennedy made a good showing in the Wisconsin and West Virginia primaries; this made him a strong contender for the party's nomination, and blocked the efforts of Senator Hubert Humphrey and others to gain the nomination. Senator Edmund Muskie's poor showing in the 1972 New Hampshire primary, on the other hand, virtually destroyed his presidential candidacy efforts even though he had been the front runner until that time.

Unless a clear party choice evolves from the preconvention campaigning, there is liable to be considerable activity within the various camps immediately prior to the convention. On the floor of the convention, many deals are made for delegates' votes, some in exchange for support of a "favorite son" for a future political post. After the selection of the party's presidential candidate, the same procedure is followed for the selection of the vice presidential candidate—although this becomes essentially a pro forma matter. The presidential candidate usually selects his own running mate and the convention simply endorses him.

In the complexities of the party convention and the preconvention campaigning, the candidates are trying to acquire the support of the majority of the party's state and local representatives and other party regulars. Regardless of how the candidates fare in the primaries, the final choice is up to the party—that is, the party regulars.

There is some danger that campaign efforts and the concern for winning will lead to questionable activities, as was the case in the 1972 presidential elections with the Committee to Reelect the President (CREEP). President Nixon and his close advisors had decided in 1971 that his campaign for reelection would be managed by this special committee. This committee was completely independent of the Republican national committee, and concentrated solely on reelecting Nixon; it was not concerned with the party's nominees for Congress and other offices. It had generally been the practice of most national party nominees in recent times to establish a separate committee. Because it was so well funded, the Committee to Reelect the President was able to utilize all the latest developments in political technology. It was responsible for handling the campaign's media effort, organizing ethnic and other special interest groups, registering potential Nixon voters, and establishing campaign headquarters across the nation in order to mobilize volunteers. The financing was a separate operation.[8]

The committee was severely criticized after the 1972 campaign. Its personnel were involved in illegal espionage activities, best illustrated by the Watergate incident. The presidential campaign was so separated from efforts on behalf of other Republican candidates that, while Nixon was reelected by a landslide, Democrats kept control of Congress.[9] On March 30, 1974 Vice President Gerald Ford criticized CREEP as "an arrogant, elite guard of political adolescents," suggesting that future Republican presidential campaigns should not be allowed to bypass the regular party organization.[10]

Other important organizational units of the parties for campaign purposes include the senatorial and congressional campaign committees. The party groups in both House and Senate maintain campaign committees which are completely separate from the national party organization. These legislative campaign committees provide assistance to party members in the legislative branches who are up for reelection. They also stimulate the local organizations to recommend promising candidates for both houses.

Each of these various party organizational elements may have a separate base of power and its own leadership, which can be strong enough to challenge the party itself. This is not a rigid hierarchical structure but rather consists of a number of organizations that in many cases are equal in power and exist in competitive relationships with one another. One can readily see why the party structure is diffused and decentralized. The county committee of the Democratic party, for example, in New England would undoubtedly have a different political perspective than a Democratic county committee in the Southwest. Each of the chairmen of the county committees to be effective would need to be a political leader in order to organize and insure some type of electoral success. And if we recall that there are about 3,000 counties in the United States one can get some idea of the breadth of the party representation and the diffusion and decentralization that is needed for any type of party structure.

The Democratic party has taken some initial steps to provide greater opportunities for participation by its members and followers. In December, 1974, a mini-convention was held in Kansas City. This was a unique happening, since conventions are normally held only during presidential election years. The purpose of the convention was to develop party guidelines, but more important to project a sense of unity in the aftermath of Watergate and the November 1974 elections. Delegates were elected by the states through a two phase process in which delegate-electors were chosen who later voted for delegates to the convention. What this mini-convention had accomplished was not clear. What impact it would have on the Democratic party was also not clear, particularly in light of the fact that little was said of the mini-convention during the early months of 1975.

The Party in Government

When we speak of the *party in government* we are referring to the party as it is represented by members of the House and the Senate as well as the President, and all of the state legislatures and state executives. On the national level in particular, the Congress and its internal workings are based primarily on party organizations, in which the party determines which of its members will be on particular committees, how they will approach various issues, and their general policy towards presidential policies. The same holds true for all state legislatures. Each of the state houses is organized and works upon the basis of party representation. Indeed, the strength of the party can be measured by the number of state houses the party controls, the number of governorships, as well as the number in Congress, and of course, who occupies the presidential chair. The same can be said of major cities, that is, whether there is a Republican or Democratic mayor, and whether or not the council at the city level is primarily Democratic or Republican. Not only may the local and state as well as federal elected positions provide the party with political strength because of its success in winning elections, but it provides a number of resources—organization, manpower, and finances.

Party in the Electorate

The third organizational element in the party is the *party in the electorate*. All of the party organizations would mean little if they were unable to nurture party support and enthusiasm and get out the vote at election time. Obviously, the voters who turn out to vote are the key to the elections so it is important for the party to ensure that registered party members do indeed turn out and vote the party line. Moreover, the party flag bearers and cadre attempt to add to party strength by appealing to uncommitted voters to support the party. This combination of affiliated party members and unaffiliated supporters constitute the party in the electorate. All the activities and efforts of party organizations are aimed at the party in the electorate to ensure enough votes to win the election. The political party that can harmoniously integrate party organization, the party in government, and the party in the electorate has the greatest chance for electoral success.

In each party organizational element there are flag bearers and a cadre, although the mix may differ. For example, the party in government is composed primarily of flag bearers since it is composed of those who have won political office and as such have a distinct appeal to the electorate. On the other hand, in the party organization, which is manned by a mix of party diehards, loyalists, and reformers, the cadre probably predominates.

Limits to the Two-Party System

We have noted that one of the significant characteristics of our political system is the two-party system. However, the limitations of this characteristic ought to be clarified. There is no question that the Democratic and Republican parties have been the main competitors for power at the national level. At the state and local levels, however, the party system ranges from the one-party to the multi-party structure. Again, this is a reflection of our dual political system. George Wallace's American Party recently struggled with both Democratic and Republican parties in some states in the South. Yet in the states of South Carolina, Georgia, and Louisiana, for example, the Democratic party has had consistent control, and at present these states are virtually one-party systems. In Kansas, Vermont, and New Hampshire, there is more or less a one-party system dominated by the Republicans. Also, in Chicago, for example, the Democratic party has controlled city politics for years. The point is that we must be very careful how we categorize our party system. We must recognize that the dual political system promotes the existence of both national and state parties, two parties, single parties, and third parties, while at the same time the party structures are influenced locally by geography and the diffusiveness and decentralization of the political and social system.

Summary

The party cannot presume the same level and intensity of support from one election to another—it must continually seek support, nurture it, and mobilize it to turn out at election time. This is particularly true in national elections. The reasons behind this have already been discussed. Additionally, the character of the political system—dual, pluralistic, diffused, and decentralized—limits the ability of any party to build a monolithic system that has effective control over its members. In this respect, the party is also influenced by its different organizational elements. Only the most committed and hard-working party organizations with intelligent and attractive leaders supported by efficient resources, can hope to achieve sufficient power to have electoral success. Once electoral success is achieved, however, that power base can be entrenched and expanded. This brings us back to the question of the power of political parties.

Political parties are a key institution in our system of government, primarily because of their acceptance as proper instruments for expressing popular sentiments and providing a link between the people and decision-makers. It should be made clear, however, that the disparate elements of the party controlled by local leaders have the significant power. The cumulative power of the party is not necessarily the simple sum of its parts, but rather a reflection of the feeling of local leaders and how much of their power they wish to grant to the national party organs.

In the final analysis, the cumulative power of the party is a function of a number of important variables, each reinforcing and expanding the other, sometimes in subtle ways, and at other times in very explicit ways. The power for the party as a whole as well as for its various parts can be expressed as follows:

$$\text{Power} = \text{Resources} + \text{Leadership} + \text{Programs} \times (\text{Historical Base} + \text{Political image} + \text{Temper of the times})$$

It also becomes clear from our discussion that any individual attempting to achieve an elected office must work through a political party. To reach the presidency, an individual must be able to weld together a number of disparate elements of the party, not only to gain the support of his own party but to win against the opposition party. Voters and workers are needed in large numbers; perhaps as important is the need for money and organizational support.

After the 1972 elections and based on surveys of voter attitudes, it appeared that a new phenomenon was emerging—an increasing number of independent voters and a propensity for ticket-splitting. Although Richard Nixon won the 1972 presidential election by a landslide, this was not reflected in other races. For example, the Democratic party increased its majority in the Senate and gained an additional governorship; only in the House of Representatives did the Republicans gain any seats, and they were still in the minority there.

Moreover, the impact of the Watergate affair and the general state of the economy fostered an increasing political skepticism in many people and a general suspicion of politics and political parties. Thus, in the middle 1970s there is likely to be a loosening of party attachments, and neither major party is likely to gain much. More than likely this will produce a new party orientation which reflects new social and economic patterns as well as a more determined focus on restoring party image and establishing a closer tie with grass roots groups.

Finally, we can see that political parties are instruments of power. "The primary function of a political party in a democracy such as ours is to control and direct the struggle for power. From this function all others derive naturally."[11] The fundamental question is whether this power has been judiciously used to effectively meet the demands of the people. Are political parties instruments for the people?

Notes

1. V. O. Key, Jr., *Politics, Parties, and Pressure Groups* (New York: Thomas Y. Crowell Company, 1960), p. 12.

2. It is difficult to accurately identify the number of patronage jobs in any government. Estimates for the city of Chicago range from 3,000 to over 40,000 including jobs associated with Cook County. There are no public records that provide information on city hall influence over jobs outside the civil service. In any case there are a number of people affected with each patronage job. The figure of 250,000 is based on turnouts for local issues that rarely attract a wide voter participation. See for example, Peter R. Knauss, *Chicago: A One-Party State* (Champaign, Ill.: Stipes Publishing Company, 1968), p. 99.

3. Clinton Rossiter, *Parties and Politics in America* (Ithaca, New York: Cornell University Press, 1960), p. 108.

4. Jim Squires, "Why the Elephant Isn't Going to Die," *Chicago Tribune*, November 10, 1974, p. 12, Perspectives.

5. *Ibid.*

6. Key, p. 225.

7. Rossiter, pp. 73–74.

8. Theodore H. White, *The Making of the President 1972* (New York: Bantam Books, Inc., 1973), pp. 366–373, 388–394, 431–435.

9. R. W. Apple, "Nixon Gives the GOP Chairman More Authority . . . ," *New York Times*, March 27, 1973, p. 27.

10. Seth S. King, "Ford Calls Campaign Unit 'An Arrogant, Elite Guard,' " *New York Times*, March 31, 1974, p. 1.

11. Rossiter, p. 11.

Selected Readings

Political parties are the main instruments for winning elections. Although Americans pride themselves on not having ideological and dogmatic parties controlled by a hard core group of professionals, nevertheless virtually all of the parties in the United States, from the major parties to the smaller, regional ones, are staffed by political cadres. These cadres provide the continuity to party structures. Parties must, of course, recruit attractive candidates and are generally led by key political leaders. More important, parties must be able to attract voters, provide reasonable platforms to achieve goals, and successfully accomplish a number of programs. If parties fail in these goals, it is likely that voters will shift their allegiance to other parties or groups. In the most recent period in American politics, there has been increasing criticism regarding the effectiveness of the major parties. A number of observers claim that neither the Democratic nor the Republican party has been able to provide the necessary policies to offer meaningful alternatives for the voters.

Allan C. Brownfeld, in his article "The Irrelevance of American Politics," is one of those observers who feels that the American two-party system has failed the voters. He states, "Over a period of time it has become increasingly evident that the two major political parties have become nothing more than vehicles for power. Their general philosophy about government cannot really be defined, and their points of difference are even more obscure." Arguing that the framers of the Constitution intended that power be diffused, Brownfeld provides a succinct historical analysis of the development of the party system in the United States, analyzing the shifting philosophical bases for the parties, and their power structure. In the 1970s a "new politics" has developed out of the disillusionment with the Vietnam war and skepticism with the government. None of the political parties has been able to effectively respond to the new politics. Moreover, according to the author, solutions that are attempted from the right and the left are either enmeshed in appeals to violence or advocate philosophies that corrupt American democracy. In the meantime, both major parties seem set on a middle path, being unable to effectively respond to either the present or the future. "Parties, as men, become frozen in time and place. In a peaceful period this is a luxury we can afford. But in this time and place irrelevance is a cardinal sin."

12.1

The Irrelevance of American Politics

ALLAN C. BROWNFELD

The American two-party system has been an enduring institution, and many observers of American democracy have made the case that without this system our society would be neither responsive to the needs of the people nor effective in fulfilling their desires. Implicit within this formulation, however, is the idea that responsiveness to the needs of society and to its desires are one and the same. It rests also on the assumption that leadership and principle could be found within each of the parties and that meaningful choices would be provided.

Over a period of time it has become increasingly evident that the two major political parties have become nothing more than vehicles for power. Their general philosophy about government cannot really be defined, and their points of difference are even more obscure. This is not new in American history, or in the history of other countries. It is only more perilous at this time.

It may be true that any society which embraces the philosophy of egalitarian, mass democracy will inevitably achieve a political system based on consensus and appeal to the lowest common denominator. This danger was recognized early in American history, and the framers of the Constitution sought in a variety of ways to prevent its occurrence.

The two conservative foundations of American liberty, the Federalist heritage from New England and the Calhoun heritage from the South, were dominant before the revolution of majority egalitarianism ushered in with the Age of Jackson.

John Adams, in 1815, expressed the long-dominant view of the framers of the Constitution that mass democracy would be as dangerous to liberty as the power of kings or emperors: "Unlimited sovereignty . . . is the same in a majority of a popular assembly . . . and a single emperor. Equally arbitrary, cruel, bloody, and in every respect diabolical."

The question of whether freedom has been the result of action by the majority,

By permission from *The Yale Review*, LX (Autumn, 1970), pp. 1-13.

or by a small and dedicated minority, is one which historians have debated for some time. In the twentieth century, the view that the majority knows what is best and proper and, through the democratic process, will almost inevitably achieve it, has gained predominance. In the eighteenth century, a different view prevailed. John Adams expressed that view in 1790:

> The nobles have been essential parties in the preservation of liberty . . . against kings and people. . . . The numbers of men in all ages have preferred ease, slumber and good cheer to liberty. . . . Blind, undistinguishing reproaches against the aristocratical part of mankind, a division which nature has made and we cannot abolish, are neither pious nor benevolent. . . . It would not be true, but it would not be more egregiously false, to say that the people have waged everlasting war against the rights of men. . . . The multitude, as well as the nobles, must have a check.

Peter Viereck says that "Modern American democracy may well envy the vigorous free speech and unlimited free debate of Burke's aristocratic parliament, a freedom unequaled by modern, mass parliaments dependent on mass elections and mass demagogy."

Those in colonial days who called for the immediate institution of direct, mass democracy were challenged in a manner that the advocates of such institutions rarely must face in this century. George Washington expressed his disagreement with this view in a letter to Thomas Jefferson. He warned that "We pour legislation in to the Senatorial saucer to cool it." The saucers included not only the then indirectly elected Senate, but a non-elective unrecallable judiciary, an electoral college for the Presidency, and a Constitution deliberately made difficult to amend and making referenda almost impossible.

The framers of the Constitution felt that freedom and liberty could best be preserved by removing them from the immediate passions of the people. H. L. Mencken, writing of George Washington, noted that "He had no belief in the infallible wisdom of the common people but regarded them as inflammatory dolts, and tried to save the Republic from them."

The framers of the Constitution did not embrace the elitism that others tended to support. They believed that power should be widely diffused, that aristocrats had no more right to arbitrary power than the unlettered and unpropertied. In a society dedicated to the utmost freedom for the individual within the ordered pattern of law, no branch of government should have a monopoly of power. Hence, the concept of checks and balances and division of powers. It was indirect democracy, representative and limited democracy, which the Founding Fathers supported. They were mindful of Plato's injunction that mass democracy would lead to tyranny as the people followed demagogues and traded liberty for security.

As time passed, the foundation which they established was radically altered. The Federalist party died with the war of 1812 and many of its ideas died with it. The advent of Andrew Jackson brought with it the success of the first American Populism. The concept that dominated the Jacksonian Revolution became the dominant concept in our politics.

It was the Age of Common Man and although there have been only sporadic enunciations of its premises, the underlying concepts became pervasive. Like Rousseau, the Populists contrasted the unspoilt Noble Savage of the Western hinterland with the corrupt overcivilized intellectual of the big city. Populist tradition rested squarely on faith in the natural goodness of man, the infinite perfectibility of the masses. If evil is viewed as external, if utopia is just around the corner, then human nature cannot be blamed for the failure of utopia to arrive. Instead, there is a temptation to blame some small aristocratic or plutocratic conspiracy. Then you have to purge them, whether they be intellectuals, Eastern bankers, or government bureaucrats. These are the same attitudes which underlay Robespierre's Committee of Public Safety.

This view was made clear by the leader of the Progressive Party, Senator Robert La Follette, in *La Follette's Magazine*. "Over and above constitutions and statutes and greater than all is the supreme sovereignty of the people!"

After the demise of the Federalists our two-party system died for a time until the Whig Party restored it.

Modern-day Democrats and Republicans have often been compared with the Democrats and Whigs of the first part of the nineteenth century. The Whig philosophy has been described by the late Richard Weaver in *The Ethics of Rhetoric:*

> It turns out to be, on examination, a position which is defined by other positions because it will not conceive ultimate goals, and it will not display on occasion a sovereign contempt for circumstances as radical parties of both right and left are capable of doing. The other parties take their bearing from some philosophy of man and society; the Whigs take their bearings from the other parties. Whatever a party of left or right proposes, they propose (or oppose) in tempered measures. Its politics is then cautionary, instinctive, trusting more to safety and to present success than to imagination and dramatic boldness of principle. It is . . . a politics without vision and consequently without the capacity to survive.

He places the modern-day Democrats and Republicans in this general frame of reference:

> there has been so violent a swing toward the left that the Democrats today occupy the position once occupied by the Socialists, and the Republicans having to take their bearings from this, now occupy the center position, which is historically reserved for liberals. . . . Democracy is a dialectical process, and unless society can produce a group sufficiently indifferent to success to oppose the ruling group on principle rather than according to opportunity for success, the idea of opposition becomes discredited. A party which can argue only from success has no rhetorical topic against the party presently enjoying success.

Alexis de Tocqueville wrote in *Democracy in America* that "The political parties which I call great are those which cling to principle rather than to their consequences, to general and not to special cases, to ideas and not to men." The American Whigs were simply the party of opposition to the militant democracy led by Andrew Jackson.

The leaders of the Whig party were among the best statesmen of the generation: Henry Clay, Daniel Webster, and John C. Calhoun. Clay's title, "The Great Compromiser," marked him as the archetypal Whig. The Whigs finally discovered a politically "practical" candidate in William Henry Harrison, soldier and Indian fighter, and through a campaign which steered very clear of issues, put him in the White House.

During the campaign his manager, Nicholas Biddle of Philadelphia, gave this advice: "Let him not say a single word about his principles or his creed—let him say nothing, promise nothing. Let the use of pen and ink be wholly forbidden." Paul Murray, in his study of Whig operations in Georgia, says: "The compelling aim of the party was to get control of the existing machinery of government to maintain that control, and in some cases to change the form of government the better to serve the dominant interest of that group."

The rising young political leader, Abraham Lincoln, began life as a Whig but later left the party. He knew that a successful party must have something more than a temperamental love of quietude or a relish of success. By founding the Republican party he hoped to stress the moral idea of freedom and the political idea of Union. The Whigs could exist in a time of tranquility, but in a time of crisis they had no solutions to the nation's pressing problems.

The Republican party proceeded to follow the path of the Whigs. For thirty or forty years its case came to this: we are the richest nation on earth with the most widely distributed prosperity. Therefore, the party advocated the status quo. Murray's judgment of the Whig party in Georgia a hundred years ago can be applied without the slightest change to the Republican party of the 1920's: "Many facts in the history of the party might impel one to say that its members regarded the promotion of prosperity as the supreme aim of government." When, with the depression, the prosperity disappeared, the party's source of argument also disappeared, and it has found none since.

For many years we have had two parties which seemed to be different only in name. Each party has considered itself more as a vehicle to power than as a repository for a particular approach to the business of government. Candidates present themselves as potential leaders not because of their ability, experience, or policy, but simply because "they can win." The Democrats and Republicans have, however, played somewhat different roles, and this may well be part of the reason for the Republicans' perpetual minority status. The Democrats, by and large, have proposed. The Republicans have, by and large, first opposed and then accepted the proposals of the Democrats. This is the current crisis of the two parties, at least on one level. The public senses no real difference between them except that each would like to be in power. Unless voters feel that the two major parties are responsive to their needs, they are left without a real choice. In such a situation, democracy itself ceases to function.

This is not strictly an American phenomenon. The Conservative party of Great Britain, much like the American Republican party, has pursued a policy of first opposing change and then accepting it. The result has been a mixture—of change which is good as well as change which has been almost disastrous.

Benjamin Disraeli lamented in the England of the nineteenth century the fact that the Conservative party had abandoned any semblance of principle. In *Coningsby*, he wrote:

> The Duke talks to me of Conservative principles, but he does not inform me what they are. I observe indeed a party in the state whose rule is to consent to no change, until it is clamorously called for, and then instantly to yield: but those are concessionary and not Conservative principles.

He gives counsel to search for something which is both lasting and meaningful:

> hold yourself aloof from political parties which from the necessity of things have ceased to have distinctive principles, and are therefore practically only factions; and wait and see, whether with patience, energy, humor and Christian faith, and a desire to look to the national welfare and not to sectional and limited interests; whether, I say, we may not discover some great principles to guide us, to which we may adhere, and which, then, if true, will ultimately guide and control others.

The modern-day Conservative party in Great Britain has all but presided over the elimination of the values which at one time it was pledged to preserve. The point is not the validity or the wrongness of given policies which the Conservative party in Great Britain or the Republican party in the United States have come to adopt. It is, instead, to make clear that a party with no basis for existence except to serve as a vehicle to power cannot truly function in a time of crisis. The fact that the two major parties, both in this country and Great Britain, do not differ in any major respect would not be so serious if the single approach which both had accepted were valid and truly intended to meet the problems of the present and the future.

In fact, liberal pundits in this country have for some time urged that both parties adopt the same middle-of-the-road approach to the major issues. James Reston, Marquis Childs, Walter Lippmann, and Joseph and Stewart Alsop have repeatedly urged the Republican party to nominate the aspirant most like that of the Democratic party. They supported Willkie, Dewey, Eisenhower, Rockefeller, and Scranton. They vigorously opposed Robert Taft, Richard Nixon and Barry Goldwater. *New York Times* columnist James Reston wrote in April 1968:

> The major political personalities and parties are not dividing and moving to the opposite extremes. They are actually coming closer together in the center. They cannot put together a winning combination in a vast and diverse continent without organizing factions of different sometimes even contradictory views. The candidates and the parties are not leading the people into a new age with a new philosophy; they are merely adjusting to the new facts of modern life created by modern science and modern economics—in short, by the fertility, intellectual and physical, of the modern human race.... The issue now is not ideological ... but personal—between men of different talents and constituencies, but of comparably similar policies. And this is an important change for the better.

But now, after having been successful in achieving a situation in which both parties reflect a generally "liberal" consensus, many of these very advocates have become disturbed and disillusioned. Walter Lippmann concludes about this situation:

> To many, it does not seem right that in this time of crisis our political system should be failing to register and reflect the issues which torment our people. What has happened, it would seem, is that the American political system, which works so well in normal times, is operating regardless of and apart from the bitter war and the urban and racial crisis at home. In the normal periods of our public life, our party system is a marvelously cohesive institution.... In normal times, the voters on election day are choosing between men and between parties who in fact say, whatever they may believe, much the same things.... Thus great masses of Americans feel themselves disfranchised and alienated from our political system.

One of the real problems is that the attitudes liberal commentators once considered valid are themselves open to serious question. Now that we do not really have one conservative party and one liberal party, but two parties of varying degrees of the same liberal philosophy, we discover that this philosophy may have outlived its usefulness.

The literature of liberal disillusionment with traditional liberal answers is voluminous. Professor Hans Morgenthau of the University of Chicago says that "The general crisis of democracy is the result of three factors: the shift of effective material power from the people to the government, and the ability of the government to destroy its citizens in the process of defending them." Morgenthau notes that "the great national decisions of life and death are rendered by technological elites and both the Congress and the people at large retain little more than the illusion of making the decisions which the theory of democracy supposes them to make."

In a speech before the National Board Meeting of Americans for Democratic Action, Daniel P. Moynihan, formerly an adviser to President Kennedy and later head of the Harvard-M.I.T. Joint Center of Urban Affairs, offered three propositions relevant to the growing dialogue:

> It is necessary to seek out and make much more effective alliances with political conservatives . . . liberals must divest themselves of the notion that the nation can be run from agencies in Washington . . . [liberals must] somehow overcome the curious condescension which takes the form of sticking up for and explaining away anything, howsoever outrageous, which Negroes individually, or collectively, might do. . . . We must begin getting private business involved in domestic programs in a much more systematic, purposeful manner. Making money is one thing Americans are good at, and the corporation is their favorite device for doing so. What aerospace corporations have done for getting us to the moon, one fears, is to enable enough men to make enough money out of doing so. It is encouraging to note how much ferment there seems to be in this direction at this time, and hopefully possible to expect that the liberal community will support the effort rather than oppose it.

The measures advocated for some time in the field of housing are an important example of the failure of an approach which tends to believe that the creation of a welfare state will solve all of our problems. Political conservatives have always opposed this approach, so that their opposition is to be expected. But today the former advocates of that approach recognize its own futility.

Jason R. Nathan, New York City Housing and Development Administration, recently told former Senator Paul Douglas's National Commission on Urban Problems that "The entire concept of Federal aid as we know it may be completely wrong." Nathan said that "Even if the Federal Government spent ten times the money they do now—which they won't—it would not be enough. After ten or fifteen years of traditional programs, for example, we have not even begun to approach the problem in Bedford-Stuyvesant in Brooklyn." Urban renewal programs, as a case in point, were meant to ease the problem of low-cost housing scarcity. Exactly the opposite has resulted.

The United States Commission on Civil Rights found that federal projects in Cleveland had drastically reduced the amount of low-rent housing in the city and contributed to the creation of a new ghetto. Out of the resentments which were produced a new bitterness grew, culminating ultimately in riots. Commenting on the Cleveland developments, Father Theodore Hesburgh, President of the University of Notre Dame and a member of the Civil Rights Commission said:

> These enormous federal programs . . . are coming in, supposedly to help the community. They want to rebuild our society. What has happened in many cases is that people who are presently in the worst situation have their houses swept out from under them by bulldozers, they are given very little help in finding houses and they generally do worse than where they came from. This is immoral.

Many former advocates of such liberal programs have come to the conclusion that they have not, in fact, solved any of the problems at which they were aimed.

In the mid-1950's two agricultural sociologists, Charles P. Loomis and I. Allan Beegle, made a survey of depressed farming areas. They were, they found, exactly where they had been in the 'thirties. The New Deal and subsequent programs had passed over these areas without touching them.

Michael Harrington has noted that the liberal approach to government has produced "socialism for the rich" and "free enterprise for the poor." In *The Other America*, he writes that "The welfare state is upside down. The protection, the guarantees, the help all tend to go to the strong and to the organized. The weakest in society are those who are always disposed of in some congressional log-rolling session."

The welfare-state philosophy has not given people a stake in their communities or the hope for a better future. Bayard Rustin, director of the A. Philip Randolph Institute in New York, said that the welfare-state philosophy inherent in the war on poverty is an "immoral bag of tricks" amounting to a new form of slavery. He stated that "The problems for Negroes, Puerto Ricans and poor whites . . . is that America has no commitment to turn muscle power into skills."

In his *Autobiography*, Malcolm X said to white liberals, those he found most guilty of supporting the idea of a dole for the ghetto:

> If . . . [they] wanted more to do, they could work on the roots of such ghetto evils as the little children out in the streets at midnight with apartment keys on strings around their necks to let themselves in, and their mothers and fathers drunk, drug addicts, thieves, and prostitutes. Or . . . [they] could light some fires under Northern city halls, unions, and major industries to give more jobs to Negroes to remove so many of them from the relief and welfare rolls, which created laziness, and which deteriorated the ghettoes into steadily worse places for humans to live . . . one thing the white man never can give the black man is self-respect. The black man never can become independent and recognized as a human being who is truly equal with other human beings until he has what they have, and until he is doing for himself what others are doing for themselves.

The fact that many liberals have dissociated themselves from the traditional politics of the New Deal and the Great Society is clear. Before his tragic death, the late Robert Kennedy was beginning to forge a coalition of those who found the older philosophy wanting. The "new politics" is a combination of disillusionment with the war in Vietnam and disillusionment with the response of government at home. But despite the gains which may be made by such a "new politics," complete with its youthful vanguard, the fact remains that the traditional two-party system has been unresponsive to change, and the two parties have found themselves to be virtually carbon copies of one another. When it still appeared that the liberal answers were valid, this was objectionable only to the right wing which disputed such answers. Now that it has become clear that the liberal answers are wanting, we have what can only be called a consensus of error. It is in this sense that American politics seems more and more irrelevant to both the present and the future.

It is not only the Populist movement of the American Independent Party which proclaims that there is not a "dime's worth of difference" between the two major parties. Liberal-left commentator I.F. Stone has made the same point, indicating that the differences which do exist and have existed have simply been matters of degree, not essence:

> The differences between the two parties just aren't that fundamental. In a democratic society it is always assumed that the people are good, as in theology it is always assumed that God is good. Evil is an accident or the work of the devil. . . . Adam's sins are still attributed to some serpent which crept into the Garden. It is the nature of the . . . majority, and of man, that brings the two-party system to the verge of breakdown when faced with the need to swallow a military defeat and to tax the whites for the benefit of the blacks.

Those who are at the political extremes, both right and left, however muddled, find that the two major parties simply echo one another. This is true. This is the result of democracy, of government by public opinion polls. This is, in large measure, the reason for the notable success of entertainers in the political arena. The reason for advancing the view that politics has become irrelevant is the fact that the points of view which are echoed by the two parties are unrelated to the crisis period ahead.

The New Left holds out as little hope for the future as the present two-party structure. This amorphous movement seems blind to the evils of Communism, blind to the fact that everything it dislikes about the American society—bureaucratization, de-humanization, an ever more powerful government, are even more true of Communism.

The New Left advocates violence, and appears more nihilistic and anarchistic than it does relevant to an infinitely complex future. While the young people in this movement often understand the defects and shortcomings of current society, they have little understanding of the technology at whose brink we now stand. In fact, Professor Zbigniew Brzezinski of Columbia University has compared their revolt with that of the Luddites at the time of the Industrial Revolution. Fearing the impact of the new machines, the Luddites sought to destroy them. Similarly, fearing the mass society of the future, young people have attempted to destroy it. But such an approach is reactionary, and as irrelevant as the old liberalism of the two major parties.

If democracy is to continue to work, it must provide an arena within which the real problems of society are discussed and debated by those who have some serious intention of solving them. Today's Republicans and today's Democrats are addicted to the liberal formula which entered our political life at the time of the New Deal. That formula has been tried to its utmost, and has now been found wanting. Today, when we are in need of a Conservative party to help us to preserve the values which really matter in the midst of a society in danger of destroying all values, we have no such party. Today, when we need a Liberal and innovative party to meet new problems with new solutions, we find no such party.

Parties, as men, become frozen in time and place. In a peaceful period this is a luxury we can afford. But in this time and place irrelevance is a cardinal sin.

Study Questions

1. What functions and roles do American political parties perform?
2. The approaches of the two major political parties in the United States have been described as being basically "programmatic" rather than "ideological," adhering to the political center in order to win the most votes. What are the advantages and disadvantages of such an approach in terms of the public interest? In the wake of the McGovern and Goldwater candidacies, the two major parties have been described as becoming more "ideological." Do you agree with this assessment, and if so, do you think it is a healthy thing?
3. Are the interests of the country best served by the political dominance of two major political parties? Or should we have a multi-party system?
4. Why has the American system of political parties been described as a decentralized one? Would greater centralization of the two major parties be desirable?
5. What are the functions of the national committees and the senatorial and congressional campaign committees of the two major parties? Should their functions be increased?
6. In this chapter, the two major parties, in general organizational terms, were divided into three elements. What are these three elements of party organization? Describe them.
7. What power do the two major political parties exercise in the American political system?
8. Based on past party realignment trends and current political circumstances, predict the future of the American party system. How will it evolve? On what facts do you base your predictions?

Bibliography

Books

Bone, Hugh A. *American Politics and the Party System.* New York: McGraw-Hill Book Company, 1971.
Burns, James MacGregor. *The Deadlock of Democracy.* Englewood Cliffs, New Jersey: Prentice-Hall, Inc., 1967.
Crothy, William J., Freeman, Donald M., and Gatlin, Douglas S., eds. *Politi-*

cal Parties and Political Behavior. Boston: Allyn and Bacon, Inc., 1967.
Goodman, William. *The Two-Party System in the United States.* Princeton, New Jersey: D. Van Nostrand Company, Inc., 1967.
Herzberg, Donald G., and Pomper, Gerald M., eds. *American Party Politics: Essays and Readings.* New York: Holt, Rinehart and Winston, Inc., 1966.
Ladd, Everett Carll. *American Political Parties: Social Change and Political Response.* Boston: Allyn and Bacon, Inc., 1967.
Owens, John R., and Staudenraus, P. J., eds. *The American Party System.* New York: The Macmillan Company, 1965.
Parris, Judith H. *The Convention Problem: Issues in Reform of Presidential Nominating Procedures.* Washington, D.C.: The Brookings Institution, 1972.
Rossiter, Clinton. *Parties and Politics in America.* Ithaca, New York: Cornell University Press, 1969.
Zucker, Norman L., ed. *The American Party Process: Readings and Comments.* New York: Dodd, Mead and Company, 1968.

Articles

Glenn, Norval D. "Class and Party Support in the United States: Recent and Emerging Trends." *Public Opinion Quarterly,* Vol. 37, No. 1 (Spring, 1973), pp. 1–20.
Ladd, Everett Carll Jr., and Hadley, Charles D. "Party Definition and Party Differentiation." *Public Opinion Quarterly,* Vol. 37, No. 1 (Spring, 1973), pp. 21–34.
Pomper, Gerald M. "Toward a More Responsible Two-Party System? What Again?" *Journal of Politics,* Vol. 33, No. 4 (November, 1971), pp. 916–940.

CHAPTER 13
Political Interest Groups

In the minds of many people, interest groups in our political system are associated with nefarious roles. We constantly hear about campaign donations and generally suspicious behavior of lobbyists, corporate interests, pressure groups, and the other interest groups trying to influence government. Most recently the excesses of the Nixon administration have given rise to the notion of a government for the influential and the privileged.

Our purpose in this chapter is to explore the role that interest groups play in the daily workings of the government. We shall also endeavor to explore the influence that interest groups and special interests have on our representatives and ultimately on ourselves. Finally, we shall explore the purpose of interest groups and try to determine whether they are destructive to the American system or are simply the result of a vibrant democratic community.

The Concept of Interest Groups

The concept of interest groups did not begin with the American political system but can be traced back to the time of Plato and Aristotle, when it was presumed that interest determined the general nature of government policies. In the writings of John Adams and James Madison, the concept of interest groups was well articulated. It was not until the early twentieth century, however, that a systematic, scholarly assessment of the American political system was made, based on the concept of group theory. In the early 1950s, the concept of the group theory of government was broadened and intellectually justified as part of the governmental process.

Americans as Joiners

Most Americans are probably members of at least one group. Indeed, we are a nation of joiners. There are bowling groups, sewing groups, social clubs, labor unions, veterans' groups, church groups, consumers' groups, and a host of other types of groups. Obviously not all of these groups are politically important, although most have the potential to become so. Our main interest here is to study those groups that are more or less consistently involved in exerting power on political actors in order to achieve their particular interest. For example, although labor unions are primarily concerned with economic considerations, they are consistently involved in the political process, exerting power in order to achieve their economic interest. On the other hand, it is unlikely that the local bowling group would be involved in the political process, except in case of the remote possibility that major bowling policies were being considered by the political system.

In commenting on the tendency for Americans to join groups, Alexis de Tocqueville in 1840 observed:

> In the United States, political associations are only one small part of the immense number of different types of associations found there. Americans of all ages, all stations in life, and all types of disposition are forever forming associations. There are not only commercial and industrial associations in which all take part, but others of a thousand different types: religious, moral, serious, futile, very general and very limited, immensely large and very minute.[1]

Group Theory

The group theory of government rests on the premise that American society is made up of a wide variety of groups diversified in their culture, life style and attitudes. This lack of homogeneity is reflected in the type of government, i.e., the federal system, and the decentralized basis of politics and power. If one goes to Chicago, San Francisco, New York, Detroit, or a host of other American cities, one can immediately detect the polyglot cultural patterns of society and the persistence of subcultures. In areas of Chicago, for example, one can find neighborhoods that are primarily Swedish, Italian, German or Jewish—to mention but a few. In practically all cases there are a number of interest groups which reflect these patterns. However, the functioning of our political system is based on the fundamental acceptance of the core values of democratic ideology. These shared core values comprise the umbrella under which a highly diversified and pluralistic system exists. In other words, subcultures and a diversity of ethnic groups can exist side by side in a system which attempts to provide equal opportunity to gain power, which is used in a way acceptable to the mass of people.

Group theorists contend that there must be a number of ways in which the values of these diversified groups can be expressed, aside from the formal government structures. Community groups, ethnic groups, labor unions, business groups, and language groups are examples of alternate channels through which they can influence political actors. For example, political power has been achieved by some Spanish-speaking peoples by organizing into Latino groups for political action. Similarly, American Indians, such as the Osage and Navajo tribes, have become involved in politics through their Indian associations.

Thus, a number of interest groups evolve, reflecting the shared values of the various groups in society. The interplay between these groups and their pursuit of power to achieve their goals are essential characteristics of the American political system. Indeed, group theorists would argue that the formal institutions of government and public politics are really surface manifestations of the complex interaction of groups.

The group concept is not limited to any particular institution, locality or interest. Groups exist, for example, in congressional politics and congressional voting, within the bureaucracy, within the executive branch of government, and even within the judicial branch of government. Groups can be both public and private, resting on social, economic, or other values.

Whether one agrees or disagrees with the group theory of politics, there seems to be no question that interest groups perform important roles in our political system. A major role, as we have already suggested, is that of providing a channel by which individual interests can be accommodated into the interests of a larger political unit, while giving the individual a more meaningful impact on the political system. It is presumed that individual political activity becomes more meaningful within the context of an organized interest group. Interest groups are also presumed to perform a participatory function in the democratic society; if we assume that a democratic system operates more effectively when there is large-scale and consistent political participation, then we must admit that interest groups provide the vehicle for such participation. Aside from the periodic elections, it is difficult for the individual to influence other political actors; however, through organized interest groups he can make his voice heard without waiting for election time. Philosophically one can argue that there is a certain amount of democratic purity in a political system based on a variety of organized interest groups. In this sense, organized interest groups are conceived as grass roots political organizations whose desires and values are articulated and eventually channeled through larger interest groups into the political structure.

It is argued that individuals are virtually powerless in the face of other political actors and it is only through organized groups that the individual's voice becomes meaningful. Indeed, it is suggested that the lack of effectively organized interest groups is an indicator of public apathy and an unhealthy sign in a democratic society.

What is an Interest Group?

In simple terms, an interest group is an association of like-minded people who have organized to bring political power to bear on political actors in order to achieve their goals. It has a formal structure, a plan of action, and a specific focus on political actors within the political system.

Fundamental to this interest group concept is the premise that there are large numbers of people who are willing to support active participation in exerting power on political actors in a political system. This doesn't necessarily mean that a large number of people must, in fact, actively participate, but at least they must lend their support to the active core group if anything is going to be accomplished in relation to political actors. In most interest groups, a rather small minority speaks in the name of the group, standing on the prestige and following of the group as a whole.

Such organizations differ widely both with respect to interests and organization. They can be small or large, permanent or temporary, rich or poor, racial or geographic, economic or social, powerful or weak. It is virtually impossible to determine their exact number, sources of strength, and specific interests. Moreover, interest groups are not always involved in trying to influence decisions of the political system, but their identity as interest groups per se becomes manifest when they try to do so.

Below is a sampling of the kinds of interest groups existing in our system. Many of those listed are also involved in lobbying activities:[2]

What is an Interest Group?

Business Groups

American Association of Nurserymen, Inc.
American Importers Association
American Mining Congress
American Paper Institute
American Retail Federation
American Trucking Association
Association of American Railroads
Coca-Cola Bottlers Association
Chambers of Commerce of the United States
Independent Bankers Association of America
National Association of Food Chains
National Association of Insurance Agents, Inc.
National Association of Manufacturers
Society of American Florists
West Virginia Railroad Association

Employee and Labor Groups

AFL-CIO Maritime Committee
International Brotherhood of Teamsters
Marine Engineers Beneficial Association
National Association of Supervisors
National Council of Agriculture Employees
United Mine Workers of America

Professional Groups

American Academy of Family Physicians
American Bar Association
American Dental Association
American Psychiatric Association
American Physicists Association
American Medical Association
American Political Science Association
American Society of Civil Engineers
American Sociological Association
Association of American Publishers
National Education Association
The Common Fund

Citizens' Groups and Miscellaneous

Action for Legal Rights
American Basketball Association
Common Cause
Homemakers United Efforts
John Birch Society
National Association for the Advancement of Colored People
National Football League
National Organization for the Reform of Marijuana Laws
National Rifle Association
National Right to Work Committee
Navajo Tribe
Osage Tribal Council
Retired Persons, Inc.
Washington Research Project Action Council

Agricultural Groups

National Association of Farmer Elected Committeemen
National Council of Farmer Cooperatives
National Cotton Council of America
National Farmers Union
National Sharecroppers Fund
National Wool Growers Association
Wheat Users Committee

Some idea of the number of associations and their variety can be gained from information available in the *Statistical Abstract of the United States*. According to this publication, in 1971 there were a total of 11,340 national associations. They included the following:[3]

Type	Number
Trade, business, commercial	2,801
Agriculture	530
Governmental, public administrative, military, legal	362
Scientific, engineering, technical	637
Educational, cultural	1,759
Social welfare	562
Health, medical	932
Public affairs	616
Fraternal, foreign interest, nationality, ethnic	470
Religious	695
Horticultural	99
Veterans, hereditary, patriotic	213
Hobby, avocational	488
Athletic, sports	392
Labor unions	234
Chambers of Commerce	106
Greek letter societies	339
General	105

The number and variety become even more impressive if we remember that this listing does not include state and local organizations.

Activities of Interest Groups

There are many examples of interest group activity in all periods of American history. One of the most notable is that of the National Rifle Association in opposing stringent federal gun laws. After the assassination of Senator Robert Kennedy in 1968, there were many efforts by citizens' groups to abolish handguns. However, through a concerted and intense mobilization of its members, the National Rifle Association was able to bring significant pressure to bear on Senators from the Midwest and West and others to defeat any proposed legislation banning handguns. Their argument was based on the fact that the Constitution gives all American citizens the right to bear arms. Thus the National Rifle Association, with an estimated membership of one million people, was able to successfully mobilize efforts against the immediate sentiments of millions of Americans. Through a cohesive organization with strong financial resources, it was able to accomplish something that millions of Americans by diffuse and uncoordinated efforts could not.

Activities of Interest Groups

Similarly, the National Association for the Advancement of Colored People (NAACP) has used the courts to bring reforms in education, business and labor unions. Operating as an interest group, it has been highly successful in focusing its resources on specific issues and political actors to bring some sense of equality to the political system.

In more recent years, Common Cause, a citizens' group with over 100,000 members, has brought pressure to bear on many political actors to make the political system more responsive to social needs and to reorder national priorities. It has been successful in exposing waste and corruption in government, particularly in the use of money to finance campaigns. For example, in 1974 Common Cause made public a list of "House and Senate candidates who in 1972 received the most contributions from registered business, health, and agriculture group committees and from registered labor group committees."[4]

In certain intances, the label "pressure group" is used instead of interest group. Pressure group suggests a more devious activity and

BUSINESS GIFTS—Senate Candidates

1. Howard H. Baker, Jr., (R., Tenn.)*#	$53,800
2. John J. Sparkman, (D., Ala.)*#	46,450
3. Ed Edmondson, (D., Okla.)	44,797
4. John G. Tower, (R., Tex.)*#	43,139
5. Jesse A. Helms, (R., N.C.(*	42,086
6. Fletcher Thompson, (R., Ga.)	38,820
7. Charles H. Percy, (R., Ill.)*#	36,742
8. James Abourezk, (D., S.D.)#	33,941
9. James A. Eastland, (D., Miss.)*#	31,850
10. James A. McClure, (R., Idaho)	31,250

House Candidates

1. Dan Kuydenall, (R., Tenn.)*#	$25,050
2. Howard Snider, (R., Calif.)	23,000
3. John Jarman, (D., Okla.)*#	20,450
4. Del Clawson, (R., Calif.)*#	20,353
5. William E. Minshall, (R., Ohio)*#	20,050
6. James Abdnor, (R., S.D.)#	20,000
7. Andrew J. Hinshaw, (R., Calif.)#	19,669
8. Stewart Bledsoe, (R., Wash.)	19,200
9. Marvin L. Esch, (R., Mich.)*#	18,400
10. John M. Zwach, (R., Minn.)*#	17,800
11. Tennyson Guyer, (R., Ohio)#	17,800
12. Allan Bloom, (R., Ind.)	17,500

*Incumbent   #Winner

LABOR GIFTS–Senate Candidates

1. Frank Kelley, (D., Mich.)	$104,589
2. David Pryor, (D., Ark.) *#	72,806
3. Clairborne Pell, (D., R.I.)*#	62,700
4. Dick Clark, (D., Iowa)#	59,940
5. Wayne Morse, (D., Ore.)	59,866
6. Lee Metcalf, (D., Mont.)*#	59,224
7. Walter (dee) Huddleston, (D., Ky.)#	59,150
8. James Abourezk, (D., S.D.)#	57,550
9. Ed Edmondson, (D., Okla.)*#	56,675
10. Walter Mondale, (D., Minn.)*#	54,850
11. Joseph Biden, (D., Del.)#	47,700
12. Barefoot Sanders, (D., Texas)	45,750

House Candidates

1. William R. Anderson, (D., Tenn.)*	$ 38,657
2. Priscilla Ryan, (Lib., N.Y.)	38,194
3. Werner Fornos, (D., Md.)	36,916
4. Peter W. Rodino, (D., N.J.) *#	28,923
5. David R. Obey, (D., Wis.)*#	26,677
6. Hugh L. Carey, (D., N.Y.)*#	26,546
7. John J. Rooney, (D., N.Y.)*#	24,995
8. Les Aspin, (D., Wis.)*#	24,490
9. Ella T. Grasso, (D., Conn.)#	24,187
10. Abner J. Mikva, (D., Ill.)*	23,997
11. Wayne Owens, (D., Utah)#	23,808
12. Ray J. Madden, (D., Ind.)*#	22,300
13. Frank Thompson, Jr, (D., N.J.)*#	21,024

*Incumbent   #Winner

is generally used by critics to indicate unethical group practices. Our main concern here is with interest groups, according to the broad concept given to the group theory of government, without moral judgment.

Functions of Interest Groups

In formal terms, interest groups perform the articulation function in the political system. Articulation means simply the rationalizing or systematic integration of individual interests into a larger group interest. Whereas political parties have a broader function and purpose, performing the aggregation role among others, interest groups have a more limited purpose and focus on specific interests and specific groups of people. This relationship is shown on the accompanying

Activities of Interest Groups

chart which is a simple representation of the operation and role of interest groups in the political system.

Certain groups of people have their economic interests represented by labor unions (e.g., AFL-CIO). The labor unions in turn attempt to place pressure on political parties (historically the Democratic party)

**Interest Groups and Their Role
in the Political System**
(simplified)

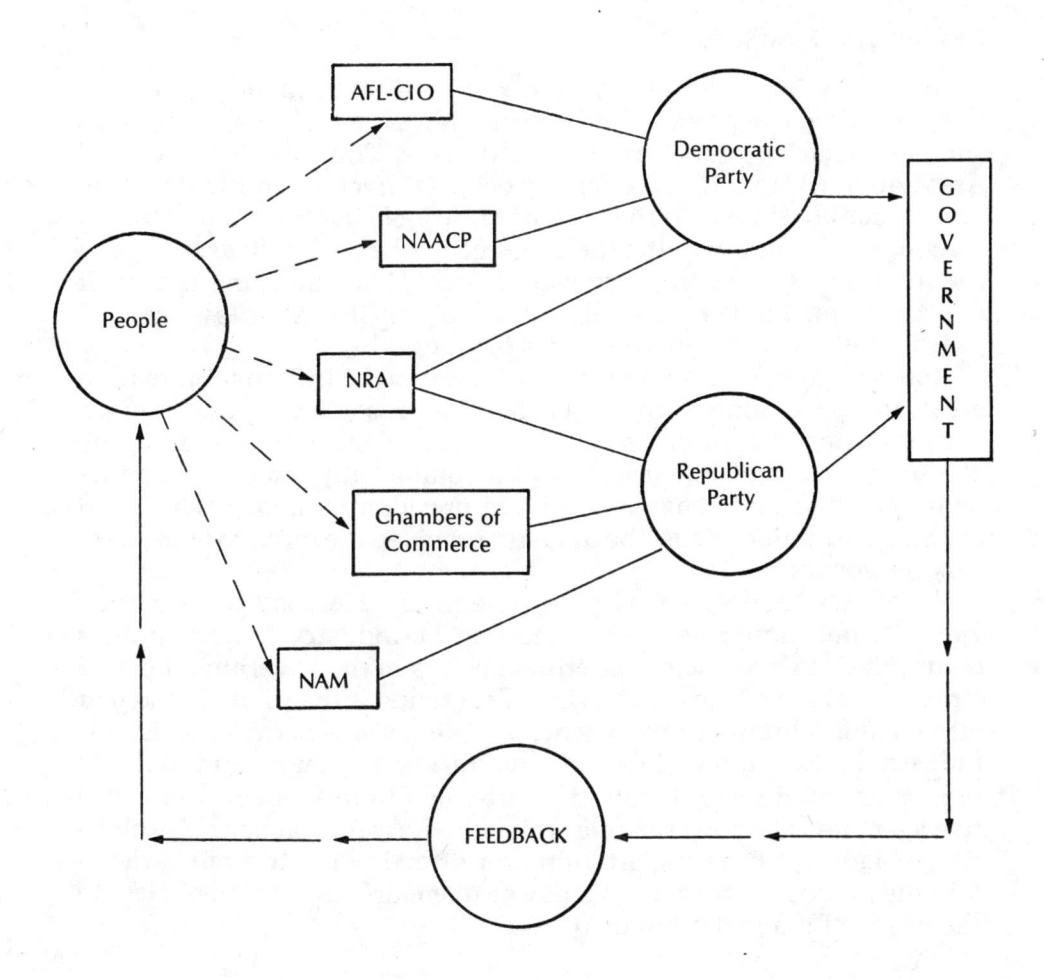

Demands ••••••••••••► Articulate ••••••••••••► Aggregate ••••••••••••► Policy

to work for legislation and policies favoring labor and the workingman. Similarly, the NAACP represents the interests of segments of the black population. It has worked mainly through the Democratic party (the Republican party has only a small black following) to bring about legislation and policies supporting the black people's drive for equality. The National Association of Manufacturers, primarily a business-oriented association, focuses much of its effort through the Republican party to gain favorable policies toward business. The chambers of commerce operate in the same manner. It should be made clear, however, that a number of groups operate through both political parties, attempting to influence legislation and policies regardless of what party is in power.

Semiofficial Functions

Interest groups can also perform semiofficial functions. That is, they provide government with a particular expertise in special areas such as medicine, dentistry, law, and labor. The American Medical Association (AMA), for example, is directly involved in the licensing process for physicians in the various states. No doctor can practice in a state without first passing the state medical examinations, which in the main must meet the approval of the AMA. The same is true of the American Bar Association and its role in licensing lawyers and passing judgment on qualifications for judgeships.

Interest groups also provide a vast amount of information to Congress and to administrative agencies. The most recent example occurred during the oil crisis in 1974. Most of the information on oil production, storage, and pricing was available only through the petroleum industry, and congressional and presidential action was based on this information. Thus, the industry provided the information necessary for government action.

Regulatory agencies play a key role in the economy of the nation and in establishing rules and regulations for industry. Interest groups realize that such agencies are critical points in the government power structure. Much of the effort of interest groups is therefore directed at influencing administrative agencies, to ensure favorable decisions. Industrial associations, labor unions, farmers' groups, and citizens' groups are all directly involved in attempts to influence administrative agencies. The power theme is clear in these interactions. Administrative agencies have important power affecting many groups; therefore the groups exert their own power to ensure favorable policies. In the words of a noted scholar:

With the growing complexity of government, legislative bodies have had to delegate authority to administrative agencies to make rules and regulations. Administrators become legislators, and pressure groups inevitably direct their activities to the point at which authority to make decisions is lodged. Where power rests, there influence will be brought to bear.[5]

Categorizing Interest Groups

For any student of American government therefore, the problem is how to study interest groups and identify their power relationships as well as their impact on other political actors and governmental policy. Groups can be studied in terms of their special interest, organization, the types of power they exert, the composition of their membership, or the main focus of their activities. No one particular way is necessarily more relevant than the others. Our approach will be in terms of types of organization, focus of activity, and presumed political power.

Categories of Interest Groups
Institutional—legislative groups, civil servant associations, policemen's unions.
Voluntary—AFL-CIO, Veterans of Foreign Wars, American Legion, local bowling league, Chamber of Commerce, American Medical Association.
Nonvoluntary—Racial groups, religious groups.
Spontaneous—Riots, some demonstrations, mobs.

There are four broad categories of interest groups: institutional, voluntary, nonvoluntary, and spontaneous.

Institutional interest groups are made up of individuals holding official positions within governmental structures; these individuals come together to act in concert to achieve certain goals. For example, scholars have clearly identified various groupings of congressmen, outside political party identification, who generally act in unison on various legislative matters and policies. A recent example of this is the Black Caucus, an organization of black congressmen. Similarly, there are individuals within the governmental bureaucracy who form subgroups to pursue certain values by placing pressure on other political actors. Institutional interest groups have a built-in power base, due to their positions in formal governmental institutions.

Voluntary interest groups are made up of individuals who voluntarily associate for a particular economic or social reason, and who are not necessarily in official governmental positions. For example, all of the labor unions would be considered voluntary interest groups, although a number of critics would argue that, due to the pressures sometimes applied, there is nothing voluntary about labor union membership. Other examples of voluntary interest groups are Veterans of Foreign Wars, the American Legion, and Common Cause.

Nonvoluntary interest groups are formed by ethnic, racial, religious or geographic characteristics. They are labeled nonvoluntary because, in the main, people have very little control over these characteristics. Generally such groups are latent or potential interest groups. For example, it is unlikely that all blacks would act as a unified interest group except in extreme circumstances where blacks as a group were threatened and this threat were clearly perceived and articulated.

Spontaneous interest groups are those interest groups that exist for a very short period of time and evolve almost overnight in response to events or to actions of other political actors. Spontaneous groups also include those anomic groups which are associated with demonstrations and riots. A spontaneous group can arise, for example, from an incident involving police brutality when crowds gather immediately in response to the event and demonstrate their disapproval. In other words, the event precipitates the temporary sharing of values, crossing other organizational lines, and brings together a group of people for a short-term association.

Each of these types of groups either exerts power or rests on a latent (potential) power base, to varying degrees influencing other political actors and the performance of the political system. It should be clear that these categorizations are not mutually exclusive or clearly delineated from one another. There are interrelationships, and complex organizational patterns between all of the categories. Interest groups that have a base cutting across all of these categories are potentially the most powerful.

The Black Caucus

The Black Caucus, a group of black congressmen, is an excellent example of an interest group that has a base of power in more than one category. It is basically institutional because it evolves from a formal government structure, Congress. It is also voluntary since it was formed to achieve certain goals shared by its members. Moreover, since its members represent a racial grouping, it can be labeled nonvoluntary. The Black Caucus also has the potential of being reinforced by spontaneous interest groups. Its power, however, is limited by the manpower and resources available to it; it is also subject to significant cross pressures.

It is interesting to examine the history of the formation of the Black Caucus. In 1970, black members of the House of Representatives asked for a meeting with President Nixon and were refused. They formed a "shadow cabinet" to review federal enforcement of civil rights legislation. The Black Caucus was organized officially in 1971. It boycotted Nixon's State of the Union message as a sign of protest against his policies in the civil rights area. The Caucus was finally able to arrange a meeting with President Nixon in March of 1971 and offered him sixty recommendations of ways to demonstrate his commitment to equal rights. Almost two months later, the President responded, asserting that his administration shared their goals.[6]

During the 93rd Congress, the Black Caucus increased its membership from thirteen to sixteen representatives—all Democrats. In the early fall of 1973, it decided to present a package of legislation; to facilitate its passage, the Caucus was willing to form coalitions even with those who previously had opposed the interests of blacks. As a result, the Caucus has sought to establish a working relationship with other congressional factions, even with Southerners.[7]

A few days after taking office, President Ford requested a meeting with the Caucus. The Chairman of the Caucus, Representative Charles B. Rangel of New York, called the new President's invitation an indication of the "seriousness of his intention to open his Administration to the advice and counsel of those of us who represent people whose views and needs were ignored by the Nixon Administration."[8]

Conflicts Between Interest Groups

Cross pressures occur among groups and parties as well as individuals. In both parties and groups the pressures generally tend to counterbalance each other. Individuals in many instances are members of two or more groups, which at times place conflicting pressures on them.

Thus, any one individual may be a homeowner, and a member of a labor union, a particular ethnic group, the Parent-Teacher Association, and the National Rifle Association. On a given issue, it is conceivable that his membership in the NRA would be contradictory to his membership in a labor union; the labor union may take a strong stand advocating gun control while the NRA may take an equally strong stand against gun control. Such cross pressures are likely to dampen any great effort on his part to support any position—unless there is a compelling reason, e.g., a crisis situation in which the individual has recently been held up by a person with a handgun.

An individual may be a member of the local policeman's association and also of the homeowners protection union. The policemen want a raise in pay which in turn may require additional real estate taxes placed on homeowners. Unless he is clearly and strongly committed in one direction, it is likely that he will not become involved in the controversy because of the uncertainty caused by the conflicting pressures.

The members of the homeowners protection union who are not policemen are likely to be opposed by policemen who are not homeowners. Each group in turn is likely to seek allies—the policemen may be joined by firemen, the homeowners by the citizens tax league, and on and on. The diagram illustrates the kinds of dynamics that groups and individuals are involved in, with particular respect to cross pressures and counterbalancing forces.

Interest Groups and Power

An important part of the power of interest groups stems from their size, leadership, composition, cohesiveness, and resources. Interest groups must be large enough in size to be worthy of some political consideration. A few hundred people would probably not make a great impact; on the other hand, a few thousand or few hundred thousand could be the basis of a powerful interest group. However, we should not assume that size alone gives power to an interest group. The millions of persons who are members of the Parent-Teacher Association, for example, do not wield a fraction of the power of the American Medical Association that numbers in the thousands.

The question of size must be qualified by a number of other factors. The leadership of an interest group is an important consideration. The political astuteness of the leaders, and their ability to articulate their group's values, have much to do with the image of the group as perceived by other political actors and groups. For example, the leadership of Martin Luther King in propelling the Southern Christian Leadership Conference to the forefront of the black rights movement has not been matched since his death. Indeed, one can argue that the SCLC has been considerably diminished in its power as a result.

The composition of the interest group likewise is an important facet of the group's power. Obviously, an interest group such as the

Importance of Group Spirit and Resources

Cross Pressures on Individuals and Groups

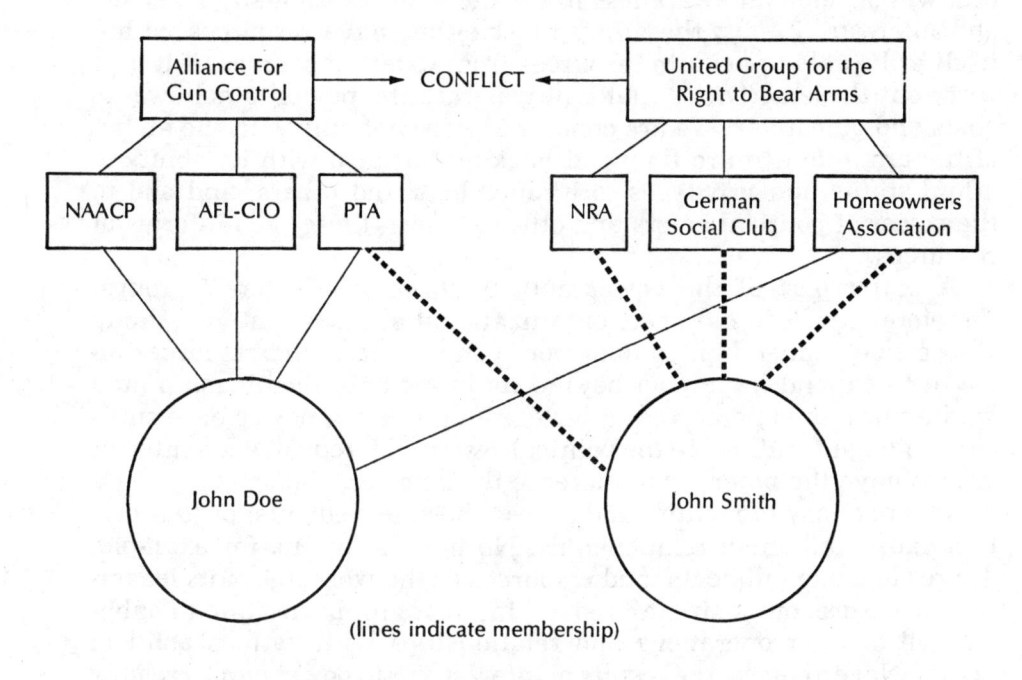

```
  Alliance For                              United Group for the
  Gun Control  ──→ CONFLICT ←──             Right to Bear Arms

 NAACP  AFL-CIO  PTA          NRA   German      Homeowners
                                    Social Club  Association

         John Doe                     John Smith
```

(lines indicate membership)

Note: The memberships and examples portrayed here do not necessarily represent existing organizations or alliances. This depicts the kinds of memberships, alliances, and pressures that are frequent in the American political system.

American Medical Association, composed of doctors who enjoy great prestige in our society and are also probably in the high income bracket, has greater power than a local sanitation workers' union. This combination of an intelligent, politically astute leadership and an educated, respected, wealthy membership contributes to the power of the group.

Importance of Group Spirit and Resources

All of these factors can do little, however, if the group is not cohesive. That is, most of the membership must actively support the leadership and the group's aim and agree on the goals to be pursued and the techniques by which they are to be achieved. This also presupposes an organizational structure, as well as a communication system that will develop an awareness in the members of their status, goals, and interests. Finally, the group must either have resources within itself or be able to acquire resources from external sources, if it is to carry out those activities that will generate the power to achieve its goals and objectives. We are concerned here not only with the ability of the group to acquire financial backing but also with its ability to afford status and privileges to its members and others, and add to the power of political actors and other groups—these are all forms of resources.

A major part of the power and functioning of interest groups, therefore, develops out of its organizational style. An interest group whose size, leadership, composition, cohesiveness and resources allow it to expand its impact beyond its immediate membership, and whose purpose is perceived to be legitimate, has a power base sufficient enough to influence the political system. Moreover, such interest groups have the potential to increase their power.

It is not easy to identify and assess those ingredients, or to ascertain cause-and-effect relationships. No interest group, for example, desires to make public its total resources or the workings of its leadership structure, or its size. Moreover, interest groups hesitate to publicize all of their operations and relationships with various political actors. Nevertheless, the results of interest group power can be readily seen in a number of instances. As already mentioned, after the assassination of Robert Kennedy, there was a significant hue-and-cry for the registration of all weapons in the hands of citizens. Serious consideration was given to such legislation in Congress. However, the National Rifle Association (NRA), a cohesive group with astute leadership, mounted a vigorous campaign against weapons registration. Concentrating on Congress, the NRA exerted tremendous pressures through organized letter-writing campaigns by local chapters. The legislation was never passed, even though a number of polls showed that the vast majority of American people approved it. One can see similar interest group activities in the case of the American Medical Association and its initial attempts to block the passage of a strong Medicare program.

Interest Groups and the Public

In what ways do interest groups function? How do they go about trying to achieve their particular objectives? Among the major concerns of any group are the attitudes of its membership and the images of the group as perceived by the public. Therefore, the leadership of an interest group has at least two major targets in an effort to mold opinions—its own membership, and the public.

A considerable amount of resources are expended by major groups on the mass media, in attempts to convince the public of the righteousness and legitimacy of their points of view and objectives. The presumption is that if public opinion is made receptive and supportive of the group's point of view, other political actors will be more likely to be influenced by group power. Additionally, every group tries to indoctrinate its own membership regarding its purposes in the hopes of developing or maintaining cohesiveness of the organization. Groups also try to place into public office those persons who are favorably disposed towards their interests. This invariably leads to expending resources for campaigns of favorable candidates and can result in a variety of campaign abuses.

As the Watergate affair has shown, a great deal of interest group activity in the 1972 presidential campaign hinted of unethical practices. Historically, there have been many cases of interest group activities which border on the unethical in trying to influence the election of candidates favoring interest group goals. In 1913 a House committee uncovered evidence that the National Association of Manufacturers controlled several members of Congress and had influence on certain key committee appointments. In the years 1928-29, the Federal Trade Commission, after investigating lobbying activities of electric utilities, concluded that company funds were spent heavily in propagandizing the public. In 1935, the Nye Committee headed by Senator Gerald P. Nye (R), investigated munitions lobby activities which seemed to favor high military appropriations. The House Armed Services Committee held hearings in 1959 on influence wielded by former military officers who were subsequently working for defense contractors. Following an investigation into his activities as secretary to the Senate (Democratic) majority, Robert (Bobby) Baker was forced to resign. Both the Senate and the House reported a code of ethics resolutions which touched on lobby activities, partly as a result of their study on abuse of lobbying laws.[9]

Campaign Financing and Campaign Reform

Interest groups, particularly those representing corporate interests, are also likely to contribute money for campaigns in the hope of receiving favors after the individual is elected to office. Of course, those in power may also urge certain interests to contribute money to campaigns. In the 1972 presidential campaign, a number of corporations were put under pressure to contribute to the reelection of Richard Nixon. American Airlines, Gulf Oil and Goodyear Tire and Rubber, for example, admitted that they illegally contributed almost half a million dollars. According to the *New York Times:*

> Many of the company's officials were asked to donate by two of President Nixon's close associates, Maurice H. Stans, formerly Secretary of Commerce, and Herbert Kalmbach, the President's personal lawyer. "I was solicited by Herbert W. Kalmbach, who said that we were among those from whom $100,000 was expected" said George A. Spater, chairman of American Airlines . . .

It was reported that seven companies publicly disclosed making illegal contributions to President Nixon's reelection campaign, in the following amounts:

American Airlines	$ 55,000
Ashland Oil	100,000
Gulf Oil	100,000
Goodyear Tire and Rubber	40,000
Minnesota Mining and Manufacturing	30,000
Phillips Petroleum	100,000
Braniff Airways	40,000

According to corporation officials, one of the reasons for these contributions was the fear that the corporations would be dealt with harshly by regulatory agencies and the fear of government reaction against noncontributors. This was particularly important since most of the corporations involved in illegal contributions had extensive dealings with the federal government.[10]

On the other hand, the need for large amounts of money to finance campaigns provides a particularly useful opportunity for a number of corporate interests and other wealthy groups to influence government. For example, it has been estimated that presidential campaigns expend anywhere from $100 million to $150 million for all participants, with the major candidates spending the greatest amount. Richard Nixon spent about $35 million in 1968 and an estimated $60 million in 1972. Congressional races in 1972 expended about $77 million.

One of the consequences of Watergate has been a campaign reform law that would limit contributions and spending in federal elections while providing subsidies for presidential candidates. The purpose is to make presidential candidates less dependent upon private contributions and to prevent financial abuses by any candidate running for federal office. Some of the specific provisions of the new law include the following:

(1) In presidential elections, the Democratic and Republican nominees would each be limited to spending $20 million for their campaigns. All of this money would be provided by the federal government. In the presidential primaries, candidates would be allowed to spend a maximum of $10 million, with the government subsidizing up to $5 million in amounts equal to what each candidate has raised.

(2) In congressional elections, "candidates for Senate will be allowed to spend up to eight cents for each voting-age person in the state or $100,000 whichever is greater," in any primary election. In the general election, the candidates would be allowed to spend up to twelve cents per voter or $150,000, and an additional 20 percent for fund-raising purposes. House candidates would be limited to $70,000 in the primary and the same amount for general elections, and up to $14,000 for fund-raising in each election.

(3) Contributors would be limited to $1,000 for any single candidate for federal office in any primary, runoff, or general election. If a number of candidates were supported by any one contributor, he would be limited to a total of $25,000 in contributions. "Organizations such as labor union political committees and industry lobbies would be limited to contributing to any one candidate no more than $5,000 for each primary, runoff, and general election—a total of $15,000." No limit is established for the total amount of contributions to various candidates.

(4) An independent commission of eight men would enforce the new law. Two members would be appointed by the President, two by the House, two by the Senate, the Senate Secretary and the Clerk of the House. The commission would be able to seek injunctions and judgments by the courts to prevent violations.[11]

The Lobbyist and His Role

A major activity of interest groups is trying to persuade public officials to adopt and enforce policies that the group thinks will be beneficial to its own interests. Lobbying is one of the primary ways that this is accomplished. This is an attempt by a person or small group of persons representing a particular interest group, to bring about defeat or passage of legislative bills or to influence their contents. Usually the lobbyist is a lawyer retained by an interest group, who operates in Washington, D.C.; he knows the intricacies of the legislative process and who the key members of Congress are with respect to any particular legislation.[12] As John F. Kennedy wrote in 1955 when he was still a senator:

> Lobbyists are in many cases expert technicians and capable of explaining complex and difficult subjects in a clear, understandable fashion. They engage in personal discussions with members of Congress in which they can explain in detail the reason for positions they advocate.[13]

Lobbying is a legal activity as long as it conforms to established rules and regulations. These are generally established in the Federal Regulation of Lobbying Act of 1946 which requires that all lobbyists register, give their expenditures, salary, and name of employer, and, quarterly, give full information of their activities for publication in *The Congressional Record*. Lobbying (as well as the Lobbying Act) has been criticized by a number of people because it gives an advantage to those groups who can afford high priced talent in Washington. Moreover, the Lobbying Act is said to be vague and with little enforcement power.

Interest groups also engage in indirect lobbying. Thus, in trying to persuade public officials, representatives of interest groups periodically testify at public hearings, write letters to officials, provide them with information, and generally try to convince them to take a certain course of action.

Limiting Interest Groups

The general attitudes of the public can limit the impact of the power of organized interest groups. Public opinion and the use of the public constituency by other political actors can do much to counterbalance the power of the interest groups. For example, public disclosure by political actors of the attempts by organized interest groups to pursue particular policy objectives may create a bad public image and thus embarrass or ridicule the involved groups. Organized interest groups can operate effectively when the public is apathetic, disinterested, or uninformed, but they wield a greater amount of power when they have the support of the public in the pursuit of their goals.

Lobbyists' Influences and Pressures on Legislators

BACK DOOR PRESSURE

Social gatherings arranged at which lobbyists meet legislators

Requests and arguments transmitted via relatives and friends of legislators

Indirect campaign contributions provided

Travel facilities provided for legislators

Job offers made to legislators

Placement of factories or other facilities in legislator's district offered to key legislator

Member of interest group placed on the staff of appropriate agency or lawmaker

FRONT DOOR PRESSURE

Arguments and data supplied to agencies, committee staffs, and legislators

Formal testimony presented at hearings by experts and executives

Model legislation formulated for government consideration

Industry-formulated legislation submitted by friendly congressmen

BACKGROUND PRESSURE

Interest group's position advertised in public media

Office of interest group established in Washington

Letters sent to legislators from interested constituents

Research findings supporting group's position financed

Associations favorable to group established nationwide to interested persons

Mass actions supported that are favorable to group's goals

Link between group's goals and national well-being developed

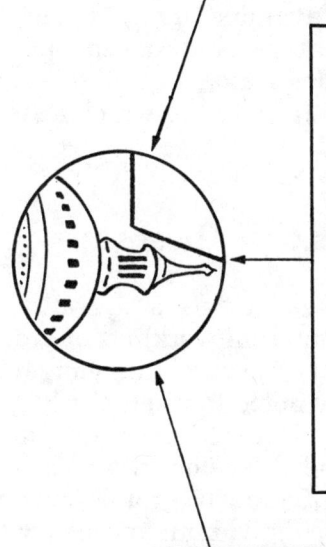

Having identified certain limitations on the power of interest groups, we ought to understand that each of these limitations can also add to their power. If the political actor has constituencies which overlap with the organized interest groups then of course the power of that particular interest group in imposing its will on the political actor increases accordingly. For example, a black congressman would find it difficult to publicly struggle against the leadership of the Southern Christian Leadership Conference if in fact a great number of his constituents are black and also members of the SCLC. Similar considerations are true with respect to countervailing interest groups (coalition of groups) and the public (public support of interest groups). Obviously, the organized interest groups attempt to present their goals and values in the most favorable light possible in order to increase their power in all of these areas. And indeed, one can argue that it is this feature of group politics which stimulates compromise and works against those interest group activities which foster extreme positions.

Interest Groups and Abuses

Obviously, there is a gap between ideals and reality. There is considerable abuse in not only the internal workings of groups but in their external behavior. The problem of election financing has already been noted. Certain labor unions are noted for their shady elections of union officials. Struggles often take place within organized groups for leadership positions. These, at times, develop into conflict ranging from political chicanery to violence. Similarly, groups can be manipulated and used by the leadership or individuals to further their own aims, with little effort to achieve the goals of the group.

Interest groups can perform valuable services in articulating the interests of a diverse social system, but this must be done within a framework of laws which minimize abuses. The recently passed Campaign Reform Bill is an example. Yet there remains much to be done, particularly in the area of consumer protection and an effective voice for consumer groups. Corporate interests still retain a significant influence in the political system. Professional groups likewise can perform valuable services, but the public must be aware that at times such groups' own professional interests take precedence. This was demonstrated by the American Medical Association's initial opposition to Medicare.

Moreover, there is always the danger that one group or coalition of groups can develop significant power in a given area with little counterbalancing power. This is particularly true in the realm of economics, whether it be the power of labor unions or industry. For example, labor unions can effectively disrupt the day-to-day business of government even over the most minor issues. On the other hand, the financial resources of corporate interests allow them a virtually free hand in influencing legislative bodies and in propagandizing the public. Moreover, corporate interests have significant influence on pricing policies affecting most Americans. The pricing policies of the petroleum industry during the oil crisis in 1974 is a case in point.

Interest groups are here to stay and the arguments about their role in a democratic society will continue. But there is a need for government to perform a counterbalancing role to insure that no single group, or coalition of interest groups, gains the upper hand at the expense of public interests.

As has been suggested throughout this book, power motivates politics. In the case of interest groups, democracy may be considerably diminished if one group acquires the power to impose its will on other political actors without regard to opposing pressures or forces. It is conceivable in such circumstances for the relatively narrow values of the interest group to subordinate the greater values of the public and political system at large. Fortunately, what has happened in our society is that most organized interest groups have limited power vis-à-vis other political actors and therefore rarely are able to impose their will for any sustained period.

One can also argue that the interest group structure is biased towards the business or upper-class values. The power of interest groups, as we discussed earlier, depends greatly on resources, intelligent leadership, composition of the membership, and cohesiveness, among other things. Most of these tend to be concentrated in the upper-class or business groups, which have the resources, education, knowledge and ability to use such structures in furthering their interests. This is not to deny that there are other groups such as labor unions that wield significant power; however, these tend to be the exception. Groups such as welfare, transient laborers, minorities, consumers, senior citizens, and women, are all underrepresented in organized interest group activities. Moreover, all individuals are not members of organized interest groups. Thus, there may be an important segment of society that is not represented.

We have suggested that the power of interest groups is determined not only by the kind of group but also by the internal characteristics. Other important facets of the extent of power of interest groups are the political actors, countervailing interest groups, and the public. Interest groups attempt to wield power in order to influence other political actors. In many instances, these political actors are insulated from the influence of organized interest groups because of their position and their own power. For example, judges are fairly well insulated from the power of interest groups. Similarly, a congressman whose constituency is predominantly white middle-class and conservative is likely to be insulated from the power of the Southern Christian Leadership Conference. Thus, the power of the interest group can be limited considerably by the particular political actor and the type of interest group involved.

We should not assume, however, that interest groups simply struggle among themselves, each counterbalancing the other, while achieving little in furthering their goals. We simply need to recall the tremendous impact of the labor union movement in our country, the power of large organized interest groups representing corporate activities and their influence on the economic policy of the United States, and the power of such groups as the American Medical Association, the American Dental Association, and the American Bar Association, in regulating and indeed determining governmental policy in the field of medicine, dentistry, and law. Regardless of whether one feels that organized interest group activity is good or evil, it cannot be denied that interest groups do perform a specific function in our political system—indeed, in any political system—and hence are basic to our understanding of American government.

Notes

1. Alexis de Tocqueville, p. 513.
2. Adapted from *Congressional Quarterly Almanac*, Vol. 29, 1973 (Washington, D. C.: Congressional Quarterly, Inc., 1973).
3. *Statistical Abstracts of the United States*, 1972.
4. As reported in *The New York Times*, March 29, 1974, p. 16.
5. V. O. Key, p. 154.
6. "Black Caucus: Sixty Recommendations for the President," *Congressional Quarterly Almanac 92nd Congress: First Session, 1971*, Vol. 27 (Washington, D.C.: Congressional Quarterly, Inc., 1972), pp. 659–660.
7. C. Gerald Fraser, "Black Caucus to Join Foes to Achieve Political Goals" *New York Times*, October 1, 1973, pp. 1, 22.
8. Paul Delaney, "Rangel Says the Black Caucus in Congress Grows Sophisticated" *New York Times*, February 13, 1974, p. 18.
9. Summarized and extracted from *The Washington Lobby*, p. 9.
10. This discussion based on Michael C. Jensen, "The Corporate Political Squeeze," in *The New York Times*, September 16, 1973, Section 3, pp. 1–2.
11. Extracted and summarized from "Out of Watergate, A Campaign Reform Bill," in *The New York Times*, October 6, 1974, Section 4, p. 2.
12. Plano and Greenberg, p. 123.
13. As quoted in *The Washington Lobby*, p. 6.

Selected Readings

Lobbying and interest group activity are integral parts of the American political landscape. For many, such activities provide a means to influence decision-makers and other political actors. For others, lobbying and interest group activity represent the seamier side of American politics. The selections for this chapter provide the student with some additional insight on this important subject. "The methods used to influence the policies of the U.S. Government vary with the interest groups and individuals involved, depending largely on their purposes, resources and political sophistication." With this observation, the selection from *The Washington Lobby* discusses the ways and means used by lobbyists to influence decision-makers. These include simple attempts to influence members of Congress to extensive and complicated attempts to defeat the President. The article also argues that a number of interest groups have little idea of how their lobbyists operate or what they do and do not accomplish. Finally, students of American politics should understand that lobbying and interest groups are an essential part of our political system and should be studied with this fact in mind.

The next selection is from the *Chicago Tribune* and describes the events that took place in a meeting of dairy farmers in Chicago's McCormick Place on September 3, 1971. The annual meeting of Associated Milk Producers, Inc. (AMPI) was addressed by President Nixon. Forty thousand dairy farmers and their friends cheered as the President and a congressional delegation of over 20 congressmen took part in the event. Richard Orr, in his article, claims that the dairymen assured President Nixon of at least 2 million dollars in campaign contributions for 1972 if he acted to impose dairy quotas. It is interesting to note that two weeks after the September meeting, the President imposed dairy quotas—although not at a level desired by dairymen. In any case, the article does show the impact of interest group activity on decision-makers and how even the President can be influenced.

13.1

Washington Lobby Employs Many Methods to Attain Objectives

CONGRESSIONAL QUARTERLY

When the Washington lobby is studied in action, certain patterns frequently recur.

The organizations that make it up and their representatives, often operating at cross-purposes, work toward these goals:
- To enact new laws or to block their passage.
- To change existing laws or to block their change.
- To affect the way laws are administered.
- To replace the Members of Congress who pass the laws—or to maintain them in office.
- To unseat the President and with him the entire hierarchy of the Executive Branch which interprets and enforces the laws—or to support his re-election or the election of a likeminded candidate, by interest group standards.

The members of the Washington lobby well know that on the election of a President, moreover, depends the appointments of scores of Federal judges from the Supreme Court down—all with lifetime tenure and together supplying the decisive factor in determining the validity of actions by the Legislative and Executive Branches.

To achieve these goals, which vary with the groups involved, organized interests resort to the whole range of stratagems found in the world of politics.

Pressure Tactics

The methods used to influence the policies of the U.S. Government vary with the interest groups and individuals involved, depending largely on their purposes, resources and political sophistication.

©1971 by Congressional Quarterly, Inc. Reprinted by permission.

The information of national policy is an endless process into which a particular interest group may choose to enter at any stage as circumstances and opportunity dictate. Lines are often difficult to draw and much overlapping is found, but the methods fall largely into these categories, as illustrated by the case studies which follow.

Committee Testimony

The starting point for many organizations in their attempt to exercise their constitutional rights to petition the Government is appearance at hearings by committees of Congress. A specific group may or may not have had a hand in getting the hearings scheduled, and witnesses need not be registered lobbyists. In the case studies, virtually all major interests availed themselves of this opportunity to place their views on record by personal appearance of spokesmen or by submission of statements.

Administrative Hearings

Organized interests promote their positions on the way laws and regulations should be administered at the many hearings by regulatory agencies and executive departments. In most cases, though spokesmen must identify their interests, they need not be registered as lobbyists. Exceptions provided by Congress are witnesses before the Federal Power Commission, Securities and Exchange Commission and the Maritime Administration.

The scope of this activity was suggested by Robert Dechert, representing the American Bar Association in 1965 Senate hearings. He testified that "in today's complex world it is a very important part of the normal practice of law for a great many attorneys to negotiate expropriation insurance provisions with the Agency for International Development, tax issues with the Treasury Department, labor problems with the Labor Department or National Labor Relations Board, antitrust questions with the Justice Department or Federal Trade Commission, and contract clauses with the Defense Department." Such appearances were common in case studies which follow, including those on drugs, education, shipping, trade and sugar.

Judicial Proceedings

While not generally considered part of the lobbying picture, efforts by organized groups to challenge Acts of Congress or executive actions through the courts are a major factor in the whole process of attempts to influence government. Particularly prominent are activities by the American Civil Liberties Union and Ralph Nader's Center for the Study of Responsive Law. The judicial process played a part in the drug and environmental studies below.

Grassroots Lobbying

Increasingly significant in the conflict of pressures are the continuous efforts of organized interests to enlist support from target sectors of the public in their activities to influence Congress and the Executive Branch. Into this category fall much of the vast outpouring of publications, newsletters, pamphlets and television-radio or platform statements, many of which appeal for letters, telephone calls or personal visits to Members of Congress.

Many kinds of groups do this to varying degrees. Nat S. Rogers, president of the American Bankers Association, said in 1970: "As part of proper lobbying activities we try to keep informed about the names of bankers who are best acquainted with their Congressmen and in turn keep them informed about current legislative activities so they may talk intelligently to their representatives. This is the prerogative of all citizens and no innuendo should leave the impression that it is improper when done by the banking community."

Its importance notwithstanding, grassroots lobbying was not covered by the 1946 Lobbying Act as interpreted by the Supreme Court. Congressional sponsors made it clear they intended such activities to be embraced by legislation covering foreign agents.

Use of grassroots lobbying tactics to influence public opinion was prominent in the education, maritime, trade, farm, supersonic transport and environmental lobbying discussed below.

Coalitions

Often closely related to grassroots pressure campaigns is the combining of forces into temporary or more or less lasting coalitions that seek to bend government to their will through the appearance of overwhelming strength. Coalitions can involve teamwork among domestic groups, between domestic and foreign groups with common interests, between elements of the Executive Branch and various groups or between interest groups and political factions. Such activity was marked in the education, maritime, trade, sugar, farm, supersonic transport and environmental case studies.

Trade-off of Support

Frequently a part of coalition formation are negotiations among interest groups and their allies in Congress leading to mutual agreement to support certain legislative goals of the participants. Informal compromises often result which prevent headon collisions in the public arenas. In its extreme form this process is known as logrolling.

Personal Lobbying

The most common concept of lobbying in the minds of public and legislators probably is personally discussing legislation with Members of Congress or staff aides. It is one step closer than committee testimony to the actual process of getting legislation enacted, changed or defeated. Personal contacts by representatives of organized interests also are frequent with executive officials outside formal hearings, although they tend to be disregarded in most Congressional consideration of lobbying.

Personal lobbying by paid representatives, under certain conditions, was the only form requiring registration under the Federal Regulation of Lobbying Act as of 1971. It played an important role in all following case studies.

Selection of Officials

One stage beyond attempts to influence the actions and thinking of persons in public office is the effort by organized interests to retain or replace them with others considered more sympathetic or susceptible. Some pressure groups make determined efforts, directly or indirectly, to influence the outcome of Federal elections to Congress or the Presidency. An *American Medical News* 1970 editorial concerning the American Medical Association's Political Action Committee (AMPAC) stated: "AMPAC is a separate organization with its own Board of Directors. It takes no position on legislation. It is involved in political education and political action, that is, electing people to office."

Also common are groups' attempts to influence the choices of committee and subcommittee chairmen and members, staff personnel and the whole range of executive and judicial appointments by the President. Such activities were conspicuous in the drug, education, maritime and trade studies below.

Pressure from Above and Below

Upon the outcome of elections and appointments can hinge the use, frequently found among some elements of the Washington lobby, of a combination of pressure from within the Government and from outside. A revolving door pattern is often pursued in which individuals switch from interest group to government and back again. This was evident, for example, in drug, trade, maritime and sugar legislation discussed in following pages.

Ignorance: Still a Factor?

By no means do all members of the Washington lobby corps employ every technique of applying pressure on public policy. Many group specialists elect to restrict their activities to reporting on Washington developments to their organizations and arranging for presentation of their positions as the need arises. This can sometimes amount to a defensive strategy. But others are more aggressive.

One reason which Bertram M. Gross gave for writing *The Legislative Struggle* was that "ignorance accounts for the failure of many Americans to do their share in making the law." Gross, in fact, questioned whether many veterans of legislative battles had "any clear idea of the forces that make for victory or defeat."

He said the downtown "office buildings of Washington are filled with organizations that have never penetrated to the inner sanctum. . . . The lobbies of Capitol Hill teem with lawyers, public-relations men, and ex-government officials who accomplish little except to wrest large fees. . . ."

Much has been revealed since Gross' attempt in 1953 to throw light from inside on the legislative process, which he called "a study in social combat." There are indications, however, that the conditions of which he spoke still exist to some degree. Elections and polls sometimes point in that direction.

There can be little question, certainly, that much ignorance persists among supporters of some organized interests concerning the pressure they make possible and their impact on the Government under which they live.

13.2

The Night the Dairymen Produced Grade-A Clout

RICHARD ORR

Looking back on it, the meeting in McCormick Place was spectacular and history-making any way you figure it.

Consider the date, Sept. 3, 1971. That evening President Nixon delivered what was billed as a "nonpolitical" speech to 40,000 dairy farmers and members of their families who jammed the vast Don Maxwell Hall to capacity. The farmers proved themselves to be an attentive and most appreciative audience, interrupting the half-hour speech 16 times with applause.

That same evening in Beverly Hills, Cal., a group of White House "plumbers" were burglarizing the office of Daniel Ellsberg's psychiatrist in search of medical records on the purloiner of the Pentagon Papers. Many months later it would be revealed that the $5,000 to pay for the burglary had come from the pockets of those very same dairy farmers who were applauding Nixon so lustily in McCormick Place.

They had contributed the money, unknowingly, as part of hundreds of thousands of dollars their leaders had given to President Nixon's reelection campaign. This particular $5,000 had gone thru a dummy Republican campaign committee named, ironically, "People United for Good Government."

All that cash, together with Presidential decisions involving dairy import quotas and price supports favorable to dairy farmers, were to tie the dairymen inextricably into the Watergate scandal. The whole web of events in the months preceding the McCormick Place meeting is yet to be unravelled by Special Watergate Prosecutor Leon Jaworski and one of his grand juries, the courts, and the House Judiciary Committee.

At least part of the story is believed to be hidden in tapes and other documents Jaworski has been trying to pry out of the White House by subpena.

The McCormick Place event was the second annual meeting of Associated Milk Producers, Inc. [A.M.P.I.], a milk marketing cooperative based in San Antonio. It was

In the *Chicago Tribune*, March 31, 1974. Reprinted, courtesy of the *Chicago Tribune*.

only a fledgling as farm organizations go. Yet, in the two years since its formation thru mergers with several smaller cooperatives, it claimed 43,000 members in 22 states from Minnesota to Texas and from Colorado to Pennsylvania.

This made it the biggest organization of its kind ever put together, with control over 12.5 per cent of the nation's milk supply, including 95 per cent of the milk for Chicago area consumers.

Still, its membership is small, compared with that of much older and, presumably, more influential general farm organizations, such as the American Farm Bureau Federation with nearly 2.3 million members, and the National Farmers Union and National Grange, with about a quarter-million members each.

So it was remarkable, indeed, when this small, new organization of dairy farmers staged the biggest, most lavish, costliest meeting in the history of American agriculture as the setting for an awesome display of political influence unrivalled by any other farm group.

Consider some other aspects of the meeting. President Nixon was, of course, the stellar attraction. But with him on the speaker's platform that evening was an all-star cast comprising his secretary of Agriculture, 11 United States senators, and 10 U.S. representatives, along with former Gov. Ogilvie and Mayor Daley.

The congressional delegation, numbering 11 Republicans and 10 Democrats, included some of the most powerful men on Capitol Hill. Many of those present had been among 125 House members [96 Democrats, 29 Republicans] and 28 senators [27 Democrats, 1 Republican] who five months earlier had sponsored dairy bills to boost milk price supports at taxpayers' expense.

And most of those present had received, or would receive later, dairy industry cash in the form of honoraria or campaign contributions.

The lineup of the dairymen's influential political friends on the platform that evening included Rep. Thomas P. O'Neill Jr. [D., Mass.], majority whip; former Rep. and now Vice President Ford [R., Mich.], then minority leader; Rep. Leslie Arends [R., Ill.], minority whip; Rep. W. R. [Bob] Poage [D., Tex.], chairman of the House Agriculture Committee; and Sen. Herman Talmadge [D., Ga.], chairman of the Senate Agriculture Committee.

Also present were two other members of the House Agriculture Committee, Rep. John Zwach [R., Minn.] and former Rep. Page Belcher [R., Okla.]; and two Senate Agriculture Committee members, Sen. Homer Curtis [R., Neb.] and former Sen. Jack Miller [R., Ia.].

Other Senators listed on the program were Sen. Stevenson [D., Ill.]; Sen. John Stennis [D., Miss.]; Sen. Clifford Hansen [R., Wyo.]; Sen. Walter Mondale [D., Minn.]; Sen. Daniel Inouye [D., Hawaii]; Sen. Ted Stevens [R., Alaska]; Sen. Marlow Cook [R., Ky.]; and Sen. Thomas McIntyre [D., N.H.]. Other congressmen listed were Rep. John Byrnes [R., Wis.]; Rep. David Pryor [D., Ark.]; former Rep. and now Sen. James Abourezk [D., S.D.]; and Rep. John Myers [R., Ind.].

Documents submitted by A.M.P.I. attorneys to a Federal District Court in Kansas City, Mo., in connection with a complicated antitrust suit against the organization, disclosed only recently that, with two exceptions, the senators and congressmen received honoraria of $1,500 each for their appearances at the meeting and for breakfast speeches the next morning. The documents pointed out that not all recipients kept their fees, naming Senators Stennis and Curtis who asked that theirs be contributed to charitable organizations.

The documents did not mention honoraria for Sen. Mondale and former Rep. Belcher.

The documents also disclosed that several politicians had received honoraria for appearances made on behalf of A.M.P.I. in 1970. Among them were Ford, $4,500; Cook, $1,500; Stevenson, $2,500; and Sen. Robert Dole [R., Kas.], former G.O.P. national chairman, $1,500. Others included two past or future Democratic Presidential candidates, Sen. Hubert Humphrey [Minn.] and Sen. George McGovern [S.D.], $2,500 each, and two past or future Democratic Vice Presidential candidates, Sen. Edmund Muskie [Me.], $3,000, and Sen. Thomas Eagleton [Mo.], $2,500.

Such fees for speeches, however, were only a dribble of the milk money that flowed like water into campaign coffers of candidates in both parties from the political slush funds of A.M.P.I. and two other large dairy cooperatives. The other two groups were Mid-America Dairymen, Inc., of Springfield, Mo., and Dairymen, Inc., of Louisville.

Precisely how much political cash was dispensed from the three funds and the identities of dozens of recipients may never be shown. However, the Nixon reelection campaign was undoubtedly the biggest winner in 1971.

Shortly before his dismissal last year, former Special Prosecutor Archibald Cox obtained a letter, dated Dec. 16, 1970, to President Nixon from a former G.O.P. congressman who at the time was an A.M.P.I. attorney. The letter said A.M.P.I. had contributed $135,000 to Republican candidates in 1970 and suggested the President could assure himself of as much as $2 million in campaign contributions if he acted promplty to impose dairy import quotas.

Two weeks later the President imposed quotas, tho not at levels desired by the dairy industry. The $2 million apparently was never contributed, but between March and mid-September of 1971 the three dairy slush funds did contribute $442,500 for the President's reelection.

Of this sum, $202,000 reportedly came from A.M.P.I.'s Committee for a Thorough Agricultural Political Education [T.A.P.E.].

Much of this cash was funneled thru 65 dummy Republican committees in Washington bearing such intriguing names as the Committee for a Better Nation, Committee for Political Integrity, Americans United for Decent Government, and Americans United for Better Leadership. The bulk of the cash flowed in just before and just after a controversial decision by the President in March, 1971, overruling Secretary of Agriculture Clifford M. Hardin and raising milk price supports.

The much publicized decision is still the subject of official investigation by Jaworski. The controversy began on March 12 when Hardin announced his refusal to accede to the requests of the three dairy groups for higher price supports on grounds it would not be in the best economic interests of dairy farmers.

On March 23 a group of 16 dairy representatives met with Nixon and other administration officials in the White House. Two days later Hardin announced he had "reevaluated" his decision and would raise price supports.

President Nixon has since revealed that the decision, in fact, was his, altho he has steadfastly denied any implication that it was a political payoff for campaign contributions.

In a White House white paper, issued last January, the President defended his decision as "totally proper" and economically "beneficial to the entire country," and said the Democrats in Congress had planned to boost supports even higher in legislation he could not veto without alienating the dairy farmers who were an essential part of his political constituency.

Whether or not the decision was "proper," the dairy farmers showed the President their appreciation when he appeared that evening in 1971 in McCormick Place.

Study Questions

1. Considering their lobbying role in our political system, do you think the term "pressure groups" is an appropriate name for what have been termed interest groups in this chapter?

2. Cite the roles or functions that interest groups play in our political system. Describe the criteria that you think must be considered when trying to determine the power and influence of different interest groups.

3. Discuss the pros and cons of the impact of interest groups on the democratic nature of our political system. Do interest groups perform a participatory function for popular expression or are they an elitist influence on the system?

4. What are the different categories of interest groups? What are the characteristics of each? Cite examples of each category.

5. Should interest groups be allowed to contribute to political campaigns? Why or why not?

6. What advantages does lobbying by interest groups have for our political system? What restrictions should be placed on lobbying? What are the factors which limit the ability of an organized interest group to influence other political actors?

7. How do you evaluate the impact of so-called citizens' lobbies, composed of interested citizens, on governmental decisions as opposed to the impact wielded by interest groups representing labor or corporate interests?

Bibliography

Books

Blaisdell, Donald H., ed. *American Political Interest Groups: Readings in Theory and Research.* New York: The Ronald Press Company, 1957, pp. 56–124.

Farkas, Suzanne. *Urban Lobbying: Mayors in the Federal Arena.* New York: New York University Press, 1971.

Holtzman, Abraham. *Interest Groups and Lobbying.* New York: The Macmillan Company, 1966.

Mahood, H. E., ed. *Pressure Groups in American Politics.* New York: Charles Scribner's Sons, 1967.
Scott, Andrew M., and Hunt, Margaret A. *Congress and Lobbies.* Chapel Hill: The University of North Carolina Press, 1966.
Zeigler, Harmon L., and Peak, Wayne G. *Interest Groups in American Society.* Englewood Cliffs, New Jersey: Prentice-Hall, Inc., 1972.
Zisk, Betty H., ed. *American Political Interest Groups: Readings in Theory and Research.* Belmont, California: Wadsworth Publishing Company, Inc., 1969.

Articles

Duscha, Julius. "Stop! In the Public Interest!" *The New York Times Magazine,* March, 1971.
Green, Mark J. "Business in Government." *New Republic,* Vol. 163, No. 20, Issue 2916 (November 14, 1970), pp. 14–16.
Kolasa, B.D. "Lobbying in the Nonpartisan Environment: The Case of March Nebraska." *The Western Political Quarterly,* Vol. XXIV (1971), pp. 65–78.
Logan, Andy. "Around City Hall." *New Yorker,* Vol. 47, No. 37 (October 30, 1971), pp. 105–112.
Ross, Robert L. "Relations Among National Interest Groups." *Journal of Politics,* Vol. 32, No. 1 (February, 1970), pp. 96–114.
Wright, Frank. "The Dairy Lobby Buys the Cream of Congress." *The Washington Monthly,* June, 1971.

Chapter 14
People and Politics

Any democracy is based on the premise that the people have a meaningful voice in selecting the leaders of government, and an influence in policy. However, the participation of people in the governmental process is an unrefined and at times rather obscure phenomenon. This is not to say that the people are not involved; indeed it is essential in a democracy that they be involved. However, the degree and scope of involvement, and the process by which this involvement takes place may vary from the complex to the very simple.

Obviously, the people's involvement in elections is the most clearly defined process, regardless of the quality of selections. Taking part in elections at any level of government is a relatively simple affair, requiring a few minutes of the citizen's time. However, when we begin to study the total process, i.e., party affiliation, development of political attitudes and familiarity with issues, the people's involvement moves into a much more complex area. Similarly, public opinion plays an important, albeit at times subtle role, in influencing the extent to which power is used by officials and in certain cases the directions of policy. In the latter case, public opinion may only react to policy already implemented, but nevertheless, it does provide a basis for accountability. This combination of political choices in elections and the nature of public opinion is the cornerstone of the democratic process. In this chapter we will briefly focus on these two factors, identifying their characteristics and relationships to the power concept of government.

Public Opinion

Pendleton Herring characterized public opinion as "The breath of life in the politics of Democracy."[1] This statement can be true only if public opinion can influence the decisions of political leaders. In order for public opinion to influence these leaders, certain conditions must be met: (1) The people must be knowledgeable about political issues; that is, they must be issued-oriented. (2) They must make their opinion known to their political representatives. (3) The representatives must be in a position to assess public opinion and feelings on policy issues of the day.

Public opinion surveys reveal, however, that most Americans are not very attentive observers of political affairs. Their interest in politics rarely extends beyond the act of voting. Gabriel Almond and Sidney Verba concluded in their study that a substantial majority of people in five Western democracies, the United States, the United Kingdom, Germany, Italy, and Mexico, show very little interest in following accounts of political and governmental affairs, and pay little attention to political campaigns.

The table shows that in five free countries, the percentage of the population which follows political issues on a regular basis is very low (27 percent in the United States). The figures for those who follow such matters from time to time are only slightly more encouraging.

Not only are the people not attentive observers of political issues, they are probably not sufficiently familiar with the structures of gov-

Following Account of Political and Governmental Affairs by Nation [in per cent]

Per Cent who Report They Follow Accounts	United States	United Kingdom	Germany	Italy	Mexico
Regularly	27	23	34	11	15
From Time to Time	53	45	38	26	40
Never	19	32	25	62	44
Other and Don't Know	1	1	1	1	1
Total Per Cent	100	100	100	100	100
Total Number	970	963	955	995	1,007

Source: THE CIVIC CULTURE: Political Attitudes And Democracy In Five Nations, by Gabriel A. Almond and Sidney Verba (Copyright 1963 by Princeton University Press), published for the Center of International Studies, Princeton University: Tables 6 and 7, p. 89.

Actual question: "Do you follow the accounts of political and governmental affairs? Would you say you follow them regularly, from time to time, or never?"

Representation for the Lawmaker

The Level of Political Information Among the Adult Public

	Year	Source
94% know the President's term is four years	1951	(AIPO)
80% know meaning of term "veto"	1947	(AIPO)
78% know what initials "FBI" stand for	1949	(AIPO)
72% know China to be "Communist"	1964	(SRC)
70% can name their mayor	1967	(AIPO)
69% can name the current Vice President	1952	(AIPO)
68% know President limited to two terms	1970	(SRC)
65% can identify Secretary of State	1966	(AIPO)
53% can name their Congressman	1970	(AIPO)
49% know there are two U.S. senators from each state	1954	(AIPO)
36% know the meaning of term "welfare state"	1950	(AIPO)
34% can name both U.S. senators from their state	1967	(ORC)
28% can name their state senator	1967	(AIPO)
19% know meaning of "no fault" insurance	1971	(AIPO)

Reproduced in part from Robert Erikson and N. Luttbeg, *American Public Opinion* (New York: Wiley, 1973), p. 25.

ernment or the identity of public officials, especially their own representatives.

Aside from the problem of a low level of public interest, even fewer people make their beliefs directly known. Only about a quarter of Americans report that they have attempted to influence local government, and less than 10 percent profess to engage in political activities by belonging to a political club or attending a political rally or meeting.

Representation for the Lawmaker

This leaves the burden of finding out what his constituents think largely upon the representative. His knowledge of public opinion must come from professional polling services, personal polls, the opinions of those close to him, the letters he receives, lobby groups, and his own sense of what the public wants.

The professional polls are generally accurate, but they have some major limitations. They usually concern themselves only with national issues; thus, state and local representatives have no professional information sources. Even for the national representative, their usefulness is limited because they do not analyze every issue, and they register the nation as a whole, rather than by individual constituencies. Polls conducted by the representative in his own district could be the most useful. Unfortunately, these are usually conducted by mail and response is poor.

The most frequent sources of public opinion for representatives seem to be letters, lobbies, and personal acquaintances. The disadvantages here are obvious. Those who write letters and join lobbies are usually those whose interest in the issue is most vital. Their feelings are not truly representative, and may actually be minority opinions. Again we refer to the letter-writing campaign of the National Rifle Association, which was instrumental in swaying the opinions of many congressmen although the mood in the country was for gun control. Similarly, the thoughts of those close to the representative are usually somewhat distorted by the very position of the opinion-holders; they often represent only one side of the partisan picture or the liberal-conservative conflict. They can also be influenced by a desire to please the representative, because of friendship or hope of personal gain.

Finally, the representative's personal sense of public opinion is a very shaky source of data. It is based upon such things as receptions in given localities, response to his speeches, etc. These things often depend more on the candidate's personality and personal popularity than on his position on issues. It is hard to gauge a whole constituency's response from a few speech tour stops or fund-raising visits. The public reaction to President Ford's pardon of former President Nixon was seen by some as an indication that Ford had misread the public mood. A Gallup poll assessing President Ford's performance, taken between September 27 and 30, 1974, after the granting of the pardon, showed a sharp decline of twenty-one points. A special poll taken by *The New York Times* immediately after the pardon showed a 62 percent disapproval of it.[2]

Representatives thus seldom have sufficient information about their constituents' opinions to translate those opinions into the laws or policies of the nation.

More Responsive Public Policy

If the voters are not informed or issue-oriented, or if the political representatives face problems in knowing their constituents' wants, then, it may be asked: is it possible to bring the public officials' actions into line with public opinion? Is it possible for public policy to be consistent with the preferences of the public?

There are five theoretical possibilities through which linkages between public opinion and leadership behavior could exist:

1. A voter could vote rationally and choose leaders whose policy positions are similar to his own. A rational choice, however, is possible only if the voter is informed, has well-formed opinions on several policy issues, and knows the positions of the various political candidates. As noted above, those conditions are not met in reality, and at best this opportunity exists only once in two or four years for most elections.
2. A voter could choose the political party which supports the general type of policy he favors. In other words, he makes a rational choice among various party platforms, finding and supporting the one which best suits him. This is the best an average voter can do; lacking the time to study every issue or every candidate's position, he picks his party to represent him. The parties would then urge their elected representatives to honor the platform pledges, in the hope that fulfilling those promises will assure electoral success again. Party platforms in most instances are made broad enough and general enough to appeal to most voters and a variety of groups. While this possibility, the "party model," seems sound in theory, in practice it does not stand up. It is found that people simply do not make a rational choice between parties. In the average presidential election, half of the voters choose their party before the platform is written and before the presidential candidate is named. The type of voter who decides how he is going to vote as early as that is hardly likely to be changed by political rhetoric. As a result the political candidate must take his direction from the expressed wishes of a minority of the voters.
3. Another possibility, the "pressure group model," involves the indirect influence of public opinion on public policy. This method recognizes that people do not participate in the determination of all public issues, but suggests that on specific issues of interest, people do form pressure groups. These pressure groups, through letter-writing campaigns and lobbying or demonstrations, are significant displays of public opinion which can effect policy changes. While pressure groups can be a significant force in creating public policy, it is questionable whether this should be considered public opinion shaping public policy. The people who join pressure groups include only a small minority of the total public. Looking at the table below the percentage of the general population who indicated they have been politically active in any way is small. Thus, no pressure group, no matter how successful, can claim to represent general public

opinion. In fact, pressure groups often run directly contrary to public opinion in their demands. The influence of the American Medical Association on the progress of Medicare legislation is a case in point. In 1962, while 55 percent of the public favored Medicare, the bill was still defeated by a small margin largely through the efforts of the AMA lobby. It can be seen that these pressure groups are more the tool of a vocal minority than a genuine vehicle of public opinion. As Schattschneider observes, "The notion that the pressure system is automatically representative of the whole community is a myth fostered by the universalizing tendencies of modern group theory."[3]

4. The two other theoretical possibilities (or models) of achieving indirect public control over public policy are similar in that they both put faith in a natural tendency which propels public officials to follow public opinion. In the "sharing model," it is believed that since the representative is an American and shares the same interests as the rest of his voters, he would naturally do what is best for the majority of the people. This view holds that the majority of the representatives usually entertain the same opinion as the majority of the people, simply because they are part of the people.

5. In the "role-playing model," the reliance is on the natural good faith of the representatives, who know in their hearts that they should answer to the people. Knowing this, they play the role of responsive representative whether they agree with the public or not.

Needless to say, these last two models are to a degree fanciful. Neither considers the fact that public officials are subject to human

Percent of Americans Professing to Having Been Active in Various Political Actions, 1952-1970

Activity	1952	1956	1960	1964	1968	1970
Belong to political club	2	3	3	4	3	5
Work for political party	3	3	6	5	5	7
Attend political rally or meeting	7	10	8	9	9	9
Contribute money to campaign	4	10	12	11	9	[a]
Use political sticker or button	[a]	16	21	16	15	9
Give political opinions	27	28	33	31	30	27
Vote in election	73	73	74	78	75	59[b]

Reproduced from Erikson and Luttberg, *op. cit.*
[a] Not asked.
[b] The 1970 elections is a midterm congressional only election, resulting in a typical lower turnout.

frailties or that they have their own motives and interests, which are not necessarily the same as the will of the people.

Presidential Conduct and Public Opinion

The President's conduct can either affect or be affected by, public opinion. President Johnson's advocacy of new civil rights legislation in 1964 apparently caused a substantial shift in public opinion favoring such a law, even though President Kennedy had made previous efforts in this direction. On the other hand, the decisions of both President Truman and President Johnson not to run for a second term of office were largely due to mounting public opinion against their conduct of unpopular wars in Asia.[4]

Yet the presidency remains the strongest of all possible positions from which to influence the direction and intensity of public opinion. On low intensity issues, such as most foreign policy matters, the President enjoys considerable latitude in tackling a situation with any of a variety of options and still receiving public support. President Nixon's trip to China provided a good example of such a case, even though the relationship with China was probably one of the more intense foreign policy opinions held by most people. Public opinion in opposition to relations with China softened substantially once Nixon's actions suggested that the time for a thaw had arrived. Similarly, presidential explanation can carry the clout to change opinion. Nixon's explanation of the rationale for sending troops into Cambodia resulted in a sudden 43 percent gain in support for the action. This high degree of responsiveness of public opinion to presidential leadership has been called by John Mueller a "rally-round-the-flag" phenomenon or effect.[5]

There is always the danger that the President can become insulated from public opinion. President Nixon's firing of special Watergate prosecutor Archibald Cox, and President Ford's pardon of Richard Nixon, are examples of the insulation of the President and consequent misreading of the public mood. If the President is not careful, his staff and the bureaucracy will try to shield him from unpleasant information. This can create beliefs and attitudes in the presidential office that do not accurately reflect the country's mood. (See Chapter 11.)

It is the intensity of public opinion on a particular issue that is most likely to influence the conduct of presidential policy. It may be theorized that the less intense public opinion is, the more autonomy the

President enjoys in policy decisions. For example, the President certainly would feel more at ease acting autonomously on a cultural exchange treaty with the Soviet Union than he would on a policy decision to commit American troops to a new ground war in Cambodia. The cultural exchange treaty would probably be an issue of far less importance than the Cambodia decision, and hence arouse far less intense opinion in a typical citizen. Similarly, civil rights and social welfare questions will evoke a greater response from the public than the question of allowing a certain singing or ballet group to perform in the United States.

Elections and Public Policy

It is a commonly held belief that the election is an effective method of demanding political accountability; it is thought that public opinion can be communicated through the ballot box and made to be felt by elected officials. Many would point out as examples the reelection of President Roosevelt in 1936, and the refusals by President Truman and President Johnson to run for reelection.

Yet, many factors mitigate the usefulness of elections as instruments through which an electorate controls public policy. Elections may not offer the voter the issues or the candidates desired. Voters may not be cognizant of or concerned with policy choices, if offered. Voters are usually subject to many psychological and social pressures, which may actually misdirect their votes toward the wrong candidate or position. An official, once elected, need not act in consonance with the opinions expressed by voters, especially if he detects apathy among them. Therefore in actual practice, the people do not completely control policy through the ballot box.

However, other factors favor elections as a means for public influence on policy decisions. Surveys show that voters frequently cross party lines in their voting, in numbers large enough to influence election outcome. Candidates must be cautious of this partisan swing vote in displaying their party attachment. By taking a position in partisanship that is palatable to weak identifiers of the opposite party, they can capture these votes. A consciousness in an elected official of these swing voters could influence policy decisions, particularly if the official perceives an election as a close one.

In many cases the candidate must also concern himself with independent voters in order to win an election. Since these independent voters are the real floaters, with a higher issue orientation than the large body of moderate-to-weak partisans, their vote can be crucial in some contests. In seeking their support, the candidate must be conscious of his constituents' issue stances.

Yet it is still true, as observed by Angus Campbell and his coauthors in *The American Voter,* that the electorate in general is politically unaware.[6] Issues are not dominant factors in elections. In presidential elections as well as others, party identification plays a consistently more important and stable role in affecting voter choices. Therefore linkage between public opinion and the conduct of public policy through the medium of the ballot box is weak or moderate at best. The ballot box has both potential and limitations as a means of communicating public sentiment.

Public Opinion and Power

Public opinion, although it has little form or substance, does exert a force in restraining or expanding the power base of elected officials. Issues which are perceived as crucial by the public are likely to develop into groundswell phenomena in which public opinion is manifested. A recent example of this was the issue of the White House tapes in the Watergate affair. President Nixon's dismissal of special Watergate prosecutor Archibald Cox, followed immediately by the resignation of Attorney General Elliot Richardson, and the firing of Deputy Attorney General Ruckelshaus, combined with Nixon's reluctance to turn over to the courts certain tapes associated with the Watergate affair, made many Americans feel that the President was acting in a questionable manner. The reaction was so great that the President reversed himself, offered the tapes to the federal circuit court, and engaged in a variety of image-making activities to regain some semblance of public trust. The President's campaign to rectify the impact of Watergate provides an exceptional example of the nature of public opinion and its relationship to the power of any particular official. Many scholars feel that the erosion of the legitimacy of the Nixon administration as a result of the Watergate revelations, diminished the President's power to conduct the business of government, both domestically and in foreign affairs.

Officials sensitive to the judgment of the public generally try to manipulate public opinion to develop the best possible support for their own position and policies. Using the mass media, and engaging in power-reinforcing activities, e.g., a call for tax reduction, law and order, or the end of unemployment, they try to create an image of legitimacy as the base for maintaining or expanding their power. It is important to note that officials who are not in the public eye or under scrutiny by other political actors may have a great base of power due to their reduced accountability. This is particularly true with respect to certain members of the bureaucracy. Indeed, the threat of public scrutiny is a key characteristic of any democratic system. However, those in government may determine what is to be scrutinized, while influencing public opinion to accept their judgment.

A receptive public atmosphere is necessary if elected officials are to maintain their present power base and it is essential if the power base is to be expanded. Public opinion establishes the general guidelines of the rules of the game, that is, how the government should act and what kinds of policies it should develop. Admittedly, the general public remains relatively ignorant of the specifics of many issues. However, the result of political decisions and the immediate issues that affect the individual's day-to-day existence and his perception of what is right, provide the basis for developing attitudes on larger political issues. Public understanding of the intricacies of the Strategic Arms Limitation Agreement is not as important as the overall impression that it will ease international tensions, since the public perceives that easing of tensions is right. Similarly, the public may not understand the complexities of fiscal and monetary policy. However, realization that inflation reduces buying power while high interest rates restrict borrowing and home ownership, provides specific reference points by which the public judges the government's policy.

When there is public apathy toward any particular issue or political behavior, the official can easily base his power on the premise that it

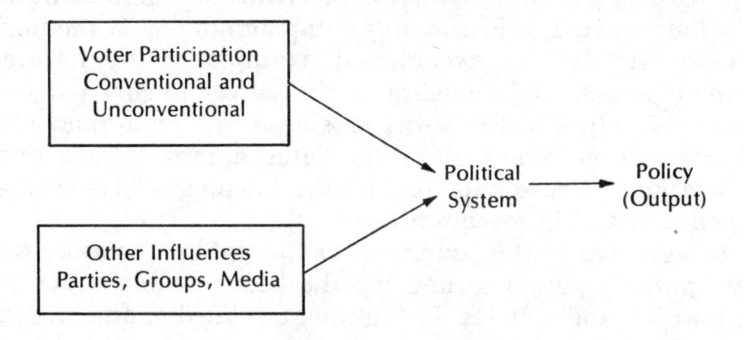

Voter Participation and Public Policy

is for the good of the people, or that the people demand it. Since there is little, if any, articulation of public attitudes, the official can use his own discretion (within limits) and by default expand his base of power. The general thesis is that public opinion, although hampered by ignorance of policy intricacies and alternatives does in the final analysis provide an ultimate judgment on the behavior of officials and the legitimacy of government.

American Voter Behavior

In American democracy elections are the basic institutional device to ensure that the government shall "derive its just powers from the consent of the governed." Therefore it is important to understand the behavior of the American voter in order to make some assessment about his possible impact on the governing process.

It should be mentioned that electoral participation is not the only way to influence governmental action. In recent years, there has been an increase in such political activities as rallies, processions, demonstrations, sit-ins, and riots. The increase has been most marked among the better educated, who have accepted the legitimacy of noninstitutional forms of political participation more readily than those who are less educated. Depending on the scope and intensity of unconventional political activity, government policy can be influenced. This heightened unconventional political participation has, for example, brought change in government policy toward military intrusions abroad. Normally, however, this kind of political activity is limited to a tiny minority.

Electoral politics have cast America into a two-party mold, the Democrats and the Republicans. But not all Democrats are strong Democrats, nor are all Republicans strong Republicans. Nor are all Democrats or all Republicans of one mind on all important issues. Given the fact that the Democrats or the Republicans are a heterogeneous lot, each of the two parties can hope to win elections only by building an electoral coalition of voters who happen to constitute a majority at the time. This necessity promotes responsiveness on the part of politicians, and gives the people a measure of power to influence policy through elections. Since each party contains supporters from the various social strata and interest groupings, the members of the two parties have overlapping interests. This provides the leaders incentives for reaching compromises where otherwise polarization or heightened political tension would be a reality. This tendency toward compromise and coalition politics helps promote stability in a democratic system. It also, however, retards the pace of social change.

There is inequality in political participation. At one end of the scale are the political activists who not only vote but also donate money (only 9 percent in 1968, see table page 474), work for the political party (5 percent in 1968), and attend meetings or rallies (9 percent in 1968). Although there is no precise estimate of the size of the politically active segment of the electorate, the activists probably do not constitute much over 5 percent of the voters. Because of their frequent and greater involvement, their knowledge of political routines, and their acquired political skills, the activists naturally wield exclusive influence in affecting the course of government policy.

V. O. Key points out that political activists are found at all income and occupational levels. This is significant for the operation of a democratic system, inasmuch as no exclusive class has monopoly over political influence. All classes have the opportunity to share the material or psychological benefits of political participation.[7]

At the other end of the political participation scale are the apoliticals or nonvoters. They constitute 30 to 40 percent. This percentage varies from local to presidential elections; in local elections as few as 20 percent of the voters may make the effective political choices. Compared with such democracies as India, Denmark, West Germany or Great Britain where 80 to 85 percent of the voters vote, the turnout in the United States is low. One consequence of this low participation is that it tends to enhance control by a tight party organization.

The degree of political participation influences politics. Authors Verba and Nie, in their recent work on political participation, find that in communities where there is a moderately high rate of participation, leaders are quite responsive to citizens, whereas in communities with very low rates of political activity, responsiveness of leaders is relatively low.[8] In the communities with low participation, the leaders feel relatively free to do as they want in regard to matters of public policy. The Verba-Nie data demonstrate that linkage between the constituents and the leaders hinges upon citizen participation in politics.

Degree of Participation

The following generalizations can be made about the rates of political participation:
1. Older voters vote proportionately more than younger voters.

2. Men are more likely to vote or participate in other political activities than women.
3. More educated citizens are more likely to participate in political activity.
4. Persons in higher income groups are more likely to vote than those in low income groups.
5. Homeowners vote more often than renters.
6. There is more voting activity in times of social crises than during normal times.
7. Persons of higher occupational status are more likely to participate in politics.
8. Differences due to religion are small. Jews are slightly more active in politics than Catholics who, in turn, are followed by Protestants.
9. Farmers are less likely to engage in political activity than city dwellers.
10. Blacks participate in politics at a much lower rate than whites.

Party Voting

The data on party voting indicate that young people include proportionately more Democrats, the old proportionately more Republicans, although a significant minority of older people have voted Democratic; in 1964 a majority of them voted so. And the young were somewhat evenly divided between Nixon and McGovern in 1972 (See Table). The young and old vote is politically significant since the population trend indicates that population at both ends of the age continuum has increased, whereas there has been a decrease in the middle category (30–39 years).

The table also shows that the difference between the sexes in their political preference is negligible. Blacks at the moment are disproportionately Democrats. So are Catholics, manual workers, and members of labor unions. The general pattern has been that high-status WASPs (White-Anglo-Saxon-Protestants) vote predominantly Republican, and low-status, minority groups, blacks, Jews and Catholics (high or low-status) vote mainly Democratic.

Most of the voters vote their party line, almost habitually. This is particularly so in periods of stability and prosperity. However, there are enough switchers (independent and weak-to-moderate party identifiers) to cause a deviating election: that is, an election in which the majority party in the electorate is not returned to power. Issues or

Social Categories and Voting Trends
(Presidential Vote, 1960–1972)
Percent Democratic of two-party vote for President *(three-party in 1968)*

	1960	1964	1968	1972
National	50	61	43	38
Men	52	60	41	37
Women	49	62	45	38
White	49	59	38	32
Non-white	68	94	85	87
College	39	52	37	37
High School	52	62	42	42
Grade School	55	66	52	49
Professional & Business	42	54	34	31
White collar	48	57	31	36
Manual	60	71	50	43
Under 30 years	54	64	47	48
30-49 years	54	63	44	33
50-plus	46	59	41	36
Protestants	38	55	35	30
Catholics	78	76	59	48
Republicans	5	20	9	5
Democrats	84	87	74	67
Independents	43	56	31	31
Members of labor union families	65	73	56	46

Source: The Gallup Poll, press release, December 14, 1972.

events can arouse citizens and decisively influence elections even when the majority of votes are regular. Independent or shifting votes thus inject an element of uncertainty in the political process, which in turn probably alerts the politicians toward public needs and concerns.

New Voting Patterns?

The 1974 congressional elections indicated a relatively wide shift to the Democratic party. It was reported that in most districts as many as 8 percent of the voters shifted to the Democrats. Equally important, it was estimated that this shift occurred in all income brackets and included Jews, Protestants, and Catholics, and professionals and laborers who had voted Republican in the last election. Democrats were quick to claim that this indicated a rebuilding of the traditional Democratic coalition which had brought victory so often in the past. On the other hand, a number of observers suggested that the vote should not be construed as a mandate for the Democrats, but rather a negative or protest vote against the Republicans, Watergate, and the economy. Moreover, vote returns indicated that less than 40 percent of the registered voters actually voted—one of the lightest turnouts in recent years. Some blamed this on voter apathy, others on protest against the Republicans and the system; still others suggested that neither party had made a great hit with the voters.[9]

Whether this new voting pattern would be a short-term or long-term one would depend on the state of the economy, Democratic accomplishments in Congress, and the ability of President Ford and the Republicans to reorganize their party. Clearly, the Democrats had the initiative and the power base to appeal to the voters and rebuild a strong political coalition. But even in victory, perceptive Democrats were cautious, knowing that the voters would expect results and would blame the Democratic party if none came.

Role of the Mass Media

In 1970 it was reported that 96 percent of all American households had a television set. The average weekly hours on the air for all television stations was about 118 out of a possible 168 hours in a week. In 1973, it was reported that there were 2,400 newspapers, both daily and Sunday, with a total circulation of over 115 million copies.[10] This gives some idea of the scope of the mass media in this country. To be sure, the number of sets in use, the total circulation of newspapers, etc., do not give us an indication of the impact, but one can certainly conclude that the mass media has significant impact on attitudes, beliefs and values of modern Americans. Indeed, the mass media, particularly television, have become key instruments in trying to influence the political attitudes of Americans. Many national candidates go to great lengths to devise television campaigns that will appeal to the most susceptible of people's beliefs, in order to develop winning campaign strategies.

There is no agreement regarding the effect of the mass media, but it is apparent that there is an impact. For example, observers agree that the John F. Kennedy-Richard M. Nixon debates in 1960 were instrumental in gaining votes for Kennedy, while portraying an image that was detrimental to Richard Nixon. Similarly, when there are issues that are not generally understood, the media can make an important impact. Candidates who are not well known can make their names household words overnight through the mass media. It is difficult, however, to measure the impact. According to some data, television has become the medium by which a majority of people follow politics and campaigns.[11] Indeed, most people would consider television as the most important medium for gaining information on politics. This influences the style of the candidate; it provides a picture of him and exposes him to public scrutiny as never before. Certainly, a bad image or a political misjudgment can have a decided impact on voters.

Television was a primary cause of the changed attitudes of Americans regarding the role of the United States in Vietnam. One observer, commenting on this, stated: "The greatest emotional force against the war was television news film coverage. As we cannot forget, television showed endless film clips of American troops being killed and injured. As one writer sardonically commented, 'Tune in at eleven and see Johnny die.'"[12]

Some critics of the mass media claim that the entire system is influenced by an elite group of top television commentators and news analysts, who interpret the news from their own perspective. These perspectives are then transmitted to a vast number of local stations and commentators, who generally follow along in their broadcasts. Similarly, the leading newspapers such as *The New York Times* and the *Washington Post* have an impact throughout the country because their lead is picked up by local newspapers. Both of these major papers serve as reference points for many other newspapers, thus increasing and intensifying their impact.

Many of the national television commentators have vast followings. People invariably associate with their favorite commentator. The news as presented by such commentators reinforces preconceived notions, expands the viewers' base of information, and in many instances motivates the viewer to accept the commentator's interpretation of events. By the slightest smirk or raising of eyebrows, or by the tone of their delivery, commentators can convey significant messages to their viewers. Thus, the commentator need not speak out against something to get the message across in his news program; he can convey the same message through broadcasting mannerisms.

As a result of increasing criticism of the use and manipulation of mass media in influencing the public, many commentators have developed a series of devices to attempt some objectivity. There now are categories such as interpretive journalism, journalistic commentary, and issue programs. However, most scholars would agree that objectivity in the mass media is an elusive goal. Regardless of attempts at unbiased news, opinions, biases, and preferences creep into newspaper stories, television programming, and the techniques used for reporting and interviewing.

On the other hand, few would deny that one of the major bastions of democracy is a free press, which is the cornerstone of the First Amendment. Indeed, it was the press that first broke the stories of the Watergate affair, the My Lai massacre, and the U.S. role in Vietnam (the Pentagon papers).

There is no question that the mass media, particularly television, have changed the political habits of voters and candidates. The media have opened up a vast area that formerly was the preserve of professional politicians, and have brought politics and government into virtually every American home. Both directly and indirectly, the mass media influence our perceptions and political behavior. The continuing dilemma in a democratic society is how to maintain a free press, yet insure a balanced and objective channel for presenting ideas and information. The dilemma becomes clearer if we recall that power is directly connected with the ability to transmit information and the ability to interpret and reach people. The mass media have power in their capacity to provide coherent views throughout the nation; this power is increased by the ability of the media to select and interpret the news. The need of a democratic society for a free press must be balanced against its need for a fair and just press. This creates a continuing conflict that can never be completely resolved.

Summary

The discussion in this chapter would indicate that voting does matter to an extent. The necessity of building majority coalitions imposes a restraint on the arbitrariness and authoritarianism of a politician. The element of uncertainty in election outcomes, due to such factors as shifting or floating votes, also tends to make politics responsive to people's concerns. However, not all qualified voters exercise their right to vote; this may be indicative of their feeling that votes are not going to make an impact on politics and policy of the country. Voter indifference gives political leaders considerable leeway in shaping policy. Leaders tend to respond to active rather than nonactive citizens. The relatively low participation of voters is therefore not likely to provoke adequate response to the needs of the nation. Also unequal political participation produces unequal political influence. Although they comprise only a tiny minority, the activists, due to their greater involvement, political skills and knowledge, are able to exert disproportionate influence on the policy-making process.

The concern for creating a politically advantageous image and winning votes, and the need to expand the political power base, makes candidates and those in office sensitive to the use of the mass media. In effect, news analysts, commentators, critics, opinion leaders, and those in office are concerned about public opinion and its capacity to limit or reinforce their power. The mass media thus become key instruments in the struggle for power. As long as the mass media try to maintain objectivity, and those struggling for an impact on public opinion operate according to acceptable standards, the conflicts remain a dynamic element of democracy.

Notes

1. Pendleton Herring, *The Politics of Democracy* (New York: W. W. Norton, 1965), p. 313.
2. Clifton Daniel, "Ford's Gallup Rating Off 21 Points After Pardon," *The New York Times*, Ocober 13, 1974, p. 1.
3. E. E. Schattschneider, *The Semi-Sovereign People: Realist's View of Democracy in America* (New York: Holt, Rinehart and Winston, 1960), p. 35.
4. Robert Erikson and N. Luttbeg, *American Public Opinion* (New York: Wiley, 1973), p. 155.
5. John Mueller, *War, Presidents, and Public Opinion* (New York: Wiley, 1973).
6. A. Campbell, et. al., *The American Voter* (New York: Wiley, 1964).
7. V. O. Key, Jr., *Politics, Parties, and Pressure Groups* (New York: Crowell, 1964), Ch. 21.
8. Sidney Verba and Norman Nie, *Participation in America* (New York: Harper and Row, 1972), pp. 316–317.
9. David E. Rosenbaum, "Wide Voter Shift From G.O.P. Shown," *The New York Times*, November 7, 1974, pp. 1 and 30.
10. *Statistical Abstract of the United States*, 1974, pp. 504–506.
11. V. O. Key, Jr., *Public Opinion and American Democracy* (New York: Alfred A. Knopf, 1971), p. 346.
12. Robert D. Novak, "The New Journalism" in Harry M. Clor (ed.), *The Mass Media and Modern Democracy* (Chicago: Rand McNally, 1974), p. 5.

Selected Readings

The power of the people in influencing decision-makers and other political actors is relatively limited in day-to-day operations of the political system. Many would even argue that the power of the people is limited not only on a day-to-day basis but in practically every aspect of the political system. Nevertheless, during elections, people do exercise one of their basic rights and it might be added, a significant amount of power in the aggregate, in deciding what persons shall have office. However, even here, people are influenced by mass media, manipulated, and virtually directed into the choices desired by certain political actors. James Moriarty, in the selection to this chapter, shows that campaigns are "generally packaged and presented by advertising specialists." Additionally, since the development of computers and the increasing sophistication of experts in the behavioral sciences, the entire political process is undergoing revolution. As a matter of fact, Moriarty argues that the complex of management-pollster-communicator, is replacing "the party structure as a buffer between the voter and the candidate." Through a sophisticated assessment of voting behavior, the complex of experts can persuade people to accept certain characteristics and assessments of the political system, and view candidates in a certain way—thus influencing voting behavior. Such a condition suggests that a candidate with a great amount of money can "buy" the necessary technology to get elected, even if opposed by the traditional party structure. The latest campaign reform bill and assessment of political ethics may provide some counterbalance to this possibility. But the serious student of democracy needs to ask whether candidates who are packaged and sold by playing upon the human subconscious are the best representatives of the people and in the best interests of American democracy.

14.1

Campaigns and the New Technology

JAMES MORIARITY

"McCluskey too picked up the pace, chiefly by increasing the number of his television appearances. . . . Skeffington, before all else, favored the direct and personal contact with the voter; this approach had left McCluskey cold. He wanted television, and—more significant—so did his principal supporters."—'The Last Hurrah."

Because he ignored the power of television in politics, Frank Skeffington, mayor of Boston in Edwin O'Connor's 1956 novel, went down in defeat.

This fictional account had its basis in fact. Ever since Dwight Eisenhower used television to overwhelm the 1952 Republican Convention, nullifying the political party power held by his rival for the nomination, Robert Taft, politicians and political scientists alike have observed that the medium brings a new dimension to politics. Instead of operating through the buffer of the party structure, the candidate on TV appeals directly to the voter. As a result, the traditional two-step process of communication, in which voters were largely influenced by local opinion leaders, has been short-circuited.

But the role of television has altered since it first proved so effective. Once merely a tool that could be used with skill, it is now part of an election technology that includes not only communications, but the increasingly precise techniques of polling, the sophisticated conclusions of research on persuasion and influence, and the versatility of computer analysis of voter patterns to pinpoint issues to emphasize and those to stay away from.

The campaign is generally packaged and presented by advertising specialists— "The campaigns can best be followed in the media trade press, where political campaigns are treated alongside beer accounts," says Dr. Harold Mendelsohn of the University of Denver. But the entire process has called into being a new group of

Reprinted with permission from *Science News*, the weekly news magazine of science and the application of science, Copyright 1970 by Science Service, Inc.

technocrats that Dr. Dan Nimmo of the University of Missouri at Columbia has termed the management-pollster-communicator complex.

This new group, in effect, has replaced the party structure as a buffer between the voter and the candidate. The professionals organize a candidate's campaign, collect data on the electorate, determine the issues and image that the candidate should put forth, and then develop strategies that the candidate should pursue if he is to be elected.

As a result, far from bringing the candidate more directly in contact with the electorate, TV, in combination with the other techniques in the system, has interposed a new buffer that is even less responsive to voter pressure than the political party.

The first step in developing a campaign according to the new technology is to profile the electorate. A potent tool in this process is census data, which yields information on social rank, based on educational and occupational levels, ethnic ratings and housing. Another source of information is the growing body of social science research on attitudes and values of voters, stimulated by the growing enthusiasm for computer-based research that is sweeping behavioral science. Correlating the census data with the research on attitudes allows the campaign director to develop his strategy on issues and communications.

Once the electorate is profiled, the optimum means of communication is chosen to reach the audience. Here several decades of communications research come into play.

Starting back in World War II, for instance, Dr. Carl Hovland and a communications study group at Yale University found that an audience with a relatively low I.Q. responds best to material in which the conclusions of an argument are stated explicitly, rather than implied.

Other studies by the Yale group indicate the importance of the order of presentation in persuasion. When conflicting views are discussed, other factors being equal, the last argument presented is the most effective. This law of primacy is a technique that President Nixon has used, probably instinctively as a good campaigner, in his public presentations. He will state a number of opposing points of view on an issue and then close with his own view: "But now I wish to make my position clear."

More recent studies have attempted to probe the relative effectiveness of television and other media. Research by Dr. Bruce Westley of the University of Kentucky, for example, indicates that women of low education and income, and with working-class status and a minimal interest in politics are particularly trusting of television. If the electorate profile showed a substantial number of such voters, then heavy TV exposure, employing the techniques developed by Hovland and others, would be an indicated strategy.

The whole process of campaigning, from traditional rallies and street meetings to the packaging of brief spot appearances on TV and radio, are thus judged on the basis of their effectiveness in the whole campaign.

Computers are useful not only for electorate profiles but also for a variety of data storage functions. Mayor John Lindsay of New York in the 1968 primary campaign catalogued the reactions of 100,000 registered Republicans to phone calls asking them to rate him and his opponent on a scale of one to five; the printout was later used in the election campaign when Lindsay was running as an independent against both a Republican and a Democrat.

Mailing lists are another tool. Sometimes they are compiled by the campaign organization, but more often they are simply bought from consultants who specialize in direct mail techniques. The lists are used not only to spread campaign literature but to solicit contributions—an increasingly important campaign function.

Funding in the new political technology is critical, and is one of the major points of controversy about modern political campaigning. Computer analysis and campaign packaging are a highly skilled, expensive business, and TV is inordinately expensive and equally important. Studies at the University of Michigan Survey Research Center show that in 1960 and 1964 television accounted for 60 percent of voters' information about Presidential elections; and Dr. Mendelsohn reports that in 1968, of the more than $50 million spent on the Presidential election, $20 million to $25 million went directly to purchase broadcast time. A new peak was reached this spring as Richard Ottinger spent $830,000 on a New York Senate primary campaign for television advertising. His total expenditure of $1.92 million was about nine times what three rivals spent.

The implications of extensive communications technology in politics are still being assessed. But some of the developments are clear.

"This means the movement into politics of high-powered media and public relations personnel," says Dr. Mendelsohn. "Because candidates can utilize their services they are displacing the political party; candidates can bypass the party with a management team and money. And of course private money in political coffers is not entirely altruistic."

Joseph Napolitan, president of a successful political consultant firm, agrees with Dr. Mendelsohn's assessment of the effect of the new technology on the political party. But he does not think the effect is bad.

"Political parties are obsolete," he says. "Technology has surpassed political parties as they function in their present status. Now instant electronic communication is the chief vehicle of comment between the voter and the candidate."

Napolitan feels that the more businesslike approach of management teams eliminates the waste of traditional political organizations. "In the past, campaigns were sloppy, poorly managed and often not staffed with professionals," says Napolitan. But more important, he feels that the new technology and use of professional management allows men who were successful in other fields to enter politics.

"Some of the best men in the Senate came in from business and the academy. Otherwise people would be deprived of their leadership," he contends.

"This development is probably more dangerous than not," says Dr. Mendelsohn. "Traditionally the party develops candidates and acts as a buffer between the public and the office. It disrupts party discipline and means that a candidate with money can be elected without being responsible to anybody, including the electorate."

"Personally I don't feel comfortable that a man could be elected without a record of public service," says Dr. Angus Campbell of the University of Michigan, an analyst of American voting behavior for the past 20 years. "It has a disruptive effect on the party and means service to the party has nothing to do with ability to get elected."

Dr. Nimmo points out in his book, "The Political Persuaders," that the increased cost of campaigning brought about by expensive communications usage will eliminate a number of candidates. He also suggests that in a period of increasing disillusionment with the political process, candidates who might appeal to disenchanted voters may be hindered from entering the arena of expensive campaigning.

But Dr. Nimmo believes that the majority of middle-class Americans are not particularly disturbed by this development. "The large number of small donations in recent campaigns," he says, "suggests that many citizens intuitively see campaign costs as a way of keeping the riffraff out of American elections; perhaps the financial contributors, large and small, prefer unregulated spending so long as it assures their interests a minimal control over elections."

As is happening in so many other fields, political behavior is being altered by technology and the technocrats who are adept in its uses. Dr. Nimmo maintains that the new technology is surpassing the importance of the political party that was the base of the old politics. But it is also in conflict with a growing movement calling for a new politics based on principle rather than party loyalty.

"Elections are approached neither as conflicts between parties nor as confrontations of principle," he states. "They are viewed instead as contests of personalities and, even more basically, they offer a choice between the sophisticated engineers working on behalf of those personalities."

Study Questions

1. Do you think that the fact that only a small percentage of citizens are politically aware is a threat to a democratic form of government? Why or why not?

2. This chapter describes five theoretical possibilities linking public opinion and leadership behavior. Summarize them, noting what you think are the merits and weaknesses of each possibility.

3. Cite examples of instances when government policy has been changed largely because of the pressure of public opinion.

4. Describe how the degree of political participation in a community or country may influence its politics and its type of leadership.

5. What are some of the generalizations that one can make about the political participation of various groups in the American electorate? What groups seem to vote or participate more than other groups? Do you think some of these patterns are gradually changing?

6. It has been asserted that most voters generally vote their party allegiance. Do you think this is a healthy situation? Why or why not?

7. What recommendations would you make to increase the level of political participation and the degree of political awareness among the American citizenry at large?

8. Should the mass media be controlled to insure that it is objective?

Bibliography

Books

Berelson, Bernard R., Lazarfeld, Paul L., and McPhee, William N. *Voting: A Study of Opinion Formation in a Presidential Campaign.* Chicago: The University of Chicago Press, 1954.

Bone, Hugh A., and Ranney, Austin. *Politics and Voters* 3d ed. Chapters 1, 2 and 3. New York: McGraw-Hill Book Company, 1971.

Burdick, Eugene, and Brodbeck, Arthur J., eds. *American Voting Behavior.* Glencoe, Illinois: The Free Press, 1959.

Campbell, Angus, Converse, Philip E., Miller, Warren E., and Stokes, Donald E. *The American Voter.* New York: John Wiley and Sons, Inc., 1960.

Campbell, Angus, Gurin, Gerald, and Miller, Warren E. *The Voter Decides.* Evanston, Illinois: Row, Peterson and Company, 1954.

Childs, Harwood L. *Public Opinion: Nature, Formation and Role.* Princeton, New Jersey: D. Van Nostrand Company, Inc., 1965.

Crotty, William J., ed. *Public Opinion and Politics: A Reader.* New York: Holt, Rinehart and Winston, Inc., 1970.

DeVries, Walter, and Tarrance, Lance Jr. *The Ticket-Splitter: A New Force in American Politics.* Grand Rapids, Michigan: William B. Eerdmans Publishing Company, 1972.

Dreyer, Edward C., and Rosenbaum, Walter A., eds. *Political Opinion and Electoral Behavior: Essays and Studies.* Belmont, California: Wadsworth Publishing Company, Inc., 1967.

Flanigan, William H. *Political Behavior of the American Electorate.* Boston: Allyn and Bacon, Inc., 1968.

Fuchs, Lawrence H., ed. *American Ethnic Politics.* New York: Harper Torch Books, Harper and Row, Publishers, Inc., 1968.

Key, V. O. Jr. *The Responsible Electorate: Rationality in Presidential Voting 1936–1960.* Cambridge, Massachusetts: The Belknap Press of Harvard University Press, 1966.

Schettler, Clarence. *Public Opinion in American Society.* New York: Harper and Row, Publishers, 1960.

Verba, Sidney, and Nie, Norman H. *Participation in America: Political Democracy and Social Equality.* New York: Harper and Row, Publishers, 1972.

Articles

Chapman, William. "The Riddle of the Young Voter." *The Progressive,* September, 1970.

Foladare, Irving S. "The Effect of Neighborhood on Voting Behavior." *Political Science Quarterly,* Vol. 83, No. 4 (December, 1968), pp. 516–529.

RePass, David E. "Issue Salience and Party Choice." *American Political Science Review,* Vol. 65, No. 2 (June, 1971), pp. 389–400.

Chapter 15
The American Political System: What Direction?

Prognostication about politics has been the downfall of many learned men. There is nothing so scientific about political behavior that allows scientifically correct predictions about the future of the American political system. Not many people, for example, could have predicted in early 1972, the revelations of the Watergate affair and their potential for a far-reaching impact on the political system. Yet, if we do not project into the future to some degree, we are left with only half the story. For what good does it do to study contemporary politics and historical lessons, if we cannot apply them to actions in the future? The most skeptical student of American politics may very well ask, "Now that we have spent so much time looking into the American political system, where do we go from here?" Without becoming embroiled in all of the rationalizations regarding intellectual capacity, understanding of one's own government, and the need for knowledgeable and involved people, we can point out that political knowledge is a direct link to political action. And political action is one basic wellspring of a democratic political system. Moreover, knowledge gained in the study of the American political system can be usefully applied to an understanding of other important subjects in the area of politics.

This background and understanding of the American political system can be used not only to assess the current political scene, but to develop a scheme that will assist in understanding the future character of American politics. It is in this light that we attempt to provide some insights into the directions that the American political system might take in the late 1970s.

No modern political system remains unchanged. Some changes are imperceptible, others quite visible. Changes are brought about from many sources—by strong pressure from the people, by the workings of the political institutions, and by the processes of politics itself. For a political system to function effectively it must be able to incorporate these changes while remaining relatively stable and operating according to the basic rules of the game. In a democratic society we assume that the political system remains open to a variety of pressures and thus is susceptible to a number of changes.

Problems in the 1970s

In the 1970s the American political system appears to be faced with a number of dilemmas, stemming primarily from a need to incorporate change while trying to maintain a traditional social and political base. The autonomy and power of the individual has clearly diminished in contrast to the power of other political actors. Yet, if the democratic condition is to be maintained, this power equation must be reversed.

In previous chapters we noted some of the major social-psychological characteristics of the American system. We tried to point out that the legitimacy and the credibility of the American political system are being questioned by a number of people. The ability of the American political system to regain the legitimacy and credibility necessary to an effective democracy rests not only on restoring the balance between individual power and the power of other political actors, but also on solving the basic problems of change and stability.

At this point the conventional textbook approach would be to list a number of major issues being faced by the American political system, followed by a discussion and possible solutions. For example, some attention would be given to such issues as energy, environment, employment, welfare, the economy, equality, individual rights and freedom, the nature of political leadership, etc. There is no question that these are major issues and they do need resolution in the immediate future. Our concern, however, is with the more fundamental issues that are the basis of the political system itself. Therefore, rather than turning our attention to all of these specific questions, discussions of which are available in many newspapers and magazines, we will concern ourselves with the basic issues of individual autonomy and power and their relationship to political actors and the political system as a whole.

Three Themes of American Politics

There are three major themes influencing the direction in which American politics and society are moving: integration and centralization, decentralization and diffusion, and social and psychological changes.

Increasing Integration and Centralization

The first theme rests on the premise that the continued industrialization of our society, its technological advances and its movement towards a computerized society motivates increasing integration of American life. As new sources of power are sought, economic institutions and processes will continue to move toward a more centralized system which is presumed to be the basis of economic efficiency. Simultaneously, there seems to be a movement towards a more unified and integrated society paralleling the economic system. Thus there appears to be a trend in which the close interrelationship between society and economy will increasingly demand specialization of the individual.

Closely related to this is the extent and scope of governmental authority at all levels. As the economic power of large corporations and institutions expands, individuals and groups will be less able to cope with the system. In our society, where economic power easily leads to political power, individuals and groups will tend to turn more and more toward government to regulate and control the economic system. In matters of social security, housing, welfare or a host of other issues, governmental institutions emerge as the only agencies able to cope with the vast conglomerate economic power. In turn government will have to expand its authority at all levels in order to deal properly with the economic and social structure. The growth of administrative agencies will probably continue and with it, the extension of bureaucratic control. Scholars who have in the past characterized the American system as a bureaucratic state were probably not far from wrong. There are no indications for the future which suggest the lessening of bureaucratic control.

One should not necessarily envision conspiracy on the part of those operating the political system. In a number of instances, the demands of the people and the inability of local governments are the real causes of the expansion of governmental authority on the higher level. The Jeffersonian ideal of a nation of stout, hard-working farmers and strong local and state governments has been clearly replaced by the Hamiltonian concept of a strong centralized national government.

Decentralization and Diffusion of Power

The second theme may appear contradictory to the first. Even though there is a definite movement towards centralization and expansion of governmental authority, there are also definite pressures for decentralization and diffusion of power within the political system. Local and state governments, political parties, and a number of political actors, reflect the heterogeneous nature of American society. This diversity provides a varied power base within the vast scope of the national system. Such power bases, stemming from local and regional constituencies, provide countervailing pressures and resistance to the centralizing trend at the national level.

Local governments and political actors who must operate at the grass roots level are much more sensitive to grievances and pressures of the people. There is a direct link that is lacking between people and the national government. These linkages will reinforce the existing power base at the local level, as people and groups turn more and more to governmental authority to cope with the increasing problems of society. Thus, while the extent of national power will expand, it will be countered by increasing power at the local levels.

Closely related to the theme of decentralization and diffusion is political participation. The phenomenon of populist politics that first emerged in nineteenth-century America had its modern counterparts in the presidential campaigns of Senator Eugene McCarthy and Senator George McGovern. Although neither man was able to reach the presidency they provided a spark which may have rekindled the concept of individual participation in politics. Coming after the significant accomplishments of the civil rights movement and the involvement of individuals in this movement, the 1972 campaign of Senator George McGovern may have provided a populist model at the national level. Perhaps more important for immediate individual impact is the expansion of this populist model at the community level. Over the past ten years there has been a proliferation of community action groups and community organizations. The civil rights groups perhaps provided the first visible method by which individuals at the local level could make some impact on the establishment.

The suspicion of political actors, and the general distrust of the workings of the American political system, have created a high degree of political skepticism within the body politic. This is probably one cause for the proliferation of community organizations and action groups. It is as if a number of people are saying, "We have to do it ourselves." For example, in the city of Chicago alone in 1973 there were over forty-two major community organizations, that is, organizations with an office and a staff of one or more persons; if one were to include all of the community organizations operating within the city (even those without office space and staff), the number would go well into the hundreds. All of these organizations attempt to scrutinize some governmental action and bring pressure to bear on some aspects of government. This relatively new phenomenon of community organization has provided new channels for the individual. It gives him a sense of power that is difficult to achieve in official institutions or political parties.

Whether this phenomenon of participatory politics will overcome the sense of skepticism and apathy is open to question. Much depends on the ability of community organizations to achieve some of their professed goals and the degree to which political leaders respond to community problems.

While conditions motivate some to move toward active involvement, they have also "turned off" a number of people—youths, people whose high hopes were dashed in the 1972 elections and even members of the regular voters who are convinced that "you can't fight city hall." Thus we see developing a unique and contradictory phenomenon—participation existing side by side with apathy and alienation.

Continuing Social and Psychological Change

The third theme, social and psychological change, is directly related to the political system and the attitudes and values associated with it. Most scholars seem to agree that there are basic changes taking place in the social pattern. Due to the impact of a generation of highly industrialized society, the civil rights movements, and the movement towards equality in all facets of our life, the social basis of society is shifting to a more egalitarian structure. The concept of middle class, for example, appears to be an increasingly vague one. Although poor and less privileged groups still exist, the increasing impetus toward an egalitarian society, buttressed by welfare assistance, Social Security, and a host of other programs, has made the distinction between the lower middle class and lower class quite hazy. The distinction between the upper middle class and lower class appears to be a much clearer one.

Indeed, our social structure is more realistically characterized in terms of ethnic groups, racial groups, youth groups, sex groups, citizens' groups, etc. Whereas not too many years ago one would speak of the vast middle class in terms of mainstream politics, one must now be aware that the middle class includes a variety of groups heretofore not considered part of the middle class. At the same time, the infusion of new groups into the traditional middle class has produced pockets of political awareness and political activity. Thus, the basic apathy of the vast number of American people is counterbalanced by a political awareness and involvement by new middle class groups.

Need for Balance

For the American political system to operate effectively while stressing the democratic condition, there must be some reconciliation of these three themes, as well as a balancing of their power and resolution of the inherent conflicts within each. This reconciliation and balance must take place at all levels of governmental authority and between the major political actors. In the main, our system expects its leaders to provide the key to this reconciliation and balance. In a study of public opinion two scholars concluded:

> Because of the pragmatic, humanitarian value system that characterizes the American political credo, the conflict between conservative ideologies and the liberal programs most people favor is understandable; but this divergence between theory and practice certainly spells caution, patience, and tact for any leader who counts, as he must, on continual popular support for legislation he believes will promote the public welfare. The effective leader in American democracy must of course formulate and communicate overall goals. But he must do more; he must plausibly demonstrate to a majority of citizens that the means by which he proposes to attain the goals are realistic, at the same time he must try to persuade them that the means are not inconsistent with their basic ideological assumptions.[1]

Political leaders, whether they be elected or appointed, are focal points or reference points from which many individuals and groups develop perceptions and attitudes on the nature of the political system.

As suggested earlier, conflict and confrontation are an inherent part of democratic political systems. Through such means issues are identified, voices heard, positions taken, and resolution achieved. Therefore, we should not assume that in a democratic system conflict is evil; on the contrary, it is necessary. Obviously we are not speaking about armed conflict or bloodshed but that conflict and confrontation that evolves between reasonable human beings, responsive institutions and wise political actors.

In our discussion so far, we have identified the general political, social, and psychological environment within which the American political system is operating. In essence what we have been suggesting is that there has been an ongoing conflict, at times implicit and at other times quite explicit, between the power of the individual and that of corporate organizations and the establishment. Moreover, there is a continuous movement in our society to make official institutions responsive to individual grievances, to recognize that the fundamental premise of democracy is individual worth and involvement. Hence, the basic issue has been and remains a struggle over power. Psychologically this seems to be reflected in a restiveness within the general mass of people, stemming from unfulfilled promises and dreams of the American political system. There appears to be a search to find some meaning in the chaos of our times—a search for renewal and revitalization. This search for the realization of unfulfilled dreams focuses mainly on the operation of the political system and on its political leaders. The decline in the legitimacy of our political system and in the credibility of its leaders is at the base of this social and political restiveness.

The major political result is the increasing recognition by individuals of the use of power to influence the political system. This has led to individual and community search for power to use on the establishment. More and more the institutions of our government will be assessed in terms of how responsive they are to the public and how effectively they articulate the power of the people. Corporations and individual political actors possessing economic power will continue to be viewed with suspicion by many. Such political actors will gain credibility mainly through an image of service to the public.

The System Continues

Peering into the future, based on our assessment to this point, we see no dramatic changes in the principles of federalism, separation of powers/checks and balances, judicial review, and limited government. Indeed, we see no dramatic changes in the acceptance of democratic ideology. Rather we see increasing pressure on the entire American political system to recapture the traditions and operations of the past while recruiting committed loyal and trustworthy political leaders to deal with the problems of the future. A political premise of a democratic system is that when the inherent flexibility and divergency are stretched to the maximum, forces will be exerted to restore the proper balance or equilibrium between contending groups and actors. This simply means that the power base of the people must be restored to maintain a balance in the democratic condition. It would appear that individuals and communities are still committed to existing institutions, but not necessarily to the way the political process has operated in the immediate past. To restore the democratic condition, institutional operations must be based on an effective accountability and responsibility to the people. This can only be done by an intensive and extensive system of public scrutiny of institutional operations and political actors. Moreover, although political parties and traditional groups must play a role in such an operation, community organizations and new channels of expressing individual power may well become important ingredients in the operation of our political system.

Cleansing the Body Politic

Associated with this restoration is the need for cleansing of the body politic. It has been said that when economic power equals political power the democratic system is well on the way to destruction, because irresponsible and unaccountable power bases are created. In many instances, political actors with unaccountable political power pursue their interests at the expense of democratic principles and procedures. Hence, there is a continuing need for individual and community political awareness, and for effective use of their power to minimize the impact of nondemocratic power bases. Political actors and the people must be aware of these nondemocratic tendencies and take some kind of political cleansing action. This should not be limited to periodic elections, but should include continual community pressure against those who would use the political system for their special purposes. Political leaders must be recruited who have a continuing commitment to the democratic condition and to the preservation of individuality and individual power.

One of the most serious issues confronting the government is the problem of inflation. In the elections of November 1974, this issue became the crucial one in achieving large-scale victories of Democratic candidates. People in every socioeconomic group, with the exception perhaps of the very rich, were confronted with an economy that was at "double digit" inflation. Some observers called it "stagflation," i.e., inflation combined with low productivity. Many observers were concerned lest continuing inflation destroy the basis for democratic society. As some would say, political ideologies and parliamentary niceties mean little in the face of a continuing and losing struggle for economic power. In any case, the individual became convinced that again he was being "squeezed" and forgotten in the massive government bureaucracy and economic power of corporate interests.

Groups and individuals in a democratic society will rarely ever achieve all that they desire. For a democratic system to work there must be reasonable and rational men who understand the process of compromise. They must understand that at times goals will not be achieved but that the opportunity must always remain for individuals and groups to be able to struggle for their goals with a reasonable chance of success.

More important, the opportunities must exist for an individual to acquire and maintain the power he needs to make his voice heard and felt in the political system. Undoubtedly there are those even in a democratic society who question the idealistic view regarding the role of the individual. They would question whether one person's power has any real impact on the operations of the political system. It is our contention that power *is* meaningful in individual terms. It is the very source of the proper operation of the American political system. We do not speak of it in idealistic terms; we have tried to provide a power perspective because we feel this is a realistic way to learn how the American political system operates. In this last chapter we have tried to provide a picture of the environment within which the American political system has evolved in the 1970s and some of those major things necessary for the continuation of the democratic condition. To reiterate, there is a need for renewal and revitalization of individual power within the political system. This generally means a recasting of traditional politics in terms of increased awareness of the need for humanism and the concept that political actors are accountable to the people. In light of the flexibility and adaptability of a democratic system, however, we feel that the leadership and the institutional framework by which the democratic condition can be restored exists.

Almost two decades ago, Eleanor Roosevelt touched upon the same issues that we are faced with now in the American political system. She stated:

> Where, after all, do universal human rights begin? In small places, close to home—so close and so small that they cannot be seen on any maps of the world. Yet they are the world of the individual person; the neighborhood; the school or college he attends; the factory, farm or office where he works. Such are the places where every man, woman or child seeks equal justice, equal opportunity, equal dignity without discrimination. Unless these rights have meaning there, they have little meaning anywhere. Without concerned citizen action to uphold them close to home, we shall look in vain for progress in the larger world.[2]

The proper operation of a democratic political system begins in the world of the individual person, his neighborhood, and his community. The individual must perceive that he has power to influence his own political system; without this perception, the democratic political system will soon decay into one in which the individual not only loses all of his power, but his autonomy as well.

Power Struggle Continues

Our assessment is not based on an idealistic notion of what a democratic system should be. We know that there is no system in the world (nor is it likely that there will ever be) that is based on absolute peace and harmony. We are also convinced that the individual will never have complete autonomy or power, even in the most democratic system. However, we are convinced that one of the most fundamental problems of the American political system is the imbalance between individual autonomy and power and that of the establishment, corporate structures, and political "fat cats" (political money-lenders). As long as politics is based on elections, accountability, and responsibility, there will always be a struggle over the power of the individual and community with respect to the other political actors. This is as it should be—but this struggle should not be allowed to shift the balance of power to unaccountable and irresponsible political actors. This imbalance is at the base of injustice. And where there is injustice, there is violence, not only to the political system, but to individual dignity.

Notes

1. Lloyd A. Free and Hadley Cantril, *The Political Beliefs of Americans* (New Brunswick, N.J.: Rutgers University Press, 1967), pp. 179–180.
2. As quoted in Joseph P. Lash, *Eleanor: The Years Alone* (New York: Signet Book, 1973), p. 72.

APPENDIX
Table of Contents

A. Voting Data For Presidential Elections

    Popular Vote Cast For President, By Political Parties, By Regions And States: 1968 And 1972

    Popular Vote Cast For President, By Major Party: 1932 To 1972

    Electoral Vote Cast For President, By Major Political Parties, By States: 1932 To 1972

    Percent Of Total And Voting-Age Population And Of Popular And Electoral Vote For President, By Regions And States: 1972

B. Data On Government Operations

    Federal Budget Receipts And Outlays: 1960 To 1974

    The Annual Federal Budget: 1970 To 1974

    Social Welfare Expenditures Under Public Programs: 1950 To 1973

    Social Welfare Expenditures Under Public Programs, Total And Per Capita, In Actual And 1973 Dollars: 1935 To 1973

    Federal Grants To State And Local Governments, By Purpose: 1950 To 1973

    Gross National Product And Personal Consumption Expenditures In Current And Constant 1958 Dollars: 1960 To 1973

    Gross National Product—Summary: 1929 To 1973

    Budget Outlays For National Defense Functions: 1960 To 1974

Most of the Data contained in Appendix A-F inclusive was taken from U.S. Bureau of the Census, *Statistical Abstract of the United States: 1974.* (95th edition.) Washington, D.C., 1974

Department Of Defense Outlays, By Branch Of Service: 1965 To 1973

C. Campaign Expenditures

Election Campaign Costs For National Offices: 1972

D. Population Data

Recent Trends

Population, By Sex, Race, Residence, And Median Age: 1790 To 1973

Percent Of Voting-Age Population Casting Votes—States: 1960 To 1972

E. Composition Of Congress

The Standing Committees

Composition Of Congress, By Political Party Affiliations, By States: 1969, 1971, And 1973

Composition Of Congress, By Political Party: 1933 To 1974

Congressional Bills, Acts, and Resolutions: 1957 to 1973

Congressional Bills Vetoed: 1913 to 1973

F. The Government Of The United States

G. Data Analysis And Statistical Exercise

Scientific Analysis

Establishing Facts And Explanations

Methods

Correlations

Exercises For The Student

Selected Data For The United States

H. United States Constitution

Appendix A

POPULAR VOTE CAST FOR PRESIDENT, BY POLITICAL PARTIES, BY REGIONS AND STATES: 1968 AND 1972

[In thousands, except percent. See also *Historical Statistics, Colonial Times to 1957*, series Y 80-128]

REGION AND STATE	1968 Total	1968 Democratic	1968 Republican	1968 Other parties	1968 % Dem.	1968 % Rep.	1972 Total	1972 Democratic	1972 Republican	1972 Other parties	1972 % Dem.	1972 % Rep.
Total	73,212	31,275	31,785	10,151	42.7	43.4	77,719	29,170	47,170	1,378	37.5	60.7
Northeast	19,239	9,657	8,278	1,304	50.2	43.0	19,953	8,277	11,483	192	41.5	57.5
North Central	22,208	9,703	10,394	2,111	43.7	46.8	23,192	9,127	13,711	353	39.4	59.1
South	19,176	6,419	6,990	5,770	33.5	36.5	20,046	6,087	13,666	295	30.4	68.2
West	12,589	5,497	6,127	966	43.7	48.7	14,529	5,679	8,309	543	39.1	57.2
Alabama	1,050	197	147	¹706	18.7	14.0	1,006	257	729	20	25.5	72.4
Alaska	83	35	38	10	42.6	45.3	95	33	55	7	34.6	58.1
Arizona	487	171	267	50	35.0	54.8	623	199	403	22	31.9	64.7
Arkansas	620	188	191	241	30.4	30.8	651	200	449	3	30.7	68.9
California	7,252	3,244	3,468	540	44.7	47.8	8,368	3,476	4,602	290	41.5	55.0
Colorado	811	335	409	67	41.3	50.5	954	330	597	27	34.6	62.6
Connecticut	1,256	622	557	78	49.5	44.3	1,384	555	811	18	40.1	58.6
Delaware	214	89	97	28	41.6	45.1	236	92	140	3	39.2	59.6
Dist. of Columbia	171	140	31	-	81.8	18.2	163	128	35	1	78.1	21.6
Florida	2,188	677	887	624	30.9	40.5	2,583	718	1,858	7	27.8	71.9
Georgia	1,250	334	380	536	26.8	30.4	1,175	290	881	4	24.6	75.0
Hawaii	236	141	91	3	59.8	38.7	270	101	169	-	37.5	62.5
Idaho	291	89	165	37	30.7	56.8	310	81	199	30	26.0	64.2
Illinois	4,620	2,040	2,175	405	44.2	47.1	4,723	1,913	2,788	22	40.5	59.0
Indiana	2,124	807	1,068	249	38.0	50.3	2,126	709	1,405	12	33.3	66.1
Iowa	1,168	477	619	72	40.8	53.0	1,226	496	706	24	40.5	57.6
Kansas	873	303	479	91	34.7	54.8	916	270	620	26	29.5	67.7
Kentucky	1,056	398	462	196	37.6	43.8	1,067	371	676	20	34.8	63.4
Louisiana	1,097	310	258	530	28.2	23.5	1,051	298	687	66	28.4	65.3
Maine	393	217	169	6	55.3	43.1	417	161	256	-	38.5	61.5
Maryland	1,235	538	518	179	43.6	41.9	1,354	506	829	19	37.4	61.3
Massachusetts	2,332	1,469	767	96	63.0	32.9	2,459	1,333	1,112	14	54.2	45.2
Michigan	3,306	1,593	1,371	343	48.2	41.5	3,490	1,459	1,962	69	41.8	56.2
Minnesota	1,589	858	659	72	54.0	41.5	1,742	802	898	41	46.1	51.6
Mississippi	655	151	89	415	23.0	13.5	646	127	505	14	19.6	78.2
Missouri	1,810	791	812	206	43.7	44.9	1,856	697	1,154	5	37.6	62.2
Montana	274	114	139	21	41.6	50.6	318	120	184	13	37.8	57.9
Nebraska	537	171	321	45	31.8	59.8	576	170	406	-	29.5	70.5
Nevada	154	61	73	20	39.3	47.5	182	66	116	-	36.3	63.7
New Hampshire	297	131	155	12	43.9	52.1	334	116	214	4	34.9	64.0
New Jersey	2,875	1,264	1,325	286	44.0	46.1	2,997	1,102	1,846	50	36.8	61.6
New Mexico	327	130	170	28	39.7	51.8	386	141	236	10	36.5	61.0
New York	6,792	3,378	3,008	405	49.7	44.3	7,166	2,951	4,193	22	41.2	58.5
North Carolina	1,587	464	627	496	29.2	39.5	1,519	439	1,055	25	28.9	69.5
North Dakota	248	95	139	14	38.2	55.9	281	100	174	6	35.8	62.1
Ohio	3,960	1,701	1,791	468	42.9	45.2	4,095	1,559	2,442	94	38.1	59.6
Oklahoma	943	302	450	192	32.0	47.7	1,030	247	759	24	24.0	73.7
Oregon	820	359	408	52	43.8	49.8	928	393	487	49	42.3	52.4
Pennsylvania	4,748	2,259	2,090	399	47.6	44.0	4,592	1,797	2,715	81	39.1	59.1
Rhode Island	385	247	122	16	64.0	31.8	416	195	220	1	46.8	53.0
South Carolina	667	197	254	215	29.6	38.1	674	187	477	10	27.7	70.8
South Dakota	281	118	150	13	42.0	53.3	307	140	166	1	45.5	54.2
Tennessee	1,249	351	473	425	28.1	37.8	1,201	357	813	31	29.7	67.7
Texas	3,079	1,267	1,228	585	41.1	39.9	3,471	1,154	2,299	18	33.3	66.2
Utah	423	157	239	27	37.1	56.5	478	126	324	29	26.4	67.6
Vermont	161	70	85	6	43.5	52.8	187	68	117	2	36.5	62.7
Virginia	1,361	442	590	329	32.5	43.4	1,457	439	988	30	30.1	67.8
Washington	1,304	616	589	100	47.2	45.1	1,471	568	837	65	38.6	56.9
West Virginia	754	374	308	73	49.6	40.8	762	277	485	-	36.4	63.6
Wisconsin	1,692	749	810	133	44.3	47.9	1,853	810	989	53	43.7	53.4
Wyoming	127	45	71	11	35.5	55.8	146	44	100	1	30.5	69.0

- Represents zero.
¹ Includes vote cast for George C. Wallace as a Democratic Party candidate.

Source: U.S. Congress, Clerk of the House, *Statistics of the Presidential and Congressional Election of Nov. 5, 1968*, and *Statistics of the Presidential and Congressional Election of Nov. 7, 1972*. (In some cases, figures have been revised by Elections Research Center, Washington, D.C.)

Appendix A

Popular Vote Cast for President, by Major Party: 1932 to 1972

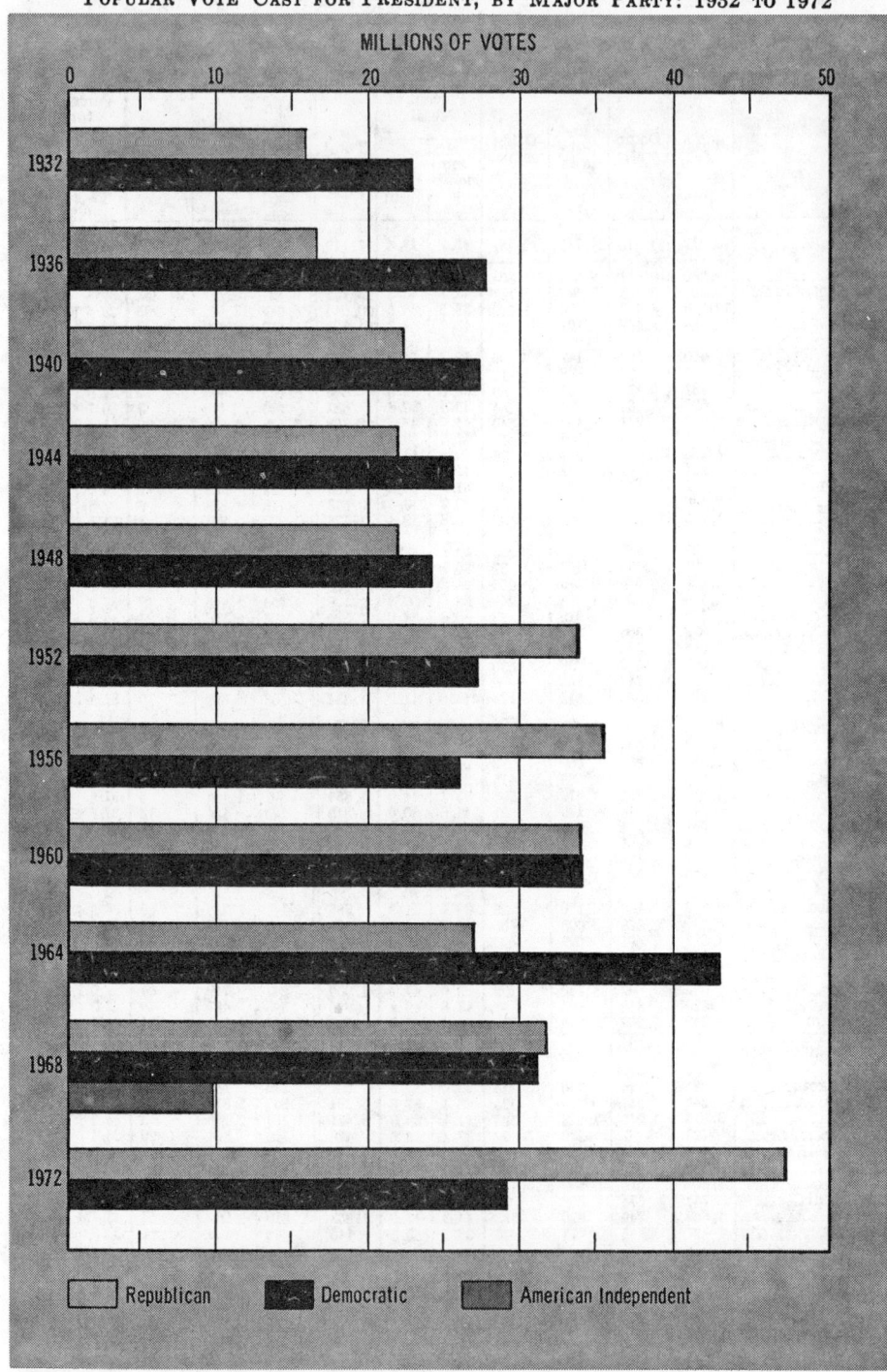

Source: Chart prepared by U.S. Bureau of the Census.

Appendix A

Electoral Vote Cast for President, by Major Political Parties, by States: 1932 to 1972

[D = Democratic, R = Republican. See also *Historical Statistics, Colonial Times to 1957*, series Y 32-79]

STATE	1932	1936	1940	1944	1948 [1]	1952	1956 [2]	1960 [3]	1964	1968 [4]	1972
Democratic	472	523	449	432	303	89	73	303	486	191	17
Republican	59	8	82	99	189	442	457	219	52	301	520
Ala.	D-11	D-11	D-11	D-11	(1)	D-11	[2] D-10	[3] D-5	R-10	(4)	R-9
Alaska	(x)	(x)	(x)	(x)	(x)	(x)	(x)	R-3	D-3	R-3	R-3
Ariz.	D-3	D-3	D-3	D-4	D-4	R-4	R-4	R-4	D-5	R-5	R-6
Ark.	D-9	D-9	D-9	D-9	D-9	D-8	D-8	D-8	D-6	(4)	R-6
Calif.	D-22	D-22	D-22	D-25	D-25	R-32	R-32	R-32	D-40	R-40	R-45
Colo.	D-6	D-6	R-6	R-6	D-6	R-6	R-6	R-6	D-6	R-6	R-7
Conn.	R-8	D-8	D-8	D-8	R-8	R-8	R-8	D-8	D-8	D-8	R-8
Del.	R-3	D-3	D-3	D-3	R-3	R-3	R-3	D-3	D-3	R-3	R-3
D.C.	(x)	(x)	(x)	(x)	(x)	(x)	(x)	(x)	D-3	D-3	D-3
Fla.	D-7	D-7	D-7	D-8	D-8	R-10	R-10	R-10	D-14	R-14	R-17
Ga.	D-12	D-12	D-12	D-12	D-12	D-12	D-12	D-12	R-12	(4)	R-12
Hawaii	(x)	(x)	(x)	(x)	(x)	(x)	(x)	D-3	D-4	D-4	R-4
Idaho	D-4	D-4	D-4	D-4	D-4	R-4	R-4	R-4	D-4	R-4	R-4
Ill.	D-29	D-29	D-29	D-28	D-28	R-27	R-27	R-27	D-26	R-26	R-26
Ind.	D-14	D-14	R-14	R-13	R-13	R-13	R-13	R-13	D-13	R-13	R-13
Iowa	D-11	D-11	R-11	R-10	D-10	R-10	R-10	R-10	D-9	R-9	R-8
Kans.	D-9	D-9	R-9	R-8	R-8	R-8	R-8	R-8	D-7	R-7	R-7
Ky.	D-11	D-11	D-11	D-11	D-11	D-10	R-10	R-10	D-9	R-9	R-9
La.	D-10	D-10	D-10	D-10	(1)	D-10	R-10	D-10	D-10	(4)	R-10
Maine	R-5	R-5	R-5	R-5	R-5	R-5	R-5	R-5	D-4	D-4	R-4
Md.	D-8	D-8	D-8	D-8	R-8	R-9	R-9	D-9	D-10	D-10	R-10
Mass.	D-17	D-17	D-17	D-16	D-16	R-16	R-16	D-16	D-14	D-14	D-14
Mich.	D-19	D-19	R-19	D-19	R-19	R-20	R-20	D-20	D-21	D-21	R-21
Minn.	D-11	D-11	D-11	D-11	D-11	R-11	R-11	D-11	D-10	D-10	R-10
Miss.	D-9	D-9	D-9	D-9	(1)	D-8	D-8	(3)	R-7	(4)	R-7
Mo.	D-15	D-15	D-15	D-15	D-15	R-13	D-13	D-13	D-12	R-12	R-12
Mont.	D-4	D-4	D-4	D-4	D-4	R-4	R-4	R-4	D-4	R-4	R-4
Nebr.	D-7	D-7	R-7	R-6	R-6	R-6	R-6	R-6	D-5	R-5	R-5
Nev.	D-3	D-3	D-3	D-3	D-3	R-3	R-3	D-3	D-3	R-3	R-3
N.H.	R-4	D-4	D-4	D-4	R-4	R-4	R-4	R-4	D-4	R-4	R-4
N.J.	D-16	D-16	D-16	D-16	R-16	R-16	R-16	D-16	D-17	R-17	R-17
N. Mex.	D-3	D-3	D-3	D-4	D-4	R-4	R-4	D-4	D-4	R-4	R-4
N.Y.	D-47	D-47	D-47	D-47	D-47	R-45	R-45	D-45	D-43	D-43	R-41
N.C.	D-13	D-13	D-13	D-14	D-14	D-14	D-14	D-14	D-13	R-12	R-13
N. Dak.	D-4	D-4	R-4	R-4	R-4	R-4	R-4	R-4	D-4	R-4	R-3
Ohio	D-26	D-26	D-26	R-25	D-25	R-25	R-25	R-25	D-26	R-26	R-25
Okla.	D-11	D-11	D-11	D-10	D-10	R-8	R-8	[3] R-7	D-8	R-8	R-8
Oreg.	D-5	D-5	D-5	D-6	R-6	R-6	R-6	R-6	D-6	R-6	R-6
Pa.	R-36	D-36	D-36	D-35	R-35	R-32	R-32	D-32	D-29	D-29	R-27
R.I.	D-4	D-4	D-4	D-4	D-4	R-4	R-4	D-4	D-4	D-4	R-4
S.C.	D-8	D-8	D-8	D-8	(1)	D-8	D-8	D-8	R-8	R-8	R-8
S. Dak.	D-4	D-4	R-4	R-4	R-4	R-4	R-4	R-4	D-4	R-4	R-4
Tenn.	D-11	D-11	D-11	D-11	[1] D-11	R-11	R-11	R-11	D-11	R-11	R-10
Tex.	D-23	D-23	D-23	D-23	D-23	R-24	R-24	D-24	D-25	D-25	R-26
Utah	D-4	D-4	D-4	D-4	D-4	R-4	R-4	R-4	D-4	R-4	R-4
Vt.	R-3	R-3	R-3	R-3	R-3	R-3	R-3	R-3	D-3	R-3	R-3
Va.	D-11	D-11	D-11	D-11	D-11	R-12	R-12	R-12	D-12	R-12	[5] R-11
Wash.	D-8	D-8	D-8	D-8	D-8	R-9	R-9	R-9	D-9	D-9	R-9
W. Va.	D-8	D-8	D-8	D-8	D-8	D-8	R-8	D-8	D-7	D-7	R-6
Wis.	D-12	D-12	D-12	R-12	D-12	R-12	R-12	R-12	D-12	R-12	R-11
Wyo.	D-3	D-3	D-3	R-3	D-3	R-3	R-3	R-3	D-3	R-3	R-3

X Not applicable.
[1] Excludes 39 electoral votes cast for States' Rights Democratic candidates as follows: Alabama 11; Louisiana 10; Mississippi 9; South Carolina 8; and Tennessee 1.
[2] Excludes 1 electoral vote cast for Walter B. Jones.
[3] Excludes 15 electoral votes cast for Harry F. Byrd as follows: Alabama 6; Mississippi 8; and Oklahoma 1.
[4] Excludes 46 electoral votes cast for George C. Wallace as follows: Alabama 10; Arkansas 6; Georgia 12; Louisiana 10; Mississippi 7; North Carolina 1. [5] Excludes 1 electoral vote cast for John Hospers.

Source: U.S. Congress, Clerk of the House, *Statistics of the Presidential and Congressional Election*.

Percent of Total and Voting-Age Population and of Popular and Electoral Vote for President, by Regions and States: 1972

REGION AND STATE	Total population [1]	Voting-age population [2]	Popular vote for President	Electoral vote for President	STATE	Total population [1]	Voting-age population [2]	Popular vote for President	Electoral vote for President
U.S.	100.0	100.0	100.0	100.0	Minnesota	1.9	1.8	2.2	1.9
					Mississippi	1.1	1.0	0.8	1.3
Northeast	23.9	24.5	25.7	22.7	Missouri	2.3	2.3	2.4	2.2
North Central	27.7	27.4	29.9	27.0	Montana	0.3	0.3	0.4	0.7
South	31.1	30.8	25.8	31.2	Nebraska	0.7	0.7	0.7	0.9
West	17.3	17.3	18.6	19.0	Nevada	0.3	0.2	0.2	0.6
Alabama	1.7	1.6	1.3	1.7	New Hampshire	0.4	0.4	0.4	0.7
Alaska	0.2	0.1	0.1	0.6	New Jersey	3.5	3.6	3.9	3.2
Arizona	0.9	0.9	0.8	1.1	New Mexico	0.5	0.5	0.5	0.7
Arkansas	0.9	0.9	0.8	1.1	New York	8.9	9.1	9.2	7.6
California	9.8	10.0	10.6	8.4	North Carolina	2.5	2.5	2.0	2.4
Colorado	1.1	1.1	1.2	1.3	North Dakota	0.3	0.3	0.4	0.6
Connecticut	1.5	1.5	1.8	1.5	Ohio	5.2	5.1	5.3	4.6
Delaware	0.3	0.3	0.3	0.6	Oklahoma	1.3	1.3	1.3	1.5
District of Col.	0.3	0.4	0.2	0.6	Oregon	1.1	1.1	1.2	1.1
Florida	3.5	3.7	3.3	3.2	Pennsylvania	5.7	5.8	5.9	5.0
Georgia	2.3	2.2	1.5	2.2	Rhode Island	0.5	0.5	0.5	0.7
Hawaii	0.4	0.4	0.3	0.7	South Carolina	1.3	1.2	0.9	1.5
Idaho	0.4	0.3	0.4	0.7	South Dakota	0.3	0.3	0.4	0.7
Illinois	5.4	5.4	6.1	4.8	Tennessee	1.9	1.9	1.5	1.9
Indiana	2.6	2.5	2.7	2.4	Texas	5.6	5.5	4.5	4.8
Iowa	1.4	1.4	1.6	1.5	Utah	0.5	0.5	0.6	0.7
Kansas	1.1	1.1	1.2	1.3	Vermont	0.2	0.2	0.2	0.6
Kentucky	1.6	1.6	1.4	1.7	Virginia	2.3	2.3	1.9	2.0
Louisiana	1.8	1.7	1.4	1.9	Washington	1.7	1.7	1.9	1.7
Maine	0.5	0.5	0.5	0.7	West Virginia	0.8	0.8	1.0	1.1
Maryland	2.0	1.9	1.7	1.9	Wisconsin	2.2	2.1	2.4	2.0
Massachusetts	2.8	2.8	3.2	2.6	Wyoming	0.2	0.2	0.2	0.6
Michigan	4.4	4.2	4.5	3.9					

[1] Estimated. As of Nov. 1. Includes Armed Forces stationed in area.
[2] Estimated. Resident population 18 years old and over.

Source: U.S. Bureau of the Census, based on data from *Current Population Reports*, series P-25, No. 479; and U.S. Congress, Clerk of the House, based on data from *Statistics of the Presidential and Congressional Election of Nov. 7, 1972*.

Appendix B

Federal Budget Receipts and Outlays: 1960 to 1974

[For years ending June 30. See table 359]

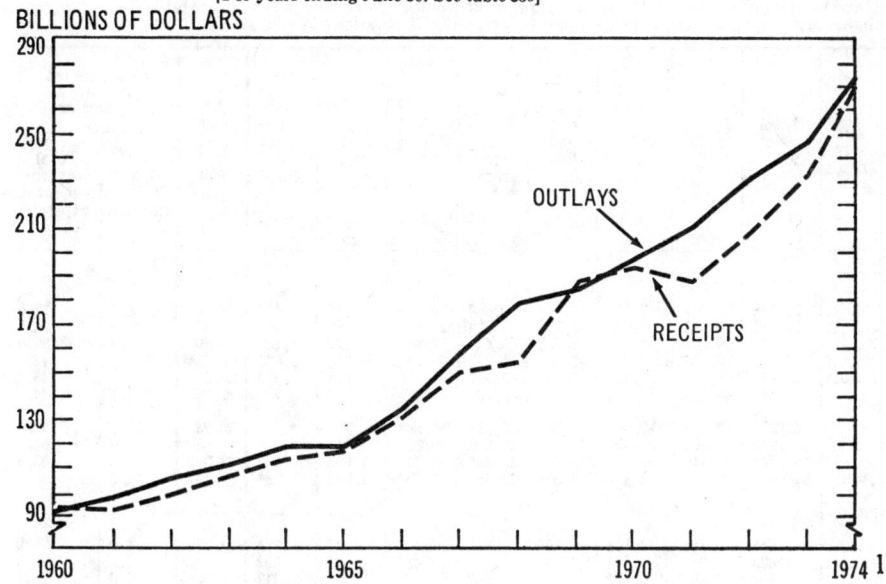

[1] Estimated.

Source: U.S. Bureau of the Census. Data from U.S. Office of Management and Budget.

The Annual Federal Budget: 1970 to 1974

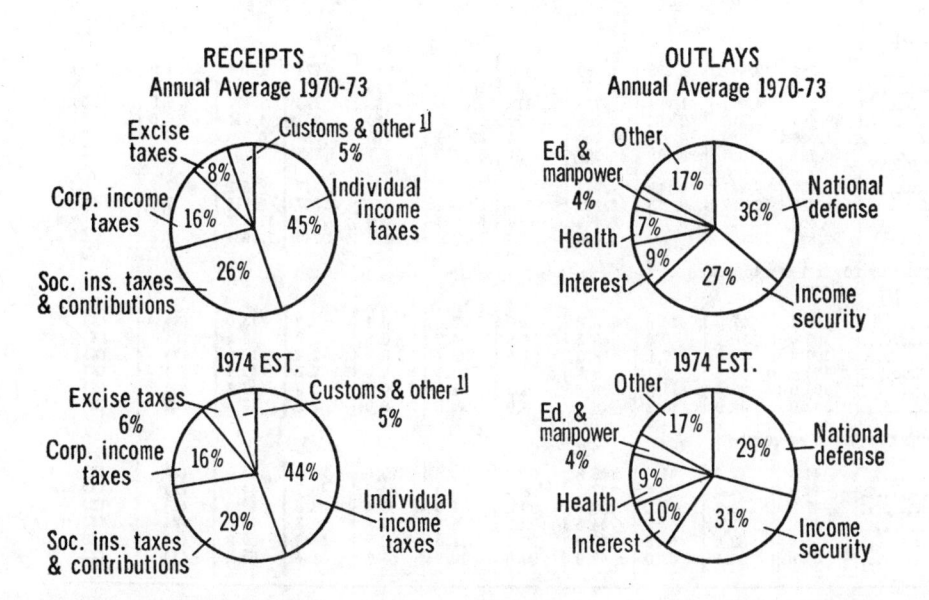

RECEIPTS — Annual Average 1970-73
- Individual income taxes: 45%
- Soc. ins. taxes & contributions: 26%
- Corp. income taxes: 16%
- Excise taxes: 8%
- Customs & other [1]: 5%

OUTLAYS — Annual Average 1970-73
- National defense: 36%
- Income security: 27%
- Other: 17%
- Interest: 9%
- Health: 7%
- Ed. & manpower: 4%

RECEIPTS — 1974 EST.
- Individual income taxes: 44%
- Soc. ins. taxes & contributions: 29%
- Corp. income taxes: 16%
- Excise taxes: 6%
- Customs & other [1]: 5%

OUTLAYS — 1974 EST.
- Income security: 31%
- National defense: 29%
- Other: 17%
- Interest: 10%
- Health: 9%
- Ed. & manpower: 4%

[1] Other includes estate and gift taxes and other receipts.

Source: U.S. Bureau of the Census. Data from U.S. Office of Management and Budget.

Appendix B

Social Welfare Expenditures Under Public Programs: 1950 to 1973

[In millions of dollars, except percent. For Federal Government, most States, and some localities, years ending June 30. Represents expenditures under public law and from trust accounts. Includes administrative expenditures and capital outlay; also includes some expenditures and payments outside U.S. See table 434 for program detail. See *Historical Statistics, Colonial Times to 1957*, series H 1–45, for related but not comparable data]

YEAR AND SOURCE OF FUNDS	Total social welfare [1]	Social insurance [1]	Public aid	Health and medical programs	Veterans programs	Education	Housing	Other social welfare	All health and medical care [2]	Gross National Product	Total Government expenditures [1]
TOTAL											
1950	23,508	4,947	2,496	2,064	6,866	6,674	15	448	3,065	8.9	37.6
1955	32,640	9,835	3,003	3,103	4,834	11,157	89	619	4,421	8.6	32.7
1960	52,293	19,307	4,101	4,464	5,479	17,626	177	1,139	6,395	10.6	38.0
1965	77,175	28,123	6,283	6,246	6,031	28,108	318	2,066	9,535	11.8	42.4
1968	113,840	42,740	11,002	8,459	7,247	40,590	428	3,285	20,039	13.8	43.2
1969	127,149	48,772	13,439	9,006	7,934	43,673	532	3,792	22,936	14.1	44.7
1970	145,894	54,676	16,488	9,753	9,018	50,848	701	4,408	25,232	15.3	47.8
1971	171,901	66,304	21,304	10,890	10,396	56,885	1,047	5,075	28,583	17.0	51.8
1972	192,749	74,715	26,092	12,771	11,465	60,741	1,396	5,569	33,392	17.5	53.4
1973 (prel.)	215,228	85,892	28,327	14,603	12,953	65,247	1,922	6,284	37,554	17.6	55.0
FEDERAL											
1950	10,541	2,103	1,103	604	6,386	157	15	174	1,362	4.0	26.2
1955	14,623	6,385	1,504	1,150	4,772	485	75	252	1,948	3.9	22.3
1960	24,957	14,307	2,117	1,737	5,367	863	144	417	2,918	5.0	28.1
1965	37,712	21,807	3,594	2,781	6,011	2,470	238	812	4,625	5.8	32.6
1968	60,314	35,390	6,455	4,233	7,214	5,000	325	1,697	13,069	7.3	35.1
1969	68,355	40,847	7,829	4,543	7,883	4,923	426	1,905	15,229	7.6	37.5
1970	77,337	45,245	9,649	4,775	8,952	5,873	582	2,262	16,600	8.1	40.1
1971	92,547	53,836	13,032	5,148	10,331	6,580	872	2,749	18,766	9.1	44.9
1972	106,186	61,163	16,304	6,322	11,405	6,699	1,196	3,097	22,065	9.6	47.0
1973 (prel.)	122,331	72,204	17,847	7,194	12,899	6,947	1,697	3,544	24,620	10.0	49.6
STATE AND LOCAL											
1950	12,967	2,844	1,393	1,460	480	6,518	(X)	274	1,704	4.9	60.1
1955	18,017	3,450	1,499	1,953	62	10,672	15	367	2,473	4.7	55.3
1960	27,337	4,999	1,984	2,727	112	16,758	33	723	3,477	5.5	58.3
1965	39,464	6,316	2,690	3,466	20	25,638	80	1,254	4,911	6.0	61.7
1968	53,526	7,350	4,636	4,226	33	35,589	103	1,589	6,970	6.5	60.0
1969	58,794	7,925	5,610	4,464	51	38,750	107	1,888	7,707	6.5	59.8
1970	68,557	9,431	6,839	4,978	67	44,975	120	2,147	8,632	7.2	62.4
1971	79,355	12,468	8,273	5,742	65	50,306	175	2,327	9,816	7.8	64.2
1972	86,563	13,552	9,788	6,449	60	54,042	200	2,472	11,327	7.9	65.4
1973 (prel.)	92,897	13,688	10,481	7,409	54	58,300	225	2,740	12,934	7.6	65.2
PERCENT OF TOTAL EXPENDITURES BY TYPE											
1950	100.0	21.0	10.6	8.8	29.2	28.4	0.1	1.9	13.0	(X)	(X)
1955	100.0	30.1	9.2	9.5	14.8	34.2	0.3	1.9	13.5	(X)	(X)
1960	100.0	36.9	7.8	8.5	10.5	33.7	0.3	2.2	12.2	(X)	(X)
1965	100.0	36.4	8.1	8.1	7.8	36.4	0.4	2.7	12.4	(X)	(X)
1970	100.0	37.5	11.3	6.7	6.2	34.8	0.5	3.0	17.3	(X)	(X)
1973	100.0	39.9	13.2	6.8	6.0	30.3	0.9	2.9	17.4	(X)	(X)
PERCENT FEDERAL OF TOTAL											
1950	44.8	42.5	44.2	29.3	93.0	2.4	100.0	38.8	44.4	(X)	(X)
1955	44.8	64.9	50.0	37.1	98.7	4.3	84.3	40.7	44.1	(X)	(X)
1960	47.8	74.1	51.6	38.9	98.0	4.9	81.4	36.6	45.6	(X)	(X)
1965	48.9	77.5	57.2	44.5	99.7	8.8	74.8	39.3	48.5	(X)	(X)
1970	53.0	82.6	58.5	49.0	99.3	11.5	82.8	51.3	65.8	(X)	(X)
1973	56.8	84.1	63.0	49.3	99.6	10.6	88.3	56.4	65.6	(X)	(X)

X Not applicable. [1] Although total welfare and insurance expenditures include workmen's compensation and temporary disability insurance payments made through private insurance carriers and self-insurers, such private payments have been omitted in computing percentages relating to all government expenditures.
[2] Combines "Health and medical programs" with medical services provided in connection with social insurance, public aid, veterans, and other social welfare programs.

Source: U.S. Social Security Administration, *Social Security Bulletin*, January 1974.

Social Welfare Expenditures Under Public Programs, Total and Per Capita, in Actual and 1973 Dollars: 1935 to 1973

[For years ending June 30. Per capita figures based on Bureau of the Census estimates of total population of the United States as of January 1, including outlying areas and Armed Forces abroad.]

YEAR	IN ACTUAL DOLLARS									IN 1973 DOLLARS			
	Total [1] (billions)	Per capita							Total [1] (billions)	Per capita		
		Total [1,2]	Social insurance	Public aid	Health and medical	Veterans	Education	Other social welfare		Total	Social insurance	Education
1935	6.5	51	3	23	3	5	16	1	20.9	162	10	50
1940	8.8	66	9	27	5	5	19	1	27.3	204	29	59
1945	9.2	65	10	7	17	8	22	1	20.1	142	22	47
1950	23.4	153	32	16	13	44	43	3	40.5	263	56	75
1955	32.5	195	59	18	19	28	67	4	49.4	296	89	101
1960	52.1	285	105	22	24	30	96	6	71.7	393	145	133
1965	76.9	391	142	32	32	30	143	10	100.0	509	185	186
1967	99.4	494	185	44	38	34	178	14	123.6	614	230	221
1968	113.5	558	209	55	42	35	199	16	137.3	675	253	241
1969	126.8	617	236	65	44	38	212	18	148.0	721	276	248
1970	145.5	701	262	79	47	43	245	21	161.7	779	292	272
1971	171.4	818	315	102	52	49	271	24	182.4	870	335	289
1972	192.2	909	351	123	60	54	287	26	198.4	938	363	296
1973 [3]	214.6	1,007	401	133	68	60	306	29	214.6	1,007	401	306

[1] Excludes expenditures within foreign countries for education, veterans payments, OASDHI, and civil service retirement benefits.
[2] Includes housing, not shown separately. [3] Preliminary.

Source: U.S. Social Security Administration, *Social Security Bulletin*, January 1974, and unpublished data.

Federal Grants to State and Local Governments, by Purpose: 1950 to 1973

[In millions of dollars, except as indicated. Includes Puerto Rico, Guam, and Virgin Islands; On basis of checks issued for years ending June 30]

YEAR	ALL GRANTS		SOCIAL WELFARE						Highways	All other
	Total	Per capita [1]	Total	Percent of all grants	Public assistance [2]	Health [3]	Education [4]	Economic opportunity, manpower [5]	Miscellaneous [6]		
1950	2,212	$14.33	1,731	78.2	1,123	123	82	–	402	429	53
1955	3,096	18.49	2,403	77.6	1,427	119	296	–	561	597	97
1960	6,838	38.08	3,610	52.8	2,059	214	441	–	896	2,942	286
1965	10,630	54.73	5,669	53.3	3,059	346	702	527	1,033	4,018	944
1967	14,820	73.97	9,845	66.4	4,175	436	2,370	1,610	1,254	4,022	953
1968	18,168	90.79	12,449	68.5	5,319	823	2,719	2,050	1,538	4,197	1,521
1969	19,771	97.49	13,802	69.8	6,280	866	2,666	2,087	1,904	4,162	1,807
1970	23,575	115.15	16,545	70.2	7,445	1,043	3,016	2,565	2,476	4,392	2,640
1971	29,215	141.42	21,067	72.1	9,640	914	3,540	2,989	3,985	4,659	3,488
1972	35,203	168.38	26,414	75.0	13,090	991	4,283	3,482	4,568	4,677	4,112
1973	[7] 43,121	204.04	26,581	61.6	11,891	1,073	4,348	3,635	5,635	4,724	5,179

– Represents zero.
[1] Based on Bureau of the Census estimates of total population, excluding Armed Forces abroad, as of July 1.
[2] Old-age assistance, medical assistance for the aged, aid to families with dependent children, aid to the blind, aid to permanently and totally disabled, the combined adult assistance program, and medical assistance.
[3] Maternal and child health services, services for crippled children, general public health services, Indian health, and construction.
[4] Colleges of agriculture and mechanic arts; agricultural extension; agricultural experiment stations through 1968; vocational education; education of handicapped; maintenance and operation of schools; school construction; defense educational activities; educational TV through 1964; elementary, secondary, and higher education activities; child development and others.
[5] Manpower development and training, economic opportunity activities, employment security administration, and public employment.
[6] Vocational rehabilitation, State soldiers' homes, child welfare services, national school lunch and special milk programs, public housing contributions, and others.
[7] Includes a grant for revenue sharing in the amount of $6,636.

Source: U.S. Social Security Administration, *Social Security Bulletin*, June 1974. (Based on data from Dept. of the Treasury.)

Appendix B

Gross National Product and Personal Consumption Expenditures in Current and Constant 1958 Dollars: 1960 to 1973

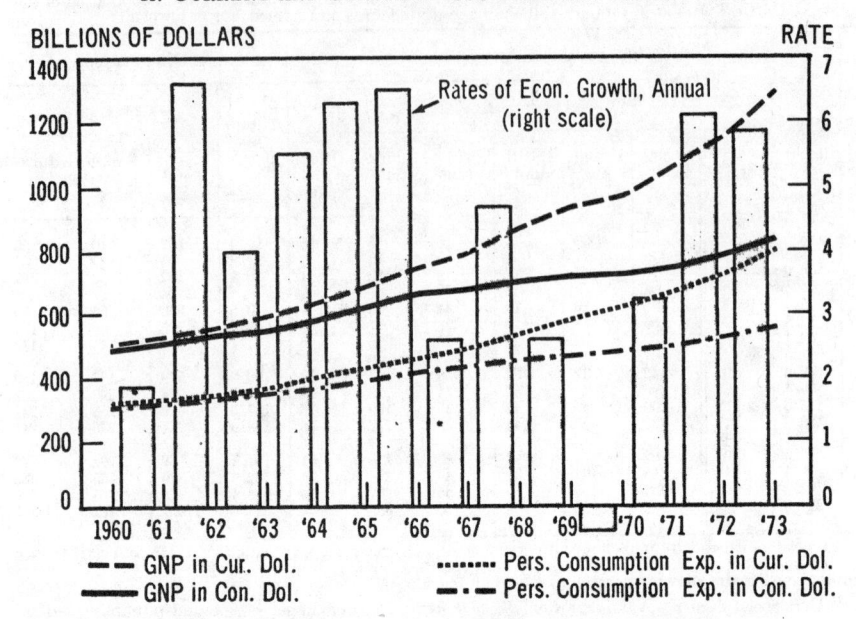

- - - GNP in Cur. Dol.
——— GNP in Con. Dol.
.... Pers. Consumption Exp. in Cur. Dol.
—·— Pers. Consumption Exp. in Con. Dol.

Source: Chart prepared by U.S. Bureau of the Census. Data from U.S. Bureau of Economic Analysis.

Gross National Product—Summary: 1929 to 1973

[In billions of dollars. Prior to 1960, excludes Alaska and Hawaii.]

ITEM	1929	1930	1933	1935	1940	1945	1950	1955
Gross national product	103.1	90.4	55.6	72.2	99.7	211.9	284.8	398.0
By type of expenditure:								
Personal consumption expenditures	77.2	69.9	45.8	55.7	70.8	119.7	191.0	254.4
Gross private domestic investment	16.2	10.3	1.4	6.4	13.1	10.6	54.1	67.4
Net exports of goods and services	1.1	1.0	.4	.1	1.7	−.6	1.8	2.0
Govt. purchases of goods and services	8.5	9.2	8.0	10.0	14.0	82.3	37.9	74.2
By major type of product:								
Goods output	56.1	46.9	27.0	39.9	56.0	128.9	162.4	216.4
Services	35.6	34.2	25.7	28.3	35.4	76.5	87.0	132.6
Structures	11.4	9.2	2.9	4.0	8.3	6.5	35.4	49.0
By sector:								
Business	95.1	82.4	48.9	64.1	89.1	172.3	256.3	352.9
Households and institutions	2.9	2.7	1.7	1.9	2.4	4.1	6.4	9.1
Rest of the world	.8	.7	.3	.4	.4	.4	1.2	1.8
General government	4.3	4.5	4.7	5.9	7.8	35.2	20.9	34.2

ITEM	1960	1965	1968	1969	1970	1971	1972	1973 (prel.)
Gross national product	503.7	684.9	864.2	930.3	977.1	1,055.5	1,155.2	1,289.1
By type of expenditure:								
Personal consumption expenditures	325.2	432.8	536.2	579.5	617.6	667.2	726.5	804.0
Gross private domestic investment	74.8	108.1	126.0	139.0	136.3	153.2	178.3	202.1
Net exports of goods and services	4.0	6.9	2.5	1.9	3.6	.8	−4.6	5.8
Govt. purchases of goods and services	99.6	137.0	199.6	210.0	219.5	234.3	255.0	277.1
By major type of product:								
Goods output	259.6	347.2	429.5	457.5	471.2	497.1	541.4	614.7
Services	187.3	262.9	346.6	377.9	410.3	447.4	487.3	534.5
Structures	56.8	74.8	88.1	94.9	95.6	110.9	126.5	139.9
By sector:								
Business	440.7	594.4	739.0	794.1	827.0	889.9	975.4	1,090.9
Households and institutions	13.2	18.5	25.5	28.1	30.8	33.5	36.8	41.1
Rest of the world	2.4	4.2	4.7	4.3	4.6	7.0	7.5	9.6
General government	47.5	67.8	94.9	103.8	114.7	125.1	135.4	147.5

Appendix B

Budget Outlays for National Defense Functions: 1960 to 1974

[In millions of dollars. For years ending June 30]

COST CATEGORY, PROGRAM, OR AGENCY	1960	1965	1967	1968	1969	1970	1971	1972	1973	1974 est.
Total	45,908	49,578	70,081	80,517	81,232	80,295	77,661	78,336	76,021	80,573
Dept. of Defense, military	41,479	45,973	67,457	77,373	77,872	77,150	74,546	75,151	73,297	78,400
Military personnel	11,044	13,387	17,956	19,859	21,374	23,031	22,633	23,036	23,246	24,081
Percent of total military	26.6	29.1	26.6	25.7	27.4	29.9	30.4	30.7	31.7	30.7
Active forces	10,390	12,662	17,054	18,988	20,482	21,977	21,428	21,629	21,722	22,448
Reserve forces	654	725	902	871	892	1,054	1,204	1,407	1,523	1,633
Retired military personnel	694	1,384	1,830	2,095	2,444	2,849	3,386	3,885	4,390	5,145
Operation [1]	10,223	12,349	19,000	20,578	22,227	21,609	20,941	21,675	21,069	23,306
Procurement	13,334	11,839	19,012	23,283	23,988	21,584	18,858	17,131	15,654	15,144
Army	(NA)	1,764	4,390	5,841	6,117	5,206	4,357	3,894	2,781	2,560
Navy (incl. Marine Corps)	(NA)	4,933	6,485	7,992	8,523	7,945	7,300	7,135	7,028	7,143
Air Force	(NA)	5,101	8,096	9,408	9,294	8,362	7,131	6,048	5,798	5,387
Defense agencies	(NA)	42	41	42	54	71	70	54	48	54
Research and development	4,710	6,236	7,160	7,747	7,457	7,166	7,303	7,881	8,157	8,414
Military construction	1,626	1,007	1,536	1,281	1,389	1,168	1,095	1,108	1,119	1,299
Family housing	(X)	563	485	495	572	614	598	688	729	966
Civil defense	(X)	93	100	108	87	80	75	75	74	83
Other [2]	−151	−885	377	1,927	−1,662	−952	−342	−327	−1,141	−38
Military assistance	1,631	1,125	858	654	789	731	999	806	531	1,100
Atomic energy program	2,623	2,625	2,264	2,466	2,450	2,453	2,275	2,392	2,393	2,328
Defense-related activities	244	136	−17	139	260	79	−70	95	177	−16
Offsetting receipts, deduct	*−69*	*−281*	*−481*	*−116*	*−138*	*−118*	*−89*	*−108*	*−377*	*−1,240*

NA Not available.   X Not applicable.   [1] Includes maintenance.   [2] Revolving and management funds, trust funds, special foreign currency program, allowances, and offsetting receipts.

Department of Defense Outlays, by Branch of Service: 1965 to 1973

[For years ending June 30. Excludes civil functions. Includes military assistance]

YEAR	Total Defense Department	OUTLAYS (mil. dol.) Army	Navy	Air Force	Other	PERCENT DISTRIBUTION Army	Navy	Air Force	Other
1965	47,098	11,552	13,339	18,146	4,061	24.5	28.3	38.5	8.6
1967	68,315	20,952	19,246	22,918	5,199	30.7	28.2	33.5	7.6
1968	78,027	25,223	22,071	25,734	4,999	32.3	28.3	33.0	6.4
1969	78,660	25,610	22,691	26,114	4,245	32.6	28.8	33.2	5.4
1970	78,349	25,147	22,656	25,233	5,313	32.1	28.9	32.2	6.8
1971	76,005	23,909	22,374	24,749	4,973	31.5	29.4	32.6	6.5
1972	76,674	23,473	22,736	24,845	5,620	30.6	29.7	32.4	7.3
1973	74,473	21,140	22,985	24,538	5,811	28.4	30.9	32.9	7.8

Source: U.S. Dept. of the Treasury, Office of the Secretary, *Combined Statement of Receipts, Expenditures, and Balances of the United States Government*, annual.

Appendix C

Election Campaign Costs for National Offices: 1972

[**Money figures in millions of dollars.** Covers some prenomination expenditures. Data are provided by the U.S. General Accounting Office, Office of Federal Elections (O.F.E.), newly created to administer the Federal Elections Campaign Act of 1971, effective as of April 7, 1972. Previously, only committees operating in two or more States were required to report receipts and expenditures. In 1968 there were 222 such committees, not all of which contributed to a presidential campaign. The new requirement of comprehensive disclosure resulted in 1,785 committees filing reports with the O.F.E. in 1972, all of which contributed in some way, but not exclusively to a presidential candidate. Except for Congressional spending, all other figures are from the O.F.E]

ITEM	1972	ITEM	1972
Campaign costs	219.0	Republican committees:	
		Number reporting	418
National spending	138.2	Spending	71.4
Congressional spending	[1] 80.8	Percent of national spending	51.7
		Third party committees:	
Democratic committees:		Number reporting	57
Number	1,048	Spending	.8
Spending	65.2	Percent of national spending	.5
Percent of national spending	47.1	Miscellaneous committees: [2]	
		Number	262
		Spending	14.0
		Percent of national spending	10.2

[1] Estimated. [2] Includes labor, business, and professional political committees.

Source: Citizens' Research Foundation, Princeton, N.J., unpublished data.

Appendix D 515

RECENT TRENDS

Subject	Unit of measure	1960	1965	1970	1972	1973[1]	Percent change, average per year 1960-65	1965-70	1970-73[1]
POPULATION[2]									
Total, incl. Armed Forces abroad	Millions	180.7	194.3	204.9	208.8	210.4	1.5	1.1	0.9
Net annual increase over previous year	Millions	2.84	2.40	2.20	1.80	1.55	-3.3	-1.7	-11.0
Resident population	Millions	180.0	193.5	203.8	208.2	209.9	1.5	1.0	1.0
Per square mile	Number	51	55	57	59	59	1.5	0.7	1.2
Northeast	Millions	44.8	47.5	49.2	49.7	49.7	1.2	0.7	0.4
North Central	Millions	51.7	54.2	56.7	57.4	57.6	1.0	0.9	0.5
South	Millions	55.2	59.6	63.0	65.1	66.0	1.5	1.1	1.5
West	Millions	28.3	32.2	34.9	36.0	36.6	2.6	1.6	1.5
Urban[3]	Millions	125.3	na	149.3	na	na	na	[4]1.8	na
Rural[3]	Millions	54.1	na	53.9	na	na	na	[4](z)	na
Male	Millions	88.6	94.8	99.2	101.5	102.2	1.4	0.9	1.0
Female	Millions	91.3	98.7	104.6	106.8	107.6	1.6	1.2	1.1
White	Millions	159	171	179	182	183	1.4	0.9	0.8
Negro and other	Millions	20.6	22.9	25.0	26.3	26.8	2.1	1.8	2.3
Negro	Millions	18.9	21.0	22.6	23.5	23.8	2.0	1.5	1.6
Percent of total population	Percent	11	11	11	11	11	ns	ns	ns
Percent in the South	Percent	60	54	53	52	52	ns	ns	ns
Persons of Spanish origin	Millions	na	na	na	na	10.6	na	na	na
Foreign born	Millions	9.7	na	9.6	na	na	na	[4]0.3	na
Native of foreign or mixed parentage	Millions	24.3	na	24.0	na	na	na	[4](z)	na
5-17 years old[3]	Millions	44	50	53	52	51	2.5	1.0	-0.7
18 years old and over[3]	Millions	115	124	134	140	142	1.4	1.6	1.7
21 years old and over	Millions	108	115	123	128	130	1.1	1.5	1.6
65 years old and over	Millions	17	18	20	21	21	2.0	1.9	2.0
Median age	Years	30	28	28	28	28	ns	ns	ns
Male, 18 years old and over:[5] [6]									
Single	Percent	25.3	17.7	19.1	19.6	19.5	ns	ns	ns
Married	Percent	69.1	76.2	75.0	74.8	74.5	ns	ns	ns
Divorced	Percent	1.9	2.5	2.5	2.8	3.0	ns	ns	ns
Female, 18 years old and over:[5] [6]									
Single	Percent	19.0	12.4	13.7	13.8	13.9	ns	ns	ns
Married	Percent	65.6	70.5	68.5	68.5	68.1	ns	ns	ns
Divorced	Percent	2.6	3.3	3.9	4.3	4.5	ns	ns	ns
Households[6]	Millions	52.8	57.4	63.4	66.7	68.3	1.7	2.0	2.5
Primary families	Millions	44.9	47.8	51.5	53.2	54.3	1.3	1.5	1.8
Primary individuals	Millions	7.9	9.6	11.9	13.5	14.0	4.0	4.5	5.4
Average size	Persons	3.33	3.29	3.14	3.06	3.01	ns	ns	ns
Families[6]	Millions	45.1	48.0	51.6	53.3	54.4	1.2	1.5	1.8
Female head	Millions	4.51	5.03	5.59	6.19	6.61	2.2	2.2	5.7
White	Millions	40.9	43.1	46.0	47.6	48.5	1.1	1.3	1.7
Female head	Percent	8.7	9.0	9.1	9.4	9.6	ns	ns	ns
Average size	Persons	3.61	3.64	3.54	3.47	3.42	ns	ns	ns
Negro and other	Millions	4.24	4.75	5.22	5.66	5.90	2.3	1.9	4.2
Female head	Percent	22.4	23.7	26.7	30.1	32.8	ns	ns	ns
Average size	Persons	4.39	4.37	4.32	4.08	4.00	ns	ns	ns
Farm	Millions	3.80	na	2.20	na	na	na	[4]-5.3	
Births, live	Millions	4.26	3.76	3.73	3.26	3.14	-2.5	-0.2	-5.6
Negro and other, percent of total	Percent	15.4	16.9	17.2	17.4	na	ns	ns	ns
Rate, all classes, per 1,000 population	Rate	23.7	19.4	18.4	15.6	15.0	-3.9	-1.1	-6.6
White	Rate	22.7	18.3	17.4	14.8	na	-4.2	-3.3	-7.8
Negro and other	Rate	32.1	27.6	25.1	21.8	na	-3.0	-1.8	-6.8
Deaths	Millions	1.71	1.83	1.92	1.96	1.98	1.3	1.0	1.0
Rate, all classes, per 1,000 population	Rate	9.5	9.4	9.5	9.4	9.4	-0.2	0.2	-0.4
Deaths per 100,000 population	Rate	955	943	945	942	na	-0.3	(z)	-0.2
Diseases of heart	Rate	369	367	362	361	na	-0.1	-0.3	-0.1
Malignancies	Rate	149	154	163	167	na	0.7	1.2	1.2
Cerebrovascular diseases	Rate	108	104	102	101	na	-0.8	-0.4	-0.5
Accidents	Rate	52	56	56	55	na	1.5	-0.3	-1.6
Infant death rate, per 1,000 live births	Rate	26.0	24.7	20.0	18.5	na	-1.0	-4.1	-3.8

Appendix D

Recent Trends

Subject	Unit of measure	1960	1965	1970	1972	1973[1]	Percent change, average per year 1960-65	1965-70	1970-73
POPULATION —Con.									
Marriages	Millions	1.52	1.80	2.16	2.27	2.28	3.4	3.7	1.8
Rate per 1,000 population	Rate	8.5	9.3	10.6	10.9	10.9	1.8	2.7	0.9
Per 1,000 unmarried women, 15 yrs. and over	Rate	74	75	77	78	na	0.4	0.6	0.5
Divorces	1,000	393	479	708	839	913	4.1	8.1	8.8
Rate per 1,000 population	Rate	2.2	2.5	3.5	4.0	4.4	2.6	7.0	7.9
Per 1,000 married women, 15 yrs. and over	Rate	9	11	15	17	na	2.9	7.2	6.5
Immigrants, total	1,000	265	297	373	385	400	2.3	4.7	2.4
HEALTH									
Life expectancy at birth, male	Years	66.6	66.8	67.1	67.4	na	0.1	0.1	0.2
Life expectancy at birth, female	Years	73.1	73.7	74.8	75.2	na	0.2	0.3	0.3
National health expenditures, total	Bil. dol	25.9	38.9	68.1	84.7	94.1	8.5	11.7	11.4
Public, percent of total	Percent	24.7	24.5	37.1	39.4	39.9	ns	ns	ns
Private consumer expenditures for health care	Bil. dol	18.0	26.8	39.5	46.7	na	8.8	8.1	8.7
Met by insurance benefits	Percent	27.8	32.6	39.8	41.7	na	ns	ns	ns
Indexes of medical care prices, total	1967=100	79.1	89.5	120.6	132.5	137.7	2.5	6.1	4.5
Physicians' fees		77.0	88.3	121.4	133.8	138.2	2.8	6.6	4.4
Semi-private room rates		57.3	75.9	145.4	173.9	182.1	5.8	13.9	7.8
Physicians, total number, M.D.'s	1,000	261	292	334	357	na	2.3	2.7	3.3
Patient care, general practice	1,000	na	66	53	52	na	na	-4.3	-1.1
Dentists, number	1,000	103	109	116	120	na	1.2	1.2	1.5
Nurses, registered, number	1,000	504	613	700	748	na	4.0	2.7	3.4
Hospitals	Number	6,876	7,123	7,123	7,061	na	0.7	(z)	-0.4
Beds	1,000	1,658	1,704	1,616	1,550	na	0.5	-1.1	-2.1
Beds per 1,000 population	Rate	9.3	8.9	8.0	7.4	na	ns	ns	na
Mentally ill patients in hospitals	1,000	na	1,566	[7]1,613	[x]1,624	na	na	[9]0.6	[10]0.3
Mentally retarded in public institutions	1,000	159	182	190	[x]190	na	2.7	0.9	na
Bed disability, days per person	Days	6.0	6.2	6.1	6.5	na	ns	ns	ns
Male	Days	5.3	5.3	5.2	5.5	na	ns	ns	ns
Female	Days	6.7	7.0	6.9	7.4	na	ns	ns	ns
Federal food program for needy families:									
Recipients	Millions	4.3	5.8	4.1	3.6	2.8	6.3	-6.7	-11.8
Cost to government	Mil. dol	59	227	289	299	241	30.7	5.0	-5.9
Federal food stamp program, total value of stamps issued	Mil. dol	(x)	85	1,090	3,309	3,893	(x)	66.6	52.9
Paid for by participants	Percent	(x)	62.4	49.5	45.7	45.2	ns	ns	ns
Average monthly participants	Millions	(x)	0.4	4.3	11.1	12.2	(x)	59.2	41.1
Federal Government cost per participant	Dollars	(x)	76	127	155	176	(x)	10.8	11.5
EDUCATION									
School enrollment, total	Millions	46.3	53.8	60.4	60.1	59.4	3.1	1.8	-0.6
Elementary (kindergarten and grades 1-8)	Millions	32.4	35.1	37.2	35.3	34.6	1.6	0.9	-2.4
High school (grades 9-12)	Millions	10.2	13.0	14.7	15.2	15.3	4.8	2.5	1.3
Higher education	Millions	3.6	5.7	7.4	8.3	8.2	9.7	5.5	3.5
Private elementary and secondary	Percent	13.0	12.6	9.4	8.7	8.2	ns	ns	ns
Enrollment in public schools	Millions	39.0	45.1	52.1	52.0	51.6	2.9	2.7	-0.4
Enrollment in private schools	Millions	7.2	8.7	8.1	8.1	7.9	3.7	-3.5	-1.3
School expenditures, total	Bil. dol	24.7	40.2	70.2	83.3	89.5	10.2	11.8	8.4
Elementary and secondary	Bil. dol	18.1	27.3	45.5	53.8	57.5	8.6	10.8	8.1
Expenditures per student	Dollars	352	478	776	956	1,042	6.3	10.2	10.3
Per student, public school	Dollars	354	487	789	966	1,047	6.6	10.1	9.9
Higher education	Bil. dol	6.6	12.9	24.7	29.5	32.0	14.3	13.9	9.0
Public	Bil. dol	19.4	31.0	56.8	68.2	73.3	9.8	12.9	8.9
Private	Bil. dol	5.3	9.2	13.4	15.1	16.2	11.8	7.8	6.5
Years of school completed, persons 25 years old and over:									
Median for all persons	Years	10.5	11.8	12.2	12.2	12.3	ns	ns	ns
Median for Negro persons	Years	8.0	9.0	9.9	10.3	10.6	ns	ns	ns
Public school pupil-teacher ratio:									
Elementary schools	Ratio	28.4	27.6	24.3	24.4	na	-0.6	-2.5	0.2
Secondary schools	Ratio	21.7	20.8	19.8	18.9	na	-0.8	-1.0	-2.3
Public school teachers, average annual salary	$1,000	5.0	6.2	8.6	9.7	10.2	4.4	6.9	5.9
High school graduates	Millions	1.9	2.7	2.9	3.0	3.1	7.4	1.7	2.0
College graduates	Millions	0.4	0.5	0.8	0.9	1.0	6.4	9.3	6.2
College (public) costs, total per full-time resident	Dollars	820	950	1,204	1,357	1,426	3.0	4.9	5.8
Federal funds for education and related activities, total	Bil. dol	3.8	7.6	12.7	16.5	16.2	14.9	10.7	8.6

Appendix D

POPULATION, BY SEX, RACE, RESIDENCE, AND MEDIAN AGE: 1790 TO 1973

[In thousands, except as indicated. Total resident population excluding Armed Forces abroad. For definition of median, see preface. See also *Historical Statistics, Colonial Times to 1957*, series A 34-50 and A 86-94]

CENSUS DATE	Male	Female	White	Negro Number	Negro Percent	Other	Urban	Rural	All classes	White	Negro
CONTERMINOUS U.S.[2]											
1790 (Aug. 2)	(NA)	(NA)	3,172	757	19.3	(NA)	202	3,728	(NA)	(NA)	(NA)
1800 (Aug. 4)	(NA)	(NA)	4,306	1,002	18.9	(NA)	322	4,986	(NA)	16.0	(NA)
1810 (Aug. 6)	(NA)	(NA)	5,862	1,378	19.0	(NA)	525	6,714	(NA)	16.0	(NA)
1820 (Aug. 7)	4,897	4,742	7,867	1,772	18.4	(NA)	693	8,945	16.7	16.5	17.2
1830 (June 1)	6,532	6,334	10,537	2,329	18.1	(NA)	1,127	11,739	17.2	17.2	16.9
1840 (June 1)	8,689	8,381	14,196	2,874	16.8	(NA)	1,845	15,224	17.8	17.9	17.3
1850 (June 1)	11,838	11,354	19,553	3,639	15.7	(NA)	3,544	19,648	18.9	19.2	17.3
1860 (June 1)	16,085	15,358	26,923	4,442	14.1	79	6,217	25,227	19.4	19.7	17.7
1870 (June 1)	19,494	19,065	33,589	4,880	12.7	89	9,902	28,656	20.2	20.4	18.5
1880 (June 1)	25,519	24,637	43,403	6,581	13.1	172	14,130	36,026	20.9	21.4	18.0
1890 (June 1)	32,237	30,711	55,101	7,489	11.9	358	22,106	40,841	22.0	22.5	17.8
1900 (June 1)	38,816	37,178	66,809	8,834	11.6	351	30,160	45,835	22.9	23.4	19.4
1910 (Apr. 15)	47,332	44,640	81,732	9,828	10.7	413	41,999	49,973	24.1	24.5	20.8
1920 (Jan. 1)	53,900	51,810	94,821	10,463	9.9	427	54,158	51,553	25.3	25.6	22.3
1930 (Apr. 1)	62,137	60,638	110,287	11,891	9.7	597	68,955	53,820	26.4	26.9	23.5
1940 (Apr. 1)	66,062	65,608	118,215	12,866	9.8	589	74,424	57,246	29.0	29.5	25.3
1950 (Apr. 1)	74,833	75,864	134,942	15,042	10.0	713	96,468	54,230	30.2	30.8	26.2
1960 (Apr. 1)	87,865	90,600	158,455	18,860	10.6	1,149	124,699	53,765	29.6	30.3	23.5
UNITED STATES											
1950 (Apr. 1)	75,187	76,139	135,150	15,045	9.9	1,131	96,847	54,479	30.2	30.7	26.2
1960 (Apr. 1)	88,331	90,992	158,832	18,872	10.5	1,620	125,269	54,054	29.5	30.3	23.5
1970 (Apr. 1)	98,926	104,309	178,098	22,581	11.1	2,557	149,325	53,887	28.0	28.9	22.4
1971 (July 1)	100,437	105,775	180,408	23,086	11.2	2,718	(NA)	(NA)	28.0	28.8	22.5
1972 (July 1)	101,471	106,759	181,899	23,471	11.3	2,860	(NA)	(NA)	28.2	29.0	22.7
1973 (July 1)	102,229	107,622	183,049	23,801	11.3	3,000	(NA)	(NA)	28.4	29.2	22.9

NA Not available. [1] Beginning 1950, current definition. For explanation of change, see p. 2.
[2] Excludes Alaska and Hawaii.

Source: U.S. Bureau of the Census, *U.S. Census of Population: 1930*, vol. II; *1940*, vol. II, part 1, and vol. IV, part 1; *1950*, vol. II, part 1; *1960*, vol. I; *1970*, vol. 1, part B; and *Current Population Reports*, series P-25, No. 519.

Appendix D

PERCENT OF VOTING-AGE POPULATION CASTING VOTES—STATES: 1960 TO 1972

[As of November 1. Resident population 21 years old and over, except as noted]

STATE	PERCENT CASTING VOTES FOR PRESIDENTIAL ELECTORS				PERCENT CASTING VOTES FOR U.S. REPRESENTATIVES						
	1960	1964	1968	1972[1]	1960	1962	1964	1966	1968	1970	1972[1]
U.S.[2]	63.1	61.8	60.7	55.7	58.7	46.3	58.1	45.6	55.2	43.8	51.0
Ala	30.8	35.9	52.7	44.2	23.7	23.9	32.2	35.9	45.7	36.3	42.8
Alaska	[3]43.7	[3]43.9	[3]49.9	47.6	[3]42.5	[3]41.9	[3]43.9	[3]41.9	[3]48.3	[3]44.9	47.7
Ariz	52.4	54.8	49.9	50.3	49.6	42.0	52.5	39.7	47.5	38.1	47.9
Ark.[4]	40.8	50.6	53.3	49.7	36.0	16.8	11.7	26.1	26.1	14.7	14.3
Calif	65.8	63.9	59.8	60.0	62.7	53.1	61.8	54.0	57.9	51.1	57.4
Colo	69.7	68.0	64.5	61.2	67.7	53.8	66.3	54.7	62.4	48.0	58.6
Conn	76.1	70.7	68.8	65.7	75.8	62.7	70.2	56.6	66.1	56.8	64.2
Del	72.2	69.0	68.3	63.5	71.7	55.1	68.1	54.1	64.0	49.2	60.9
D.C.	(X)	38.7	34.4	31.5	(X)	(X)	(X)	(X)	(X)	(X)	(X)
Fla	48.6	51.2	53.0	50.6	39.3	27.6	39.1	27.5	42.9	28.1	37.8
Ga	[1]29.2	[1]43.3	[1]43.4	37.8	[1]22.9	[1]13.3	[1]31.7	[1]31.2	[1]33.1	[1]29.5	28.7
Hawaii	[5]49.7	[5]51.3	[5]53.8	50.9	[5]49.2	[5]50.0	[5]56.9	[5]50.0	[5]55.3	[5]44.0	51.8
Idaho	79.7	77.2	73.3	64.8	77.0	66.6	75.1	65.5	69.6	56.0	63.0
Ill	75.5	73.2	69.3	62.6	73.1	57.1	71.2	57.1	66.3	51.3	58.1
Ind	76.3	73.5	70.7	60.6	75.8	64.2	72.9	57.4	67.9	55.7	60.1
Iowa	76.5	72.9	69.8	64.2	73.6	49.2	70.3	53.6	67.2	45.5	62.6
Kans	69.7	65.1	64.8	59.4	65.3	46.9	61.7	50.2	60.7	52.2	57.0
Ky	[1]57.6	[1]53.3	[1]51.2	48.4	[1]46.8	[1]32.9	[1]48.6	[1]33.9	[1]41.9	[1]22.2	44.7
La	44.6	47.3	54.8	45.0	28.7	18.8	31.7	28.0	31.4	17.6	29.0
Maine	71.7	65.1	66.4	62.6	69.5	48.7	63.2	53.1	64.9	52.9	62.1
Md	56.5	54.1	54.4	50.4	52.5	37.1	49.0	35.2	44.9	37.3	45.3
Mass	75.6	70.0	67.4	62.2	69.2	60.3	63.0	53.5	59.5	50.9	54.6
Mich	72.2	67.9	65.7	59.4	70.1	58.3	64.8	48.4	60.5	49.3	55.7
Minn	76.4	75.8	73.8	68.0	75.1	59.4	74.2	58.6	71.2	59.4	66.0
Miss	25.3	33.9	53.2	46.0	21.9	13.5	29.9	31.5	36.5	24.9	41.9
Mo	71.5	67.1	64.3	56.8	68.1	45.3	65.6	38.0	61.2	41.1	56.1
Mont	70.3	69.4	68.0	69.0	69.0	62.4	68.9	64.3	65.3	60.8	68.5
Nebr	70.6	66.4	60.9	56.4	66.9	50.7	63.8	54.5	59.3	49.5	55.6
Nev	58.3	52.1	54.4	52.2	56.3	42.1	50.3	47.7	50.9	45.4	51.9
N.H.	78.7	71.8	69.5	64.1	75.7	57.7	70.1	56.1	66.2	47.4	60.4
N.J.	70.8	68.7	66.0	59.6	67.8	49.0	65.7	49.6	61.9	46.6	56.4
N. Mex	61.7	61.9	60.7	60.7	59.8	52.4	65.9	49.8	57.5	50.2	58.7
N.Y.	67.3	64.8	59.9	56.1	64.0	50.6	61.1	49.5	53.8	47.2	51.7
N.C.	52.9	52.8	54.3	43.9	50.4	31.0	47.9	32.7	47.9	30.6	39.0
N. Dak	77.9	71.4	70.1	69.8	71.8	60.8	68.8	55.1	64.8	58.4	66.8
Ohio	70.7	66.6	63.3	57.0	65.3	51.0	62.6	45.9	58.2	47.4	53.4
Okla	63.1	63.4	61.2	56.8	58.6	42.7	57.1	42.7	52.6	42.1	45.1
Oreg	71.8	68.9	66.4	61.9	70.6	57.5	67.3	56.1	63.9	49.9	58.0
Pa	70.3	67.9	65.3	56.3	69.6	62.1	63.7	55.4	62.9	48.7	54.7
R.I.	75.2	71.6	67.2	61.8	72.7	59.2	68.5	58.1	63.7	54.6	57.7
S.C.	30.4	39.4	46.7	39.5	25.8	20.3	32.9	26.5	44.0	28.7	37.0
S. Dak	77.6	74.1	73.2	70.8	76.3	63.1	72.8	58.4	70.7	60.4	69.4
Tenn	49.8	51.7	53.7	44.3	30.5	28.2	46.8	35.4	43.6	41.0	40.6
Tex	41.2	44.6	48.7	45.2	36.4	26.1	44.4	20.9	37.9	27.5	37.6
Utah	78.2	78.2	76.7	69.4	77.1	63.3	77.3	57.9	75.5	63.9	72.7
Vt	72.4	70.4	64.0	60.5	71.8	53.0	70.5	56.4	62.3	57.5	60.2
Va	32.8	41.1	50.1	45.6	27.2	18.4	36.6	26.2	46.7	32.0	39.8
Wash	71.9	71.7	66.0	62.0	65.1	50.4	68.2	51.2	61.0	49.2	54.9
W. Va	78.0	75.5	71.1	64.5	76.3	58.5	73.4	47.2	67.1	40.7	61.0
Wis	72.9	69.5	66.5	62.7	70.1	52.3	67.7	46.5	64.5	50.7	61.0
Wyo	72.7	74.2	67.1	64.7	69.8	61.1	72.4	64.6	65.0	58.6	65.0

X Not applicable.
[1] Population 18 years old and over.
[2] Excludes District of Columbia except for presidential elections of 1964, 1968, and 1972.
[3] Population 19 years old and over.
[4] According to Arkansas law, it is not required to tabulate votes for unopposed candidates.
[5] Population 20 years old and over.

Source: U.S. Bureau of the Census, *Current Population Reports*, series P-25, No. 479, and unpublished data. Based on votes cast as presented in U.S. Clerk of the House, *Statistics of the Presidential and Congressional Election* and *Statistics of the Congressional Election*.

Appendix E

The Standing Committees (94th Congress)

Senate Committees	Chairman	State	Age[1]
Aeronautical & Space Sciences	Frank E. Moss	Utah	62
Agriculture & Forestry	H. E. Talmadge	Ga.	60
Appropriations	J. L. McClellan	Ark.	77
Armed Services	John C. Stennis	Miss.	72
Banking, Housing & Urban Affrs.	William Proxmire	Wis.	58
Commerce	W. G. Magnuson	Wash.	68
District of Columbia	Thos. F. Eagleton	Mo.	44
Finance	Russell B. Long	La.	55
Foreign Relations	J. J. Sparkman	Ala.	74
Government Operations	Abraham Ribicoff	Conn.	63
Interior & Insular Affairs	Henry M. Jackson	Wash.	61
Judiciary	J. O. Eastland	Miss.	69
Labor & Public Welfare	H. O. Williams, Jr.	N. J.	54
Post Office & Civil Service	Gale W. Mcgee	Wyo.	58
Public Works	Jennings Randolph	W. Va.	71
Rules & Administration	Howard W. Cannon	Nev.	61
Veterans' Affairs	Vance Hartke	Ind.	54

House Committees			
Agriculture	Thomas Foley	Wash.	45
Appropriations	George Mahon	Tex.	73
Armed Services	Melvin Price	Ill.	70
Banking & Currency	Henry Reuss	Wis.	62
District of Columbia	C. D. Diggs, Jr.	Mich.	51
Education & Labor	Carl D. Perkins	Ky.	61
Foreign Affairs	T. E. Morgan	Pa.	67
Government Operations	Jack Brooks	Tex.	51
House Administration	Wayne L. Hays	Ohio	62
Interior & Insular Affairs	J. A. Haley	Fla.	74
Internal Security	R. H. Ichord	Mo.	47
Interstate & Foreign Commerce	H. O. Staggers	W. Va.	66
Judiciary	P. W. Rodino, Jr.	N. J.	64
Merchant Marine & Fisheries	Leonor K. Sullivan	Mo.	70
Post Office & Civil Service	David N. Henderson	N. C.	52
Public Works	Robert E. Jones	Ala.	61
Rules	Ray J. Madden	Ind.	81
Science & Astronautics	Olin E. Teague	Tex.	63
Standards of Official Conduct	Melvin Price	Ill.	69
Veterans' Affairs	Ray Roberts	Tex.	60
Ways & Means	Al Ullman	Ore.	60

[1] Ages of chairmen as of 1/3/74. Because Democrats were in the majority in both houses in the 94th Congress, all committee chairmen were Democrats.

Appendix E

COMPOSITION OF CONGRESS, BY POLITICAL PARTY AFFILIATIONS, BY STATES: 1969, 1971, AND 1973

[Figures are for the beginning of the session. Dem.=Democratic; Rep.=Republican]

STATE	REPRESENTATIVES 91st Congress (1969)[1] Dem.	Rep.	92d Congress (1971)[2][3] Dem.	Rep.	93d Congress (1973)[4][5] Dem.	Rep.	SENATORS 91st Congress (1969) Dem.	Rep.	92d Congress (1971)[2] Dem.	Rep.	93d Congress (1973)[4] Dem.	Rep.
Total	[1]243	[2]192	254	180	239	192	57	43	54	44	56	42
Alabama	5	3	5	3	4	3	2	-	2	-	2	-
Alaska	-	1	1	-	-	-	1	1	1	1	1	1
Arizona	1	2	1	2	1	3	-	2	-	2	-	2
Arkansas	3	1	3	1	3	1	2	-	2	-	2	-
California	21	17	20	18	23	20	1	1	2	-	2	-
Colorado	3	1	2	2	2	3	-	2	-	2	1	1
Connecticut	4	2	4	2	3	3	2	-	1	1	1	1
Delaware	-	1	-	1	-	1	-	2	-	2	1	1
Florida	9	3	9	3	11	4	1	1	1	1	1	1
Georgia	8	2	8	2	9	1	2	-	2	-	2	-
Hawaii	2	-	2	-	2	-	1	1	1	1	1	1
Idaho	-	2	-	2	-	2	1	1	1	1	1	1
Illinois	[1]12	12	12	12	9	14	-	2	1	1	1	1
Indiana	4	7	5	6	4	7	2	-	2	-	1	1
Iowa	2	5	2	5	3	3	1	1	1	1	2	-
Kansas	-	5	1	4	1	4	-	2	-	2	2	-
Kentucky	4	3	5	2	5	2	-	2	-	2	1	1
Louisiana	8	-	8	-	6	1	2	-	2	-	2	-
Maine	2	-	2	-	1	1	1	1	1	1	2	-
Maryland	4	4	5	3	4	4	1	1	-	2	-	2
Massachusetts	[1]7	[1]5	8	4	8	3	1	1	1	1	1	1
Michigan	7	12	7	12	7	12	1	1	1	1	1	1
Minnesota	3	5	4	4	4	4	2	-	2	-	2	-
Mississippi	5	-	5	-	3	2	2	-	2	-	2	-
Missouri	9	1	9	1	9	1	2	-	2	-	2	-
Montana	[1]1	[1]1	1	1	1	1	2	-	2	-	2	-
Nebraska	-	3	-	3	-	3	-	2	-	2	-	2
Nevada	1	-	1	-	-	1	2	-	2	-	2	-
New Hampshire	-	2	-	2	-	2	1	1	1	1	1	1
New Jersey	9	6	9	6	8	7	1	1	1	1	1	1
New Mexico	-	2	1	1	1	1	2	-	2	-	1	1
New York	26	15	24	17	22	17	-	2	-	1	-	1
North Carolina	7	4	7	4	7	4	2	-	2	-	1	1
North Dakota	-	2	1	1	-	1	1	1	1	1	1	1
Ohio	6	18	7	17	7	16	1	1	-	2	-	2
Oklahoma	4	2	4	2	5	1	1	1	1	1	-	2
Oregon	2	2	2	2	2	2	-	2	-	2	-	2
Pennsylvania	14	13	14	13	13	12	-	2	-	2	-	2
Rhode Island	2	-	2	-	2	-	2	-	2	-	2	-
South Carolina	5	1	4	1	4	2	1	1	1	1	1	1
South Dakota	-	2	2	-	1	1	1	1	1	1	2	-
Tennessee	5	4	5	4	3	5	1	1	-	2	-	2
Texas	20	3	20	3	20	4	1	1	1	1	1	1
Utah	-	2	1	1	2	-	1	1	1	1	1	1
Vermont	-	1	-	1	-	1	-	2	-	2	-	2
Virginia	5	5	4	6	3	7	2	-	1	-	-	1
Washington	5	2	6	1	6	1	2	-	2	-	2	-
West Virginia	5	-	5	-	4	-	2	-	2	-	2	-
Wisconsin	[1]3	[1]7	5	5	5	4	2	-	2	-	2	-
Wyoming	-	1	1	-	-	1	1	1	1	1	1	1

– Represents zero. [1] Changes as of the beginning of the 2d session, 1970: Total, 245 Dem., 189 Rep.; Ill., 11 Dem., 12 Rep., 1 vacancy; Mass. 8 Dem., 4 Rep.; Mont., 2 Dem., 0 Rep.; and Wis., 4 Dem., 6 Rep. [2] S.C. had 1 vacancy at beginning of session; N.Y. had 1 Senator classified Conservative-Republican and Va. had 1 classified Independent. [3] Changes as of the beginning of the 2d session, 1972: Total, 255 Dem., 177 Rep., 3 vacancies; Ill., 12 Dem., 11 Rep.; Pa., 14 Dem., 12 Rep.; S.C., 5 Dem., 1 Rep.; Vt., vacant. [4] Alaska, Ill., and La. each had 1 vacancy; Mass. had 1 Representative classified as Independent-Democrat; N.Y. had 1 Senator classified Conservative-Republican and Va. had 1 Senator classified Independent. [5] Two new members: Delegates from Guam and the Virgin Islands.

Source: U.S. Congress, Joint Committee on Printing, *Congressional Directory*.

Appendix E

COMPOSITION OF CONGRESS, BY POLITICAL PARTY: 1933 TO 1974

[D=Democratic, R=Republican. Figures are for beginning of first session of each Congress, except 1974, which are for beginning of second session. See also *Historical Statistics, Colonial Times to 1957*, series Y 139–145]

YEAR	Party and President	Congress	HOUSE Majority party	HOUSE Minority party	HOUSE Other	SENATE Majority party	SENATE Minority party	SENATE Other
1933	D (F. Roosevelt)	73d	D-310	R-117	5	D-60	R-35	1
1935	D (F. Roosevelt)	74th	D-319	R-103	10	D-69	R-25	2
1937	D (F. Roosevelt)	75th	D-331	R-89	13	D-76	R-16	4
1939	D (F. Roosevelt)	76th	D-261	R-164	4	D-69	R-23	4
1941	D (F. Roosevelt)	77th	D-268	R-162	5	D-66	R-28	2
1943	D (F. Roosevelt)	78th	D-218	R-208	4	D-58	R-37	1
1945	D (F. Roosevelt) / D (Truman)	79th	D-242	R-190	2	D-56	R-38	1
1947	D (Truman)	80th	R-245	D-188	1	R-51	D-45	–
1949	D (Truman)	81st	D-263	R-171	1	D-54	R-42	–
1951	D (Truman)	82d	D-234	R-199	1	D-49	R-47	–
1953	R (Eisenhower)	83d	R-221	D-211	1	R-48	D-47	1
1955	R (Eisenhower)	84th	D-232	R-203	–	D-48	R-47	1
1957	R (Eisenhower)	85th	D-233	R-200	–	D-49	R-47	–
1959 [1]	R (Eisenhower)	86th	D-283	R-153	–	D-64	R-34	–
1961	D (Kennedy)	87th	D-263	R-174	–	D-65	R-35	–
1963	D (Kennedy) / D (Johnson)	88th	D-258	R-177	–	D-67	R-33	–
1965	D (Johnson)	89th	D-295	R-140	–	D-68	R-32	–
1967 [2]	D (Johnson)	90th	D-247	R-187	–	D-64	R-36	–
1969	R (Nixon)	91st	D-243	R-192	–	D-57	R-43	–
1971 [2][3]	R (Nixon)	92d	D-254	R-180	–	D-54	R-44	2
1973 [4]	R (Nixon)	93d	D-239	R-192	1	D-56	R-42	2
1974 [5]	R (Nixon)	93d	D-243	R-188	–	D-57	R-41	2

– Represents zero. [1] Excludes Hawaii; 2 Senators (1-R, 1-D) and 1 Representative (D) seated August 1959.
[2] House had 1 vacancy at beginning of session.
[3] Senate had 1 Independent member and 1 Conservative-Republican. [4] House had 3 vacancies at beginning of session, and 1 member classified Independent-Democrat. [5] House had 4 vacancies at beginning of session.

Source: U.S. Congress, Joint Committee on Printing, *Congressional Directory*.

CONGRESSIONAL BILLS, ACTS, AND RESOLUTIONS: 1957 TO 1973

[Excludes simple and concurrent resolutions. See also *Historical Statistics, Colonial Times to 1957*, series Y 129–138]

ITEM	85th Cong.	86th Cong.	87th Cong.	88th Cong.	89th Cong.	90th Cong.	91st Cong.	92d Cong.	93d Cong.
Period of session	1957–58	1959–60	1961–62	1963–64	1965–66	1967–68	1969–70	1971–72	1973
Measures introduced	19,112	18,261	18,376	17,480	24,003	26,460	26,303	22,969	14,064
Bills	18,205	17,230	17,230	16,079	22,483	24,786	24,631	21,363	13,010
Joint resolutions	907	1,031	1,146	1,401	1,520	1,674	1,672	1,606	1,054
Measures enacted	1,854	1,292	1,569	1,026	1,283	1,002	941	768	295
Public	1,009	800	885	666	810	640	695	607	245
Private	845	492	684	360	473	362	246	161	50

Source: U.S. Congress, *Calendars of the U.S. House of Representatives and History of Legislation*.

CONGRESSIONAL BILLS VETOED: 1913 TO 1973

PERIOD	President	VETOED BILLS Total	VETOED BILLS Regular	VETOED BILLS Pocket	Vetoes sustained	Bills passed over veto
1913–1921	Wilson	44	33	11	38	6
1921–1923	Harding	6	5	1	6	–
1923–1929	Coolidge	50	20	30	46	4
1929–1933	Hoover	37	21	16	34	3
1933–1945	F. Roosevelt	635	372	263	626	9
1945–1953	Truman	250	180	70	238	12
1953–1961	Eisenhower	181	73	108	179	2
1961–1963	Kennedy	21	12	9	21	–
1963–1969	Johnson	30	16	14	30	–
1969–1973	Nixon	41	23	18	36	5

– Represents zero.
Source: U.S. Congress, Senate Library, *Presidential Vetoes . . . 1789–1968*; U.S. Congress, *Calendars of the U.S. House of Representatives and History of Legislation*.

The Government of the United States
[As of June 1, 1974. Only the more important agencies are shown.]

THE CONSTITUTION

LEGISLATIVE

THE CONGRESS

Senate   House

Architect of the Capitol
General Accounting Office
Government Printing Office
Library of Congress
United States Botanic Garden
Cost Accounting Standards Board

EXECUTIVE

THE PRESIDENT

Executive Office of the President

White House Office
Office of Management and Budget
Council of Economic Advisers
National Security Council
Office of Economic Opportunity
Energy Policy Office
Council on Economic Policy
Federal Property Council

Office of the Special Representative for Trade Negotiations
Council on International Economic Policy
Council on Environmental Quality
Domestic Council
Office of Telecommunications Policy
Special Action Office for Drug Abuse Prevention

DEPARTMENT OF STATE
DEPARTMENT OF THE TREASURY
DEPARTMENT OF DEFENSE
DEPARTMENT OF JUSTICE
DEPARTMENT OF THE INTERIOR

DEPARTMENT OF AGRICULTURE
DEPARTMENT OF COMMERCE
DEPARTMENT OF LABOR
DEPARTMENT OF HEALTH, EDUCATION, AND WELFARE
DEPARTMENT OF HOUSING AND URBAN DEVELOPMENT
DEPARTMENT OF TRANSPORTATION

JUDICIAL

The Supreme Court of the United States
Circuit Courts of Appeals of the United States
District Courts of the United States
United States Court of Claims
United States Court of Customs and Patent Appeals
United States Customs Court
Territorial Courts
Federal Judicial Center
Administrative Office of the United States Courts
United States Tax Court

INDEPENDENT OFFICES AND ESTABLISHMENTS

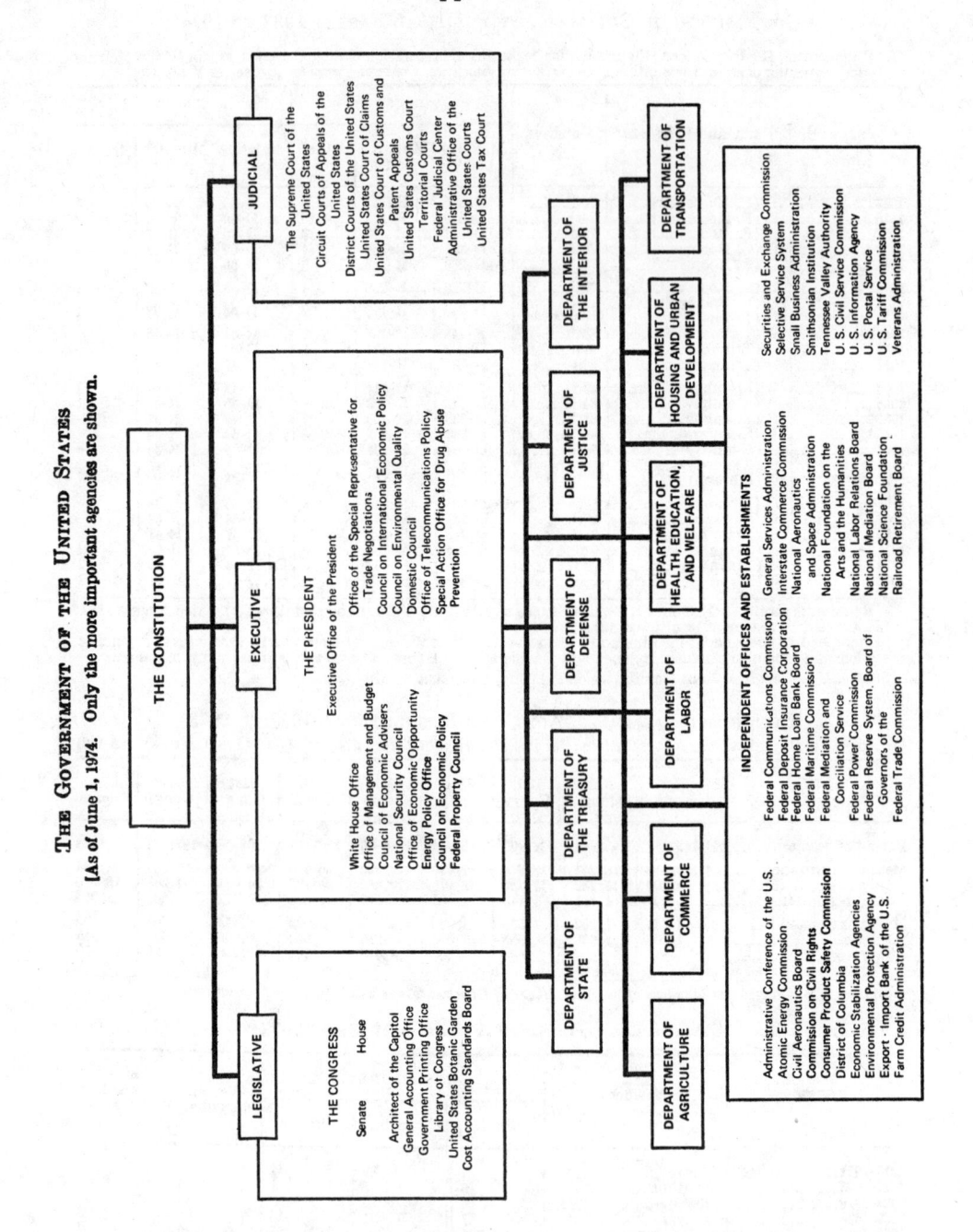

Administrative Conference of the U.S.
Atomic Energy Commission
Civil Aeronautics Board
Commission on Civil Rights
Consumer Product Safety Commission
District of Columbia
Economic Stabilization Agencies
Environmental Protection Agency
Export - Import Bank of the U.S.
Farm Credit Administration

Federal Communications Commission
Federal Deposit Insurance Corporation
Federal Home Loan Bank Board
Federal Maritime Commission
Federal Mediation and Conciliation Service
Federal Power Commission
Federal Reserve System, Board of Governors of the
Federal Trade Commission

General Services Administration
Interstate Commerce Commission
National Aeronautics and Space Administration
National Foundation on the Arts and the Humanities
National Labor Relations Board
National Mediation Board
National Science Foundation
Railroad Retirement Board

Securities and Exchange Commission
Selective Service System
Small Business Administration
Smithsonian Institution
Tennessee Valley Authority
U.S. Civil Service Commission
U.S. Information Agency
U.S. Postal Service
U.S. Tariff Commission
Veterans Administration

Source: U.S. General Services Administration, National Archives and Records Service.

Appendix G
DATA ANALYSIS AND STATISTICAL EXERCISE

A. Scientific Analysis:

The business of science is to systematically generate explanations by bringing theory and fact to bear upon one another. Empirical facts are found in the real world and theory is found in the world of ideas. The facts are not facts apart from a conceptual framework. A statement of fact is an empirically verifiable statement about phenomena in terms of a conceptual scheme.

Operational definitions of concepts, controlled observation, statistical generalization, and empirical verification constitute the basic principles of scientific inquiry.

B. Establishing Facts and Explanations:

The procedures political scientists use to establish facts or test explanations are several. Basically they include:
 (a) Systematic Observation
 (b) Experimental Method
 (c) Correlational and Causal Analysis

C. Methods:

(a) Systematic Observation is of two kinds: participant and non-participant. The former involves for the investigator spending time in the actual setting to be studied. But to guide his observations, the investigator must use some conceptual framework. Otherwise, he would be lost in the numerous activities that might be taking place in a particular observational setting. The thing observed becomes significant only if the observer relates it to something he knows or to his past experience; or, if reflecting upon it, he hits upon some useful hypothesis. Non-participant observation involves the techniques of personal interviewing and survey analysis used frequently by such organizations as Gallup Poll.

(b) **Experimental Design:** In an experiment, the researcher manipulates or controls some variable and studies systematically the effect of manipulated variable on some other dependent variable. In order to persue this kind of investigation, two or more similar groups may be selected. One, the **control group** is held as a yardstick for comparison, while the other, the **test group** is exposed to the experimental factor whose effect the researcher wishes to determine.

(c) **Correlational and Causal Analysis:** Correlational or co-variate procedure is widely used in contemporary political science. Two things are said to correlate when they co-vary or vary together. Thus for example, the extent of poverty in cities may be related to the degree of crime or violence in them. The degree of party competition in different states may be related to welfare expenditures there. Or military takeovers of governments may be related to decline in economic development in certain countries.

But while two variables may be associated, the association is not enough to say that one variable is a cause of the other. For establishing a causal relation, two additional requirements must be met. First, the independent or causal variable whose effect we are studying on the dependent variable must occur first or change prior to the dependent variable. Second, care must be taken to insure there is no third variable or factor that intervenes to cause the observed association. If there is a third variable that when held constant makes the original relation between two particular variables disappear, then we will have to conclude that the observed association or correlation is spurious.

D. Correlations:

Although it is not important for our present study, it is possible to calculate the degree of association between two variables (correlation coefficient). Numerically the results of such a calculation will vary within the limits of -1.0 to $+1.0$. The former indicates a perfect negative correlation, and the latter indicates a perfect positive correlation.

LINEAR RELATIONSHIP

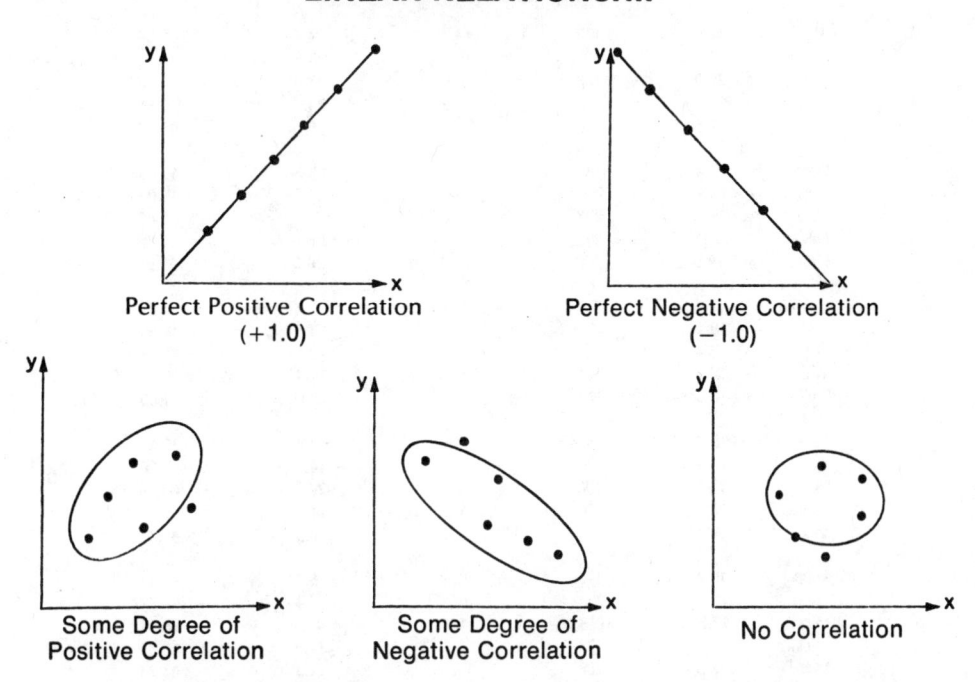

Perfect Positive Correlation (+1.0)

Perfect Negative Correlation (−1.0)

Some Degree of Positive Correlation

Some Degree of Negative Correlation

No Correlation

1. In a positive correlation when one variable increases, the other also increases.
2. In a negative correlation when one variable increases, the other decreases.

The above diagrams are known as "scattergrams" or scatterplots. Each dot in the scattergram represents one observation (say, a state or a country) placed in the graph according to its values on the two variables whose association one is investigating.

EXERCISES FOR THE STUDENT

In the Appendix there is a variety of statistical data. For example, there is data on the characteristics of states and the vote for the U.S. President.

1. Draw a scattergram relating any one state characteristic (such as labor union membership) to the 1968 vote for President Nixon.
2. Draw a scattergram indicating the relation between Nixon-Wallace vote by state in 1968 and Nixon vote by state in 1972. What does the scattergram indicate to you?
3. Note: Allow enough room on your graph for 50 plots.

SELECTED DATA FOR THE UNITED STATES

State	Birth Rate[1]	Expend. for Education[2]	Murder Rate[3]	% Pop. below Poverty Level[4]	Expend. for Public Assistance[5]
Ala.	17.8	179	13.7	24.7	60.04
Alaska	24.2	390	10.6	13.5	43.92
Ariz.	20.0	288	6.0	13.4	13.72
Ark.	16.7	157	9.9	21.1	59.60
Calif.	17.8	276	7.1	9.6	98.74
Colo.	19.0	283	5.3	17.2	59.45
Conn.	16.4	221	2.9	5.7	45.09
Del.	19.3	298	7.2	15.7	62.47
Fla.	18.4	215	11.3	20.5	36.04
Ga.	19.6	200	11.9	20.0	69.23
Hawaii	19.8	265	3.4	6.7	51.28
Idaho	18.1	195	1.9	8.6	38.68
Ill.	17.4	225	8.6	8.4	70.78
Ind.	17.9	243	4.9	11.1	27.73
Iowa	17.2	273	1.4	9.0	31.00
Kans.	15.4	232	3.5	8.2	36.69
Ky.	17.9	201	10.4	14.1	53.86
La.	19.9	198	9.5	22.2	64.08
Maine	17.9	190	1.6	14.1	67.87
Md.	16.1	257	9.3	10.3	45.35
Mass.	18.2	190	3.5	6.7	85.11
Mich.	18.7	292	8.3	9.4	59.57
Minn.	17.8	288	1.9	8.5	58.28
Miss.	20.0	173	8.1	34.9	68.80
Mo.	17.5	208	10.4	14.3	43.71
Mont.	16.8	237	3.6	16.7	38.14
Nebr.	16.8	244	2.5	10.4	36.67
Nev.	19.5	255	9.0	8.6	30.15
N.H.	17.3	201	2.5	9.6	30.14
N.J.	16.0	211	5.2	7.1	52.34
N. Mex.	21.6	295	6.1	17.8	52.05
N.Y.	17.1	278	7.2	9.7	140.45
N.C.	18.1	182	10.7	16.0	41.11
N. Dak.	18.4	262	0.2	14.3	48.90
Ohio	17.2	200	6.4	10.2	30.50
Okla.	16.2	204	5.8	16.3	79.26
Oreg.	17.0	295	4.0	10.3	44.03
Pa.	15.8	213	4.1	10.7	48.71
R.I.	17.4	211	3.1	10.4	65.47
S.C.	18.7	179	12.5	17.4	29.36
S. Dak.	17.3	279	2.0	15.7	39.97
Tenn.	18.5	175	9.6	18.2	46.26
Tex.	19.6	203	11.3	17.7	49.73
Utah	23.6	312	2.5	5.9	44.09
Vt.	17.8	251	2.5	12.4	77.81
Va.	16.8	203	5.9	13.6	34.89
Wash.	16.7	295	3.6	8.4	54.23
W. Va.	16.2	195	5.6	15.0	45.79
Wis.	17.4	291	2.1	6.5	52.04
Wyo.	18.5	336	10.3	14.4	20.80

Source: Bureau of the Census, *Pocket Data Book USA 1971* (Washington, D.C.: U.S. Government Printing Office, 1971). Bureau of the Census, *Statistical Abstract of the United States, 1972* (Washington, D.C.: U.S. Government Printing Office, 1972). Bureau of the Census, *Statistical Abstract of the United States, 1973* (Washington, D.C.: U.S. Government Printing Office, 1973). *Congressional Quarterly Guide to the 1972 Elections.*

NUMBER OF REGISTERED VOTERS[6]

State	18-24 Yrs. Old	Over 65 Yrs. Old	Black Population[7]	Labor Union Membership[7]
Ala.	18%	14%	26.2%	20.2%
Alaska	26	02	2.9	25.0
Ariz.	19	14	3.0	17.6
Ark.	17	18	18.3	17.8
Calif.	18	13	7.0	30.5
Colo.	21	13	3.0	20.5
Conn.	16	14	6.0	24.2
Del.	18	12	14.3	22.5
Fla.	15	21	15.3	13.8
Ga.	20	12	25.9	16.3
Hawaii	30	06	1.0	28.1
Idaho	18	15	0.3	18.5
Ill.	17	14	12.8	35.7
Ind.	18	14	6.9	35.6
Iowa	17	18	1.2	21.1
Kans.	18	17	4.8	16.5
Ky.	19	15	7.2	27.4
La.	20	13	29.8	18.4
Maine	17	17	0.3	18.4
Md.	18	11	17.8	23.3
Mass.	18	16	3.1	25.6
Mich.	18	13	11.2	40.2
Minn.	18	16	0.9	28.9
Miss.	19	16	30.8	13.2
Mo.	17	17	10.3	35.9
Mont.	18	15	0.3	36.4
Nebr.	18	18	2.7	17.8
Nev.	17	09	5.7	32.8
N.H.	18	16	0.3	17.3
N.J.	17	16	10.7	29.5
N. Mex.	20	11	1.9	14.8
N.Y.	16	15	11.9	35.6
N.C.	21	12	22.2	7.9
N. Dak.	19	17	0.4	17.2
Ohio	18	14	9.1	36.3
Okla.	18	17	6.7	16.1
Oreg.	17	16	1.3	30.8
Pa.	16	15	8.6	37.1
R.I.	19	16	2.7	26.0
S.C.	22	11	30.5	9.7
S. Dak.	18	19	0.2	12.0
Tenn.	18	14	15.8	20.6
Tex.	19	13	12.5	14.4
Utah	23	12	0.6	20.9
Vt.	19	16	0.2	16.2
Va.	20	11	18.5	16.7
Wash.	19	14	2.1	40.0
W. Va.	17	16	3.9	43.0
Wis.	18	16	2.9	31.4
Wyo.	18	14	0.8	17.7

[1]Per 1,000 population in 1969.
[2]Per capita expenditures in dollars (1969).
[3]Known offenses per 100,000 population (1969).
[4]Percent based upon civilian resident population in 1969.
[5]Per capita expenditures in dollars (1972).
[6]Percentage of registered voters (1972).
[7]Percentage of state population (1970).

The Constitution of the United States

We the People of the United States, in Order to form a more perfect Union, establish Justice, insure domestic Tranquility, provide for the common defence, promote the general Welfare, and secure the Blessings of Liberty to ourselves and our Posterity, do ordain and establish this Constitution for the United States of America.

Article I

Section 1. All legislative Powers herein granted shall be vested in a Congress of the United States, which shall consist of a Senate and House of Representatives.

Section 2. The House of Representatives shall be composed of Members chosen every second Year by the People of the several States, and the Electors in each State shall have the Qualifications requisite for Electors of the most numerous Branch of the State Legislature.

No Person shall be a Representative who shall not have attained to the Age of twenty five Years, and been seven Years a citizen of the United States, and who shall not, when elected, be an Inhabitant of that State in which he shall be chosen.

Representatives and direct Taxes shall be apportioned among the several States which may be included within this Union, according to their respective Numbers, which shall be determined by adding to the whole Number of free Persons, including those bound to Service for a Term of Years, and excluding Indians not taxed, three fifths of all other Persons. The actual Enumeration shall be made within three Years after the first Meeting of the Congress of the United States, and within every subsequent Term of ten Years, in such Manner as they shall by Law direct. The Number of Representatives shall not exceed one for every thirty Thousand, but each State shall have at Least one Representative; and until such enumeration shall be made, the State of New Hampshire shall be entitled to chuse three, Massachusetts, eight, Rhode-Island and Providence Plantations one, Connecticut five, New-York six, New Jersey four, Pennsylvania eight, Delaware one, Maryland six, Virginia ten, North Carolina five, South Carolina five, and Georgia three.

When vacancies happen in the Representation from any State, the Executive Authority thereof shall issue Writs of Election to fill such Vacancies.

The House of Representatives shall chuse their speaker and other Officers; and shall have the sole Power of Impeachment.

Section 3. The Senate of the United States shall be composed of two Senators from each State, chosen by the Legislature thereof, for six Years; and each Senator shall have one Vote.

Immediately after they shall be assembled in Consequence of the first Election, they shall be divided as equally as may be into three Classes. The Seats of the Senators of the first Class shall be vacated at the Expiration of the Second Year, of the second Class at the Expiration of the fourth Year, and of the third Class at the Expiration of the sixth Year, so that one third may be chosen every second year; and if Vacancies happen by Resignation, or otherwise, during the Recess of the Legislature of any State, the Executive thereof may make temporary Appointments until the next Meeting of the Legislature, which shall then fill such Vacancies.

No person shall be a Senator who shall not have attained to the Age of thirty years, and been nine Years a Citizen of the United States, and who shall not, when elected, be an Inhabitant of that State for which he shall be chosen.

The Vice President of the United States shall be President of the Senate, but shall have no Vote, unless they be equally divided.

The Senate shall chuse their other Officers, and also a President pro tempore, in the Absence of the Vice President, or when he shall exercise the Office of President of the United States.

The Senate shall have the sole Power to try all Impeachments. When sitting for that Purpose, they shall be on Oath or Affirmation.

When the President of the United States is tried, the Chief Justice shall preside: And no Person shall be convicted without the Concurrence of two thirds of the Members present.

Judgment in Cases of Impeachment shall not extend further than to removal from Office, and disqualification to hold and enjoy any Office of honor. Trust or Profit under the United States: but the Party convicted shall nevertheless be liable and subject to Indictment, Trial, Judgment and Punishment, according to law.

Section 4. The Times, Places and Manner for holding Elections for Senators and Representatives, shall be prescribed in each State by the Legislature thereof; but the Congress may at any time by law make or alter such Regulations, except as to the Places of chusing Senators.

The Congress shall assemble at least once in every Year, and such Meeting shall be on the first Monday in December, unless they shall by Law appoint a different Day.

Section 5. Each House shall be the Judge of the Elections, Returns and Qualifications of its own Members, and a Majority of each shall constitute a Quorum to do Business, but a smaller Number may adjourn from day to day, and may be authorized to compel the Attendance of absent Members, in such Manner, and under such Penalties as each House may provide.

Each House may determine the Rules of its Proceedings, punish its Members for disorderly Behaviour, and, with the Concurrence of two thirds, expel a Member.

Each House shall keep a Journal of its Proceedings, and from time to time publish the same, excepting such Parts as may in their Judgment require Secrecy; and the Yeas and Nays of the Members of either House on any question shall, at the Desire of one fifth of those Present, be entered on the Journal.

Neither House, during the Session of Congress, shall, without the Consent of the other, adjourn for more than three days, nor to any other Place than that in which the two Houses shall be sitting.

Section 6. The Senators and Representatives shall receive a Compensation for their Services, to be ascertained by Law, and paid out of the Treasury of the United States, be privileged from Arrest during their Attendance at the Session of their respective Houses, and in going to and returning from the same, and for any Speech or Debate in either House, they shall not be questioned in any other Place.

No Senator or Representative shall, during the Time for which he was elected, be appointed to any civil Office under the Authority of the United States, which shall have been created, or the Emoluments whereof shall have been encreased during such time; and no Person holding Office under the United States, shall be a Member of either House during his Continuance in Office.

Section 7. All Bills for raising Revenue shall originate in the House of Representatives; but the Senate may propose or concur with Amendments as on other Bills.

Every Bill which shall have passed the House of Representatives and the Senate, shall, before it become a Law, be presented to the President of the United States; If he approve he shall sign it, but it not he shall return it, with his Objections to that House in which it shall have originated, who shall enter the Objections at large on their Journal, and proceed to reconsider it. If after such Reconsideration two thirds of that House shall agree to pass the Bill, it shall be sent, together with the Objections, to the other House, by which it shall likewise be reconsidered, and if approved by two thirds of that House, it shall become a Law. But in all such Cases the Votes of both Houses shall be determined by yeas and Nays, and the Names of the Persons voting for and against the Bill shall be entered on the Journal of each House respectively. If any Bill shall not be returned by the President within ten Days (Sundays excepted) after it shall have been presented to him, the Same shall be a Law, in like Manner as if he had signed it, unless the Congress by their Adjournment prevent its Return, in which Case it shall not be a Law.

Every Order, Resolution, or Vote to which the Concurrence of the Senate and House of Representatives may be necessary (except on a question of Adjournment) shall be presented to the President of the United States; and before the Same shall take Effect, shall be approved by him, or being disapproved by him, shall be repassed by two thirds of the Senate and House of Representatives, according to the Rules and Limitations prescribed in the Case of a Bill.

Section 8. The Congress shall have Power To Lay and collect Taxes, Duties, Imposts and Excises, to pay the Debts and provide for the common Defence and general Welfare of the United States; but all Duties, Imposts and Excises shall be uniform throughout the United States.

To Borrow Money on the Credit of the United States;

To regulate Commerce with foreign Nations, and among the several States, and with the Indian Tribes;

To establish an uniform Rule of Naturalization, and uniform Laws on the subject of Bankruptcies throughout the United States;

To coin Money, regulate the Value thereof, and of foreign Coin, and fix the Standard Weights and Measures;

To provide for the Punishment of counterfeiting the Securities and current Coin of the United States;

To establish Post Offices and post Roads;

To promote the Progress of Science and useful Arts, by securing for limited Times to Authors and Inventors the exclusive Right to their respective Writings and Discoveries;

To constitute Tribunals inferior to the supreme Court;

To define and punish Piracies and Felonies committed on the high Seas, and Offences against the Law of Nations;

To declare War, grant Letters of Marque and Reprisal, and make Rules concerning Captures on Land and Water;

To raise and support Armies, but no Appropriation of Money to that Use shall be for a longer Term than two Years;

To provide and maintain a Navy;

To make Rules for the Government and Regulation of the land and naval Forces;

To provide for calling forth the Militia to execute the Laws of the Union, suppress Insurrections and repel Invasions;

To provide for organizing, arming, and disciplining, the Militia, and for governing such Part of them as may be employed in the Service of the United States, reserving to the States respectively, the Appointment of the Officers, and the Authority of training the Militia according to the discipline prescribed by Congress;

To exercise exclusive Legislation in all Cases whatsoever, over such District (not exceeding ten Miles square) as may, by Cession of particular States, and the Acceptance of Congress, become the Seat of the Government of the United States, and to exercise like Authority over all Places purchased by the Consent of the Legislature of the State in which the Same shall be for the Erection of Forts, Magazines, Arsenals, dock-Yards, and other needful Buildings;—And

To make all Laws which shall be necessary and proper for carrying into Execution the foregoing Powers, and all other Powers vested by this Constitution in the Government of the United States, or in any Department or Officer thereof.

Section 9. The Migration or Importation of such Persons as any of the States now existing shall think proper to admit, shall not be prohibited by the Congress prior to the Year one thousand eight hundred and eight, but a Tax or duty may be imposed on such Importation, not exceeding ten dollars for each person.

The Privilege of the Writ of Habeas Corpus shall not be suspended, unless when in Cases of Rebellion or Invasion the public Safety may require it.

No Bill of Attainer or ex post facto Law shall be passed.

No Capitation, or other direct, Tax shall be laid, unless in Proportion to the Census or Enumeration herein before directed to be taken.

No Tax or Duty shall be laid on Articles exported from any State.

No Preference shall be given by any Regulation of Commerce or Revenue to the Ports of one State over those of another: nor shall Vessels bound to, or from, one State, be obliged to enter, clear, or pay Duties in another.

No Money shall be drawn from the Treasury, but in Consequence of Appropriations made by Law; and a regular Statement and Account of the Receipts and Expenditures of all public Money shall be published from time to time.

No title of Nobility shall be granted by the United States: And no Person holding any Office of Profit or Trust under them, shall, without the Consent of the Congress, accept any present, Emolument, Office or Title, of any kind whatever, from any King, Prince, or foreign State.

Section 10. No State shall enter into any Treaty, Alliance, or Confederation; grant Letters or Marque and Reprisal; coin Money; emit Bills of Credit; make any Thing but gold and silver Coin a Tender in Payment of Debts; pass any Bill of Attainder, ex post facto Law, or Law impairing the Obligation of Contracts, or grant any Title of Nobility.

No State shall, without the Consent of Congress, lay any Imposts or Duties on Imports or Exports, except what may be absolutely necessary for executing it's inspection Laws: and the net Produce of all Duties and Imposts, laid by any State on Imports or Exports, shall be for the Use of the Treasury of the United States; and all such Laws shall be subject to the Revision and Control of the Congress.

No State shall, without the Consent of Congress, lay any Duty of Tonnage, Keep Troops, or Ships of War in time of Peace, enter into any Agreement or Compact with another State, or with a foreign Power, or engage in War, unless actually invaded, or in such imminent Danger as will not admit of delay.

Article II

Section 1. The executive Power shall be vested in a President of the United States of America. He shall hold his Office during the Term of four Years, and together with the Vice President, chosen for the same term, be elected, as follows

Each State shall appoint, in such Manner as the Legislature thereof may direct, a Number of Electors, equal to the whole Number of Senators and Representatives to which the State may be entitled in the Congress: but no Senator or Representative, or Person holding an Office of Trust or Profit under the United States, shall be appointed an Elector.

The Electors shall meet in their respective States, and vote by Ballot for two Persons, of whom one at least shall not be an Inhabitant of the same State with themselves. And they shall make a List of all the Persons voted for, and of the Number of Votes for each; which List they shall sign and certify, and transmit sealed to the Seat of the Government of the United States, directed to the President of the Senate. The President of the Senate shall, in the Presence of the Senate and House of Representatives, open all the Certificates, and the Votes shall then be counted. The person having the greatest Number of Votes shall be the President, if such Number be a Majority of the whole Number of Electors appointed; and if there be more than one who have such Majority, and have an equal Number of Votes, then the House of Representatives shall immediately chuse by Ballot one of them for President: and if no Person have a Majority, then from the five highest on the List the said House shall in like Manner chuse the President. But in chusing the President, the Votes shall be taken by States, the Representation from each State having one Vote; A quorum for this Purpose shall consist of a Member or Members from two thirds of the States, and a Majority of all the States shall be necessary to a Choice. In every Case, after the Choice of the President, the Person having the greatest Number of Votes of the Electors shall be the Vice President. But if there should remain two or more who have equal Votes, the Senate shall chuse from them by Ballot the Vice President.

The Congress may determine the Time of chusing the Electors, and the Day on which they shall give their Votes; which Day shall be the same throughout the United States.

No person except a natural born Citizen of the United States, at the time of the Adoption of this Constitution, shall be eligible to the Office of the President; neither shall any Person be eligible to that Office who shall not have attained to the Age of thirty five Years, and been fourteen Years a Resident within the United States.

In Case of the Removal of the President from Office, or of his Death, Resignation, or Inability to discharge the Powers and Duties of the said Office, the Same shall devolve on the Vice President, and the Congress may by Law provide for the Case of Removal, Death, Resignation or Inability, both of the President and Vice President, declaring what Officer shall then act as President, and such Officer shall act accordingly, until the Disability be removed, or a President shall be elected.

The President shall, at stated Times, receive for his Services, a Compensation, which shall neither be encreased nor diminished during the Period for which he shall have been elected, and he shall not receive within that Period any other Emolument from the United States, or any of them.

Before he enter on the Execution of his Office, he shall take the following Oath or Affirmation:—"I do solemnly swear (or affirm) that I will faithfully execute the Office of President of the United States, and will to the best of my Ability, preserve, protect and defend the Constitution of the United States."

Section 2. The President shall be Commander in Chief of the Army and Navy of the United States, and of the Militia of the several States, when called into the actual Service of the United States; he may require the Opinion, in writing, of the principal Officer in each of the executive Departments, upon any Subject relating to the Duties of their respective Offices, and he shall have Power to grant Reprieves and Pardons for Offences against the United States, except in Cases of Impeachment.

He shall have Power, by and with the Advice and Consent of the Senate, to make Treaties, provided two thirds of the Senators present concur; and he shall nominate, and by and with the Advice and Consent of the Senate, shall appoint Ambassadors, other public Ministers and Consuls, Judges of the supreme Court, and all other Officers of the United States, whose Appointments are not herein otherwise provided for, and which shall be established by Law: but the Congress may by Law vest the Appointment of such inferior Officers, as they think proper, in the President alone, in the Courts of Law, or in the Heads of Departments.

The President shall have Power to fill up all Vacancies that may happen during the Recess of the Senate, by granting Commissions which shall expire at the End of their next Session.

Section 3. He shall from time to time give to the Congress Information of the State of the Union, and recommend to their Consideration such Measures as he shall judge necessary and expedient; he may, on extraordinary Occasions, convene both Houses, or either of them, and in Case of Disagreement between them, with Respect to the Time of Adjournment, he may adjourn them to such Time as he shall think proper; he shall receive Ambassadors and other public Ministers; he shall take Care that the Laws be faithfully executed, and shall Commission all the Officers of the United States.

Section 4. The President, Vice President and all civil Officers of the United States, shall be removed from Office on Impeachment for, and Conviction of, Treason, Bribery, or other High Crimes and Misdemeanors.

Article III

Section 1. The judicial Power of the United States, shall be vested in one supreme Court, and in such inferior Courts as the Congress may from time to time ordain and establish. The Judges, both of the supreme and inferior Courts, shall hold their Offices during good Behavior, and shall, at stated Times, receive for their Services, a Compensation, which shall not be diminished during their Continuance in Office.

Section 2. The judicial Power shall extend to all Cases, in Law and Equity, arising under this Constitution, the Laws of the United States, and Treaties made, or which shall be made, under their Authority;—to all Cases affecting Ambassadors, other public Ministers and Consuls;—to all Cases of admiralty and maritime Jurisdiction;—to Controversies to which the United States shall be a Party;—to Controversies between two or more States; between a State and Citizens of another State;—between Citizens of different States;—between Citizens of the same State claiming Lands under Grants of different States, and between a State, or the Citizens thereof, and foreign States, Citizens or Subjects.

In all Cases affecting Ambassadors, other public Ministers and Consuls, and those in which a State shall be Party, the supreme Court shall have original Jurisdiction. In all other Cases before mentioned, the supreme Court shall have appellate Jurisdiction, both as to Law and Fact, with such Exceptions, and under such Regulations as the Congress shall make.

The Trial of all Crimes, except in Cases of Impeachment, shall be by Jury; and such Trial shall be held in the State where the said Crimes shall have been committed; but when not committed within any State, the Trial shall be at such Place or Places as the Congress may by Law have directed.

Section 3. Treason against the United States, shall consist only in levying War against them, or in adhering to their Enemies, giving them Aid and Comfort. No Person shall be convicted of Treason unless on the Testimony of two Witnesses to the same overt Act, or on Confession in open Court.

The Congress shall have Power to declare the Punishment of

Treason, but no Attainder of Treason shall work Corruption of Blood, or Forfeiture except during the Life of the Person attained.

Article IV

Section 1. Full Faith and Credit shall be given in each State to the public Acts, Records, and judicial Proceedings of every other State. And the Congress may be general Laws prescribe the Manner in which such Acts, Records and Proceedings shall be proved, and the Effect thereof.

Section 2. The Citizens of each State shall be entitled to all Privileges and Immunities of Citizens in the several States.

A Person charged in any State with Treason, Felony, or other Crime, who shall flee from Justice, and be found in another State, shall on Demand of the executive Authority of the State from which he fled, be delivered up, to be removed to the State having Jurisdiction of the Crime.

No Person held to Service or Labour in one State, under the Laws thereof, escaping into another shall, in Consequence of any Law or Regulation therein, be discharged from such Service or Labour, but shall be delivered up on Claim of the Party to whom such Service of Labour may be due.

Section 3. New States may be admitted by the Congress into this Union; but no new State shall be formed or erected within the Jurisdiction of any other State; nor any State be formed by the Junction of two or more States, or Parts of States, without the Consent of the Legislatures of the States concerned as well as of the Congress.

The Congress shall have Power to dispose of and make all needful Rules and Regulations respecting the Territory or other Property belonging to the United States; and nothing in this Constitution shall be so construed as to Prejudice any Claims of the United States, or of any particular State.

Section 4. The United States shall guarantee to every State in this Union a Republican Form of Government, and shall protect each of them against Invasion; and on Application of the Legislature, or of the Executive (when the Legislature cannot be convened) against domestic Violence.

Article V

The Congress, whenever two thirds of both Houses shall deem it necessary, shall propose Amendments to this Constitution, or, on the

Application of the Legislatures of two thirds of the several States, shall call a Convention for proposing Amendments, which, in either Case, shall be valid to all Intents and Purposes, as Part of this Constitution, when ratified by the Legislatures of three fourths of the several States, or by Conventions in three fourths thereof, as the one or the other Mode of Ratification may be proposed by the Congress; Provided that no Amendment which may be made prior to the Year One thousand eight hundred and eight shall in any Manner affect the first and fourth Clauses in the Ninth Section of the first Article; and that no State, without its Consent, shall be deprived of its equal Suffrage in the Senate.

Article VI

All Debts contracted and Engagements entered into, before the Adoption of this Constitution, shall be as valid against the United States under this Constitution, as under the Confederation.

This Constitution, and the Laws of the United States which shall be made in Pursuance thereof; and all Treaties made, or which shall be made, under the Authority of the United States, shall be the supreme Law of the Land; and the Judges in every State shall be bound thereby, any Thing in the Constitution or Laws of any State to the Contrary notwithstanding.

The Senators and Representatives before mentioned, and the Members of the several State Legislatures, and all executive and judicial Officers, both of the United States and of the several States, shall be bound by Oath or Affirmation, to support this Constitution; but no religious Test shall ever be required as a Qualification to any Office or public Trust under the United States.

Article VII

The Ratification of the Conventions of nine States, shall be sufficient for the Establishment of this Constitution between the States so ratifying the Same.

Amendments

[The first 10 Amendments were ratified December 15, 1791, and form what is known as the "Bill of Rights"]

Amendment 1

Congress shall make no law respecting an establishment of religion, or prohibiting the free exercise thereof; or abridging the freedom of speach, or of the press; or the right of the people peacably to assemble, and to petition the Government for a redress of grievances.

Amendment 2

A well regulated Militia, being necessary to the security of a free State, the right of the people to keep and bear Arms, shall not be infringed.

Amendment 3

No Soldier shall, in time of peace be quartered in any house, without the consent of the Owner, nor in time of war, but in a manner to be prescribed by law.

Amendment 4

The right of the people to be secure in their persons, houses, papers, and effects, against unreasonable searches and seizures, shall not be violated, and no Warrants shall issue, but upon probable cause, supported by Oath or affirmation, and particularly describing the place to be searched, and the persons or things to be seized.

Amendment 5

No person shall be held to answer for a capital, or otherwise infamous crime, unless on a presentment or indictment of a Grand Jury, except in cases arising in the land or naval forces, or in the Militia, when in actual service in time of War or public danger; nor shall any person be subject for the same offence to be twice put in jeopardy of life or limb; nor shall be compelled in any criminal case to be a witness against himself, nor be deprived of life, liberty, or property, without due process of law; nor shall private property be taken for public use, without just compensation.

Amendment 6

In all criminal prosecutions, the accused shall enjoy the right to a speedy and public trial, by an impartial jury of the State and district wherein the crime shall have been committed, which district shall have been previously ascertained by law, and to be informed of the nature and cause of the accusation; to be confronted with the witnesses against him; to have compulsory process for obtaining witnesses in his favor, and to have the Assistance of Counsel for his defence.

Amendment 7

In Suits at common law, where the value in controversy shall exceed twenty dollars, the right of trial by jury shall be preserved, and no fact tried by a jury, shall be otherwise re-examined in any Court of the United States, than according to the rules of the common law.

Amendment 8

Excessive bail shall not be required, nor excessive fines imposed, nor cruel and unusual punishments inflicted.

Amendment 9

The enumeration in the Constitution, of certain rights, shall not be construed to deny or disparage others retained by the people.

Amendment 10

The powers not delegated to the United States by the Constitution, nor prohibited by it to the States, are reserved to the States respectively, or to the people.

Amendment 11 (Ratified February 7, 1795)

The Judicial power of the United States shall not be construed to extend to any suit in law or equity, commenced or prosecuted against one of the United States by Citizens of another State, or by Citizens or Subjects of any Foreign State.

Amendment 12 (Ratified July 27, 1804)

The Electors shall meet in their respective states and vote by ballot for President and Vice-President, one of whom, at least, shall not be an inhabitant of the same state with themselves; they shall name in their ballots the person voted for as President, and in distinct ballots the person voted for as Vice-President, and they shall make distinct lists of all persons voted for as President, and of all persons voted for as Vice-President, and of the number of votes for each, which lists they shall sign and certify, and transmit sealed to the seat of the government of the United States, directed to the President of the Senate;—The President of the Senate shall, in the presence of the Senate and House of Representatives, open all the certificates and the votes shall then be counted;—The person having the greatest number of votes for President, shall be the President, if such number be a majority of the whole number of Electors appointed; and if no person have such majority, then from the persons having the highest numbers not exceeding three on the list of those voted for as President, the House of Representatives shall choose immediately, by ballot, the President. But in choosing the President, the votes shall be taken by states, the representation from each state having one vote; a quorum for this purpose shall consist of a member or members from two-thirds of the states, and a majority of all the states shall be necessary to a choice. And if the House of Representatives shall not choose a President whenever the right of choice shall devolve upon them, before the fourth day of March next following, then the Vice-President shall act as President, as in the case of the death or other constitutional disability of the President—The person having the greatest number of votes as Vice-President, shall be the Vice-President, if such number be a majority of the whole number of Electors appointed, and if no person have a majority, then from the two highest numbers of the list, the Senate shall choose the Vice-President; a quorum for the purpose shall consist of two-thirds of the whole number of Senators, and a majority of the whole number shall be necessary to a choice. But no person constitutionally ineligible to the office of President shall be eligible to that of Vice-President of the United States.

Amendment 13 (Ratified December 6, 1865)

Section 1. Neither slavery nor involuntary servitude, except as a punishment for crime whereof the party shall have been duly convicted, shall exist within the United States, or any place subject to their jurisdiction.

Section 2. Congress shall have power to enforce this article by appropriate legislation.

Amendment 14 (Ratified July 9, 1868)

Section 1. All persons born or naturalized in the United States, and subject to the jurisdiction thereof, are citizens of the United States and of the State wherein they reside. No State shall make or enforce any law which shall abridge the privileges or immunities of citizens of the United States; nor shall any State deprive any person of life, liberty, or property, without due process of law; nor deny to any person within its jurisdicition the equal protection of the laws.

Section 2. Representatives shall be apportioned among the several States according to their respective numbers, counting the whole number of persons in each State, excluding Indians not taxed. But when the right to vote at any election for the choice of electors for President and Vice President of the United States, Representatives in Congress, the Executive and Judicial officers of a State, or the members of the Legislature thereof, is denied to any of the male inhabitants of such State, being twenty-one years of age, and citizens of the United States, or in any way abridged, except for participation in rebellion, or other crime, the basis of representation therein shall be reduced in the proportion which the number of such male citizens shall bear to the whole number of male citizens twenty-one-years of age in such State.

Section 3. No person shall be a Senator or Representative in Congress, or elector of President and Vice President, or hold any office, civil or military, under the United States, or under any State, who having previously taken an oath, as a member of Congress, or as an officer of the United States, or as a member of any State legislature, or as an executive or judicial officer of any State, to support the Constitution of the United States, shall have engaged in insurrection or rebellion against the same, or given aid or comfort to the enemies thereof. But Congress may by a vote of two-thirds of each House, remove such disability.

Section 4. The validity of the public debt of the United States, authorized by law, including debts incurred for payment of pensions and bounties for services in suppressing insurrection or rebellion, shall not be questioned. But neither the United States nor any State shall assume or pay any debt or obligation incurred in aid of insurrection or rebellion against the United States, or any claim for the loss or emancipation of any slave; but all such debts, obligations and claims shall be held illegal and void.

Section 5. The Congress shall have power to enforce, by appropriate legislation, the provisions of this article.

Amendment 15 (Ratified February 3, 1870)

Section 1. The right of citizens of the United States to vote shall not be denied or abridged by the United States or by any State on account of race, color, or previous condition of servitude.

Section 2. The Congress shall have power to enforce this article by appropriate legislation.

Amendment 16 (Ratified February 3, 1913)

The Congress shall have power to lay and collect taxes on incomes, from whatever source derived, without apportionment among the several States and without regard to any census or enumeration.

Amendment 17 (Ratified April 8, 1913)

The Senate of the United States shall be composed of two Senators from each State, elected by the people thereof for six years; and each Senator shall have one vote. The electors in each State shall have the qualifications requisite for electors of the most numerous branch of the State Legislatures.

When vacancies happen in the representation of any State in the Senate, the executive authority of such State shall issue writs of election to fill such vacancies: *Provided,* That the legislature of any State may empower the executive thereof to make temporary appointments until the people fill the vacancies by election as the legislature may direct.

This amendment shall not be so construed as to affect the election or term of any Senator chosen before it becomes valid as part of the Constitution.

Amendment 18 (Ratified January 16, 1919)

Section 1. After one year from the ratification of this article the manufacture, sale, or transportation of intoxicating liquors within, the importation thereof into, or the exportation thereof from the

United States and all territory subject to the jurisdiction thereof for beverage purposes is hereby prohibited.

Section 2. The Congress and the several States shall have concurrent power to enforce this article by appropriate legislation.

Section 3. This article shall be inoperative unless it shall have been ratified as an amendment to the Constitution by the legislatures of the several States, as provided in the Constitution, within seven years from the date of the submission hereof to the States by the Congress.

Amendment 19 (Ratified August 18, 1920)

The right of citizens of the United States to vote shall not be denied or abridged by the United States or by any State on account of sex.

Congress shall have power to enforce this article by appropriate legislation.

Amendment 20 (Ratified January 23, 1933)

Section 1. The terms of the President and Vice President shall end at noon on the 20th day of January, and the terms of Senators and Representatives at noon on the 3d day of January, of the years in which such terms would have ended if this article had not been ratified; and the terms of their successors shall then begin.

Section 2. The Congress shall assemble at least once in every year, and such meeting shall begin at noon on the 3d day of January, unless they shall by law appoint a different day.

Section 3. If, at the time fixed for the beginning of the term of the President, the President elect shall have died, the Vice President elect shall become President. If a President shall not have been chosen before the time fixed for the beginning of his term, or if the President elect shall have failed to qualify, then the Vice President elect shall act as President until a President shall have qualified; and the Congress may by law provide for the case wherein neither a President elect nor a Vice President elect shall have qualified, declaring who shall then act as President, or the manner in which one who is to act shall be selected, and such person shall act accordingly until a President or Vice President shall have qualified.

Section 4. The Congress may by law provide for the case of the death of any of the persons from whom the House of Representatives may choose a President whenever the right of choice shall have devolved upon them, and for the case of the death of any of the persons from whom the Senate may choose a Vice President whenever the right of choice shall have devolved upon them.

Section 5. Sections 1 and 2 shall take effect on the 15th day of October following the ratification of this article.

Section 6. This article shall be inoperative unless it shall have been ratified as an amendment to the Constitution by the legislatures of three-fourths of the several States within seven years from the date of its submission.

Amendment 21 (Ratified December 5, 1933)

Section 1. The eighteenth article of amendment to the Constitution of the United States is hereby repealed.

Section 2. The transportation or importation into any State, Territory, or possession of the United States for delivery or use therein of intoxicating liquors, in violation of the laws thereof, is hereby prohibited.

Section 3. This article shall be inoperative unless it shall have been ratified as an amendment to the Constitution by conventions in the several States, as provided in the Constitution, within seven years from the date of the submission hereof to the States by the Congress.

Amendment 22 (Ratified February 27, 1951)

Section 1. No person shall be elected to the office of the President more than twice, and no person who has held the office of President, or acted as President, for more than two years of a term to which some other person was elected President shall be elected to the office of the President more than once. But this Article shall not apply to any person holding the office of President when this Article was proposed by the Congress, and shall not prevent any person who may be holding the office of President, or acting as President, during the term within which this Article becomes operative from holding the office of President or acting as President during the remainder of such term.

Section 2. This article shall be inoperative unless it shall have been ratified as an amendment to the Constitution by the legislatures of three-fourths of the several States within seven years from the date of its submission to the States by the Congress.

Amendment 23 (Ratified March 29, 1961)

Section 1. The District constituting the seat of Government of the United States shall appoint in such manner as the Congress may direct:

A number of electors of President and Vice President equal to the whole number of Senators and Representatives in Congress to which the District would be entitled if it were a State, but in no event more than the least populous State; they shall be in addition to those appointed by the States, but they shall be considered, for the purposes of the election of President and Vice President, to be electors appointed by a State; and they shall meet in the District and perform such duties as provided by the twelfth article of amendment.

Section 2. The Congress shall have power to enforce this article by appropriate legislation.

Amendment 24 (Ratified January 23, 1964)

Section 1. The right of citizens of the United States to vote in any primary or other election for President or Vice President, for electors for President or Vice President, or for Senator or Representative in Congress, shall not be denied or abridged by the United States or any State by reason of failure to pay any poll tax or other tax.

Section 2. The Congress shall have power to enforce this article by appropriate legislation.

Amendment 25 (Ratified February 10, 1967)

Section 1. In case of the removal of the President from office or of his death or resignation, the Vice President shall become President.

Section 2. Whenever there is a vacancy in the office of the Vice President, the President shall nominate a Vice President who shall take office upon confirmation by a majority vote of both Houses of Congress.

Section 3. Whenever the President transmits to the President pro tempore of the Senate and the Speaker of the House of Representatives his written declaration that he is unable to discharge the powers and duties of his office, and until he transmits a written declaration to the contrary, such powers and duties shall be discharged by the Vice President as Acting President.

Section 4. Whenever the Vice President and a majority of the principal officers of the executive departments, or such other body as Congress may by law provide, transmit to the President pro tempore of the Senate and the Speaker of the House of Representatives their written declaration that the President is unable to discharge the powers and duties of his office, the Vice President shall immediately assume the powers and duties of the office of Acting President.

Thereafter, when the President transmits to the President pro tempore of the Senate and the Speaker of the House of Representatives his written declaration that no inability exists, he shall resume the powers and duties of his office unless the Vice President and a majority of the principal officers of the executive departments, or such other body as Congress may by law provide, transmit within two days to the President pro tempore of the Senate and the Speaker of the House of Representatives their written declaration that the President is unable to discharge the powers and duties of his office. Thereupon Congress shall decide the issue, assembling within forty-eight hours for that purpose if not in session. If the Congress, within ten days after the receipt of the written declaration of the Vice President and a majority of the principal officers of the executive departments, or such other body as Congress may by law provide, determines by two-thirds vote of both Houses that the President is unable to discharge the powers and duties of the office, the Vice President shall continue to discharge the same as Acting President: otherwise, the President shall resume the powers and duties of his office.

Amendment 26 (Ratified June 30, 1971)

Section 1. The right of citizens of the United States, who are eighteen years of age or older, to vote shall not be denied or abridged by the United States or by any State on account of age.

Section 2. The Congress shall have power to enforce this article by appropriate legislation.

INDEX

Abbott Laboratories, 177
Acheson, Dean, 206, 216
Act to Regulate Commerce, 176
Active-negative presidential character, 115
Active-positive presidential character, 115
Action, Lord, 55
Adams, John, 76, 183, 295, 433
Adams, John Quincy, 405
Adams, Samuel, 76
AFL-CIO, 177, 365, 441
Agency for International Development, 206
Agnew, Spiro, resignation of, 9, 114, 183
Allende, Salvador, 205
Almond, Gabriel, 470
American Bar Association (ABA), 442, 456
American Confederation, 79, 110
American Dental Association, 456
American Farm Bureau Federation, 168, 365
American Legion, 162, 444
American Medical Association (AMA), 442, 446, 456
  opposition to Medicare, 448

American party, 417
American society, nature of, 8–9
American system:
  bases of power in, 3
  core values of, 84
  democracy in, 83
  diffusion of power in, 90
  judiciary in, 321–322
  operation of, 16–17
  power in, 80
  problems of, 1
  role of courts in, 292
  role of presidency in, 109
American Voter, The, 477
Aristotle, 49
Arms Control and Disarmament Agency, 206
Articles of Confederation, 75–76

Bailey, F. Lee, 336
Baker, Robert (Bobby), 449
Baker v. *Carr*, 298, 307, 308, 342
Barber, James David, 115
Bill of Rights, 83, 84
Black Caucus, 443–445
Blackmun, Harry, 308
Brezhnev, Leonid, 162
Brokerage politics, 90

549

Brookings Institution, 214
Brown v. Board of Education, 87, 293, 298, 299, 300, 307, 342
Burger, Warren E., 302, 308
Burger Court, 299, 302, 308–309, 342
Burke, Edmund, 229
Burns, James McGregor, 169
Burr, Aaron, 404

Campbell, Angus, 477
Carswell, G. Harrold, 308
Central Intelligence Agency (CIA), 123, 205, 210
Chambers of Commerce, 177
Checks and balances, 75, 78, 81, 82, 110
"Chicago Seven," 336
Civil Aeronautics Board, 377
Civil law, 324, 327
Civil Rights Act of 1875, 300
Civil Rights Act of 1964, 87
Civil Service Reform Act, 380
Clark, Ramsey, 341
Clausewitz, Karl von, 49
Clay, Henry, 405
Committee to Reelect the President (CREEP), 414
Common Cause, 439, 444
Common law, 322
Congress:
  committee on committees in, 257
  committee system in, 167, 260–264
  composition of, 227–229
  interest groups and, 168
  leadership in, 255–260
  legislation, process of, 269–271
  legislative oversight, 267–269
  majority floor leader in, 257
  party whips in, 257
  relations with president, 167–168, 267
  representational styles in, 230–238
  Rules Committee, 257
  seniority system and, 167, 261–263
  Speaker of the House, 256
Congressional elections, 1974, 10, 180, 183, 265, 407–408, 482
Constitutional Convention, 76–78, 109
Constitutionalism, concept of, 82
Converse, Philip, 2

Coolidge, Calvin, 114
Corcoran, Thomas, 131
Council of Economic Advisors, 212
Council of Foreign Relations, 214
Court system, 324–326
Cox, Archibald, 475, 477
Criminal law, 324, 326
Cuban Blockade, 123

Dahl, Robert, 90
Daley, Richard J., 412
Davidson, Roger, 230, 231
Declaration of Independence, 84
Democracy:
  American, 3
  as core value, 51
  definition of, 3, 15, 85
  "representative," 3
Democracy in America, 11
Democratic party, 406, 411, 415
Democratic-Republicans, 404
Democratic society:
  basis of, 2, 4
  conformity in, 13
  individual in, 9
  political activity in, 8–9
  problems of, 87
  use of coercion in, 55
Democratic Steering and Policy Committee, 263
Department of Agriculture, 201
Department of Defense, 181, 201, 208, 362, 375
Department of Health, Education and Welfare, 181
Department of Housing and Urban Development, 181
Department of State, 201, 205–206

Egalitarianism, 13
Eisenhower, Dwight D.:
  heart attacks of, 183
  as passive-negative president, 115
  and Vietnam, 130, 159
Engle v. Vitale, 307
Escobedo v. Illinois, 301, 307, 340
Executive agreements, 202
Executive power, limits on, 125

Federal bureaucracy, 127, 174
  defined, 361
Federal Communications Commission, 377
Federal Energy Office, 366
Federal Power Commission, 175, 176, 366
Federal Regulation of Lobbying Act of 1946, 452
Federalism, 75, 78, 80
  growth of, 110
  and "reserved" powers, 80
Federal Trade Commission, 377, 449
Federalist, The, 294
Federalists, 404
Food and Drug Administration, 126
Ford, Gerald, 113, 116, 117
  accession to presidency of, 183
  and Black Caucus, 445
  as Congressman, 238
  and CREEP, 414
  and meeting with Brezhnev, 124
  and Nixon pardon, 118, 472, 475
Fortas, Abe, 308
Fourteenth Amendment, 300
Fuller, Melville, 302

Garner, John Nance, 183
Gellhorn, Walter, 238
Gibbons v. *Ogden,* 304
Gideon v. *Wainwright,* 301, 307, 340
Goldberg, Arthur J., 307–308
Goldwater, Barry, 162, 403, 411
Great Depression of 1930's, 179
"Great Society," 125
Group theory, 434–436
Grund, Francis J., 11

Haig, Alexander, 172
Halberstam, David, 165
Hamilton, Alexander, 294, 404
Hancock, John, 76
Harding, Warren, 110, 114
Haynsworth, Clement F., 308
Hebert, F. Edward, 264
Henry, Patrick, 76
Herring, Pendleton, 470

Hilsman, Roger, 215
Hoffman, Julius, 336
Hoover, Herbert, 114
Hoover, J. Edgar, 111
House Armed Services Committee, 449
House Judiciary Committee, 87, 169
House of Representatives, 87
House Ways and Means Committee, 261
Hughes, Charles Evans, 289, 306
Hughes, Emmet John, 109
Humphrey, Hubert, 413

Ideology:
  American, 2
  definition of, 2, 52
  democratic, 85, 86, 88
  as foundation of political system, 51–52
Interstate Commerce Commission, 175, 377

Jackson, Andrew, 110, 386, 405
  and Democratic party, 411
  and populist politics, 405
Jackson State University, 55
Javits, Jacob, 407
Jay, John:
  as Chief Justice, 303
  and *The Federalist,* 294
Jefferson, Thomas, 4, 76, 77, 295
  and Democratic-Republicans, 404
  and presidential roles, 124
Johnson, Lyndon B., 114, 302
  as active-negative president, 115
  decision not to seek reelection, 55, 214
  and Gulf of Tonkin Resolution, 164
  and public opinion, 125
  relations with Congress, 81
  as Senate Majority Leader, 268
  and sending of troops into Dominican Republic, 208
  and Vietnam, 130, 159, 160
Judicial review, 75, 78, 126, 296
Judicial supremacy, concept of, 83
Judiciary Act of 1789, 295
Jury system, 324
Justinian Code, 322

Kennedy, John F., 114, 452
  assassination of, 183
  and Cuban Blockade, 123
  appointment of federal judges by, 329
  and Southern Democrats, 169
  and State Department, 127
  and relations with Adlai Stevenson in 1960 campaign, 165
  and Vietnam, 130, 159
  in 1960 Wisconsin and West Virginia primaries, 413
Kennedy, Robert F., 127
  assassination of, 438
  and National Rifle Association, 448
Kent State, 55
Kerner, Otto, 338
Key V. O., 6, 480
King, Martin Luther, 446
Kissinger, Henry, 362
  and efforts for Mideast Peace, 205
  and resignation of President Nixon, 205
  as special assistant for national security, 211, 372
  visit to Peking, 172

Lincoln, Abraham, 4, 110, 123
Lipset, Seymour Martin, 8
Lobbying, 451–452
Lodge, Henry Cabot, 203
"Lonely crowd," 17
Long, Russell B., 366

MacArthur, Douglas A., 208–209
McCarthy, Eugene, 408
McCulloch v. *Maryland*, 126, 303
McDonald, Myron, 14
McGinniss, Joe, 13, 117
McGovern, George, 403, 411
McKinley, William, 208
McNamara, Robert S., 375
Madden, Ray J., 258
Madison, James, 294, 433
Mansfield, Mike, 117, 259
Marbury v. *Madison*, 83, 292, 294, 303
Marshall, John, 83, 295, 303
Mass media:
  and the courts, 335–337
  growth of, 116
  impact of, 110
  and presidency, 126
  role of 14–15, 483–485
  use of, 117
  and Watergate, 14, 132
  and winning elections, 117
Miller, Warren, 234
Miller v. *California*, 308, 342
Mills, C. Wright, 16
Missouri Compromise (1820), 305
Mondale, Walter F., 266
Monroe, James, 405
Montesquieu, 6
Morgenthau, Hans, 54
Moyers, Bill, 8
Moynihan, Daniel Patrick, 178
Mueller, John, 475
Muskie, Edmund, 413

Napoleonic Code, 322
National Aeronautics and Space Council, 212
National Association for the Advancement of Colored People (NAACP), 439, 441
National Association of Manufacturers, 177, 442, 449
National Industrial Recovery Act, 126, 293
National Labor Relations Act, 293
National Labor Relations Board, 377
National Rifle Association, 438, 472
National Rural Elected Cooperative Association, 365
"National security," 159
National Security Act, 209
National Security Council, 209, 210
New Deal, 123, 306
Nixon, Richard M., 114, 403
  as active-negative president, 115
  appointments of federal judges by, 329
  appointments to the Supreme Court by, 308
  and CREEP, 414
  corporate contributions to reelection of, 450
  and detente, 160
  and election campaign of 1972, 162
  and firing of Archibald Cox, 475

foreign policy of, 114, 129, 130
isolation of, 82
and meeting with Brezhnev, 162
resignation of, 132, 183
and "silent majority," 164
and television debates with John F. Kennedy, 116, 117
and trip to China, 475
and Vietnam, 130, 159, 160
and White House staff, 172
Nixon administration:
  and black population, 178
  and problems of welfare and poverty, 178
North Atlantic Treaty Organization (NATO), 215
Nye, Gerald P., 449

Office of Emergency Preparedness, 212
Office of Management and Budget, 211
Office of Science and Technology, 212
Office of Special Representative for Trade Negotiations, 212
Oil embargo, 179
Organization of American States (OAS), 215

Paine, Thomas, 76
Participatory democracy, 83
Passive-negative presidential character, 115
Passive-positive presidential character, 115
Peace Corps, 206
Pericles, 3
Plessy v. *Ferguson*, 300
Pluralism, concept of, 82
Pluralists, 16
Poage, W. R., 264
Political interest groups, 433
  activities of, 438–440
  categories of, 443–444
  conflicts between, 445–446
  lobbying by, 451–452
  and political contributions, 442–451
  and public, 448–449
Political parties:
  characteristics of, 409–411
  and national conventions, 413–414

organization of, 401, 412–413
power of, 400–403
rise of, 110
roots of, 409
third parties, 409
types of, 399
Political system:
  and community, 51
  concept of, 50–51, 53
  and Constitution, 75
  and ideology, 51
  judiciary in, 321–322
  power and, 54, 80, 89
  power holders in, 56
  presidency in, 109, 111
Politics, definition of, 49
Politics Among Nations, 54
Popular sovereignty, 82
Population, composition of American, 5
Power:
  in American political system, 80
  coercive, 54–55
  concept of, 6, 53
  consensus, 54–55
  misuse of, 55–56
Power elite, 16
Power model, and American political system, 89
Presidency:
  "active," 113
  basic structure of, 110
  Buchanan model of, 113
  and Cabinet, 173–174
  constitutional basis of, 112
  Eisenhower model of, 114
  informal grants of power to, 161
  and legislative liaison staff, 170
  Lincoln model of, 113
  "passive," 113
  political basis of, 112
  power of, 112
  public opinion and, 125
  and regulatory agencies, 175–177, 181
  relationship with Congress, 167–168
  role of, in American political system, 109, 122, 123
Presidential power:
  and appointments, 170
  Congressional checks on, 126, 167
  in domestic affairs, 157
  Executive office and, 171

in foreign affairs, 160
  limits on, 214–215
  and morals and ethics, 161
  and span of control, 127
  symbolic, 213
  veto and, 178
Presidential roles:
  chief bureaucrat, 174
  chief diplomat, 123, 201
  chief executive, 119
  chief legislator, 123, 167
  chief politician, 124, 166
  commander in chief, 122, 201, 206, 208–209, 212
Public opinion, 470
  and presidential power, 477–478
  and presidential conduct, 475, 476

RAND Corporation, 214
Rangel, Charles B., 445
Reich, Charles A., 7
Republican party, 406, 442
Republicans, *see* Democratic-Republicans
Retired Servicemen's Associations, 162
Richardson, Elliot, 477
Ridgway, Matthew B., 209
Riesman, David, 13
Robinson, James, 264
Rockefeller, Nelson A., 14
Roman law, 322
Roosevelt, Eleanor, 501
Roosevelt, Franklin D., 110, 114
  appointment of federal judges by, 329
  and federal bureaucracy, 364, 374
  and New Deal, 123
  as Secretary of the Navy, 127
  and Supreme Court, 126, 292
Roosevelt, Theodore, 110, 114
Rosenthal, Benjamin S., 366
Rossiter, Clinton, 118, 403, 409
  and roles of the president, 118, 131, 132
Rourke, Francis E., 367
Rowan, Carl, 177
Ruckelshaus, William, 477
Rusk, Dean, 57

Schenck v. *United States*, 305
Schlesinger, Arthur M., 13, 111

Scott v. *Sanford*, 305
Secretary of Defense, 206
Secretary of State, 205–206
Selling of the President, The, 13, 117
Senate Foreign Relations Committee, 203
"Separate but equal" doctrine, 87, 300
Separation of powers, 75, 78, 81, 110
Sheppard, Sam, 335
Smyth v. *Ames*, 305
Socialist party, 409
Southeast Asian Treaty Organization (SEATO), 159
Southern Christian Leadership Conference, 446, 454, 456
Spirit of the Laws, The, 6
Stare decisis, 323
Statistical Abstract of the United States, 437
Stevenson, Adlai, 165
Stokes, Donald, 234
Stone, Harlan F., 306
Stone, W. Clement, 57
Strategic Arms Limitation Agreement, 478
Strategic Arms Limitation Talks (SALT), 130
Strauder v. *West Virginia*, 305
Supreme Court, 83, 123, 126
  functioning of, 290–293
  judicial activism, 301–302
  judicial restraint, 301–302
  major periods of, 303–309
  role of Chief Justice, 290
  and Watergate tapes, 81

Taft, William Howard, 110, 114
  as Chief Justice, 304
Taney, Roger, 304
Terkel, Studs, 8
Third parties, 409
Thomas, Norman, 409
Tobacco Institute, 168
Tocqueville, Alexis de, 11, 12, 85–86, 344, 434
Totalitarian system, use of coercion in, 55
Treaties, 202
Truman, Harry S., 110, 111, 114, 183, 201
  and role of president, 118, 120

Index

and decision not to run for second
 term, 475
and Korea, 208
and removal of Gen. MacArthur,
 208–209

United States:
 constitution of, 81, 84
 economic growth of, 5
 free enterprise system in, 179
 growth rate in, 5
 mixed economic system in, 179
 political system, impersonality of, 13
 population, composition of, 5
United States Information Agency, 206
United States v. Curtiss-Wright Export Corporation, 202

Vantage Point, The, 131
Verba, Sidney, 470
Veterans of Foreign Wars, 162, 444
Vice President:
 as president of Senate, 258
 role of, 183
Vietnam War, 9, 126, 130
 attitude of American people to, 214
 and presidency, 158
 and U.S. involvement, 159, 160
Vinson, Fred, 306, 307

Waite, Morrison, 302
Wallace, George, 417
Warren, Earl, 293, 299, 306
Warren Court, 293, 298, 302, 306–307
Washington, George, 110, 173, 399
Watergate, 3, 9, 14, 17, 87, 158, 167, 169, 493
 House Judiciary Committee and, 69, 87
 Senate Select Committee on, 169
 voter reaction to, 182
Whig Party, 405
White, Edward D., 302
White, Theodore, 116, 379
White House staff, 170 –172
Wilson, Woodrow, 110, 114
 and League of Nations, 202–203
 observations on Congress, 265
Working, 8

Zero population growth, 5